EXECUTIVES AND MANAGERS
THEIR RIGHTS & DUTIES

STIKEMAN, ELLIOTT

Butterworths

Toronto and Vancouver

Executives and Managers: Their Rights & Duties

The Butterworth Group of Companies
Canada:
Butterworths Canada Ltd.,
75 Clegg Road, MARKHAM, Ontario L6G 1A1
and 17th Floor, 808 Nelson Street, Box 12148, VANCOUVER, B.C. V6Z 2H2
Australia:
Butterworths Pty Ltd., SYDNEY, ADELAIDE, BRISBANE, CANBERRA, MELBOURNE, and PERTH
Ireland:
Butterworth (Ireland) Ltd., DUBLIN
Malaysia:
Malayan Law Journal Sdn Bhd, KUALA LUMPUR
New Zealand:
Butterworths of New Zealand Ltd., WELLINGTON and AUCKLAND
Singapore:
Butterworths Asia, SINGAPORE
South Africa:
Butterworths Publishers (Pty), DURBAN
United Kingdom:
Butterworth & Co. (Publishers) Ltd., LONDON and EDINBURGH
United States:
Butterworth Legal Publishers, CARLSBAD, California; SALEM, New Hampshire

Executives and Managers: Their Rights & Duties is reprinted in part from the Butterworths looseleaf service **Executive Employment Law**, authored by Stikeman, Elliott.

EXECUTIVES AND MANAGERS
THEIR RIGHTS & DUTIES

STIKEMAN, ELLIOTT

Montreal, Toronto, Ottawa, Calgary, Vancouver, New York,
Washington, D.C., London, Sydney, Budapest, Prague,
Hong Kong, Singapore, Taipei

CONTRIBUTING AUTHORS

John F. Anderson
A. Edward Aust
S. Jason Baxendale
Jean-Pierre Belhumeur
Patrick L. Benaroche
Hélène Bussières
Jean Carrier
Lyse Charette
Edward B. Claxton
Lorna A. Cuthbert
Lily Germain
Margaret E. Grottenthaler
Paul D. Hayward
Mélanie Hébert

Catherine Jenner
Derek N. Linfield
Stuart C. McCormack
Gary Nachshen
Frédéric Pierrestiger
Eveline Poirier
Andra M. Pollak
R. Bruce Pollock
Pierre A. Raymond
Steeve Robitaille
André J. Roy
H. Heward Stikeman
Alison J. Youngman

ASSOCIATE EDITORS

John F. Anderson   Hélène Bussières   Catherine Jenner

Andra M. Pollak   A. Edward Aust
General Editor   Editor-in-Chief

* We wish to thank Céline Bastien, Robert Mason, John McLean and Patricia Rivers for
their assistance.

The views expressed herein summarize many of the main issues arising in the contributors' respective areas of the law; they are not and should not be construed as an expression of a legal opinion on any of the matters discussed herein.

PREFACE

The purpose of this text is to assist executives and other interested parties to understand and appreciate the legal framework in which executives operate. In doing so, it refers to many of the principal laws of Ontario, Quebec and British Columbia as well as the decisions that interpret the extent and nature of executive rights and duties.

For the purposes of understanding the scope of this book we have used the term "executive" in its broadest sense. It includes an employee whose position, when considered in respect of the overall organization in which he or she functions, carries with it the right of independent action, autonomy and discretion, including the power to direct or administer something. However, different laws may have their own definitions of the term.

Executive behaviour is increasingly subjected to legal limits and an evolving body of case law. The attention paid to this area of law by legislators and the courts is to some extent a recognition of the importance of executive decisions to their organizations and society as a whole. It is also fueled by the rapid pace of change management faces due in part to technological advances, competitiveness and the financial pressures to which so many companies are subjected. Both the electronic and written media report almost daily on corporate leadership issues.

The growing number of stakeholders, including shareholders, employees, pension fund and mutual fund managers, with an interest in corporate behaviour are contributing to the attention paid to what executives receive as compensation and what they contribute to their organizations.

The roles of executives and senior managers have evolved from the time when public companies were dominated by their directors, owners or principal shareholders. In today's world, many corporate executives, especially in public companies where there is no dominant shareholder, often play an equal or more influential role than the board of directors.

The increased mobility of executives between organizations and different countries has increased the use of written employment contracts for executives with respect to specific terms. However, all executives, even those without a written contract, must acquaint themselves with the interpretation of their common law rights and duties.

The rights and duties concerning executives' behaviour as senior management employees according to the numerous statutory obligations legislated by provincial and federal governments under corporate, securities, tax, pension and immigration laws, place a myriad of additional restrictions on their actions.

Be it fraudulent acts, insider trading, permitting a worker not entitled to work in Canada to enter the workplace, allowing workers to perform their duties in unsafe circumstances or simply being incompetent, the legal consequences can be severe and may have significant penal sanctions attached to them.

The courts have paid increasing attention to what type of executive behaviour constitutes cause for the lawful termination of their relationship. This area of the law has seen dramatic changes over the past decade with the influx of women, different ethnic groups, and a more diverse group of judges evaluating such behaviour. Executives who sexually harass subordinates can incur company liability.

The circumstances surrounding the termination of an executive's services are often of interest to stakeholders in their organizations, not only with respect to how much they receive in severance pay, but also as indication of the corporate stability, values and culture. Exclusion of someone from the workplace unlawfully has caused the Supreme Court of Canada to remind society of the importance of the employment relationship in our times and of the impact on an employee's emotional, financial and physical well-being.

Special thanks must go to our fellow lawyers who practice in our different offices and legal jurisdictions, who authored and integrated the various subjects in the numerous areas of the law in this work. Our firm, Stikeman, Elliott, has supported this work with the belief that by providing the comparative approaches of the laws and decisions in Quebec, Ontario and British Columbia, in English and in a French book on this subject, that there are substantial benefits for the positive evolution of the law.

We would also like to recognize the contribution and assistance of Butterworths Canada Limited who, since our first discussions in 1991 with Mary Anne Logan concerning this book, had the foresight and determination for this initiative. Her colleagues, John Yates and Philip Waxman, have now taken the next step to make this work available beyond the legal profession marketplace in an accessible format, for all, to which surely they are entitled.

Hopefully this work will inspire subsequent attempts at providing the public with a synthesis of digestible and timely legal information.

A. Edward Aust
Editor-in-Chief
October 23, 1997

TABLE OF CONTENTS

Preface.   v

PART I: INTRODUCTION

CHAPTER 1: AN OVERVIEW

		Para.
A.	INTRODUCTION.	1.1
B.	FOUNDATIONS OF THE EMPLOYMENT CONTRACT.	1.9
	1. The Notion of "Employment"	1.9
	2. Origins: Rome	1.14
	3. History of Employment in Europe.	1.17
C.	DEFINING AND REDEFINING THE ROLE AND RESPONSIBILITIES OF THE CORPORATE EXECUTIVE	1.20
	1. From Colonization to Economic Liberalism: The Emergence of the Joint-Stock Company	1.20
	2. Management in the Early Canadian Company	1.21
	3. The Evolution of the Corporate Manager in Limited Liability Joint-Stock Companies.	1.27
	4. Corporate Executives in the 20th Century	1.32
	(a) The Role of the Director Juridically Defined.	1.34
	(i) Common Law.	1.34
	(ii) Civil Law.	1.37
	(b) Attempts to Define the Role of Executives in Law. .	1.40
	(i) Common Law.	1.40
	(ii) Civil Law.	1.42
	(c) Situation of Executives in Practice	1.47
	(d) Re-examining the Juridical Status of Executives . . .	1.51
	(i) The Executive and the Contract.	1.51
	(ii) The Executive Contract and Article 1434 of the Civil Code of Quebec	1.54
	(1) Equity and the Obligation of Good Faith .	1.55
	(2) Custom (Usage) and the Obligations of the Executive	1.57
D.	CONCLUSION — THE CORPORATE EXECUTIVE TODAY: MASTER AND SERVANT?.	1.65

CHAPTER 2: DETERMINATION OF LAWS GOVERNING THE EMPLOYMENT RELATIONSHIP

Para.

A. JURISDICTIONAL ISSUES: RULES GOVERNING THE CONTENT
AND INTERPRETATION OF THE EMPLOYMENT CONTRACT 2.1
1. Civil Law 2.7
2. The Common Law 2.9
3. Other Employment Law Issues 2.12
    (a) Public Order Laws 2.12
    (b) Pension Plan Laws 2.13
4. Application of Constitutional Law Principles in the
Employment Context 2.14
B. SOURCES OF EMPLOYMENT LAW 2.22
1. Legislation 2.23
    (a) Civil Code 2.23
    (b) Statutes 2.25
        (i) Labour Standards 2.26
        (ii) Human Rights 2.27
        (iii) Health and Safety 2.28
        (iv) Workers' Compensation 2.29
2. Case Law 2.30
3. Doctrine 2.31
C. CONCLUSION 2.32

CHAPTER 3: THE FORMATION OF THE EMPLOYMENT CONTRACT

A. INTRODUCTION 3.1
B. REQUISITES TO THE VALIDITY OF AN EMPLOYMENT CONTRACT . 3.2
1. Offer and Acceptance 3.2
2. Consideration 3.7
    (a) Negotiated Terms of Employment Contract 3.7
    (b) Non-Negotiated Terms of Employment: Company
    Policies or Manuals 3.13
3. Intention to Create Legal Relations 3.19
C. DEFECTS IN CONSENT 3.20
1. Mistake/Error 3.21
2. Fraud 3.26
3. Duress, Undue Influence and Unconscionability/Fear . . . 3.33
D. CONTENT OF THE EMPLOYMENT CONTRACT 3.36

		Para.
E.	CONCLUSION	3.38

CHAPTER 4: THE NATURE OF EMPLOYMENT, THE EMPLOYER AND THE EMPLOYEE

A.	INTRODUCTION	4.1
B.	ESSENTIAL ELEMENTS OF THE EMPLOYMENT RELATIONSHIP	4.3
	1. The Individual Must Work for Another	4.5
	2. The Individual Must Receive Remuneration	4.6
	3. The Individual Must Be Subordinate to the Employer	4.8
C.	DEFINING THE EMPLOYER AND THE EMPLOYEE WITHIN VARIOUS CORPORATE STRUCTURES	4.14
	1. Who Is the Employer?	4.14
	(a) Companies with the Same Administration	4.16
	(b) Third Party Control (Personnel Agencies)	4.23
	(c) Seconding Agreements	4.24
	(d) Limited Partnership	4.33
	(e) Joint Venture	4.35
	2. Who Is the Employee?	4.37
	(a) Employee, Partner, Officer and Director	4.38
	(b) Who Has the Authority to Represent the Employer?	4.43
D.	CONCLUSION	4.46

CHAPTER 5: PRE-EMPLOYMENT OBLIGATIONS

A.	INTRODUCTION	5.1
B.	LIMITATIONS IMPOSED DURING THE RECRUITMENT PHASE	5.2
	1. Advertisements, Applications and Interviews	5.2
	2. Negligent Misrepresentation	5.5
C.	CONCLUSION	5.20

PART II: OBLIGATIONS ARISING FROM THE EMPLOYMENT RELATIONSHIP UNDER COMMON AND CIVIL LAW

A. EMPLOYER'S OBLIGATIONS

CHAPTER 6: PROVIDE THE WORK

		Para.
A.	INTRODUCTION	6.1
B.	TYPE OF WORK	6.3
C.	AUTHORITY AND RESPONSIBILITIES	6.15
D.	PLACE OF WORK	6.23
E.	DIRECTIVES AND ASSISTANCE	6.30
F.	RESPECT	6.35
G.	TOOLS, MATERIALS, EQUIPMENT AND SPACE	6.37
H.	HOURS OF WORK	6.40
I.	DURATION	6.42
	1. Fixed-Term Contract or Indeterminate Contract	6.42
	2. Term Contract — Automatic Renewal Clause	6.49
	3. Term Contract — Tacit Renewal	6.51
J.	CONCLUSION	6.55

CHAPTER 7: PROVIDE REMUNERATION

A.	INTRODUCTION	7.1
B.	REMUNERATION DEFINED	7.3
C.	MODIFICATION OF REMUNERATION	7.9
D.	COMPONENTS OF REMUNERATION	7.16
	1. Salary	7.16
	2. Salary Increases	7.22
	3. Vacation Pay and Statutory Holidays	7.25
	4. Advances	7.29
	5. Commissions	7.33
	6. Bonuses	7.39
	7. Profit Sharing	7.50
	8. Stock Purchase and Option Plans	7.52
	9. Retirement Benefits, Deferred Compensation, Life and Health Insurance Benefits	7.55
	10. Expatriate Allowance	7.61

Para.

11. Private Club Membership Fees. 7.62
12. Expense Accounts. 7.64
13. Company Cars. 7.65
14. Subsidized Housing and Loans 7.67

CHAPTER 8: SAFETY OF EXECUTIVES

A. CONTENT OF OBLIGATION. 8.1
B. LEGAL BASIS OF OBLIGATION 8.5
C. VICARIOUS LIABILITY. 8.7
D. STATUTORY OBLIGATION TO ENSURE SAFETY 8.11
   1. Employers 8.12
   2. Officers and Supervisors 8.14
   3. Employees 8.15
   4. Strict Liability Offence/Due Diligence Defence 8.18
E. SEXUAL HARASSMENT. 8.27
F. STATUTORY OBLIGATION TO PROTECT DIGNITY 8.43

B. EMPLOYEE'S OBLIGATIONS

CHAPTER 9: EXECUTE THE WORK

A. INTRODUCTION. 9.1
B. EXECUTIVE'S ROLE WITHIN THE EMPLOYER'S ORGANIZATION . . 9.4
C. COMPONENTS OF THE OBLIGATION TO EXECUTE THE WORK . . . 9.6
   1. Behavioural Component 9.10
      (a) Attitude. 9.10
      (b) Conduct. 9.14
      (c) Obedience to Directives 9.23
      (d) Personality Conflicts 9.38
   2. Physical Component. 9.41
      (a) Presence at Work. 9.41
      (b) Absenteeism. 9.45
      (c) Mental or Physical Incapacity 9.49
      (d) Substance Abuse 9.60
   3. Competence. 9.69

CHAPTER 10: LOYALTY

		Para.
A.	INTRODUCTION	10.1
B.	DISHONESTY	10.5
C.	DAMAGE TO EMPLOYER'S INTERESTS AND REPUTATION	10.13
D.	FIDUCIARY DUTY	10.22
	1. General	10.22
	2. The "Canaero" Decision	10.27
	3. Who Owes a Fiduciary Duty?	10.32
E.	TESTS FOR DETERMINING WHO OWES A FIDUCIARY DUTY	10.37
	1. Key Personnel Test	10.37
	2. Key Person in a Department Test	10.38
	3. Employer's Vulnerability as a Factor	10.39
	4. Length of Employment as a Factor	10.45
	5. Lower-Level Employees: Fiduciary Breach by Association	10.46
	6. Contract	10.47
F.	THE POSITION OF INDEPENDENT CONTRACTORS	10.50
G.	FIDUCIARY OBLIGATIONS DURING EMPLOYMENT	10.54
	1. Conflict of Interest	10.55
	2. Whistle-Blowing	10.70
	3. Obligation to Report Fellow Employees' Harmful or Disloyal Conduct	10.76
	4. Obligation to Account	10.81
	5. Fiduciary Obligations After Termination of Employment	10.85
	(a) The "Canaero" Decision	10.85
	(b) Post-Employment Competition	10.94
H.	DUTY OF CONFIDENTIALITY	10.106
	1. Types of Information	10.108
	(a) Information of a Trivial Nature	10.109
	(b) Limited Confidential Information	10.110
	(c) Trade Secrets	10.112
	(i) Characteristics of a Trade Secret	10.114
	2. The Springboard Theory	10.116
I.	PATENTS AND OTHER INTELLECTUAL PROPERTY RIGHTS	10.120
	1. Assignment Contracts	10.125
	2. Validity of Inventions	10.129
J.	COPYRIGHTS	10.130
K.	INDUSTRIAL DESIGN ACT	10.140
L.	INTEGRATED CIRCUIT TOPOGRAPHY ACT	10.143
M.	PUBLIC SERVANTS INVENTIONS ACT	10.145

CHAPTER 11: THE WRITTEN EMPLOYMENT CONTRACT AND SOME SPECIFIC PROVISIONS

		Para.
A.	INTRODUCTION	11.1
	1. Common Law	11.3
	2. Civil Law	11.5
	3. Illegal, Void or Unenforceable Clauses	11.7
	(a) Severability	11.8
	(b) Independent Legal Advice	11.9
B.	DEFINING THE EXECUTIVE'S POSITION	11.11
C.	DURATION PROVISIONS	11.12
D.	PLACE OF WORK	11.14
E.	NON-COMPETITION	11.16
	1. Civil Law	11.17
	2. Common Law	11.18
	3. Reasonableness	11.19
	(a) Duration	11.22
	(b) Territory	11.25
	(c) Nature of the Prohibited Activities	11.27
	4. Onus of Proving the Covenant Unreasonable	11.31
F.	NON-SOLICITATION OF CLIENTS	11.35
G.	NON-SOLICITATION OF EMPLOYEES	11.41
H.	CONFIDENTIALITY PROVISIONS	11.42
H.1	SURVIVAL OF COVENANT UPON TERMINATION OF EMPLOYMENT	11.45.1
I.	REMEDIES FOR BREACH	11.46
	1. Injunction	11.46
	2. Breach of Contract	11.47
	3. "Liquidated Damages" Clause	11.48
	4. Rights to Relief	11.49
J.	REMUNERATION AND BENEFIT CLAUSES	11.51
K.	NOTICE OF TERMINATION AND SEVERANCE PAYMENT	11.55
	1. Scope of Contract	11.55
	2. Contracting out of Notice Requirements	11.57
	3. Monetary Indemnity in lieu of Notice	11.58
	4. Obligation to Mitigate Damages	11.61
	5. Termination Payment	11.63
L.	EXECUTIVE PROTECTION FROM CHANGE IN CONTROL	11.67
	1. Elements of a Golden Parachute Agreement	11.69
	(a) Change in Control	11.70
	(b) Loss of Employment or Resignation for Good Reason	11.72

Para.

2. Advantages and Criticism of Golden Parachute
   Agreements 11.75
   (a) Advantages 11.75
   (b) Criticism. 11.80
3. Golden Parachute Compensation 11.81
   (a) Business Judgment Rule 11.82
   (b) Fiduciary Duty 11.83
   (c) Enforceability and Validity of a Golden Parachute
       Clause. 11.87
   (d) Taxing Provisions. 11.88
       (i)   In the United States 11.88
       (ii) In Canada. 11.90
   (e) Surviving Judicial Scrutiny. 11.91
       (i)   Timing 11.92
       (ii) Origin of Proposal 11.93
       (iii) Relationship to the Services Performed 11.94
       (iv) Employee Obligation to Search for Alternative
             Employment 11.95
       (v)   Summary 11.96
M. ARBITRATION PROVISIONS 11.97

PART III: TERMINATION OF THE EMPLOYMENT RELATIONSHIP

CHAPTER 12: TERMINATION OF EMPLOYMENT

A. INTRODUCTION 12.1
B. TERMINATION UPON THE OCCURRENCE OF AN EVENT 12.2
   1. Expiry of Term. 12.2
   2. Frustration/Impossibility of Performance 12.3
      (a) Illness 12.4
      (b) Fortuitous Event and Financial Difficulties 12.5
      (c) Change of Employer 12.8
      (d) Death 12.11
C. REPUDIATION BY THE EXECUTIVE 12.13
   1. Resignation. 12.13
   2. Constructive Resignation. 12.19
D. REPUDIATION BY THE EMPLOYER. 12.21
   1. Dismissal. 12.21
      (a) Dismissal for Cause 12.22

		Para.
(i)	Theft, Fraud or Dishonesty	12.29
(ii)	Insubordination	12.32
(iii)	Intoxication	12.33
(iv)	Breach of Company Rules or Policies	12.34
(v)	Incompetence	12.35
(vi)	Disloyalty	12.36
(vii)	Other Causes	12.38
(viii)	Condonation	12.39
(b)	Dismissal Without Cause	12.41
(i)	Fixed-Term Contract	12.41
(ii)	Contract of Indeterminate Duration	12.42
(iii)	Establishing Reasonable Notice of Termination	12.43
(1)	Position	12.46
(2)	Age	12.48
(3)	Induced to Leave Stable Employment	12.49
(4)	Finding Similar Employment	12.52
(5)	Length of Service	12.59
(6)	Other Factors	12.61
(7)	"Ball Park" Doctrine	12.68
(iv)	Statutory Limitations on the Right to Dismiss Without Cause	12.69.1
2.	Constructive Dismissal	12.70
(a)	Remuneration and Benefits	12.74
(b)	Duties and Responsibilities	12.77
(c)	Status	12.83
(d)	Geographical Transfer	12.85
(e)	Employer Conduct	12.91

CHAPTER 13: DAMAGES AWARDED FOR WRONGFUL DISMISSAL

A.	INTRODUCTION	13.1
B.	LENGTH OF NOTICE PERIOD	13.2
1.	The Fixed-Term Employment Contract	13.4
2.	The Indeterminate Employment Contract	13.6
C.	HEADS OF DAMAGES	13.8
1.	Salary	13.12
2.	Increase in Salary	13.14
3.	Commissions	13.17
4.	Bonuses and Profit Sharing	13.20

		Para.
5.	Pensions.	13.26
6.	Insurance and Medical Plans and Other Marginal Benefits	13.31
7.	Club Membership Fees, Company Car or Car Allowance	13.36
8.	Moving Expenses and Other Expenses Incurred in Searching for Alternative Employment	13.39
9.	Vacation Pay	13.44
10.	Expense Accounts	13.45
11.	Severance Pay / Termination Pay	13.46
12.	Share Option Plans and Share Purchase Plans	13.51
13.	Director's Fees	13.54
14.	Income Tax Deduction Benefits.	13.55
15.	Other Claims	13.56

CHAPTER 14: AGGRAVATED/MORAL AND PUNITIVE/EXEMPLARY DAMAGES

A.	INTRODUCTION	14.1
B.	LEGAL BASIS OF THE AWARD	14.6
C.	HUMILIATION	14.21
D.	ANXIETY AND MENTAL DISTRESS	14.24
E.	LOSS OF REPUTATION	14.29
F.	REFERENCES AND OTHER VERBAL OR WRITTEN COMMUNICATIONS REGARDING A TERMINATED EMPLOYEE	14.35
G.	PUNITIVE AND EXEMPLARY DAMAGES	14.37

CHAPTER 15: EMPLOYER RECOURSES FOR BREACH OF CONTRACT BY EXECUTIVES

A.	INTRODUCTION	15.1
B.	DAMAGES FOR AN EXECUTIVE'S PREMATURE RESIGNATION	15.3
C.	NULLITY OF THE EMPLOYMENT CONTRACT	15.15
D.	EXECUTIVE LIABILITY IN TORT	15.17
E.	PROFITS AND EXPENSES WRONGFULLY ACQUIRED	15.20

CHAPTER 16: OTHER ISSUES CONCERNING WRONGFUL TERMINATION AND DAMAGE AWARDS

		Para.
A.	NEAR CAUSE/CONTRIBUTORY FAULT	16.1
B.	BUSINESS EXPENSES PERSONALLY INCURRED IN EARNING REMUNERATION	16.7
C.	MITIGATION	16.9
	1. Nature of the Obligation	16.9
	2. Alternative Employment	16.20
	3. Geographic Area of Search	16.30
	4. Starting a Business (Self-Employment)	16.36
	5. Termination Provision	16.44
	6. Anticipated Mitigation	16.44.2
D.	PENSION, DISABILITY OR UNEMPLOYMENT BENEFITS RECEIVED DURING THE NOTICE PERIOD	16.45
	1. Pension Benefits	16.45
	2. Disability Benefits	16.52
	3. Employment Insurance	16.54
E.	TERMINATION PACKAGES AND RELEASE AND DISCHARGE TRANSACTIONS	16.58
F.	PERSONAL LIABILITY OF THE PERSON WHO TERMINATES	16.69

PART IV: OTHER EXECUTIVE EMPLOYMENT-RELATED STATUTES

CHAPTER 17: IMMIGRATION AND EMPLOYMENT

A.	INTRODUCTION	17.1
B.	RESPONSIBILITIES OF THE CANADIAN EMPLOYER	17.5
C.	COMING TO CANADA	17.10
	1. Visitor or Immigrant?	17.12
	2. Visa Requirements	17.16
	3. Admissibility	17.19
	4. Passport Requirements	17.22
D.	EMPLOYMENT	17.23
	1. What is "Employment"?	17.24
	2. The Employment Authorization Requirement	17.27
	3. Selected Exceptions to the Employment Authorization Requirement	17.30

			Para.
4.	The Validation Requirement		17.34
5.	Selected Exceptions to the Validation Requirement		17.38
	(a) Intra-Company Transferees		17.39
		(i) The Intra-Company Transferee under the FTA	17.41
		(ii) The E-15	17.45
	(b) Professional Category		17.48
E.	PERMANENT RESIDENCE IN CANADA		17.51
	1. An Overview		17.51
	2. The Province of Quebec		17.56
	3. Family Class		17.58
	4. Independent Applicants		17.60
		(a) Entrepreneurs	17.63
		(b) Investors	17.66
			(i) Privately Administered Investment Syndicate	17.70
			(ii) Government-Administered Venture Capital Fund	17.71
			(iii) Quebec	17.72
		(c) Persons with Arranged Employment in Canada	17.73
F.	MAINTAINING PERMANENT RESIDENCE IN CANADA		17.76

CHAPTER 18: TAX CONSIDERATIONS

A.	TAX PLANNING AND THE EMPLOYMENT CONTRACT	18.1
B.	THE TAXPAYER	18.5
	1. Employee or Independent Contractor?	18.7
	(a) Common Law Jurisdictions	18.11
	(b) Quebec	18.13
	(c) Contractual Implications	18.14
	2. Personal Services Corporations	18.16
C.	SITUS OF EMPLOYMENT	18.25
D.	PLACE OF RESIDENCE	18.29
	1. The Domestic Rules of Residency	18.34
	2. International Tax Treaties	18.39
E.	THE TAXATION OF EMPLOYMENT INCOME	18.42
	1. Salary, Wages and Other Remuneration	18.43
	(a) The Basic Inclusion Rules	18.43
	(b) Timing of Income Inclusion	18.47
	(c) Indirect Payments	18.50
	2. Employment Benefits	18.51
	(a) Automobiles	18.58
	(b) Aircraft	18.63

Para.

    (c) Club Memberships 18.64
    (d) Legal Services Plans 18.66
    (e) Child Care................................... 18.67
    (f) Employer-Paid Vacations...................... 18.68
    (g) Sickness or Accident Benefits and Disability
        Income Benefits 18.70
    (h) Insurance Premiums 18.71
    (i) Sales for Less than Fair Market Value 18.73
    (j) Loans and Advances.......................... 18.74
    (k) Retirement Plans 18.79
    (l) Private Health Services Plans 18.80
    (m) Supplementary Unemployment Benefit Plans 18.83
    (n) Health and Welfare Trusts..................... 18.84
    (o) Flexible Benefit Plans 18.87
    (p) Counselling Services.......................... 18.91
    (q) Relocation Expenses 18.93
    (r) Reimbursement of Employment-Related Costs 18.97
  3.   Allowances.................................... 18.102
  4.   Directors' Fees 18.104
  5.   Employees' Profit Sharing Plans 18.105
  6.   Deferred Compensation.......................... 18.108
F. THE EMPLOYEE AS A SHAREHOLDER OR QUASI-SHAREHOLDER. 18.115
  1.   Stock Option Plans 18.120
  2.   Stock Purchase Plans 18.125
  3.   Phantom Stock Plans 18.126
  4.   Share Appreciation Rights........................ 18.131
G. TERMINATING EMPLOYMENT 18.132
H. DEPARTING FROM CANADA 18.136
I. ENTERING CANADA 18.141
J. WITHHOLDING AND CONTRIBUTION OBLIGATIONS 18.144

CHAPTER 19: RETIREMENT INCOME PROVISIONS

A. INTRODUCTION... 19.1
B. TAX-SHELTERED RETIREMENT SAVINGS VEHICLES 19.3
  1.   Registered Retirement Savings Plan 19.7
    (a) Individual RRSP............................. 19.7
    (b) Group RRSP 19.10
    (c) Creditor Protection 19.13
  2.   Registered Pension Plan.......................... 19.15
    (a) Standard Plan.............................. 19.18

Para.

      (i)   Contribution Limits 19.18

      (ii) Enrolment 19.22

      (iii) Vesting and Locking-in 19.23

      (iv) Portability 19.25

      (v) Residual Surplus Entitlement upon

           Termination 19.26

   (b) Individual Plan 19.28

  3. Deferred Profit Sharing Plan 19.33

C. SUPPLEMENTARY EXECUTIVE RETIREMENT PLANS. 19.35

  1. Retirement Compensation Arrangement 19.38

  2. Secular Trust 19.42

  3. Unfunded Retirement Income Arrangement 19.44

D. RETIREMENT COUNSELLING SERVICES 19.50

E. POST-RETIREMENT INSURANCE COVERAGE 19.52

CHAPTER 20: DUTIES AND LIABILITIES OF CORPORATE DIRECTORS AND OFFICERS

GENERAL PRINCIPLES

A. INTRODUCTION 20.1

B. DIRECTORS AND OFFICERS 20.11

  1. Directors 20.11

    (a) The Concept 20.11

    (b) Independent Directors and Liability 20.17

  2. Officers 20.20

C. LEGAL DUTIES OF DIRECTORS AND OFFICERS. 20.25

  1. Framework 20.25

  2. Duty to Exercise Care, Diligence and Skill 20.29

    (a) General Nature 20.29

    (b) Standards of Care, Diligence and Skill 20.31

  3. Duty of Fairness to Shareholders, Creditors and Others 20.36

  4. Fiduciary Duties of Directors and Senior Officers 20.39

    (a) Conflicts of Duty and Interest 20.43

    (b) Misappropriating Corporate Opportunities 20.47

CIVIL LIABILITY RELATED TO EMPLOYMENT LAW

A. INTRODUCTION 20.50

B. LIABILITY TOWARDS EMPLOYEES. 20.51

  1. Directors' Liability for Wages 20.51

    (a) The Debtor 20.53

    (b) The Creditors 20.60

    (c) The Nature of the Debts 20.67

       (i)   What Can Be Claimed 20.67

Para.

(ii) What Cannot Be Claimed 20.77
(iii) A Special Case: Executive Termination and
"Golden Parachutes" 20.79
(iv) Alternate Liability 20.93
(v) Joint and Several Liability 20.95
(vi) Statutory Limitation Periods 20.96
2. Liability for Wrongful Dismissal 20.100
3. Liability for Inducement to Breach a Contract......... 20.103
4. New Legislation 20.106
C. LIABILITY TO OTHER CONSTITUENCIES.................... 20.108
1. General Rules.................................... 20.109
2. Liability for Excessive Executive Compensation....... 20.114
D. STATUTORY LIABILITIES 20.138
1. Income and Other Tax Legislation.................. 20.139
2. Employment Insurance 20.149
3. Statutory Health Insurance 20.150
4. Pension Plans................................... 20.154
5. Other Common Law Liabilities 20.156
PENAL AND CRIMINAL LIABILITIES AND EMPLOYMENT
A. INTRODUCTION....................................... 20.160
B. PERSONS AT RISK 20.163
C. AREAS OF RISK 20.167
1. Discrimination.................................. 20.167
2. Immigration..................................... 20.168
3. Occupational Health............................. 20.169
4. Competition Law 20.172
5. Environmental Law 20.175
(a) The Importance of Environmental Law........... 20.175
(b) The Prohibitions.............................. 20.178
(c) The Implementation of Policies Respecting
Environmental Law.......................... 20.184
D. DEFENCES 20.192
1. General Principles............................... 20.192
2. A Practical Case: Due Diligence in Environmental Law .. 20.197
E. CRIMINAL CODE LIABILITY 20.205
1. Introduction.................................... 20.205
2. Aiding and Abetting a Criminal Offence 20.207
3. Secret Commissions 20.209
4. Manipulation of Stock Exchange Transactions 20.212
5. Affecting the Public Market 20.213
6. False Prospectus, Statement or Account or False
Statement Concerning Financial Status.............. 20.214
7. Fraud.. 20.217

		Para.
8.	Criminal Liability for Theft	20.218
9.	Criminal Liability in Gaming in Stocks or Merchandise	20.220
10.	Criminal Liability for Forging Trademarks	20.221
11.	Criminal Liability Concerning Trade Unions	20.222
12.	Falsification of Books and Documents	20.223

CHAPTER 21: LIABILITY OF SENIOR EXECUTIVES UNDER SECURITIES LEGISLATION

A.	INTRODUCTION		21.1
B.	POTENTIAL LIABILITY ARISING FROM ISSUER'S DISCLOSURE OBLIGATIONS		21.6
	1.	Civil Liability	21.6
		(a) Failure to Deliver a Prospectus or a Bid Circular	21.6
		(b) Securities Transactions Effected with Documents Containing a Misrepresentation	21.15
	2.	Statutory Offences	21.35
	3.	Criminal Liability	21.50
C.	USE OF PRIVILEGED INFORMATION		21.53
	1.	Liability	21.70
		(a) Civil Liability	21.70
		(b) Statutory Offences	21.74
	2.	Defences	21.76
	3.	Damages and Fines	21.93
		(a) Damages	21.93
		(b) Fines	21.99
	4.	Statutory Limitation Periods	21.103

CHAPTER 22: DEFENSIVE STRATEGIES

A.	INTRODUCTION	22.1
B.	UNANIMOUS SHAREHOLDER AGREEMENT	22.2
C.	INDEMNIFICATION	22.5
D.	INSURANCE	22.16
E.	RELIANCE ON EXPERTS	22.20
F.	DILIGENCE	22.23
G.	CONCLUSION	22.31

TABLE OF CONTENTS

CHAPTER 23: CORPORATE GOVERNANCE

		Para.
A.	GENERAL PRINCIPLES	23.1
B.	THE TSE COMMITTEE ON CORPORATE GOVERNANCE	23.4
C.	PRACTICAL ADVICE	23.12
D.	CONCLUSION	23.15

INDEX

PART I
INTRODUCTION

CHAPTER 1

AN OVERVIEW*

A. INTRODUCTION

§1.1 With the industrialization of most western societies, employment has become one of the most important social relationships for a majority of Canadians. This was eloquently stated by Chief Justice Dickson of the Supreme Court of Canada:

> Work is one of the most fundamental aspects in a person's life, providing the individual with a means of financial support and, as importantly, a contributory role in society. A person's employment is an essential component of his or her sense of identity, self-worth and emotional well-being.[1]

As the ranks of employees have swollen, especially in larger business organizations, the influence of executives upon such employees and our citizenry as a whole has increased. Few members of modern-day society, with the exception of the highest ranks of government, exercise as much power and influence as the corporate executives who control corporations:

> To speak of the powers of a corporation is to speak in reality of the powers of a handful of corporate executives who exercise an ever-increasing influence on modern society through the means put at their disposal by the corporation.[2]

[1] *Reference re Public Service Employee Relations Act (Alta.)*, [1987] 1 S.C.R. 313, at 368.
[2] James A. Smith, *Corporate Executives in Quebec* (Montreal: Centre d'Édition Juridique, 1978), p. 19.

§1.2 Few experts would contest the fact that the directors of many public corporations have seen significant portions of their power pass on to their executives.[1] This work discusses the legal rights and obligations of executives of publicly held corporations in which no one person holds a controlling interest, as well as executives who are controlling shareholders of corporations.

[1] James M. Gillies, *Boardroom Renaissance: Power, Morality and Performance in the Modern Corporation* (Toronto: McGraw-Hill Ryerson, 1992).

---

* The authors wish to thank George Sopel, student-at-law, for his valuable contribution to this chapter.

§1.3 In the late 1980s and early 1990s, there was a re-evaluation of the role and responsibility of those who have traditionally been set apart from the "labouring" class, *i.e.* those who are entrusted with the senior management of our business institutions: the corporate *executives*. While some statutory law has focused on the duties of directors and, to a lesser extent, officers, the thrust of this introductory chapter is to demonstrate how relatively little attention has been paid to executives in the civil and common law. As Professor Bruce Welling recently noted, "the other half of corporate management is legally under-analyzed; the officers of a typical corporation are by far the more important group in the business world."[1] With an increasing awareness of the impact felt by society as a result of the unrestrained behaviour of executives, as well as an understanding of the freedom of movement required to compete in an increasingly competitive marketplace, the law and its interpretation have expanded and, to a certain extent, clarified the role and responsibilities of the corporate executive.

[1] Bruce L. Welling, *Corporate Law in Canada*, 2nd ed. (Toronto: Butterworths, 1991), p. 300.

§1.4 Many have contended that the harsh times we are experiencing are, to some extent, due to the way in which corporations have been run by executives. As early as 1932, Adolf A. Berle and Gardiner C. Means, in their seminal study *The Modern Corporation and Private Property*,[1] set forth the following warning to shareholders: The dispersion of ownership evinced in the corporation of the 20th century would have the inevitable effect of placing ultimate power over the affairs of the company into the hands of the board of directors, if not into the hands of the officers themselves. By the 1980s, it was clear that executives as a whole (as opposed to directors) had claimed a virtual stranglehold over control of some of the most important corporations in North America — with predictable (and certain unpredictable) results.

[1] (New York: Harcourt, Brace, Jovanovich, 1968).

§1.5 Law is not a static, immutable entity. It continually evolves. A full understanding of the dynamics of such a system requires at least a summary review of legal history. The aim of this introductory chapter is thus to explain briefly the origins of the notion of *employment*, both in its general sense and in so far as such a term may be applied to the senior executive. In order to do this, we will first review the origins of employment relations in Europe. This analysis will reveal the ways in which the work relationships in these early civilizations were later integrated into the systems of civil and common law in their respective territories. This should encourage a coherent understanding of the evolution of the laws governing executive employment as they currently exist in reference to the laws of Canada's three most populous provinces: Ontario, Quebec and British Columbia.

§1.6 In a sole proprietorship, there may be a single executive responsible for all corporate decision-making as well as the more mundane administrative tasks. In a larger corporation, there may be several executives with different degrees of responsibility and decision-making power with respect to the company.

§1.7 Of course, an executive's principal objective is to enhance shareholder value, but in doing so he or she is subject to many other obligations. This work aims at defining the various components of the executive employment contract including the rights and obligations of each of the parties to the employment contract under civil and common law. It also examines those other statutory aspects which may be of particular concern to executives. This book will deal with the executive's right to work in light of immigration law and the consequences of tax law and pensions law for the executive. As well, for executives who are officers and directors, their obligations under corporate and securities legislation are discussed. Where appropriate, we will emphasize how the executive's employment contract may differ from that of a non-executive employee's employment contract.

§1.8 For the purposes of this work, we have used the term "executive" in its broadest sense in the context of employment. The executive is the employee whose position, when considered in respect of the overall organization in which he or she functions, carries with it the right of independent action, autonomy and discretion, including the power to direct or administer something.[1] An executive may or may not be an officer or director of a corporation. Where an executive is an employee and holds an office, certain obligations may overlap or emanate from legal sources other than the employment contract. Conversely, a director or officer is not necessarily an employee. What characterizes the executive is the authority to decide certain issues, even though this autonomy may not be absolute, as in cases where the executive is subordinate to a board of directors.

---

[1] *Lee-Shanok v. Banca Nazionale del Lavoro of Canada Ltd.*, [1987] 3 F.C. 578 (C.A.).

B. FOUNDATIONS OF THE EMPLOYMENT CONTRACT

1. The Notion of "Employment"

§1.9 In the civil law of Quebec, the notion of "employment" is defined in article 2085 of the Civil Code of Quebec:

> A contract of employment is a contract by which a person, the employee, undertakes for a limited period to do work for remuneration, according to the instructions and under the direction or control of another person, the employer.[1]

Thus, three requirements exist for the formation of a contract of employment:

(1) An individual must work for another;
(2) He or she must receive remuneration; and
(3) The individual must be subordinate to the employer.[2]

---

[1] *Civil Code of Quebec*, 1991, c. 64 (Bill 125), (hereafter "C.C.Q."), replacing the *Civil Code of Lower Canada*, Que. 1866, as amended (hereafter "C.C.L.C.").

[2] A. Edward Aust and Lyse Charette, *The Employment Contract* (Cowansville: Éditions Yvon Blais, 1993, 2nd ed.), pp. 17 *et seq.* See also *Van Alstyne v. Rankin*, [1952] C.S. 12 (Que. S.C.), at 15, cited in Aust and Charette, at 27.

§1.10 The first two conditions are, for the most part, self-evident. The third element in the employment relationship, however, remains the most crucial when analyzing the status of the corporate executive. An executive who has employment status is, as a matter of law, subordinate to the board of directors which appointed him or her to this position. In practice, however, the activities of a high-ranking executive often seem to fall beyond the scrutiny of the board. Likewise, when the executive functions as a member of the board, his or her authority has an even greater propensity to remain unchecked.

§1.11 In any case, the jurisprudence in Quebec courts has made it clear that:

> A chairman of the board, a president of a corporation or in fact any of its officers or employees all stand in the same relative position with regard to their *employment* by a corporation.[1]

---

[1] *Van Alstyne v. Rankin*, [1952] C.S. 12 (Que. S.C.), at 15 (emphasis added).

§1.12 To understand the nature of the obligation an executive may have in civil law, it is necessary to refer to article 1434 of the Civil Code of Quebec:

> A contract validly formed binds the parties who have entered into it not only as to what they have expressed in it but also as to what is incident to it according to its nature and in conformity with usage, equity or law.[1]

Indeed, it may be argued that this article of the Code is the foundation on which lies every contract of employment in the civil law. In order, then, to appreciate the peculiarities of the employment relationships between executives and their companies, it will be necessary to understand the source of these obligations. This understanding will allow us to derive the *implicit*, as well as explicit, obligations of the corporate executive today.[2]

[1] A similar provision existed at CCLC, art. 1024.
[2] See chapter 4, "The Nature of Employment, The Employer and the Employee".

§1.13 In the following section, we will take a brief look at the historical developments in law and society which have helped to shape the current law of employment.

2. Origins: Rome

§1.14 Any historical review of the law of contract inevitably leads us back to the laws of Rome — the foundation of our civil law — and much of our common law. Our knowledge of the employment relationship in regard to these times of antiquity is rather sketchy. The reason is quite simple. In Rome, contracts of lease and hire of services were just that: what was hired by the "employer" (*locator*) was not so much the "manpower" of any particular citizen, but rather, that person's expertise, his skill in a particular craft. This type of hiring resembles what we have come to know in the civil law today as the "contract of enterprise":

> As opposed to the employment contract, the contract of enterprise is characterized by the debtor's autonomy in the realization of an obligation of result.[1]

This was the case, for instance, when a blacksmith was commissioned to perform work upon a metal, or where landscapers or architects were hired to perform work upon an estate. This is similar to the status of professionals today, such as doctors or notaries. These professionals are not usually considered employees and are, therefore, not always governed by the ordinary rules of employment contracts.[2]

[1]   Comité, *R.D.* Titre Immobiliers — Doctrine — Doc. 1, numéro 38; cited in *Dictionnaire de droit privé* (Cowansville: Éditions Yvon Blais, 1991), p. 134 (translation).

[2]   *Cf. Lapointe v. Hôpital Le Gardeur*, [1992] 1 S.C.R. 382.

§1.15 In Rome, the practice of "hiring" another person for a fixed period of time was not common. Slaves were often used for domestic work; artisans benefited from the assistance of apprentices. Instances of the actual subordination of one Roman to another for a lengthy period of work were rare. Indeed, this was antithetical to the ancient notion of citizenship. The emperor Justinian provides a short section in his *Institutes* governing the "hire of services" (*locatio operarum*) under the Book of *Obligations*:

> *Locatio conductio operarum* was where one party (*locator*) let out his services to the other (*conductor*) in return for a money payment. The services so let could only be *operae illiberales*, and therefore advocates and physicians, surveyors, professors of law, and other skilled professional men could not conclude this contract.[1]

[1]   R.W. Leage, *Roman Private Law* (London: MacMillan, 1932), p. 331.

§1.16 This lease of services (*locatio operarum*) differed very little from the lease and hire of a thing:

> The contract of letting on hire approaches very nearly to that of sale, and is governed by the same rules of law.
> Contracts of sale and contracts of letting on hire are so nearly connected, that in some cases it is questioned whether the contract is one or the other.[1]

With such little recognition of the status of an "employee" in Roman law, it stands to reason that such a relationship was not highly regarded in theory, and occurred infrequently in practice.

[1]   Justinian, *Institutes*, Bk. III, Title XXIV (Sandars ed.).

3. History of Employment in Europe

§1.17 The true birth of the employment contract, it may be argued, can be traced to the early Renaissance.[1] The plagues of the 14th century which reduced the available manpower in France fostered a need to re-evaluate and formalize the relationship between those who co-ordinated or delegated work (be they artisans, petit bourgeois, etc.) and those who performed the work. This formalization of the status of employee was not made for the benefit of the worker but rather to facilitate the *employer's* burden of obtaining sufficient labourers to suit his needs.[2]

[1] *Cf.* Maurice Bouvier-Ajam, *Histoire du travail en France* (Paris: Librairie générale de droit et de jurisprudence, 1981), p. 108. This book is particularly noteworthy for its comprehensive and splendid exposition of the history and influence of the work relationship on French civilization.

[2] *Cf.* Maurice Bouvier-Ajam, *Histoire du travail en France* (Paris: Librairie générale de droit et de jurisprudence, 1981) at 328 *et seq.*

§1.18 The advent of the medieval "corporation" helped to fashion a more formal relationship between employer and employee which resembles the "contract of enterprise." A worker is given a mandate to execute a specific task and has ultimate discretion to decide how the task will be executed.[1]

[1] Maurice Bouvier-Ajam, *Histoire du travail en France* (Paris: Librairie générale de droit et de jurisprudence, 1981), pp. 231 et seq.

§1.19 The modern conception of employment finds its true start with the beginnings of the first companies and the rise of large-scale private enterprise.

C.   DEFINING AND REDEFINING THE ROLE AND RESPONSIBILITIES OF THE CORPORATE EXECUTIVE

1.   From Colonization to Economic Liberalism: The Emergence of the Joint-Stock Company

§1.20 The notion of *compagnie* may be traced back to the earliest history of Canada as business ventures emanating from Europe were chiefly responsible for the settling of New France.[1] These companies were given access and monopolies to certain areas of commerce in New France in exchange for promising to colonize the areas where their trade took place.[2] Although some groupings of entrepreneurs had existed before these corporations made their way into the Canadian territory,[3] it was the few incorporated associations that paved the way for later company law in the colony. The following question is thus raised: Who actually controlled and/or managed these associations?

[1] "Famous names like *La Compagnie des Cent Associés* (1627), *La Compagnie des Habitants de la Nouvelle France* (1645), *La Compagnie du Canada* (1700), *La Compagnie d'Occident ou des Indes* (1717), are linked with the expansion of the French colony": James A. Smith, *Corporate Executives in Quebec* (Montreal: Centre d'Édition Juridique, 1978), p. 4.

² *La Compagnie des Cent Associés* (1627), *La Compagnie des Habitants de la Nouvelle France* (1645), *La Compagnie du Canada* (1700), *La Compagnie d'Occident ou des Indes* (1717). James A. Smith, *Corporate Executives in Quebec* (Montreal: Centre d'Édition Juridique, 1978), p. 4.

³ Fishermen, especially. See E.E. Palmer, "Directors' Powers and Duties", in *Studies in Canadian Company Law*, Jacob S. Ziegel, ed. (Toronto: Butterworths, 1967), p. 365.

2. Management in the Early Canadian Company

§1.21 The status of corporate officers in the civil law of Quebec may be traced back to the founding companies of New France.

§1.22 Whereas most commercial groupings which emanated from France were not recognized in law as such — that is, they benefited from no independent juridical personality beyond that of their controlling partners — the first few actual corporations (those recognized by Royal Charter) held many rights and powers by virtue of their privileged status, as conferred on them by the king.

§1.23 It was only in the mid-19th century that the company in Canada took on the look of the British and American "joint-stock" companies.[1] Until then, even chartered companies operated much like partnerships.

¹ On the history of the joint-stock company, see the following texts: John P. Davis, *Corporations* (New York: Burt Franklin, 1971); Ronald Ralph Formoy, *The Historical Foundations of Modern Company Law* (London: Sweet & Maxwell, 1923); William Robert Scott, *The Constitution and Finance of English, Scottish, and Irish Joint-Stock Companies to 1720* (Gloucester: Cambridge University Press, 1968); Shaw Livermore, *Early American Land Companies* (New York: The Commonwealth Fund, 1939); A.B. Levy, *Private Corporations and their Control* (London: Routledge & Kegan Paul Ltd., 1950); H.P. Biggar, *The Early Trading Companies of New France* (St. Clair Shores: Scholarly, 1977).

§1.24 The managers of such joint-stock companies were always associates, holding more stock in the company than most of the other shareholders.[1] In fact, when directors were chosen from outside the ranks of the company, they were immediately given shares.[2] Thus, even when such a manager was given an honorarium — as was usually the case[3] — he was generally entrusted with a mandate (to serve as the acting organ of all partners) rather than being considered a strict "servant" of the company.[4] In the presence of this active role in the affairs of the company — that is, serving not merely as manager, but as partner as well — these early officers clearly escape the view we have today of an employee. Early corporate managers may be thus characterized juridically as mandataries.

[1] Henri Lévy-Bruhl, *Histoire juridique des sociétés de commerce en France aux XVIIe et XVIIIe siècles* (Paris: Éditions Domat-Montchrestien, 1938), p. 207.

[2] Henri Lévy-Bruhl, *Histoire juridique des sociétés de commerce en France aux XVIIe et XVIIIe siècles* (Paris: Éditions Domat-Montchrestien, 1938), at 205.

[3] Henri Lévy-Bruhl, *Histoire juridique des sociétés de commerce en France aux XVIIe et XVIIIe siècles* (Paris: Éditions Domat-Montchrestien, 1938), at 206.

[4] *Cf.* the example of the Buanderie du Pont de Sèvres, whose "administrateur-directeur" was given the duty "d'être le *représentant* du comité d'administration, de faire exécuter les décisions de l'assemblée générale et du comité, de surveiller l'entreprise, de diriger la correspondance ainsi que la comptabilité": Henri Lévy-Bruhl, *Histoire juridique des sociétés de commerce en France aux XVIIe et XVIIIe siècles* (Paris: Éditions Domat-Montchrestien, 1938), at 207.

§1.25 It was often difficult to discern between a shareholders' meeting and a managers' meeting since these positions were frequently held by the same people. "[Especially] in small businesses comprised of a small number of shareholders, these two functions were merged."[1] Over and above these functions, the title of corporate administrator (*"administrateur-directeur"*) entailed many privileges for its beneficiary. Sometimes, the director was appointed to his office for life.[2] In addition, directors were often granted the *"droit de bourgeoisie"* and, on occasion, even noble status by a monarchy which saw in the companies a virtually costless means of expanding an empire and garnering great sums of wealth in a most expedient way.

[1] Henri Lévy-Bruhl, *Histoire juridique des sociétés de commerce en France aux XVIIe et XVIIIe siècles* (Paris: Éditions Domat-Montchrestien, 1938), p. 192 (translation).

[2] Henri Lévy-Bruhl, *Histoire juridique des sociétés de commerce en France aux XVIIe et XVIIIe siècles* (Paris: Éditions Domat-Montchrestien, 1938), at 206.

§1.26 All disputes of a private nature which might have arisen between partners were to be settled by an administrative tribunal, whose members were to have been chosen by the partners in dispute.[1] The role of the King's Court extended, at most, to the nomination of a head arbitrator to intercede in situations where the members of the tribunal could not agree to a conclusion, or where one party refused to appoint an administrator on its own.[2] Since the manager of a company was invariably also a partner, any contentions between him and the company would have been resolved by arbitration as well. This, in part, could serve to explain the absence of jurisprudence regarding the relationship between the directors and companies in this period of history.

[1] Henri Lévy-Bruhl, *Histoire juridique des sociétés de commerce en France aux XVIIe et XVIIIe siècles* (Paris: Éditions Domat-Montchrestien, 1938), p. 274.

[2] Henri Lévy-Bruhl, *Histoire juridique des sociétés de commerce en France aux XVIIe et XVIIIe siècles* (Paris: Éditions Domat-Montchrestien, 1938), p. 274.

3. The Evolution of the Corporate Manager in Limited Liability Joint-Stock Companies

§1.27 The limited liability joint-stock company[1] was slow to emerge in France and its colonies. Both in practice and as a juridical entity, this type of commercial association was virtually non-existent in French-dominated areas prior to the late 19th century. The leading powers were hesitant to grant the exceptional statutory recognition which was required,[2] preferring the partnership, which allowed for a greater degree of state supervision and control than did the joint-stock company ("société en commondite" or "société anonyme").

> [1] On the development of limited liability, see Bishop Carleton Hunt, *The Development of the Business Corporation in England, 1800-1867* (New York: Russell & Russell, 1969), pp. 116-44; Ronald Ralph Formoy, *The Historical Foundations of Modern Company Law* (London: Sweet & Maxwell, 1923), pp. 115-30.
>
> [2] Charles E. Freedeman, *Joint Stock Enterprise in France, 1807-1867* (Chapel Hill: University of North Carolina Press, 1979), at 4-5.

§1.28 The *société anonyme* stood as an excellent way for an investor to pursue ventures while maintaining a low profile, both for political reasons (in the case of aristocrats, who were not meant to engage in the "bourgeis" practices of trade and commerce), as well as to minimize liability. However, these *sociétés* operated in much the same way as the more traditional partnerships of the past; only now, liability of the shareholders was limited (often simply because the identity of the partners was not made public).

§1.29 The managing directors (*gérants*) of these companies remained, for the most part, important shareholders, whose position entailed an element of risk (unlimited liability), at least in principle.[1]

> [1] Nonetheless, Lévy-Bruhl notes that *all* shareholders were in principle liable *in infinitum* and *in solidum* toward these companies: Henri Lévy-Bruhl, *Histoire juridique des sociétés de commerce en France aux XVIIe et XVIIIe siècles* (Paris: Éditions Domat-Montchrestien, 1938), p. 50.

§1.30 Canada preceded Britain in establishing a statutory basis providing for the incorporation of limited liability companies. The general incorporation statute of 1850[1] predated by five years the first British laws granting all shareholders limited liability for the debts incurred by the company,[2] and represented a significant step in the evolution of corporate managers by allowing them to easily modify their status from that of "partner" to that of "employee."

> [1] 13-14 Vict., c. 28 (Can., 1850).

² Maurice Martel and Paul Martel, *La compagnie au Québec* (Ottawa: Wilson & Lafleur, 1990), p. 52; James Smith and Yvon Renaud, *Droit québécois des corporations commerciales* (Montreal: Juridico, 1974), pp. 21 *et seq.*

§1.31 During the Industrial Revolution, allowing a non-partner to hold executive office permitted the entrepreneurs of the time to diversify their interests by freeing them to seek out new ventures in which to invest, rather than confining them to the rigours of managing the day-to-day affairs of companies. Limited liability, which required stockholders to relinquish direct control over the affairs of the corporation, also served as a convenient theoretical justification to allow all stockholders, no matter how important their share, to be absolved from liability. Henceforth, only those exercising direct control over the daily affairs of the company, that is, the corporate directors and, to a lesser extent, the officers could be held responsible.

4. Corporate Executives in the 20th Century

§1.32 Early Canadian incorporation acts stipulated that the president of an incorporated company was to be elected from among the members of the board of directors who had to be shareholders.[1] In this way, the Canadian corporation of the mid-19th century followed its French predecessor: the principal officer of the company remained at once the mandatary of the body which appointed him — the board — while concurrently sitting as a member of that very same body while still retaining ownership (at least in part) of the company. It was thus difficult to assimilate the position of "president" into the ranks of the other employees of the company, and the title of president was often granted merely to designate a figurehead, so as to comply with incorporation regulations requiring that those responsible for the affairs of the company be designated.[2]

¹ F.E. LaBrie and E.E. Palmer, "The Pre-Confederation History of Corporations in Canada", in *Studies in Canadian Company Law*, Jacob S. Ziegel, ed. (Toronto: Butterworths, 1967), p. 33, at 47.
² *Ibid.*, at 54. "The said persons shall give notice of their formation into a company and the name of their President and Secretary": 12 Vict., c. 56 (Can., 1849).

§1.33 At approximately the same time (the middle of the 19th century), stipulations in incorporation acts exonerating shareholders of companies from unlimited liability for the debts of their companies emerged. However, few cases regarding the role and responsibilities of corporate managers were reported until the mid 1950s.

(a)   The Role of the Director Juridically Defined

(i)   Common Law

§1.34 While the role of the executive was discussed very little until quite recently, British case law has analyzed the authority of corporate directors since at least the middle of the 18th century. The early common law decisions attributed the responsibilities of "trustee", "agent", or "fiduciary" to the directors of companies. As noted by Lord Chancellor Hardwicke in the early decision of *Charitable Corp. v. Sutton*:[1]

> . . . committee-men [directors] are most properly agents to those who employ them in this trust, and who empower them to direct and superintend the affairs of the corporation.

As early as 1859, in a Canadian decision, *Grimes v. Harrison*,[2] the directors of a building society were held in breach of trust for the mismanagement of the society's funds.

---

[1]   (1742), 2 Atk. 400 at 405, 26 E.R. 642.
[2]   (1859), 26 Beav. 435, 53 E.R. 966, cited in E.E. Palmer, "Directors' Powers and Duties", in *Studies in Canadian Company Law*, Jacob S. Ziegel, ed. (Toronto: Butterworths, 1967), p. 365, at 367, note 11.

§1.35   Palmer explains that the view of corporate directors as trustees in this country stems from an historical source in Canadian law:

> The modern corporation director . . . is the direct descendant of the trustees named in the deeds of settlement that provided the constitution of 18th and 19th century unincorporated partnerships and who, by that time, had also come to be described as directors.[1] [. . .] It was only natural, then, that initially the courts turned to the law of trusts to map out the duties of directors at common law adapting it to meet the needs of the time.[2]

---

[1]   E.E. Palmer, "Directors' Powers and Duties", in *Studies in Canadian Company Law*, Jacob S. Ziegel, ed. (Toronto: Butterworths, 1967), p. 365, at 366.
[2]   E.E. Palmer, "Directors' Powers and Duties", in *Studies in Canadian Company Law*, Jacob S. Ziegel, ed. (Toronto: Butterworths, 1967), at 366-67.

§1.36   Later decisions in the common law introduced the idea that corporate directors would be more aptly described as fiduciaries,[1] or other unique roles.[2]

---

[1]   L.C.B. Gower, *Principles of Modern Company Law* (London: Stevens & Sons, 1979), p. 575. *Cf.* Mortimer Feuer, *Personal Liabilities of Corporate Officers and Directors* (Englewood Cliffs: Prentice-Hall, 1961), p. 11.
[2]   *Cf.* Clément Fortin, "De la nature juridique de la fonction d'administrateur et d'officier en droit québécois des compagnies" (1970), 1 R.D.U.S. 129, at 145, 147; E.E.

Palmer, "Directors' Powers and Duties", in *Studies in Canadian Company Law*, Jacob S. Ziegel, ed. (Toronto: Butterworths, 1967), p. 365, at 367.

(ii) Civil Law

§1.37 In Quebec, the cases which called upon the court to decide on the role and duties owed by *"directeurs"* of a bank arose in 1890.[1] In *McDonald v. Rankin*,[2] a director of a bank was sued for damages by shareholders who alleged mismanagement of the bank's funds following the loss of a very considerable sum due to poor investments. The court was first brought to consider what type of function was exercised by the directors of the bank. Since, through the bank's Charter, they held virtually all powers to decide on all matters relating to the company, the directors were held to be mandataries by virtue of article 1710 of the Civil Code of Lower Canada,[3] they were assigned the task of executing "their mandate with the skill and the care of a *'bon père de famille'* ".[4] Pagnuelo J. cited Wharton, *On Negligence*, to support his conclusion:

> Whatever be the consideration which induces a person to undertake the control of another's affairs, he is required, if there is confidence bestowed and accepted, to show the diligence a good man of business is accustomed to show in the exercise of such a trust. A man holding himself out to the public as a business man, capable of properly acting as a bank director, is liable for *culpa levis* in not showing the diligence a good bank director should. What this diligence is, is of course determined in part by the charter of the bank, in part by general commercial law, in part by business usage.[5]

[1] "Cette question s'est rarement présentée dans ce pays et l'on ne trouve guère de précédents parmi nous qui puissent nous guider": per Pagnuelo J. in *McDonald v. Rankin* (1890), 7 M.L.R. 44 (Que. S.C.), at 45, discussed *infra*. For a thorough evaluation of the status of middle management in France, see Alain Le Bayon, *Notion et statut juridique des cadres de l'entreprise privée* (Paris: L.G.D.J., 1971).

[2] *McDonald v. Rankin* (1890), 7 M.L.R. 44 (Que. S.C.).

[3] *McDonald v. Rankin* (1890), 7 M.L.R. 44 (Que. S.C.), at 66 *et seq.* This article has been replaced by C.C.Q., art. 1309.

[4] *McDonald v. Rankin* (1890), 7 M.L.R. 44 (Que. S.C.), at 66 (translation).

[5] *McDonald v. Rankin* (1890), 7 M.L.R. 44 (Que. S.C.), at 89. *Cf.* also *Banque d'Épargne de la Cité et du District v. Geddes* (1890), 6 M.L.R. 243 (Que. S.C.), decided earlier in the year, also by Pagnuelo J., with a similar conclusion.

§1.38 Thus, the law has imposed a rather stringent duty upon the directors of corporations in Canada. This might seem somewhat ironic, considering how little control is effectively exerted by directors in certain corporations. Often, it would seem that the directors exist merely to ensure the smooth, uninterrupted reign of a C.E.O. who holds the real power over the decision-making process.

§1.39 What has been said of the duties and responsibilities of corporate officers in Canadian courts? Surprisingly little. Early corporate law tended to ignore the role played by officers in favour of that played by directors, and the relationship between the directors and shareholders. In some jurisdictions in Canada, most notably federally and in Ontario, this vacuum has been filled, and the fiduciary duty and the duty of care prescribed for directors have now been extended to officers.[1] Nor is the role of officers defined by statute, although s. 1(1) of the Ontario Act specifies the holders of nine positions as officers, and further includes in that definition any other individual designated an officer or any other individual who performs functions for a corporation similar to those normally performed by an individual occupying any such office.[2] In contrast to the duties prescribed for directors, we may gather only a confused picture of executive law from what jurisprudence exists.

---

[1] *Canada Business Corporations Act*, R.S.C. 1985, c. C-44, as am., s. 122; *Business Corporations Act*, R.S.O. 1990, c. B.16, as am., s. 134.

[2] Bruce L. Welling, *Corporate Law in Canada*, 2nd ed. (Toronto: Butterworths, 1991), p. 326.

(b) Attempts to Define the Role of Executives in Law

(i) Common Law

§1.40 Common law courts frequently attribute fiduciary responsibilities to high-ranking corporate executives. In *Canadian Aero Service Ltd. v. O'Malley*,[1] the Supreme Court of Canada held that, even though the senior officers of a company were, in principle, under the control of the directors of a parent company, the nature of their work, which allowed them a considerable amount of freedom to manage the affairs of their corporation, necessitated that they exercise their work within the scope of duties prescribed for fiduciaries. As explained by Laskin J.:

> Although they were subject to supervision of the officers of the controlling company, their positions as senior officers of a subsidiary which was a working organization, charged them with initiatives and with responsibilities far removed from the obedient role of servants.
>
> It follows that O'Malley and Zarzycki stood in a fiduciary relationship to Canaero, which in its generality betokens loyalty, good faith and avoidance of a conflict of duty and self-interest.[2]

---

[1] [1974] S.C.R. 592. See also *Canadian Industrial Distributors Inc. v. Dargue* (1994), 7 C.C.E.L. (2d) 60 (Ont. Ct. (Gen. Div.)).

[2] [1974] S.C.R. 592, at 606.

§1.40.1 An employee must have a "directing hand" over the business or the "power and ability to direct and guide the affairs of the company" before the employee will qualify and be obligated as a fiduciary.[1]

> [1] *R.W. Hamilton Ltd. v. Aeroquip Corp.* (1988), 65 O.R. (2d) 345 (H.C.J.). *Cf.*, however, *EII Ltd. (c.o.b. Gerrard-Ovalstrapping) v. Dutko*, [1997] M.J. No. 225, File No. CI 97-01-01902 (Man. Q.B.); at para. 20, where Morse J. rejected the "very strict test referred to in *R.W. Hamilton*" in favour of a "more pragmatic test" based upon whether the employee was in a position of trust with access to the confidential information and customers of the employer.

§1.41 As noted above, the director's fiduciary duties stem from the degree of control which, according to his or her position, the director of the company ought to exert over the management of the business. The recent trend has been that high-ranking executives usually hold such powers over the affairs of the company. In this regard, the responsibilities of the executive may be safely defined as being analogous to those of directors.[1]

> [1] This view has been confirmed by the courts in *Abbey Glen Property Corp. v. Stumborg*, [1976] 2 W.W.R. 1 (Alta. S.C.), affd [1978] 4 W.W.R. 28 (C.A.); *Motherwell v. Motherwell*, [1976] 6 W.W.R. 550 (Alta. C.A.); *Wilcox v. G.W.G. Ltd.*, [1984] 4 W.W.R. 70 (Alta. Q.B.), revd on other grounds [1986] 1 W.W.R. 567 (C.A.).

§1.41.1 Consideration of a manager's position, experience and authority will be made by a court in determining whether a fiduciary duty arose out of the employment relationship. A manager generally breaches his fiduciary duty by using confidential information about his previous employer in pursuit of a subsequent business opportunity, especially in soliciting the previous employer's suppliers and customers.[1]

> [1] *Canadian Industrial Distributors Inc. v. Dargue* (1994), 7 C.C.E.L. (2d) (Ont. Ct. (Gen. Div.)); *Naylor Group Inc. v. Cece* (1994), 57 C.P.R. (3d) 349 (Ont. Ct. (Gen. Div.)).

(ii) Civil Law

§1.42 Until recently, the doctrine and jurisprudence in the civil law were uncertain as to the exact status of the senior officers of a company in Quebec. Earlier decisions in the 20th century demonstrated the courts' willingness to borrow freely from the common law notion of officers as trustees[1] or fiduciaries[2] of the company. In the Supreme Court of Canada decision, *Ghimpelman v. Bercovici*,[3] Abbott J. stated the following proposition:

> I share the view . . . that the board of directors and the officers of a company incorporated under the *Quebec Companies Act*, are respectively the agents or *mandataries* of the company. As such, they are subject to the provisions of the Title "Of

Mandate" in the *Civil Code*, except in so far as these are rendered inapplicable by any general or special law relating to corporations as such.

¹ *Tanguay v. Royal Paper Mills Co.* (1907), 31 C.S. 397 (Que. S.C.), at 404; *Maison Morin v. J.A. Marceau Ltée* (1924), 62 C.S. 301 (Que. S.C.).
² *Barry v. Larocque* (1934), 72 C.S. 70 (Que. S.C.); *Ringuet v. Bergeron*, [1960] S.C.R. 672.
³ [1957] S.C.R. 128, at 140-41.

§1.43 This view of officers as mandataries, and therefore subject to the appropriate provisions of the Civil Code,¹ had been adopted in the doctrine as well as in the jurisprudence.² Yet, it would seem odd to characterize one whose responsibilities derive, in principle, from the directives of another (the board) as a mandatary. Indeed, the definition of mandate provided in article 2130 of the Civil Code of Quebec states:

> Mandate is a contract by which a person, the mandator, empowers another person, the mandatory, to represent him in the performance of a judicial act with a third person and the mandatory, by his acceptance, binds himself to exercise the power to perform it.

¹ C.C.L.C., arts. 1701 *et seq*; now C.C.Q., arts. 2130 *et seq.*
² James A. Smith, *Corporate Executives in Quebec* (Montreal: Centre d'Édition Juridique, 1978), pp. 123 *et seq.*

§1.44 While a director may readily be designated a mandatary (of the owners — the shareholders — of the corporation), the same would not seem to be so in the case of an executive who is not a director of the company. Since only directors may be entrusted with the management of a business by the shareholders, it is they who are ultimately responsible for the liabilities of the company under Canadian law.¹

¹ Both federal law (see the *Canada Business Corporations Act*, R.S.C. 1985, c. C-44) as well as the various company laws which exist in each of the provinces and territories. See Chapter 20, "Duties and Liabilities of Corporate Directors and Officers".

§1.45 What elements in their status of employment make executive officers different from other employees? As noted above, the principal features of employment are: (1) performing work for another; (2) receiving remuneration; and (3) subordination. Of the three, it seems that the last feature, subordination, remains the characteristic which differentiates an executive from lower-level employees. This seems odd, considering that officers remain, in principle, subordinate to the directors of the company.

§1.46 Over the last half of the century, executives have gained increasing control over the complete management of companies, by caring for the implementation of directives, and preparing the long-range goals. As stated by Gonthier J. in the Supreme Court of Canada decision, *Bank of Montreal v. Kuet Leong Ng:*[1]

> The obligations of directors and senior officers are imposed upon them *not because they are true mandataries of their corporation* or of the shareholders, *but because of the nature of the control* they exercise over the affairs of the corporation.

---
[1] [1989] 2 S.C.R. 429, at 442 (emphasis added).

(c) Situation of Executives in Practice

§1.47 Recent studies support the contention that in the course of their daily activities (and even long-range planning), corporate officers are frequently subordinate to no one. Indeed, as noted by Professor Bruce Welling:

> Practically speaking, for the largest and most financially important corporations in Canada, the managers have virtually free reign in determining the corporate destiny. This is a somewhat cruel joke of the business world to which the law has yet to respond in any effective manner. Many full-time corporate managers effectively appoint the board of directors, select themselves and their protégés for management positions, and regard the shareholders as a necessary rubber stamp in accomplishing their long-term managerial goals.[1]

---
[1] Bruce L. Welling, *Corporate Law in Canada*, 2nd ed. (Toronto: Butterworths, 1991), pp. 300-301.

§1.48 As Adolf A. Berle and Gardiner C. Means concluded in their very influential treatise, *The Modern Corporation and Private Property*,[1] the way in which public corporations have evolved in the last century has led to a strengthening of the position of corporate officers, and a consolidation of powers in their hands. The authors demonstrate how the large stock-company of the 20th century, having far too many shareholders to qualify any one (or even group of them) as a controlling interest, has placed power squarely in the hands of the boards of directors and senior officers. This stands in contradistinction to the earlier companies, where the owners were the ones who exercised decision-making power.

---
[1] (New York: Harcourt, Brace, Jovanovich, 1968).

§1.49 In the *New Industrial State*,[1] John Kenneth Galbraith found that the complexities of modern corporate management often required officers to be versed in the specialized skills exercised throughout the company. Thus, such positions have been increasingly filled with engineers, scientists, and specialists in the field of corporate organization, leaving the directors of the company often quite clueless as to what should be the proper decision to take at any given moment. The full burden of decision-making is thereby shifted almost exclusively to the upper-level officers, those who supposedly possess the knowledge required to come to such conclusions.

[1] (Boston: Houghton Mifflin, 1967). See also Terence H. White, *Power or Pawns: Boards of Directors in Canadian Corporations* (Don Mills: CCH, 1978), a study of this phenomenon in Canada.

§1.50 The effect of this revolution in the management of companies has been to give senior officers ever-growing powers to guide their companies, with little effective control being placed on their behaviour. Faced with such a phenomenon, the courts have had to refine their view of the legal status of executives to determine their rights and obligations.

(d) Re-examining the Juridical Status of Executives

(i) The Executive and the Contract

§1.51 The express stipulations included in the executive's employment contract often fail to cover all possible implications which might arise out of the agreement between the parties. Thus, the codifiers of 1866, following on the model of the *Code Napoléon* (article 1135), included in article 1024 of the *Civil Code of Lower Canada* a rule designed to supplement any lacunae in the contract formed between persons:

> The obligation of a contract extends not only to what is expressed in it, but also to all the consequences which, by equity, usage or law, are incident to the contract, *according to its nature.* [Emphasis added.]

§1.52 The new Civil Code of Quebec also recognizes the need for the inclusion of implicit obligations in the contractual relationship which it expresses as follows:

> A contract validly formed binds the parties who have entered into it not only as to what they have expressed in it but also as to what is incident to it according to its nature and in conformity with usage, equity or law.[1]

[1] C.C.Q., art. 1434.

§1.53 As we see, then, the *nature* of each person's contract with the company must be examined in order to identify the implied obligations imposed upon the parties stemming from the nature of the services for which the individual is being hired.[1] Obviously, the obligations of certain executives will differ from those of an assembly-line worker. Nevertheless, both will have to respect certain fundamental obligations derived from "equity, usage or law." (The Supreme Court of Canada, in *Machtinger v. HOJ Industries Ltd.*,[2] confirmed that the same issues apply for the common law as well.)

[1] Paul-André Crépeau, "Le contenu obligationnel d'un contrat" (1965), 43 Can. Bar Rev. 1.
[2] [1992] 1 S.C.R. 986.

(ii) The Executive Contract and Article 1434 of the Civil Code of Quebec[1]

§1.54 The historical survey of the status of directors and officers given above reveals that such persons have traditionally been treated as mandataries by the courts and, as such, have been subject to the rules of mandate. The most authoritative case in the civil law, *Bank of Montreal v. Kuet Leong Ng*,[2] clearly likens the obligations of senior officers to those of a mandatary, even though officers are not true mandataries since they do not exercise complete control over the affairs of the corporation.

[1] The discussion which follows is based on case law decided with respect to art. 1024 of the Civil Code of Lower Canada. However, the authors believe that this interpretation would apply to the current successor provision of art. 1024 of the C.C.L.C. (C.C.Q., art. 1434).
[2] [1989] 2 S.C.R. 429.

(1) Equity and the Obligation of Good Faith

§1.55 In *Bank of Montreal v. Kuet Leong Ng*,[1] Gonthier J. stated:

> The fiduciary obligation [imposed on senior officers] in the common law translates in the civil law into terms of good faith and loyalty of the employee to the employer . . .

Gonthier J. seems to imply here that the obligation of good faith imposed on an executive should be different from that imposed on another employee. In reality, however, the obligation of good faith is implicit in every contract of employment, as it is with every contract in general.

[1] [1989] 2 S.C.R. 429, at 443.

§1.56 As explained by L'Heureux-Dubé J. in the Supreme Court of Canada decision, *National Bank of Canada v. Houle*:[1]

> . . . at a general level, it seems indisputable that an implicit obligation of good faith exists in every contract in Québec civil law. This obligation is derived from a long civil law tradition formulated in art. 1024 *C.C.L.C.*; it mandates that rights be exercised in a spirit of fair play.

The spirit of "fair play" which L'Heureux-Dubé describes here stems from the moral concept of equity found in article 1434 of the Civil Code, which promotes a spirit of fairness in regard to contracted relationships[2] rather than stemming from their capacities as "mandataries" or "fiduciaries" (as argued by Gonthier J. in *Kuet Leong*).

---

[1] [1990] 3 S.C.R. 122, at 158.
[2] See Paul-André Crépeau, "Le contenu obligationnel d'un contrat" (1965), 43 Can. Bar Rev. 1, at 23 *et seq.*

(2) Custom (Usage) and the Obligations of the Executive

§1.57 Rather than assigning different degrees of loyalty to employees based solely on the title which they hold, the courts should instead look to the degree of control the employee exercises in his or her assigned task to assess the extent of his or her obligations. Thus, for example, the same level of confidence can be asked from a secretary as from a high-ranking executive in the safeguarding of volatile corporate files, even though their rank may differ. Both must maintain a strict level of confidentiality in such circumstances, due to the nature of the specific obligations they both hold in regard to such files. This brings us to a re-evaluation of the obligations of employees based on the circumstances of the functions which they execute, rather than simply on their hierarchy within the corporate structure.

§1.58 Based on the nature of their work, executives benefit from a much greater leeway in their daily management of the business. Today, many executives thrive in an atmosphere of significant freedom; their decisions usually become the final word which serves to guide the company. While in the past, directors exercised a much greater control over the conduct of their appointed officers, the situation today has almost been reversed. An ever-increasing number of board directors are being appointed on the recommendation of the C.E.O., who is often a member, if not chairman, of this same board.

§1.59 Of course, there remain a significant number of corporations where the directors have maintained their traditional role — that of close supervision of the officers' dealings. In such cases, directors actually do keep the latter in check. In such situations, it would seem only logical for the courts to assign a lesser degree of responsibility to a president who, in truth, finds himself or herself subordinate to and bound by a board's directives. In such a case, it would seem easier to absolve the malfeasant officer from the entire burden of responsibility. But, in the case of the officer who retains a virtual free hand in managing the company's affairs, a much greater burden of responsibility should be assigned.

§1.60 Since the obligations arising from a contract may be implied according to "usage," that is, "a practice established over time and adhered to in a given place or in a particular milieu, and which may become obligatory",[1] we must look to what the courts have said over time concerning the role and responsibilities of persons in such a position to quantify these obligations.

[1] Quebec Research Centre of Private and Comparative Law, *Private Law Dictionary* (Cowansville: Éditions Yvon Blais, 1991), p. 448.

§1.61 The implications of such a process are truly formidable. Since business practices throughout Canada are virtually the same — as indeed they are throughout most liberal democracies — the view of executives propounded by the courts in one province may equally apply to those employed in another province. In this way, the designation of usage (or custom) as a source of obligations in the civil law allows a rapprochement to be formed with jurisdictions adhering to the juridical system of the common law.

§1.62 To understand the executive's obligations, it is necessary to understand the reasoning of the courts in the decisions defining the implied obligations in the contract of employment. There exists no exhaustive statutory list of the obligations of employment in the common law nor in civil law. Essentially, in both civil and common law, most of the implied obligations arise from the nature and uniqueness of each employment relationship.

§1.63 To better understand how a court will look at the obligations of an employer and executive in any given executive employment contract, it is important to appreciate that for an employment relationship to exist in law there must be salary paid, work done, and subordination. It is this last aspect, subordination, which will be focused upon by the court in determining the extent of a particular obligation. Specifically, in both the *Canadian Aero* and *Kuet Leong Ng* cases,[1] the Supreme Court of Canada has implied an obligation of good faith and loyalty from the nature of the contract and specifically held that the higher the degree of control an executive and/or senior employee exercises, the greater the degree of the obligation. Looked at inversely, the less subordinate the (executive-)employee is to a higher authority, the greater the degree of the obligation.

[1]   See §§1.40, 1.41 and 1.55, *supra*.

§1.64 These implied employment obligations apply to all employees in varying degrees. However, employees who are also officers have additional statutory duties of care[1] which may or may not add additional obligations. For instance, the Canada Business Corporations Act[2] contains the following explicit duties imposed upon directors and officers: honesty, prudence, care, diligence and skill. Similarly, employees who are officers and also directors will have even greater responsibility, as the degree of control exerted by such executives rises. Understanding the sources of these obligations and the interpretation placed on them by the courts is a fundamental necessity for every executive who as executives are deemed to have knowledge of their obligations.

[1]   For examples, see Chapter 20, "Duties and Liabilities of Corporate Directors and Officers".) See also J.M. Wainberg and Mark I. Wainberg, *Duties and Responsibilities of Directors in Canada* (Don Mills: CCH, 1987).

[2]   See s. 122(1)(*a*) of the *Canada Business Corporations Act*, R.S.C. 1985, c. C-44.

D.   CONCLUSION — THE CORPORATE EXECUTIVE TODAY: MASTER *AND* SERVANT?

§1.65 The rise of the modern corporate executive sprang from a need in the business community. The professional executive allows investors the opportunity to diversify their interests and expand their holdings without having the burden of managing the day-to-day affairs of their companies. Control of the company is taken from the shareholders and effectively given to the executives. This development provides a more or less ideal way to justify the notion of limited liability, so essential to the growth of capitalism and the corporation in the 20th century. While we have clearly experienced dramatic change in our employment laws over the last few centuries, the last ten years have sparked a re-evaluation of the role of the executive.

§1.66 We may conclude that, while more has been written about executives recently, the notion and status of corporate executives in Canada has yet to be clearly defined in law. The status of executives has evolved principally out of practice, and often in spite of certain legislation. It is hoped that this introductory chapter will allow a better understanding of how the role of executives has evolved to date, as well as shed light on the rather lengthy historical process which led to their rise as employed corporate managers.

§1.67 Nearly half a century ago, Georges Ripert wrote the following note concerning the influence of the modern corporation on contemporary society:

> For over a century, it is no longer men who hold the powerful positions in commerce and industry; rather, they have been eliminated by widely held shareholdings in corporations. No fact is more important than this one for the comprehension of the capitalist regime.[1]

With the utmost respect, we disagree with this assertion. While the modern corporation has undeniably exerted a profound influence on contemporary society, it would be erroneous to deny those who control the activities of such great organizations their share of attention. With the increased responsibilities and degrees of control that executives have gained over corporations in the last half-century, the law has moved toward assigning greater duties upon them. It is the status which corporate executives presently hold in Canadian law — and the additional responsibilities which seem inevitable in light of recent judicial pronouncements — that we have set out to examine in the pages that follow.

[1] Georges Ripert, *Aspects juridiques du capitalisme moderne* (Paris: L.J.D.G., 1951), p. 51.

CHAPTER 2

DETERMINATION OF LAWS GOVERNING THE EMPLOYMENT RELATIONSHIP

A. JURISDICTIONAL ISSUES: RULES GOVERNING THE CONTENT AND INTERPRETATION OF THE EMPLOYMENT CONTRACT

§2.1 It is important to ascertain at the outset of any legal inquiry which jurisdiction's laws regulate any particular matter and, in this case, the employment relationship. This determination will circumscribe which elements must be present for the relationship to exist, the obligations that flow from it, and the effects of the relationship on third parties: indeed, these may differ from one jurisdiction (province, state, country) to another.

§2.2 In an era of globalization, it is increasingly common for companies to conduct inter-company, interprovincial or international transfers of executives or to hire executives who work or reside in foreign countries, provinces or states. This means that a particular employment relationship may have contacts with several jurisdictions, which complicates the issue of identifying the applicable law. Moreover, the employment relationship may, in these cases, be governed by the laws of more than one jurisdiction.

§2.3 In Canada, where the parties have expressly agreed in advance that the employment contract will be governed by the laws of a particular jurisdiction, these laws will be applied by the courts as the proper law of the employment contract,[1] so long as this does not offend local precepts of public order and includes provisions as favourable to the executive as local laws.[2]

---

[1] Art. 3111 C.C.Q. and *Nike Informatic Systems Ltd v. Avac Systems Ltd*, [1980] 1 W.W.R. 528 (B.C.S.C.); *Smith Transport Ltd v. IN-TRA-CO INC.*, [1974] C.S. 265 (Que. S.C.); *Hill v. W.P. London & Associates Ltd.* (1986), 13 C.C.E.L. 194 (Ont. H.C.J.); *Vita Food Products Inc. v. Unus Shipping Co.*, [1939] A.C. 277 (P.C.).

[2] Art 3118 C.C.Q.. The designation by the parties may not result in depriving the executive of the protection to which he or she is entitled under the mandatory provisions of the law of the jurisdiction where the executive habitually carries on his or her work.

§2.4   Since employment and labour laws are generally regarded as policing laws or laws of immediate application, a court will not hesitate to apply such laws to any employment relationship evolving within its jurisdiction. As a result, the employment contract will be regulated by two legislative systems: local law will regulate any matter of public order and the designated law will regulate all other aspects of the relationship.

§2.5   The parties' choice of governing law may be disregarded by the courts if their selection is not *bona fide* (in the sense that it is made to avoid the application of a law with a closer connection to the transaction) or is illegal or if the application of the chosen law is against a public policy of the jurisdiction in which the contract is sought to be enforced.[1] So long as there is some connection with the chosen law, the *bona fides* of the choice is unlikely to be questioned.

> [1]   See J.-G. Castel, *Canadian Conflict of Laws*, 3d ed. (Toronto: Butterworths, 1994). See also *Fleming v. Samuelsohn Ltd* (1990), 49 B.C.L.R. (2d) 391 (S.C.).

§2.6   In the absence of an express choice, or if the courts cannot invalidate the parties' choice of law, the determination of the proper law lies in applying more objective criteria. Firstly, it is necessary to identify the particular legal issue under consideration. For example, does the issue involve rights under a pension plan or does it involve the interpretation of certain terms of the employment contract? Once the issue is identified, the second step consists of applying the principles of conflicts of laws of the jurisdiction in which it is sought to enforce the particular right or obligation in issue in order to determine which jurisdiction's laws apply to that issue. These conflicts of laws rules may differ depending on the province where the action is instituted in Canada. In addition, constitutional law principles may be relevant in determining the applicable choice of law rule.

1. Civil law

§2.7   If an unlawful termination suit is instituted in Quebec and the parties have not designated the proper law governing the contract, the court will apply the law of the place where the executive habitually works. If the executive does not habitually work in the same place, then the law of the place where the employer has its domicile or establishment is applicable to the employment contract.[1]

> [1]   Art. 3118 C.C.Q.. Prior to the coming into force of the new Civil Code of Quebec, the applicable law, if none was specifically designated by the parties, was the law of the jurisdiction where the parties had concluded the employment contract. See

Soupes Campbell Ltée v. Cantin, D.T.E. 91T-741 (Que. C.A.). See also chapter 3, "The Formation of the Employment Contract".

§2.8 If the Quebec court decides that foreign law applies, it generally hears the case in accordance with the applicable foreign law[1] with the same reservations mentioned above as pertains to designated law.[2] Therefore, if the result of applying foreign law is manifestly inconsistent with public order (as understood in international relations) the foreign law may be disregarded.[3] Finally, though foreign law may govern the legal issues opposing the parties, the procedural rules of the Quebec courts apply.[4]

[1]   *Aberman v. Solomon*, [1986] R.D.J. 385 (Que. C.A.).
[2]   See §2.3 to §2.5.
[3]   Art. 3080 and 3081 C.C.Q..
[4]   Art. 3132 C.C.Q., which states that procedure is governed by the law of the court seized of the matter.

2. The Common Law

§2.9 If an executive institutes proceedings in a Canadian province other than Quebec and failing an express designation by the parties as to which law should apply to their contract, the common law choice of law rules apply. The common law requires the application of a "nexus test" in order to determine the governing law.[1] This text requires that the court determine which jurisdiction is most closely connected with the transaction. In *Hill v. W.P. London & Associates Ltd,*[2] the court held that a correct statement of the law is as follows:

> Eventually the Canadian courts adopted the "proper law" doctrine which may be defined as the system of law by which the parties intended the contract to be governed. Where their intention is neither expressed nor able to be inferred from the circumstances, the proper law is the system of law with which the transaction has its closest and most real connection. . . .
>
> Where the parties have expressly selected the proper law, in the absence of any vitiating factors, the choice will be upheld. Where the parties have not selected the proper law the court will ascertain the proper law objectively in the light of the facts and circumstances of each case having regard to the place of contracting, the place of performance, the place of residence or chief place of business of the parties, the subject matter of the contract, the form of the contract, the language and money used: in short, any factor which connects the contractual relationship to a particular system of law.

[1]   *Imperial Life Assur. Co. of Canada v. Colmenares*, [1967] S.C.R. 443. See also *Cansulex Ltd. v. Reed Stenhouse Ltd.* (1986), 8 B.C.L.R. (2d) 397 (S.C.).
[2]   (1986), 13 C.C.E.L. 194 (Ont. H.C.J.), at 202.

§2.10   In *Campbell v. Pringle & Booth Ltd.*,[1] the court was forced to determine the proper law applicable to an employee of a Canadian company who had moved to Chicago to establish a branch office of the employer. The employer alleged that the proper law was the law of the state of Illinois since the plaintiff was an employee of an American corporation. The court rejected this view and concluded that the employee was an employee of an Ontario-based corporation and at no time had he ever been advised that the defendant intended the law of the state of Illinois to apply to the employment relationship. Hence, the law of Ontario was the applicable law.

   [1]   (1988), 30 C.C.E.L. 156 (Ont. H.C.J.).

§2.11   The determination of the governing law of an employment contract can be a complex issue for the parties. Consequently, and particularly in the context of an executive employment contract, employers and executives are well advised to acquaint themselves with the differences between potentially applicable laws and, possibly, to incorporate within a written employment contract a clause which specifically provides for the law which will govern the employment relationship. Although their choice remains subject to laws of immediate application, it may nevertheless regulate other key and complex aspects of their contract, such as remuneration.

3.   Other Employment Law Issues

(a)   Public Order Laws

§2.12   As we mentioned above, not all employment law issues are governed by the laws of the applicable foreign jurisdiction. Certain employment law matters are governed by the laws of public order of the place where the employment services are performed. Consequently, these matters may add to or supersede the express terms of a written employment contract or normally applicable by foreign law.[1] For example, a province's labour standards (concerning hours of work, statutory holidays, vacation and minimum notice of termination), human rights laws, occupational health and safety legislation, workers' compensation laws and laws governing trade unions would apply to the employee performing his or her duties in that province, even though the parties may have agreed that the laws of another Canadian province or any other state govern the employment contract because these laws are public order.[2] The same is true of certain provisions of the Civil Code of Quebec, for example, regarding restrictive covenants such as non-competition agreements.

[1] C.C.Q., art. 3118
[2] C.C.Q., art. 3118.

(b) Pension Plan Laws

§2.13 Issues relating to employee pension plans also raise special choice of law issues. Canadian jurisdictions each have specific pension plan legislation relating to employee pension plans. Which jurisdiction's laws will apply to the particular employment plan depends on a nexus between the plan and the relevant jurisdiction. Where a particular pension fund relates to an employer involved in a federally regulated industry (such as banking, railways, airlines, etc.), federal pension fund legislation will be applicable. Where the pension fund has beneficiaries in one or more provinces, the relevant provincial pension fund legislation may also be applicable. Canadian pension fund legislation is not uniform and pension regulatory authorities in Canada have reciprocal arrangements for enforcement of pension legislation where beneficiaries are employed in more than one province. Generally, the applicable legislation will be that of the jurisdiction where the majority of the beneficiaries are employed. For example, in Ontario, persons employed in the province are subject to provincial pension legislation.[1]

[1] *Pension Benefit Act*, R.S.O. 1990, c. P.8.

4. Application of Constitutional Law Principles in the Employment Context

§2.14 In addition to any issues of governing jurisdiction, the Canadian constitutional context requires us to determine whether provincial or federal statutes regarding employment generally regulate the employment relationship. Authority to make laws in Canada originates from the *Constitution Act, 1867*.[1] This Act divides authority to enact laws between the Parliament of Canada[2] and the provincial legislatures[3] according to the subject-matter involved. The federal Parliament has authority over subjects of general or national interest such as atomic energy, banking, postal services, interprovincial railways and transportation, aeronautics, telecommunications, criminal law or navigation and shipping. The provinces have the power to regulate matters of a more local concern such as education, social welfare, property and civil rights.

[1] Enacted as the *British North America Act, 1867*, 30 & 31 Vict., c. 3.
[2] *Constitution Act, 1867*, s. 91.
[3] *Constitution Act, 1867*, s. 92.

§2.15   The *Constitution Act, 1867* does not expressly distribute exclusive jurisdiction over employment and labour matters to either the federal or the provincial level. Consequently, many conflicts have arisen between the provincial and federal governments over which level of government can legislate with respect to these matters. The courts have concluded that no one level of government has exclusive authority over the subject of employment and labour relations: legislative powers in this area are divided between the Parliament of Canada and the provincial legislatures.[1]

> [1]   *Canada (A.G.) v. Ontario (A.G.)*, [1937] A.C. 326 (P.C.); *Toronto Electric Commrs. v. Snider*, [1925] A.C. 396 (P.C.). See also *Ontario Hydro v. Ontario (Labour Relations Board)*, [1993] 3 S.C.R. 327.

§2.16   Jurisdiction with respect to regulating employer-employee relations in terms of working conditions (such as hours of work, statutory holidays, vacation, notice of termination, standards of health and safety in the workplace, workers' compensation, trade unions, discrimination and human rights) is divided between the Parliament of Canada and the provinces on the basis of whether the industry in which the work is done is itself subject to federal or provincial jurisdiction.[1]

> [1]   *Bell Canada v. Québec (Commission de la santé et de la sécurité du travail)*, [1988] 1 S.C.R. 749; *Letter Carriers' Union of Canada v. C.U.P.W. and M. & B. Enterprises Ltd.*, [1975] 1 S.C.R. 178; *Commission du salaire minimum v. Bell Telephone Co. of Canada*, [1966] S.C.R. 767; *Reference re Industrial Relations and Disputes Investigation Act (Can.)*, [1955] S.C.R. 529; *Reference re Minimum Wage Act of Saskatchewan*, [1948] S.C.R. 248. See also *The Bay v. U.S.W.A., Local 898* (1995), 26 C.L.R.B.R. (2d) 161 (B.C.); *Ontario Hydro v. Ontario (Labour Relations Board)*, [1993] 3 S.C.R. 327.

§2.17   Because they are considered an essential aspect of the business, employment and labour relations are thus regulated by the jurisdiction which governs the business itself. Consequently, an executive, working for a federally regulated industry, who wishes to take maternity or parental leave would look to the *Canada Labour Code*[1] to determine her or his rights, while an executive working for a company subject to provincial laws would look at the legislation of the relevant province to determine her or his rights.

> [1]   R.S.C. 1985, c. L-2.

§2.18   The courts have repeatedly stated that federal jurisdiction over employment and labour relations extends to industries which, although they are not *per se* under federal legislation, are an "integral part or necessarily incidental" to an undertaking within federal jurisdiction. This principle applies mostly to businesses that are accessory to, or that provide services to, a federal undertaking.

§2.19 As an illustration of the doctrine of "integral part or necessarily incidental", the courts have held that federal jurisdiction over maritime transportation gives the federal government power to regulate the employment relations of the stevedoring industry because the activities of the stevedoring industry are an integral part of shipping.[1] The courts have also ruled that the employees of a company constructing an airport runway are subject to provincial legislation because, unlike aeronautics, a construction company is not a federal undertaking and, further, the work performed by these employees is not an integral part of the operation of an airport.[2]

---

[1] *Reference re Industrial Relations and Disputes Investigation Act (Can.)*, [1955] S.C.R. 529.

[2] *Construction Montcalm Inc. v. Commission du salaire minimum*, [1979] S.C.R. 754. See also *Teamsters Local 879 v. G.S. Dunn & Co.* (1995), O.L.R.B. Rep. 128; *Ontario Hydro v. Ontario (Labour Relations Board)*, [1993] 3 S.C.R. 327; *Canadian Pacific Ry. v. British Columbia (A.G.)*, [1950] A.C. 122 (P.C.); *International Brotherhood of Electrical Workers, Local 348 v. Alberta (Labour Relations Board)* (1995), 28 Alta. L.R. (3d) 172 (Q.B.).

§2.20 In summary, provincial laws regulating the employment relationship, such as labour standards legislation and health and safety legislation apply to the businesses in that province under provincial jurisdiction, but do not apply to works, undertakings or businesses within federal jurisdiction. Furthermore, it has been judicially determined that provincial codes or charters regulating discrimination in the workplace apply to provincially regulated businesses but do not apply to federal undertakings and vice versa.[1]

---

[1] *Forest Industries Flying Tankers Ltd. v. Kellough*, [1980] 4 W.W.R. 13 (B.C.C.A.); *Canadian Pacific Ltd. v. Alberta (A.G.)* (1980), 108 D.L.R. (3d) 738 (Alta. C.A.).

§2.21 A more delicate problem arises in Quebec by reason of the adoption of the new Civil Code, particularly regarding the provisions on employment law and the protection of privacy. Will these provisions be applied to federally regulated undertakings or must one refer to federal common law (including the Civil Code of Lower Canada) for the solution?

The courts will have one of four options, namely: (1) applying new law as enacted by the new Civil Code; (2) applying the Civil Code of Lower Canada as it was in 1866; (3) applying the Civil Code of Lower Canada as amended from time to time since 1866 or (4) noting a juridical void (or the absence of any positive rule of law). We believe it is probable that any provision of the new Civil Code which enacts new

law regarding employment matters will be inapplicable to federal undertakings as the latter will continue to be governed by provisions of
the Civil Code of Lower Canada and the court decisions which have
interpreted these provisions.[1]

[1]   Indeed, it can be argued that the Civil Code of Quebec (or at least any provision
enacting new law), as a postconfederative law, could not apply to a field of exclusive federal jurisdiction such as employment and labour relations in a federally
regulated undertaking. This principle of interjurisdictional immunity has been
recognized many times by the Supreme Court of Canada and reaffirmed in the
case of *Bell Canada v. Québec (CSST)*, [1988] 1 S.C.R. 749. Provincial laws of general
application may not, even incidentally, impact on employment and labour relations of a federally regulated undertaking. As a result, certain provisions of health
and safety laws, the Quebec Charter of Rights and Freedoms (*Kealty v. SITA*,
[1991] R.J.Q. 397 (S.C.)) and the Quebec French Language Law (*Joyal v. Air Canada*,
[1976] C.S. 1211 (Qué. S.C.)) were held inoperative with regard to federally regulated undertakings.

Concurrently, courts recognized that the expression "employment and labour
relations" or "working conditions" includes anything which is susceptible of being the object of an agreement between employer and employee regarding their
relationship. These are "conditions under which a worker or workers, individually or collectively, provide their services, in accordance with the rights and obligations included in the contract of employment by the consent of the parties or by
operation of law, and under which the employer receives those services" (*Bell
Canada v. Québec (CSST)*, [1988] 1 S.C.R. 749, at pages 798 and 799). These "conditions" are at the heart of Parliament's exclusive jurisdiction.

The 1866 Civil Code of Lower Canada (constituting at the very least a preconfederative law) avoided this rigorous test because of article 129 of the Constitution Act of 1867 (Hogg Peter, *Constitutional Law of Canada*, 3d ed. vol. 1, Thomson
Canada Limited, Scarborough, 1992 at pages 2 to 11, where the author identifies
five sources of preconfederative law). Article 129 allowed preconfederative laws
to apply to fields declared to be exclusively under federal jurisdiction, until the
law was modified or restricted by the new federal parliament or a provincial legislature acting within its postconfederative area of jurisdiction.

This created a "mirror" effect. See H. Brun & G. Tremblay, *Droit constitution-
nel*, 2d ed. Yvon Blais, Cowansville, 1990, at p. 433, where the authors illustrate
the effects described above with the rules related to marriage: "in Quebec, the
preconfederative provisions of the Civil Code of Lower Canada have continued to
date to regulate marriage by virtue of section 129 of the *Constitution Act of 1867*.
Quebec cannot modernize any relevant provisions since this area of law is within
exclusive federal jurisdiction. Parts of the Civil Code of Quebec which were enacted in 1980 and pertained to marriage (and divorce) will only become operative
if by constitutional amendment, competence over this matter is handed over to
the provinces (or to Quebec)." The objective of section 129 was clearly to avoid a
void in the law with respect to matters under federal jurisdiction. Subsequently,
Parliament enacted statutes within its jurisdiction, which statutes impliedly repealed the preconfederative laws as they related to subjects within the competence of Parliament. See for example, *Moore v. Johnson*, [1982] 1 S.C.R. 115.

If one accepts that the effect of section 129 has been to render certain parts of
the Civil Code of Lower Canada federal law, then one can object to the provincial
government's power to modify these laws as they affect federal undertakings. In
other words, applying the interjurisdictional immunity theory and the wider defi-

nition of "working conditions", certain provisions of the Civil Code of Quebec, such as articles 2088 and following, and articles 35 and following of the Civil Code of Quebec, which would appear to regulate employment relations in a federal undertaking, would be inapplicable to these undertakings inasmuch as they are postconfederative provisions.

This conclusion creates yet another important and delicate issue. What rule of law is thus applicable to a federal undertaking? Indeed, many reject the idea that the new Civil Code does not apply to federal undertakings for the reasons that there would be a juridical void from the absence of any applicable federal law governing these matters. This position fails to consider a fundamental fact. If article 129 made the Civil Code of Lower Canada the applicable federal law until validly replaced by Parliament, the Quebec government could not by repealing the Code and replacing it by a new one, repeal the "mirror" which section 129 initially created. In the *Moore* case mentioned above, the Supreme Court stated that although preconfederative law dealing with a matter within federal jurisdiction did not become *stricto sensu* federal law, only Parliament could repeal, abolish or modify it (pages 121 to 123).

The 1866 Civil Code of Lower Canada remains alive as federal common law until it is repealed or replaced "expressly or implicitly" by Parliament.

Two other objections to our reasoning must also fail. The first has to do with the exceptional nature of the Civil Code which would escape the division of powers and section 129 and apply *proprio motu* to all. If this theory is followed, this would mean that any new rules of law adopted under the Civil Code should apply to federal undertakings and the Quebec government could insert in the Code all its laws to render them applicable to federal undertakings (including the French Language Charter and the Charter of Human Rights and Freedoms, which are clearly inapplicable to federal undertakings).

The second objection has to do with "property and civil rights" which are within exclusive provincial jurisdiction. Some see in this field of jurisdiction an exclusive provincial power to adopt laws governing the formation and drafting of a contract. We believe, however, that it is a mistake to restrict employment and labour relations to meaning only normative aspects (hours of work, minimum salary, etc.). Since Parliament rightly adopted provisions regarding the termination of the employment contract (for example, article 240 of the Canada Labour Code which provides for reinstatement), what prevents Parliament from requiring, for example, that any individual employment contract must, in a federal undertaking, be in writing? It is erroneous to distinguish between Parliament's power over collective employment relations and individual employment relations. Inasmuch as exclusive power to legislate over property and civil rights was meant to protect Quebec civil law, (see G. Beaudoin, *La constitution du Canada*, Wilson & Lafleur, Montréal, 1990, at p. 6) it cannot in our view lead to the result desired by those who oppose our view that new law under the Civil Code of Quebec is inoperative with respect to federal undertakings.

See also R. Bonhomme, G. Gascon and L. Lesage, *Le contrat du travail en vertu du Code civil du Québec*, Cowansville, Yvon Blais, 1994, at p. 29.

B. SOURCES OF EMPLOYMENT LAW

§2.22 Once the relevant jurisdiction governing the particular employment law issue under consideration is determined, its laws apply to the issue. A broad review of the sources of employment law will be identified in this section. Specifically, these sources include legislation, case law, and doctrine.

1. Legislation

(a) Civil Code

§2.23 In Quebec, the primary source of law since January 1, 1994, is the Civil Code of Quebec;[1] the Civil Code of Lower Canada may nevertheless be the proper source of rights and obligations with respect to certain aspects of an employment relationship which began prior to that date.[2]

> [1] S.Q., 1991, c. 64 (Bill 125).
>
> [2] See *Emballages Dawson Inc. v. Béland*, D.T.E. 94T-741 (Que. S.C.) one of the first decisions on this matter. With regards to the law as it applies under the Civil Code of Lower Canada, see A.E. Aust and L. Charette, *The Employment Contract*, 2d ed. Cowansville, Yvon Blais, 1993.

§2.24 Article 2085 of the Civil Code of Quebec defines the contract of employment as a contract by which a person, the employee, undertakes for a limited time to do work for remuneration, according to the instructions and under the direction of the employer. Article 1377 of the Civil Code of Quebec states that the general rules in the chapter regarding contracts apply to all contracts, regardless of their nature. As such these rules apply to the employment relationship.[1] Although the new Civil Code of Quebec has many more provisions regarding the employment contract than its predecessor, the Civil Code of Lower Canada had, it is submitted that the new code continues to be merely a skeleton of the law relating to the employment relationship and that case law will continue to be heavily relied upon by the courts to determine employment law issues.

> [1] These rules are discussed more fully in Chapter 3, "The Formation of the Employment Contract."

(b) Statutes

§2.25 The most important statutes are those which address labour standards, human rights, French language (Quebec),[1] health and safety in the workplace and workers' compensation. These statutes may or may not apply to the particular employment terms of an executive employee.

> [1] *Charter of the French Language*, R.S.Q., c. C-11.

(i) Labour Standards

§2.26 Labour standards legislation[1] generally provides minimum guarantees for the individual worker. It may include minimum wage requirements, maximum hours of labour, overtime rates of pay, vacation with pay, fair employment practices, minimum notice requirements, maternity and parental benefits, statutory holidays, equal pay provisions, and other similar protection.

[1] See, *e.g.*, in Quebec, *An Act respecting Labour Standards*, R.S.Q., c. N-1.1; in Ontario, the *Employment Standards Act*, R.S.O. 1990, c. E.14; in British Columbia, the *Employment Standards Act*, R.S.B.C. 1996, c. 113; and, at the federal level, the *Canada Labour Code*, R.S.C. 1985, c. L-2. See also *Wilks v. Harrington, Division of Ingersoll-Rand Canada Inc.* (1987), 18 C.C.E.L. 100 (Que. S.C.); *Sandner v. British Columbia (Director of Employment Standards)* (1987), 17 C.C.E.L. 71 (B.C. Co. Ct.), affd 35 C.C.E.L. 273 (C.A.); *Mills-Hughes v. Raynor* (1988), 19 C.C.E.L. 6 (Ont. C.A.); *Stevens v. Globe & Mail* (1996), 28 O.R. (3d) 481 (C.A.); *Standard Commercial Tobacco Co. of Canada v. C.U.O.E.* (1988), 24 C.C.E.L. 57 (Ont. Div. Ct.); *Fenton v. British Columbia (Forensic Psychiatric Services Comm.)* (1991), 37 C.C.E.L. 225 (B.C.C.A.), leave to appeal denied (1992), 39 C.C.E.L. 289n (S.C.C.).

(ii) Human Rights

§2.27 Human rights legislation[1] will generally serve to protect an employee from discriminatory practices based on sex, national or ethnic origin, colour, religion, race, age, mental or physical disability. It may also provide for affirmative action programs or pay equity provisions. The Quebec Charter offers more protection than other provinces' legislation as it extends to liberty of expression, right to privacy and protection of reputation.

[1] See, *e.g.*, in Quebec, the *Charter of Human Rights and Freedoms*, R.S.Q., c. C-12; in Ontario, the *Human Rights Code*, R.S.O. 1990, c. H.19; in British Columbia, the *Human Rights Code*, R.S.B.C. 1996, c. 210; and, at the federal level, the *Canadian Human Rights Act*, R.S.C. 1985, c. H-6. See also *Ontario Human Rights Comm. v. Ontario Liquor Control Bd.* (1988), 19 C.C.E.L. 172 (Ont. Div. Ct.); *Consumers' Distributing Co. v. Ontario Human Rights Comm.* (1987), 15 C.C.E.L. 256 (Ont. Div. Ct.), leave to appeal denied (1987), 15 C.C.E.L. 256n (C.A.); *Roosma v. Ford Motor Co. of Canada* (1987), 19 C.C.E.L. 243 (Ont. Bd. of Inq.), affd (1988), 66 O.R. (2d) 18 (Div. Ct.). See also *Wong v. Ottawa Board of Education* (1995), 95 C.L.L.C. §230-003 (Ont. Bd. of Inq.); *Underwood v. Smiths Falls Bd. of Commrs. of Police* (1985), 10 C.C.E.L. 212 (Ont. Bd. of Inq.); *Brown v. Waterloo Regional Bd. of Commrs. of Police* (1986), 13 C.C.E.L. 45 (Ont. Bd. of Inq.); *Lord v. Haldimand-Norfold Police Services Board* (1995), 95 C.L.L.C. §230-023 (Ont. Human Rights Bd. of Inq.); *Keshen v. Carrier Canada Ltd.* (1989), 30 C.C.E.L. 107 (B.C.S.C.); *Ontario Human Rights Comm. v. Ontario Teachers' Federation* (1994), 19 O.R. (3d) 371 (Div. Ct.); *Olivier v. Jules A. Roberge Inc.*, D.T.E. 95T-635 (Qué. Q.C.).

(iii)   Health and Safety

§2.28   The object of health and safety legislation[1] is the elimination, at their source, of dangers to the health, safety and physical well-being of workers. These laws also deal with training and informing employees regarding safe work methods. Refusal to perform dangerous work, protective reassignment in case of danger to one's health and protective reassignment of a pregnant or breast-feeding worker, are also regulated by these laws.

[1]   See, *e.g.*, in Quebec, *An Act respecting Occupational Health and Safety*, R.S.Q., c. S-2.1; in Ontario, the *Occupational Health and Safety Act*, R.S.O. 1990, c. O.1. See also *R. v. Cancoil Thermal Corp.* (1986), 11 C.C.E.L. 219 (Ont. C.A.); *R. v. Rio Algom Ltd.* (1988), 23 C.C.E.L. 85 (Ont. C.A.). Refer to Chapter 8, "Safety of Executives", for a more complete discussion of this issue.

(iv)   Workers' Compensation

§2.29   Workers' compensation legislation[1] has been established to ensure that an employee who sustains a personal injury as a result of an accident arising from, and in the course of, his or her employment, or who is disabled by a specified industrial disease, is entitled to compensation. In addition, each of these laws has numerous regulations which serve to implement the aims of the legislation.

[1]   See, *e.g.*, in Quebec, *An Act respecting Industrial Accidents and Occupational Diseases*, R.S.Q., c. A-3.001; in Ontario, the *Workers' Compensation Act*, R.S.O. 1990, c. W.11 [Note that Bill 99, which received royal assent on October 10, 1997, will repeal the *Workers' Compensation Act* and replace it with the *Workplace Safety and Insurance Act, 1997*, in force January 1, 1998. The amendments include certain new restrictions on a worker's entitlement to benefits for mental stress, chronic pain and occupational disease.]; in British Columbia, the *Workers' Compensation Act*, R.S.B.C. 1996, c. 492; and, at the federal level, the *Government Employees Compensation Act*, R.S.C. 1985, c. G-5. See also *Kuntz v. Ontario Workers' Compensation Bd.* (1985), 12 C.C.E.L. 50 (Ont. Div. Ct.), revd on other grounds 31 D.L.R. (4th) 630 (C.A.); *Roncato v. O'Brien* (1987), 17 C.C.E.L. 290 (Ont. H.C.J.); *Kooner v. British Columbia Workers' Compensation Bd.* (1991), 35 C.C.E.L. 14 (B.C.C.A.).

2.   Case Law

§2.30   Case law or jurisprudence refers to the body of decisions rendered by the courts which define and interpret the express and implied rights and obligations of the parties to the employment relationship. This source of law is most important to an executive. What one particular court rules may be relied on as a precedent for an executive in his or her own particular circumstances. In addition, there are numerous decisions rendered by administrative and quasi-judicial bodies which apply and interpret the statutory law with respect to employment but which are not necessarily binding on other administrative, quasi-judicial or judicial bodies. These decisions serve as a yardstick, and illustrate the extent of the rights and obligations created by legislation.

3. Doctrine

§2.31 Doctrine refers to texts or articles written by legal scholars which transmit their knowledge and understanding of the law. Doctrine is a useful aid in drawing the legal community's attention to lapses in the law and the confusion which exists regarding particular issues. It may also be used as an aid in interpreting the law.

C. CONCLUSION

§2.32 Once it has been determined which jurisdiction's laws govern the employment relationship, issues of formation of the employment contract must be analyzed. This subject is treated in the next chapter.

CHAPTER 3

THE FORMATION OF THE EMPLOYMENT CONTRACT

A. INTRODUCTION

§3.1 The law of contract is the basis of the legal relationship between an employee and his or her employer. A contract of employment is the agreement between the employer and executive which sets out their respective rights and obligations. The requisite elements of formation of a common law contract are (1) offer and acceptance; (2) consideration; and (3) the intention to create legal relations. The requisite elements of the formation of a valid contract in Quebec deal with similar issues and are generally described as (1) parties legally capable of contracting; (2) their consent legally given; (3) something which forms the object of the contract; and (4) a lawful cause.[1]

[1] C.C.Q., art. 1385 (previously C.C.L.C., art. 984).

B. REQUISITES TO THE VALIDITY OF AN EMPLOYMENT CONTRACT

1. Offer and Acceptance

§3.2 Capacity to contract refers to the ability to enter into binding legal relations. In Quebec, every person is capable of entering into juridical acts unless the law specifically declares otherwise.[1] The capacity to contract is intertwined with the notion of consent in that it requires each party to have the ability to give enlightened and free consent to enter into a contractual relationship. Where one is incapable of giving consent at the time of formation of the contract, it will be unenforceable.[2] Consent is obtained through the acts of offer and acceptance.

[1] C.C.Q., art. 4; see also C.C.Q., art. 1409 (previously C.C.L.C., art. 985). Those legally incapable of contracting in matters pertaining to their employment are persons under fourteen years of age (C.C.Q., art. 156) and incapable persons of full age (Q.C.Q., art. 256). Incapable persons of full age are those whose capacity is limited by express provision of law and those in respect of which judgment has been rendered, ordering the institution of protective supervision (C.C.Q., art. 154). Protective supervision may be obtained for a person of full age who is incapable of caring for him/herself or of administering his/her property by reason, *inter*

alia, of illness, deficiency or debility due to age which impairs his/her mental facilities or physical ability to express his/her will (C.C.Q., art. 258).
² C.C.Q., art. 1398. *Ross v. Hawker Siddeley Canada Inc.*, D.T.E. 88T-589 (Que. C.A.).

§3.3 In Quebec, as well as in the common law provinces, an offer is a
unilateral act that demonstrates the intention of the offeror to enter
into a contract and the willingness to be bound by the terms of the offer should those terms be accepted by the offeree.[1] An offer may be express or tacit, written or verbal, addressed specifically to one party or
to the world at large. An offeror may revoke the offer at any time prior
to its acceptance unless a term is attached.[2] Even if not revoked, an offer will not be considered to be open indefinitely because an offeror
cannot be said to have reasonably intended to be bound to outdated
terms. Unless the offeror stipulates a specific time at which the offer
will lapse, an offer will lapse after a reasonable period of time.[3] Once
revoked or lapsed, an offer cannot be accepted.

[1] C.C.Q., art. 1388 to 1390.
[2] C.C.Q., art. 1390(2).
[3] C.C.Q., art. 1392(1). *Boxer v. Norvan Properties Ltd.* (1988), 25 B.C.L.R. (2d) 231
    (C.A.); *Barrick v. Clark*, [1951] S.C.R. 177; *Vitra Glass Ltée v. Lavigueur Ltée*, [1959]
    B.R. 799 (Que. C.A.).

§3.4 At common law, the contract is formed when the offeree accepts
the offer and such acceptance is communicated to the offeror. Acceptance is an unequivocal act which demonstrates the intention to accede
to the terms of an offer and thereby create a relationship of mutual
rights and obligations with the co-contracting party. In Quebec, under
the new provisions of the Civil Code of Quebec, the contract is formed
when and where acceptance is received by the offeror, regardless of
the method of communication used, and even though the parties have
agreed to reserve agreement as to secondary terms.[1]

[1] C.C.Q., art 1387. Note that this new provision eliminates the confusing results
    which used to occur based on the method of communicating acceptance.

§3.5 In most employment relationships, there is no written employment contract. The prospective employee is typically offered a position
of employment with the employer. Such an offer may be accepted
either expressly, by the offeree stating that he or she agrees to take the
job, or tacitly, by the offeree commencing the work which is the subject
of the offer. When the offeree commences this work, it can be inferred
that he or she has accepted to perform the services, and a binding contract will have been formed.[1] When negotiations precede the formation
of the contract of employment, it may be that the contract is not
formed until the execution of the written agreement, notwithstanding

the commencement of work by the employee. In *Bowen v. Canadian Tire Corp.*,[2] despite the plaintiff's attendance at meetings of the board of directors and executive committee meetings, as well as the defendant's efforts to assist the plaintiff in securing a suitable residence, the court held that no contract was formed prior to the approval of the executive's employment by the defendant's board of directors which the plaintiff knew not to be a mere formality. In addition, since essential terms had not been agreed upon, there could be no contract.

[1] *Sherwood v. Merrill Lynch Canada Inc.*, unreported, March 5, 1990 (Ont. C.A.); *Carlill v. Carbolic Smoke Ball Co.*, [1893] 1 Q.B. 256 (C.A.).

[2] (1991), 35 C.C.E.L. 113 (Ont. Ct. (Gen. Div.)).

§3.6 An example of the difficulty that may be involved in determining when an offer has been accepted arose in *Parte v. Rogers Cablesystems Ltd.*[1] In that case, the court examined the situation where the plaintiff employee had made the following response to an offer:

> I look forward to any questions or comments you have and to your agreement in principle to the first option.[2]

The court held that it was clear from the evidence that the offer had only been conditionally accepted by the plaintiff, by electronic letter dated May 24, 1990, subject to agreement by the employer's representative to the plaintiff's somewhat ambiguous condition. The court then found that the plaintiff's conditional acceptance was in fact a counter-offer of his own rather than an acceptance of the defendant's offer and that he had never received a reply to his counter-offer from anyone else on behalf of the defendant. Although he saw his superior nearly every day, the latter had never discussed it with him either. The court then determined:

> I therefore find from the evidence that there was no effective acceptance by the Plaintiff of the Defendant's offer of May 9, 1990 nor was there acceptance by the Defendant of the Plaintiff's counter-offer, and that, therefore, there was no agreement between them, there being no consensus *ad idem*.[3]

[1] (1992), 37 A.C.W.S. (3d) 664 (Alta. Q.B.); affd/judicial review refused, [1994] A.W.L.D. 057 (Alta. C.A.).

[2] (1992), 37 A.C.W.S. (3d) 664 (Alta. Q.B.), at 9.

[3] (1992), 37 A.C.W.S. (3d) 664 (Alta. Q.B.), at 10.

2. Consideration

(a) Negotiated Terms of Employment Contract

§3.7 The common law concept of consideration requires that there be a bargain between the parties. In other words, each party must promise to give something to the other party in order to form a binding contract. In a contract of employment, the employee agrees primarily to perform services and the employer agrees to pay for these services. This exchange is the essence of the consideration in the employment contract.

§3.8 The issue of consideration is of particular importance where the parties seek to amend the terms of their relationship. For a contractual amendment to be enforceable, it must be supported by fresh consideration from both parties so that one party may not unilaterally alter the employment relationship. Thus, an agreement by an employee to take on additional responsibility will be enforceable if there is consideration from the employer, such as the promise to increase the employee's salary. Where an employer attempts to unilaterally alter the terms of employment, without consideration from the employee, the issue of "constructive dismissal" may arise.[1]

[1] See Chapter 12, "Termination of Employment".

§3.9 The principle of consideration is of particular relevance when one considers the effect of a written employment contract signed after the employee commences his or her employment, or when an employer attempts to assert that the content of a company manual, policy directive or internal regulation forms part of the terms of the employment contract. With respect to the former, where the executive has commenced work and, subsequently, the employer requires the executive to sign a written employment contract, a concern will arise if the terms of this written contract differ from the oral terms of employment established at the time of hiring.[1]

[1] *Francis v. Canadian Imperial Bank of Commerce* (1994), 7 C.C.E.L. (2d) 1 (Ont. C.A.).

§3.10 In *Baker v. British Columbia Ins. Co.,*[1] an employee and an employer entered into a renewed employment contract. This contract was identical to the previous contract except for a clause which gave the employer the right to terminate the employee's employment, without cause, on 90 days' notice. The court held that the clause was ineffective as there was no consideration given for the new term. The employee was entitled to reasonable notice which, in this case, was 12 months.

[1] (1992), 41 C.C.E.L. 107 (B.C.S.C.); affd/judicial review refused (1993), 46 C.C.E.L. 211 (B.C.C.A.).

§3.11 Furthermore, in *Monarch Messenger Services Ltd. v. Houlding,*[1] subsequent to the employee's commencement of work, the employer sought to have the employee sign a standard form contract which contained a restrictive covenant prohibiting employees from soliciting any of the employer's customers for a period of one year following termination. The proposed agreement also placed restrictions on the ability of an employee to disclose confidential information gained as a result of employment. Houlding refused to sign this contract and his employment was terminated. He then established a rival messenger service, contrary to the terms of the restrictive covenant, and was held to be liable for the improper use, for his own benefit, of confidential information acquired in the course of his employment. This liability, however, was not based on breach of the restrictive covenant. In fact, since Houlding was not aware of the covenant at the time of hiring, this covenant could not be imposed after the work commenced without consideration flowing from the employer.[2]

[1] (1984), 5 C.C.E.L. 219 (Alta. Q.B.); affd/judicial review refused (1986), 13 C.C.E.L. xxxvi *n* (Alta. C.A.).

[2] See also *Puiia v. Occupational Training Centre* (1983), 43 Nfld. & P.E.I.R. 283 (P.E.I.C.A.). See also *MacDonald v. Royal Canadian Legion* (1995), 12 C.C.E.L. (2d) 211 (N.S.S.C.).

§3.12 To avoid any uncertainty as to whether there is consideration for entering into an employment contract, it is advisable that the written contract be executed before the employee commences work.[1] Of course, in all circumstances it will be necessary to prove that any given clause did indeed form part of the employment contract. In one case, for example, the notice provisions were merely incorporated on the employment form which the employee was requested to sign on his first day of work and the provisions were not explained to him. The court held that the employee was entitled to view the form as a mere administrative document as opposed to an employment contract, the terms of which were not binding on the employee.[2]

[1] *Bowen v. Canadian Tire Corp.* (1991), 35 C.C.E.L. 113 (Ont. Ct. (Gen. Div.)).

[2] *Burden v. Eastgate Ford Sales & Service (82) Co.* (1992), 44 C.C.E.L. 218 (Ont. Ct. (Gen. Div.)).

(b) Non-Negotiated Terms of Employment: Company Policies or Manuals

§3.13 Regarding the enforceability of company manuals, policy directives or internal regulations, the inquiry is similar to the above. The issue is whether the terms of the employee policy manual form part of the employment contract. This is a question of fact to be determined in each case.[1]

[1]   *Hill v. Peter Gorman Ltd.* (1957), 9 D.L.R. (2d) 124 (Ont. C.A.); *Wiebe v. Central Transport Refrigeration (Man.) Ltd.* (1994), 3 C.C.E.L. (2d) 1 (Man. C.A.); revg in part 45 C.C.E.L. 1 (Q.B.); *Sagkeeng Educational Authority Inc. v. Guimond* (1995), 16 C.C.E.L. (2d) 259 (F.C.T.D.); *Thibault v. Auger*, [1950] C.S. 343 (Que. S.C.).

§3.13.1   The courts have nevertheless adopted certain guidelines in this area. Generally, employer handbooks and policies were not considered to bind employers and employees since they had not been mutually agreed upon. However, where such documents establish rights for the employees and have, with time, become rules which are known and accepted by all of the parties, some contractual force may be attributed to them. This is especially true where the employee may have been influenced in his or her decision to join the company or to remain with an employer because of such rights.

§3.13.2   Where an employer attempts to alter or vary the terms of a contract with an employee, the employee has a number of choices. On the one hand, the employee may accept, either expressly or impliedly, the variation. In this case, there is a new contract. On the other hand, if the change is material, the employee may refuse the variation and argue that he has been constructively dismissed by his employer. We refer you to Chapter 12 for an analysis of the constructive dismissal issue.

§3.14   In the case of a verbal employment contract, recent cases have held that an employee is not subject to the provisions of a manual unless the employee was made aware of its terms at the time employment commenced.[1] However, where handbook or policies grant additional rights to employees, the courts increasingly tend to view these rights as binding work conditions. For example, in *Prince v. T. Eaton Co.*,[2] the court, while dealing with the impact of an injury suffered by the terminated employee during the reasonable notice period, held that the employer's policy manual could reasonably be perceived as the source of a term of the employment contract because it was a document "common" to both the employer and the employee.

[1]   *Starcevich v. Woodward's Ltd.* (1991), 37 C.C.E.L. 46 (B.C.S.C.); *Wiebe v. Central Transport Refrigeration (Man.) Ltd.* (1994), 3 C.C.E.L. (2d) 1 (Man. C.A.); *Ewasiuk v. Estevan Area Home Care District 9 Inc.* (1985), 9 C.C.E.L. 267 (Sask. Q.B.); *Rahemtulla v. Vanfed Credit Union* (1984), 4 C.C.E.L. 170 (B.C.S.C.).

[2]   (1992), 41 C.C.E.L. 72 (B.C.C.A.); leave to appeal refused, [1993] 2 S.C.R. xi.

§3.15 In *Adams v. Comark Inc.*,[1] the court decided that a "policy" concerning the use of frequent flyer points accumulated while travelling in the course of duties, which allowed the employee to utilize the points for his personal benefit, had become a condition of employment as it was a significant benefit enjoyed over a sustained period of time. This decision may allow an executive to argue that a "practice" or "custom" amounts to a policy or even to a condition of employment.

[1]   (1992), 42 C.C.E.L. 15 (Man. C.A.).

§3.16 In *King v. Gulf Canada Ltd.*,[1] the court was asked to determine whether a letter addressed "To All Employees" constituted a contract. The court found that the letter was not a contract, even though it stated that it was "binding on all employees", since there was an absence of evidence indicating that either party intended the statements in the letter to be contractual.[2]

[1]   (1992), 37 A.C.W.S. (3d) 663 (Ont. C.A.); application for leave to appeal dismissed, [1993] 2 S.C.R. viii.
[2]   (1992), 37 A.C.W.S. (3d) 663 (Ont. C.A.), at 2-6.

§3.17 Whether a handbook or policy of a contractual nature is enforceable will depend upon the particular wording used.[1] In *Rahemtulla v. Vanfed Credit Union*,[2] the contractual effect of a policy manual for employees was discussed. McLachlin J. stated the following principles:

> . . . if the terms of the policy manual are to be binding, it must be concluded that they have contractual force. The usual elements of a contract must be established: a concluded agreement; consideration; and contractual intention.
>
> The agreement consists of "an outward expression of common intention and of expectation": Anson on the Law of Contract (24th ed.), p. 23. Inward concurrence of intention is not enough for the formation of a contract; there must be an outward manifestation of assent by each party such as to induce a reasonable reliance in the other: S.J. Waddams, The Law of Contracts (1977), p. 18. Both offer and acceptance must be communicated by one party to the other.
>
> The evidence in the case at Bar does not establish that the parties expressed a common intention to be bound by the terms of the policy manual. The usual method of indicating assent to written documents is by signature; this was not done. Nor was assent manifested by conduct. It may be that the defendant's assent can be inferred from the act of giving the manual to the plaintiff. But, while the plaintiff may have privately accepted the terms of the manual, there is no evidence that this acceptance was ever communicated by her to the defendant. Communication of assent cannot be inferred from the fact that the plaintiff continued to work after being given the manual. She had contracted to work for the defendant prior to receiving the manual. The fact that she continued to fulfil this obligation after being given the manual cannot be taken as an assent to its terms.[3]

[1]   See *Rinaldo v. Canada Trust Co.*, unreported, March 1, 1989 (Ont. Dist. Ct.), where the written policy or handbook expressly recognized the employer's discretion in dealing with the benefit, including the possibility of unilateral termination of the benefit.

[2]   (1984), 4 C.C.E.L. 170 (B.C.S.C.). See also *Jones v. Consumers Packaging Inc.* (1995), 14 C.C.E.L. (2d) 273 (Ont. Gen. Div.).

[3]   (1984), 4 C.C.E.L. 170 (B.C.S.C.), at 177-78.

§3.18   In written employment contracts, one frequently finds a provision that the written contract contains all the terms of employment between the employee and the employer. In such a circumstance, if the provisions of a manual are to be considered part of the employment contract, there should be a provision which expressly incorporates the manual into the contract. An attempt by an employer to impose the terms of a manual or policy directive after the commencement of the employee's work may amount to an attempt to unilaterally amend the employment contract, and will raise the issue of constructive dismissal.[1]

[1]   See Chapter 12, "Termination of Employment".

3. Intention to Create Legal Relations

§3.19   An offer exists only where the offeror intends to be bound by the terms of the offer, if accepted. It is for this reason that job advertisements and other "invitations to treat" are not considered offers. Instead, an advertisement for an available job represents the desire of the employer to solicit applications from prospective employees. It is only after the employer considers the applications and makes an offer of employment, with the intent to be bound thereby, that a contract of employment may be formed upon acceptance by the offeree.

C. DEFECTS IN CONSENT

§3.20   Fundamental to the enforceability of any contract is the existence of a consent given freely and voluntarily.[1] At common law, the circumstances under which a court may deny enforcement of a contract as a result of failure to obtain a free and voluntary consent can be broken down into three categories. These are (1) mistake; (2) fraud; and (3) duress, undue influence and unconscionability. In Quebec, (1) error; (2) fear; and (3) lesion invalidate consent.[2] Lesion will not be discussed as it is a cause of nullity only in certain cases with respect to minors and interdicted persons.[3]

[1] C.C.Q., art. 1399; Ville de Montréal-Est v. Gagnon, [1978] C.A. 100 (Que.), leave to appeal to S.C.C. refused 42 N.R. 88*n*.
[2] C.C.Q., art. 1399 (previously C.C.L.C., art. 991).
[3] C.C.Q., art. 1405 to 1408.

1. Mistake/Error

§3.21 In the common law provinces, this principle essentially addresses the issue of which party is to assume the risk of loss. Although variously described by legal scholars, for these purposes it can be broken down into two categories.

§3.22 The first category involves the failure to accurately record in writing the terms of the agreement. Thus, if the executive and the employer agree to an annual base salary of $100,000 but the subsequent written agreement provides for an annual base salary of $90,000, the executive could rely on the principle of mistake where the employer failed to remunerate the executive at the base rate of $100,000 per annum. It is important to note, however, that this remedy is very narrowly construed by the courts.

§3.23 The second category involves the situation where one party has made a mistake in payment. In an employment context, mistakes often occur where the employer has overpaid the employee in respect of bonuses, commissions, or other entitlements. It is generally recognized that the employee, in these circumstances, has been unjustly enriched and therefore the employer can require repayment. The unilateral withholding by the employer of the amount overpaid from the employee's wages may be prohibited under various provincial employment standards statutes.[1]

[1] See, *e.g.*, the Ontario *Employment Standards Act*, R.S.O. 1990, c. E.14, s. 8, and the British Columbia *Employment Standards Act*, R.S.B.C. 1996, c. 113, s. 21(1).

§3.24 Under Quebec law, article 1400 of the Civil Code of Quebec enumerates three types of errors which are a cause of nullity: error (1) in the nature of the contract, (2) in the substance of the thing which is the object of the prestation, or (3) anything that was essential in determining that contract. An inexcusable error does not vitiate a contract.

§3.25 For a contract to be void because of an error related to its consideration, the contracting party must make it clear from the start that this element is a main consideration for the contract. A party invoking an error relating to the substance of the contract must show that this specific quality was an agreed requirement. A quality which is merely accessory is insufficient to justify a declaration of nullity.[1]

[1]   *Ville d'Anjou v. Patry*, D.T.E. 88T-125 (Que. S.C.).

2. Fraud

§3.26   Fraud exists when a false representation is made knowingly, without belief in its truth, or recklessly, without caring whether it is true or false.[1] An error on the part of one party induced by fraud committed by the other party or with his or her knowledge vitiates consent whenever, but for that error, the party would not have contracted or would have contracted on different terms.[2] Fraud is never presumed and must be proven. Of particular interest in the employment context is the situation in which the employee misleads the employer on the application for employment. Generally, the position of the courts is that, where there is evidence of such a misrepresentation by the employee, the contract of employment may be rendered null and void.[3] In other cases, the employer has relied on this fraud as a just cause for terminating the employment relationship.[4]

[1]   *Derry v. Peek* (1889), 14 App. Cas. 337 (H.L.).
[2]   C.C.Q., art. 1401.
[3]   *Bridgewater v. Leon's Mfg. Co.* (1984), 6 C.C.E.L. 55 (Sask. Q.B.).
[4]   *Werle v. SaskEnergy Inc.* (1992), 103 Sask. R. 241 (Q.B.).

§3.27   In *Ville de Montréal-Est v. Gagnon*,[1] the Quebec Court of Appeal dealt with this issue. In that case, the City of Montreal had hired a fireman on the basis of an application form for employment. The form in question required the applicants to make solemn affirmations about themselves, having the same force and effect as if they were made under oath. One applicant affirmed that he had no criminal record. Upon investigation, however, it was discovered that he did in fact have a criminal record at the time he made his affirmation. To make matters worse, he was found guilty of shoplifting while the investigation was being carried out. He was fired on the basis of his dishonesty. Mr. Justice Bélanger, on behalf of the court, wrote:

> . . . it was not a question of dismissing an employee because of an act committed during the course of a valid contract for the lease and hire of services but rather, to cease recognizing and giving effect to a contract the consent for which was improperly obtained.[2]

[1]   [1978] C.A. 100 (Que. C.A.).
[2]   [1978] C.A. 100 (Que. C.A.), at 101.

§3.28 The problem of proper representation at the time of hiring is of particular relevance to executives who are often referred to prospective employers through "head-hunters", or executive placement agencies. Often, the *curriculum vitae* describing the executive is prepared by the third party agency, obviously with the consent of the executive, but along the form and guidelines recommended by the third party. The executive should be cautious not to unduly embellish his qualifications or experience. Generally, however, when a *curriculum vitae* exaggerates the qualities of an employee but contains no untruths, courts will consider this insufficient to invalidate the consent.[1]

[1] *Tanquay v. Scanway Corp.*, D.T.E. 85T-65 (Que. S.C.); *Bridgewater v. Leon's Mfg. Co.* (1984), 6 C.C.E.L. 55 (Sask. Q.B.).

§3.29 Similarly, the executive should not conspicuously neglect to reveal a relevant characteristic which he or she knows or ought to know would be an important consideration for the employer. There is often a fine line between presenting one's attributes in a favourable way, which is permissible, and providing false information or purposely omitting key information, which is not permissible. For example, an executive who, at the time he was hired, concealed the fact that he had been fired by his previous employer for unauthorized use of company funds, was properly dismissed when his new employer discovered this fact.[1] Similarly, it was a breach of the obligation of loyalty for an employee to neglect to reveal to her employer that she had previously been fired, thus leading her employer to believe that she was still working at the time of hiring when, in fact, she was not.[2]

[1] *Jarret v. Henry Morgan & Co.* (1881), 12 R.L. 58 (Que. S.C.).
[2] *Gobeil v. C.L.S.C. Saguenay-Nord*, J.E. 82-524 (Que. S.C.).

§3.30 The question of pre-employment dishonesty also raises the issue of executives with criminal records and the extent to which they must reveal this. The Quebec *Charter of Human Rights and Freedoms*[1] prohibits an employer from dismissing, refusing to hire, or otherwise penalizing a person in his or her employment simply because he or she has been convicted of a penal or criminal offence, if the offence was in no way connected with the employment or if the person has obtained a pardon for the offence. Many other provincial and federal laws include similar prohibitions.[2] However, with the exception of the *Canadian Human Rights Act*, no law precludes an employer from asking the employee whether he has a criminal record, even if unrelated to his work.[3] Although the authors do not believe that an executive need go so far as to volunteer the existence of a criminal record unrelated to his or her employment, he or she is certainly under an obligation not to deny the existence of such a record when questioned in this regard by a potential employer at the time of hiring. False representations at hiring may justify termination of employment.[4]

1   R.S.Q., c. C-12, s. 18.2 [en. 1982, c. 61, s. 5; am. 1990, c. 4, s. 133].
2   See the *Criminal Records Act*, R.S.C. 1985, c. C-47, the *Canadian Human Rights Act*, R.S.C. 1985, c. H-6, the British Columbia *Human Rights Code*, R.S.B.C. 1996, c. 210 and the *Human Rights Code*, R.S.O. 1990, c. H.19.
3   For a complete discussion of discrimination on the basis of a criminal record in Canada, see T.J. Singleton, *"La discrimination fondée sur le motif des antécédents judiciaires et les instruments anti-discriminatoires canadiens"* (1993), 72 R. du B. Can. 456.
4   See *Ville de Montréal-Est v. Gagnon*, [1978] C.A. 100 (Que.); *Les Biscuits Associés du Canada Ltée v. Commission des droits de la personne du Québec*, [1981] C.A. 521 (Que.); *Renda v. Lachine*, J.E. 83-368 (Que. S.C.).

§3.31   In view of the fact that standards applied to executives are high and reflect their greater responsibilities to the organization, any dishonest conduct in the course of employment would likely constitute a clear breach of the employment agreement, and be cause for termination.

§3.32   The obligation not to mislead also applies to employers. In British Columbia, labour standards legislation[1] specifically provides that employers cannot induce or persuade persons to become their employees by means of certain deceptive or false representations, advertising, or pretences. In particular, employees may not be misled with regard to the availability of a position, the nature of the work to be done, the wages to be paid for the work, or the conditions of employment.[2]

1   *Employment Standards Act*, R.S.B.C. 1996, c. 113, s. 8.
2   With respect to the employer's duty of care regarding employment opportunities, see chapter 5, "Negligent Misrepresentation."

3.   Duress, Undue Influence and Unconscionability/Fear

§3.33   The concepts of duress and undue influence are part of the general law of unconscionability by which a contract may be set aside if its proposed terms are patently unfair or unreasonable toward one of the parties. The principle of unconscionability recognizes that there may be circumstances in which the inequality of bargaining power between parties to a contract may allow the stronger party to impose unfair contractual provisions on the weaker party. In such cases, an unfair contract may be set aside as unconscionable.

§3.34   The issue of unconscionability has arisen in connection with the enforceability of notice provisions in an employment contract. The Ontario Court of Appeal, in *Jobber v. Addressograph Multigraph of Canada Ltd.*[1] and *Wallace v. Toronto-Dominion Bank,*[2] accepted that the doctrine of unconscionability may work to render provisions of employment contracts unenforceable.

[1] (1980), 1 C.C.E.L. 87.
[2] (1983), 145 D.L.R. (3d) 431; leave to appeal dismissed (1983), 52 N.R. 157*n* (S.C.C.).

§3.35 In Quebec, the civil law principle of fear vitiating consent is similar to the common law principles of duress and undue influence. Fear of serious injury to the person or property of one of the parties vitiates consent given by that party where the fear is induced by violence or threats exerted or made by or known to the other party. Apprehended injury may also relate to another person or his property and is appraised according to the circumstances.[1] In addition, the Civil Code of Quebec also stipulates that fear induced by the abusive exercise of a right or a power or the threat of such exercise vitiates consent.[2]

[1] C.C.Q., art. 1402.
[2] C.C.Q., art. 1403.

D. CONTENT OF THE EMPLOYMENT CONTRACT

§3.36 As is the case for most contracts, the employment contract does not have to be written in order to be valid.[1] In practice, the great majority of employment agreements are not embodied in a written document. Consequently, it is sometimes difficult to determine what is the extent and content of the employment contract.[2] One of the primary reasons executives will enter into a written employment contract is to avoid this uncertainty. Generally, however, all employment contracts implicitly include the employer's obligation to provide work, provide remuneration, and ensure the safety of its employee, as well as the employee's obligation to execute the work and be loyal to his or her employer. Each of these implied employment obligations is examined more fully later in this work.[3]

[1] Except in Quebec, in the specific case of a stipulation of non-competition: C.C.Q., art. 2089.
[2] Regarding the application of manuals, see, *supra,* at §§3.13 *et seq.*
[3] See Chapters 6 to 10.

§3.37 The parties are also free to set out particular provisions through express terms of the employment contract. Such terms may include productivity levels, attendance requirements, non-competition agreements, entitlement to sick leave, and employer's contributions to pension and other benefit plans and termination provisions. These terms are discussed in more detail later in this work.[1]

[1]   See Chapter 11, "The Written Employment Contract and Some Specific Provisions".

E. CONCLUSION

§3.38 As we have seen, an employment contract exists once specific technical requisites of formation of a contract are met. In the next chapter, we will examine the essential elements of a validly formed employment contract and the parties to such contract.

CHAPTER 4

THE NATURE OF EMPLOYMENT, THE EMPLOYER AND THE EMPLOYEE

A. INTRODUCTION

§4.1 What sets the employment contract apart from all other contracts is the nature of the benefits exchanged by the parties, which include personal, mental and physical abilities.[1] This personal aspect has led to the characterization of an employment contract as *intuitu personae:*[2] one party contracts because of the identity of the other. Because of this characterization, the courts, except in the Province of Quebec,[3] have held that in case of wrongful termination of an employment contract, specific performance or, in other words, forcing the parties to continue the employment relationship should not be ordered[4] and that the employment contract cannot be assigned.[5]

---

[1] In Quebec, art. 2085 of the Quebec Civil Code (previously 1665a of the C.C.L.C.). Article 2085 defines a contract of employment as a contract by which a person, the employee, undertakes for a limited period to do work for remuneration, according to the instructions and under the direction and control of another person, the employer.

[2] Of a personal nature which cannot be transferred.

[3] In Quebec, the *Labour Standards Act* creates a recourse for reinstatement available to employees who are not part of upper management and who feel that they have been dismissed without just and sufficient cause.

[4] *Semchuk v. Regina Bd. of Education* (1986), 15 C.C.E.L. 223 (Sask. Q.B.), affd 57 Sask. R. 34 (C.A.); *Savoie v. Roy*, [1983] C.A. 513 (Que.); *Savage v. United Elastic Ltd.* (1979), 105 D.L.R. (3d) 571 (N.S.S.C.); *Union des employés de commerce, local 500 v. Légaré Automobiles Inc.*, [1973] C.A. 577 (Que.); *Dupré Quarries Ltd. v. Dupré*, [1934] S.C.R. 528. But see the J.A. Vallerand's *obiter dictum* in *Rock-Forest (Ville de) v. Gosselin*, [1991] R.J.Q. 1000 (C.A.) to the effect that the law has evolved since the case of *Dupré Quarries* and that in some cases reinstatement could be ordered; and *Boivin v. L'Orchestre symphonique de Laval 1984 Inc.*, D.T.E. 92T-822 (Que. S.C.), where interlocutory injunctions ordering the reinstatement of a wrongfully dismissed employee were granted. See also *Computertime Network Corp. v. Zucker*, D.T.E. 94T-1367 (Que. C.A.).

[5] Although recently courts have recognized the validity of seconding agreements (see, *infra*, §§4.24 *et seq.*).

---

§4.2 It is the nature of the relationship that will determine a person's legal status as one of employee or other (such as independent contractor or partner) and not the title or status that an individual is given in a contract or letter.[1]

---

[1]   *National Financial Brokerage Center Inc. v. Investors Syndicate Ltd.* (1986), 9 C.P.R. (3d) 497 (Que. C.A.); *Wiebe Door Services Ltd. v. M.N.R.*, [1986] 5 W.W.R. 450 (F.C.A.) *Doyle v. London Life Ins. Co.* (1985), 23 D.L.R. (4th) 443 (B.C.C.A.), leave to appeal to S.C.C. refused 64 N.R. 318*n*; *MacPhail v. Tackama Forest Products Ltd.*, [1994] 3 W.W.R. 36 (B.C.S.C.).

B.   ESSENTIAL ELEMENTS OF THE EMPLOYMENT RELATIONSHIP

§4.3   Regardless of the way the parties have characterized their relationship, employment exists when the following three elements are present: the individual (1) works for another, (2) receives remuneration for his or her work, and (3) is subordinate to another, the employer. The question of whether an employment relationship exists can usually be settled only by examining all of the various elements of the relationship.[1]

---

[1]   In Quebec, C.C.Q., art. 2085. *MacKenzie v. Jevco Ins. Management Inc.* (1986), 9 B.C.L.R. (2d) 127 (S.C.), affd 24 B.C.L.R. (2d) 360 (C.A.); *Montreal v. Montreal Locomotive Works Ltd.*, [1947] 1 D.L.R. 161 (P.C.). See also *McGuire v. Wardair Canada Ltd.* (1969), 71 W.W.R. 70 (Alta. S.C.); *Johnston v. Northwood Pulp Ltd.* (1968), 70 D.L.R. (2d) 15 (Ont. H.C.J.); *Lingelbach v. James Tire Centres Ltd.* (1995), 7 C.C.E.L. (2d) 297 (Sask. C.A.). See also *Allish v. Allied Engineering of B.C. Ltd.* (1957), 22 W.W.R. 641 (B.C.C.A.) where an employment contract was found not to exist.

§4.4   The issue of whether or not a person is an employee may arise in situations other than wrongful dismissal claims or in actions opposing the alleged employer and alleged employee. For example, a third party may seek to have this issue determined in cases where the third party claims compensation from an employer based on vicarious liability for the acts or omissions of an employee in the course of employment.[1] This issue of whether or not a person is an employee may also be raised in the context of a particular statute. However, the statutory definition of who is an employee may be different than that under the Civil Code of Quebec or common law and, consequently, the elements which must be present may not be the same. This is so because some legislation limits the definition of employee in order to restrict the application of the legislation. Thus, when determining whether someone is an employee, and when referring to case law, we must pay attention to the specific context in which the issue was raised.

---

[1]   *Côté v. Turmel*, [1967] B.R. 309 (Que. C.A.). Article 1463 of the Civil Code of Quebec stipulates that "[t]he principal is liable to reparation for injury caused by the

fault of his agents and servants in the performance of their duties; nevertheless, he retains his recourses against them." Regarding the extent of this obligation, see Jean-Louis Baudouin, *La responsabilité civile délictuelle*, 3rd ed. (Cowansville: Éditions Yvon Blais, 1990), pp. 251-96. See also Chapter 8, "Safety". Similar liability exists in common law; see *Plains Engineering Ltd. v. Barnes Security Services Ltd.* (1987), 19 C.C.E.L. 205 (Alta. Q.B.).

1. The Individual Must Work for Another

§4.5 An individual may work for another person, a partnership, a corporation or any other legal entity or group of persons. A person may even be an employee of a corporation of which he happens to be the sole or the majority shareholder. An individual who incorporates his or her own company which undertakes by a contract to provide services to another company is generally not an employee of the latter company.[1] However, the courts have held that where an employer tells an employee to incorporate himself or herself and continues to hire that person's company to do the same function, that person may continue to be an employee, notwithstanding the incorporation.[2] Incorporating oneself does not prevent a court from finding that the incorporated individual is really the employee.[3]

[1] *Habitabec Inc. v. Cloutier*, D.T.E. 90T-1266 (Que. S.C.); *Dazé v. Messageries dynamiques*, J.E. 90-678 (Que. C.A.); *Vachon v. Martin*, D.T.E. 88T-606 (Que. S.C.), affg. *Vachon v. Prudentielle Cie d'assurance Ltée*, D.T.E. 88T-221 (Que. T.A.); *Donaldson v. C.F.C.F. Inc.*, D.T.E. 84T-658 (Que. S.C.); *Watchstraps Inc. v. Poupart Ltée*, [1962] C.S. 273 (Que. S.C.).

[2] *Systèmes de communication Incotel Ltée v. Marcotte*, D.T.E. 88T-355 (Que. Prov. Ct.); *Queensbury Enterprises Inc. v. J.R. Corporate Planning Associates Inc.* (1989), 27 C.C.E.L. 56 (Ont. C.A.); *Mayer v. Technologies Industrielles S.N.C. Inc.*, D.T.E. 95T-1258 (Que. S.C.).

[3] *MacPhail v. Tackama Forest Products Ltd.*, [1994] 3 W.W.R. 36 (B.C.S.C.).

2. The Individual Must Receive Remuneration

§4.6 What constitutes remuneration is a question of fact.[1] Remuneration may be in the form of money, goods or materials. Each set of facts must be analyzed in order to ensure that remuneration does exist. A person offering services to another gratuitously will generally be regarded as a volunteer worker, not an employee.[2] The form or means used to calculate the remuneration does not affect the employment relationship. Remuneration may be awarded as a rate for piecework, an hourly rate, or entirely by commission.

[1] See Chapter 7, "Provide Remuneration".

[2] However, where an employer alleges that a position is a volunteer position, employment standards referees and the courts will examine the facts surrounding

the position closely in order to determine whether there has been a genuine volunteering of services or whether the worker is in fact an employee. Factors which may receive consideration include the extent to which the worker views the position as being in pursuit of his or her livelihood; the extent to which a benefit is conferred upon the recipient of the worker's services; the relative equality or inequality of the parties and the manner in which the relationship came about.

§4.7 Remuneration serves as one of the indicia in determining whether or not an employment relationship exists. Where the employee receives compensation in a profit/loss-sharing arrangement, the courts are more likely to find that the individual is an independent contractor.[1]

---

[1] *Doyle v. London Life Ins. Co.* (1985), 23 D.L.R. (4th) 443 (B.C.C.A.), leave to appeal to S.C.C. refused 64 N.R. 318*n*; *Isabelle v. Dame Isabelle*, [1967] C.S. 498 (Que.); *Montréal v. Montreal Locomotive Works Ltd.*, [1947] 1 D.L.R. 161 (P.C.).

3.   The Individual Must Be Subordinate to the Employer

§4.8 The essence of the employment relationship is the employee's state of subordination to the employer and the latter's concurrent right of control over the work to be done by the employee and how it is to be done.[1] This characteristic distinguishes the employment contract or the lease-and-hire of personal services from entrepreneurship, as well as from other contracts, notably from mandate.[2] The obligation to submit to lawful direction and to obey orders is distinctive of an employment relationship.[3] The employer has the right to give orders and expect compliance with these orders.

That the courts will consider subordination as a hallmark of the employment relationship is well illustrated in *Jaremko v. A.E. LePage Real Estate Services Ltd.*[4] In this case, the court held that a real estate salesman was an employee despite the fact that he had a considerable amount of control over his hours, that he was paid entirely by commission and that he considered himself to be "self-employed" for income tax purposes. The court held that the company nevertheless maintained "substantial control" given that, among other things, the salesman was subject to the company's policy regarding discipline and dismissal.

---

[1] *Preston Developments Inc. v. The Canadian Surety Co.* (1993), 1 C.C.E.L. (2d) 1 (Sask. C.A.). *Doyle v. London Life Ins. Co.* (1985), 23 D.L.R. (4th) 443 (B.C.C.A.), leave to appeal to S.C.C. refused 64 N.R. 318*n*; *Re Nelson and Byron Price & Associates Ltd.* (1981), 122 D.L.R. (3d) 340 (B.C.C.A.); *Lemay Construction Ltée v. Poirier*, [1965] B.R. 565 (Que. C.A.); *Montréal v. Montreal Locomotive Works Ltd.*, [1947] 1 D.L.R. 161 (P.C.); *Grimaldi v. Restaldi*, [1933] S.C.R. 489.

[2] *Verochio Ltd. v. Temiscouata Ry. Co.* (1941), 71 B.R. 311 (Que. C.A.).

[3] Art. 2085 of the Civil Code of Quebec states that the work is to be done "accord-

ing to the instructions and under the direction or control" of the employer, which is the translation of an earlier version of the French text. In French, the article now says simply that the work is to be done "under the direction or control" of the employer. The English version will surely be corrected shortly to more accurately reflect the French text.

4 (1989), 60 D.L.R. (4th) 762 (Ont. C.A.), affg (1987), 17 C.C.E.L. 262 (H.C.J.).

§4.9 While the degree of control or direction may vary according to the nature of the occupation and circumstances, some degree of subordination must be present for the court to conclude that the individual is an employee. This degree of subordination is sometimes known as the "control test". The principal's authority to fire, the control exercised over the work performed, and the degree of supervision are elements to defining an employer-employee relationship.[1] Obviously, the degree of subordination of a closely supervised employee differs substantially from a professional or skilled employee who operates more freely and is loosely supervised or even self-managed.[2]

[1] *Trans-Quebec Helicopters Ltd. v. Heirs of Lee*, [1980] C.A. 596 (Que.).
[2] In *Brosseau v. Villeneuve*, D.T.E. 90T-850 (Que. S.C.), the court held that a person who had an obligation to report to work daily from 8:00 a.m. to 4:00 p.m. and whose work was supervised hourly via a "Stop wait" time sheet was an employee. See also *Marotta v. R.* (1986), 11 C.C.E.L. 53 (F.C.T.D.) where the court held that the traditional test for "control" is not the decisive test where a high degree of latitude is afforded to a highly skilled professional and that resort must therefore be had to other tests in order to determine whether an employer-employee relationship exists. See also *Re Becker Milk Co. Ltd. and Director of Employment Standards of the Ontario Ministry of Labour* (1973), 1 O.R. (2d) 739 (Div. Ct.).

§4.10 One who contracts to do a specific piece of work, furnishes his or her own equipment, and executes the work either entirely in accordance with his or her own ideas or in accordance with a plan previously given to him or her by the person for whom the work is done, without being subject to the orders of the latter in respect to the details of the work, is generally an independent contractor, and not an employee.[1] Other aids to determining if a person is an independent contractor or an employee include whether that person is limited exclusively to providing services for the party with whom the work is contracted; whether, in the performance of his or her duties, the person bears any risk of loss; and whether the person expects to realize profits from providing those services other than by way of a fixed commission.[2]

[1] *Imperial Taxi Brandon (1983) Ltd. v. Hutchison* (1987), 46 D.L.R. (4th) 310 (Man. C.A.); *Kranz v. J.H. Whittome & Co.* (1988), 14 A.C.W.S. (3d) 16 (B.C. Co. Ct.); *Lambert v. Blanchette* (1926), 40 B.R. 370 (Que. C.A.); *Taboika v. Produits asphalte du Québec Ltée.*, D.T.E. 95T-1259, on appeal.
[2] *Jaremko v. A.E. LePage Real Estate Services Ltd.* (1989), 60 D.L.R. (4th) 762 (Ont. C.A.); *Doyle v. London Life Ins.* (1985), 23 D.L.R. (4th) 443 (B.C.C.A.), leave to ap-

peal to S.C.C. refused 64 N.R. 318*n*; *Quebec Asbestos Corp. v. Couture*, [1929] S.C.R. 166.

§4.11   The new Civil Code of Quebec now defines the contract of enterprise as a contract by which one party, the contractor, undertakes to carry out physical or intellectual work for another party, the client, for a price. The contractor is free to choose the means of performing the contract and no relationship of subordination exists between the contractor and the client in respect of such performance.[1]

[1]   Art. 2098 and 2099 C.C.Q.

§4.12   The fact that the contract of hire for services describes the employee as an independent contractor is not sufficient to determine that he or she is in fact an independent contractor. In *Rousell v. Prairie Implement Manufacturers Assn.*,[1] the plaintiff, who was 64 years old, was hired as a consultant under a contract which described him as an independent contractor. At trial, it was found that he was an employee as he had to devote his full time to the employer, his contract could not be assigned, and his hours, travel and activities were carried out under the direction of the general manager.

[1]   (1992), 36 A.C.W.S. (3d) 809 (Sask. Q.B.).

§4.13   In *Beaulieu v. Picard*,[1] Mr. Justice Greenshields declared, with respect to an unskilled employee:

> I take it as a fair statement of our law and jurisprudence that it is immaterial whether the workman is paid by the piece or by the foot, as in this case, provided the work was done on the premises and under the supervision of the defendants.
>
> In order to be an independent contractor, as pretended by the defendants, a workman must be free from orders and must not be subject to the orders of anyone as to the manner in which the work is to be done.

[1]   (1912), 42 C.S. 455 (Que. Ct. of Rev.), at 458.

C.   DEFINING THE EMPLOYER AND THE EMPLOYEE WITHIN VARIOUS CORPORATE STRUCTURES

1.   Who Is the Employer?

§4.14   Although it is usually easy to identify who the employer is, this is not always the case. The general rule is that the employer is the one who controls and directs the employee. In some circumstances, there may appear to be two employers. In those cases, one may have to refer to the fundamental elements which make up the employment relationship to properly identify the employer.

§4.15 Determining who is the true employer is particularly important when an employee seeks to recover compensation for wrongful dismissal or improper breach of the employment contract. However, one court has held that, in a case where the identity of the real employer is unclear and the plaintiff sues two alleged employers, the defendants may have the burden of proving which of the two is in fact the real employer.[1]

[1] *Léger v. Groupe S.M. Inc.*, D.T.E. 90T-147 (Que. S.C.).

(a) Companies With the Same Administration

§4.16 In *Castagna v. Design Hydraulics Inc.*,[1] two companies (Design Hydraulics "DH" and Normont Hydraulics "NH") were held jointly liable for the losses flowing from the breach of Castagna's employment contract even though Castagna was employed only by NH. The court held that the two companies were joint employers because of the following facts: DH was NH's agent; both companies had the same president who wrote to Castagna using, alternately, NH's letterhead and DH's letterhead. Moreover, the president had offered Castagna employment with DH after his mandate with NH was completed.

[1] D.T.E. 88T-1006 (Que. S.C.).

§4.17 Similarly, in *Denis Pépin Automobiles Ltée v. Longchamps*,[1] the Quebec Court of Appeal rejected an appellant company's submission that it should not be held liable to pay the employee's wrongful dismissal award because it was no longer the employee's employer following a corporate reorganization. The court found that this reorganization did not absolve the original employer of responsibility where the employee had the same duties and reported to the same individuals before and after the reorganization. Consequently, both companies were held liable for the damages arising from the breach of the employment.

[1] D.T.E. 88T-852 (Que. C.A.). See also *Sinclair v. Dover Engineering Services Ltd.* (1988), 49 D.L.R. (4th) 297 (B.C.C.A.); *Bagby v. Gustavson Int. Drilling Co.* (1980), 24 A.R. 181 (C.A.).

§4.18 In *Choquette v. F.O.I.S.I. Forces immobilières & stratégies d'investissement Inc.*,[1] the agent of one of the three defendant companies had met with the plaintiff in order to inquire as to his interest in becoming the sales manager of the company. Choquette left his current employment and, upon joining the company in October 1986, discovered that another sales manager had been hired. Three months later, at the end of January 1987, he was transferred to another position at the same salary due to the abolition of his position. In March 1987, he was terminated. His termination documents identified another of the defendants as employer. In an action for wrongful dismissal, he claimed notice and damages. The court determined that, when three defendants acting with each other have the same administration and are linked according to their financial statements, which do not reveal the identity of the employer to the person whose services they retain, they must be regarded as joint and several employers and must bear the responsibility of the acts of their agents together.

[1]   D.T.E. 91T-1187 (Que. S.C.).

§4.19   One court has stated:

> As long as there exists a sufficient degree of relationship between the different legal entities who apparently compete for the role of employer, there is no reason in law or in equity why they ought not all to be regarded as one for the purpose of determining liability for obligations owed to those employees who, in effect, have served all without regard for any precise notion of to whom they were bound in contract. What will constitute a sufficient degree of relationship will depend, in each case, on the details of such relationship, including such factors as individual shareholdings, corporate shareholdings and interlocking directorships. The essence of that relationship will be the element of common control.

· · · · ·

> It must be kept in mind that one may be employed by a number of companies at different times for different purposes, or even at the same time. That is a matter of agreement reached between the employee and his respective employers and as long as they are aware of the employee's various activities or roles it is a matter with respect to which the parties can reach what they consider the most commercially convenient arrangement.[1]

[1]   *Johnston v. Topolinski* (1988), 23 C.C.E.L. 285 (Ont. Dist. Ct.), at 290-91; citing *Sinclair v. Dover Engineering Services Ltd.* (1987), 11 B.C.L.R. (2d) 176 (S.C.), affd 49 D.L.R. (4th) 297 (B.C.C.A.).

§4.20   In *Boccia v. Bata Industries Ltd.*,[1] the parent company had very close control over the subsidiary and the plaintiff himself. When the parent company ordered its subsidiary to terminate the plaintiff's employment, the plaintiff was able to successfully sue the parent company for inducing breach of contract.

[1] (1989), 4 D.E.L.D. 10 (Ont. H.C.J.); *contra*, see *Sauer v. S.N.C.-Lavelin Inc.*, D.T.E. 93-1275 (Que. S.C.).

§4.21 If it is found that related enterprises are so closely intertwined as to be virtually one business enterprise, the court will allow liability to fall beyond the nominal employer.[1] Among the various factors that will be examined by the courts are the following: (a) whether the parent company was in constant control of the subsidiary, including the hiring and firing of the subsidiary's employees; (b) the purpose of the subsidiary corporation; (c) who appointed the management of the subsidiary; and (d) the similarities between the boards of directors.

[1] *Manley Inc. v. Fallis* (1977), 2 B.L.R. 277 (Ont. C.A.).

§4.22 The judicial trend has been to consider that if an employee has been transferred between subsidiaries, the real employer is the parent or the corporate group as a whole. Also, if there is evidence that an employee could easily be confused as to who is the real employer, the court may award damages against the entire corporate conglomerate.[1] Nowhere is this more clearly expressed than in *Bagby v. Gustavson Int. Drilling Co.*:[2]

> . . . the realities of modern business life . . . require us to recognize the existence of the modern corporate conglomerate and its business practices. It is common place for an employee to spend a lifetime with essentially one employer. Yet from time to time he is transferred to the employ of one associated company after another as the interests of the group as a whole may require. If at some point in his career, the employee finds that the particular corporate entity which is at the moment his nominal employer is bankrupt, it would be unrealistic as well as unjust to ignore his past service with other entities of the conglomerate. The law must . . . recognize the reality that though he may have worked only a few months for the bankrupt subsidiary, he has served the group as a whole for a lifetime. We are entitled to ask: In substance who is his employer? Liability for contractual obligations should flow from that answer.

[1] *Sullivan v. Mack Maritime Ltd.* (1982), 39 N.B.R. (2d) 298 (Q.B.); *Kennedy v. Junsen Holdings Ltd.* (1981), 1 D.E.L.D. 23 (Ont. H.C.J.).

[2] (1980), 24 A.R. 181 (C.A.), at 199. See also *Olson v. Sprung Instant Greenhouses Ltd.* (1985), 12 C.C.E.L. 8 (Alta. Q.B.) and *Holmes v. British Steel Canada Inc.* (1984), 25 A.C.W.S. (2d) 19 (B.C.S.C.).

(b) Third Party Control (Personnel Agencies)

§4.23 In certain circumstances, the employer may transfer the control of an employee to a third party. This is most frequent with personnel agencies who lease the services of temporary workers. In these cases, day-to-day control over the work done is only one element in deciding who is the employer. The selection process, hiring, discipline, training, evaluation, remuneration, assignment of functions and duration of service are of critical importance in determining the true employer in three-party relationship situations.[1] So too, the court held that the effective subordination could be transferred to a third party by the one who engages and pays the salary of the employee.[2] This occurred in *Syndicat des fonctionnaires provinciaux du Québec Inc. v. Québec (Procureur général)*,[3] where the Quebec Labour Tribunal found that the worker was the employee of the company where he was working. One of the tribunal's main reasons for this decision was the preponderance of work for the lessee rather than for the agency. The conclusion may have been different if employees had been supplied to many employers and not just to one employer.

[1] See *Royal Victoria Hospital v. Vassart*, [1990] R.J.Q. 1961 (Que. S.C.). See also *Zellers Inc. v. Agences de personnel Cavalier inc.*, D.T.E. 94T-550 (Que. C.A.L.P.); *Canadian Offshore Marine Ltd v. Seafarers International Union of Canada* (1973), 1 N.R. 292 (F.C.A.).

[2] Also, with respect to determining who has control over the employee, see *Watchstraps Inc. v. Poupart Ltée*, [1962] C.S. 273 (Que.).

[3] [1984] T.T. 353 (Que. Lab. Trib.).

(c) Seconding Agreements

§4.24 The question as to who the employer is may also have to be addressed in cases where employees are seconded by their original employer to another person or organization. The issue raised is whether the seconding (lending) employer remains the employer or whether it has passed that status on to the person or organization to whom it has seconded its employee (*i.e.*, the receiving employer).

§4.25 The term "secondment" is little known in employment law. The term "second" as a verb is defined as "to transfer (an employee) temporarily to another branch or department". *Webster's Third New International Dictionary*[1] defines secondment as "the detachment of a person from his regular organization for temporary assignment elsewhere."

[1] (Springfield, Mass.: G. & C. Merriam Co., 1967), p. 2051.

§4.26 Not surprisingly, the case law in Canada on the secondment of employees and/or secondment agreement is sparse. American and British doctrines and case law provide little guidance in determining the relevant features of the relationship between the secondor, the receiving employer and the secondee. While Canadian case law reveals several relevant considerations, it establishes neither a uniform "test" which can be used to determine who is the actual employer of the seconded personnel nor the extent of each party's obligation.

§4.27 In *Alberta Union of Provincial Employees v. Farran*,[1] the Alberta Court of Appeal distinguished between permanent positions within a department's general organization and a secondment position. The secondment position is "clearly designed for what might be described as a projects study".[2] The appointed employee to the secondment position was to retain her previous classified position during the tenure of the project study. "Upon the project's termination, the appointee would return to, and continue with, the duties assigned to her before assuming the [secondment] position".[3] The court's decision emphasized that a secondment position was one in which the seconded employee performed "a special duty of a temporary nature". The decision cited, and closely followed, the definition of "secondment" found in *Webster's Third New International Dictionary*.

[1] (1980), 110 D.L.R. (3d) 183 (Alta. C.A.).
[2] (1980), 110 D.L.R. (3d) 183 (Alta. C.A.) at 187.
[3] (1980), 110 D.L.R. (3d) 183 (Alta. C.A.) at 188.

§4.28 In *Belisle v. Public Service Commn. Appeal Bd.*,[1] the Federal Court of Appeal held that staff seconded to the Canada Employment and Immigration Commission from the Department of External Affairs did not, by that fact alone, become appointed to new positions with the Commission. When comparing the duties and authority of the Commission and the Department of External Affairs, it was found that External Affairs exercised "personnel management authority" over seconded officers. However, during the secondment period "the seconded officer [fell] under the authority of his or her superior in the Commission."[2] One could not take disciplinary measures without first consulting External Affairs, and appraisal reports on the seconded officers would be prepared according to External Affairs' instructions. Seconded assignments were determined by the Commission, but External Affairs had final say as to the selection of officers. An agreement was drafted specifying an agreed-to predetermined fixed period. This secondment agreement also provided that, upon expiry of the term, the employee would be at the disposal of the Department of External Affairs. This case would seem to indicate that the seconding employer remains the real employer notwithstanding a seconding agreement, at least in cases when it maintains a certain control over the employee as to discipline and appraisals, for instance.

[1] (1983), 149 D.L.R. (3d) 352 (F.C.A.).
[2] (1983), 149 D.L.R. (3d) 352 (F.C.A.), at 355.

§4.29 In these earlier cases, the courts have closely assimilated the notion of "secondment" to that of a "temporary transfer" of an employee to a specific assignment, upon completion of which the employee is reintegrated to the previous position. More recently, in *Atkinson v. Gulf Canada Ltd.*,[1] the Ontario High Court held the seconding employer responsible for the salary due upon termination of employment before the end of the secondment period. In so determining the employer's obligations, the court emphasized that the aggrieved employee was an employee of the seconding employer (Gulf Canada) in every real sense of the word. He was paid by Gulf, his pension contributions went to the Gulf pension plan and he received benefits extended to Gulf employees by way of health plans and other fringe benefits.

[1] (1986), 36 A.C.W.S. (2d) 433 (Ont. H.C.J.).

§4.30 In the case of *Snead v. Agricultural Development Corp. of Saskatchewan*,[1] the Saskatchewan Court of Queen's Bench (Regina) focused on the language of the secondment agreement. In reading the agreement, it seemed evident to the court that the seconding employer regarded the plaintiff as its employee. In addition, the court viewed as critical evidence a number of telexes sent to the employee by the seconding employer concerning specific instructions vis-à-vis the employee's work with the joint-venture company to which he had been seconded. The court accordingly held the seconding employer liable for the termination of employment by the joint-venture company.

[1] (1990), 33 C.C.E.L. 179 (Sask. Q.B.).

§4.31 In a third case, *Commission scolaire de Sept-Îles v. Club de ski Gallix*,[1] the Quebec Superior Court held that the receiving employer could not dismiss the seconded employee without cause. This case could perhaps be used to establish that the veritable employer is the receiving employer in the context of a seconding agreement.[2]

[1] D.T.E. 91T-653 (Que. S.C.) (presently on appeal).
[2] The court does not, however, comment on the liability of the seconding employer who in fact paid the employee's salary to later be reimbursed by the receiving employer.

§4.32 Because there are relatively few cases available on this subject, it remains difficult to predict with certainty the outcome before the courts on any one set of facts. Nevertheless, the authors believe the courts will look to the following elements to ascertain who is the true employer in the case of a seconding agreement:

- who issues directives to the employees;
- the existence and content of a contract of secondment;
- whether the parties have acted in such a way as to denounce their intention of secondment;
- who pays, disciplines and evaluates the employees;
- who represents itself as the employer to third parties;
- whether a pension plan covering the seconded employees is maintained and, if so, by whom;
- who decides upon salary increases for the employees, as well as any other relevant information.

(d) Limited Partnership

§4.33 Limited partnership consists of one or more persons called "general partner" and one or more persons called "special partner", where the special partner makes a contribution to the common stock while the general partner is authorized to administer the business and to bind the partnership.[1]

[1] In Quebec, see Civil Code of Quebec, art. 2236 (previously C.C.L.C., arts. 1871 *et seq*).

§4.34 Whether a special partner or a general partner can be an employee or whether the limited partnership itself can be an employer is a question which has been raised more frequently in recent years. Since only the general partners are authorized to administer the business and to bind the partnership, it is apparent that the limited partners cannot be considered employers as they cannot contract on behalf of the partnership with an employee nor can they direct, hire, fire or otherwise control the employee,[1] roles traditionally held by employers.

[1] Gagnon v. Beaulieu, [1977] C.P. 250 (Que. Prov. Ct.).

(e) Joint Venture

§4.35 One case has held that, should an employee and an employer decide to enter into a joint venture, then the nature of the relationship is altered and the initial employment relationship severed, notwithstanding the fact that the duties of the former employee may remain unchanged.

> When the plaintiff adopted the joint-venture relationship he ceased to be one of the defendant's employees. Surely he cannot be looked upon as an employee of the joint venture. Together with the defendant, he became a co-adventurer.[1]

Consequently, when the parties are bound by a joint-venture agreement, upon termination of this agreement there is no action for wrongful dismissal. The application of this principle would seem to be limited to more senior employees who are able to contract on a relatively equal basis with their employer. In the case mentioned above, for example, the former employee was a drug manager.

[1]   *Semenoff v. Saskatoon Drug & Stationery Co.* (1988), 49 D.L.R. (4th) 102 (Sask. Q.B.), at 106.

§4.36   Although the general rule is that the joint venturer is not an employee, the court may, in some cases, look beyond the apparent contractual relationship to examine if the joint venturer is in reality acting as an independent contractor. Where the court concluded that the plaintiff was acting not as an independent businessman but rather as an employee, the court held that the franchisee was in reality an employee.[1]

[1]   *Head v. Inter Tan Canada Ltd.* (1991), 33 C.C.E.L. 159 (Ont. Ct. (Gen. Div.)).

2.   Who Is the Employee?

§4.37   The employee must be a specific individual. A fundamental aspect of the employment contract is the personal nature of the services. An employee cannot, without the consent of the employer, assign someone else to render the services in his or her place. A person may be an employee of several different employers simultaneously.

(a)   Employee, Partner, Officer and Director

§4.38   It is not uncommon today for an individual to hold several positions and titles while being employed in an organization. Frequently, management of smaller firms and senior executives of larger organizations wear as many hats as roles they perform. For example, an officer, a shareholder and an employee may be one and the same. He or she may not, however, be both an employee and a partner simultaneously.

§4.39   A partner cannot be an employee of the partnership since he or she is self-employed.[1] As is clear from corporate and tax law, a partnership is not a separate legal entity and thus, a partner is his own "employee" so he cannot have true employee status. However, the fact that a person shares in the profits of the business does not necessarily entail that the relationship is that of partnership. The real intent of the parties must be examined to determine whether the profit-sharing is simply a form of employee remuneration in light of the fact that a shareholder of an incorporated company may be an employee as may the directors and officers of the company.[2] Moreover, where a partnership agreement appears to exist but one of the partners retains all of the shares while the others receive a monthly salary non-related to performance, one could conclude that the "partner" receiving the allowance is indeed an employee.[3]

[1] *Craig Brothers v. Sisters of Charity*, [1940] 4 D.L.R. 561 (Sask. C.A.); *Ellis v. Joseph Ellis & Co.*, [1905] 1 K.B. 324 (C.A.). See also *Dockrill v. Coopers & Lybrand Chartered Accountants* (1994), 111 D.L.R. (4th) 62 (N.S.C.A.).

[2] *Guildford v. Anglo-French Steamship Co.* (1883), 9 S.C.R. 303.

[3] *Rooney v. Creative Laminating Concepts*, unreported, Feb. 23, 1988, File No. 181/87/CA (N.B.C.A.).

§4.40 Whereas a director or officer of a company is elected and may, by resolution to that effect, be dismissed, such a person may not be removed from his or her position as employee, if such is also the case, without notice. A person who is simultaneously a director or officer and an employee is entitled to receive notice of termination of the employment contract if there is no cause to end his or her employee services. Mr. Justice Collins of the Quebec Superior Court stated in *Van Alstyne v. Rankin*:[1]

> A chairman of the board, a president of a corporation or in fact any of its officers or employees all stand in the same relative position with regard to their employment by a corporation. Their employment can be terminated for cause at any time, subject to whatever legal claim for damages any such party whose employment is so terminated may have against the corporation in respect of such termination and subject always of course to the terms of any special contract which may exist. The difference in rank and occupation is of no consequence in so far as the right to terminate is concerned. The fact that the plaintiff was elected or appointed directly by the directors gave him no greater right than any other employee of the corporation defendant, except that he could only be dismissed by the directors themselves.

[1] [1952] C.S. 12 (Que.), at 15.

§4.41 Finally, removal from office of a person who is both director or officer and employee does not end the employment relationship unless there is an agreement to the contrary.

§4.42 An interesting discussion with respect to the rights of a shareholder-employee to the profits of a company was raised in *Carlson v. Trans-Pac Industries Corp.*[1] As compensation for his services, Carlson was to receive a monthly salary, a percentage of profits and, initially, a 25% share in Trans-Pac Industries Corp., to be followed by additional shares from time to time. Carlson invoked a "shotgun" provision that was part of a shareholders' agreement whereby he attempted to buy out other shareholders of Trans-Pac Industries Corp. His employment was thereafter terminated. By this time, he held 52% of Trans-Pac Industries Corp. The Court of Appeal ruled that while the shares of Carlson would have permitted him to participate in the management and profits of Trans-Pac Industries Corp., they could not be used to wrest control from, to the exclusion of, his ultimate employer. The decision supports the proposition that even though an employee may be given shares in a company, the employee does not acquire more rights than the employer to the business.

[1]   (1990), 2 B.L.R. (2d) 70 (B.C.C.A.).

(b)   Who Has the Authority to Represent the Employer?

§4.43   The issue of whether someone can validly represent and bind his or her employer in its dealings with employees is a question of fact and depends in each case on the responsibilities and powers granted to that person by those authorized to grant or bestow them. In some cases, a statute will limit one's capability of binding the employer. In *Mignault v. Commission d'appel en matière de lésions professionnelles du Québec*,[1] the Quebec Superior Court held that Mignault, a lawyer hired by the president of the Commission at a salary agreed upon by the president, could not be paid that salary since it was in excess of the policies prepared by the treasury counsel which have force of law. Although the president of the Commission had authority to hire Mignault, he did not have authority to bind the Commission to pay a higher salary than that provided by law, as he was not an agent of the state.

[1]   D.T.E. 91T-105 (Que. S.C.).

§4.44   A person who is not employed by the employer may properly represent the employer before its employees if he or she has duly received this power. In *DeCoster v. Econosult Inc.*,[1] the Quebec Superior Court held that DeCoster had been dismissed by his employer even though the letter of termination was issued by someone not employed by Econosult. Econosult demonstrated that, by written contract, the parties had agreed that the resident engineer would represent Econosult in its dealings with DeCoster. The person who had signed the termination notice was in fact the resident engineer of the project although not an employee of Econosult.

¹ D.T.E. 89T-119 (Que. S.C.).

§4.45 In *Québec (Procureur général) v. Corriveau,*¹ Corriveau's employment was terminated by the Social Affairs Minister, the latter believing in good faith, although erroneously, that the C.L.S.C.-employer was still under trusteeship. The Quebec Court of Appeal confirmed the Superior Court's decision that, at the time of termination, the trusteeship no longer existed and the Minister therefore had no authority to terminate Corriveau's employment. Furthermore, the "authority *de facto*" doctrine did not validate the Minister's decision. Briefly stated, the *de facto* doctrine prevents one from annulling a judge's or other agent of the Crown's decision on the mere ground that there was an irregularity in the nomination of such judge or agent, who otherwise appears to have received his or her authority according to law. This doctrine did not prevent Corriveau from disputing his termination since the doctrine aims to protect the administrator and not the other party. Hence, Corriveau was successful in his claim for damages for breach of his term contract.

¹ [1989] R.J.Q. 1 (C.A.).

D. CONCLUSION

§4.46 The particular nature of the employment relationship explains its changing nature and adaptability. One is often required to go back to the basic elements and tests to ensure that the parties to this relationship have been properly identified.

§4.47 The next chapter will examine situations where a potential employer has obligations towards a person even before the conclusion of the employment relationship.

CHAPTER 5

PRE-EMPLOYMENT OBLIGATIONS

A. INTRODUCTION

§5.1 Provincial and federal human rights legislation[1] as well as rules developed by common law impose some restrictions upon the employment relationship even before an employment contract is entered into between employer and employee. These obligations will be referred to as pre-employment obligations; that is, those restrictions and liabilities which may be placed upon either party during the formative stages of the employment relationship. Pre-employment obligations include those which arise during the recruitment process as well as liabilities which may be imposed upon either of the parties as a result of negotiations with respect to the particular terms of the employment contract.[2]

---

[1] See, *e.g.*, *Human Rights Code*, R.S.B.C. 1996, c. 210; *Human Rights Code*, R.S.O. 1990, c. H.19; *Charter of Human Rights and Freedoms*, R.S.Q., c. C-12; *Canada Act, 1982*, c. 11 (U.K.) (now R.S.C. 1985, App. II, No. 44); *Canadian Human Rights Act*, R.S.C. 1985, c. H-6.

[2] Droits et obligations de l'employeur face au recrutement d'employés et aux références après emploi, P.L. Benaroche (1995) Dev. Recent Droit du Travail, 101-142.

B. LIMITATIONS IMPOSED DURING THE RECRUITMENT PHASE

1. Advertisements, Applications and Interviews

§5.2 Federal and provincial human rights legislation prohibits discrimination in employment advertisements, applications and interviews. An example is section 23 of the Ontario *Human Rights Code*,[1] which states:

> *Discriminatory employment advertising*
>
> 23(1) The right under section 5 to equal treatment with respect to employment is infringed where an invitation to apply for employment or an advertisement in connection with employment is published or displayed that directly or indirectly classifies or indicates qualifications by a prohibited ground of discrimination.
>
> *Application for employment*
>
> (2) The right under section 5 to equal treatment with respect to employment is

infringed where a form of application for employment is used or a written or oral inquiry is made of an applicant that directly or indirectly classifies or indicates qualifications by a prohibited ground of discrimination.

¹ R.S.O. 1990, c. H.19; see also *Human Rights Act*, S.B.C. 1984, c. 22, s. 6; *Charter of Human Rights and Freedoms*, R.S.Q. c. C-12, s. 18.1 [as amended], *Canadian Human Rights Act*, R.S.C. 1985, chap. H-6, s. 8.

§5.3 None of the recruitment steps should seek to obtain information related to prohibited grounds of discrimination. The prohibited grounds of discrimination may include ethnic origin, sex, sexual orientation, marital or family status, age, race, colour, religion, creed, citizenship and mental or physical disability.[1] Many human rights commissions have published guidelines with respect to applications for employment and employment interviews, which outline both appropriate and discriminatory questions.[2] However, if the marital status, age, sex or other prohibited ground of discrimination is a genuine and reasonable requirement because of the nature of the particular job, the employer will be exempt from the relevant prohibition and such inquiry will be allowed.[3]

¹ See, e.g., R.S.O. 1990, c. H.19, s. 5; see also *Human Rights Code*, R.S.B.C. 1996, c. 210, s. 6; *Charter of Human Rights and Freedoms*, R.S.Q. c. C-12, s. 10 [as amended], *Canadian Human Rights Act*, R.S.C. 1985, chap. H-6, ss. 7, 10.

² Although the guidelines are not legally binding, they do represent the commissions' views as to the types of questions that are appropriate or inappropriate on employment application forms and at employment interviews, and accordingly may be given considerable weight by the courts. The range of prohibited questions suggested by the guidelines can be quite extensive, including not only questions which directly identify an applicant by a prohibited ground but also questions which may indirectly identify such an applicant. For example, the Ontario Human Rights Commission guidelines prohibit enquiries on application forms as to the name and location of schools attended.

³ See, *e.g.*, *Human Rights Code*, R.S.B.C. 1996, c. 210, ss. 6, 11; *Human Rights Code*, R.S.O. 1990, c. H.19, s. 24(1)(b); *Charter of Human Rights and Freedoms*, R.S.Q., c. C-12, s. 20 [am. 1982, c. 61, s. 6], *Canadian Human Rights Act*, R.S.C. 1985, chap. H-6, s. 15.

§5.4 Employers are not alone in the obligation to comply with human rights legislation prohibiting discrimination in employment advertisements. In British Columbia, a newspaper which advertised employment opportunities and specified preferences as to age and sex was ordered by a human rights board of inquiry to cease such advertising. Further, the board (making use of its extensive remedial powers) ordered the newspaper to publish in its classified advertisements section an article about prohibited discrimination in employment advertising and the provisions of the legislation.[1]

[1] *Hope v. Gray-Grant* (1980), 2 C.H.R.R. D/256 (B.C. Bd. of Inq.).

2. Negligent Misrepresentation

§5.5 An interesting issue which has arisen in the context of pre-employment obligations is that of negligent misrepresentation. Negligent misrepresentation is a tort and is considered independently actionable from any contractual relationship between the parties. In this regard, the courts have ruled that a person who owes another a duty of care (often referred to as being in a special relationship) and gives advice or information to that person with the intention of inducing him or her to enter into a contract, including an employment contract, must exercise reasonable care to ensure that the advice or information is correct and can be relied upon. A person may be held liable for the resulting economic losses if he or she negligently makes a misleading representation, or negligently fails to tell the person who was induced to enter into the contract of some fact that should have been stated at the pre-employment stage.[1] The key element in the employment context is that the employer, or a representative of the employer, was negligent in making the statement or representation. The Supreme Court of Canada has suggested that there is a special relationship between the employer and the prospective employee.[2] The following cases highlight the issue of negligent misrepresentation in the employment context.

[1] *Esso Petroleum Co. v. Mardon*, [1976] 2 All E.R. 5 (C.A.); *Hedley Byrne & Co. v. Heller & Partners Ltd.*, [1964] A.C. 465 (H.L.); *De Groot v. St. Boniface Hospital* (1993), 48 C.C.E.L. 271 (Man. Q.B.), appeal allowed in part (1994), 3 C.C.E.L. (2d) 280 on the issue of the amount of damages.
[2] *Queen v. Cognos Inc.* (1993), 99 D.L.R. (4th) 626, at 648 (S.C.C.).

§5.6 In *H.B. Nickerson & Sons Ltd. v. Wooldridge*,[1] Wooldridge, a foreigner, was advised by the employer that, if he came to Canada, he could easily expect to obtain the Canadian qualifications necessary for his employment. The Canadian regulations with respect to these qualifications were subsequently changed, but the employer failed to advise Wooldridge, who accepted employment and immigrated to Canada. On arrival, Wooldridge realized he did not meet the qualifications. The court held that the employer was in breach of its duty of care in failing to advise Wooldridge of the changes in the regulations. However, the court also held that Wooldridge was contributorily negligent in failing to make his own inquiries. The court equated the contributory negligence as 40% of Wooldridge's loss.

[1] (1980), 115 D.L.R. (3d) 97 (N.S.C.A.).

§5.7 Inaccurate and misleading information regarding an employer's true financial situation, which induces a prospective employee to accept employment, may amount to negligent misrepresentation.[1]

---

[1] *Steer v. Aerovox Inc.* (1984), 5 C.C.E.L. 130 (N.S.S.C.). See also *Boudreault v. Centre Hospitalier St-Vincent de Paul*, D.T.E. 90T-771 (Que. S.C.).

§5.8 In *Pettit v. Prince George District Credit Union*,[1] the plaintiff made inquiries with the defendant regarding the availability of employment. The defendant advised the plaintiff that a job was available, but that the defendant was still working out some details and the job would possibly be available as early as the following January or late March. The plaintiff discussed neither salary nor the creation of an employment contract. The job subsequently became available the following June. The British Columbia Supreme Court dismissed the plaintiff's claim of negligent misstatement and held that, although a position had not become available as soon as the defendant had said it would, there was no proof that the defendant was negligent in making its statement. The court stated that the offer in June was in reasonable compliance with what had been promised, particularly in light of the evidence that no specific start date, position or salary had ever been held out to the plaintiff.

---

[1] (1991), 35 C.C.E.L. 140 (B.C.S.C.).

§5.9 In *Williams v. Saanich School District No. 63*,[1] the defendant school board offered the plaintiff a position and informed the plaintiff that the employees' union had initiated a grievance over his selection for the position. The board assured the plaintiff that there was nothing to worry about. The board of arbitration ruled against the school board and forced it to hire a union member to fill the position. The school board was unsuccessful in finding alternative employment for the plaintiff and ultimately terminated his employment. The court held that the board had not failed in its duty of care since it did not know and could not have known the ultimate outcome of the arbitrator's ruling. The representative of the board who had assured the plaintiff that he should not worry had expressed an honest opinion, believing it to be true because of similar previous experiences. The court added that the plaintiff should have realized that it was impossible to predict the outcome of litigation. By placing so much reliance on the board representative's remarks, the plaintiff had failed to take reasonable care to protect his own interests.

---

[1] (1986), 11 C.C.E.L. 233 (B.C.S.C.), affd 17 C.C.E.L. 257 (C.A.).

§5.10 The issue at stake in *Gravino v. Gulf Canada Ltée*[1] was whether an executive was entitled to claim damages for constructive dismissal when he was not named to the position of vice-president after moving to Toronto. The Quebec Superior Court held that the plaintiff had the burden of proving that he had actually been promised the position within a particular time frame. In the absence of clear evidence, mere speculation did not constitute a true promise upon which the plaintiff could base a claim, particularly since he knew that the person who had made the alleged promise did not have the authority on his own to satisfy the promise.

[1] D.T.E. 91T-1059 (Que. S.C.).

§5.11 In *Queen v. Cognos Inc.*,[1] the manager of Cognos, a computer software company, with the full knowledge of the company's senior management, advertised for an accountant to help with the development of accounting software. Queen, a chartered accountant, applied and was interviewed for the position. During the job interview, the manager told Queen that the project in question was a major one which would be developed over a period of two years and maintained thereafter and that the position being interviewed for would be needed throughout this period. The manager also advised Queen that additional staff would be required. At no point during the interview was Queen advised that there was no guaranteed funding for the project described to him or that the position for which he was applying was subject to budgetary approval. Upon being offered the position, he immediately accepted it and signed a written employment contract which allowed Cognos to terminate his employment at any time "without cause" upon one month's notice or payment in lieu thereof.

[1] [1993] 1 S.C.R. 87; revg 30 C.C.E.L. 1 (Ont. C.A.); revg 18 C.C.E.L. 146 (Ont. H.C.J.).

§5.12 Queen commenced his employment in April 1983 and was advised in September that there would be a reassignment of personnel involved in the project due to a decrease in research and development funding. He was notified of the termination of his employment, but this notice was later rescinded. In July 1984, Queen received a second notice, effective October 25, 1984, that his employment would be terminated. He worked until that day and was paid until November 15, 1984.

§5.13 The Supreme Court of Canada rendered a judgment declaring that Cognos, and its representative, owed Queen a duty of care with respect to the representations made about Cognos and the nature and existence of the employment position being offered and, hence, were liable for payment of the damages caused as a result of that representation. In rendering this decision, the Court made the following analysis:

(1) The fact that the alleged negligent misrepresentations were made in a pre-contractual setting, such as during negotiations or in the course of an employment hiring interview, and the fact that a contract is subsequently entered into by the parties do not, in themselves, invalidate an action in tort for damages caused by the misrepresentations.

(2) The duty or liability of the defendant with respect to negligent misrepresentation may in some cases be limited or excluded by a term of the subsequent contract so as to diminish or extinguish the plaintiff's remedy in tort.

(3) The first and only question should be whether there is a specific contractual duty created by an express term of the contract which is coextensive with the common law duty of care which the representee alleges the representor has breached.

(4) If the pre-contractual representation relied on by the plaintiff became an express term of the subsequent contract, then absent any overriding considerations arising from the context in which the transaction occurred, the plaintiff cannot bring a concurrent action in tort for negligent misrepresentation and is confined to whatever remedies are available under the law of contract.

(5) If there exists a "special relationship" between the parties, the employer and its representative, the manager, accordingly owed a duty of care to the appellant to exercise reasonable care and diligence in making representations as to the employer and the employment opportunity being offered.

(6) The misrepresentations by the manager during the interview were made negligently, and the duty of care was therefore breached. It is not sufficient that the manager was truthful during the interview and that he believed in what he was representing. The applicable standard of care should be the one used in every negligence case, namely the universally accepted "reasonable person".

§5.14 The standard of care required by a person making representations is an objective one: it is a duty to exercise such reasonable care as the circumstances require to ensure that representations made are accurate and not misleading. In this case, it was found that the manager had negligently misrepresented the nature and existence of the employment opportunity being offered. In fact, it was the existence, or reality, of the job being interviewed for, and not the extent of the appellant's involvement therein, which was at the heart of the action. Thus, by breaching this duty of care, and negligently misrepresenting the employment opportunity, the employer, Cognos, and its representative were liable for the damages caused to the employee.

§5.15 It should be noted that the court held that, in some cases, the terms of the employment agreement could limit the employer's liability, but such was not the case here as the disclaimer in the employment agreement had neither expressly nor impliedly stated that there might be no job of the sort described during the interview after the appellant's arrival but referred rather to certain other terms and conditions which were included in the employment contract.

§5.15.1 Subsequent to *Queen v. Cognos Inc.*,[1] a number of courts have considered what constitutes an untrue, negligently made representation. Where financial decisions are not finalized, budgets are subject to revision and where it is reasonably foreseeable that a prospective employee's decision-making authority will be circumscribed, the employee will have a difficult time proving that negligent misrepresentations were made during the hiring process.[2] Also, where an employee had been shown a position profile reflecting the duties and responsibilities of a position prior to employment and, due to a personality conflict between the employee and management, the employee did not work in a position which reflected this profile, this was found as not being negligent misrepresentation since things had developed differently than as originally intended or envisaged solely due to the personality conflict.[3]

[1]   (1993), 99 D.L.R. (4th) 626 (S.C.C.).
[2]   *Dixon v. British Columbia Transit* (1995), 9 B.C.L.R. (3d) 108 (S.C.).
[3]   *Skidd v. Canada Post Corporation* (1993), 47 C.C.E.L. 169 (Ont. Ct. (Gen. Div.)), vard on other grounds [1997] O.J. No. 712, Feb. 26, 1997, Appeal No. C14894 (C.A.).

§5.15.2 An unanticipated change in the employer's operations which negatively affects an employee will not necessarily be grounds for a successful action for negligent misrepresentation.[1]

[1]   *Buerman v. Canada (Attorney General)* (1996), 19 C.C.E.L. (2d) 127 (Ont. Ct. (Gen. Div.)).

§5.15.3 The mere fact that an employer may induce an employee to relocate or that the employer assists with that relocation is not *prima facie* evidence of a representation of long-term or permanent employment. Rather, a court will examine the nature of the employment when determining whether an employee had a reasonable expectation of permanent employment.[1]

[1] *Ellams v. Kilborn Western Inc.* (1994), 91 Man. R. (2d) 279 (Q.B.).

§5.15.4 If an employer has offered employment to a person (future employee) and subsequently reneges on that offer without communicating this information to the future employee, these actions by the employer may support a finding of negligent misrepresentation.[1]

[1] *De Groot v. St. Boniface General Hospital* (1994), 22 C.C.L.T. (2d) 163 (Man. C.A.).

§5.15.5 Also, subsequent to *Queen v. Cognos Inc.*,[1] the courts have considered what constitutes "reasonable reliance" on statements made by a potential employer. Generally, when assessing what constitutes "reasonable reliance", a reviewing court will look at what the employee knew, or should have known, about industry practice.[2]

[1] (1993), 99 D.L.R. (4th) 626 (S.C.C.).
[2] *Horton v. Rio Algom Ltd.* (1995), 9 C.C.E.L. 180 (Ont. Ct. (Gen. Div.)); *Beauchemin v. Universal Handling Equipment Co.* (unreported), [1996] A.J. No. 128 (Q.B.). See also *Jacks v. U & R Tax Services Ltd.* (1995), 33 C.P.C. 201 (Man. Q.B.), affd (1995), 41 C.P.C. (3d) 321 (C.A.).

§5.16 An example of the application of a disclaimer clause which protected the employer's representatives from an action in tort based on negligent misrepresentation arose in the case of *Steele v. SNC Inc.*[1] In this case, the plaintiff, Steele, a geophysicist, was steadily employed when he was approached by a representative of the defendant and offered a position on a mineral development project in Thailand. There was some talk of the employment contract being five years. The final letter of agreement was for a term of up to two years, renewable every two years. The agreement also contained a disclaimer clause which stated that the employee certified that the terms and conditions set out in the contract constituted the entire agreement, that no promises or understandings were made other than those stated in the contract, and that the agreement was subject to modification only by written instruments signed by both the employer and the employee.

[1] (1992), 41 C.C.E.L. 257 (Ont. Ct. (Gen. Div.)).

§5.17 When the employee was advised of his termination to be effective in January 1987, he brought an action in contract for damages for breach of a collateral warranty, arguing that an oral agreement had been reached between the parties which amended the written contract by providing for a five-year term of employment and that the defendant's representatives were liable for negligent misrepresentations which had induced the plaintiff to enter into the agreement.

§5.18 At trial, the court held that the statement of the defendant's representative did not and could not alter the terms of the written agreement which contained a clear statement of the contract term and a disclaimer clause. The negotiation of the case had been directed toward and resulted in the making of a contract of employment which dealt specifically with the term of the contract. Any independent representations regarding the term of the agreement could not be found under a separate head of liability and tort. To hold otherwise would in effect permit the plaintiff to negate the disclaimer clause in the agreement. The court held that where there is a disclaimer clause, a negligent misrepresentation merges with the signed agreement. It should be noted that this case relied on the Court of Appeal's decision in *Queen v. Cognos Inc.*,[1] which was later overturned by the Supreme Court of Canada.[2] However, we wish to mention that although the Supreme Court of Canada overturned the decision in *Queen v. Cognos*, this was based not on the fact that there was a disclaimer clause, but rather on the fact that the disclaimer clause did not specifically address the issue in question. Hence, where a disclaimer clause specifically addresses an issue such as the term of the contract, it may be relied upon to protect the employer from an action in negligent misrepresentation. It is imperative, however, that there be a direct link between the alleged tort and the action which the disclaimer clause aims at protecting.

[1] (1990), 30 C.C.E.L. 1.
[2] [1993] 1 S.C.R. 87.

§5.18.1 In British Columbia, labour standards legislation specifically provides that employers cannot induce or persuade employees to become employees by means of deceptive advertising or false pretences. In particular, employers may not mislead with regard to the availability of a position, the nature of the work to be done or the conditions of employment.[1]

[1] *Employment Standards Act*, R.S.B.C. 1996, c. 113, s. 8.

§5.18.2 Although the employer has an obligation not to mislead the employee as to the duration of employment, this does not mean that the employer is obligated in each case to advise each candidate, before hiring, of the possibility that there could be a staff reduction or lay-offs which are situations which may occur from time to time in all types of undertakings and which everyone applying for a position should be aware of. In accepting employment, an employee accepts certain risks inherent to this decision.[1]

> [1] *Lessard v. Federation des producteurs de volailles du Quebec (Volbec)*, D.T.E. 93T-593 (Que. S.C.).

§5.18.3 However, in a case where an employee was advised that she would be a probationary employee for a nine month period before becoming a permanent employee, the employer could not terminate her at will during the probationary period without providing reasonable notice. Where the employee had completed three months of her nine month probationary period she was entitled to receive a month notice of termination even though she was a probationary employee.[1]

> [1] *Lessard v. Federation des producteurs de volailles du Quebec (Volbec)*, unreported, file no. D.T.E. 93T-593 (Que. S.C.), at 13; see also *Newman v. Stokes Inc.*, D.T.E. 93T-553 (Que. S.C.).

§5.19 With respect to the damages that may be awarded for negligent misrepresentation, generally the employee will be restored to the economic position he or she was in before the representation was made. However, the court may award damages for lost profits if such were reasonably foreseeable at the time the misrepresentation was made negligently.

C. CONCLUSION

§5.20 The foregoing cases demonstrate the importance of the recruiting process as it relates to the rights of both the employer and employee. The employer must avoid conduct which is discriminatory in nature in the hiring process, and it must also take care to ensure that representations made to induce prospective employees to accept employment are honestly believed to be accurate and reliable and that relevant information is not negligently omitted when such statements are made. The employer would also be well advised to include in a written employment contract, a disclaimer with respect to pre-employment representations.

§5.21 The next five chapters will review the rights and obligations of the employer and the executive which stem from the employment relationship: the employer's obligation to provide the work, provide remuneration and provide a safe working environment, and the executive's obligation to execute the work and be loyal.

PART II

OBLIGATIONS ARISING FROM THE EMPLOYMENT RELATIONSHIP UNDER COMMON AND CIVIL LAW

CHAPTER 6

PROVIDE THE WORK

A. INTRODUCTION

§6.1 An employer has the obligation to provide an executive with work in accordance with the terms and conditions of employment that have been agreed to or which can reasonably be implied. In Quebec, this obligation is expressly provided for at art. 2087 of the Civil Code of Quebec. The employer must ensure that the executive is provided the assistance necessary to properly execute his or her mandate. The standard of performance expected of the executive must be clearly explained and the employer must delegate sufficient authority and leeway in order for the executive to achieve those goals. The terms and conditions of employment must be complied with for the duration of the contract, which may be for a fixed or an indeterminate term, unless the parties expressly or tacitly agree otherwise. If such terms and conditions, whether express or implied, are not complied with, an executive may, if the breaches are material, be in a position to sue the employer for constructive or wrongful dismissal, as discussed in Chapter 12.

§6.2 An employer is generally not obligated to provide a specific amount of work. In some cases, however, it may be inferred from the basis of the executive's remuneration that he or she is to receive a certain workload and number of responsibilities. This is especially true of the employee who is paid on commission or on a piecework basis. Indeed, the employee must be assigned a reasonable territory and/or amount of work to benefit from the chosen method of payment. In the case of an executive eligible for a bonus on sales or profit, the employer must act in good faith and use reasonable efforts to ensure that the level of sales or profit impacting the bonus is reasonably attainable.

B. TYPE OF WORK

§6.3 It is often difficult to determine and describe the type of work an executive is entitled to receive and execute. Numerous factors must be considered. Is the executive hired with the understanding that he or she will perform technical work as opposed to hands-on work, or is he or she expected to be a troubleshooter? Is the type of work envisaged purely managerial in nature? Another consideration may be whether the executive is to work with a group of hard-driving individuals and provide for their leadership, or whether his or her role is mostly focused on public relations activities. The answers to these questions will assist in determining what type of work must be provided to the executive.

§6.4 As previously mentioned, the employer's right to change the terms and conditions of employment, such as the nature of the executive's work, is established by the agreement between the parties. The applicable test is well summarized by the British Columbia Court of Appeal in *Orth v. Macdonald Dettwiler & Associates Ltd.*:[1]

> . . . if an employee asserts he has been constructively dismissed, he must establish there has been conduct on the part of the employer which breaches an express or an implied term of the contract of employment going to the very root of the contract. One term which, if not express, may be implied in a contract of employment is that the employer will not make such a substantial change in the duties and status of the employee as to constitute a fundamental breach of the contract.

[1] (1986), 16 C.C.E.L. 41, at 55-56.

§6.5 The difficulty in determining an employer's right to unilaterally change the work is increased by the business undergoing rapid change. Often, the nature of the work may remain relatively stable for long periods of time. Then, abruptly, external or internal challenges to the viability of the organization require skills that the executive has not sharpened. For instance, an executive who for years was required to operate the existing business and did so successfully may, in the face of a shrinking market or more aggressive competition, be requested to develop new products or new markets. In so doing, the organization provides a different type of work than that for which the executive was hired. In particular situations, the change may be such as to amount to a significant breach of the conditions of employment.

§6.6 The removal of all management functions or a clear demotion without cause will likely breach the employment agreement in an irreparable fashion.[1] The effect of assigning part of the executive's managerial functions to others is not as clear, however, particularly when hierarchy and remuneration are unchanged.[2] In *Lavigne v. Sidbec-Dosco Inc.*,[3] a transfer which had the effect of rendering an executive incidental constituted a constructive dismissal.

[1] *Moser v. Farm Credit Corp.* (1992), 44 C.C.E.L. 213 (Sask. Q.B.); *Pelliccia v. Pink Pages*

Advertising Ltd. (1989), 28 C.C.E.L. 261 (B.C.S.C.); *Saint John Shipbuilding Ltd. v. Perkins* (1989), 24 C.C.E.L. 106 (N.B.C.A.); *Elliott v. Southam Inc.* (1988), 59 Alta. L.R. (2d) 376 (Q.B.); *Administration de pilotage des Laurentides et la Guilde de la marine marchande du Canada v. Gagnon*, [1981] C.A. 431 (Que.).

2   *Charbonnier v. Air Canada Touram*, D.T.E. 90T-407 (Que. C.A.), where the court held that there was no express or implied right in the employee's contract not to be assigned to another managerial position with the same remuneration.

3   D.T.E. 85T-4 (Que. S.C.); affd, unreported, May 4, 1988, C.A.M. 500-09-001556-844.

§6.7 Defining the limits of the employer's right to change the type of work can be further complicated when jobs evolve quickly by reason of technological improvements or expansion of the employer's services. Complications may also arise when an employer's workforce is reduced resulting in redistribution of the work and dismissals. In such situations, it may be difficult to assess whether the change is such that it amounts to a significant breach of the conditions of employment, which allows the executive to claim a constructive dismissal.

§6.8 The Ontario High Court has recognized the employer's dilemma in facing economic difficulties. In *Pullen v. John C. Preston Ltd.,*[1] the company began experiencing severe financial difficulties from a lack of sales. As a result, Pullen's salary was reduced. He was taken off the company profit-sharing program and given a new job description with lesser responsibilities. The court held that the elimination of several, but not all, of Pullen's former managerial responsibilities in his proposed new job description was a "genuinely required redirection of his efforts necessitated by the company's financial needs, and not a deliberate elimination of his managerial functions".[2] In so finding, the court rejected his claim for constructive dismissal.

1   (1985), 7 C.C.E.L. 91 (Ont. H.C.J.); affd (1987), 16 C.C.E.L. xxiii (C.A.).

2   (1985), 7 C.C.E.L. 91 (Ont. H.C.J.), at 96. See also *Orth v. Macdonald Dettwiler & Associates Ltd.* (1986), 16 C.C.E.L. 41 (B.C.C.A.).

§6.9 In *Lesiuk v. B.C. Forest Products Ltd.,*[1] the plaintiff was a plant engineer with management functions. In a management restructuring, the plaintiff's duties in the organization were changed though he retained the same salary. Using an objective test, Taggart J.A. of the British Columbia Court of Appeal compared Lesiuk's duties before and after the unilateral change to determine whether a fundamental term of the contract had been breached and found that, indeed, there were substantial changes. The employer's motives in changing the duties were also considered. The court found that the employer was compelled by economic circumstances to make the management changes it did. Taggart J.A. stated:

> The economic facts cannot be ignored, though they ought not to be given more
> than an appropriate share of consideration. With respect, I think [the trial judge]
> gave too little weight to that aspect and placed too much emphasis on the extent
> to which the plaintiff's duties were changed.[2]

Having given credence to the economic motives of the employer, the
court went on to draw a distinction between "substantial change" and
"breach of a fundamental term". In essence, only the breach of a fundamental term is a breach of the employment contract; substantial
change to one's working conditions would not lead to this same conclusion. The court concluded that changes were made to the executive's duties as a result of economic circumstances, and found that this
did not breach a fundamental term of the employment contract.

[1]   (1986), 15 C.C.E.L. 91 (B.C.C.A.).
[2]   (1986), 15 C.C.E.L. 91 (B.C.C.A.), at 99. See also *Podas v. Pacific Press Ltd.* (1991), 61
B.C.L.R. (2d) 196 (C.A.); *Henderson v. Westfair Foods Ltd.* (1990), 32 C.C.E.L. 152
(Man. Q.B.), revd on other grounds 40 C.C.E.L. 81 (C.A.).

§6.10   In *Mifsud v. MacMillan Bathurst Inc.*,[1] the question of demotion
with no change in salary was considered. Interestingly, the court
found that the contract of employment contained, as an implied term,
the right of the employer to demote an employee for inadequate performance. Consequently, a demotion for unsatisfactory performance
could not be said to be a breach of a fundamental term of the contract.

[1]   (1989), 28 C.C.E.L. 228 (Ont. C.A.).

§6.11   In *Jervis v. Raytheon Canada Ltd.*,[1] the court found that there was
an implied term in the employment contract that the defendant could
reorganize its operations from time to time in order to remain competitive. The executive in that case was found to have the obligation to
consider a new position in the reorganization and by his failure to do
so he had impliedly agreed to his demotion. In another decision, the
same court found that the corporate reorganization resulted in a demotion and constructive dismissal.[2]

[1]   (1990), 35 C.C.E.L. 73 (Ont. Ct. (Gen. Div.)), affd (1997), 26 C.C.E.L. (2d) 101 (C.A.).
[2]   *Greaves v. Ontario Municipal Employees' Retirement Board* (1995), 15 C.C.E.L. (2d) 94
(Ont. Ct. (Gen. Div.)).

§6.11.1   The Ontario Court of Appeal has held that situations regarding an employee who has risen through the ranks in his company
should be distinguished from those where a supervisory or executive
employee was originally hired away from another employer to fill a
specific position. In *Davidson v. Allelix Inc.*,[1] the latter situation arose. In

this case, it was found that a senior microbiologist who had been engaged by the defendant to supervise the construction of a biotechnical plant and to manage it, rightfully resigned from his position and sued for constructive dismissal when the defendant abandoned the plan to build the plant and asked the plaintiff to do research there.

[1]   (1991), 86 D.L.R. 542 (Ont. C.A.); 7 O.R. (3d) 581, 54 O.A.C. 241.

§6.11.2   In certain cases, the sale of a company may give rise to a claim for constructive dismissal of an employee against the vendor company even if the employee continues to work with the new company.[1]

[1]   *Novosel v. Riegl* (1993), 46 C.C.E.L. 245 (Ont. Ct. (Gen. Div.)).

§6.11.3   In *Taylor v. Dallas Investments Inc.,*[1] the sale agreement between the defendant and the previous employer provided that the defendant would employ all present staff with new compensation packages similar to those which they were already receiving. The principal of the defendant discussed the plaintiff's duties with him along with the changes in procedures, authorities and methods of management and casually commented that all the employees were on probation. Several months later when the employee was terminated without notice, he sued the defendant-purchaser for wrongful dismissal. The court held that unless employees are advised otherwise, it is an implied term of the employment contract that a change of ownership does not break their service. A purchaser/employer who does not wish to contract on this basis must advise the employees accordingly and give them the option of becoming a new employee or declining employment and suing the former employer for wrongful dismissal. If the purchaser/employer does not specifically discuss this matter with the employees being taken over, he or she will be fixed with the implied term if the issue is not squarely raised.[2] In Quebec, the Civil Code explicitly provides for continuation of service.[3]

[1]   (1993), 8 Alta. L.R. 181 (Q.B.)
[2]   See also *Sorel v. Tomenson, Saunders Whitehead Ltd.* (1985), 9 C.C.E.L. 226, vard (1987), 39 D.L.R. (4th) 460 (B.C.C.A.).
[3]   C.C.Q., art. 2097.

§6.12   If a change in employment is contemplated, the employer has an obligation to inform the executive of the extent of the change contemplated. In the case of *Stevens v. Globe & Mail,*[1] the plaintiff was removed from a management position in Toronto and offered an analyst's position in Washington, D.C. The court found that the employer had an obligation to present alternative postings in sufficient detail, particularly with respect to the issue of compensation and other benefits, so that they could be fairly evaluated by the employee. Gibson J. stated:

> In my view, in law, Stevens was entitled to full and fair particulars of any proposed change in his employment . . . [T]o be advised that he was expected to move to Washington for some sort of a new writing job, with no discussion of compensation, and that he would no longer be part of the management committee (with a substantial loss of bonus), in my view, Stevens could reasonably consider this change to be, in fact and in law, a demotion, and certainly not suitable equivalent or alternative employment. In my view, therefore, he was constructively dismissed in law.[2]

[1]   (1992), 7 O.R. (3d) 520 (Gen. Div.); appealed on separate grounds (1996), 28 O.R. (3d) 481 (C.A.).
[2]   (1992), 7 O.R. (3d) 520 (Gen. Div.) at 524.

§6.13 Some common law courts have decided that in order to maintain the employment relationship, the employer need not provide actual work to its employees,[1] so long as the employer continues to pay the agreed salary and benefits. The British Columbia Court of Appeal has recently stated that there are exceptions to this proposition and that a chief executive officer is one of them. In *Park v. Parsons Brown & Co.*,[2] the court stated:

> One exception relates to contracts of employment where there is a benefit to the employee, such as an actress, or a radio or television performer, from the performance of the work. A second is where the employee's remuneration is by commission.
> I have no difficulty in fitting this case into both exceptions. Park was employed as a chief executive officer and a part of his remuneration was a bonus in the form of a percentage of the yearly income of Parsons Brown.
> As the chief executive officer, he was primarily responsible for the operations of the company, and the success or failure of the company was a reflection of his performance in that role. If he was not allowed to perform the role of chief executive officer, that part of his remuneration in the form of a bonus would reflect, not his abilities, but those of a management committee. Further, his reputation in the business community as a manager would suffer when it became known that he was without duties to perform or powers to exercise.[3]

The employer was not allowed to remove the executive's functions during the reasonable notice period.

[1]   *Suleman v. British Columbia Research Council* (1990), 52 B.C.L.R. 138 (C.A.); *Turner v. Sawdon & Co.*, [1901] 2 K.B. 653 (C.A.); *Emmens v. Elderton* (1853), 4 H.L.C. 624, 10 E.R. 606.
[2]   (1989), 27 C.C.E.L. 224 (B.C.C.A.).
[3]   (1989), 27 C.C.E.L. 224 (B.C.C.A.) at 230.

§6.14 Hence, for some types of jobs, failure to provide the work agreed upon amounts to constructive dismissal even if salary, benefits and title remain unaffected. In these particular cases, the opportunity to work is an integral part of employment, as, for example, when the executive requires the challenge to demonstrate and enhance his abilities. This aspect takes on an increased importance for an executive who is side-tracked and given insignificant work after a reorganization.

§6.14.1 In Quebec, article 2087 of the Civil Code of Quebec specifically provides that the employer is bound to allow the performance of the work agreed upon. Hence, the failure to provide the work agreed upon to an executive or any other employee is a breach of the employment obligations, even if remuneration is maintained.

C. AUTHORITY AND RESPONSIBILITIES

§6.15 Inherent in the employer's obligation to furnish work is an executive's right to be given the authority and responsibility for the activities involved. For example, a vice-president of marketing should be given the responsibility for marketing activities and have the authority generally to choose the means to meet required objectives. Furthermore, the executive must be given and be seen to have authority over those who are involved in his or her sphere of responsibility. The lines where such authority and responsibilities begin or end are often blurred, especially in areas where there is joint authority with the chief executive.

§6.16 In order to define what authority or responsibilities were agreed upon, it is necessary to examine the particular circumstances of each employment relationship. While many organizations have documentation which defines such terms, others do not. In some cases, such documentation does not reflect reality. The courts will usually review the intention of the parties by referring to actual practice. Such an inquiry may be difficult when there is no pattern of behaviour and the executive has been allowed to assume or refuse assignments.

§6.17 If the employer provides an executive with a title but fails to allow the executive to perform the duties normally associated with the title, its obligations may not be met. Similarly, one's employment contract may be breached when the employer reduces an executive's authority to such an extent that it amounts to a fundamental change or prevents the executive from properly carrying out his or her duties.[1] Likewise, an employer who erodes the responsibilities and authority of an executive may be subject to a claim in constructive dismissal.[2] For example, when the head office specialists of a holding company constantly interfere with a related organization's own senior specialist, such interference may constitute a fundamental change in one's level of authority.

[1] See *Drayton v. W.C.W. Western Canada Water Enterprises Inc.* (1991), 36 C.C.E.L. 157 (B.C.S.C.), where the executive vice-president and chief financial officer alleged that his participation and strategies were ignored or frustrated by the employer's principals, but the court found no breach of contract.

[2] *Colasurdo v. CTG Inc.* (1988), 18 C.C.E.L. 264 (Ont. H.C.J.); *Lavigne v. Sidbec-Dosco Inc.*, D.T.E. 85T-4 (Que. S.C.), affd, unreported, May 4, 1988, C.A.M. 500-09-001556-844; *Allard v. Procureur général du Québec*, D.T.E. 84T-173 (Que. Prov. Ct.). No such constructive dismissal was found in *Podas v. Pacific Press Ltd.* (1991), 61 B.C.L.R. (2d) 196 (C.A.).

§6.18 In *Campbell v. Merrill Lynch Canada Inc.*,[1] the court examined the effect of corporate downsizing on an employment relationship. In this case, the plaintiff, a corporate debt financing specialist, maintained that the infrastructure which had previously supported her position was eliminated as a result of the corporate reorganization and downsizing. She alleged that because the defendant was no longer a full-service firm, she no longer had access to those prospective clients who might otherwise have sought the services of a specialist in corporate debt financing. With the loss of the Corporate Finance Group there were no longer "relationship managers" capable of providing introductions to clients with whom the defendant had previously done business. Clients would be inclined to look to competitors for services which the defendant, through the plaintiff, might have otherwise provided. The plaintiff stated that the effect of these changes upon her position was such that she could no longer be sure of earning the bonuses or other incentive income which she had previously received, and that if she continued in her employment with no prospect of success, her reputation in the investment industry would be damaged. The court held as follows:

> I have concluded that the removal of all effective infrastructures for the discharge of the plaintiff's duties as a corporate debt financing specialist, effectively made it impossible for her to fulfil a productive role for the defendant. While this would not have deprived her of all opportunity to bonus income, the loss of the chance to succeed in the role for which she was hired, for a significant period of time, amounts in my view to a breach of the fundamental term of the contract of employment. I am therefore of the view that there was a constructive dismissal of the plaintiff as she contends. (See *Park v. Parsons Brown and Company et al.* (1989), 39 B.C.L.R. (2d) 107 (B.C.C.A.) at pp. 112-13).[2]

[1] (1992), 36 A.C.W.S. (3d) 812 (B.C.S.C.).
[2] (1992), 36 A.C.W.S. (3d) 812 (B.C.S.C.), at p. 10 of the judgment.

§6.19 Changes in an executive's reporting functions may also constitute the basis of a successful claim by the executive for constructive dismissal where having to report to another person, in effect, amounts to a demotion. In *Snyders v. Saint John Shipbuilding Ltd.*,[1] the plaintiff was hired as vice-president and general manager under an executive employment agreement which provided that he would report directly to the chairman. The plaintiff had been employed for two years when he was informed he would report to a newly hired vice-president instead of the chairman. The plaintiff resigned and sought damages on the basis of constructive dismissal. On appeal, the court found that the change in reporting functions reduced the role of the plaintiff to that of a junior vice-president with substantial loss in authority, thereby breaching a fundamental term of the employment contract.

[1] (1989), 29 C.C.E.L. 26 (N.B.C.A.), leave to appeal to S.C.C. refused 103 N.B.R. (2d) 89n. See also *Wilding v. Qwest Foods Ltd.*, unreported, April 2, 1992, Vancouver No. C908657 (B.C.S.C.).

§6.20 Unilateral changes that cause loss of prestige for the executive, including changes in title or level of authority, when these factors were an important consideration in the executive's decision to enter into the employment relationship, may constitute constructive dismissal. In some cases, this may be brought about by the introduction of an additional level of authority between the executive and the president. Constructive dismissal was found to exist when the promotion of a colleague resulted in a major reduction of the plaintiff's authority and thus constitutes a demotion.[1] It is to be noted that a demotion can constitute a constructive dismissal even if there is a legitimate business justification for the reorganization.[2]

[1] *Plitt v. P.P.G. Canada Inc.* (1992), 34 A.C.W.S. (3d) 82 (Ont. Ct. (Gen. Div.)).
[2] *Greaves v. Ontario Municipal Employees' Retirement Board* (1995), 15 C.C.E.L. (2d) 94 (Ont. Ct. (Gen. Div.)).

§6.21 Numerous other cases have also concluded that a change in reporting functions amounts to a constructive dismissal.[1] In *Moore v. University of Western Ontario*,[2] the reporting change was not seen as fundamental. The plaintiff in that case was responsible for information and relations with other universities. From 1972 to 1983, he reported directly to the president of the university. Following an internal reorganization, a new position was created. The plaintiff was not allowed to apply for this new position but was assured that his position and remuneration would not be affected by the changes. Following the reorganization, the plaintiff was required to report to the person holding this new position instead of to the president. The court held that

> ... many factors are to be taken into account in deciding how important a job is in the structure of the university. Reporting status is not the sole criterion to decide on the indication of status in a job or position.[3]

In this particular case, the change was not fundamental and therefore did not constitute a constructive dismissal.

[1]   *Ally v. Institute of Chartered Accountants of Ontario* (1992), 42 C.C.E.L. 118 (Ont. Ct. (Gen. Div.)); *McNeil v. Presstran Industries* (1992), 37 A.C.W.S. (3d) 350 (Ont. C.A.); *Vanderleest v. City of Regina* (1992), 42 C.C.E.L. 67 (Sask. Q.B.); *Kidd v. Southam Press Ltd.* (1983), 1 C.C.E.L. 167 (Ont. H.C.J.); *Burton v. MacMillan Bloedel Ltd.*, [1976] 4 W.W.R. 267 (B.C.S.C.).

[2]   (1985), 8 C.C.E.L. 157 (Ont. H.C.J.).

[3]   (1985), 8 C.C.E.L. 157 (Ont. H.C.J.) at 171. See also *Johnston v. Co-Van International Trucks Inc.* (1993), 48 C.C.E.L. 147 (B.C.S.C.).

§6.22   Finally, it should be noted that a unilateral modification in job content which has the effect of humiliating the executive in front of his or her peers or subordinates has in some cases constituted constructive dismissal.[1] In all cases, reference should be made to the employment agreement to determine if the employer has a contractual right to unilaterally impose the change in working conditions.[2]

[1]   *Gravino v. Gulf Canada Ltée*, D.T.E. 91T-1059 (Que. S.C.), appeal abandoned Sept. 25, 1991, C.A.M. 500-09-001184-910.

[2]   *Macaulay v. Imperial Life Assur. Co. of Canada*, D.T.E. 84T-395 (Que. S.C.). See also *Atkinson v. Equity Silver Mines Ltd.*, [1994] B.C.J. No. 260 (B.C.S.C.).

D.   PLACE OF WORK

§6.23   The geographic location at which the employer must provide the work may be expressly agreed to, but is usually accepted or implied from the circumstances. For many employees, it is implied that the place of work will remain unchanged for the duration of the employment relationship.[1] In these cases, a forced transfer to another location may amount to a breach of the employment contract by the employer. However, an offer to consider a transfer should be distinguished from an order to transfer.[2]

[1]   *Morris v. International Harvester Canada Ltd.* (1984), 7 C.C.E.L. 300 (Ont. H.C.J.).

[2]   *Marleau v. Overnite Express (1980) Inc.*, D.T.E. 87T-754 (Que. C.A.).

§6.24   Some executives work regularly at several locations, while others are obliged to travel periodically. In other cases, an executive may not initially need to travel, but as the organization grows and its needs change, the evolution of the executive's responsibilities may require him or her to travel.

§6.25 As the number of employers who have national or international operations increases, the issue of where the work is to be performed gains importance. In conjunction with this development, courts more readily recognize the *bona fide* requirements of transfers, as discussed below.

§6.26 In the context of an executive employment contract, it is increasingly common for an individual to be transferred to other locations. In fact, a contract of employment may include an implied term that the executive must accept a request to transfer to another location because of the executive's particular activities or the national or international nature of the employer's activities. This issue is of particular importance because of possible conflicting interests between those of the employer requiring the transfer of an executive to another location and those of the executive whose family or other needs dictate that the move, at that particular time, is not desirable.

§6.27 A transfer to another geographic location can involve a loss of prestige and position which effectively constitutes a demotion and therefore a fundamental breach of the contract of employment.[1] In *Gravino v. Gulf Canada Ltée*,[2] the court recognized that mobility is customarily required of executives in corporations operating throughout Canada and held that a tacit condition of the plaintiff's employment required that he accept postings to other locations from time to time, which in this case was from Montreal to Toronto. The court added that ambitious employees such as the plaintiff must have understood that in order to be promoted to the more senior positions, they would have to acquire experience in several of the different aspects of the defendant's operations, which meant that the executive had to work in different parts of the country. The court cited *Durrant v. Westeel-Rosco Ltd.*,[3] a decision of the British Columbia Supreme Court, where Murray J. stated:

> It is my view that it was an implied term in the plaintiff's contract of employment with the defendant that he would accept all regional transfers not involving a demotion. I fail to see how large national or international corporations can operate effectively without such an implied term in their contracts of employment.[4]

Since the company's head office was in Toronto, officers of the company would ordinarily be required to reside there. Head office experience was considered an integral part of an executive's future training and, as such, executives should expect to be posted there at one time or another.[5]

[1] *Springer v. Merrill Lynch, Royal Securities Ltd.* (1984), 4 C.C.E.L. 81 (Ont. H.C.J.).

[2] D.T.E. 91T-1059 (Que. S.C.), appeal abandoned Sept. 25, 1991, C.A.M. 500-09-001184-910. See also *Owens Illinois Canada Inc. v. Boivin* (1988), 23 C.C.E.L. 255 (Que. C.A.); *Lever v. Bic Sport Canada Inc.*, unreported, Oct. 10, 1989, C.S.M. 500-05-004174-877; *Smith v. Viking Helicopter Ltd.* (1989), 24 C.C.E.L. 113 (Ont. C.A.); *Bélair v. Communications Radiomutuel Inc.*, D.T.E. 88T-268 (Que. S.C.); *Karjanlahti v. Tamrock Canada Inc.*, [1993] B.C.J. No. 1029 (B.C.S.C.).

[3] (1978), 7 B.C.L.R. 14.

[4] (1978), 7 B.C.L.R. 14, at 20.

[5] See also *Morris v. International Harvester Canada Ltd.* (1984), 7 C.C.E.L. 300 (Ont. H.C.J.).

§6.28 Failure to accept a transfer in cases where the request was within the employer's rights or where the executive received proper notice, may amount to insubordination, and accordingly constitute cause for dismissal without notice.[1] Where the Defendant company underwent a downsizing forced by economic conditions and offered the plaintiff the opportunity to relocate from England to Texas, the court held that it was an implied term of the contract that the plaintiff would accept all reasonable transfers that were not demotions and that were not demanded in bad faith. Consequently, the employee's failure to accept the transfer constituted a breach of employment and the defendant was entitled to terminate the plaintiff for this breach.[2]

[1] *Page v. Jim Pattison Industries Ltd.*, [1984] 4 W.W.R. 481 (Sask. C.A.).

[2] *Froese v. Horton CBI Ltd.*, unreported, Nov. 10, 1993, File No. 41348/89 (Ont. Ct. (Gen. Div.)).

§6.29 The question of whether to accept or refuse a transfer to another location, as well as whether one should accept the possibility of a transfer as a condition of employment, has become increasingly difficult in light of the many cases where both members of a household work and earn income. In order to convince key executives to accept transfers to other locations, employers frequently offer assistance to their spouses in finding employment at the new location.[1]

[1] *Henderson v. Westfair Foods Ltd.* (1990), 32 C.C.E.L. 152 (Man. Q.B.), revd on other grounds 40 C.C.E.L. 81 (C.A.). An opposite view seems to have been retained in *Holgate v. Bank of Nova Scotia* (1989), 27 C.C.E.L. 201 (Sask. Q.B.).

E. DIRECTIVES AND ASSISTANCE

§6.30 Depending on the type of work and the level of authority in the company, the amount of assistance and/or direction that an executive may need to carry out his or her functions will vary considerably. The employer has an obligation to ensure that the executive is clearly instructed on the duties and responsibilities of the position. The employer must provide sufficient instructions or information to allow the executive to meet the required standards. The employer must ensure that the information is communicated, facilities are provided and specialists and/or consultants are assigned where necessary. Likewise, the executive may be entitled to training, and supervision to some degree, if such is inherently agreed to or required.

§6.31 Should an employer fail significantly to provide the necessary assistance, direction and/or objectives, the employer may be considered to have breached its obligations under the employment contract. In such circumstances, the employer may be prevented from relying on incompetence as a cause for terminating the employment relationship without notice. In *E.H. Freund Ltd. v. Cogasa Mining Corp.*,[1] the employee's inability to get instructions from his director frustrated his efforts to fulfil the employment contract. The court found that the employer's failure to communicate constituted a fundamental breach of the employment contract.

[1] (1983), 4 C.C.E.L. 60 (B.C.C.A.).

§6.32 Courts have on many occasions held that to establish cause for dismissal, the employer must show that the employee was informed of the unsatisfactory performance, was given an explanation of the required standard and was afforded opportunity to improve his or her shortcomings.[1] It must also be demonstrated that the employee was warned or was aware that failure to improve or to correct the unacceptable performance could lead to dismissal.[2] In *Anderson v. Pirelli Cables Inc.*,[3] Mr. Justice Walsh stated:

> Particularly at the executive level of employment, courts should be cautious in the determination of what is "properly required" by an employer of its employee.

He continued:

> This in my view is especially so in cases where there is no clear and unequivocable evidence that the employee was warned of his shortcomings, and that his performance must improve or his services would be terminated, and that he clearly understood this to be the situation.

[1] *Lindquist v. People's Co-operative Ltd.* (1985), 12 C.C.E.L. 134 (Man. Q.B.); *Manning v. Surrey Memorial Hospital Society* (1975), 54 D.L.R. (3d) 312 (B.C.S.C.). See also *Regan v. Chaleur Entrepreneurship Centre Inc.* (1994), 7 C.C.E.L. (2d) 46 (N.B.Q.B.).

² *Champagne v. Club de Golf Lévis Inc.*, D.T.E. 87T-548 (Que. Prov. Ct.).
³ (1984), 5 C.C.E.L. 156 (Ont. H.C.J.), at 159.

§6.33 Obviously, an executive is expected to be able to improve or compensate for shortcomings. Courts do not require employers or boards of directors to warn or discipline an executive to the same extent or degree required of employers in their relations with employees occupying lower levels in the hierarchy.

§6.34 Certain behaviour may not require that the employee be given a chance to rectify the situation. Indeed, serious faults such as fraud, conflict of interest, unauthorized use of funds, as well as taking property belonging to another without permission may entitle the employer to dismiss the employee without notice.[1] Whether or not an isolated act will constitute just cause for summary dismissal is a matter to be decided on the specific facts and severity of the misconduct.[2]

[1] *Guillemette v. Simpsons Sears Ltd.*, D.T.E. 85T-901 (Que. S.C.). See also *Aasgaard v. Harlequin Enterprises* (1993), 48 C.C.E.L. 192 (Ont. Ct. (Gen. Div.)), affd [1997] O.J. No. 1112, No. C16138 (C.A.).
[2] *Atkins v. Windsor Star* (1994), 2 C.C.E.L. (2d) 229 (Ont. Ct. (Gen. Div.)); *Croxford v. London Jeep Eagle Ltd.* (1995), 11 C.C.E.L. (2d) 308 (Ont. Ct. (Gen. Div.)).

F.   RESPECT

§6.35 An employer's obligation to provide the work includes the obligation to do so in a respectful manner as an employer must treat employees with courtesy. What constitutes failure by an employer to respect an executive is a question of fact since, in most instances, the executive represents the employer. The difficulty often lies in the ability to prove abusive treatment which, although subtle, is humiliating. One court has held that a worker was justified in asking that his employment contract be recognized as having been terminated because an officer of the company had manifested his dislike of the employee through insults and other offending remarks.[1]

[1] *Talbot v. Jos. Dufresne & Fils Ltée*, J.E. 79-778 (Que. Prov. Ct.).

§6.36 A situation which may also constitute a breach of contract is where an employer creates or permits a hostile work environment to continue for an employee, for example, by tolerating disrespectful remarks or gestures by the employee's peers or superiors. The Ontario Court of Appeal has upheld the claim for constructive dismissal of a senior psychiatrist because of the behaviour and remarks of his superior.[1] These included public questioning of the psychiatrist's integrity and honesty, criticizing the quality of his work without cause, and attempting to get the employee to give up long-established and accepted work habits. The trial judge stated:

> Certainly, no employer is required by law to retain the services of an employee who is no longer performing adequately within the job he has been hired to do. However, if the problem has been caused by another employee whom the employer prefers to retain, then the dismissal, although perhaps necessary in the interests of the employer, is wrongful from the point of view of the employee, and must be compensated for. Such is the case here.[2]

[1] *Paitich v. Clarke Institute of Psychiatry* (1988), 19 C.C.E.L. 105 (Ont. H.C.J.), upheld on appeal 30 C.C.E.L. 235 (C.A.).

[2] (1988), 19 C.C.E.L. 105 (Ont. H.C.J.), 19 C.C.E.L. at 134.

G. TOOLS, MATERIALS, EQUIPMENT AND SPACE

§6.37 An employer has the obligation to provide the tools, materials, equipment and space necessary for the full execution of the work. The extent of the obligation depends on the nature of the employment. In some cases, the employer may have to provide a chauffeur, an expense account, technological support, competent staff or any other necessary factor for the position.

§6.38 Should the employer fail to discharge this obligation and the executive be unable to accomplish the work satisfactorily, the executive may rely on the employer's breach as the cause of the failure. Such was the case in *Turcot v. Conso Graber Inc.,*[1] where Turcot was fired from Conso Graber Inc. for alleged unsatisfactory performance. The court concluded that Turcot, a sales representative, had sold less than what was expected of him and that he had failed to bring in new clients. However, the court held that the employee's poor performance was probably due to the company's failure to furnish the employee with the materials he required to do the job properly. Delays in the delivery of goods which were to be sold, the absence of a merchandise catalogue and even the poor quality of some of the company goods were held to explain his poor performance and inability to recruit new clients.

[1] D.T.E. 87T-668 (Que. S.C.).

§6.39 The employer cannot unilaterally and without notice cease to provide the executive with the tools necessary to perform the work or cease to provide the materials agreed upon. In *Reilly v. Hotels of Distinction (Canada) Inc., Hotel le Grand/Grand Hotel,*[1] the employer took away Reilly's company car and moved her to a smaller office. The court held that these actions, among others, by the employer amounted to a fundamental change in Reilly's working conditions and allowed Reilly to successfully claim she had been constructively dismissed.

[1]   D.T.E. 87T-645 (Que. S.C.). See also *Occhionero v. Roy*, D.T.E. 92T-632 (Que. S.C.).

H. HOURS OF WORK

§6.40 While in many occupations hours of work are clearly defined and must be adhered to by both employee and employer, for the vast majority of executives there is no legal definition of hours of work. Rarely do the parties to an executive employment relationship anticipate such terms; in fact, they are rarely even discussed. The employer's organizational culture and the requirements of the position will generally dictate the range of working hours that are acceptable. Most executives are usually evaluated on their efforts as a whole as opposed to their hours at work as a single variable.

§6.41 Where an executive's functions may be described to a large extent as intellectual, it may be difficult to determine when an executive is in fact working. However, should an executive's functions imply or express the intention that he or she will be available to other employees or third parties during specific time frames, hours of work may become an issue to be examined more closely. Clearly, where an employer agrees to specific hours of work, they must be respected.

I. DURATION

1. Fixed-Term Contract or Indeterminate Contract

§6.42 An employment contract may be for a definite or indeterminate term,[1] subject to the statutory exceptions discussed below. A person hired for a fixed period, to complete a certain project or until a predetermined event occurs, is employed under a fixed-term contract. The employer has an obligation to provide work for the duration of the term unless the contract specifically provides otherwise.[2] All employees hired other than for a fixed term or undertaking are parties to an employment contract of indeterminate duration.

[1]   Article 2086 of the Civil Code of Quebec expressly provides for this.
[2]   *Paddon v. Phillips Barratt Kaiser Engineering Ltd.* (1987), 18 B.C.L.R. (2d) 170 (S.C.).

§6.43 In Quebec, the term of the employment contract is limited by article 2085 of the Civil Code of Quebec, which stipulates that the employee undertakes *for a limited period* to do work for another which means that the employee may not promise to provide services for his or her lifetime. However, there exists no upper limit on the duration of a fixed term contract. In Ontario however, section 2 of the *Employers and Employees Act*[1] provides:

> No voluntary contract of service or indenture is binding for longer than a term of nine years from the date thereof.[2]

The Ontario Court of Appeal confirmed that section 2 of the Act does not apply to an indefinite term contract but does pose an upper limit to the duration of a fixed term contract.[3] It is noteworthy that pursuant to regulations under the Ontario *Employment Standards Act*, where a person is employed for a term or a task and such term or task exceeds a period of 12 months, the employment is deemed not to be for a definite term.[4]

[1] R.S.O. 1990, c. E.12.
[2] See *Pelletier v. Caisse Populaire Lasalle Sudbury Ltd.* (1984), 5 C.C.E.L. 1 (Ont. H.C.J.), affd 56 O.R. (2d) 784 (C.A.).
[3] *Hine v. Susan Shoe Industries Ltd.* (1994), 3 C.C.E.L. (2d) 119 (Ont. C.A.); *Leonetti v. Hussmann Canada Inc.* (1995), 12 C.C.E.L. (2d) 249 (Ont. Ct. (Gen. Div.)). See also *Charlton v. B.C. Sugar Refining Co.*, [1925] 1 WW.R. 546 (B.C.C.A.), regarding a similar provision in B.C. legislation.
[4] *Termination of Employment Regulations*, R.R.O. 1990, Reg. 327, s. 15(1).

§6.44 The courts have frequently been called upon to distinguish between a fixed-term contract and a contract of indeterminate duration.[1] The relevance of the distinction is twofold. First, there is the right of the parties to expect certainty in the duration of the employment relationship. The fixed-term contract, by its very nature, lends itself to greater certainty. Secondly, there are the consequences arising from a decision to terminate the employment relationship.

[1] *Laliberté v. Viceroy Homes Ltd.* (1990), 32 C.C.E.L. 117 (Ont. H.C.J.); *Shawinigan Lavalin Inc. v. Espinosa*, D.T.E. 90T-261 (Que. C.A.); *Riddell v. City of Vancouver* (1985), 11 C.C.E.L. 288 (B.C.C.A.); *Boilard v. Aciers Pitt (Québec) Ltée*, D.T.E. 84T-657 (Que. S.C.); *Landry v. Radio du Pontiac Inc.*, D.T.E. 83T-200 (Que. S.C.); *Pacifique Plante v. Ville de Montréal*, [1976] C.A. 95 (Que.).

§6.45 An employment contract is presumed to be in force for an indeterminate period, unless proven otherwise.[1] The party alleging the existence of a fixed-term contract has the burden of proving it.[2] In *Nicholls v. Richmond*,[3] McLachlin J. of the British Columbia Supreme Court stated:

Probably both parties at the time of making the contract expected that Mr. Nicholls would stay with the municipality to retirement age. But they made no agreement, express or implied, to that effect. There is a difference between a vague expectation and a binding contractual term.

1   *Mattson v. ALC Airlift Canada Inc.* (1993), 18 C.P.C. (3d) 310 (B.C.S.C.); *Couture v. Entreprise de Navigation de l'Isle Inc.*, J.E. 79-160 (Que. S.C.); *MacDonald v. White Rock Waterworks Co.* (1973), 38 D.L.R. (3d) 763 (B.C.S.C.) ("permanent" employment was interpreted as meaning employment for an indeterminate period); *Richardson v. Koefod*, [1969] 1 W.L.R. 1812 (C.A.); *Chadburn v. Sinclair Canadian Oil Co.* (1966), 57 W.W.R. 477 (Alta. S.C.); *Henderson v. Canadian Timber & Saw Mills Ltd.* (1904), 12 B.C.R. 294 (C.A.); *Mattson v. ALC Airlift Canada Inc.*, unreported, Dec. 15, 1993, File No. C905815 (B.C.S.C.).

2   *Turcot v. Conso Graber Inc.*, D.T.E. 87T-668 (Que. S.C.); *Bryan v. University of British Columbia* (1987), 16 C.C.E.L. 269 (B.C.S.C.), affd 64 D.L.R. (4th) 175 (C.A.).

3   (1984), 52 B.C.L.R. 302 (S.C.), at 308.

§6.46   The fact that an employee is employed in a project having a specific duration does not necessarily mean that the employee is hired for the full duration of the project or that the employment will automatically come to an end upon completion of the project.[1] Remuneration in the form of an annual salary does not necessarily lead to the presumption that employment is for a fixed one-year period. There is a distinction between agreements that establish the duration of the employment relationship[2] and agreements which determine the conditions of employment for a particular period of time.[3] Employment contracts which establish the terms of remuneration for the first year of employment or for a specific number of years of employment do not necessarily create fixed-term contracts. These provisions merely guarantee a minimum salary, thereby providing the executive with a sense of security as to remuneration but not as to the length of the employment relationship.[4]

1   *Mattson v. ALC Airlift Canada Inc.* (1993), 18 C.P.C. (3d) 310 (B.C.S.C.); *Ostick v. Novacorp Int. Consulting Inc.* (1989), 27 C.C.E.L. 286 (B.C.S.C.); *Hubler v. Geneva Cosmetics Inc.* (1984), 4 C.C.E.L. 318 (Ont. Co. Ct.); *Boivin v. Corp. des Loisirs de Taschereau Inc.*, J.E. 82-767 (Que. Prov. Ct.).

2   *Bélair v. Communications Radiomutuel Inc.*, D.T.E. 88T-268 (Que. S.C.).

3   *Ballard v. Alberni Valley Chamber of Commerce* (1992), 39 C.C.E.L. 225 (B.C.S.C.); *Boilard v. Aciers Pitt (Québec) Ltée*, D.T.E. 84T-657 (Que. S.C.); *Careau v. Sogemec Inc.*, [1981] C.S. 862 (Que.).

4   *Carignan v. Infasco Division Ivaco Inc.*, D.T.E. 89T-118 (Que. S.C.); *Turcot v. Conso Graber Inc.*, D.T.E. 87T-668 (Que. S.C.); *Tanguay v. Scanway Corp.*, D.T.E. 85T-65 (Que. S.C.); *Jasmin v. Jean-Luc Surprenant Inc.*, J.E. 83-683 (Que. S.C.); *Dubois v. J. René Ouimet Ltée*, [1959] C.S. 573 (Que.); *Levesque v. J.B. Renaud & Cie*, [1954] B.R. 22 (Que. C.A.); *Thibault v. Cie d'Autobus de l'Abitibi Ltée*, [1952] R.L. 371 (Que. Mag. Ct.); *L'Héreault v. Mathieu*, [1943] C.S. 12 (Que.); *Stewart v. Hanover Fire Ins. Co.*, [1936] S.C.R. 177; *Asbestos Corp. Ltd. v. Cook*, [1933] S.C.R. 86; *Cité de Montréal v. Davis* (1897), 6 B.R. 177 (Que. C.A.), affd 27 S.C.R. 539.

§6.47 In *Major v. Compagnie d'assurances Provinces-unies,*[1] certain clauses of the employment contract read as follows:

> 1. The Company retains the services of Major who agrees, in the capacity of president, for a period of ten years from January 1st, 1973 to December 31st, 1982 . . .

> • • • • •

> 12. After age sixty-five (65), Major may, for a period which may continue until 1982 (unless premature death occurs), exercise the "function" of Chairman of the Board or other less important functions according to the needs of the Company. This will permit him to reduce his responsibilities and activities and he will keep an office and a secretarial service supplied by the Company and, depending on the responsibilities exercised, remuneration to be defined. In addition, Major maintains his eligibility for benefits from group insurance, sickness and hospital, the costs of representation that are necessary for the function. [Authors' translation]

The Quebec Court of Appeal confirmed the Superior Court's decision that the clause did not create an obligation for the company to employ Major for a further ten-year term, as the conditions of such employment, after 1982, were not defined.

§6.47.01 Furthermore, agreeing on a term of employment does not automatically amount to the conclusion of a fixed-term contract if the parties have also reserved their right to prematurely terminate the contract by providing notice to the other party.[2]

---

[1] D.T.E. 89T-414 (Que. C.A.); affg, unreported, Dec. 6, 1986, C.S.M. 500-05-010713-830.

[2] *Thibodeau v. Ste-Julienne (Corp. Municipale),* [1994] R.J.Q. 2819 (Que. C.A.).

§6.47.1 Furthermore, the fact that the parties to an employment contract have agreed upon a specific period of employment does not necessarily mean that they are bound by a fixed term contract if at the same time they have agreed on the right to prematurely terminate the contract upon providing notice to the other party.[1]

---

[1] *Thibodeau v. Ste-Julienne (Corp. municipale de),* D.T.E. 94T-1252 (Que. C.A.); *Shawinigan Lavalin Inc. v. Espinosa,* [1990] R.L. 27 (Que. C.A.); *Gagné v. Produits forestiers Portbec ltée,* D.T.E. 97T-293 (S.C.).

§6.48 With respect to probationary employees, Quebec decisions vary as to whether the probationary period is equivalent to a fixed-term contract, that is, that the employee is entitled to the full benefit of the probation period as a guaranteed term of employment.[1]

[1] Term contract: *Potvinc v. G. & W. Freightways Ltd.*, D.T.E. 88T-644 (Que. Prov. Ct.). Not term contract: *Beauchemin v. Hôpital d'Youville de Sherbrooke*, D.T.E. 89T-239 (Que. S.C.); *Serapiglia v. Eastern Provincial Airways (1963) Ltd.*, J.E. 79-242 (Que. S.C.), appeal dismissed, unreported, Dec. 4, 1979, C.A.M. 500-09-000237-792; *Anthony v. Hopital général juif, Sir Mortimer B. Davis*, D.T.E. 94T-16 (Ct. of Que.).

2. Term Contract — Automatic Renewal Clause

§6.49 Employment contracts frequently provide that the term of employment will renew automatically. To avoid misunderstandings, the parties should clearly indicate under what conditions the contract will be renewed, and whether a notice of non-renewal will be required to prevent the contract from being automatically renewed. Failure to give timely notice of non-renewal, an irregular notice or one emanating from a person lacking the necessary authority will lead to the automatic renewal of the contract.[1]

[1] *Cadorette v. O.G.I.S. Inc.*, D.T.E. 88T-575 (Que. S.C.); *Boldrini v. Université du Québec*, [1975] C.S. 749 (Que.).

§6.50 An issue that arises is whether a fixed-term contract which is automatically renewed on several occasions remains a fixed-term contract or becomes an employment contract of indeterminate duration. In *Québec (Procureur général) v. Corriveau*,[1] the Quebec Court of Appeal held that a four-year contract, which provided for automatic renewal as long as the board of directors did not give notice in writing of its intention not to renew, was properly characterized as a fixed-term contract.

[1] [1989] R.J.Q. 1 (C.A.). See also *Saunders v. Fredericton Golf & Country Club Inc.* (1994), 151 N.B.R. (2d) 184 (C.A.); revg (1993), 140 N.B.R. (2d) 387 (Q.B.).

3. Term Contract — Tacit Renewal

§6.51 A term contract of employment is tacitly renewed for an indeterminate term, where the employee continues to carry on his or her work after the expiry of the term, without further agreement between the parties.[1]

[1] *Erlund v. Quality Communication Products Ltd.* (1972), 29 D.L.R. (3d) 476 (Man. Q.B.); *Hague v. St. Boniface Hospital*, [1936] 3 D.L.R. 363 (Man. Q.B.); *Normandin v. Solloway Mills & Co.* (1931), 40 O.W.N. 429 (H.C.J.); *Messer v. Barrett Co.*, [1927] 1 D.L.R. 284 (Ont. C.A.); *Parker v. Beeching*, [1923] 4 D.L.R. 35 (Alta. C.A.).

§6.52 In Quebec, article 2090 C.C.Q. provides that the contract is tacitly renewed where the employee continues to work for five days after the expiry of the term without objection from the employer.[1]

> [1] Under the former Civil Code, the Civil Code of Lower Canada, the employment contract was tacitly renewed for a period equal to the original term, up to a maximum of one year, so long as the employee worked for more than eight days after the expiry of the term: see articles 1667 and 1641 C.C.L.C.; *Stewart v. Hanover Fire Insurance Co.* [1936] S.C.R. 177; *Bergeron v. Mines d'amiante Bell Ltée*, D.T.E. 88T-870 (Que. P.C.). Furthermore, the parties were bound by a contract for an indeterminate term only where terms and conditions of employment after expiry of the term contract differed from those enjoyed during the term contract. See for example, *Jean v. Groupe Promodor Inc.*, D.T.E. 85T-64 (Que. S.C.); *Roy v. Centre Hospitalier de l'Université Laval*, [1976] C.S. 1120 (Que. S.C.).

§6.53 Quebec courts have held that tacit renewal is not possible if the employee is incapable of furnishing his or her services immediately following the expiration of the term.[1]

> [1] *Lapointe v. Québec Propane Inc.*, D.T.E. 84T-546 (Que. S.C.); *Caisse Populaire de la Cité de Shawinigan v. Beaulac*, [1980] C.A. 154 (Que.).

§6.54 In Ontario, regulations pursuant to the *Employment Standards Act* deal with the issue of renewal. Section 15 of Regulation 327 provides:

> (2) Where a person who is employed for a definite term or task continues to be employed for a period of three months or more after completion of the term or task, the employment of that person shall be deemed not to be employment for a definite term or task and his or her employment shall be deemed to have commenced at the beginning of the term or task.[1]

Section 65(2) of the British Columbia *Employment Standards Act*[2] is similar to section 15(2) above.

> [1] *Termination of Employment Regulations*, R.R.O. 1990, Reg. 327, subs. 15(2).
> [2] R.S.B.C. 1996, c. 113.

J. CONCLUSION

§6.55 The employer's obligation to furnish the work is multi-facetted, including to provide the work agreed upon and delegate the authority and responsibilities necessary to carry on such work. This obligation exists throughout the full duration of the employment relationship, whether the contract is for a fixed term or an indeterminate term. The next chapter will review the employer's second obligation: pay the remuneration.

CHAPTER 7

PROVIDE REMUNERATION

A. INTRODUCTION

§7.1 The employer's obligation to provide the executive with remuneration or with the agreed-upon consideration is one of the principal employment obligations and is an essential element of the employment contract.[1] Clearly, a key element in attracting and retaining the best executives is the compensation package offered by the employer. Indeed, most employers seek to design their remuneration package in a way to motivate the executive to achieve peak performance.

---

[1] *Employment Standards Act*, R.S.O. 1990, c. E.14, s. 7; Civil Code of Quebec, art. 2087; *Vapomatic Inc. v. Tremblay*, [1975] R.D.T. 204 (Que. Prov. Ct.); *Tremblay v. Beliveau*, [1955] R.L. 57 (Que. Mag. Ct.).

§7.2 Where the obligation to pay is not specifically set out in a contract, it will be implied by the courts. In Quebec, article 2085 of the Civil Code of Quebec (previously C.C.L.C., art. 1665a), imposes upon the employer an obligation to provide remuneration for the employee's work. In addition to the common law obligation to pay remuneration due for services rendered, most Canadian jurisdictions have enacted labour standards legislation which specifically covers the employer's obligation to pay remuneration and, to some extent, establishes administrative and quasi-judicial procedures for enforcement.[1]

---

[1] See, *e.g.*, *Employment Standards Act*, R.S.O. 1990, c. E.14, s. 7; *Act Respecting Labour Standards*, R.S.Q., c. N-1.1; *Employment Standards Act*, R.S.B.C. 1996, c. 113.

B. REMUNERATION DEFINED

§7.3 Remuneration has a broader meaning than salary. Salary usually refers to periodically paid fixed compensation, while remuneration designates any benefit or advantage having a pecuniary value to which the employee is entitled as a result of executing the work furnished by his or her employer. This may include payment of a salary, commissions, bonuses, a car allowance, discount purchase plans, the provision of group insurance plans and pension plans, as well as stock options or other benefits which cater to the executive's needs.

§7.4 The importance of determining what constitutes remuneration between the parties to an executive employment contract is in the identification of what the executive is entitled to claim from his or her employer in exchange for executing the work at any given time. This may be particularly significant upon termination of the employment contract when all the respective debts are accrued and claimed.[1]

---

[1] The issue of what constitutes remuneration is also relevant in the context of wrongful dismissal. See Chapter 13, "Damages Awarded for Wrongful Dismissal".

§7.5 As an employee ascends the organization's hierarchy, the components of his or her remuneration are often modified in such a way as to be based on more than just straight salary. It may include such components as stock options, profit-sharing plans and/or bonuses. Disputes relating to the characterization of a particular benefit as a gift, a discretionary payment, or an integral part of remuneration frequently arise since it is only when the benefit is an integral part of the remuneration that the employer may not unilaterally and without notice cease to provide it.

§7.6 It is not necessary that the remuneration or method for calculating it be predetermined. If there is evidence that neither the executive nor the employer considered leasing or receiving the services for free, the parties may be deemed to have tacitly agreed that remuneration would be determined by usage or by ulterior agreement.[1] Alternatively, the executive may be paid on a *quantum meruit* basis for services actually rendered.[2]

---

[1] *Tremblay v. Beliveau*, [1955] R.L. 57 (Que. Mag. Ct.).
[2] *Hill v. Develcon Electronics Ltd.* (1991), 37 C.C.E.L. 19 (Sask. Q.B.); *Marquis Road Veterinary Medical Centre Ltd. v. Goebel* (1985), 39 Sask. R. 170 (C.A.); *Shell Canada Resources Ltd. v. Sayers* (1985), 41 Alta. L.R. (2d) 197 (C.A.), leave to appeal to S.C.C. refused Jan. 27, 1986; *Syhlonyk v. Syhlonyk* (1982), 20 Sask. R. 354 (Q.B.).

§7.7 In *Zinman v. Hechter*,[1] an employee had worked for the company from 1943 until the sale of the business in 1978, and had accepted a lower salary in consideration of the promise that he would be taken care of for life if the company was sold. He had been paid a salary of $9,000 for a position with a market value of $25,000 to $35,000. When the business was sold, the company provided the employee with a house worth $17,000 and an annual rental income of $1,500. The court found that the agreement to pay an additional sum upon the company being sold was vague and uncertain so as to render it unenforceable. However, the court cited the principle in *Deglman v. Guaranty Trust Co.*

of Canada,[2] that an employer must pay reasonable remuneration for services rendered under a void or unenforceable contract if the employee's services were accepted by the employer. As there was evidence to support a finding that the employee had been underpaid by $120,000, this constituted a reasonable measure of remuneration and the employee was awarded $120,000 less the value of the house he had been given.

[1] (1980), 9 Man. R. (2d) 129 (Q.B.), vard 130 D.L.R. (3d) 183 (C.A.), leave to appeal to S.C.C. refused 41 N.R. 488.
[2] [1954] S.C.R. 725.

§7.8 On the other hand, an executive may not later claim remuneration from the employer on the basis of unjust enrichment when he or she has voluntarily provided services without hope of receiving any particular or additional remuneration for them.[1] This is also true of the particularly diligent executive who has devoted enormous time and effort to his or her employer without first having established his or her right to remuneration for such work. In such cases, the executive may not subsequently tabulate his or her time and claim payment.[2]

[1] *Henri v. Garderie La Gaminerie Inc.*, D.T.E. 89T-162 (Ct. of Que.).
[2] *Leahy v. Marlborough Productions Ltd.*, [1991] B.C.W.L.D. 895 (S.C.); *Maheu, Noiseux & associés v. Ronéo Vickers Canada Ltd.*, D.T.E. 88T-588 (Que. C.A.).

C. MODIFICATION OF REMUNERATION

§7.9 The employer must continue to provide the entire remuneration for the duration of the employment relationship unless the parties mutually agree otherwise. A unilateral and abrupt change to an executive's remuneration may lead a court to conclude that the executive has been constructively dismissed, thereby entitling him or her to compensation.[1] Although a substantial reduction in salary has clearly been identified as a constructive dismissal,[2] some courts have recognized that a "relatively minor" change or reduction in the consideration to be paid for services is not sufficient to constitute constructive dismissal.[3] These cases lead us to believe that the courts will be more inclined to examine the extent to which a person's remuneration has been reduced rather than holding outright that any change or reduction is a fundamental breach of the employment contract. In *Hamilton & Olsen Surveys Ltd. v. Otto,*[4] the Alberta Court of Appeal reversed a trial judge's decision which had found that the employees were constructively dismissed when the employer unilaterally reduced their vacation entitlement from six to four weeks per year and suspended its matching contributions to the group R.R.S.P. savings plan ultimately reducing the plaintiffs' annual compensation by between 6.5 and 8 per cent. On appeal, the Court held that a reduction in benefits due to external economic pressures, where salaries are maintained, does not constitute a fundamental breach of an employment contract, is readily compensable by damages and does not amount to constructive dismissal.

[1] See Chapter 12, "Termination of Employment" and Chapter 13, "Damages Awarded for Wrongful Termination".

[2] *Boyd v. Whistler Mountain Ski Corp.* (1990), 20 A.C.W.S. (3d) 518 (B.C.S.C.); *Farquhar v. Butler Brothers Supplies Ltd.* (1988), 23 B.C.L.R. (2d) 89 (C.A.); *Pearl v. Pacific Enercon Inc.* (1985), 7 C.C.E.L. 252 (B.C.C.A.).

[3] *Purdy v. Vancouver Island Helicopters Ltd.* (1988), T.L.W. 747-034-3 (W.D.P.M.) (B.C.S.C.); *Poole v. Tomenson Saunders Whitehead Ltd.* (1987), 18 C.C.E.L. 238 (B.C.C.A.) ($100,000 salary and bonus effectively reduced by $4,500); *Oxman v. Dustbane Enterprises Ltd.* (1986), 13 C.C.E.L. 209 (Ont. H.C.J.), revd on other grounds 23 C.C.E.L. 157 (C.A.).

[4] (1993), 12 Alta. L.R. (3d) 431 (C.A.); leave to appeal to S.C.C. refused (1994), 15 Alta. L.R. (3d) lii.

§7.10   Although remuneration is an essential element of the employment contract, it would appear that once an executive reaches a substantial level of remuneration, what is fundamental — unless expressly or implicitly agreed otherwise — is that the executive remain within a range rather than having him or her maintain the same individual components of remuneration.

§7.11   In *Adams v. Comark Inc.*,[1] the Manitoba Court of Appeal examined whether an executive had been wrongfully dismissed for refusing to sign a code of business ethics which standardized policies and practices applicable to all the employer's divisions. The executive objected to the loss of personal use of frequent flyer points that he had enjoyed up until then. The court held that the issue was not whether the frequent flyer benefit was a *fundamental* term of employment, but whether it was a term at all. The court decided in the affirmative. Thus, the term could not be unilaterally changed by the employer. The court upheld the executive's action for wrongful dismissal.

[1] (1992), 42 C.C.E.L. 15 (Man. C.A.).

§7.12   The manner in which the remuneration is calculated may not be changed without notice by the employer unless the executive agrees to the modification. Accordingly, an employer may not unilaterally change the mode of remuneration from a fixed salary to a piecework rate.[1] Nor can the employer unilaterally change the mode of remuneration from commission to fixed salaries or vice versa, especially when the effect of the modification is a reduction in salary.[2] It has been held that the introduction of a completely new compensation package constitutes a fundamental change in the employment relationship amounting to constructive dismissal.[3]

[1] *Marchand v. Jean* (1918), 54 C.S. 279 (Que. S.C.).

[2] *Sherrard v. Moncton Chrysler Dodge (1980) Ltd.* (1990), 29 C.C.E.L. 158 (N.B.Q.B.), vard 33 C.C.E.L. 72 (C.A.); *Nyveen v. Russell Food Equipment Ltd.*, D.T.E. 88T-294 (Que. S.C.). See also *Blewett v. White Oaks Realty Ltd.* (1994), 4 C.C.E.L. (2d) 160 (Ont. Ct. (Gen. Div.)); *Cook v. Royal Trust* (1990), 31 C.C.E.L. 6 (B.C.S.C.); *Jeffrey v. Plant Forest Products Corp.* (1990), 32 C.C.E.L. 237 (Sask. Q.B.); and *McPhee v. Torino Motors (1975) Ltd.* (1989), 28 C.C.E.L. 68 (B.C. Co. Ct.). For a contrary view, see *George v. Morden & Helwig Ltd.* (1988), 20 C.C.E.L. 29 (Ont. H.C.J.), where the court concluded that since the employer's modification of the employee's remuneration from a salary-plus-bonus basis to a commission-only basis would have made the employee better off financially, the employee had acted prematurely in considering himself constructively dismissed; *Rebitt v. Pacific Motor Sales & Service Ltd.* (1988), 20 C.C.E.L. 239 (B.C.C.A.); *Graves v. Okanagan Trust Co.* (1956), 20 W.W.R. 17 (B.C.S.C.); *Farber v. Royal Trust Co.*, unreported, Aug. 11, 1989, C.S.M. 500-05-004698-856 (Que. S.C.) (on appeal, C.A.M. 500-09-001201-896).

[3] *Cook v. Royal Trust* (1990), 31 C.C.E.L. 6 (B.C.S.C.); *Ager v. Motorola Canada Ltd.* (1989), 89 C.L.L.C. 14,042 (B.C.S.C.); *Rémi Carrier Inc. v. Nolan*, D.T.E. 86T-370 (Que. C.A.); *Olson v. Sprung Instant Greenhouses Ltd.* (1985), 12 C.C.E.L. 8 (Alta. Q.B.); *Young v. Huntsville District Memorial Hospital* (1984), 5 C.C.E.L. 113 (Ont. H.C.J.); *Martin v. City of Woodstock* (1979), 8 B.L.R. 124 (Ont. H.C.J.), affd 3 A.C.W.S. (2d) 119 (C.A.).

§7.13 Executive and employer alike should be particularly careful to agree on the meaning of words or expressions used to determine remuneration. Otherwise, the courts may be called upon to draw conclusions which may not necessarily correspond to the parties' original understanding.[1]

[1] For example, in *D.H. Howden & Co. v. Sparling*, [1970] S.C.R. 883, the Court held that the literal meaning of the words "gross profit" was the net selling price less the total of the defendant's incoming invoices and the incoming freight costs.

§7.14 An employer's poor financial situation will not validate a unilateral change in the contract of employment.[1] When the employer has a contractual commitment to the employee, it is bound by the commitment[2] unless the contract is changed either in writing or by some other form of express agreement. Until such an agreement occurs, any decision to change, reduce, or eliminate bonus provisions or benefits is illegal.

[1] *Farquhar v. Butler Brothers Supplies Ltd.* (1988), 23 B.C.L.R. (2d) 89 (C.A.).

[2] *Johnstone v. Harlequin Enterprises Ltd.* (1991), 36 C.C.E.L. 30 (Ont. Ct. (Gen. Div.)).

§7.15 The following sections briefly describe some of the components of remuneration. The tax treatment for each of the components which make up an executive's remuneration should be analyzed so that both the employer and the executive may maximize their earnings.[1]

> [1] The tax implications are examined more fully in Chapter 18, "Tax Considerations".

D. COMPONENTS OF REMUNERATION

1. Salary

§7.16 As previously mentioned, the obligation to provide remuneration may encompass more than the mere payment of salary. Although payment of a fixed salary is the principal method of compensating executives, employment contracts frequently lay out elaborate and sophisticated mechanisms for providing incentive compensation to the executive. Very often these mechanisms tie into the performance or profits of the business.

§7.17 Although an employer may not impose a reduction in salary, circumstances may bring an employee to expressly or impliedly agree to a reduction in salary. For example, the employer may be experiencing difficult financial times requiring a temporary or permanent reduction in overhead costs. In such cases, the executive may prefer a reduced salary to being unemployed. So, too, an executive may agree to a change in the components of his or her remuneration from straight salary to profit-sharing or a reduction in salary in exchange for the increase of other benefits of employment such as longer vacation time or a company car. In all cases, where the executive expressly or implicitly accepts the new terms of remuneration, he or she may not later insist on the benefits of the previous terms, or allege constructive dismissal, should the modifications prove unsatisfactory. Forgoing immediate payment of salary in consideration of the financial difficulties of the business does not suggest that the executive has agreed to new terms of employment. Indeed, one court has held that this may be interpreted as granting the debtor-employer a delay.[1]

> [1] *Cogear Corp. v. Cormier*, J.E. 79-107 (Que. C.A.).

§7.18 Under the Ontario *Employment Standards Act*[1] and similar legislation in other provinces, vacation pay due and accruing is deemed to be held in trust for the employee. However, a Saskatchewan decision[2] suggests that if the employer does not hold such monies separate and apart from its general operating funds so that they cannot be traced, such monies cease to be a trust and are susceptible to subordination under the *Bankruptcy Act*.[3]

[1] R.S.O. 1990, c. E.14, s. 15.

[2] *Robinson, Little & Co. (Trustee) v. Saskatchewan (Minister of Labour)*, [1990] 1 W.W.R. 354 (Sask. C.A.).

[3] R.S.C. 1985, c. B-3 (now the *Bankruptcy and Insolvency Act*).

§7.19 Depending on the nature of the job, it may be important for both employer and employee to thoroughly discuss the possibility, frequency, and payment of work done in excess of the employee's normal work week or normal work day.

§7.20 Most provincial employment standards legislation and the *Canada Labour Code* provide for payment, at a premium rate, for work performed in addition to the regular work week for certain categories of employees. However, this is not particular cause for concern to executives, because they may not be covered by premium rate provisions (as is the case in Quebec) or, as in most cases, hours of work are not an issue since it is generally understood that executives, as representatives of the employer, will be available for work as needed, and since, in any event, the decision to work overtime is the executive's alone.[1] For example, in Ontario, certain professionals[2] and persons whose only work is "supervisory or managerial in character"[3] are exempt from the overtime provisions of the *Employment Standards Act*.[4]

[1] *Poon, Wong & Associates Inc. v. Wong*, [1991] B.C.W.L.D. 1186 (S.C.).

[2] Employment Standards Act Reg., R.R.O. 1990, Reg. 325, s. 3(1)(*a*), exempts professionals such as architects, dentists, lawyers, doctors, pharmacists, professional engineers and others from the overtime provisions of the *Employment Standards Act*.

[3] Employment Standards Act Reg., R.R.O. 1990, Reg. 325, s. 4(*b*). Note, however, that the exemption applies to a person "whose *only* work is supervisory or managerial in character" (emphasis added). Several employment standards decisions in Ontario have suggested that, where an employee performs other duties in addition to those of a managerial or supervisory nature, the exemption will not apply. See, *e.g.*, *Hogan and Greenfield Design-Build Ltd. (Re)*, (May 18, 1990) E.S.C. 2695 (Betcherman); *D & V Traders Ltd. (Re)*, (March 20, 23, 1990) E.S.C. 2655 (Baum).

[4] R.S.O. 1990, c. E.14.

§7.21 Payment of salary must be made in the place expressly or implicitly agreed upon by the parties. Usually, employees receive their salaries at the place of employment. When an executive works for two related corporations or is to be paid in different countries, the details of such an agreement should be clearly documented to avoid misunderstanding.

2. Salary Increases

§7.22 Salary increases are generally discretionary, unless the parties mutually intended regular increases to be part of the working conditions. Nevertheless, as is the case with bonuses, the courts have held that where increases are routinely granted, as opposed to being rewards for performance, they may form part of remuneration and be claimed as such. As with profit-sharing plans, when a salary increase is proposed, it becomes a new contractual term by reason of the executive's continued employment, failure to protest the changes, and acceptance of benefits.[1]

[1] *King v. Solna Offset of Canada Ltd.* (1984), 3 O.A.C. 178 (C.A.).

§7.23 Some contracts provide, in advance, for a specific increase in salary.[1] Other agreements acknowledge that the salary will be adjusted periodically or according to a merit system or in accordance with the cost of living as established by Statistics Canada or some other agency. Still other employment arrangements contemplate an automatic increase in salary. In such cases, denying an executive the automatic increase to which he or she is entitled amounts to a reduction in salary. In *Lavigne v. Sidbec-Dosco Inc.*,[2] a comptroller was demoted with a negligible reduction in salary. However, he did not receive the automatic increase all other employees received. The court held that the 4.6% reduction in his pay, added to the general increase in salaries budgeted at the rate of 11% which he failed to receive, combined to reduce the plaintiff's expected salary by 15.6%. This reduction, coupled with the plaintiff's reduced authority and responsibility, amounted to a constructive dismissal. In *Landry v. Radio du Pontiac Inc.*,[3] the employee's salary was fixed at $21,000, to be increased to $25,000 retroactive to the date of hiring as soon as the employer's finances would permit it. The court rejected the employee's claim that the employer had failed to give the agreed-upon increase when proof was submitted by the employer that its financial situation could not support a $25,000 annual salary.

[1] *Atlas Refuse Collectors Inc. v. Baehr*, [1965] B.R. 195 (Que. C.A.).
[2] D.T.E. 85T-4 (Que. S.C.), confirmed on appeal, unreported, May 4, 1988, C.A.M. 500-09-001556-844.
[3] D.T.E. 83T-200 (Que. S.C.).

§7.24 Although the executive may not be entitled to a specific salary increase, the process of "red-circling" or freezing his or her salary, and ultimately impacting negatively pension benefits, may amount, in certain circumstances, to constructive dismissal.[1]

[1] *Dibbin v. Canada Trust Co.* (1988), 18 C.C.E.L. 113 (N.S.S.C.); *Taylor v. C.B.C.*, unreported, Nov. 7, 1984, No. 15243/82 (Ont. H.C.J.); *Cole v. Dresser Canada Ltd.* (1983), 4 C.C.E.L. 230 (Ont. H.C.J.); *Malone v. Ontario* (1983), 3 C.C.E.L. 61 (Ont. H.C.J.).

3. Vacation Pay and Statutory Holidays

§7.25 Vacation with pay and statutory holidays are regulated by provincial statutes which create liabilities for the employer that do not exist at common law. In Ontario, the *Employment Standards Act* stipulates that every employer shall give to each employee, including executives, a vacation with pay for at least two weeks upon the completion of each 12 months of employment, whether such employment is active or not.[1] Holiday pay constitutes "wages" under provincial employment standards statutes. In addition, section 25 of the *Employment Standards Act* requires that every employer give each employee a public holiday with pay on the 8 days set out in the definition section of the Act.

[1] See, *e.g.*, the *Employment Standards Act*, R.S.O. 1990, c. E.14, s. 28; *An Act respecting Labour Standards*, R.S.Q., c. N-1.1, ss. 66 *et seq.* [am. 1990, c. 73, ss. 22-28]. Similar legislation exists in the other provinces.

§7.26 The *Employment Standards Act*[1] also provides for the manner in which vacation pay is to be calculated and the year when it is to be granted by the employer. The Ontario Court of Appeal has held that, under the Act, vacation pay constitutes a debt due to employees for services rendered and not merely an amount claimed or flowing from termination of employment.[2] A lien for vacation pay under the Act has priority over the rights of secured creditors upon liquidation.[3]

[1] R.S.O. 1990, c. E.14.
[2] *Mills-Hughes v. Raynor* (1988), 19 C.C.E.L. 6, additional reasons at 47 D.L.R. (4th) 381 (Ont. C.A.); revg in part 10 C.C.E.L. 180 (H.C.J.). See also *Brown v. Shearer* (1995), 12 C.C.E.L. (2d) 54 (Man. C.A.), affg (1994), 96 Man. R. (2d) 34 (Q.B.).
[3] *National Bank of Canada v. McArthur* (1986), 11 C.C.E.L. 179 (Ont. Div. Ct.), leave to appeal to C.A. refused 6 P.P.S.A.C. xxx.

§7.27 In Quebec, no legislation stipulates the minimum annual vacation entitlement for an executive. Indeed, the relevant provisions of the labour standards legislation exclude senior managerial personnel from its application. Furthermore, there is no legal requirement with respect to what indemnity must be paid to an executive during his or her vacation. In fact, there is no legal obligation to continue the executive's remuneration or to pay a percentage of the previous year's earnings. It is unlikely that any employer would consider preventing an executive from going on vacation, but since there is no minimum entitlement prescribed by law, the employer's policies and practice should be discussed at the outset of the relationship. Because of the legislative void, issues such as whether any commissions,[1] bonuses,[2] or other earnings are to be factored into the executive's vacation pay should be discussed before they result in misunderstandings or litigation.

[1]   *Grossman v. Rosemount Knitting Inc.*, J.E. 81-123 (Que. S.C.) (appeal abandoned April 13, 1981, C.A.Q. 200-09-000065-81).
[2]   *Lemieux v. Lois Canada Inc.*, D.T.E. 88T-647 (Que. Prov. Ct.).

§7.28   With respect to statutory holidays, it would appear that Quebec's *National Holiday Act*[1] sets out the only guaranteed holidays for the executive working in Quebec. On the other hand, employees other than senior managerial personnel are guaranteed a minimum of eight legal holidays (including the National Holiday).[2]

[1]   R.S.Q., c. F.1.1.
[2]   *An Act respecting Labour Standards*, R.S.Q., c. N-1.1, s. 60, and *National Holiday Act*, R.S.Q., c. F.1.1..

4. Advances

§7.29   Many employers provide advances to employees paid partly or wholly on a commission basis. An issue that often arises before the courts is whether or not the employee is obliged to repay such advances. Essentially, the question that is asked is whether advances are to be considered against commissions earned or whether they are in fact a base salary. To establish whether an advance is salary, one must look to the implied terms of the agreement and the surrounding circumstances.[1] Obviously, if the parties have expressly agreed that such advances are loans, as opposed to a guaranteed salary, or are to be deducted from earnings, they must be reimbursed. If they constitute a base salary, they need not be reimbursed.[2] In *Royal Guardians v. Neilson*,[3] the Quebec Superior Court held that, in general, advances on commissions are loans subject to reimbursement.

[1]   *Wuraftic v. Triad Creations Ltd.*, [1971] C.A. 83 (Que.).
[2]   *Menuiserie de Scott Inc. v. Boissinot*, J.E. 82-503 (Que. Prov. Ct.).
[3]   [1959] C.S. 316 (Que. S.C.). See also *Bourque v. Compuset Business Forms & Systems Analysis Inc.*, unreported, Aug. 22, 1990, 500-02-045671-851 (Ct. of Que.).

§7.30   Another issue is whether the executive must reimburse the portion of the advances which exceeds the commissions earned. For example, earnings may fall short of advances at the time of termination of employment. In other cases, an executive may simply fail to earn enough commissions to cover the advances received in any particular year. Some courts have held that, in the absence of an express or implied agreement to the contrary, contracts of employment providing for payments from time to time of sums of money as advances against commissions to be earned impose no liability to repay if the commissions fall short of the amount of the advance. In *Labrosse v. Creadis Inc.*,[1] the Quebec Court of Appeal held that, in the absence of an express clause stating that advances were to be reimbursed, these advances became non-reimbursable salary, particularly where all legal deductions had been made.[2] Consequently, unless otherwise agreed, the contract will be interpreted to provide that the reimbursement to the employer will be deducted from the commissions earned, if any.

[1] D.T.E. 91T-138 (Que. C.A.).
[2] The same ruling is found in *Olympic Industries Inc. v. McNeil* (1993), 86 B.C.L.R. (2d) 273 (C.A.) and *Barnard v. T.M. Energy House Ltd.*, [1982] 4 W.W.R. 619 (B.C. Co. Ct.).

§7.31 Other decisions have required that the executive reimburse any advance in excess of commissions earned, unless agreed otherwise. These courts have decided that the word "advance" implies a notion of refund.[1] In *Newton v. W. Rodgerson's Insulators Ltd.*,[2] the employer successfully counterclaimed for advances against sales commissions that the employee had overdrawn during two years of employment.

[1] See *Bourque v. Compuset Business Forms & Systems Analysis Inc.*, unreported, Aug. 22, 1990, 500-02-045671-851 (Ct. of Que.); *André Lacroix Publicité Inc. v. Tremblay*, unreported, June 11, 1990, 200-02-007090-873 (Ct. of Que.); *Cusin & associés v. Lessard*, unreported, Jan. 6, 1990, 650-02-000002-897 (Ct. of Que.); *145074 Canada Ltée v. Rivard*, D.T.E. 87T-644 (Que. Prov. Ct.); *Machines Automatiques Laniel Co. (Ste-Adèle) Inc. v. Beausoleil*, [1985] C.P. 189 (Que. Prov. Ct.); *Nordmende (Québec) Ltd. v. Kiwitt*, [1966] C.S. 465 (Que. S.C.); *Graff Brushes Ltd. v. Marvin*, [1962] C.S. 72 (Que. S.C.); *Mérette v. Presto Oil Co.*, [1957] B.R. 262 (Que. C.A.).
[2] (1983), 59 N.S.R. (2d) 409 (S.C.). See also *Bell Rinfret & cie v. Bernard*, D.T.E. 88T-297 (Que. C.A.).

§7.32 A third school of thought is that the question of whether the employee must return any advances in excess of earned commissions is one of fact, and each case is different.[1] In these instances, an advance is recoverable if there is an express or implied term to repay the advance to the employer. This implication may arise if the parties discuss repayment without dispute by the employee.[2]

[1] *Systèmes de communication Incotel Ltée v. Marcotte*, D.T.E. 88T-355 (Que. Prov. Ct.); *Gilbert v. Taylor* (1940), 78 C.S. 18 (Que. S.C.).

² See *Bayside Sales Ltd. v. Maitland*, [1977] 4 W.W.R. 443 (Man. C.A.).

5. Commissions

§7.33 In the sales business, executives are frequently paid commissions based on the earnings of the sales staff reporting to them. When and under what conditions commissions become payable is of significant importance and should be clearly specified. For example, if a contract states that the executive is entitled to a commission on "net sales" defined as "products sold and actually delivered", no commission is owing for his or her having merely obtained orders and having had them confirmed by the employer.[1]

¹ *West Coast Woolen Mills Ltd. v. Engel*, [1971] C.A. 20 (Que.). An opposite conclusion was reached in *Don Giustino Inc. v. Collection L.S.M. Inc.*, J.E. 82-666 (Que. S.C.), where the court determined that the employer's evidence was insufficient to prove that there had been an agreement that the employee should receive commissions only on that which had been actually invoiced.

§7.34 A reduction in commissions may constitute wrongful dismissal.[1] Similarly, if the employer imposes a ceiling on the employee's commission earnings, the employer may have made a unilateral variation of the contract, giving the employee a cause of action for the balance of the commission.[2] Moreover, where the employer is consistently late in the payment of commissions, this may amount to breach of contract.[3]

¹ *Dunse v. Quadra Wood Products Ltd.* (1983), 18 A.C.W.S. (2d) 208 (B.C.S.C.).
² *Luchuk v. Sport B.C.* (1984), 3 C.C.E.L. 117 (B.C.S.C.).
³ *Heuman v. Spartan Agencies Ltd.* (1987), 5 A.C.W.S. (3d) 24 (B.C.S.C.).

§7.35 An employer must not cause the executive's commissions to be reduced through no fault of the executive. Hence, in *Bégin v. Versabec Inc.*,[1] the Quebec Superior Court ordered that an employee be compensated for loss of sales and, consequently, for the reduction in commissions which he suffered because his employer had transferred client accounts to a related company.

¹ Unreported, July 4, 1990, C.S.M. 500-05-010341-889 (Que. S.C.).

§7.36 As a rule, the employer may not unilaterally change the territory over which the executive is entitled to receive commissions if such a change would have the effect of decreasing the executive's earning potential. Reducing the potential for sales and commissions has been held to be a fundamental breach of contract.[1]

[1] *Vassallo v. Crosbie Enterprises Ltd.* (1981), 9 A.C.W.S. (2d) 335 (Nfld. S.C.). The same may be said of the employer's decision to reassign its employees with the intent of reducing or defeating their right to a commission. See *Prozak v. Bell Telephone Co. of Canada* (1984), 46 O.R. (2d) 385 (C.A.), revg in part 37 O.R. (2d) 761 (H.C.J.).

§7.37 It may be prudent for the parties to discuss in advance the executive's right to commissions after his or her dismissal, and the terms of their payment. This is particularly true in cases where a number of commissions are earned as a result of a client's repeat orders for the product sold, or when commissions are paid after the product has been delivered or paid for by the customer. In a case where the employment contract stipulated that the payment of commissions on sales completed after the termination of the employee's employment was at the sole discretion of the employer, the court held that the employer had to act reasonably, honestly, and in good faith in exercising its discretion.[1]

[1] *Greenberg v. Meffert* (1985), 18 D.L.R. (4th) 548 (Ont. C.A.), leave to appeal to S.C.C. refused 30 D.L.R. (4th) 768n.

§7.38 Although the courts have recognized that the payment of remuneration on a commission basis is a valid method for satisfying the employer's obligation to provide remuneration, it may not be unilaterally imposed by the employer on an already existing employment relationship where the executive is entitled to a fixed salary. Where remuneration was changed from a salary-plus-commission basis to a commission-only basis, such modification constituted constructive dismissal.[1] The same result occurred where remuneration was changed from straight salary to salary plus commission.[2] This is the case even where the employer's proposition is for *bona fide* reorganization purposes.[3]

[1] *Blewett v. White Oaks Realty Ltd.* (1994), 4 C.C.E.L. (2d) 160 (Ont. Ct. (Gen. Div.)); *Sherrard v. Moncton Chrysler Dodge (1980) Ltd.* (1990), 29 C.C.E.L. 158 (N.B.Q.B.), vard 33 C.C.E.L. 72 (C.A.). See also *Cook v. Royal Trust* (1990), 31 C.C.E.L. 6 (B.C.S.C.); *Jeffrey v. Plant Forest Products Corp.* (1990), 32 C.C.E.L. 237 (Sask. Q.B.), and *McPhee v. Torino Motors (1975) Ltd.* (1989), 28 C.C.E.L. 68 (B.C. Co. Ct.). For a contrary view, see *George v. Morden & Helwig Ltd.* (1988), 20 C.C.E.L. 29 (Ont. H.C.J.), where the court concluded that since the employer's modification of the employee's remuneration from a salary-plus-bonus basis to a commission-only basis would have made the employee better off financially, the employee acted prematurely in considering himself constructively dismissed.
[2] *Rebitt v. Pacific Motor Sales & Service Ltd.* (1988), 20 C.C.E.L. 239 (B.C.C.A.).
[3] *Hart v. Bogardus Wilson (1984) Ltd.* (1987), 13 B.C.L.R. (2d) 269 (C.A.).

6. Bonuses

§7.39 A bonus, whether a flat amount or a percentage of sales or profits, may or may not be considered an integral part of an executive's renumeration. Generally, if it is an integral part of the wage structure, it will constitute a legal term of the contract of employment;[1] otherwise, it will not.

---

[1] *Poon, Wong & Associates Inc. v. Wong,* [1991] B.C.W.L.D. 1186 (S.C.); *Sandelson v. International Vintners Ltd.* (1987), 18 B.C.L.R. (2d) 86 (S.C.); *Clifton v. Ground Engineering Ltd.* (1982), 19 Sask. R. 181 (Q.B.).

§7.40 When the bonus is not a discretionary decision, such as when it is calculated according to an established formula or practice, or when it is given with great regularity, it will most likely be considered as salary.[1] In these instances, *de facto* payments of bonuses establish a contractual basis to claim the bonus as a right.

---

[1] *Reynolds v. First City Trust Co.* (1989), 27 C.C.E.L. 194 (B.C.S.C.); *Sandelson v. International Vintners Ltd.* (1987), 18 B.C.L.R. (2d) 86 (S.C.); *Comité Paritaire du Camionnage du District de Québec v. Cartier Ready Mix Inc.,* [1966] C.S. 430 (Que. S.C.). Such a bonus will therefore be considered by the court when assessing damages: *Ryshpan v. Burns Fry Ltd.* (1995), 10 C.C.E.L. (2d) 235 (Ont. Ct. (Gen. Div.)), appeal dismissed (1996), 20 C.C.E.L. (2d) 104 (Ont. C.A.); *Roscoe v. McGavin Foods Ltd.* (1983), 2 C.C.E.L. 287 (B.C.S.C.); *Gillespie v. Ontario Motor League Toronto Club* (1980), 4 A.C.W.S. (2d) 87 (Ont. H.C.J.).

§7.41 Frequently, bonus payments comprise the greater part of an executive's renumeration. If the amount of the bonus is undetermined, the court will seek to uphold the promise of a bonus and pay what is considered equitable. In *King v. Harris,*[1] the managing directors of the company received a salary in the amount of $10,920 per year and a "substantial bonus", though there was no formula to determine the amount of the bonus. In a claim for arrears of the bonus, the court found that the executives would not have worked as managing directors for the salary alone. Since the contract did not provide a formula for calculating the bonus, the court awarded arrears in bonuses on a *quantum meruit* basis.[2]

---

[1] (1980), 30 Nfld. & P.E.I.R. 118 (Nfld. S.C.).
[2] The same result occurred for a "mutually agreeable bonus" in *Johnson v. Foundation Co. of Canada* (1980), 29 N.B.R. (2d) 314 (Q.B.).

§7.42 If there is a bonus or profit-sharing plan which vests on a deferred basis, the employer has the obligation to inform the employee of the time when vesting occurs.[1]

¹ *Fletcher v. Cliffcrest Enterprises Ltd.* (1985), 9 C.C.E.L. 45 (Alta. Q.B.).

§7.43 In *Terrasses Holdings D.W.S./ Holdings v. Saunders,*[1] although the bonus was held not to be an integral part of the remuneration structure since no ascertainable amount had been stipulated by the parties, the fact that it had been promised created a quasi-contract which was binding on the employer. Consequently, the employer could be held liable in a claim for unjust enrichment if he failed to pay it.

¹ D.T.E. 89T-415 (Que. C.A.).

§7.44 In *CJMS Radio Montréal Ltée v. Audette,*[1] a clause entitled the employee to a bonus to be calculated and paid at the end of the employer's fiscal year. The clause also provided for a *pro rata* bonus in the case of discharge for cause. The employer claimed that since employment had been terminated by mutual agreement before the end of the fiscal year and the contract did not contemplate this situation, the employee was not entitled to any bonus. However, the court held that a bonus due even following a dismissal for cause was not discretionary or a gratuity and was, instead, an integral part of the employee's remuneration. The employee was thus entitled to receive a bonus, on a *pro rata* basis, to be paid at the end of the employer's fiscal year in the event his termination was without cause or by mutual consent before the end of any fiscal year.

¹ [1966] B.R. 756 (Que. C.A.).

§7.45 At common law, the court came to a similar conclusion in *Daniels v. Canadian Tire Corp.*[1] where the court concluded that the employer could not impose as a condition of awarding the bonus that the employee still work for him at the end of the fiscal year unless such a condition had been made known to be a condition of the original employment contract.

¹ (1991), 39 C.C.E.L. 107 (Ont. Ct. (Gen. Div.)). See also *Grace v. Reader's Digest Assn. (Canada) Ltd.* (1995), 14 C.C.E.L. (2d) 109 (Ont. Ct. (Gen. Div.)).

§7.46 However, in *Nugent v. Midland Doherty Ltd.,*[1] the employee had a remuneration package that consisted of salary plus a discretionary bonus reflecting national profits and personal performance calculated and paid at the end of the employer's fiscal year. The employee resigned before the end of the fiscal year and, as a result, the court found that he was not entitled to the percentage bonus. This finding was based on the rule of law relating to partial performance of contracts which states that, under an employment contract in which remuneration is not to be paid until the end of a term, the employee is bound to complete the term before he or she becomes entitled to anything.

[1] (1989), 31 C.C.E.L. 235 (B.C.C.A.). See also *Pimlott v. Marbridge Investments Ltd.* (1967), 61 D.L.R. (2d) 309 (B.C.C.A.); *Lyons v. Speton* (1993), 89 B.C.L.R. (2d) 268 (C.A.).

§7.47 If the method or formula for calculating the bonus is changed during the course of the employment contract thereby reducing the employee's remuneration, such modification may amount to wrongful breach of contract. In *Cardwell v. Young Manufacturer Inc.,*[1] the court held that, whether or not the parties were consensual as to the calculation of the bonus, the terms as expressed by the employer and as understood by the employee when he was hired were clear, and that the later change in bonus structure amounted to constructive dismissal.

[1] (1988), 20 C.C.E.L. 272 (Ont. Dist. Ct.). See also *Fyfe v. Olshansky,* unreported, Dec. 18, 1990, 700-02-001107-896 (Ct. of Que.).

§7.48 An employer is obligated to advise an employee of disentitlement to benefits if the employee leaves before the year end. Failure to do so may estop the employer from denying the executive's claim to the funds.[1] Some contracts specifically provide for the bonus to be paid only if the executive is still employed at the date on which the bonus becomes payable or on the last day of the employer's fiscal or calendar year. These agreements have been enforced, and are not contrary to law or public order.[2]

[1] *Malinowski v. Nault Sawmill & Lumber Co.* (1985), 41 Alta. L.R. (2d) 334 (Q.B.); *Daniels v. Canadian Tire Corp.* (1991), 39 C.C.E.L. 107 (Ont. Ct. (Gen. Div.)); *Grace v. Reader's Digest Assn. (Canada) Ltd.* (1995), 14 C.C.E.L. (2d) 109 (Ont. Ct. (Gen. Div.)).
[2] *Mahoney v. Alliance, Cie mutuelle d'assurance-vie,* D.T.E. 91T-431 (Que. S.C.); *Tremblay v. Entreprises minières Redpath Ltée,* D.T.E. 89T-305 (Ct. of Que.); *Brower v. Baskill Electrical Services Ltd.* (1985), 6 C.C.E.L. 36 (Alta. Q.B.).

§7.49 Failure to pay the full amount of a bonus will not always amount to repudiation of the contract. Failure to pay the full amount of a bonus was held not to be a fundamental breach in one case since the bonus was a relatively minor part of the consideration which was to be paid for services to be rendered over a prolonged period of time.[1]

[1] *Poole v. Tomenson Saunders Whitehead Ltd.* (1987), 18 C.C.E.L. 238 (B.C.C.A.). See also *Hamilton & Olsen Surveys Ltd. v. Otto* (1993), 12 Alta. L.R. (3d) 431 (C.A.), leave to appeal to S.C.C. refused (1994), 15 Alta. L.R. (3d) lii and *Pathak v. Jannock Steel Fabricating Co.* (1996), 21 C.C.E.L. (2d) 12 (Alta. Q.B.).

7. Profit Sharing

§7.50 Many employers today have profit-sharing plans for their executives. Such plans vary significantly in form, in substance, and with respect to the formula used to determine entitlement. As a method of providing remuneration, profit-sharing plans, like bonuses and commissions, attempt to stimulate the executive to achieve peak performance.[1] Moreover, they have an additional advantage in that they encourage employee interest in the company's overall objectives (development, cost-cutting measures, etc.).

---

[1] *Nolan v. Rémi Carrier Inc.*, J.E. 83-829 (Que. S.C.), affd D.T.E. 86T-370 (C.A.); *Carey v. F. Drexel Co.*, [1974] 4 W.W.R. 492 (B.C.S.C.).

§7.51 Again, the method of calculating the executive's share in the profits may not be significantly altered or removed if it reduces the employee's entitlement without the employee's consent. Otherwise, the executive may have a basis to allege wrongful dismissal.[1] As for assessing the employee's entitlement to a share of the profits, the same rules apply as those for verifying entitlement to bonuses.[2] If it is expressly understood that the executive must be employed at the fiscal year end in order to benefit from a profit-sharing plan, no prorated profits will be owed to the executive who resigns from his or her employment before that date.[3]

---

[1] *Pullen v. John C. Preston Ltd.* (1985), 7 C.C.E.L. 91 (Ont. H.C.J.).
[2] Compensation was refused where the plan was discretionary in *Jolicoeur v. Lithographie Montréal Ltée*, [1982] C.S. 230 (Que. S.C.); affd, unreported, April 15, 1987, C.A.M. 500-09-000314-823. See also *Longchamps v. Denis Pépin Automobiles Ltée*, J.E. 83-495 (Que. S.C.), affd D.T.E. 88T-852 (C.A.).
[3] *Daniels v. Canadian Tire Corp.* (1991), 39 C.C.E.L. 107 (Ont. Ct. (Gen. Div.)).

8. Stock Purchase and Option Plans

§7.52 Some employers provide their employees with the right to purchase company stock. Others provide "phantom stock plans" which are similar to stock plans except that they do not give a proprietary interest in the corporation. The phantom stock plan is a monetary incentive plan in which the monetary award is determined in accordance with a formula based on actual stock prices and dividends.

§7.53 Generally, a stock purchase or option plan forms an integral part of the wage structure. Depending on the wording of the plan and whether it includes wording giving discretion to the employer to amend or discontinue the plan, the employer may or may not unilaterally make significant changes which would affect a beneficiary of the plan. If a stock option scheme is offered during employment, this constitutes an inducement to executives to continue in their employment. By continuing their employment, they accept what constitutes a unilateral contract making the stock option enforceable.[1]

> [1] *Maier v. E & B Exploration Ltd.,* [1986] 4 W.W.R. 275 (Alta. C.A.).

§7.54 In the executive employment contract, stock options often represent a substantial part of the employee's remuneration or potential remuneration. An employer may not prevent an executive from participating in a plan that is open to a group of employees of which the executive is a part. If an executive is to receive no remuneration except for stock options, he or she may not claim payment for his or her time and effort in the event the options prove worthless.[1]

> [1] *Leahy v. Marlborough Productions Ltd.,* [1991] B.C.W.L.D. 895 (S.C.).

9. Retirement Benefits, Deferred Compensation, Life and Health Insurance Benefits

§7.55 The benefits that an employee enjoys as a condition of employment, whether a pension plan, medical insurance plan, or accident and disability insurance plan, are generally considered an obligation the employer must continue to fulfil during the life of the agreement.[1] These benefits may not be unilaterally decreased by the employer any more than other components of remuneration.[2] In many cases, entitlement to benefits will depend on the interpretation of a written employment contract, company policy or other document[3] and, in some cases, applicable legislation.[4]

> [1] See *Bergeron v. Mines d'amiante Bell Ltée,* D.T.E. 88T-870 (Que. Prov. Ct.); *Kenzie v. Standard Motors (77) Ltd.* (1985), 8 C.C.E.L. 173 (Sask. Q.B.).
> [2] *Ronalds Federated Ltd. v. Zgodzinski,* D.T.E. 88T-371 (Que. C.A.); *Bergeron v. Mines d'amiante Bell Ltée,* D.T.E. 88T-890 (Que. Prov. Ct.); *Reincke v. Ernst & Whinney Inc.* (1992), 16 Alta. L.A. (3d) 213 (Q.B.), affd/judicial review refused (1993), 14 Alta. L.R. (3d) 64 (C.A.).
> [3] *Pendleton v. Deschênes & fils (1969) Ltée,* D.T.E. 88T-591 (Que. S.C.); *Bradley v. Saskatchewan Wheat Pool* (1984), 3 C.C.E.L. 304 (Sask. Q.B.).
> [4] *Castagna v. Design Hydraulics Inc.,* D.T.E. 88T-1006 (Que. S.C.).

§7.56 Commonly, pension benefits are paid for by wage deductions, and are treated in the employment contract as part of remuneration of employment.[1] Pensions are usually payable as an annuity upon retirement and, in some cases, early retirement. Deferred compensation generally refers to that part of the executive's salary which is earned during employment but deferred until a later period (retirement or termination of employment) when it becomes payable in instalments over a fixed period or in a lump sum.

[1] *Dickinson v. Northern Telecom Canada Ltd.* (1985), 7 C.C.E.L. 139 (Ont. Co. Ct.).

§7.57 In a fragile economy, pension plans merit increased consideration because they not only provide a means for ensuring future earnings for the employee, but also serve as an instrument upon which the employer may eventually rely when attempting to reduce its workforce through early retirement.

§7.58 Claims by employees for pension benefits after termination from employment have met with success in the courts. In *Mosier v. Linden-Alimak Inc.,*[1] an employee was dismissed without cause after 20 years of service to the company. The employee claimed for loss of future benefits under the pension plan. The court allowed the claim, finding that an implied term of the employee's pension plan was that employees terminated without cause prior to retirement age are entitled to a pension calculated on full past service.

[1] (1985), 8 C.C.E.L. 45 (B.C.S.C.).

§7.59 In *MacPherson v. Canadian Javelin Ltd.,*[1] the plaintiff, who had joined the defendant company as an exploration geologist in May 1957 and resigned in August 1976, proved to the court the existence of a written contract providing health and life insurance benefits which were to take effect upon the employee's retirement. No specific figures had been agreed upon. The preponderance of evidence established that the company had no defined or fixed retirement policy for any of its officers or employees during the relevant period of time, *i.e.,* between 1957 and 1976. Each case of retirement had been dealt with on an individual basis on conditions usually determined *ad hoc* by management with some regard, however, to conditions set in prior retirement cases. In the circumstances, the court determined the extent of the geologist's claim on a somewhat equal basis to that previously used by the company for the retirement of other senior employees. The employee was thus entitled to receive retirement benefits in the amount of $2,000 per month for the first year and $1,000 per month thereafter for a period of 204 months (*i.e.,* a total of 216 months which corresponded to 18 years' service) as well as life and health insurance benefits for an equivalent period.

[1] [1982] C.S. 563 (Que.).

§7.60 The Ontario High Court has held that an employer who provides long-term disability benefits to its employees has a duty of care to advise them of their right to make a claim. In *Tarailo v. Allied Chemical Canada Ltd.*,[1] the employer was liable for the benefits which a former employee would have received under the company long-term disability policy because it failed to advise the employee of his right to make a claim. The court found that the employee may well have been so mentally ill that he did not appreciate that he had a claim. Conversely, the employer had information that should have alerted it to the fact that its employee might have a claim for disability benefits.

[1]   (1989), 26 C.C.E.L. 209 (Ont. H.C.J.), appeal settled on consent of the parties 7 O.R. (3d) 318 (C.A.).

§7.60.1   The fact that an employee's unused sick days accumulate from year to year, and may be used in a subsequent year does not imply that they are convertible into cash upon termination of employment.[1]

[1]   *Société canadienne d'hypothèques et de logement v. Hudon*, D.T.E. 94T-1398 (Que. C.A.).

10.   Expatriate Allowance

§7.61   Of specific interest to certain executives is the consideration of expatriate allowances as an integral part of the remuneration. It is increasingly customary for companies to expatriate their key employees to other locations in the hope that these employees will be able to apply their particular skills or learn new ones at these places. The expatriation allowance aims to compensate the executive for the inconvenience or increase in the cost of living which may be suffered from working abroad. It may also serve as an incentive to encourage employees who are hesitant to work abroad, particularly when the acceptance of a transfer is not a term of the executive's employment agreement. In *Allison v. Amoco Production Co.*,[1] the court stated:

> The payment of the basic salary plus expatriate allowance or compensation plus other employee benefits were, taken together, by common law a term of the employment contract between the defendant and the loanee. Although in labour negotiations wages, fringe benefits and special allowances may be dealt with separately, the aggregate amounts settled upon are all considered as terms of the contract of employment and taken together constitute the remuneration paid or payable to the employee for his services.

[1]   [1975] 5 W.W.R. 501 (Alta. S.C.), at 505-6.

11. Private Club Membership Fees

§7.62 If club dues were paid by the employer purely for the executive's personal use, they may constitute part of the executive's remuneration.[1] However, if club dues are intended to assist the employee in promoting the employer's business, they do not form part of remuneration; clearly, they were designed not as a "perk", but rather as a tool to carry on business.[2]

[1] *Carey v. F. Drexel Co.*, [1974] 4 W.W.R. 492 (B.C.S.C.).
[2] *Douglas v. Sandwell & Co.* (1977), 81 D.L.R. (3d) 508 (B.C.S.C.).

§7.63 The issue is not as clear when club fees are intended for the benefit of both the employer and the executive. In these cases, it is hard to establish what part of the benefit constitutes remuneration. The issue is relevant in cases of unilateral modification by the employer which affects this benefit, and in cases of damages for wrongful termination.

12. Expense Accounts

§7.64 Little has been written regarding expense accounts as a form of remuneration. Where expense accounts are provided solely for company business-related events or expenses, they do not constitute part of an executive's remuneration.[1] However, if the executive is provided with a fixed-rate expense account, whether or not this payment constitutes remuneration is not as clear, particularly in cases where the executive is not required to provide receipts. One may consider whether the amount of the expense account exceeds the executive's business-related disbursements and, consequently, whether the excess payment serves to increase the remuneration. In such cases, it may be argued that such excess payment does indeed constitute remuneration. Furthermore, the handling of such payments from a tax perspective may be indicative of the parties' intentions.

[1] *Villa v. John Labatt Ltée*, [1990] R.J.Q. 2247 (S.C.); revd in part on another issue *La Brasserie Labatt Limitée v. Villa*, [1995] R.J.Q. 73 (C.A.).

13. Company Cars

§7.65 Many executives are provided with cars or allowances for the use of their cars. Such benefits are part of remuneration if the vehicle is partly or wholly intended for the executive's personal use. In such cases, removing the vehicle or the allowance is tantamount to a reduction in salary and, as such, its unilateral withdrawal may constitute a fundamental breach of the contract. In *Reilly v. Hotels of Distinction (Canada) Inc., Hotel Le Grand/Grand Hotel*,[1] the director of sales was deprived of a company car. This was held to be a breach of the employer's obligation, and the loss of a fringe benefit of such significant value was held to constitute a constructive dismissal.[2]

> [1] D.T.E. 87T-645 (Que. S.C.).
> [2] See also *Schwann v. Husky Oil Operations Ltd.* (1989), 27 C.C.E.L. 103 (Sask. C.A.); *Nerada v. Hobart Canada Inc.* (1982), 1 C.C.E.L. 116 (B.C.S.C.); *Brown v. OK Builders Supplies* (1987), 14 C.C.E.L. xxxi (B.C.C.A.), affg 11 C.C.E.L. 243 (S.C.).

§7.66 Conversely, an automobile allowance which compensates only job-related expenses does not constitute remuneration.[1] However, even if the vehicle or allowance is not remuneration (*i.e.*, the vehicle or allowance is exclusively for business purposes), the unilateral removal of such a business tool may amount to constructive dismissal if it is a fundamental change to the executive's working conditions.

> [1] *Salmi v. Greyfriar Developments Ltd.* (1983), 1 C.C.E.L. 82 (Alta. Q.B.), affd on this point (1985), 7 C.C.E.L. 80 (C.A.).

14. Subsidized Housing and Loans

§7.67 An executive employment agreement may occasionally provide for subsidized or actual housing or assistance with the mortgage. In *Hawkins v. Ontario*,[1] the employer agreed to pay the employee's accommodation costs for a reasonable time after relocation. When the employee was subsequently dismissed, the court awarded the accommodation expenses in the claim for wrongful dismissal since it was an integral part of the remuneration. In *Bower v. J.M. Schneider Inc.*,[2] the employee was offered a mortgage subsidy for a nine-year term as part of the employment contract. Upon termination, the court limited a claim for continuation of the mortgage subsidy to the end of the reasonable notice period and not to the end of the subsidy program.

> [1] (1985), 8 C.C.E.L. 183 (Ont. H.C.J.).
> [2] (1986), 16 C.C.E.L. 129 (B.C.C.A.).

§7.68 If company-paid housing is provided in part to support business-related events, the actual portion of the benefit to the executive, which should be computed as forming part of the remuneration, may be difficult to determine.

§7.69 Interest-free or low-interest loans granted to the executive by the employer, including loans for the purchase of a house or company stock, is another benefit which may form part of the executive's remuneration. The British Columbia Court of Appeal has said that it is an implied term that a preferred loan rate granted to an employee will end upon the termination of the employment contract.[1] Again, the parties must clearly stipulate the purpose of the monetary payment and the terms of repayment. This will avoid situations such as in the case of *Poon, Wong & Associates Inc. v. Wong*,[2] where the employer alleged that a monthly payment was a loan while the employee contended it was an advance on bonus. The court ruled in favour of the employer.

[1] *Bank of Nova Scotia v. Horgan* (1985), 9 C.C.E.L. 288 (B.C.C.A.).
[2] [1991] B.C.W.L.D. 1186 (S.C.).

CHAPTER 8
SAFETY OF EXECUTIVES

A. CONTENT OF OBLIGATION

§8.1 The rights and obligations of employers and employees regarding safety are now extensively regulated by statute. Each of the provinces and the federal government have enacted occupational health and safety legislation applicable to employees within their respective jurisdictions. In addition, each of the provinces has a comprehensive workers' compensation system funded by employers which provides benefits to injured workers on a no-fault basis. However, even prior to the advent of such legislation, the employer's obligation to ensure safety was impliedly included in the employment contract.

§8.2 The extent of this obligation means that employers must ensure their employees' safety, regardless whether this is expressly stipulated in a written employment contract.[1] This obligation implies that the employer has to take every reasonable step to foresee potential dangers or hazards which the employee may face because of his or her particular position and take all necessary measures to avoid such dangers or hazards.[2] To do so, the employer must furnish the employee with a safe workplace,[3] including proper equipment and tools,[4] and ensure that the workforce is competent and properly instructed.[5]

---

[1] *Richard v. Gauthier and Breton*, [1964] C.S. 307 (Que. S.C.); *Guillemette v. Lafontaine*, [1962] C.S. 660 (Que. S.C.); *Whitton v. Jesseau*, [1962] C.S. 309 (Que. S.C.); *Canadian Shade Tree Service v. Diabo*, [1961] B.R. 501 (Que. C.A.); *Laramée v. Boucher*, [1944] R.L. 300 (Que. C.A.); *Boiteau v. Bernard* (1941), 70 B.R. 237 (Que. C.A.); *Marois v. Syndicat Coopératif Immobilier* (1939), 77 C.S. 279 (Que. S.C.).

[2] *Marois v. Syndicat Coopératif Immobilier*, (1939), 77 C.S. 279 (Que. S.C.); *Boiteau v. Bernard*, (1941), 70 B.R. 237 (Que. C.A.); *Robitaille v. Vancouver Hockey Club Ltd.* (1979), 19 B.C.L.R. 158 (S.C.), vard 30 B.C.L.R. 286 (C.A.).

[3] *Landry v. Charles Duranceau Ltée*, [1962] C.S. 583 (Que. S.C.); *Conseil des ports nationaux v. Commission des accidents du travail*, [1989] R.J.Q. 792 (C.A.); *Caron v. Delisle* (1940), 47 R.L. 143 (Que. S.C.).

[4] *Whitton v. Jesseau*, [1962] C.S. 309 (Que. S.C.); *Marois v. Syndicat Coopératif Immobilier*, (1939), 77 C.S. 279 (Que. S.C.).

[5] *Canadian Shade Tree Service v. Diabo*, [1961] B.R. 501 (Que. C.A.); *St-Arnaud v. Palmer Bros. Ltd.*, [1961] R.L. 379 (Que. S.C.); *Laramée v. Boucher*, [1944] R.L. 300 (Que. C.A.); *Côté v. Sidbec-Dosco Ltée*, J.E. 84-390 (Que. S.C.).

---

§8.3 While the common law duty to ensure safety arises most often in the context of production or line employees, an executive is also entitled to the benefit of the employer's obligation to provide safety. Because of the executive's different responsibilities and duties, however, the employer's obligation to ensure safety may take a somewhat different twist from furnishing safe tools and equipment. For example, the employer who wishes to send an executive to a country with an unstable political climate, or where there is danger of contracting a disease, may have to provide for the safe entry and evacuation of the plant by the executive in the event of a strike by employees or political uprising. His safety or his family's safety may also be at risk because of public representations the executive must make for the benefit of the employer or simply because the executive heads a company which is the subject of controversy. For example, it is not uncommon for groups of individuals to institute demonstrations against a business that has operations in or maintains business relations with countries having deplorable humanitary conditions. In some cases, the executives of these businesses become the target of the population's discontent. In some cases, their security or their family's security is at risk from unscrupulous demonstrators. The employer's obligation of safety may include, among other measures, the provision to the executive and his family of the services of a bodyguard. The employer must ensure that this person is well-trained and competent to deal with emergency situations.

§8.4 With the advent of no-fault benefits under workers' compensation legislation, the implied duty of care has assumed a lesser importance. However, it should be noted that, depending upon the language of the workers' compensation legislation involved, it may retain its importance since executives may in some cases not be included within the ambit of statutory coverage. For example, in Ontario, compensation benefits are available to any worker, but the definition of "worker" specifically excludes an executive officer of a corporation.[1] An officer may elect to be deemed to be a worker for the purposes of the Act and included within the scheme of benefits, but this requires action on the part of the executive or the corporation and does not occur automatically by operation of the Act.[2] The same is true in Quebec.

---

[1] *Workers' Compensation Act*, R.S.O. 1990, c. W.11, s. 1(1). Note that Bill 99, which received royal assent on October 10, 1997, will repeal the *Workers' Compensation Act* and replace it with the *Workplace Safety and Insurance Act, 1997*, in force January 1, 1998. Subsection 1(1) of the present Act expressly excludes "an executive officer of a corporation" from the definition of "worker". Section 11(2) of the new Act provides that "[s]ubject to section 12, the insurance plan does not apply to workers who are executive officers of a corporation". Section 12(2) of the new Act provides that "the [Workplace Safety and Insurance] Board may declare that an executive officer of the corporation is deemed to be a worker to whom the insurance

plan applies. The Board may make the declaration only if the executive officer consents to the application."

2 *Workers' Compensation Act*, R.S.O. 1990, c. W.11, s. 13(1).

B. LEGAL BASIS OF OBLIGATION

§8.5 Prior to the advent of statutory regulation, the common law imposed a duty on employers to provide employees with safe tools and equipment, a safe system of work, and fellow employees who would not foreseeably endanger them, *i.e.*, properly trained individuals.[1] This common law obligation was said to have arisen either in tort or as an implied term of the contract of employment. The latter seems to be the preferred view.[2]

1 *Wilsons & Clyde Coal Co. v. English*, [1938] A.C. 57 (H.L.).
2 *Marshment v. Borgstrom*, [1942] S.C.R. 374; *Matthews v. Kuwait Bechtel Corp.*, [1959] 2 Q.B. 57 (C.A.).

§8.6 Until recently, the legal basis of the obligation to ensure safety remained controversial in Quebec. Some jurists were of the view that the failure to ensure adequate safety was a breach of an implied contractual obligation while others considered that such an act was a delictual fault (similar to a tort).[1] Article 2087 of the Civil Code of Quebec puts this issue to rest. This section provides that the employer has the obligation to take all necessary measures to ensure the health, safety and dignity of its employees. Hence, the obligation to provide safety will be an implied term of every contract of employment, with the consequences that the executive who alleges that the employer breached the obligation to provide a safe work place may sue for damages for breach of contract.

1 *Valois v. Caisse Populaire Notre-Dame-de-la-Merci*, [1991] R.J.Q. 1057 (Que. S.C.) (contractual liability) and Agropur, *Coopérative Agro-Alimentaire v. Lamothe*, [1989] R.J.Q. 1764 (Que. C.A.) (delictual liability).

C. VICARIOUS LIABILITY

§8.7 The common law has long recognized the concept of vicarious liability, whereby an employer is jointly and severally responsible for any tortious actions or inactions of its employees acting within the scope of their duties and responsibilities. A classic statement of vicarious liability, adopted by a number of courts in Canada, is set out in Salmond on the *Law of Torts* as follows:

> ... it is clear that the master is responsible for acts actually authorised by him: for

liability would exist, in this case, even if the relation between the parties was merely one of agency, and not one of service at all. But a master, as opposed to the employer of an independent contractor, is liable even for acts which he has not authorised, provided they are so connected with acts which he has authorised that they may rightly be regarded as modes — although improper modes — of doing them. In other words, a master is responsible not merely for what he authorises a servant to do, but also for the way in which he does it. If a servant does negligently that which he was authorised to do carefully, or if he does fraudulently that which he was authorised to do honestly, or if he does mistakenly that which he was authorised to do correctly, his master will answer for that negligence, fraud or mistake. On the other hand, if the unauthorised and wrongful act of the servant is not so connected with the authorised act as to be a mode of doing it, but is an independent act, the master is not responsible: for in such a case the servant is not acting in the course of his employment but has gone outside of it.[1]

[1] *Salmond & Heuston on the Law of Torts*, 19th ed. by R.F.V. Heuston and R.A. Buckley (London: Sweet & Maxwell, 1987), p. 521.

§8.8 The common law in Canada does not yet recognize the concept of vicarious immunity, although it has been applied by some American courts. Under such a concept, an employee who is negligent in the performance of his or her duties is entitled to the protection of any immunity in favour of the employer contained in a contract between the employer and the injured party. While not adopting the vicarious immunity doctrine, the Supreme Court of Canada has recently relaxed the rules of privity of contract to provide that employees, including executives, may be third party beneficiaries of contractual limitation of liability provisions in contracts between their employer and another party provided:

(1) the clause, either expressly or impliedly, extends its benefits to the employee or employees seeking to rely on it; and

(2) the employee or employees seeking the benefit of the clause must have been acting in the course of their employment and must have been performing the very services provided for in the contract when the loss occurred.[1]

[1] *London Drugs Ltd. v. Kuehne & Nagel Int. Ltd.* (1992), 143 N.R. 1 (S.C.C.), at 76.

§8.9 Further, if an executive, acting *bona fide* and within the scope of his or her authority, procures or causes a breach of contract between the employer and a third party, such executive is not personally liable in tort for his or her actions since they are deemed to be the acts of the company itself.[1]

[1] *Said v. Butt*, [1920] All E.R. Rep. 232 (K.B.); *Levi v. Chartersolf Canada Inc.* (1994), 8 C.C.E.L. (2d) 10 (Man. Q.B.).

§8.10 Under Quebec civil law, an employer is also responsible for damages caused by the acts of its executives acting within their functions and responsibilities. This liability is based on article 1463 of the Civil Code of Quebec (previously C.C.L.C., art. 1054(7)), which provides for the employer's vicarious liability for the acts of its servants. To trigger the employer's liability, a victim must demonstrate that the author of the injury was an employee and that this employee committed a fault while in the performance of his or her duties. The employer may, of course, claim from the faulty employee the compensation which had to be paid to the victim. However, as at common law, the liability does not attach where the employee is not under the employer's control at the time of the faulty conduct, or if the employee committed no actual fault.[1] The employer will also be liable when its employee's acts cause injury to another employee. This principle was reaffirmed in *Côté v. Sidbec-Dosco Ltée*,[2] where an employer was held responsible for the harassment by one of its foremen of another employee. The court awarded the harassed employee $6,500 in damages.

[1] *Perras v. Mongeau*, [1942] B.R. 167 (Que. C.A.); *Huddleston v. Ramzan* (1988), 26 B.C.L.R. (2d) 266 (S.C.); *Rainbow Industrial Caterers Ltd. v. Canadian National Ry.* (1988), 30 B.C.L.R. (2d) 273 (C.A.); *Veronneau v. Gregory* (1979), 11 B.C.L.R. 121 (S.C.); *Roed v. Tahsis Co.* (1977), 4 B.C.L.R. 176 (S.C.); *Rheaume v. Gowland* (1978), 8 B.C.L.R. 93 (S.C.).

[2] J.E. 84-390 (Que. S.C.); *Marshment v. Borgstrom*, [1942] S.C.R. 374; *Conseil des ports nationaux v. Commission des accidents du travail du Québec*, [1989] R.J.Q. 792 (C.A.).

D. STATUTORY OBLIGATION TO ENSURE SAFETY

§8.11 One area of the employment relationship drawing a growing amount of attention from both a legislative and judicial perspective is health and safety. All of the provinces and the federal government have enacted comprehensive legislative schemes regulating the health and safety of employees.[1] In the following paragraphs, we will briefly discuss some of the rights and obligations which exist in Ontario. Similar provisions exist in the other provinces. However, the reader should refer to the specific statute for particular details regarding health and safety rights and obligations.

[1] *Canada Labour Code*, R.S.C. 1985, c. L-2, Part II, ss. 122-165; *Occupational Health and Safety Act*, R.S.O. 1990, c. O.1; *An Act respecting Occupational Health and Safety*, R.S.Q., c. S-2.1; *Occupational Health and Safety Act*, R.S.A. 1980, c. O-2; *Workers' Compensation Act*, R.S.B.C. 1996, c. 492; *Workplace Safety and Health Act*, R.S.M. 1987, c. W210; *Occupational Health and Safety Act*, S.N.B. 1983, c. O-0.2; *Occupational Health and Safety Act*, R.S.N. 1990, c. O-3; *Occupational Health and Safety Act*, R.S.N.S. 1989, c. 320; *Occupational Health and Safety Act*, R.S.P.E.I. 1988, c. O-1; *Occupational Health and Safety Act, 1993*, S.S. 1993, c. O-1.1.

1. Employers

§8.12 In Ontario, the *Occupational Health and Safety Act* imposes duties and responsibilities on each of the three principal levels within the workplace hierarchy. The broadest and most extensive are imposed on the employer, which is not surprising given that it is the employer who has the greatest financial resources as well as the necessary authority to ensure compliance in the workplace.[1] The Act is a paternalistic statute. It operates on the underlying premise that employers are in the best position to ensure and enforce safety in the workplace and that workers cannot always be trusted to do what is in their best interest as far as safety is concerned. Therefore the employer, its officers and supervisors must bear the most significant responsibilities. The more important duties of an employer are:

(1) to provide the protective devices required and prescribed by the regulations under the Act;

(2) to maintain the protective devices in proper working order;

(3) to ensure that the protective devices are in fact used by the employees;

(4) to ensure that all measures and procedures prescribed by the Act are carried out in the workplace;

(5) to acquaint a worker or a person in authority over a worker with the hazards in the workplace of which the employer is aware;

(6) to take every precaution reasonable in the circumstances for the protection of a worker;

(7) to appoint as supervisors competent persons as defined in the Act;[2]

(8) to maintain records of biological, chemical and physical agents as prescribed by the regulations;

(9) to respond in writing within 21 days to any recommendations from the joint health and safety committee with either a schedule for implementing the recommendation, if the employer agrees, or the reasons for disagreement if such is the case; and

(10) to prepare and review, at least annually, a written occupational health and safety policy and a program to implement that policy.[3]

---

[1] *Occupational Health and Safety Act*, R.S.O. 1990, c. O.1, ss. 25 and 26.

[2] According to s. 1(1), a "competent person" must be:

    (a) qualified because of knowledge, training and experience to organize the workplace and its performance;

    (b) familiar with the provisions of the Act and the regulations that apply to the work; and

(c) have knowledge of any potential or actual danger to health or safety in the workplace.

[3] Similar obligations exist in Quebec under the *Act respecting Occupational Health and Safety*, R.S.Q., c. S-2.1, ss. 50-62 [am. 1985, c. 6, ss. 530, 531; 1992, c. 21, s. 303].

§8.13 The detailed requirements of the Act are contained in the regulations. There is one set of regulations for each of the industrial, mining and construction sectors.[1]

[1] See R.R.O. 1990, Regs. 851, 854 and 213/91 respectively.

2. Officers and Supervisors

§8.14 Both officers and supervisors have specific duties under the Act. An officer must take all reasonable care to ensure that the company complies with the Act and the regulations as well as any orders issued by inspectors and directors of the Ministry of Labour. Supervisors, who are defined as those individuals having authority over a workplace or charge of a workplace, have the following duties:

(1) to ensure that workers use the devices and equipment prescribed under the Act and regulations;
(2) to advise workers of any potential or actual danger to their health and to provide, where prescribed, written instructions as to protective measures to be taken; and
(3) to take every precaution reasonable in the circumstances for the safety of workers under their care and control.[1]

[1] R.S.O. 1990, c. O.1, s. 27.

3. Employees

§8.15 Employees have the duty to, amongst others:

(1) work in compliance with the provisions of the Act and the regulations;
(2) use or wear the equipment, protective devices or clothing that the employer requires to be worn; and
(3) not render any safety device ineffective.[1]

[1] R.S.O. 1990, c. O.1, s. 28.

§8.16 The maximum penalty for an individual is a fine of $25,000 and up to one year in prison; the maximum fine for a company has recently been increased to $500,000.[1] Fines in excess of $100,000 are now commonplace for serious offences, particularly those involving fatalities.

¹ R.S.O. 1990, c. O.1, s. 66.

§8.17 The Act also provides an employee with the right to refuse to perform unsafe work.¹ Although the circumstances necessary to trigger this right are less likely to arise at senior levels within the organization, any employee, including an executive, has the right to refuse to perform work when he reasonably believes that any equipment or device he operates may endanger himself or other employees, that the physical condition of the workplace may endanger himself or other employees, or that any activity he is required or asked to engage in may endanger himself or any other employees. Once an employee has exercised this right, a statutory scheme of investigation is mandated. This involves both a first-level internal investigation and a second-level investigation by representatives of the Ministry of Labour. It is important to note that it is the reasonable, subjective belief at the time that is determinative. It is not necessary to objectively prove that the danger exists as is the case with the common law right to refuse unsafe work. For example, a truck driver may refuse to drive a particular vehicle if he or she honestly and reasonably believes that the vehicle is unsafe. The mere fact that another employee drives the vehicle without incident is not proof that the initial employee's refusal was unreasonable.

¹ R.S.O. 1990, c. O.1, Part V.

4. Strict Liability Offence/Due Diligence Defence

§8.18 Statutes in the health and safety fields are normally referred to as public welfare enactments, *i.e.*, for the greater good of the citizenry as a whole. As such, they create strict liability offences and there is no requirement, as there is in criminal offences, that the accused intended the consequences of his or her actions or inactions. The limited mental element of the charge is satisfied upon proof that the proscribed act or omission occurred and that an accused was negligent, inattentive or indifferent to his or her responsibilities.

§8.19 It is a defence to charges of this nature for an individual to prove, on a balance of probabilities, that he or she acted with due diligence. Due diligence exists where a person takes all precautions reasonable in the circumstances to prevent or avoid the commission of the offence or, alternatively, where a person reasonably believed in a mistaken set of facts which, if true, would have rendered the act or omission innocent.¹

¹ *R. v. City of Sault Ste. Marie*, [1978] 2 S.C.R. 1299.

§8.20 The onus is on the accused to establish on a balance of probabilities that he or she acted with due diligence. As a result, in any prosecution, the prosecutor must establish that the act or omission proscribed by the legislation occurred. Thereafter, the burden of proof shifts to the accused to establish that he or she acted with due diligence. Until recently, it was arguable that imposing a burden on an accused to prove due diligence on a balance of probabilities was a violation of an individual's Charter right to be presumed innocent until proven guilty. The Supreme Court of Canada has now definitively determined that, while the placing of an onus on the defence to establish due diligence beyond a reasonable doubt violates an accused's Charter right, any such violation is a reasonable limit in a free and democratic society.[1] The Court's conclusion is premised on the public welfare nature of such offences and the fact that the actions or inactions of a defendant are uniquely within the defendant's knowledge. The Court held that the requirement that the defendant prove the defence of due diligence on a balance of probabilities did not impose an unfair burden.

¹ *R. v. Wholesale Travel Group Inc.*, [1991] 3 S.C.R. 154.

§8.21 As to the first branch of the due diligence defence, *i.e.*, verifying whether every precaution reasonable in the circumstances was taken, the court considers a number of factors including whether the officers or the company created a system, sufficient within the terms and practices of its industry, to prevent the commission of the offence and whether reasonable steps were taken to ensure the effective operation of that system. Officers cannot establish due diligence simply by showing that they delegated all aspects of compliance to subordinates. They must go further and establish that the subordinates were properly trained and equipped to handle the task and that the system was being monitored to ensure it was working.

§8.22 Due diligence based on a reasonable belief in a mistaken set of facts does not include a mistake of law. A mistake of law, *i.e.*, an error as to what was required of an individual in a given set of circumstances, is not a defence recognized at common law. The mistaken belief must be in a set of facts which, if they were true, would render the act or omission innocent. For example, the defence has been successfully invoked where a statute prohibited duck hunting within a specified radius of any baited area.[1] An individual who was found hunting within such an area argued that she was unaware that the area was baited. As her evidence was believed, it constituted a defence since she believed in a mistaken set of facts which, had they been true — that is to say, had the area not been baited — would have rendered her act or omission innocent. However, if she had pleaded that she was unaware that the law prohibited her from hunting in a baited area, then she would have been relying on a mistake of law, which would not have been a defence.

¹ *R. v. Chapin*, [1979] 2 S.C.R. 121.

§8.23 The defence of due diligence has most recently been examined in the Ontario case of *R. v. Bata Industries Ltd.*¹ In this case, Thomas Bata, the Chairman of the Board, and two executives/directors of the company's plant in Batawa, Ontario were charged with offences under the *Ontario Water Resources Act*. The company had stored certain contaminants, by-products of its operation, in storage drums outside the plant proper. The drums had, from time to time, overflowed and contaminants had leaked into the ground and subsequently into adjacent rivers and bodies of water. Both the president of the company and the general manager of the plant were found guilty of violating their duties under the Act, and each was eventually fined $16,000. The court specifically ordered that the individuals not be reimbursed by the company for the fines levied.

¹ (1992), 9 O.R. (3d) 329 (Prov. Div.); vard (1993), 14 O.R. (3d) 354 (Gen. Div.); revd
   (1995), 25 O.R. (3d) 321 (C.A.).

§8.24 With respect to the president, the court found that the storage problem had been brought to his attention but that there was no evidence that he had taken any steps thereafter to view the site and assess the problem. The court concluded that due diligence would have required the president to exercise a degree of supervision and control that demonstrated that "he was exhorting those whom he may normally be expected to influence or control to an accepted standard of behaviour".¹ He had a responsibility not only to give instructions, but also to see to it that those instructions were carried out in order to minimize the harmful effects of the damage.

¹ (1992), 9 O.R. (3d) 329 (Prov. Div.) at 365.

§8.25 Insofar as the general manager was concerned, the court held that, since he was on site, he had a responsibility to personally inspect the area on a regular basis and if he decided to delegate responsibility for the problem, he had to ensure that the delegate received the training necessary to enable him or her to do the job, to follow up by way of detailed reports and to ensure that the appropriate action was in fact taken. Other factors which the court indicated were considerations in assessing whether due diligence was established included:

(1) the general standard of care common to the business activity in question;
(2) the gravity of the potential harm;
(3) alternatives available to minimize the harm;
(4) the likelihood of harm; and
(5) the ability of the officer to control the conduct in question.

§8.26 In Quebec, the Labour Tribunal examined the criteria and elements of a valid due diligence defence in great detail in *Commission de la santé et de la sécurité du travail du Québec v. Mines Sigma (Québec) Ltée.*[1]

---

[1] [1992] T.T. 391. See also *Commission de la santé et de la sécurité du travail du Québec v. Société d'électrolyse et de chimie Alcan Ltée*, D.T.E. 83T-803 (Que. Lab. Trib.) ($5,000 fine); *Commission de la santé et de la sécurité du travail du Québec v. Achille de la Chevrotière Ltée*, D.T.E. 85T-571 (Que. Lab. Trib.); *Commission de la santé et de la sécurité du travail du Québec v. J.M. Asbestos Inc.*, D.T.E. 89T-759 (Que. Lab. Trib.); *Commission de la santé et de la sécurité du travail du Québec v. Ben Blackburn Inc.*, D.T.E. 89T-725 (Que. Lab. Trib.) ($8,000 fine); *Commission de la santé et de la sécurité du travail du Québec v. Extraction R.M. Ltée*, D.T.E. 89T-869 (Que. Lab. Trib.); *Commission de la santé et de la sécurité du travail du Québec v. Entreprises Lagacé (1982) Inc.*, D.T.E. 90T-163 (Que. Lab. Trib.) ($10,000 fine).

E. SEXUAL HARASSMENT

§8.27 In Canada, two types of harassment are recognized. The first involves vexatious comments or conduct that is known or ought reasonably to be known to be unwelcome. The second involves sexual solicitations or advances made by a person in a position to confer, grant or deny a benefit or advancement where the person making the solicitation or advance knows or ought reasonably to know that it is unwelcome.

§8.28 With respect to the first type of harassment, one isolated incident is not normally enough to establish the harassment. Rather, a course of conduct is required.[1] This form of harassment involves both a subjective element, in that the affected individual must be distressed, annoyed, embarrassed or otherwise intimidated by the course of conduct, and an objective element, in that the perpetrating party must have known or reasonably ought to have known that the recipient felt distressed, annoyed or embarrassed. Conduct may amount to sexual harassment even though it has nothing to do with sexual attraction or advances so long as it is directed at a person because of his or her gender.[2]

[1] *Cuff v. Gypsy Restaurant* (1987), 8 C.H.R.R. D/3972 (Ont. Bd. of Inq.); but see, *contra, Purdy v. Marwick Mfg. Co.* (1987), 9 C.H.R.R. D/4840 (Ont. Bd. of Inq.).

[2] *Shaw v. Levac Supply Ltd.* (1990), 14 C.H.R.R. D/36 (Ont. Bd. of Inq.).

§8.29 With respect to the more direct form of harassment, sexual solicitations or advances, a number of evidentiary issues often arise in light of the fact that one rarely encounters a situation where the alleged offence takes place in the open and in full view of other individuals. As a general rule, such events take place in private one-on-one situations where the only available evidence is from the direct parties who invariably recount diametrically opposed stories. As a result, tribunals tend to rely on circumstantial evidence, drawing inferences from the conduct of the parties, including whether the complainant told anyone else of the incidents shortly after they occurred.[1] In addition, human rights tribunals have tended to allow similar fact evidence to be introduced more frequently than is the norm in criminal proceedings.[2]

[1] *Graesser v. Porto* (1983), 4 C.H.R.R. D/1569 (Ont. Bd. of Inq.); *Morano v. Nuttall* (1988), 9 C.H.R.R. D/4876 (Ont. Bd. of Inq.); *Noffke v. McClaskin Hot House* (1989), 11 C.H.R.R. D/407 (Ont. Bd. of Inq.).

[2] *Commodore Business Machines Ltd. v. Ontario (Minister of Labour)* (1984), 49 O.R. (2d) 17 (Div. Ct.); *Piazza v. Airport Taxi Cab (Malton) Assn.* (1985), 7 C.H.R.R. D/3196 (Ont. Bd. of Inq.), vard on other grounds (1987), 24 O.A.C. 8 (Div. Ct.); affd on other grounds (1989), 69 O.R. (2d) 281; *Cuff v. Gypsy Restaurant* (1987), 8 C.H.R.R. D/3972 (Ont. Bd. of Inq.); *Graesser v. Porto, supra,* note 1; but see, *contra, Mehta v. MacKay* (1990), 15 C.H.R.R. D/232 (N.S.C.A.).

§8.30 Sexual harassment in the workplace is strictly prohibited under the *Canadian Human Rights Act,*[1] the *Canada Labour Code,*[2] and the Quebec *Charter of Human Rights and Freedoms*[3] as well as under most human rights legislation in the individual provinces.[4] In fact, the Quebec Charter prohibits all forms of harassment, not only sexual harassment.

[1] R.S.C. 1985, c. H-6, ss. 3 and 7.

[2] R.S.C. 1985, c. L-2, ss. 247.1 *et seq.* [en. R.S.C. 1985, c. 9 (1st Supp.), s. 17].

[3] R.S.Q., c. C-12, ss. 10 and 10.1. [en. 1982, c. 61, ss. 3 and 4].

[4] See *Janzen v. Platy Enterprises Ltd.,* [1989] 1 S.C.R. 1252.

§8.31 Sexual harassment can exist in many forms, as stated by Chairman Shime in *Bell v. Ladas:*[1]

> The forms of prohibited conduct that, in my view, are discriminatory run the gamut from overt gender-based activity, such as coerced intercourse to unsolic-

ited physical contact to persistent propositions to more subtle conduct such as gender-based insults and taunting, which may reasonably be perceived to create a negative psychological and emotional work environment.

[1]   (1980), 1 C.H.R.R. D/155 (Ont. Bd. of Inq.), at para. 1389.

§8.32 Arjun P. Aggarwal gives the following examples, among others, of what may constitute sexual harassment:

1. Verbal Behaviour
   — continuous idle chatter of a sexual nature and graphic sexual descriptions;
   — offensive and persistent risqué jokes or jesting and kidding about sex or gender specific traits; . . .
   — staged whispers or mimicking of a sexual nature about the way a person walks, talks, sits, etc; . . .
   — innuendos or taunting;
   — unwelcome remarks;
   — jokes that cause awkwardness or embarrassment;
   — gender-based insults or sexist remarks; . . .

2. Gestures and Other Non-Verbal Behaviour
   — licking lips or teeth;
   — lewd gestures, such as hand or sign language to denote sexual activity; . . .

3. Visual Sexual Harassment
   — display of pornographic or other offensive, derogatory and/or sexually explicit pictures, photographs, cartoons, drawings, symbols and other material; . . .

4. Physical Behaviour
   — touching that is inappropriate in the workplace such as patting, pinching, stroking or brushing up against the body;
   — hugging;
   — cornering or mauling;
   — invading another's "personal space"; . . .

5. Psychological Sexual Harassment
   — repeated unwanted social invitations, for dinner, drinks, or movies;
   — relentless proposal of physical intimacy beginning with subtle hints which may lead to overt requests for dates and/or sexual intercourse; . . . [1]

[1]   *Sexual Harassment in the Workplace*, 2nd ed. (Toronto: Butterworths, 1992), pp. 11-13. See also *Commission des droits de la personne du Québec v. Linardakis*, [1990] R.J.Q. 1169 (Ct. of Que.).

§8.33 The contravention of this prohibition will entitle the victim of harassment to obtain the cessation of such interference and compensation for the moral or material prejudice resulting therefrom. In addition, the court may condemn the person guilty of harassment to pay exemplary damages in the case of unlawful and intentional acts of harassment.[1]

[1]   *Charter of Human Rights and Freedoms*, R.S.Q., c. C-12, s. 49. See *Halkett v. Ascofigex*

Inc., [1986] R.J.Q. 2697 (S.C.); *Foisy v. Bell Canada,* [1984] C.S. 1164 (Que. S.C.); *Augustus v. Gosset,* [1990] R.J.Q. 2641 (S.C.); and the *Canadian Human Rights Act,* R.S.C. 1985, c. H-6, s. 53.

§8.34 The employer's obligation to provide a safe workplace includes the obligation to provide an environment free of harassment.[1] Accordingly, an employer which has been duly notified of the harassment of its employees by other employees may be liable if it fails to take the appropriate steps to stop that harassment. The rank of the author of the harassment and whether he or she is a member of management is irrelevant to the issue of the employer's liability. This was reaffirmed in *Thessaloniki Holdings Ltd. v. Saskatchewan Human Rights Commn.*[2] In this case, the plaintiff was a waitress who informed her employer that she was a victim of harassment by the cook. The employer did nothing, and a board of inquiry condemned him to pay $2,500 to the plaintiff. The Court of Queen's Bench upheld this condemnation against the employer and stated that "even subtle tolerance of sexual discrimination in the workplace is unacceptable."[3]

---

[1] K. Schucher, "Achieving a workplace free of sexual harassment: The Employer's Obligations" (1995), 3 Can. Lab. E.L.J. 171-200.
[2] [1991] 6 W.W.R. 590 (Sask. Q.B.).
[3] [1991] 6 W.W.R. 590 (Sask. Q.B.), at 595.

§8.35 In *Halkett v. Ascofigex Inc.,*[1] the Quebec Superior Court condemned the employer jointly and severally with the employee who committed sexual harassment toward another employee. The court based its judgment on article 1054(7) of the Civil Code of Lower Canada (as it then was), which provides for the liability of the employer for the faults committed by its servants.[2]

---

[1] [1986] R.J.Q. 2697 (S.C.).
[2] Now see C.C.Q., art. 1463; see also *Foisy v. Bell Canada,* [1984] C.S. 1164 (Que. S.C.).

§8.36 In *Augustus v. Gosset,*[1] the Quebec Superior Court decided that the employer should not be vicariously liable for exemplary damages "unless the employer has expressly or implicitly authorized or ratified the employee's reprehensible act".

---

[1] [1990] R.J.Q. 2641 (S.C.), at 2656.

§8.37 In *Robichaud v. Canada (Treasury Bd.),*[1] the Supreme Court of Canada concluded that, under the *Canadian Human Rights Act,* the employer is liable for the sexual harassment committed by a foreman upon one of its employees. As the Supreme Court put it:

... the statute contemplates the imposition of liability on employers for all acts of their employees "in the course of employment", interpreted in the purposive fashion outlined earlier as being in some way related or associated with the employment.[2]

[1] [1987] 2 S.C.R. 84. See also *Gervais v. Agriculture Canada*, D.T.E. 88T-533 (Can. H.R.T.).
[2] *Robichaud*, [1987] 2 S.C.R. 84 at 95.

§8.38 Although the employer's intention is not relevant to determine liability, the Supreme Court of Canada has said that it will take the employer's attitude into account when assessing the damages to be awarded to the victim:

For example, an employer who responds quickly and effectively to a complaint by instituting a scheme to remedy and prevent recurrence will not be liable to the same extent, if at all, as an employer who fails to adopt such steps.[1]

[1] *Robichaud v. Canada (Treasury Bd.)*, [1987] 2 S.C.R. 84, at 96.

§8.39 In *Dupuis v. British Columbia (Min. of Forests)*;[1] the complainant, a graduate student, was hired by the Minister of Forests to coordinate bird surveys in the Queen Charlotte Islands as an employee subordinate to her supervisor. The complainant and her supervisor had sexual intercourse on several occasions. At trial, the complainant testified that she did not wish to have sexual intercourse with her supervisor but felt that she did not have a choice. Her supervisor testified that he believed she had voluntarily agreed to do so. In determining whether sexual harassment occurred, two issues were considered: whether the complainant's actions were consistent with her allegation that the conduct of her supervisor was unwelcome, and whether the alleged harasser knew or ought to have known that the conduct was unwelcome. While the complainant had the option to travel with fellow workers, she did choose to travel alone with her supervisor, who made arrangements to share a room. Since prior to sleeping together on the first evening, she had indicated that she was opposed to having intercourse, the adjudicator found that the complainant had not welcomed the sexual acts. He so concluded after taking into account all the facts, including that the complainant had not opposed the sexual encounters later that night and during the days that followed. With respect to the second part of the analysis, the adjudicator considered the vulnerable position of the complainant in dealing with her supervisor, especially with respect to the level, degree and circumstances of the control that he exercised over her. It led the adjudicator to conclude that the supervisor should have known that the complainant was not comfortable with his sexual conduct. In his analysis of the control that the supervisor had over the complainant, the adjudicator focused on the particulars such as the fact: (a) that she reported directly to the supervisor; (b) that the supervisor was responsible within the government for the area of her academic interest; (c) that the supervisor had a role in funding decisions with respect to the research she might carry out; (d) that the supervisor was affiliated with the university where she intended to undertake a Master's program in the Department of Zoology; (e) that in the isolated areas they were exploring, the complainant had no other contacts. In concluding that sexual harassment had occurred and the employer was responsible, the adjudicator relied upon the reasoning of the Supreme Court of Canada in *Robichaud v. Canada (Treasury Board)*, [1987] 2 S.C.R. 84 and the United States Supreme Court in *Meritor Savings Bank v. Vinson* (1986), 106 S. Ct. 2399. The adjudicator ordered the respondent to: (1) cease contravention, namely sexual harassment and refrain from committing same; (2) pay compensation in the amount of $5,000 for emotional injury; (3) pay compensation in the amount of $14,976 for lost wages and $594 for tuition fees incurred by contravention; and (4) search the Ministry's files and remove any evaluation done by the supervisor.

[1]   (1993), 20 C.H.R.R. D/87 (B.C. Council of Human Rights).

§8.40 In addition to a condemnation for the acts, the "author of harassment" can have his or her employment terminated by the employer. If the sexual harassment is proven, the courts will generally dismiss a complaint for unlawful dismissal since sexual harassment will often be deemed to constitute a just cause for dismissal without notice.[1] However, it is not necessarily the case that a finding of sexual harassment for the purposes of a human rights complaint will automatically give rise to a finding of sexual harassment for wrongful dismissal purposes. Different considerations are said to be involved, and there would appear to be a stricter standard upon an employer dismissing an employee for sexual harassment than for an employee alleging such harassment under human rights legislation. In the dismissal context, there is generally a heightened concern that the alleged harasser has received fair warning about the offending conduct and has been treated fairly during the investigation process. The fact that the individual is a member of management is an aggravating factor.[2] The same reasoning applies in the case of sexual harassment against a client.[3] For instance, in the case of *W. (G.) v. Pharmacy C*,[4] a pharmacist was dismissed for, among other reasons, sexually harassing employees. After reminding the employer that it must act diligently when confronted with a possible situation of sexual harassment in the workplace, the arbitration tribunal dismissed the employee's action stating that his dismissal for sexual harassment was wholly justified.

¹ *Mackie v. Genesco Canada Ltd.* (1991), 34 A.C.W.S. (3d) 796 (Ont. Ct. (Gen. Div.));
*Syndicat des travailleurs(euses) de la Société des alcools du Québec et Société des alcools
du Québec,* D.T.E. 90T-1330 (T.A.); *Canadian National Ry. Co. v. Canadian Brotherhood of Railway, Transport & General Workers,* D.T.E. 88T-1070 (T.A.); *Gravel v. Messageries de Presse Benjamin Enr.,* D.T.E. 86T-847 (Commr. of Lab.); *Himmelman v.
King's-Edgehill School* (1985), 7 C.C.E.L. 16 (N.S.S.C.). For a contrary finding, see
Gonsalves v. Catholic Church Extension Society of Canada (1996), 20 C.C.E.L. (2d) 106
(Ont. Ct. (Gen. Div.)).
² *Tellier v. Bank of Montreal* (1987), 17 C.C.E.L. 1 (Ont. Dist. Ct.); *Vachon v. American
Motors of Canada,* [1987] T.A. 605; *Commission des droits de la personne v. Lemay*
(1995), R.J.Q. 1967, D.T.E. 95T-816 (Human Rights Trib.).
³ *Granada Location de T.V. Ltée v. Syndicat des salariés de systèmes de location du Québec,*
[1987] T.A. 690.
⁴ [1991] T.A. 438.

§8.41 Even though sexual harassment in the workplace is prohibited,
this does not mean that normal social involvement between employees
or between management and employees is prohibited. This was reaffirmed by Arbitrator Shime in *Bell v. Ladas:*¹

> The prohibition of such conduct is not without its dangers. One must be cautious that the law not inhibit normal social contact between management and employees or normal discussion between management and employees. It is not
> abnormal, nor should it be [a] prohibited activity for a supervisor to become socially involved with an employee. An invitation to dinner is not an invitation to a
> complaint. The danger or the evil that is to be avoided is coerced or compelled social contact where the employee's refusal to participate may result in loss of employment benefits. . . .
>
> Again, the Code ought not to be seen or perceived as inhibiting free speech. If
> sex cannot be discussed between supervisor and employee neither can other values such as race, colour or creed, which are contained in the Code, be discussed.

¹ (1980), 1 C.H.R.R. D/155 (Ont. Bd. of Inq.), at paras. 1390-1391. See also *Foisy v.
Bell Canada,* [1984] C.S. 1164 (Que.).

§8.42 Thus, in the case of *Shiels v. Saskatchewan Government Ins.,*¹ an action for wrongful dismissal was upheld, and the employee awarded 12
months' notice, because his conduct did not amount to sexual harassment. His actions had consisted of touching and kissing a fellow employee during a convention. The court decided that, since these actions
were not "unwanted" by the co-employee, they could not constitute
sexual harassment.

¹ (1988), 20 C.C.E.L. 55 (Sask. Q.B.). See also *Bannister v. General Motors of Canada
Ltd.* (1994), 8 C.C.E.L. (2d) 281 (Ont. Ct. (Gen. Div.)); *Tse v. Trow Consulting Engineers Ltd.* (1995), 14 C.C.E.L. (2d) 132 (Ont. Ct. (Gen. Div.)).

§8.42.1   In *Au v. Lyndhurst Hospital*,[1] a worker made a claim under the Ontario *Occupational Health and Safety Act* because she alleged that she was sexually harassed by her supervisor. In an interim decision, it was found that sexual harassment can constitute a health and safety issue for the purposes of the *Occupational Health and Safety Act*, in addition to or as an alternative to, meriting a claim under the *Human Rights Code* (Ontario). The Ontario Labour Relations Board ruled that Ms Au was not fired as a result of her sexual harassment complaint but rather was let go as part of an internal restructuring. However, the Board confirmed that sexual harassment could be considered a health and safety issue and that the Board therefore had jurisdiction over complaints asserting reprisals for behaviour protected by the *Occupational Health and Safety Act*, including cases involving allegations of sexual harassment. In such cases, it was held, the Board will need to determine whether the Board ought to exercise such jurisdiction in light of the explicit coverage of sexual harassment by the *Human Rights Code*. As a result of this decision, more employees may be expected to take the OHSA route due to the considerable backlog of cases and significant delays associated with the Human Rights Commission.

---

[1]   [1995] O.L.R.B. Rep. Nov. 1371 and [1996] O.L.R.B. Rep. May/June 456 and [1997] O.L.R.D. No. 2523, File No. 1517-94-OH.

F.   STATUTORY OBLIGATION TO PROTECT DIGNITY

§8.43   Under the new Civil Code of Quebec, the employer is not only statutorily bound to protect the health and safety of the executive but is also bound to protect his or her dignity[1] There is no express definition of dignity in the Code but the authors are of the view that reference may be made to Chapter III of the Civil Code of Quebec, "Respect of Reputation and Privacy."[2] These articles essentially provide that every person is entitled to the right to the respect and privacy of his reputation and that no one may invade this privacy without his or her consent. In addition, article 37 of the new code stipulates that every person who establishes a file on a person must have a legitimate reason for doing so and may only gather information which is relevant to the stated objective of the file and that he or she may not, without the authorization or consent of the person concerned, reveal this information to a third party. In all cases the person upon whom a file has been established may examine and receive copy of the file. Although it is impossible at this time to define the exact impact of these provisions, certain issues must be considered: Can the employer give a reference about or discuss an employee without the employee's consent? What will constitute valid consent? Is the fact that the former employee gave the former employer's name as a reference sufficient? Until these questions are cleared up, the most prudent course would probably be to obtain the written consent of the employee before discussing his or her work with a third party and, unless the consent is totally unqualified, ensuring that all communications are in writing and that the employee has been notified of their content before any mailings have been done. This will probably result in more reference letters being prepared upon the termination of employment and given to the employee at that time, and fewer oral references.

[1]   C.C.Q., art. 2087.
[2]   C.C.Q., articles 35 to 41.

CHAPTER 9

EXECUTE THE WORK

A. INTRODUCTION

§9.1 Pursuant to the employment contract, the executive, like all other employees, has the obligation to do the work for which he or she was hired. What exactly constitutes "doing the work"?

§9.2 To properly satisfy the obligation to execute the work, the executive must be present at work, be physically and mentally fit and be competent to do the assigned work. The executive must also follow directions and observe the rules of good conduct. An executive must personally do the work assigned and may not delegate it to another unless so authorized.

§9.3 Refusal or failure to execute the work may amount to legal cause for dismissal. If so, it justifies the employer's decision to put an end to the employment contract without notice.[1] Although the employer may occasionally require the executive to temporarily execute functions somewhat different from those for which he or she was hired, the employer may be prevented from introducing conditions of employment which, in effect, require that the executive perform a job other than that to which he or she initially agreed.[2]

---

[1] *Erlund v. Quality Communication Products Ltd.* (1972), 29 D.L.R. (3d) 476 (Man. Q.B.); *Babcock v. C & R Weickert Enterprises Ltd.* (1993), 50 C.C.E.L. 1 (N.S.C.A.).

[2] See Chapter 12, "Termination of Employment".

B. EXECUTIVE'S ROLE WITHIN THE EMPLOYER'S ORGANIZATION

§9.4 The executive's obligation to execute the work is determined by examining the executive's role within the organization. Although this role has not been clearly defined by the courts, the factors generally referred to include the executive's relationship with and accountability to the employer, shareholders, partners, subordinates, customers, public and governmental authorities.

§9.5 The executive's specific job functions with respect to these different factors necessarily vary according to the type of job, place of work and the specifics of the employment contract. These factors help determine the content of the obligation to execute the work. For example, certain conduct which may not amount to cause for dismissal in a large office may be held to be such in a smaller one where the same behaviour causes greater interpersonal difficulties.[1] In many cases, the executive must be perceived as a role model in the eyes of his or her subordinates.[2] The executive may also be expected to favourably represent the employer in the business world as well as within the public domain.[3] Whether or not the executive fulfils his or her obligation to do the work will be examined in relation to every aspect of the executive's role.

[1]   *Essery v. John Lecky & Co.* (1986), 60 Nfld. & P.E.I.R. 219 (P.E.I.S.C.).
[2]   See for example *Sauvé v. Banque Laurentienne du Canada*, [1994] R.J.Q. 1679 (Que. S.C.), in appeal; *Bertrand v. Aliments Ashley-Koffman*, D.T.E. 94T-523 (Que. S.C.).
[3]   *Boisvenue v. Town of St. Stephen* (1987), 22 C.C.E.L. 116 (N.B.Q.B.) (dismissal for cause — high standard of behaviour required of person in position of public confidence); *Murchison v. Grosfillex*, unreported, March 20, 1991, C.S.M. 500-05-009627-868 (Que. S.C.).

C.   COMPONENTS OF THE OBLIGATION TO EXECUTE THE WORK

§9.6   Once the executive's role within the organization is determined, different components come into play in assessing whether or not the executive meets his or her obligation to execute the work. The first component is one we will refer to as the "behavioural component". The behavioural component infers attitude, conduct, use of discretion and avoidance of personality conflicts.

§9.7   The second component is a physical component. The executive is expected to attend work regularly and punctually and to be physically and emotionally fit to execute the work. This second component will be discussed more fully under the specific headings "Absenteeism", "Mental or Physical Incapacity" and "Substance Abuse".

§9.8   The third component, which is the qualitative, and occasionally quantitative, component, requires that the executive carry out his or her responsibilities satisfactorily. This component will be discussed further under the heading "Competence".

§9.9   The executive's obligation to act in good faith is implicit in the employment contract. It can also evolve in respect to the executive's status and responsibilities.

> One difficulty in wrongful dismissal cases arises from the tendency to look at all cases as if they were in the same category and to apply the same principles to

the dismissal of a senior executive as one would to an hourly-rated employee on an assembly line. This fails to recognize that once an employee reaches a certain level, he can stand in a fiduciary position to his employer and must be considered apart from the usual master and servant relationship.[1]

---

[1] *Helbig v. Oxford Warehousing Ltd.* (1985), 9 C.C.E.L. 75 (Ont. C.A.), at 85; leave to appeal to S.C.C. refused 52 O.R. (2d) 754*n*. This obligation will be examined more fully in Chapter 10, "Loyalty".

1. Behavioural Component

(a) Attitude

§9.10 An important aspect of the executive's obligation is to display a fitting attitude. The executive must demonstrate interest in the work to be performed. The courts have recognized that, just as a positive or constructive approach can improve the work environment, a negative attitude can hinder it.

§9.10.1 In this regard, a disruptive personality may warrant termination of employment, where the effect of such personality is to create a dysfunctional working environment.[1]

---

[1] *Croome v. Worthington Canada Inc.* (1986), 34 A.C.W.S. (2d) 494 (Ont. Dist. Ct.); *Fonceca v. McDonnell* (1983), 1 C.C.E.L. 51 (Ont. H.C.J.).

§9.11 In *Ma v. Columbia Trust Co.,*[1] a 28-year-old vice-president of finance was dismissed because of his poor interpersonal skills and his attitude toward subordinates. The vice-president was described by witnesses at trial as a hard-driving professional who had high expectations of his subordinates. He was also described as being loud, using abusive language, and occasionally throwing tantrums. The British Columbia Supreme Court upheld his dismissal because of the "accumulative effect of incidents".[2] Similarly, in *Beyea v. Irving Oil Ltd.,*[3] a 47-year-old plant foreman was dismissed because of his resistance to change his attitude despite written warnings. The court considered his behaviour in light of the substantial number of employees who reported to him and who would take his actions as the standard for their own behaviour. The court upheld the dismissal, concluding that the foreman's behaviour was "incompatible" with his continued employment.

---

[1] (1985), 9 C.C.E.L. 300 (B.C.S.C.).
[2] (1985), 9 C.C.E.L. 300 (B.C.S.C.), at 310.
[3] (1985), 8 C.C.E.L. 128 (N.B.Q.B.), affd 14 C.C.E.L. 67 (C.A.).

§9.12 In *Drolet v. Ville de l'Ancienne-Lorette,*[1] the Quebec Provincial Court upheld a decision to dismiss an employee who had been hired to work on a project which had to be completed within a specific time frame. The success of the project was contingent upon the team working successfully together as a whole. In view of the employee's refractory attitude toward authority and his systematic refusal to work with his co-workers, his dismissal was upheld. In *Bazinet v. Radiodiffusion Mutuelle Ltée,*[2] the Quebec Court of Appeal held that an undisciplined attitude, even in the face of otherwise competent work, may constitute cause for dismissal. In that case, the plaintiff manager was perceived as a difficult, inflexible and intractable person, difficult to work with and for, intent on pursuing his "profondes convictions" and maintaining control and, accordingly, was held not to satisfy his employment obligations.[3]

---

[1]   D.T.E. 88T-585 (Que. Prov. Ct.).

[2]   D.T.E. 89T-1081 (Que. C.A.). See also *Poulin v. Immeubles Québec West Wakefield Ltée,* D.T.E. 88T-370 (Que. S.C.); *Lavoie v. Squibb Canada Inc.,* D.T.E. 88T-267 (Que. C.A.), leave to appeal to S.C.C. refused Oct. 6, 1988.

[3]   *Bazinet v. Radiodiffusion Mutuelle Ltée,* D.T.E. 89T-1081 (Que. C.A.) at 5 of the judgment. See also *Goulet v. Equipement de Bureau Astro-Tech Ltée,* J.E. 84-364 (Que. S.C.). On the other hand, in *Carle v. Comité paritaire du vêtement pour dames* (1987), 22 C.C.E.L. 281 (Que. S.C.), the court held that a lawyer's strong personality, eagerness to do the work assigned and attempts to reorganize the legal department did not warrant dismissal.

---

§9.13 Dedication to and interest in work is expected from an executive. However, personal ambition must not upset the smooth management of the business or undermine the corporate culture. For example, in *Green v. Confederation Life Ins. Co.,*[1] the executive, upon hearing of the company's intention to promote a colleague, advised his employer that if this were to occur, it would amount to his own constructive dismissal. The court, in finding that the employer had ample and just cause to terminate the plaintiff's employment, held:

> I appreciate that ambition is or can be a laudatory trait, but it is also my view that ambition must not, in a corporate setting, become counter productive to the smooth management of a company.[2]

---

[1]   (1985), 10 C.C.E.L. 109 (Ont. H.C.J.).

[2]   (1985), 10 C.C.E.L. 109 (Ont. H.C.J.) at 119-20.

---

§9.13.1 Finally, unpopularity by reason of a controversial personality or an authoritarian style of management is generally not cause for termination.[1]

[1] *Beaulac v. London Life, compagnie d'assurance-vie,* J.E. 93-1486 (Que. S.C.); *Corriveau v. P.G. Québec,* [1986] R.J.Q. 2349 (S.C.) affd in part [1989] R.J.Q. 1 (C.A.).

(b) Conduct

§9.14 Employees must treat their employer and their employer's representatives with respect. The violation of this obligation may lead a court to find that the employee has violated the obligation to execute the work.[1] The obligation to treat one's employer with respect exists during and, in certain aspects, after working hours.[2]

[1] *Fournier v. Tout Rôti Ltée,* D.T.E. 90T-131 (Que. S.C.).
[2] *Bousquet v. Nellis* (1908), 35 C.S. 209 (Que. Ct. of Rev.); *Montreal Watch Case Co. v. Bonneau* (1892), 1 B.R. 433 (Que. C.A.). See also *Clément v. Simpsons Sears Ltée,* J.E. 83-844 (Que. S.C.).

§9.15 Employees have a duty to exercise proper conduct in the workplace, including the obligation to follow reasonable employer rules defining appropriate conduct. Rules of conduct may be express or implied from the circumstances or corporate culture. Minor defects in conduct or errors of judgment will not usually justify dismissal. Failure to respect explicit rules will be discussed at length under the heading "Obedience to Directives".[1]

[1] See, *infra,* §§9.23 *et seq.*

§9.16 What constitutes proper conduct will depend greatly on where the employee works and what functions he or she performs at the time. Particularly in the case where it is imperative that the employer maintain an irreproachable public image (*e.g.* non-profit organizations whose funding depends on its public image) an employee's conduct must be commensurate with this responsibility and his integrity, and the appearance of integrity must be flawless.[1] In the specific context of the executive employment contract, for the executive to fulfil his or her obligation, he or she may be required to assimilate and use proper etiquette at all times.[2] Cases of misconduct will be examined individually to determine whether there exists a breach of the obligation to execute the work.

[1] *Lemieux v. Association pulmonaire du Quebec,* D.T.E. 93T-552 (Ct. of Que.).
[2] The court may occasionally accept indiscreet conduct when this would not offend the employer: *Murchison v. Grosfillex,* unreported, March 20, 1991, C.S.M. 500-05-009627-868 (Que. S.C.).

§9.17 The length of time an employee has been working for the employer may play an important part in evaluating the employee's performance. In *Tremblay v. Gaz Inter-Cité Québec Inc.*,[1] the employee had only been with the company two months. Yet, within that short time frame, he had refused to work with his superior, had insulted company managers and had threatened his superior during his last interview. Furthermore, he had shown no willingness to remedy his lack of productivity. The court concluded the dismissal was for cause.

[1] J.E. 84-935 (Que. S.C.).

§9.18 The duty to exercise proper conduct may extend to activities which are outside actual job duties. Aggressive behaviour at a party which may not amount to breach in one case may, in a different context, be a grave enough fault to give rise to dismissal without notice.[1] For instance, the court may examine whether the incident had a negative impact on future employment relations within the company, whether the company's reputation was damaged, and whether clients were offended.

[1] *Clément v. Simpsons Sears Ltée*, J.E. 83-844 (Que. S.C.).

§9.19 In *Chamberlain v. Maisonneuve Broadcasting Co.*,[1] the court held that a sales representative had been discharged for cause when he made an unflattering remark about one of the employer's clients during an off-duty reception. The remark was overheard by an employee of the client who reported it to the client who then refused to do further business with the employer. In *Boilard v. Aciers Pitt (Québec) Ltée*,[2] a sales representative with three months' service was inebriated at a cocktail party held for clients and cried in front of the clients. The following day he did not show up at a meeting his superiors had requested him to attend and did not justify his absence. Noting the employee's recent hiring and the attitude of aloofness he demonstrated during and after the party, the court concluded he had been rightfully dismissed.

[1] D.T.E. 87T-669 (Que. S.C.).
[2] D.T.E. 84T-657 (Que. S.C.).

§9.20 The examination of an executive's off-duty conduct may even, in some cases, extend to the examination of his personal relationships. For example, in *Canadian Imperial Bank of Commerce v. Boisvert*,[1] the respondent was an assistant supervisor in a Montreal branch of the bank at the time of her dismissal. The employee was cohabiting with a convicted armed robber who had recently been charged with the robbery of two banks. The employer suggested she resign, barring which dismissal would ensue. She refused and was subsequently dismissed without notice. The Federal Court of Appeal referred the matter back to the adjudicator but adopted the principle that, in some special cases, marriage or cohabitation with a particular person can create just cause for dismissal, as it did in this case.

[1] (1986), 13 C.C.E.L. 264 (F.C.A.). See also *Yeomans v. Simon Fraser University* (1996), 20 C.C.E.L. (2d) 224 (B.C.S.C.).

§9.21 The courts may also consider the executive's conduct as a "revelation of character".[1] If the employee's conduct, even off company premises, reveals that he or she is unworthy of the company's trust, then there may be cause for dismissal.[2] In *Altschul v. Tom Davis Management Ltd.*,[3] the plaintiff was a comptroller and financial adviser. In the course of his employment, he advised another employee of the company to pay bribes if it attracted contracts for the defendant. In reaching its conclusion, the court stated:

> I concur with the defendant's arguments for, in this instance, the person fully in charge of the financial management of the company, counselled the doing of an illegal act to a new employee. The revelation of character of such a senior employee and officer of the company should not have to be countenanced by responsible business. Mr. Davis, in evidence, stated that if word got around in the business community that his company was party to illegal acts, such as bribes, his chances of expanding a new line and the business itself would be severely handicapped. There was no specific evidence to support this, but I have no hesitation in accepting his opinion. In my view, the conduct of Mr. Altschul, in counselling the offering of bribes and his support for same, demonstrated a character so flawed as to be no longer worthy of trust by his employer.[4]

[1] *Jewitt v. Prism Resources Ltd.* (1980), 110 D.L.R. (3d) 713 (B.C.S.C.), affd 127 D.L.R. (3d) 190 (C.A.). But see *Rock v. The Canadian Red Cross Society* (1994), 5 C.C.E.L. (2d) 231 (Ont. Ct. (Gen. Div.)). For a revelation of character including alcohol abuse, see *Bell v. General Motors of Canada* (1989), 27 C.C.E.L. 110 (Ont. H.C.J.), discussed, *infra*, at §9.63.
[2] *Granoff v. National Trust Co.* (1986), 38 A.C.W.S. (2d) 195 (B.C.S.C.).
[3] (1985), 6 C.C.E.L. 180 (Ont. Dist. Ct.).
[4] (1985), 6 C.C.E.L. 180 (Ont. Dist. Ct.), at 183.

§9.22 As will be discussed in the section below entitled "Obedience to Directives", an executive, notwithstanding his or her authority to exercise a significant degree of discretion, must not act in contravention of lawful policies established by the employer. Accordingly, the editor of a newspaper, which had always been known to support a particular political party, had no right to write an article, unknown to the owner, which unmistakably attacked the political party in question. Only the owner could change the political colour of his paper, with the employee's discretion being restricted to commenting on his own personal political views.[1]

---

[1] *Bélanger v. Bélanger* (1895), 24 S.C.R. 678.

(c) Obedience to Directives

§9.23 An employee must follow employer directives which are lawful and not contrary to good morals.[1] An employee who neglects or refuses to carry out his or her employer's lawful and proper instructions and requests could be subject to termination for cause. In order for directives or internal regulations to be enforceable, they must be clearly set out and communicated to the employee.[2] Doubts in that regard are generally interpreted in favour of the employee.[3]

---

[1] In *Dooley v. C.N. Weber* (1994), 3 C.C.E.L. (2d) 95 (Ont. Ct. (Gen. Div.)), affd (1990), 80 O.A.C. 234 (C.A.), a middle management employee was ordered not to be involved sexually with his female subordinates. He did not follow the order and was fired. The court held that the dismissal was without cause because the order he had been given was not reasonable in today's world and was not within the scope of his employment contract. There was no evidence that the company suffered in any way whatsoever, either financially or otherwise, arising out of the conduct of the plaintiff. In *English v. Toyota Plaza* (1995), 13 C.C.E.L. (2d) 239 (Nfld. S.C.), a salesman was directed to either take a personal development course and finance it personally, or "face the consequences". The employee failed to register for the course and was subsequently dismissed. He then launched a wrongful dismissal suit against the employer and was successful.
[2] Regarding the inclusion of manuals as part of the employment contract, see Chapter 3, §§3.13 *et seq.*
[3] See, e.g., *Malabre v. IDI Electric (Canada) Ltd.*, J.E. 84-524 (Que. S.C.); *Lefrançois v. Hydro-Québec*, D.T.E. 88T-551 (Que. S.C.).

§9.24 *R. v. Arthurs* is cited in this context in *Kellas v. CIP Inc.*[1] The plaintiff was employed by the defendant to build a road into a new timber area. The employer, after consultations with government ministries, chose a creek-crossing site believed to be least harmful to the environment. The plaintiff moved the crossing 15 feet, did not inform his superiors of the change, left the site before clean-up was over, and failed to return for inspection. The court upheld summary dismissal.

---

[1] (1990), 32 C.C.E.L. 196 (B.C.S.C.).

§9.25 In *Stein v. British Columbia (Housing Management Commn.)*,[1] the court held that the executive's failure to do that which was required of him was inconsistent with the continuation of his contract of employment:

When the appellant, as a regional manager, agreed to do something which he knew his superiors considered important and the importance of which he himself recognized, his superiors were entitled, until informed to the contrary, to assume that the system had been put in place and was operational. It may be that their failure to make further inquiries and badger the appellant to put the system in operation (which some might consider nagging) was a failure of competence on their part and, thus, a breach of duty by them to the respondent. But that question does not bear on the issue before us.

• • • • •

A judge sitting in his chambers may well consider that a procedure laid down for the operation of an enterprise is silly, time-consuming and generally useless, and he may be right. But it is not a judge's business to decide, when the question is obedience or disobedience to lawful orders, on the wisdom or lack of wisdom of those orders.[2]

---

[1] (1992), 41 C.C.E.L. 213 (B.C.C.A.).
[2] (1992), 41 C.C.E.L. 213 (B.C.C.A.) at 225.

§9.26 In *Lavoie v. Ville de Fossambault sur le lac*,[1] a municipal inspector whose duties included the surveillance, maintenance and operation at a waterworks and sewer system was held to have been rightfully dismissed because he did not, even though he had been warned repeatedly, maintain the equipment properly. His conduct with respect to his superior's instructions amounted to insubordination and his negligence had caused his employer damage.[2]

---

[1] J.E. 81-368 (Que. S.C.).
[2] See also *Drolet v. Ville de l'Ancienne Lorette*, D.T.E. 88T-585 (Que. Prov. Ct.), where the employee's constant refusal to obey directives, thereby causing delays in production, was a cause for dismissal.

§9.27 In *Beaulieu v. Services Financiers Avco Canada Ltée*,[1] the assistant manager was hired with the understanding that she might have to make field calls which would require her to visit the residences of the finance company's customers. When the assistant manager subsequently refused to perform the field calls on the basis that they made her nervous and ill, the Quebec Superior Court upheld her dismissal without notice because she had refused directives and failed to perform the normal functions of her job.

---

[1] J.E. 85-78 (Que. S.C.).

§9.28 In *Donaldson v. Philippine Airlines Inc.*,[1] the plaintiff was the district sales manager of the defendant corporation. In 1979, the company instituted a policy not to extend credit to Plaza Air, their customer. The employee-plaintiff subsequently extended substantial credit to Plaza Air and withheld reports from the defendant. The court held:

> . . . it is clear from his own evidence that the plaintiff certainly knew . . . that he had no right to extend credit of any kind to Plaza Air, and he did so clearly contrary to his instructions. Indeed, while trying to get payment for the amount due from Plaza, he advised the manager of Plaza that in extending credit he was acting contrary to his instructions.

• • • • •

> In our opinion, the plaintiff wilfully disobeyed his employer in a manner essential to the operation of its business by extending credit to Plaza Air, and in deliberately withholding information from the company which they were entitled to receive. For these reasons, on the basis of the evidence of Mr. Donaldson himself, we think the defendant has shown adequate cause for his dismissal . . .[2]

[1] (1985), 7 C.C.E.L. 229 (Ont. C.A.).
[2] (1985), 7 C.C.E.L. 229 (Ont. C.A.) at 232, 233-34. See also *Sauvée v. Banque Laurentienne du Canada*, [1994] R.J.Q. 1679 (Que. S.C.), in appeal.

§9.28.1 However, in *Rock v. The Canadian Red Cross Society*, the court held that the breach of policy which had led to the termination of the medical director of the defendant's transfusion centre in Ottawa was serious but did not justify termination.[1] The Canadian Red Cross Society policy prohibited its blood transfusion centres from maintaining their own bank accounts or sources of funding. The evidence clearly showed that the plaintiff had breached the policy of the Canadian Red Cross in maintaining separate accounts and in charging alcohol to these accounts for staff activities. The court concluded that the accounts were maintained in an open fashion by the plaintiff with two signatures required and all the records were kept at the Ottawa Centre Office. They were not concealed in any way or hidden from inspection. Furthermore, the plaintiff did not derive any personal benefit and did not expose the Canadian Red Cross to any financial loss because of her misconduct. The court concluded that, in view of the plaintiff's position and extensive contribution to the Canadian Red Cross in scientific research, the breach of policy could have been dealt with by other forms of discipline rather than by an immediate termination.

[1] (1994), 5 C.C.E.L. (2d) 231 (Ont. Ct. (Gen. Div.)).

§9.29 An executive must also recognize the authority of his or her superiors. A failure to do so constitutes insubordination. In order to justify dismissal without notice, the insubordination must be serious. As well, insubordination may be found in an executive's refusal to accomplish a task within his or her scope of responsibilities.

§9.30 In *Bratti v. F & W Wholesale Ltd.*,[1] the plaintiff was told well in advance that his preferred vacation dates would conflict with a period during which the defendant would be understaffed. The plaintiff took the time off anyway and was dismissed. Taking vacation without notice during a busy time when the defendant was understaffed, and in the face of refusals by the defendant to allow him to take vacation at that time amounted to insubordination, going to the root of the employer-employee relationship. The court stated:

> . . . if the situation is characterized as F & W having dismissed him, such dismissal was not wrongful but for cause because of the insubordination . . .
>
> I have no doubt that in this case the disobedience of Bratti to the reasonable requirement of Perri [the manager] that he not go for vacation, at that particular time, was wilful disobedience and a deliberate flouting of an essential contractual condition . . .
>
> Although, in hindsight, the operations of F & W were not prejudiced to the extent that they had to be discontinued or curtailed, the potential for that to happen was present throughout all of the deliberations between Bratti and Perri and, I find, it was only due to good fortune that Perri was able to obtain . . . [a replacement]. His unilateral decision, therefore, to take his vacation when he did was to the prejudice of the proper conduct of F & W's business and had the potential for putting the whole operation of the company considerably at risk.[2]

---

[1] (1989), 28 C.C.E.L. 142 (B.C. Co. Ct.).
[2] (1989), 28 C.C.E.L. 142 (B.C. Co. Ct.) at 149-50. A similar result was reached in *Ehmcke v. Penetang Bottling Co.* (1992), 41 C.C.E.L. 251 (Ont. Ct. (Gen. Div.)).

§9.31 In assessing whether there is cause for dismissal, the court will examine the corporate culture. For example, if the hierarchical relationship within the company is strictly enforced, there may be cause for dismissal if an employee fails to respect the same.[1] However, in *Bell v. Cessna Aircraft Co.*,[2] an employee, threatened with dismissal, bypassed his immediate superiors and presented his case to a higher officer. The court found that the employee's actions did not constitute cause:

> In my opinion, the learned trial judge erred in law in holding that the only ground for bypassing middle management was to expose a fraud or a malevolent conspiracy likely to affect the operations of a company. While it may be wrong to go over the head of one's immediate supervisors for the purpose of criticizing business or administrative decisions made by middle management and thus afford grounds for immediate dismissal, different considerations apply where an employee's job is at stake. In my view, simple justice requires that where a junior executive on reasonable grounds and acting in good faith believes that he is about to be discharged, he should have the opportunity to present his side of the case to top management.[3]

[1] *Bell v. Cessna Aircraft Co.* (1982), 131 D.L.R. (3d) 551 (B.C.C.A.), motion for leave to appeal to S.C.C. dismissed (1982), 43 N.R. 167.
[2] (1982), 131 D.L.R. (3d) 551 (B.C.C.A.).
[3] (1982), 131 D.L.R. (3d) 551 (B.C.C.A) at 558.

§9.32 An isolated act of disobedience or a single error may or may not be sufficient to justify a summary discharge. In other words, not every breach of an employer directive, albeit serious, will give rise to a right of justifiable dismissal.

§9.33 In *Taweel v. T.R.A. Foods Ltd.,*[1] the plaintiff was summarily dismissed from his position as manager of a grocery store when he violated his own rules, which he had made for employees, by shopping for his groceries on Sunday when the store was closed. He always paid for the groceries on Monday and there were no allegations of dishonesty or fraud. The plaintiff brought an action for damages for wrongful dismissal. In allowing the action, the court found that the manager had displayed poor judgment but that there were no reasonable grounds for summary dismissal. The court concluded:

> In assuming an exclusive privilege to shop on Sunday, Mr. Taweel, at most, displayed poor judgment in setting an example for other employees; but in all the circumstances, I cannot see that he revealed a tainted character nor provided reasonable or justifiable grounds for his summary dismissal.[2]

[1] (1990), 32 C.C.E.L. 230 (P.E.I.S.C.).
[2] (1990), 32 C.C.E.L. 230 (P.E.I.S.C.), at 235.

§9.34 In *Gagnon v. Golden Eagle Refining Co. of Canada Ltd.,*[1] a single act of insubordination was sufficiently serious to justify the employee's dismissal. The employee had agreed to rent one of the company's gas stations to an individual despite his superior's refusal to authorize the arrangement. Dismissal was held to be for cause due to the failure of the employee to respect the vice-president's choice of a lessee-distributor. In another case, a sales manager was dismissed for cause for having taken a new company motor home for his personal use contrary to the instructions received from the vice-president that only used vehicles were available for this purpose.[2]

[1] [1971] C.A. 743 (Que.).
[2] *Vacanciers Mobiles (1979) Inc. v. Duchesne*, D.T.E. 85T-15 (Que. C.A.).

§9.35 In *Dupras v. Gagnair Consultants Ltée,*[1] a vice-president who owned 25% of the shares of the company was wrongfully dismissed when he refused to vote according to the president's preference. According to the court, the voting rights on shares were attached to his status of shareholder and not to his employee status or to his employment contract.

¹ D.T.E. 86T-805 (Que. S.C.), affd 90T-869 (C.A.).

§9.36 It has been determined that differing opinions and priorities of the executive employee with his or her employer are not insubordination when they arise from a different conception of the undertaking.[1]

> ¹ *Girco Inc. v. Girardeau*, D.T.E. 89T-738 (Que. S.C.). See also *Habitations populaires Desjardins de Lanaudière Inc. v. Boyer*, D.T.E. 88T-550 (Que. C.A.); *Mainville v. Brasserie Michel Desjardins Ltée*, D.T.E. 88T-292 (Que. S.C.), appeal abandoned Sept. 16, 1988, C.A.M. 500-09-000185-884; *Murchison v. Grosfillex*, unreported, March 20, 1991, C.S.M. 500-05-009627-868 (Que. S.C.).

§9.37 Insubordination is generally not found when an executive exercising his or her discretion obtains poor results provided he or she was acting in the best interests of the company.[1] It is also worthy of note that the executive has the right to, and should, refuse orders that are contrary to his or her professional ethics.[2]

> ¹ *Mainville v. Brasserie Michel Desjardins Ltée*, D.T.E. 88T-292 (Que. S.C.), appeal abandoned Sept. 16, 1988, C.A.M. 500-09-000185-884.
> ² *Clement v. Phoenix Ins. Co. of Hartford* (1894), 6 C.S. 502 (Que. Ct. of Rev.).

(d) Personality Conflicts

§9.38 As a general rule, given that employees often have a very limited role in selecting co-workers, they are not obliged to maintain positive relationships with fellow employees. Accordingly, an employee's personality conflict with another employee or his or her superior may not in itself permit the employer to dismiss the employee without prior notice.[1] However, the executive's obligation in this regard is generally greater.

> ¹ See the case of *Banville v. Procureur général du Québec*, D.T.E. 84T-172 (Que. S.C.); *Bibeau v. C.L.S.C. du Marigot*, D.T.E. 86T-2 (Que. S.C.); *Thorneloe v. Commission scolaire Eastern Townships*, D.T.E. 84T-870 (Que. S.C.).

§9.39 In *Blackburn v. Coyle Motors Ltd.*,[1] the plaintiff was 62 years of age at the time of his termination. He had been employed for 27 years as a bookkeeper with the defendant car dealership. Upon the death of the principal owner of the company, his wife assumed control. There was a serious personality conflict between the plaintiff and the effective new owner of the company. The plaintiff's conduct toward the new owner was inappropriate but had improved since she originally took control of the company. The plaintiff was advised on April 2, 1982 that his termination would be effective June 28, 1982. The plaintiff sued for wrongful dismissal. The plaintiff was found to have called the new owner "Blondie" behind her back and to her face. Further, the plaintiff had insisted that Mrs. Coyle not speak to him directly but through the general manager. According to the court:

> . . . having said all that about the difficulties between the plaintiff and Mrs. Elenor Coyle, he did do his job. . . . There was never any complaint about his work, really, it was only his manners and his truculence. He was never ordered to change the way he did his work. He was never warned that if he did not do something differently he would be fired. What it really boils down to is a personal repugnance that Mrs. Coyle had toward the plaintiff. I have come to the conclusion that he was terminated, that he was fired, and he was fired without just cause.[2]

---

[1] (1983), 3 C.C.E.L. 1 (Ont. H.C.J.).
[2] (1983), 3 C.C.E.L. 1 (Ont. H.C.J.) at 4-5.

§9.40 However, if the conflict is such that it becomes disruptive, affecting other employees and the efficient operation of the employer's business, it may constitute legal cause for dismissal.[1] The size of the office may be relevant since conduct which may not constitute cause for dismissal in a large office may do so in a smaller office where it creates greater interpersonal difficulties.[2] Furthermore, executives have a greater obligation to get along with superiors as well as subordinates because they are role models.

---

[1] In *Ma v. Columbia Trust Co.* (1985), 9 C.C.E.L. 300 (B.C.S.C.), referred to earlier (see §9.11), poor interpersonal skills and inability to co-operate with fellow employees justified dismissal of a 28-year-old vice-president of finance. See also *Maheu v. Catalytic Enterprises Ltd.*, D.T.E. 84T-636 (Que. S.C.); *Banville v. Procureur général du Québec*, D.T.E. 84T-172 (Que. S.C.); *Bibeau v. C.L.S.C. du Marigot*, D.T.E. 86T-2 (Que. S.C.); *Thorneloe v. Commission scolaire Eastern Townships*, D.T.E. 84T-870 (Que. S.C.).
[2] *Holden v. Phase Electric Ltd.* (1986), 39 A.C.W.S. (2d) 478 (N.B.Q.B.).

§9.40.1 In *Woolley v. Ash Temple Ltd.*,[1] the British Columbia Supreme Court recognized that an employee's cumulative record of insubordination, combined with his alienation of the staff, might indeed afford sufficient grounds for dismissal where the continuation of the plaintiff's employment would prejudice the proper conduct of the employer's business. In this case, it was demonstrated that if Woolley, a branch manager, had not been terminated, some of the staff were seriously considering leaving the company to join competitors. This would have threatened the continued proper conduct of Ash Temple's business.

¹ (1991), 36 C.C.E.L. 257 (B.C.S.C.).

2. Physical Component

(a) Presence at Work

§9.41 Generally, the obligation to be present at work means that an employee is expected to attend work regularly, be punctual, and be fit to perform.

§9.42 The executive's obligation to be present at work may differ from that of an employee occupying a lower position in the hierarchy. For example, whereas the non-executive employee may have relatively fixed working hours, the executive may be called upon to work a more irregular and often extended schedule. This may include being present at social events and gatherings to promote the employer's interests. Of note in this regard are the provisions of employment standards legislation (Ontario and Quebec, for instance) which set minimum standards regarding various employment matters including hours of work and overtime and which expressly exclude persons whose work is exclusively managerial and supervisory in nature from the application of the hours of work and overtime provisions.[1]

¹ *Act Respecting Labour Standards*, R.S.Q., c. N-1.1, s. 3(6); *General Regulation* under *Employment Standards Act*, R.R.O. 1990, Reg. 325 [as amended], s. 3 & 4, R.R.O. 1990, Reg. 325, s. 4(b).

§9.43 The issue of executive relocation also forms part of the physical component of the obligation to execute the work.[1] The executive may be obliged to relocate with the business operations. If the executive expressly agreed, in the employment contract, to relocate or if it can be reasonably implied from the nature of the employer's business (*e.g.*, worldwide corporate operations, prior history of executive transfers) and all the surrounding circumstances that such an obligation exists, then the executive will be required to meet those demands. The converse is also true. Where an implied term of the employment contract is that the employment with the company will remain permanently in the same city, dismissal for failure to relocate may only be done upon giving proper notice.[2] Recently, courts have shown an inclination to find as an implied term in the employment contract that the employee will accept regional transfers not involving a demotion or undue hardship. For example, in *Durrant v. Westeel-Rosco Ltd.*,[3] the British Columbia Supreme Court stated that it failed to see "how large national or international corporations can operate effectively without such an implied term in their contracts of employment".[4]

¹ *Gravino v. Gulf Canada Ltée*, D.T.E. 91T-1059 (Que. S.C.), appeal abandoned Sept. 25, 1991, C.A.M. 500-09-001184-910; *Stefanovic v. SNC Inc.* (1988), 22 C.C.E.L. 82 (Ont. H.C.J.); *Henderson v. Westfair Foods Ltd.* (1990), 32 C.C.E.L. 152 (Man. Q.B.), revd on other grounds 40 C.C.E.L. 81 (C.A.); *Holgate v. Bank of Nova Scotia* (1989), 27 C.C.E.L. 201 (Sask. Q.B.); *Owens Illinois Canada Inc. v. Boivin* (1988), 23 C.C.E.L. 255 (Que. C.A.). See also Chapter 6, "Furnish the Work". This mobility does not, however, apply to the employee's family: *Villa v. John Labatt Ltée*, [1990] R.J.Q. 2247 (Que. S.C.); revd in part on another issue *La Brasserie Labatt Limitée v. Villa*, [1995] R.J.Q. 73 (C.A.).
² See *Morris v. International Harvester Canada Ltd.* (1984), 7 C.C.E.L. 300 (Ont. H.C.J.).
³ (1978), 7 B.C.L.R. 14 (S.C.), at 20.
⁴ See also *Rose v. Shell Canada Ltd.* (1985), 7 C.C.E.L. 234 (B.C.S.C.); *Canadian Bechtel Ltd. v. Mollenkopf* (1978), 1 C.C.E.L. 95 (Ont. C.A.); *Reber v. Lloyds Bank Int. Canada* (1985), 61 B.C.L.R. 361 (C.A.). The employer has no obligation to accommodate the employee's family in offering relocations: *Froese v. Horton CBI Ltd.*, unreported, Nov. 10, 1993 (Ont. Ct. (Gen. Div.)).

§9.44 Several factors may be important in persuading a court that such an implied term exists. In *Stefanovic v. SNC Inc.*,¹ the defendant was an engineering and construction company with offices across Canada and worldwide. The plaintiff engineer was originally hired as an on-sight project planner. In 1981, he was offered and accepted the position of Manager of Planning and Scheduling in the defendant's office and moved his family to Toronto with the defendant's assistance. Due to a downturn in the economy in 1982, the defendant decided that those employees in the Toronto office whom it wished to keep were to be given temporary layoffs, and others were to be terminated. The plaintiff was placed on temporary layoff and expressed his displeasure. He was then given the option of transferring to the head office in Montreal and was subsequently offered a position on a Baie Comeau project. The plaintiff refused both of these offers and was dismissed. The court found that there was no bad faith on the part of the defendant and that the refusal of the plaintiff to accept either of the job offers was cause for termination of his employment.

¹ (1988), 22 C.C.E.L. 82 (Ont. H.C.J.).

§9.44.1 However, in *Jeffrey v. Purolator Courier*,¹ the plaintiff employee was successful in an action for damages for wrongful dismissal. The employee took a ten-week leave of absence from her job based in Ottawa, and when she was ready to return to work, she found that her position had been filled. When she refused an offer to manage the Cornwall office, she was dismissed. The court considered the reduction of responsibilities and lessening of prestige, and found that the transfer offer was akin to constructive dismissal.

¹ (1995), 8 C.C.E.L. (2d) 205 (Ont. Ct. (Gen. Div.)).

(b) Absenteeism

§9.45 Temporary illness or absence from work for legitimate reasons does not constitute cause for dismissal. However, excessive absence, failing to offer reasonable explanations for absence, or failing to notify of an absence may be cause for dismissal. It is a question of degree.

§9.46 The practical question of degree has been considered in many cases. In *Riley v. Crown Trust Co.*,[1] MacDonald J. of the Alberta Supreme Court said:

> The termination of the plaintiff's employment was not caused by one incident or even an occasional incident but by more or less a consistent failure to report to work on time. The expectation of the defendant was known and recognized by the plaintiff but it cannot be said it was respected by him.

> • • • • •

> The defendant was more than patient with the plaintiff in encouraging him to cure his failing and in giving him warning that he was jeopardizing his position if his tardiness continued.
> The conduct of the plaintiff must be considered, in my opinion, as a wilful act of disobedience to not only a lawful and reasonable but also to a necessary order of the defendant. In a business office such as operated by the defendant, it is inconceivable that employees should choose to come to work at a time of their own choosing. Repetitious aberration on the part of the employee would understandably disaffect good employee relations as well as relations with customers and organization of work by staff members.[2]

---

[1] (1977), 5 A.R. 1 (S.C.), at 3.
[2] See also *McIntyre v. Hockin* (1889), 16 O.A.R. 498; *Cardenas v. Canada Dry Ltd.* (1985), 10 C.C.E.L. 1 (Ont. Dist. Ct.).

§9.47 Excessive absences, failing to offer a reasonable explanation for the absences or failing to notify of an absence may be a cause for dismissal. That being said, the employee must be offered the opportunity to explain his or her absence.[1]

---

[1] *Côté v. Cie Nationale de Forage et Sondage Inc.*, J.E. 84-1046 (Que. S.C.).

§9.48 A different approach to absenteeism for executives may be justified because of the greater leadership and decision-making role they have in their organization. Indeed, an executive's presence or absence from work usually affects the business' or department's functioning in a manner different than would the presence or absence of a less senior employee. In order to determine if an executive's absence is cause for dismissal, the court will examine whether this absence seriously disrupts the employer's business.[1] Again, this is a fact-specific inquiry.

[1] *Petit v. Pajar Production Ltée*, D.T.E. 90T-1298 (Que. C.A.); *Proulx v. Taxis Coop Québec*, D.T.E. 89T-1178 (Que. S.C.); revd in part D.T.E. 94T-254 (Que. S.C.); *Yeager v. R.J. Hastings Agencies Ltd.* (1984), 5 C.C.E.L. 266 (B.C.S.C.) (misconduct due to illness causing incapacity to work).

(c) Mental or Physical Incapacity

§9.49 The executive must be physically and mentally fit to do his or her work. The executive must fulfil any physical and/or mental requirements which the employer has established in good faith as being required for the performance of the work.[1] Courts have held that physical and mental requirements must be reasonable in accordance with the nature and demands of the job. For example, a physical education teacher may reasonably be required to be physically fit. However, a temporary leave of absence due to medical problems may not be seen as a physical or psychological unfitness for a job regardless of the employer's demand.[2]

[1] *Tarailo v. Allied Chemical Canada Ltd.* (1989), 26 C.C.E.L. 209 (Ont. H.C.J.), appeal settled by consent of the parties 7 O.R. (3d) 318 (C.A.).

[2] *Thom v. Goodhost Foods Ltd.* (1987), 17 C.C.E.L. 89 (Ont. H.C.J.).

§9.50 It is important to note that each provincial jurisdiction as well as federal law provides protection from discrimination for employees suffering from a "handicap" or a "disability".[1] To varying degrees, these statutes require the employer to "accommodate" the employee's disability or handicap. In Ontario, the *Human Rights Code*[2] places a duty of reasonable accommodation, limited by undue hardship, on employers. In determining whether the employer has complied with this obligation, the Ontario Human Rights Commission, a board of inquiry or a court will take into account any standards prescribed by regulations, the cost of the accommodation, outside sources of funding, if any, and the safety requirements, if any. In Quebec, the existence of such an obligation is still a matter of great debate.

[1] See, e.g., Ontario *Human Rights Code*, R.S.O. 1990, c. H.19, s. 5; *Charter of Human Rights and Freedoms*, R.S.Q. 1977, c. C-12, s. 10.

[2] Ontario *Human Rights Code*, R.S.O. 1990, c. H.19, s. 17(2).

§9.51 Although the circumstances of an individual operating with a permanent physical impairment is readily covered by the *Human Rights Code* in Ontario, the issue is not as clear where an executive, as a result of an illness, is incapable of regular attendance at work. For example, in *Rivest v. Canfarge Ltd.*,[1] the plaintiff had been employed by a concrete company and its predecessors for 19 years and had an exemplary work record. At the time he was dismissed, the plaintiff was a vice-president and general manager. Due to the pressures of work and the long hours, the plaintiff had taken several days off without notice. The defendant terminated his employment and the plaintiff claimed wrongful dismissal. Bowen J. of the Alberta Supreme Court found that there was no ground for summary dismissal. There is English authority for the proposition that a full-time employee who, because of illness, becomes able to perform only on a part-time basis may be dismissed without notice.[2] Essentially, as demonstrated in recent case law, the test of just cause to be applied is whether or not the incapacity of an employee due to illness puts an end "in the business sense, to their business engagement".[3]

[1] [1977] 4 W.W.R. 515 (Alta. S.C.).
[2] *Condor v. Barron Knights Ltd.*, [1966] 1 W.L.R. 87 (Assizes).
[3] *Yeager v. R.J. Hastings Agencies Ltd.* (1984), 5 C.C.E.L. 266 (B.C.S.C.), at 288.

§9.52 An employee who falls permanently ill and is unable to perform his or her duties may be dismissed for failing to fulfil his or her obligations in the contract. An employer must, however, carefully examine whether the insurance benefits, if any, to which the employee is entitled will affect the employer's right to terminate employment. Technically, permanent or prolonged illness frustrates the contract as opposed to constituting a breach of the contract.[1] As well, the "belief of the employee or his medical adviser that the former's disability was only temporary cannot affect the question in light of the subsequent knowledge which revealed its permanency."[2]

[1] *Burgess v. Central Trust Co.* (1988), 19 C.C.E.L. 193 (N.B.Q.B.); *MacLellan v. H.B. Contracting Ltd.* (1990), 32 C.C.E.L. 103 (B.C.S.C.).
[2] *Dartmouth Ferry Commn. v. Marks* (1903), 34 S.C.R. 366, at 375.

§9.53 While the permanent affliction cases may be clear, the difficult situations arise in the case of intermittent or lengthy illness. *Marshall v. Harland & Wolff Ltd.*[1] lists certain aspects that a court would likely examine to determine whether or not the ill employee has fulfilled his or her obligation to attend work regularly:

(a) *The terms of the contract, including the provisions as to sickness pay* — ... When the contract provides for sick pay, it is plain that the contract cannot be frustrated so long as the employee returns to work, or appears likely to return to work, within the period during which such sick pay is payable. ...

(b) *How long the employment was likely to last in the absence of sickness* — The relationship is less likely to survive if the employment was inherently temporary in its nature or for the duration of a particular job, than if it was expected to be long term or even lifelong.

(c) *The nature of the employment* — Where the employee is one of many in the same category, the relationship is more likely to survive the period of incapacity than if he occupies a key post which must be filled and filled on a permanent basis if his absence is prolonged.

(d) *The nature of the illness or injury and how long it has already continued and the prospects of recovery* — The greater the degree of incapacity and the longer the period over which it has persisted and is likely to persist, the more likely it is that the relationship has been destroyed.

(e) *The period of past employment* — A relationship which is of long standing is not so easily destroyed as one which has but a short history. This is good sense and, we think, no less good law, even if it involves some implied and scarcely detectable change in the contract of employment year by year as the duration of the relationship lengthens. The legal basis is that over a long period of service the parties must be assumed to have contemplated a longer period or periods of sickness than over a shorter period.

[1]   [1972] 2 All E.R. 715 (N.I.R.C.), at 718-19.

§9.53.1 Furthermore, some legislative provisions prohibit terminating an employee for illness when the absence from work is less than a certain number of weeks.[1]

[1]   See *An Act Respecting Labour Standards*, R.S.Q., c. N-1.1, art. 122.2. This article does not apply to senior managerial personnel (art.3(6)).

§9.54 In the presence of a clause indicating that an executive may be dismissed if he or she is absent for a given period, it will be difficult to dismiss the executive who is absent for frequent or prolonged periods but whose combined absence is not greater than that permitted by the employment contract.[1] In *Thom v. Goodhost Foods Ltd.*,[2] the plaintiff advised the Chief Executive Officer of the defendant of his state of health and stated that he was taking a medical leave of absence. A little over a week later, he received a termination letter. The court found that while the plaintiff's decision to take an immediate leave of absence on hearing his doctor's diagnosis may have been an overreaction, it did not constitute grounds for dismissal either by itself or in conjunction with earlier conduct. The employment contract expressly provided him with the right to take time off with pay so long as the business was operating efficiently.

[1]   *Burmeister v. Regina Multicultural Council* (1983), 24 Sask. R. 284 (Q.B.), revd in part on other grounds 40 Sask. R. 183 (C.A.); *Bull v. Realty Capital Corp.* (1981), 8 C.C.E.L. 229 (Ont. C.A.); *Petit v. Pajar Production Ltée*, D.T.E. 90T-1298 (Que. C.A.).
[2]   (1987), 17 C.C.E.L. 89 (Ont. H.C.J.).

§9.55 Prior to the decision of the Supreme Court of Canada in

Sylvester v. British Columbia,[1] courts had differed on whether an employee who becomes disabled during the notice period should receive reasonable notice in addition to disability pay or sick leave benefits. At least one court had concluded that these two entitlements were quantitatively different and for different purposes; therefore the payment of one should not preclude or offset the payment of the other. Such was the case in *McKay v. Camco Inc.*[2] In a 2:1 decision, the Ontario Court of Appeal set out the purpose of each of those benefits:

> The rights conferred on the appellant by the express and implied terms of his contract of employment are, in my respectful opinion, quantitatively different. The disability plan provided for the maintenance of the appellant's income during the period of disability. It was a benefit which formed part of the bargain between the appellant and the respondent. . . .
>
> The breach of the implied term requiring reasonable notice gives rise to an entirely different right. The employee is entitled to damages measured by the salary and other benefits to which he would have been entitled during the notice period but subject to his duty to mitigate. . . .
>
> The appellant's rights under the contract of employment to disability payments and to proper notice of dismissal are not only different in kind but also serve different purposes. The right to disability payments is intended to provide income to the appellant when he is unable to work. The purpose of requiring reasonable notice is to give the dismissed employee an opportunity to find other employment.[3]

[1] (1997), 146 D.L.R. (4th) 207 (S.C.C.).

[2] (1983), 43 O.R. (2d) 603 (H.C.J.), revd on other grounds (1986), 53 O.R. (2d) 257 (C.A.). See also *Datardina v. Royal Trust Corporate of Canada* (1995), 6 B.C.L.R. (3d) 1 (C.A.); *Bohun v. Similco Mines Ltd.* (1995), 6 B.C.L.R. (3d) 22 (C.A.).

[3] *McKay v. Camco Inc.* (1986), 53 O.R. (2d) at 267.

§9.55.1 In its decision in *Sylvester v. British Columbia*[1] the Supreme Court clarified that disability benefits received by an employee during his or her notice period should be deducted from damages for wrongful dismissal. A B.C. government employee was terminated during a period when he was receiving disability benefits. He sued for wrongful dismissal and at trial was awarded damages equivalent to 15 months' notice less the amount of the benefits received during that time.

[1] (1997), 146 D.L.R. (4th) 207 (S.C.C.).

§9.55.2 The Court of Appeal allowed an appeal from that judgment, awarded damages equivalent to 20 months' salary and found him also entitled to the disability benefits received during that period. Lambert J.A. concluded that a disability benefits plan should be considered a contract distinct from the basic employment contract and that once an employee is given notice of termination, the employer is required to comply both with its obligation to pay salary during the notice period and with its obligation to pay disability benefits. There was no challenge to the finding that Sylvester was entitled to 20 months' notice and the only issue before the Supreme Court was whether the disability benefits received by the employee should be deducted from the award for wrongful dismissal.

§9.55.3   Mr. Justice Major reasoned that since disability benefits are contractual, the question of deductibility turned on the terms of the employment contract and the intention of the parties. It was held that the disability plans "should not be considered contracts which are distinct from the employment contract, but rather as integral components of it".[1] He went on to find that in this case, the contract did not provide for the respondent to receive both disability benefits and damages for wrongful dismissal and that no such intention could be inferred. Damages for wrongful dismissal are based on the premise that the employee would have worked during the notice period, while disability benefits are payable only when the employee is unable to work. The court reasoned that the contractual right to damages and the contractual right to benefits are "based on opposite assumptions about his ability to work and it is incompatible with the employment contract for the employee to receive both amounts".[2] In contrast to the Court of Appeal, Major J. "fail[ed] to see how both contractual provisions can operate simultaneously when each is based on a contrary assumption about the ability of the employee to work".[3] The principle to be applied in awards for wrongful dismissal was stated as:

> ... absent an intention by the parties to provide otherwise, an employee who is dismissed while not working but receiving disability benefits and an employee who is dismissed while working should be treated equally ... Deducting disability benefits ensures that all affected employees receive equal damages, i.e., the salary the employee would have earned had the employee worked during the notice period.[4]

Major J. expressed a fear that if disability benefits were not deductible, then this would serve as a deterrent to employers establishing such plans. It is notable that the court left open the possibility of recovery of benefits in addition to damages where the benefits are akin to a private insurance plan for which the employee has provided consideration. This was clearly not the case here since the employee did not make any contribution to the disability plans.

[1]   *Sylvester v. British Columbia* (1997), 146 D.L.R. (4th) 207 (S.C.C.) at 211.
[2]   *Sylvester v. British Columbia* (1997), 146 D.L.R. (4th) 207 (S.C.C.) at 212.
[3]   *Sylvester v. British Columbia* (1997), 146 D.L.R. (4th) 207 (S.C.C.) at 213.
[4]   *Sylvester v. British Columbia* (1997), 146 D.L.R. (4th) 207 (S.C.C.) at 213-14.

§9.55.4 The decision in *Sylvester* has already proven influential. In *Dowsley Estate v. Viceroy Fluid Power International Inc.,*[1] the Ontario Court of Appeal followed *Sylvester* and deducted workers' compensation benefits from damages for wrongful dismissal. Even though Major J. had expressly distinguished statutory benefits such as employment insurance and workers' compensation from contractual disability benefits, the Ontario C.A. found that the principle of deductibility from *Sylvester* was still applicable. In the wake of this decision, it now appears that statutory benefits are also deductible from wrongful dismissal awards, at least in Ontario.

[1] (1997), 34 O.R. (3d) 57 (C.A.).

§9.56 *Yeager v. R.J. Hastings Agencies*[1] is another leading case on this issue. A salesman was employed with the defendant company for 30 years. His performance had been satisfactory over 27 years and he had handled some of the agency's largest and most important accounts. In the final 15 months of his employment, the plaintiff's performance deteriorated considerably. Various complaints arose concerning his inability to handle his accounts and those accounts were eventually taken from him. The plaintiff was finally dismissed for cause. At the time of the dismissal, the plaintiff was erroneously diagnosed as suffering from an incurable form of brain disease. In fact, the plaintiff's condition improved steadily subsequent to his dismissal and, at the time of trial, he was no longer disabled. The court found that the plaintiff was incapacitated for two years but that such an incapacity, in the circumstances, did not frustrate the contract. The court stated:

> Whether or not the incapacity of an employee due to illness will result in the frustration of a contract of employment will depend, in each case, on the relationship of the term of the incapacity or absence from work to the duration of the contract itself.[2]

The court held that, although two years is a long period of disability, that alone is not determinative of the issue. The permanency of this relationship, the court found, was exemplified not only by the 30 years of service given by the plaintiff but also by the fact that over the years the plaintiff was invited to, and did, become a significant shareholder of the company's stock.

[1] (1984), 5 C.C.E.L. 266 (B.C.S.C.).
[2] (1984), 5 C.C.E.L. 266 (B.C.S.C.) at 287.

§9.57 If a provision of the employment contract specifies that an employee who becomes disabled is entitled to receive salary for a specified period, the disabled person remains an employee for the duration of that period following his or her disability. The fact that the employee cannot furnish any personal services does not immediately end the contract between the employer and the employee.[1]

> [1] *Sylvestre v. Mines Sigma Québec Ltée*, D.T.E. 83T-372 (Que. Prov. Ct.).

§9.58 Conversely, in the context of a fixed-term contract, which was tacitly renewable on a yearly basis, one court held that the employment contract had not been tacitly renewed in May since the long absences due to illness had precluded the plaintiff from furnishing his personal services to the bank. Thus, as he had been absent since January, it was unreasonable to hold that in May his contract had been renewed.[1] In another case of a fixed-term contract, the employment contract was terminated since the employee's absence amounted to a substantial part of the entire contract period.[2]

> [1] *Caisse Populaire de Shawinigan v. Beaulac*, J.E. 80-44 (Que. C.A.).
> [2] *Vachon v. Cotton*, [1953] C.S. 167 (Que. S.C.) (3 months' absence during 12 months' contract).

§9.59 The court will also consider other circumstances, including the nature of the accident, the length of time an employee was absent from his or her job, the fact that he or she had been a faithful employee for a great many years, and the assurance given by the employer to the employee that the position would be kept for him or her.[1] It should be noted, however, that if the absence is due to a work accident, the employee may not be penalized for exercising a right pursuant to workers' compensation legislation.[2]

> [1] *Bruneau v. Caverhill* (1909), 37 C.S. 271 (Que. Ct. of Rev.); *Shaw v. Ecole E.C.S. Inc.*, J.E. 85T-560 (Que. S.C.).
> [2] See, *e.g.*, *An Act respecting Industrial Accidents and Occupational Diseases*, R.S.Q., c. A-3.001, s. 32.

(d) Substance Abuse

§9.60 An executive who is under the influence of alcohol or drugs to such an extent that it affects his or her ability to be alert in mind and body may be considered by the courts to suffer from an illness or disability. If such is the case, the employer must deal with this situation similarly to any case of physical or psychological illness. For example, an employer may be well advised to encourage executives suffering from such an illness to seek professional help.

§9.61 Upon being advised that an executive has followed the required treatment for such illness and is believed to be able to continue work and function normally, an employer may allow the executive to return to work. Should the executive then not be able to fulfil his or her obligations, an employer would usually be held to have "cause" to sever the employment relationship. In one case, the employer fired an employee because the latter refused to follow a detoxication treatment. The court held that the employee had been wrongfully dismissed because it was not shown that he had a drinking problem.[1]

---

[1] *Clément v. Simpsons Sears Ltée*, J.E. 83-844 (Que. S.C.).

§9.61.1 The extent to which management can require employees to submit to alcohol and drug testing remains unclear. While such policies reflect management's legitimate interest in maintaining a safe and productive workplace and limiting the employer's potential vicarious exposure to third parties, such policies can be highly intrusive into the dignity and privacy interests of individual employees. Recent human rights decisions illustrate some of the limits human rights tribunals will impose in order to protect employee privacy interests.

§9.61.2 In *Esso Petroleum Canada C.E.P., Loc. 614, Re*,[1] the employer's decision to implement a policy on the use of drugs and alcohol in the workplace, in response in part to the 1989 Exxon Valdez oil spill, was grieved by the union. The policy provided for, amongst other things, random urine testing for drugs and random alcohol breath testing for employees in jobs determined to be "safety sensitive", mandatory periodic medical examinations and blood testing to detect chemical dependency, obligatory disclosure of present or past substance abuse problems, and drug and alcohol testing for all employees for reasonable cause and after a significant work accident.

---

[1] (1994), 56 L.A.C. (4th) 440, upheld by the B.C. Labour Relations Board in a decision dated August 2, 1996 (B.C.L.R.B. File No. B257/96).

§9.61.3 After a thorough review of the jurisprudence, the Board[1] distilled a two-step test: first, is there justification or adequate cause? In other words, is there evidence of a drug and/or alcohol problem in the workplace? Is there a need for management's policy? Secondly, what are the alternatives available and can the problem be combatted in a less invasive way? In the result, the Board found much of the policy to be unacceptable. However, rules focusing on use and possession on company premises and upon the employee's unfitness for work were acceptable, as were certain disclosure requirements for employees in safety/sensitive positions, and mandatory random testing in a rehabilitation context, with reasonable and probable grounds or after a significant work accident or near miss.

---

[1]   (1994), 56 L.A.C. (4th) 440, upheld by the B.C. Labour Relations Board in a decision dated August 2, 1996 (B.C.L.R.B. File No. B257/96).

§9.61.4   A similar policy came under scrutiny in *Martin Entrop v. Imperial Oil Limited*.[1] In *Entrop*, the complainant alleged that his right to equal treatment with respect to employment had been infringed because of his "handicap and perceived handicap", contrary to the Code. The policy mandated that employees in "safety sensitive" positions disclose to management any past or present problems with alcohol or drug abuse. As Mr. Entrop was employed in such a position and had previously experienced a problem with alcohol, he was forced to disclose this to Imperial Oil. However, Mr. Entrop had not touched alcohol for more than seven and a half years at the time. Upon disclosure, Mr. Entrop was reassigned to a different, "less desirable" position with no loss in pay. A revised policy was introduced allowing those who abstained from alcohol or drugs for five years and had completed a mandatory rehabilitation program to work in "safety sensitive" positions. Mr. Entrop applied for reinstatement to his initial position and was forced to provide numerous letters from people all testifying to his sobriety. As well, he had to complete numerous physical and psychological tests. The diagnosis from these tests was consistent that he had "alcohol dependence in remission" and "no psychological or psychiatric reasons that would prevent the patient from resuming his full duties at this time". Mr. Entrop was reinstated to his "safety sensitive" position on condition that he agreed to sign an undertaking regarding post reinstatement controls. The undertaking included such provisions as an agreement to undergo unannounced alcohol testing at least twice per quarter, continued abstinence from alcohol, and an annual mandatory medical examination including medical screening for alcohol and drug abuse. The conditions placed upon Mr. Entrop in the undertaking were different from other employees engaged in "safety sensitive" positions. However, the policy did require all employees in the "safety sensitive" or "specified employee" positions to undergo random mandatory testing for drugs and alcohol. Following consistently negative test results, Imperial Oil in January 1995 revised the conditions of Mr. Entrop's undertaking to delete the yearly medical examinations, the additional unannounced alcohol tests, the quarterly review meetings, and the stipulation that his reinstatement was conditional upon "maintaining satisfactory job performance". However, the undertaking continued to state that Mr. Entrop would continue to abstain from any alcohol. In addition, he would report to his supervisor any alcohol or drug related charges, and report any changes in his circumstances that may increase his risk of relapse.

[1] (1995), 24 C.C.E.L. (2d) 87 (Ont. Bd. of Inquiry).

§9.61.5 The Board[1] found that there was *prima facie* evidence of discrimination against Mr. Entrop on three separate grounds under the *Ontario Human Rights Code*:

(1) The obligation to self disclose the past or present alcohol-related problems;
(2) Mr. Entrop's removal from his job;
(3) Mr. Entrop's reinstatement process that required ongoing controls.

The Board held that Imperial Oil met the subjective standard of "good faith" and honesty in developing their Alcohol and Substance Policy. The Board stated that Imperial Oil's motives, such as trying to reduce costly accidents, were legitimate aspects of a good faith appraisal of measures to enhance workplace safety. The Board considered, first, whether there was objective evidence to support Imperial Oil's claim that it had the right to ensure that employees in "safety sensitive" positions remained free from alcohol impairment. The evidence indicated that Imperial Oil had relied on the results of an extensive survey in implementing the Policy. Second, the Board considered whether Imperial Oil had established an objective standard of reasonable necessity in Mr. Entrop's case, where there was a past alcohol abuse problem. A few expert witnesses testified on the likelihood of relapse of alcoholics. Through their testimonies it was clear that in Martin Entrop's position, the risk of relapse was extremely unlikely. Thus, the Board concluded that the Respondent's decision to single out Martin Entrop under its policy was objectively unjustified. The findings of the Board can be summarized as follows:

(1) Alcoholism is accepted as a handicap under the *Ontario Human Rights Code*.
(2) In accommodating an employee's problems, an employer must use the least intrusive means possible.
(3) Provisions of the company policy that provide for pre-employment drug testing, and random alcohol and drug testing, are unlawful.
(4) For cause, post-incident drug and alcohol testing, with certification to a safety-sensitive position, and post-reinstatement (follow-up) drug testing may be permissible, but only if the company can establish that the testing is necessary as one facet of a larger process of assessment of drug and alcohol abuse.

[1]   *Entrop v. Imperial Oil Ltd.* (1995), 24 C.C.E.L. (2d) 87 (Ont. Bd. of Inquiry).

§9.61.6   In another important decision relating to drug testing, *Canadian Civil Liberties Assn. v. Toronto Dominion Bank*,[1] the Canadian Human Rights Tribunal held that a policy of mandatory drug testing for new and returning employees did not constitute discrimination on the basis of disability. The policy provided, amongst other things, that all applicants for employment, as a condition of employment, were required to submit to a drug-screening test. In the event of a positive result, further testing was required together with counselling and/or treatment. If a third test was positive, or if the employee refused such a test, then the employee's employment would be terminated. The Tribunal held that there was nothing in the *Canadian Human Rights Act* to prohibit such a requirement. When employment was terminated, the termination was based on a breach of a condition of employment (prohibition on illegal drug use) rather than a perceived disability (drug dependence).

[1]   (1994), 6 C.C.E.L. (2d) 196 (Can. Hum. Rts. Trib.); set aside (1996), 22 C.C.E.L. (2d) 229 (F.C.T.D.).

§9.61.7   In the alternative, the Canadian Human Rights Tribunal[1] held that, if the policy was discriminatory, the discrimination affected only a small class of employees, did not constitute direct discrimination, and the employer was making reasonable efforts to accommodate such employees by referring employees for assessment, paying for whatever treatment was necessary and maintaining the employees on the payroll. Finally, the Tribunal held that, in the event it was mistaken in its conclusion that any discrimination did not constitute direct discrimination, the Tribunal concluded that the bank's defence that the policy represented a "bona fide occupational requirement" would not have succeeded. No evidence was presented to support the conclusion that there might be a drug problem among the bank employees sufficient to justify such an intrusive policy.

[1]   (1994), 6 C.C.E.L. (2d) 196 (Can. Hum. Rts. Trib.); set aside (1996), 22 C.C.E.L. (2d) 229 (F.C.T.D.).

§9.61.8   The Federal Court of Canada, Trial Division, has issued its decision[1] in the appeal of this ruling. The court held that the policy was discriminatory against drug-dependent employees and that the bank had a duty of reasonable accommodation for these employees. The court further held that the bank had a duty of reasonable accommodation to the point of "undue hardship" for these drug-dependant employees. The court further held that the point of undue hardship is reached for the bank when the bank is faced with the continued presence of an employee who cannot be rehabilitated and who persists in criminal acquisition and use of illegal drugs. The court further set aside the decision of the Canadian Human Rights Tribunal and directed the Tribunal for a further hearing only on the issue of whether the policy is "rationally related to the performance of the job".

¹ *Canadian Civil Liberties Assn. v. Toronto Dominion Bank* (1996), 22 C.C.E.L. (2d) 229 (F.C.T.D.); setting aside (1994), 6 C.C.E.L. (2d) 196 (Can. Hum. Rts. Trib.).

§9.62 When the abuse of alcohol leads to misconduct on the part of an employee, there may be cause for dismissal. In *Dupré Quarries Ltd. v. Dupré*,¹ the employee had, on several occasions, been unable to perform his functions due to his state of drunkenness and had signed company cheques in blank. This was found to be cause for dismissal.

¹ [1934] S.C.R. 528.

§9.63 The revelation of character which may result from an intoxicated employee's conduct may also justify summary dismissal. Such was the case in *Bell v. General Motors of Canada*,¹ where the drunken plaintiff assaulted a secretary from his department by punching and kicking her. The employer terminated the employee for cause, even though the alleged misconduct had taken place off company premises, on the basis that it affected company morale. Assaulting a fellow employee, even off company property and outside work hours, was inconsistent with the duties of a supervisor and the obligation of respect owed by one employee to another.

¹ (1989), 27 C.C.E.L. 110 (Ont. H.C.J.). However, it is the revelation of character laid bare by the assault, rather than the assault itself, which will justify dismissal. Where employee misconduct, such as an assault, does not reveal such character, dismissal may not be warranted. See *Yeomans v. Simon Fraser University* (1996), 20 C.C.E.L. (2d) 224 (B.C.S.C.).

§9.64 Courts in recent cases have stated that the effect of intoxication on the job depends on the extent of the drunkenness and the prejudice caused to the employer's business.¹ Conversely, it is conceivable that, in some types of employment, a certain amount of drinking is contemplated and at least two Canadian courts have taken account of that fact. In *Hardie v. Trans-Canada Resources Ltd.*,² the Alberta Court of Appeal adopted the following from the reasons for judgment at trial:

> It is my considered opinion that we have a situation here where salespeople in this organization are encouraged to engage in convivial pursuits, namely drink-

ing with the clients, and that they cannot now be heard to complain that the result of this gives them cause for termination.[3]

The court arrived at the same conclusion in *Commission des normes du travail v. Pavage Jérômien Inc.*[4]

[1] *Marystown Shipyard Ltd. v. Rose* (1985), 6 C.C.E.L. 220 (Nfld. C.A.); *Anstey v. Canadian National Ry. Co.* (1980), 27 Nfld. & P.E.I.R. 95 (Nfld. C.A.).
[2] (1976), 2 A.R. 289 (C.A.).
[3] (1976), 2 A.R. 289 (C.A.) at 294. See also *Pelletier v. Caisse Populaire Lasalle Sudbury Ltd.* (1984), 5 C.C.E.L. 1 (Ont. H.C.J.), vard 56 O.R. (2d) 784 (C.A.).
[4] D.T.E. 83T-735 (Que. Prov. Ct.). See also *Côté v. Cie Nationale de Forage et Sondage Inc.*, J.E. 84-1046 (Que. S.C.).

§9.65 Some consideration will also be given to mitigating factors and the employment history of the employee. In *Robinson v. Canadian Acceptance Corp.*,[1] an employee, having given ten years of generally satisfactory service, suffered a personal and emotional crisis which interfered seriously with his work. After several warnings, the employer dismissed him without notice. The court found that the executive had been wrongfully dismissed:

> . . . the plaintiff began to experience difficulties. He became emotionally involved in an extramarital affair, with which he was unable to cope. As a result, he sought refuge, firstly, in excessive drinking and, finally, in emotional collapse. . . .
>
> During this period immediately before the plaintiff's dismissal, which was short compared to his 10 years of service with the company, there is no evidence that he wilfully intended to disobey the dictates of his superiors or to neglect his work. . . . *The plaintiff was going through the type of experience which many executives encounter some time during their business career, and for which many companies make allowance through their personnel policies. There cannot be many executives who work under years of constant pressure who do not at some time go through a period of emotional upset, during which they cease to function as efficiently as they would at normal times.*[2]

[1] (1973), 43 D.L.R. (3d) 301 (N.S.S.C.), affd 47 D.L.R. (3d) 417 (C.A.).
[2] (1973), 43 D.L.R. (3d) 301 (N.S.S.C.) at 309, affd 47 D.L.R. (3d) 417 (C.A.) (emphasis added).

§9.66 However, where alcoholism is the source of serious deterioration in job performance and where, although warned, the executive is unable or unwilling to help himself or herself, there may be grounds for dismissal without notice. For example, in *Visentin v. Shell Canada Ltd.*,[1] the plaintiff was employed by the defendant and after two years was promoted to the position of field operator. Three years later the quality of the plaintiff's work began to decline because of his financial and marital problems and his alcoholism. The plaintiff was warned several times that if his performance did not improve, disciplinary action would be taken. He enrolled for counselling in the defendant's employee assistance program on several occasions but always failed to follow up on his treatment and did not stop drinking. The employer dismissed the plaintiff without notice. The court upheld the dismissal. Although none of the incidents cited by the defendant was an example of gross incompetence, their cumulative effect was a source of concern to the defendant. It was the frequency of the errors, not their individual gravity, that caused concern and ultimately rendered the plaintiff unfit for employment.

[1] (1989), 29 C.C.E.L. 65 (Alta. Q.B.).

§9.67 A further consideration in any termination of an employee for reasons related to substance abuse are certain human rights statutes. In fact, under the *Canadian Human Rights Act*,[1] "disability" is defined to include a "previous or existing dependence on alcohol". Thus, the employer's efforts to accommodate the employee's "disability" will be considered by various human rights commissions and tribunals in substantiating a termination which is based in whole or in part on the employee's improper use of alcohol. For example, in *Niles v. Canadian National Ry. Co.*,[2] a Canadian Human Rights Tribunal found that Mr. Niles was discriminated against when he was terminated because of alcohol dependency. Mr. Niles had been suspended because of absenteeism resulting from an increasing dependence on alcohol. CN informed him that he would not be reinstated until CN was totally convinced that he was able to resume his duties. Seven months later Mr. Niles was fired because CN did not believe that he had made the necessary efforts to rehabilitate himself from his alcohol dependency. The tribunal found that CN had discriminated against Mr. Niles on the basis of a disability, which was contrary to the *Canadian Human Rights Act*.

[1] R.S.C. 1985, c. H-6, s. 25.
[2] (1991), 14 C.H.R.R. D/327 (Can. H.R.T.).

§9.68 The tribunal then considered the application of section 15 of the Act, where it is stated that it is not a discriminatory practice to dismiss an employee based on a *bona fide* occupational requirement:

> The Tribunal can certainly recognize that there may exist numerous situations where an employee's dependence, or perhaps even use, of alcohol or drugs could constitute a serious employment offence and provide ample basis for dismissal.[1]

In the end, the tribunal found that, while CN's policy on drinking problems and alcoholism was a fair recognition of the legitimate interests of both the employer and employee, and quite properly provided a level of accommodation for the affected employee, CN had failed to comply with its terms and to accommodate the complainant in accordance with that policy.

[1]   *Niles v. Canadian National Ry. Co.* (1991), 14 C.H.R.R. D/327 (Can. H.R.T.), at D/336, para. 43.

3. Competence

§9.69   The employee's obligation to execute the work implies that he or she must have the necessary competence and appropriate qualities to do so. The failure to execute the work because of lack of competence is cause for dismissal.[1]

[1]   *Allcroft v. Adams* (1907), 38 S.C.R. 365; *Denhoff v. B & L Lumber Ltd.* (1987), 53 Alta. L.R. (2d) 300 (Q.B.).

§9.70   How exactly can we define competence and how much competence is required of an employee?

> *A contract of employment usually embodies obligations of means.* Competence refers to the ability of the employee to use the means necessary to fulfil the objects of the contract, *i.e.* render the services required by the employer. Incompetence is difficult to appreciate, as it entails a subjective assessment, depending on circumstances. An imperfection in the form of a mistake does not, *per se*, constitute incompetence authorizing dismissal without notice. It is a question of degree, extent, content and effect. Incompetence is the implicit refusal or the incapacity to use the reasonable means of achievement that any other average employee would use in similar circumstances. Non-performance will derive from gross and continued indifference, disregard for instructions and carelessness, tantamount to a wilful rupture of the contractual relationship or the impossibility to execute an essential obligation of the contract.[1]

[1]   *Barth v. B & Z Consultants Inc.*, [1989] R.J.Q. 2837 (Que. S.C.), at 2841 (emphasis added).

§9.71   To define what constitutes competence requires that the parties examine the specific employment contract. Pre-employment representations made by the employee regarding his or her qualifications may be relevant considerations, as well as the importance of these representations in the formation of the employment contract. In fact, if these representations were the actual cause of the contract, the issue of frustration may even arise. However, what constitutes cause is generally less clear-cut in the case of an executive.[1]

[1]   *Werle v. SaskEnergy Inc.* (1992), 103 Sask. R. 241 (Q.B.) (the court held that the ex-

ecutive's misrepresentations as to his qualifications constituted cause for dismissal). See also *Warren v. Super Drug Markets Ltd.* (1965), 53 W.W.R. 25 (Sask. Q.B.), at 34.

§9.72 How much competence is required of an executive? Is competence measured by efforts or results? Must he or she achieve certain standards of productivity? The difficulty arises particularly in cases where, for example, an executive is hired to turn a company around. What if the economic context prevents the company and the executive from reaching their objectives? Is there cause for dismissal? Is there an additional level of competence required of an executive as opposed to a lower-level employee? Although these issues have not been fully discussed by the courts, in one case,[1] for example, the Chairman of the Board of Directors for a group of financial institutions and manager of one of the operations was lawfully dismissed when his handling of loans was shown to be a grossly negligent administration of public funds. It was also proved that three of the operations he was responsible for showed substantial losses.[2]

[1] *Ligue des Caisses d'Économie du Québec v. King*, J.E. 83-61 (Que. S.C.).
[2] See also *Webster v. Grand Trunk Ry. Co. of Canada* (1857), 1 L.C.J. 223 (S.C.). With respect to imprudence, see *Ruel v. Banque Provinciale du Canada*, [1971] C.A. 343 (Que.).

§9.72.1 In *Gravel v. Fernand Gravel Assurances Inc.*,[1] the Court held that if the employer expects certain *results* to be obtained, he must make such an expectation clear to the executive.

[1] D.T.E. 93T-1243 (Que. S.C.) (on appeal).

§9.73 In the context of a wrongful dismissal claim pursuant to labour standards legislation, at least one arbitrator has held that:

> *Even though there may not be specific criteria to evaluate the competence of an executive, case law has established that he must not be evaluated in the same way as a regular employee. Even though he may not necessarily be required to show exceptional competence, the employer is entitled to expect that he be more productive and that he provide more results than the other employees.*[1]

[1] *Services techniques informatiques S.T.I. Inc. v. Tessier*, D.T.E. 91T-304 (Que. T.A.), at 21 of the award (translation) (emphasis added). A recent amendment to the Quebec *Labour Standards Act*, R.S.Q., c. N-1.1, s. 3(6) [en. 1990, c. 73, s. 3] excludes senior management from its application.

§9.74 However, mere dissatisfaction with an executive's performance is not sufficient reason for dismissal.[1] The employer must show real misconduct or incompetence on a balance of probabilities.[2] In these cases it is incumbent upon the employer to clearly communicate the objective standard of performance and to warn the executive to improve substandard performance.[3]

[1] *Côté v. Cie Nationale de Forage et Sondage Inc.*, J.E. 84-1046 (Que. S.C.).

[2] *English v. NBI Canada Inc.* (1989), 24 C.C.E.L. 21 (Alta. Q.B.); *Chalifour v. Hallmark Automotive Centres Ltd.*, [1976] R.D.T. 586 (Que. Prov. Ct.); *Jolicoeur v. Lithographie Montréal Ltée*, [1982] C.S. 230 (Que. S.C.), confirmed on appeal, unreported, April 15, 1987, C.A.M. 500-09-000314-823; *Desrochers v. Centre des Langues Feuilles d'érables Ltée*, J.E. 80-635 (Que. S.C.), appeal abandoned Aug. 25, 1981, C.A.M. 500-09-000892-802.

[3] *Erlund v. Quality Communication Products Ltd.* (1972), 29 D.L.R. (3d) 476 (Man. Q.B.); *Ferguson v. Allstate Ins. Co. of Canada* (1991), 35 C.C.E.L. 257 (Ont. Ct. (Gen. Div.)); *Strickland v. Tricom Associates (1979) Ltd.* (1982), 38 Nfld. & P.E.I.R. 451 (Nfld. S.C.); *Bridgewater v. Leon's Mfg. Co.* (1984), 6 C.C.E.L. 55 (Sask. Q.B.); *Babcock v. C & R Weickert Enterprises Ltd.* (1993), 50 C.C.E.L. 1 (N.S.C.A.).

§9.75   Negligence in the execution of one's functions, lack of personal discipline, and output inferior to that agreed upon by the employee are elements capable of becoming legitimate reasons for dismissing an employee.[1] The difficulty lies in establishing the objective standard of performance. To evaluate competence or to set standards of performance, an employer may establish sales objectives, production quotas or goals. Once these standards are established by the company, known by the employee and adhered to by the company as a whole, an employee's ability to execute the work and fulfil the objectives of the job is much easier to evaluate. An employee who cannot attain the required volume of sales or production output may be dismissed unless he or she is able to prove that those standards have never been adhered to or enforced.[2]

[1] *Ross v. Willards Chocolates Ltd.*, [1927] 2 D.L.R. 461 (Man. K.B.); *French v. Morton* (1909), 14 O.W.R. 243 (H.C.J.).

[2] *Gignac v. Radio Futura Ltée*, D.T.E. 86T-205 (Que. S.C.).

§9.76   In *Matheson v. Matheson International Trucks Ltd.*,[1] the court summed up the challenge facing the employer: "It is not enough for the employer to dismiss for what he honestly believes to be just cause; the true test is whether just cause existed". Consequently, if incompetence is alleged, the employer must prove that the employee's performance fell below an objective standard. It is clearly beneficial for the employer to respond to substandard performance early by giving warnings and communicating the consequences of continued substandard performance. This eases the burden of proving, on a balance of probabilities, that the employee's performance did not meet this objective standard.

[1] (1984), 4 C.C.E.L. 271 (Ont. H.C.J.), at 275.

§9.77 An employer is entitled to expect that an employee's quality of work will not deteriorate with time. In fact, as the employee gains experience, failure to improve may justify dismissal.[1] The employer's failure to warn the employee that his or her performance is unsatisfactory and to advise him or her of what must be proved may invalidate an otherwise justified dismissal. In fact, the employer's failure to comment on minor incidents may amount to condonation of the employee's conduct on which the employer will not then be able to rely.[2] In terminating an employee for cause, a company must also examine whether its own actions created the employee's difficulties.[3]

[1] *Martel v. Dozois*, [1960] C.S. 344 (Que. S.C.).
[2] *McIlveen v. British Columbia* (1988), 24 C.C.E.L. 197 (B.C.S.C.); *Champagne v. Club de Golf Lévis Inc.*, D.T.E. 87T-548 (Que. Prov. Ct.); *Bourasse v. C.S.R. de Chauveau*, D.T.E. 87T-107 (Que. Prov. Ct.); *Marcotte v. Assomption Cie Mutuelle d'Assurance-Vie*, [1981] C.S. 1102 (Que. S.C.); *Brunelle v. Ballets Jazz de Montréal Inc.*, D.T.E. 88T-619 (Que. S.C.).
[3] *Casey v. General Inc.* (1988), 24 C.C.E.L. 142 (Nfld. S.C.).

§9.78 In *Larose v. T. Eaton Co.*,[1] the plaintiff had been employed by the defendant for 17 years. As a function of employment, the plaintiff was subject to a number of performance reviews concerning attendance, appearance, attitude, productivity, etc. These performance reviews indicated that the plaintiff's rating with respect to overall performance, with one exception, was never above satisfactory. The plaintiff was given written warnings indicating, among other things, that future unsatisfactory work would constitute sufficient grounds for termination. Finally, the plaintiff was dismissed with 8 weeks' notice. The court found in favour of the defendant, noting that after 17 years of service, an employee should not be dismissed without a warning or following a brief and unreasonable warning. Conversely, the court went on to say that an employee with 17 years' service is without protection under the law if, after sufficient warnings and a reasonable opportunity to improve his service, he fails to meet reasonable performance requirements which are within his demonstrated ability:

> On the other hand, an employee who has muddled along for 17 years without having had his potential seriously tested has no valid complaint if, after being given a reasonable opportunity, his failure to measure up to reasonable requirements which are within his demonstrated ability results in his dismissal.[2]

[1] (1980), 3 C.C.E.L. 51 (Ont. Co. Ct.).
[2] (1980), 3 C.C.E.L. 51 (Ont. Co. Ct.), at 56.

§9.79 Negligence in the execution of one's functions, lack of personal discipline, output inferior to that agreed upon and that the employee is capable of have been held to be legitimate reasons for dismissing an employee.[1]

> [1] *Martel v. Dozois*, [1960] C.S. 344 (Que. S.C.); *Lavoie v. Squibb Canada Inc.*, D.T.E. 88T-267 (Que. C.A.), leave to appeal to S.C.C. refused Oct. 6, 1988; *R. v. Arthurs, ex parte Port Arthur Shipbuilding Company*, [1969] S.C.R. 85.

§9.80 Giving bonuses, gifts or additional vacation days are common methods used by employers to motivate and reward their employees' competence or productivity. An employer may have difficulty dismissing an employee for reasons of incompetence or lack of productivity when the latter has recently or consistently received awards or some other form of recognition by the company[1] or has been consistently praised in company evaluations or references.[2]

> [1] *Lemyre v. J.B. Williams (Canada)*, D.T.E. 84T-752 (Que. S.C.); *Arnold v. Univers Pontiac-Buick Ltée*, D.T.E. 85T-478 (Que. Prov. Ct.); *Faule v. Sun Life du Canada*, J.E. 84-363 (Que. S.C.).
> [2] *Laperrière v. Transports Kingsway Ltée*, D.T.E. 88T-617 (Que. S.C.).

§9.81 Of particular interest in Quebec is article 2087 of the Civil Code of Quebec which stipulates that in executing the employment contract:

> The employee is bound not only to carry on his work with prudence and diligence, but also to act faithfully and honestly and not to use any confidential information he may obtain in carrying on or in the course of his work. [. . .]

This definition of the employee's obligations would seem to indicate that the duty to execute the work goes beyond merely doing the work and requires prudence and diligence in carrying out the work. This raises the question as to whether the prudence and diligence required is a positive obligation or merely an obligation not to be negligent. It is suggested that this is a positive obligation to act in a way as to actively avoid any risk of damage to the employer's reputation, workplace or otherwise.

CHAPTER 10

LOYALTY

A. INTRODUCTION

§10.1 The duty of loyalty goes to the heart of the executive's employ-ment relationship.[1] Courts have consistently held that the intensity of this obligation increases in direct proportion to the degree of responsi-bility assumed by the employee in the organizational hierarchy.[2] Thus, although every employee owes a duty of loyalty (which, in Quebec, is implied from article 1434 of the Civil Code of Quebec and also flows from the employment contract itself),[3] courts have frequently held that the privileged rapport which executives have with their employer re-sults in a stricter test of what constitutes loyal conduct both during and after employment.

---

[1] Insofar as the obligations of directors and senior officers are concerned, the Supreme Court of Canada has held that the fiduciary obligation at common law translates in the civil law into terms of good faith and loyalty of the employee to the employer. See, e.g., *Bank of Montreal v. Kuet Leong Ng*, [1989] 2 S.C.R. 429 at 443.

[2] *Valcourt v. Maison L'Intervalle*, D.T.E. 95T-322 (Que. S.C.); *Ref-Com Commercial Inc. v. Holcomb*, D.T.E. 91T-989 (Que. S.C.); *Bank of Montreal v. Kuet Leong Ng*, [1989] 2 S.C.R. 429; *P. Brunet Assur. Inc. v. Mancuso*, unreported, Feb. 17, 1988, C.S.M. 500-05-008530-873 (Gonthier J.); *Montour Ltée v. Jolicoeur*, [1988] R.J.Q. 1323 (S.C.); *National Financial Brokerage Center Inc. v. Investors Syndicate Ltd.* (1986), 9 C.P.R. (3d) 497 (Que. C.A.); *Piché, Charron & associés v. Perron*, J.E. 84-756 (Que. S.C.); *A.P.G. Analyse, Programmation et Gestion Canada Inc. v. Tremblay*, D.T.E. 89T-1 (Que. S.C.); *Johnson & Higgins, Willis Faber Ltée v. Picard*, unreported, Nov. 6, 1987, C.S.Q. 200-05-002075-872 (Doiron J.), vard [1988] R.J.Q. 235 (C.A.).

[3] C.C.Q., art. 2088. *Guillemette v. Simpsons-Sears Ltd.*, D.T.E. 85T-901 (Que. S.C.); *Positron Inc. v. Desroches*, [1988] R.J.Q. 1636 (S.C.); appealed and settled out of court, unreported, Sept. 16, 1991, C.A.M. 500-09-000620-880.

---

§10.2 The obligation of loyalty is broad and its particulars depend on the specific employment relationship. In essence, the executive's duty to be loyal means that he or she must at all times act faithfully, hon-estly and in such a way that his or her conduct does not reflect poorly on or contrary to the employer's interests. It also means that the execu-tive may not place himself or herself in conflict with the employer's in-terests during the term of employment and, in certain circumstances, even after the employment relationship has ended.

§10.3   This chapter will examine the scope and intensity of the executive's obligation to be loyal. Can an employer intervene to control an executive's conduct if it is not illegal but it is immoral? What are the limits to the executive's right to compete with his prior employer after termination of employment in the absence of a restrictive covenant?

§10.4   Since, as a result of their privileged role in the organization, executives frequently have access to a wide array of confidential information belonging to their employer, we will also explore the various types of information normally accessible to executives in an organization, the extent to which executives can lawfully make use of such information following termination of employment, and the protection afforded by law to such information as well as to other forms of intellectual property.

§10.4.1   The analysis of this obligation is more important than ever since the coming into force of article 2088 of the Civil Code of Quebec which stipulates that:

> The employee is bound not only to carry on his work with prudence and diligence, *but also to act faithfully and honestly* and not to use any confidential information he may obtain in carrying on or in the course of his work. [. . .] [emphasis added]

Although the courts have not yet analyzed the meaning and extent of the duty to act faithfully and honestly, the authors are of the view that one may refer to existing case law which has imposed an implicit duty of loyalty on the employee. In fact, it may be appropriate to refer to the French version of the Civil Code of Quebec which speaks of the employee's obligation to act *"avec loyauté"* (with loyalty).[1]

---

[1]   See *Service d'entretien Serca v. Choquette*, D.T.E. 96T-699 (Que. S.C.), which was rendered on the basis of article 2088 of the Civil Code of Quebec.

B.   DISHONESTY

§10.5   An employer is entitled to expect and demand that executives employed in the organization will act with the utmost good faith, honesty and integrity. It is a patent breach of the obligation of loyalty, and of the employment contract itself, when an executive fails to serve his or her employer faithfully. Dishonest conduct consists of any behaviour that is untrustworthy.

§10.6   Dishonesty related to employment may exist even before the executive's contract is formed. Offences of this nature usually take the form of misrepresention at the time of hiring or omitting to reveal characteristics of the executive which may influence the employer's decision to retain his or her services. Strictly speaking, this issue concerns the actual formation of the contract itself.[1]

¹ See Chapter 3, "The Formation of the Employment Contract".

§10.7 In view of the fact that high standards are applied to executives and reflect their greater responsibilities to the organization, any dishonest conduct in the course of employment, such as theft, fraud, taking bribes or kickbacks and embezzling company funds, likely constitutes a clear breach of the employment agreement and ought to be cause for termination.[1] Even a simple thing such as subsequently inserting the wrong date on a previously signed but undated letter has been found to be dishonest to the point of constituting a breach of the duty of loyalty.[2]

¹ For a more complete list of examples of dishonest conduct in Canadian jurisprudence as it pertains to the employment relationship, see Ellen E. Mole, *Wrongful Dismissal Practice Manual* (Toronto: Butterworths, looseleaf), §§4.120 *et seq.*
² *Lake Ontario Portland Cement Co. v. Groner*, [1961] S.C.R. 553.

§10.8 In the case of *Nadeau v. Produits Industriels Canado Ltée*,[1] a corporate secretary's conduct was characterized as "unforgivable" by the court when it was determined that the secretary had falsely informed the company's bank manager that a resolution had been passed requiring two signatures on cheques, his intention being only to maliciously prevent the president of the company (albeit his own father) from continuing to draw cheques on the company account.

¹ D.T.E. 87T-755 (Que. S.C.).

§10.9 Any untruthful conduct, in general, will be cause for dismissal if the conduct is such as to undermine, or seriously impair, the essential trust and confidence the employer is entitled to expect in the circumstances of the particular relationship.[1] However, where the untruth was not premeditated, but simply "blurted out" in answer to a question about a branch manager's personal life, such conduct did not warrant dismissal without notice.[2]

¹ *Ennis v. Canadian Imperial Bank of Commerce* (1986), 13 C.C.E.L. 25 (B.C.S.C.).
² *Black v. FCA International Ltd.* (1989), 27 C.C.E.L. 277 (B.C.S.C.). However, see *Richardson v. Davis Wire Industries Ltd.* (1997), 28 C.C.E.L. (2d) 101 (B.C.S.C.).

§10.10 Misuse or misappropriation of an employer's property may also be cause for dismissal.[1] Where an employee is dismissed for theft but is acquitted on a charge of theft at a criminal trial, the acquittal is irrelevant for the purposes of any wrongful dismissal trial. The employer need only establish that the theft occurred on a balance of probabilities, not beyond a reasonable doubt, and one isolated theft is cause for dismissal.[2] Temporarily "borrowing" funds from the employer is strictly prohibited unless this practice has been approved by internal policy or unless such conduct has previously been condoned by the employer. Even where the employee has since reimbursed the money which was wrongfully withdrawn from his or her employer's account, dismissal may be judged appropriate.[3]

[1]   *Valcourt v. Maison L'Intervalle*, D.T.E. 95T-322 (Que. S.C.); *Seulnick v. Services Ltd.*, unreported, May 17, 1976, C.P.M. 500-02-029774. See also *Byl v. West Wind Aviation Inc.* (1987), 4 A.C.W.S. (3d) 368 (Sask. Q.B.).

[2]   *Kong v. Oshawa Group Limited* (1993), 46 C.C.E.L. 181 (Ont. Ct. (Gen. Div.)).

[3]   *Sauvé v. Banque Laurentienne du Canada*, [1994] R.J.Q. 1679 (Que. S.C.) in appeal; *Guillemette v. Simpsons-Sears Ltd.*, D.T.E. 85T-901 (Que. S.C.); *Boulanger v. Canadian Seafarers' Welfare Plan*, [1970] C.A. 941 (Que.).

§10.11   Executives cannot, however, be dismissed without notice on a mere suspicion.[1] In one case, the Quebec Superior Court awarded an extra sum of $10,000 as compensation for moral damages to a commercial loans manager because he had been dismissed on the basis of what turned out to be false accusations of corruption and dishonesty.[2] The court held that such allegations made it more difficult for the plaintiff to obtain a position with another bank. More recently, the Newfoundland Court of Appeal in *Trask v. Terra Nova Motors Ltd.*[3] affirmed a trial judgment awarding additional damages because the defendant, after dismissing the plaintiff, had informed other prospective employers that the plaintiff had committed theft. The trial judge found that the allegation of theft was false, and, in awarding damages in lieu of notice, doubled the notice period that otherwise would have been appropriate, from nine months to 18 months, to reflect the plaintiff's diminished prospects at finding other employment. In addition, the Court of Appeal affirmed the trial judge's award of $4,000 for mental suffering. Moreover, behaviour previously condoned by the employer cannot later be used as a reason for dismissal.[4]

[1]   *Côté v. Placements M & A Brown Inc.*, D.T.E. 87T-956 (Que. Prov. Ct.); *Ratel v. Tarter*, [1952] C.S. 87 (Que.).

[2]   *Delorme v. Banque Royale du Canada* (1987), 19 C.C.E.L. 298 (Que. S.C.).

[3]   (1995), 9 C.C.E.L. (2d) 157 (Nfld. C.A.). Also on damages for mental suffering, see *Kempling v. Hearthstone Manor Corp.* (1996), 137 D.L.R. (4th) 12 (Alta. C.A.).

[4]   *Dupuis v. Datagram Inc.*, D.T.E. 87T-936 (Que. S.C.).

§10.11.1 The principle that employer misconduct, such as a false allegation of theft, may lead to an increase in the period of reasonable notice to reflect diminished employment prospects resulting from such misconduct has not been accepted by all courts. The courts in British Columbia, for example, have held that such employer misconduct is not a proper consideration in the determination of what constitutes reasonable notice. The British Columbia Supreme Court, for example, has held:[1]

> Counsel for [the plaintiff] asked that I lengthen the period of notice because of the difficulty of finding new employment caused by the unfounded "thief" accusation. In support of this submission, he cited *Rahemtulla v. Vanfed Credit Union*, [1984] 3 W.W.R. 296 (B.C.S.C.). I find, however, that *Rahemtulla* has been overruled on this point by the British Columbia Court of Appeal in *Lojstrup v. British Columbia Buildings Corp.*, [1989] 4 W.W.R. 605. Macdonald J.A. for the court said at p. 610:
>
> > As I have stated earlier, the consequence of an unfounded allegation of theft against a dismissed employee is that he or she will have greatly increased difficulties in finding employment. But the employer's conduct cannot be taken into account under the rubric of "the availability of similar employment, having regard to the experience, training and qualification of the servant". The employee's reputation has been damaged but not his or her qualifications. And I do not think there is any other basis upon which the employer's misconduct can be taken into account with respect to period of notice. The test for implication of a term must be met. The parties, "had their attention been drawn to the matter at the time of making the contract", would not have "manifestly agreed" that if in terminating the employer misconducted himself in some way amounting to a tort or at least a non-actionable wrong, the period of notice would be lengthened.
>
> The Manitoba Court of Appeal has taken a conflicting point of view in *Wallace v. United Grain Growers Ltd.* (1995), 95 C.L.L.C. 210-046, 356 at 141, 365-66 where the court took into account the manner of dismissal and the likely adverse impact it would have upon the plaintiff's employment prospects as a factor in determining the required notice period.

Of course, a false allegation of employee misconduct may expose the employer to liability for aggravated or punitive damages or damages for mental distress.[2]

---

[1] *Larsen v. A & B Sound Ltd.* (1996), 18 C.C.E.L. (2d) 237 (B.C.S.C.) at 241-42.

[2] See, *e.g.*, *Dixon v. British Columbia Transit* (1995), 13 C.C.E.L. (2d) 272 (B.C.S.C.), where the employer was held to have committed the torts of deceit and defamation, and was found liable, *inter alia*, for aggravated damages in the amount of $50,000 and punitive damages in the amount of $75,000.

§10.12 It should be noted, however, that criminal conduct during employment, if not related to employment, does not prevent an employee from claiming and obtaining benefits and other employment-related advantages otherwise due to the employee.[1]

[1] *Drolet v. Ville de Chibougamau*, D.T.E. 90T-905 (Ct. of Que.).

C. DAMAGE TO EMPLOYER'S INTERESTS AND REPUTATION

§10.13 The executive's duty to act in good faith vis-à-vis the employer implies that he or she will not, either deliberately or negligently, behave in a manner that will harm the employer's business affairs and reputation. Indeed, a company's reputation is often reflected in the behaviour of its representatives, namely, its executives. This means that an executive's conduct can, to a certain extent, be scrutinized even if it is off-duty and unrelated to work.

§10.14 In one case,[1] for example, a part-time lecturer was hired by the University of Western Ontario's School of Business Administration. Although the terms and conditions of employment were arranged earlier in the year, he was scheduled to start work the following September. Prior to the actual start of school, the university administrators discovered that the individual had been charged with participating in a fraudulent scheme involving insurance claims and terminated his employment, following which the employee sued the university for wrongful dismissal. In deciding that the dean of the school had no other alternative than to dismiss the plaintiff, the Ontario County Court held that the reputation of the university would be at stake if the fraudulent conduct of the plaintiff became public knowledge.

[1] *Pliniussen v. University of Western Ontario* (1983), 2 C.C.E.L. 1 (Ont. Co. Ct.).

§10.15 Although most executives understand the impact that their off-duty behaviour may have on the employer's organization, some still believe that their behaviour away from the job is simply of no concern to the employer. Courts have tended to strike a balance between the employee's fundamental right to privacy[1] and the employer's right to protect its legitimate business interests. Hence, courts will allow a certain level of intrusion by the employer if the off-duty conduct of the executive clearly affects the employer's reputation, the executive's job performance or other employees.[2] However, this intrusion must not be abusive. In the early '80s, a California court ordered the IBM corporation to pay one of its sales executives $200,000 in punitive damages in addition to $100,000 for other damages because of the shoddy manner in which she had been dismissed; the executive had been given one hour to clear out her desk and leave the premises after 12 years with the company simply because it was discovered that she had been carrying on an off-hours romance with an executive of one of IBM's main competitors.[3]

[1] See Quebec *Charter of Human Rights and Freedoms*, R.S.Q., c. C-12, s. 5: "Every person has a right to respect for his private life". See also Richard M. Howe, " 'Minding Your Business': Employer Liability for Invasion of Privacy", *The Labour Lawyer*, Vol. 7 (1991), p. 315.

[2] *Reilly v. Steelcase Canada Ltd.* (1979), 26 O.R. (2d) 725 (H.C.J.); *Chamberlain v. Maisonneuve Broadcasting Co.*, D.T.E. 87T-669 (Que. S.C.); *Dooley v. C.N. Weber Ltd.* (1994), 3 C.C.E.L. (2d) 95 (Ont. Ct. (Gen. Div.)), affd (1990), 80 O.A.C. 234 (C.A.), application for leave to appeal dismissed [1995] S.C.C.A. No. 264; *Yeomans v. Simon Fraser University* (1996), 20 C.C.E.L. (2d) 224 (B.C.S.C.).

[3] Brian A. Grossman, *The Executive Firing Line* (Toronto: Carswell/Methuen, 1982), p. 42.

§10.16 Misrepresenting the employer's financial status can critically injure the employer's business if creditors get wind of the information and believe it to be true without further verification.[1]

[1] Surprisingly, the court in one case excused the employee because of the absence of malice: *MacLellan v. Liné Canada Machine-Outil Ltée*, D.T.E. 83T-540 (Que. S.C.).

§10.17 Implication in off-duty criminal activity may not, for the ordinary employee, be sufficient to constitute a breach of the obligation of loyalty. However, the status of "executive" renders such conduct much more objectionable because of the direct reflection it has on the employer. In the case of non-executive employees, off-duty criminal conduct which reflects on the employee's ability to do the work or the trust required in him or her will generally be cause for dismissal. In one case,[1] the court confirmed the dismissal of a transit bus driver who had pleaded guilty to the attempted sexual assault of a ten-year-old girl. The gravity of the offence was sufficient to lead the court to conclude that public trust in the employer would be irreparably damaged if the accused were permitted to continue in his employment. In another case,[2] a bank teller who had not in any way committed a disloyal act but was living with a convicted bank robber was found to be properly dismissed. Among other things, the type of business, the nature of her job and the image that the whole situation would convey to the public with respect to the employer's trustworthiness, were all important considerations in the decision.

[1] *Fraternité des chauffeurs d'autobus v. C.T.C.U.M.*, D.T.E. 86T-100 (Que. C.A.).

[2] *Canadian Imperial Bank of Commerce v. Boisvert* (1986), 13 C.C.E.L. 264 (F.C.A.).

§10.18 With respect to treatment of an executive's conduct which could be qualified as "immoral", much depends on the existing community standards of morality.[1] In the case of *Carrick v. Cooper Canada Ltd.*[2], for example, the vice-president of operations for the employer company told his wife that he was leaving on a business trip to Barbados for a week with other company executives. In reality, the vice-president was vacationing in Bermuda with a girlfriend. The matter became "sticky" when, while trying to reach the vice-president during his absence, his colleagues were informed by his wife that he was on business in Barbados with other executives of the company. The employer dismissed the vice-president, who then sued the company for wrongful dismissal. The Ontario High Court held in favour of the executive, stating that the moral aspect of his conduct, although it could be viewed in different ways by different people, did not, in a material way, directly or indirectly affect the operations and management of the company or its credibility.

[1]   See, *e.g.*, *Denham v. Patrick* (1910), 20 O.L.R. 347 (C.A.), where the court held that an employee was properly dismissed after confessing to having slept with several young women. However, see *Reilly v. Steelcase Canada Ltd.* (1979), 26 O.R. (2d) 725, in which Keith J. concluded that adultery by an employee with the wife of a fellow employee, the interest and reputation of the employer being unaffected, is not in modern times sufficient cause for dismissal.

[2]   (1983), 2 C.C.E.L. 87 (Ont. H.C.J.).

§10.19 However, the Ontario Supreme Court held in favour of a company that had dismissed an employee for having used its premises for sexual purposes, given the employee's high-profile position with the organization.[1]

[1]   *Manolson v. Cybermedix Ltd.* (1985), 5 C.P.C. (2d) 291 (Ont. S.C., Master).

§10.20 In another case, a court held that a sales representative was properly dismissed for having referred to a client of the employer in a racist fashion during the course of an off-duty conversation.[1]

[1]   *Chamberlain v. Maisonneuve Broadcasting Co.*, D.T.E. 87T-669 (Que. S.C.). In another context, see the case of *Fraser v. Commission des relations de travail*, [1985] 2 S.C.R. 455; (1985), 23 D.L.R. (4th) 122; (1985), 9 C.C.E.L. 233, where the Supreme Court of Canada reviewed the extent to which civil servants are permitted to criticize the government that employs them.

§10.21 Although each case is decided on its own facts, there are a variety of factors which will influence a court's decision in determining whether an act of dishonesty, illegality or immorality during employment, but not necessarily in the course of work, is a breach of the obligation of loyalty. In summary, we can say that the following factors have been considered in deciding whether an employee has breached his or her duty of loyalty by bringing his or her employer into disrepute:

(1) the type of business of the employer;
(2) the nature of the employee's activities;
(3) the extent to which the employee is publicly visible;
(4) the degree of responsibility of the employee for the wrongful act;
(5) whether the reproached conduct contravenes moral standards of the community; and
(6) the likelihood of adverse pecuniary impact on the employer.

One thing is certain: the standard the executive must meet is a rigorous one; conduct by the executive which reflects poorly on the employer generally amounts to a disloyal repudiation of the employment contract.

D. FIDUCIARY DUTY

1. General

§10.22 At common law, a fiduciary relationship is said to exist when one person is in a position of "trust" vis-à-vis another.[1] Since executives are normally charged with initiative and responsibility far greater than that of ordinary employees, they stand in a fiduciary relationship to their employer and, hence, are bound by a fiduciary duty to their employer and subject to fiduciary obligations.

[1] The courts have frequently struggled with the proper scope of the definition of fiduciary relationship, and a comprehensive definition has proven elusive. However, the following general proposition was accepted as correct by La Forest J. in the recent Supreme Court of Canada decision of *Hodgkinson v. Simms* (1994), 117 D.L.R. (4th) 161 at 168:

> a fiduciary relationship exists where one party agrees to act on behalf of, or in the best interests of another person and, as such, is in a position to affect the interests of that other person in a legal or practical sense. As such, fiduciary relationships are marked by vulnerability in that the fiduciary can abuse the power or discretion given him or her to the detriment of the beneficiary.

§10.23 In Quebec,[1] the concept of "fiduciary duty" has been the subject of much confusion. This is due largely to the fact that the law regarding "fiduciaries" originates from the common law of "trusts"[2] and, although the principles have been applied in Quebec, the way in which they have been incorporated into Quebec law has been awkward at best.

¹ For a general discussion of this subject from the Quebec law perspective, see
   François Guay, "Les obligations contractuelles des employés vis-à-vis leur ex-em-
   ployeur: La notion d'obligation fiduciaire existe-t-elle en droit québécois?" (1989),
   49 Rev. du Bar. 739; Glen Bowan, "Senior Managers of Quebec and their Fiduciary Obligations" (1990), 4 Nat. Lab. Rev. 62.
² Indeed, the Civil Code does not recognize the concept of a "trust" other than
   when it is created by gift or will: C.C.L.C., arts. 981a-981n.

§10.24 This does not mean that executives in Quebec have a lesser obligation towards their employer than their common law counterparts.
Rather, Quebec civil law and Canadian common law impose a virtually identical duty on executives acting on behalf of their employer
both during and after employment. However, each legal system pos-
sesses, even though it does not always use it, a different mechanism to
achieve this result. Although in the past, when Quebec judges have attempted to apply common law principles to problems arising in Quebec, this has resulted in what some have termed the "undue influence
of the common law on the civil law system".¹ With the coming into
force of article 2088 of the Civil Code of Quebec, this should no longer
cause a problem.

¹ James A. Smith, *Corporate Executives in Quebec* (Montreal: Centre d'Edition Juridique, 1978), pp. 118 *et seq.*

§10.25 Although historically, Quebec civil law defined the relationship between a business and the person who managed it as one of
"mandate"¹ which resulted in requiring the mandatary to apply, in the
execution of the mandate, the "reasonable skill and all the care of a
prudent administrator"², the new Civil Code now makes the obligation to act faithfully and honestly an explicit obligation of the employment contract. It is no longer necessary to rely on the law of mandate
to find such a duty.

¹ *Entreprises Rock Ltée v. Habitations C.J.C. Inc.*, [1986] R.J.Q. 2671 (S.C.). The Quebec
   courts, as early as 1891, treated senior officers and directors as mandataries of the
   company which employed them: *McDonald v. Rankin* (1890), 7 M.L.R. 44 (S.C.), relied on in *Bank of Montreal v. Kuet Leong Ng*, [1989] 2 S.C.R. 429.
² C.C.L.C., art. 1710.

§10.25.1 Although the concept of "loyalty" has most frequently been
the subject of discussion in Quebec, in *Kucey v. Gelfant*,¹ the British Columbia Supreme Court made it clear that such a duty is also an implied term of the employment contract at common law. In this case the
Court held that:

It seems clear that any contract for services, and particularly here between dental specialists, there is an implied term that the employee will "faithfully, honestly and diligently serve his employer"[2]

In rendering its decision, the Court relied on an earlier decision by the British Columbia Court of Appeal[3] which had held that:

> As my learned brother has referred to the implied term of the contract of employ-ment, however one puts it, it is a promise by the employee that he will faithfully, honestly and diligently serve his employer. If he commits a fundamental breach of that term the employer is entitled to say "I have no further obligations to per-form and that includes the obligation of giving you reasonable notice."

Hence, the court held that the employee who frequently criticized the skill and training of his employers to others was rightfully dismissed.

[1] (1993), 48 C.C.E.L. 121 (B.C.S.C.).
[2] (1993), 48 C.C.E.L. 121 (B.C.S.C.) at 125.
[3] *Durand v. Quaker Oats Co. of Canada* (1990), 45 B.C.L.R. (2d) 354 (C.A.).

§10.26 Whether the duty owed by an executive to his or her employer is called "fiduciary duty" or "greater duty of loyalty", the result throughout Canada is the same. It is a duty which imports a strict ethic in business and personal conduct for executives, the intensity of which lies on a continuum which varies depending upon the degree of con-trol or independent authority exercised by the executive in the course of his or her work. Quite often this is reflected in the level or position which the individual holds within the hierarchy of the employer's or-ganization. Prior to tracing the evolution of the "fiduciary duty" both in Quebec and in the common law provinces, a brief historical survey is in order.

2. The "Canaero" Decision

§10.27 In *Canadian Aero Service Ltd. v. O'Malley, Zarzycki, Wells, Terra Surveys Ltd.*,[1] the Supreme Court of Canada purported to clarify the re-sponsibility of fiduciaries with respect to corporate opportunities. Ca-nadian Aero Service Ltd. ("Canaero") was in the business of topographical mapping and geophysical exploration. The defendants O'Malley and Zarzycki developed long and fructuous careers with the company, ultimately holding the positions of President/Chief Execu-tive Officer and Executive Vice-President, respectively. Both defen-dants were very much involved on behalf of Canaero in a Government of Canada project for the topographical mapping and aerial photo-graphing of parts of Guyana. The defendants themselves had actively pursued the Guyana project on behalf of Canaero until July 25, 1966.

Roughly one month later, they incorporated their own company, and three days after that, they resigned from their positions at Canaero. They then made their own proposal to the Canadian government for the Guyana project and successfully obtained it. Canaero sued O'Malley and Zarzycki for breach of "fiduciary duty" and claimed the profits that had been made by the two defendants as a result of their theft of an opportunity which properly belonged to the company.

¹ [1974] S.C.R. 592.

§10.28 On behalf of the Supreme Court of Canada, Justice Bora Laskin stated that whether the defendants were directors of the company or not was of little importance since, as "top management", their duty to their employer was more exacting than that of a mere employee whose only duty, unless enlarged by contract, consists of respecting trade secrets and the confidentiality of customer lists. The duty of these senior officers was similar to that owed to a corporation by its directors. Justice Laskin added that "their positions as senior officers . . . charged them with initiatives and with responsibilities far removed from the obedient role of servants".¹

¹ [1974] S.C.R. 592, at 606.

§10.29 The Court went on to conclude that O'Malley and Zarzycki stood in a fiduciary relationship to Canaero, which "in its generality betokens loyalty, good faith and avoidance of a conflict of duty and self-interest".¹ In the Court's view, the fiduciary relationship goes at least as far as precluding a senior officer from obtaining for himself, either secretly or without the approval of the company, any property or business advantage belonging to the company or for which it had been negotiating; this is especially so where the senior officer is himself a participant in the negotiations on behalf of the company.

¹ [1974] S.C.R. 592, at 606.

§10.30 The Court clearly imposed a stricter application of the general standards of loyalty, good faith and avoidance of a conflict of duty and self-interest on directors and senior management of a company, stating that this was simply a

> . . . recognition of the degree of control which their positions give them in corporate operations, a control which rises above day-to-day accountability to owning shareholders and which comes under some scrutiny only at annual general or at special meetings. It is a necessary supplement, in the public interest, of statutory regulation and accountability which themselves are, at one and the same time, an

acknowledgment of the importance of the corporation in the life of the community and of the need to compel obedience by it and by its promoters, directors and managers to norms of exemplary behaviour.[1]

---

[1] [1974] S.C.R. 592, at 610.

§10.31 The Court went on to canvass old English law to confirm and conclude that a fiduciary's obligations preclude him or her from acting in breach thereof *even after* resignation; otherwise, it would be too easy for a person in a fiduciary position to avoid his or her responsibilities by simply resigning.[1] The Court ordered "the faithless fiduciaries to answer for their default according to their gain" by forcing O'Malley and Zarzycki to account for their profits.[2] Recent Canadian case law with respect to the "fiduciary duty" owed by executives, usually senior management, and more particularly as concerns the scope of acceptable conduct after employment vis-à-vis their former employers has evolved within this framework.

---

[1] [1974] S.C.R. 592, at 613-16.
[2] [1974] S.C.R. 592, at 622.

3. Who Owes a Fiduciary Duty?

§10.32 Canadian courts have tended to adopt a somewhat pejorative distinction between "mere employees" and "top management" or "senior managerial officers".[1] Since the latter are very much involved in managing the corporate affairs of the organization they are often seen as "fiduciaries"; the former are not.[2] As was pointed out by Mr. Justice Gonthier of the Superior Court of Quebec (as he then was), the jurisprudence has always maintained a clear distinction between, on the one hand, "senior management" of a corporation who are, for these purposes, treated much like directors and, on the other hand, "mere employees".[3]

---

[1] Although this distinction has been applied quite regularly in Quebec, the same cannot be said for common law jurisdictions. For a critique on how the jurisprudence subsequent to *Canaero* has unjustifiably supported the extension of the fiduciary obligations to a variety of non-fiduciary relationships, see Peter C. Wardle, "Post-Employment Competition — *Canaero* Revisited" (1990), 69 Can. Bar Rev. 233.
[2] *Koné Inc. v. Dugré*, J.E. 91-1392 (Que. S.C.).
[3] *P. Brunet Assur. Inc. v. Mancuso*, unreported, Feb. 17, 1988, C.S.M. 500-05-008530-873.

§10.33 Another judge has noted that "one must be careful not to 'stretch' the *ratio decidendi* [reasoning] of this [*Canaero*] decision beyond the factual framework within which it was rendered".[1] The learned judge added the following:

> It is essential to note that the *Canaero* decision did *not* extend the obligations of "mere employees", whose duty to their former employer (unless enlarged by contract) consists only of respect for trade secrets and for confidentiality of customer lists, whether or not such mere employees were key employees or long-time employees who may have enjoyed a close relationship with the "top management" or directors of their former employer.[2]

In that case, the court went on to hold that the defendant, who worked as a sales representative, was not a senior managerial officer and thus not in a position where he had a degree of control in the operation of the plaintiff corporation so that the "strict ethic" of the *Canaero* decision did not apply to him.

---

[1]   *Montour Ltée v. Jolicoeur*, [1988] R.J.Q. 1323 (Que. S.C.), at 1327.

[2]   *Montour Ltée v. Jolicoeur*, [1988] R.J.Q. 1323 (Que. S.C.), at 1328.

§10.34   In deciding who is a "mere employee", it should be noted that the title held by an individual within an organization, in and of itself, may be quite meaningless.[1] We must examine whether, *factually*, the individual in question exercises any degree of authority or control over the affairs of the company in order to determine whether fiduciary obligations will be imposed on him or her. Accordingly, the defendant in one case was not held to "strict ethic" conduct since his titles as president and director were only on paper, the defendant having no real authority to bind the company or make any decisions on its behalf.[2]

---

[1]   *National Financial Brokerage Center Inc. v. Investors Syndicate Ltd.* (1986), 9 C.P.R. (3d) 497 (Que. C.A.).

[2]   *Compagnie des Attractions de Montréal Ltée v. Van Godbout*, [1977] C.S. 365 (Que. S.C.); affd, unreported, March 26, 1980, C.A.M. 500-09-000646-778.

§10.35   The determining principle in this area is well stated by Spencer J. of the British Columbia Supreme Court who, in *57134 Manitoba Ltd. v. Palmer*[1] observed:

> I am of the opinion that the imposition of the sort of fiduciary duty found in *Can. Aero Services Ltd. v. O'Malley*, is not to be tested so much by what the defendant did *not* do with the former employer, as suggested by defence counsel before me, but rather what he did. Nominal titles are not determinative. The Court must examine the actual level of functions and responsibility held by the employee.[2]

In *Empire Stevedores (1973) Ltd. v. Sparringa*,[3] for instance, the court disregarded the employee's designation as Vice-President and found that, notwithstanding his nominal title, the employee exercised very little executive authority. Similarly, in *Tomenson Saunders Whitehead Ltd. v. Baird*,[4] an employee who held the title of Vice-President was found not to be a fiduciary employee on the basis of the actual level of functions and responsibilities that his employment entailed. In *Genesta Mfg. Ltd. v. Babey*,[5] an employee designated as a branch manager was held not to be top management since he possessed no autonomous decision-making authority and his actions were subject to approval by his superiors.

[1]   (1985), 8 C.C.E.L. 282 (B.C.S.C.), at 286.

[2]   At trial, Palmer was held to have breached his fiduciary duty to his former employer, and damages were awarded against both Palmer and a company controlled by Palmer. In addition, Palmer's new employer was also held liable for the plaintiff's damages sustained while Palmer was with the new employer under a theory of vicarious liability. On appeal, Esson J.A. for the court questioned whether Palmer had in fact been in a fiduciary relationship with his former employer but nevertheless affirmed the damage awards against the defendants on the basis of the general duty of good faith of any employee. See *57134 Manitoba Ltd. v. Palmer* (1989), 37 B.C.L.R. (2d) 50 (C.A.). See also *Investors Syndicate Ltd. v. Vandenberg* (1986), 10 C.C.E.L. 153 (Ont. H.C.J.); *Helbig v. Oxford Warehousing Ltd.* (1985), 9 C.C.E.L. 75 (Ont. C.A.), leave to appeal to S.C.C. refused 52 O.R. (2d) 754*n*.

[3]   (1978), 19 O.R. (2d) 610 (H.C.J.); leave to appeal to C.A. refused *loc. cit.*

[4]   (1980), 7 C.C.E.L. 176 (Ont. H.C.J.).

[5]   (1984), 2 C.P.R. (3d) 32 (Ont. H.C.J.).

§10.36   As we have previously mentioned, some courts of the common law jurisdictions appear to have moved from this rigorous interpretation of which employees fall under the rubric of top management. The tendency in a number of more recent decisions has been to hold much lower functionaries than those in *Sparringa* and *Genesta* to be fiduciaries.

That the distinction has been relaxed in Ontario may be seen, for example, in cases such as *Sure-Grip Fasteners Ltd. v. Allgrade Bolt & Chain Inc.*[1] and *Canadian Industrial Distributors Inc. v. Dargue.*[2]

In *Dargue*, for example, MacPherson J. at p. 64 summarized the law on fiduciaries in the employment context as follows:

> The law does not lightly impose the mantle of fiduciary on an employee. This is so because the duties that a person who is found to be a fiduciary must perform are exacting duties indeed.
> The leading Canadian case dealing with when an employee becomes a fiduciary is *Canadian Aero Service Ltd. v. O'Malley*, [1974] S.C.R. 592 ("Canaero"), which stands for the proposition that *some* employees in *some* circumstances will be deemed to be fiduciaries.

MacPherson J. then set out at p. 65 a passage from *Canaero* in which Laskin J. described the nature of fiduciary duty in the employment context and some of the factors to be considered in determining whether it exists. Interestingly, in the passage quoted, Laskin J. mostly referred to "the general standards of loyalty, good faith and avoidance of a conflict of duty and self-interest" to which a *director or senior officer* must adhere.

MacPherson J. then cited at p. 65, as a useful summary of the law, the following passage from the *Sure-Grip Fasteners* case:

> It is clear that the generic relationship between employer and employee does not per se give rise to fiduciary responsibilities. . . .
> In general, the relationship becomes elevated to the fiduciary level when the employer reposes trust and confidence in the employee on a continual basis, relying upon the employee in reaching business decisions. It is the trust and reliance transferred by the employer which gives the employee the power, and in some cases, the discretion, to make business decisions, on the employer's behalf.

MacPherson J. concluded that the defendant, formerly the manager of a territory accounting for 40% of the national sales of the company, in view of his position, experience and authority, and the trust and reliance reposed in him by his employer, was a fiduciary.

Given the very onerous obligations that a fiduciary must accept, many have criticized this development as placing obligations which are simply too onerous on a number of employees who should properly be classified as mere employees.

Another reason for perhaps questioning the expansion of the class of employees subject to fiduciary obligations and thus reaffirming the distinction between "directors and senior officers" and "mere employees" is the Supreme Court of Canada's decision in *LAC Minerals Ltd. v. International Corona Resources Ltd.*[3]

The *LAC Minerals* decision dealt with a relationship that has not traditionally been recognized as giving rise to fiduciary duties: a contractual relationship between two sophisticated commercial entities.

In *LAC Minerals*, a junior mining company, Corona, owned mining rights on certain lands on which it was carrying out exploratory drilling. *Lac Minerals* approached Corona with a view to a possible joint development of the mine. Corona revealed the results of its drilling to *LAC Minerals*, which results indicated that certain adjacent property contained sizeable deposits, and *LAC Minerals* proceeded to acquire and develop the mine for its own account.

Both the trial judge and the Court of Appeal held that there had been a breach of fiduciary duty. However, the Supreme Court of Canada in a 3:2 split found there to have been no fiduciary relationship. Instead, the Court found that *LAC Minerals* had breached a duty not to misuse confidential information and dismissed *LAC Minerals'* appeal.

[1] (1993), 45 C.C.E.L. 276 (Ont. Ct. (Gen. Div.)).

[2] (1994), 7 C.C.E.L. (2d) 60 (Ont. Ct. (Gen. Div.)).

[3] [1989] 2 S.C.R. 574.

§10.36.1 According to Hallett J.A. for the Nova Scotia Court of Appeal in the recent case of *Trophy Foods Inc. v. Scott*,[1] the Supreme Court in *LAC Minerals*, "in overturning a judgment of the Ontario Court of Appeal is suggesting to the courts to put out a sea anchor and not find that a fiduciary relationship exists every time a party has imposed a trust or confidence in dealing with another". It should be noted that, under the new Civil Code of Quebec, *all* employees are bound to act faithfully and honestly. No distinction is made between top management and "mere" employees with respect to the existence of the obligation. However, it is submitted that courts may distinguish (as they have in the past) between the *extent* of the obligation of each employee depending upon his or her level in the hierarchy of the undertaking. This next section examines the jurisprudential mechanisms adopted by the common law courts to extend the fiduciary duty to lower-level employees.

[1] (1995), 60 C.P.R. (3d) 231 (N.S.C.A.), at p. 240.

E. TESTS FOR DETERMINING WHO OWES A FIDUCIARY DUTY

1. Key Personnel Test

§10.37 The substantive test of top management set out in *Canaero* has been greatly broadened by the adoption in some court decisions of the "key personnel" test. This outcome stems from the fact that key employees can exist at all levels of the corporation, and not just at the top management level. An application of this looser test can be seen in *Demarco Agencies Ltd. v. Merlo*,[1] where the court held that a salesman was a key person in the company. The court based its conclusion on the fact that (1) the employee had some incidental contact with the firm's corporate clients, and (2) his selling territory and accounts amounted to over 50% of the company's business.

[1] (1984), 48 Nfld. & P.E.I.R. 227 (Nfld. Dist. Ct.), vard 62 Nfld. & P.E.I.R. 248 (C.A.). See also *57134 Manitoba Ltd. v. Palmer* (1985), 8 C.C.E.L. 282 (B.C.S.C.) and *Extermination P.E. Tremblay et Lemieux Inc. v. Extermination Agrolac Inc.*, D.T.E. 95T-1104 (Que. S.C.) (motion for appeal rejected 200-09-000431-954).

2. Key Person in a Department Test

§10.38 A variation of the "key personnel" test, and one which makes further inroads on the rationale of *Canaero*, was adopted in *Hudson's*

Bay Co. v. McClocklin.[1] The Manitoba Court of Queen's Bench held that the head of the Bay Optical department was a fiduciary on the basis that he was a key employee within his department although not within the store as a whole. It was held that by directly soliciting the department's hearing aid clientele he had breached his fiduciary duty to the Bay. The court acknowledged that its decision represented a departure from the top management test. Jewers J. relied on a number of factors in holding the employee a fiduciary:

> ... the key position occupied by the defendant in the hearing aid department; his long and close personal association with the plaintiff's hearing aid customers; his personal knowledge of them and access to their personal records and needs; the fact that he resigned and was not discharged; and the fact that so soon after leaving he commenced the solicitation complained of.[2]

[1]   [1986] 5 W.W.R. 29 (Man. Q.B.); see also *Genesis Canada Inc. v. Hill* (1994), 56 C.P.R. (3d) 419 (Ont. Gen. Div.).
[2]   [1986] 5 W.W.R. 29 (Man. Q.B.), at 34.

3. Employer's Vulnerability as a Factor

§10.39 Several decisions have suggested that the vulnerability of the employer is a factor to be applied. In *EJ Personnel Services Inc. v. Quality Personnel Inc.*,[1] the judge noted:

> Where an employer by the nature of its business is particularly vulnerable to loss by the soliciting of that employer's clients, an employee stands in a fiduciary relationship to the employer and owes a duty to the employer to not solicit those clients after leaving the business.

[1]   (1985), 6 C.P.R. (3d) 173 (Ont. H.C.J.), at 176. See also *Edgar T. Alberts Ltd. v. Mountjoy* (1977), 79 D.L.R. (3d) 108 (Ont. H.C.J.); *Quantum Management Services Ltd. v. Hann* (1989), 25 C.P.R. (3d) 218 (Ont. H.C.J.), affd (1992), 11 O.R. (3d) 639*n* (Ont. C.A.). See further the Supreme Court of Canada's consideration of vulnerability as a factor in fiduciary relationships in *Hodgkinson v. Simms*, discussed at §10.55.1.

§10.40 A contrary decision is *Tomenson Saunders Whitehead Ltd. v. Baird*,[1] where the court declined to base the finding of a fiduciary duty on the employer's vulnerability. To do so, the court noted, would be to make the employee captive to his or her employer. The court held that the employer must bear the risk inherent in its choice of business.

[1]   (1980), 7 C.C.E.L. 176 (Ont. H.C.J.).

§10.40.1 In *Anderson, Smyth & Kelly Customs Brokers Ltd. v. World Wide Customs Brokers Ltd.*[1] Moshansky J. acknowledged the competing lines of cases and held that a key consideration was therefore the manner in which former clients were notified of the employee's departure.

Moshansky J. then quoted with approval at p. 70 the following statement of the law from *Metropolitan Commercial Carpet Ltd. v. Donovan:*[2]

> . . . it is clear that an employee, even of senior management status, is permitted to enter into competition with a former employer in the absence of any contractual stipulation to the contrary and in the course of pursuing his new business would be entitled to take all of the usual steps to advertise his new venture.... . On the other side, if an employee leaves his employment with the purpose of securing a prospective contract which his former employer was pursuing and affirmatively seeking that contract would undoubtedly constitute a gesture of bad faith.

Moshansky J. in the *World Wide Customs Brokers* case concluded that the clients had followed the defendant by virtue of their personal relationship with him and thus the defendant's actions, in contacting clients whom he had personally served as a customs broker while with his former employer and asking them whether they wished for him to continue as their broker, did not constitute a breach of the defendant's obligations to his former employer.

[1]   (1993), 1 C.C.E.L. (2d) 57 (Alta. Q.B.), revd 20 C.C.E.L. (2d) 1 (C.A.). See §10.40.2.
[2]   (1989), 42 B.L.R. 306 (N.S.T.D.).

§10.40.2   The decision of Moshansky J. in the *World Wide Customs Brokers* case was, however, overturned on appeal,[1] and the departing employee in that case, Kelly, was held to have breached his fiduciary duty to his former employer. The fiduciary relationship was held to have arisen not only through Kelly's former status as a director and senior officer of his former employer but also through his status as a key employee. Kelly had been the manager of the appellant company's Edmonton office, "a position of trust with attendant power to affect the economic interests of the Appellant. As will be seen, Kelly's position as a key employee was sufficient in itself to give rise to fiduciary obligations".[2]

Central to the Court of Appeal's decision was the issue of employer vulnerability.

> Here, the evidence clearly indicates that in his capacity as an employee of the Appellant, Kelly was a fiduciary. He was the manager of the Appellant's Edmonton office and one of three employees at that location. Kelly was responsible for the day-to-day operation of the Edmonton office from 1985 until his departure on August 25, 1989. The other employees were clerical staff. As the Appellant's key employee in Edmonton, Kelly was in a position to unilaterally exercise his delegated authority to affect the Appellant's legal and economic interests. To put it another way, in his capacity as a director and officer and manager of the Appellant's Edmonton office, Kelly possessed the kind of authority typically found in a relation-

ship of dependency or vulnerability. It was the kind of relationship in which equity will intervene to protect the dependant or vulnerable party by acting on the
conscience of the fiduciary.[3]

The Court of Appeal held that, in the circumstances, direct solicitation
of the former employer's clients would place the departing employee
in breach of his fiduciary obligations, and that Kelly "should have kept
his distance from these clients long enough to allow the Appellant to
minimize its vulnerability to solicitation. He should not have actively
directed the Appellant's clients to his new affiliation".[4] Notwithstanding the absence of any written non-competition or non-solicitation
agreement, the court held that Kelly should have refrained from such
solicitation for a period of one year after his departure.

[1]   *Anderson, Smyth & Kelly Customs Brokers Ltd. v. World Wide Customs Brokers Ltd.*
       (1996), 20 C.C.E.L. (2d) 1 (Alta. C.A.).
[2]   *Anderson, Smyth & Kelly Customs Brokers Ltd. v. World Wide Customs Brokers Ltd.*
       (1996), 20 C.C.E.L. (2d) 1 (Alta. C.A.) at 7.
[3]   *Anderson, Smyth & Kelly Customs Brokers Ltd. v. World Wide Customs Brokers Ltd.*
       (1996), 20 C.C.E.L. (2d) 1 (Alta. C.A.) at 8.
[4]   *Anderson, Smyth & Kelly Customs Brokers Ltd. v. World Wide Customs Brokers Ltd.*
       (1996), 20 C.C.E.L. (2d) 1 (Alta. C.A.) at 13.

§10.41   Vulnerability has also been considered a factor outside of the
employer-employee relationship. In *Lac Minerals Ltd. v. International
Corona Resources Ltd.*,[1] the Supreme Court of Canada accepted that the
vulnerability of the party seeking to assert that the other was subject to
a fiduciary duty is a factor to be considered. In that case, the central issue to be decided was whether two corporations with an arm's-length
relationship could be subject to a fiduciary relationship. Although on
the facts of the case there was disagreement in the Court on this point
(the majority of the Court holding that a fiduciary relationship existed), there was no disagreement with the sentiment expressed by La
Forest J. in his dissenting judgment that

> . . . when determining if new classes of relationship should be taken to give rise to
> fiduciary obligations then the vulnerability of the class of beneficiaries of the obli-
> gation is a relevant consideration.[2]

[1]   [1989] 2 S.C.R. 574.
[2]   [1989] 2 S.C.R. 574, at 662.

§10.42   Thus, it might be argued that *Lac Minerals* supports the view
expressed in *EJ Personnel*. However, *Lac Minerals* may be distinguished
on the basis that the Court used this as a factor to determine if new
classes of relationship (there, an arm's-length commercial relationship)
should be subject to a fiduciary duty. This is not the same issue that

was dealt with in *EJ Personnel*. It is already clearly established that the employer-employee relationship is one in which fiduciary duties can exist.

§10.43 The corresponding effect of looking to the employer's vulnerability when applied to larger commercial operations is that middle management might not be termed fiduciaries. *Reed Stenhouse Ltd. v. Foster*[1] provides a useful recent illustration of this perspective. In this case, the employee in question was a middle manager of one of three major sales and service units. The Alberta Court of Queen's Bench held that given the employee's position in the company hierarchy — in which he operated basically as a salesman — he did not owe a fiduciary duty. The fact that he had the title of Vice-President was not borne out by his actual duties and hence his job description was given no weight in the decision.

[1] (1989), 27 C.P.R. (3d) 419 (Alta. Q.B.).

§10.44 This case illustrates both the functional approach adopted to the characterization of an employee as top management or senior management and an implicit rejection of the "key to the department" test. Under this theory, seen in *Hudson's Bay Co. v. McClocklin*,[1] the employee might have been found to be a fiduciary in light of his position as department head.

[1] [1986] 5 W.W.R. 29 (Man. Q.B.). See, *supra*, §10.38.

4. Length of Employment as a Factor

§10.45 Common sense suggests that a certain period of time must pass before the employee acquires the necessary element of employer trust that is at the heart of a fiduciary relationship. This was seen in *Gordon Trailer Sales & Rentals Ltd. v. Lenton*,[1] where the court held that 12 days of employment was too short for trust to be reposed in the employee.

[1] (1989), 25 C.P.R. (3d) 1 (Ont. S.C.).

5. Lower-Level Employees: Fiduciary Breach by Association

§10.46 A lower-level employee may be transformed into a fiduciary by virtue of his or her association with a senior officer. A case illustrating this proposition is *Edgar T. Alberts Ltd. v. Mountjoy*.[1] In this case, a senior employee, Mountjoy, left to set up a business competing with his former employer. A number of subordinate employees also left, of their own volition, and went to work for Mountjoy. Chief Justice Estey of the Ontario High Court (as he then was) held that the subordinate employees were subject to a fiduciary duty by virtue of their association with Mountjoy.

[1] (1977), 79 D.L.R. (3d) 108 (Ont. H.C.J.). See also *Sure-Grip Fasteners Ltd. v. Allgrade Bolt Chain Inc.* (1993), 45 C.C.E.L. 276 (Ont. Ct. (Gen. Div.)); *Canadian Industrial v. Dargue* (1994), 7 C.C.E.L. 60 (Ont. Ct. (Gen. Div.)).

6. Contract

§10.47 Fiduciary obligations can also be created by contract. For example, in *Burgess v. Industrial Frictions & Supply Co.*,[1] the defendant, the major shareholder of the company, agreed to sell his shares back to the company. In the agreement setting this out, the defendant was bound to conduct himself as a fiduciary of the company.

[1] (1987), 12 B.C.L.R. (2d) 85 (C.A.).

§10.48 It is important to note that these contractually created obligations exist alongside the pre-existing implied fiduciary obligations. Thus, if a contract setting out the scope of an employee's fiduciary duties is rendered invalid, by virtue of legal disability or otherwise, the employee will still be subject to fiduciary obligations if he or she falls within the common law definition of a fiduciary. This is the clear rubric of *Wallace Welding Supplies Ltd. v. Wallace.*[1] There, an employee was held in breach of a fiduciary duty notwithstanding that his non-competition agreement with his employer was rendered invalid by reason of imprecision in drafting. The Ontario High Court stated:

> . . . the duty [to act fairly] may co-exist with a non-competition covenant. The latter is an agreed restraint on the right of a former employee to compete. The former is a common law duty that is owed to a competitor who is a former employer. They are independent of each other.[2]

[1] (1986), 11 C.C.E.L. 108 (Ont. H.C.J.). See also *Empire Stevedores (1973) Ltd. v. Sparringa* (1978), 19 O.R. (2d) 610 (H.C.J.), leave to appeal to C.A. refused *loc. cit.*
[2] *Wallace Welding* (1986), 11 C.C.E.L. 108 (Ont. H.C.J.) at 114.

§10.49 The fiduciary duty may even extend beyond the contractual duty. This occurred in *Wallace Welding Supplies Ltd. v. Wallace,*[1] where it was held that the duty not to compete extended beyond the terms of a negotiated non-competition agreement.

[1] (1986), 11 C.C.E.L. 108 (Ont. H.C.J.).

F. THE POSITION OF INDEPENDENT CONTRACTORS

§10.50 Independent contractors, like employees, may also be subject to a fiduciary duty. Thus, a person cannot seek to rely on a contract which states that he or she is an independent contractor to relieve that person of his or her fiduciary responsibilities.[1]

---

[1] *Professional Court Reporters v. Carter* (1993), 46 C.C.E.L. 281 (Ont. Ct. (Gen. Div.)).

§10.51 In *Investors Syndicate Ltd. v. Versatile Investments Inc.*,[1] the Ontario Court of Appeal held that a sales representative was an "employee" notwithstanding the language of his contract which designated him as an independent contractor. The court held that the relevant question was whether the sales representative was an agent. The court defined the relationship of agency as follows:

> Agency is the relationship which exists between two persons, one of whom expressly or impliedly consents that the other should represent him or act on his behalf, and the other of whom similarly consents to represent the former or so to act.[2]

It was held that the independent contractor fell within this definition and was therefore a fiduciary.

---

[1] (1983), 73 C.P.R. (2d) 107 (Ont. C.A.).
[2] (1983), 73 C.P.R. (2d) 107 (Ont. C.A.), at 112, citing *Bowstead on Agency*, 14th ed. (London: Sweet & Maxwell, 1976), p. 1.

§10.52 The same result was reached in *Tri-Associates Ins. Agency Ltd. v. Douglas*,[1] where it had been contended that the "employee" was in fact a sub-agent and therefore not subject to the imposition of fiduciary responsibilities. The court rejected this argument, stating:

> Whether he was technically an employee or not does not appear to me to be important. The contract [the alleged sub-agent] entered into with Tri-Associates and the fact that he was the commercial representative and in charge of that department placed him in a fiduciary relationship with Tri-Associates.[2]

---

[1] (1985), 15 C.C.L.I. 61 (Ont. H.C.J.).
[2] (1985), 15 C.C.L.I. 61 (Ont. H.C.J.), at 65.

§10.53 Accordingly, it is not open to a suitably-minded executive employee, who would otherwise be classified as "top management" or "senior management", to avoid the fiduciary responsibilities that go with that classification by simply declaring that he or she is not an employee. This view is consistent with the functional standard adopted for the imposition of fiduciary duties, which focuses not on the individual's designation within the company but on his or her actual role in corporate affairs.

G.   FIDUCIARY OBLIGATIONS DURING EMPLOYMENT

§10.54   Since the *Canaero* decision, courts have had occasion to decide the scope and intensity of this "fiduciary duty". Certain Quebec judges have applied the principles emanating from the *Canaero* case outright, referring to a "fiduciary duty" in Quebec, without bothering to explain how they incorporate the common law of trusts into Quebec law. Others, wishing to avoid reliance on the "foreign" concept of "fiduciaries", have nonetheless recognized and applied the same duties, but on the basis of both the general obligation of loyalty and the general principle that the more senior the position and responsibilities held in the hierarchy of an organization, the more intense will be the obligation of loyalty attached thereto. The justification for the analysis is no longer relevant in Quebec as the new Civil Code now provides that all employees are bound to act faithfully and honestly.[1]

---

[1]   C.C.Q., art. 2088.

1.   Conflict of Interest

§10.55   Fiduciaries are precluded from placing themselves in a conflict of interest position or from carrying out any activity which could potentially place them in a conflict of interest situation. Thus, any executive who deals on his own account without his employer's knowledge while purporting to act in the employer's interest breaches his or her duty of loyalty. The same would apply to an individual who diverts company business to himself or herself. Also, it need not be proven that the employer has in fact suffered damage by the conflict created by the executive; the mere potential for conflict and damage is sufficient to rupture the bond of trust which must exist between an executive and his or her employer. The most common illustration of this type of breach is secret commissions or "kickbacks". In fact, any executive who fraudulently accepts a reward, advantage or benefit of any kind in exchange for doing or forbearing to do any act relating to his or her employer's business is guilty of a criminal offence.[1]

---

[1]   *Criminal Code*, R.S.C. 1985, c. C-46, s. 426 [am. R.S.C. 1985, c. 27 (1st Supp.), s. 56].

§10.55.1   The failure of a person in a fiduciary position to disclose a material conflict of interest was at the heart of the Supreme Court's recent examination of fiduciary duties in *Hodgkinson v. Simms*.[1] The facts of the case briefly were as follows: Hodgkinson, a stock broker, approached Simms, a partner in the accounting firm Simms & Waldman, for tax-related advice. Simms advised investment in certain residential tax shelters (Multiple Unit Residential Buildings or "MURBs"), but failed to disclose an arrangement under which he received fees from the developers of MURBs in question when clients of Simms invested in their projects. Hodgkinson invested in the MURBs recommended by Simms and suffered significant losses due to a general decline in the real estate market. Upon subsequently learning of the arrangement, Hodgkinson sued Simms and at trial Simms was held liable for the full amount of the loss as damages for breach of contract and breach of fiduciary duty. The British Columbia Court of Appeal set aside the finding of breach of fiduciary duty and reduced the damages to the amounts paid by the developers to the respondent, on the basis that the losses suffered by the appellant were caused by the collapse of the real estate market rather than the failure to disclose. Hodgkinson appealed.

[1] (1994), 117 D.L.R. (4th) 161 (S.C.C.).

§10.55.2 As with its earlier decision in *LAC Minerals*,[1] the Supreme Court was almost evenly divided as to whether the relationship in question was a fiduciary one. La Forest J., L'Heureux-Dubé and Gonthier JJ. concurring and Iacobucci J. concurring in the result, concluded that there was a fiduciary relationship; Sopinka and McLachlin JJ., Major J. concurring, concluded there was not.

[1] [1989] 2 S.C.R. 574.

§10.55.3 La Forest J. held that, in view of the professional relationship of the parties requiring trust, confidence and independence, and the plaintiff's reliance on the defendant's advice, the relationship was a fiduciary one. La Forest J. concluded that the appellant was entitled to recover his losses in full, since he would not have made the investments had the arrangement been disclosed.

§10.55.4 Sopinka and McLachlin JJ. in dissent took a somewhat different view of the facts and concluded that since the decision to invest lay entirely with the appellant, the relationship was not a fiduciary one. In their view, the respondent's liability should be restricted to damages flowing from breach of contract, and would have maintained the damage award ordered by the Court of Appeal.

§10.55.5   A central issue on which the Court split was the question of the need to show vulnerability to establish the existence of a fiduciary relationship. La Forest J. at p. 192 cautioned against overemphasizing vulnerability in assessing whether a fiduciary relationship existed. Rather, in the context of independent professional advisory relationships at least, the relationship becomes a fiduciary one when the client reposes trust and confidence in the adviser and relies on the advice given. Where this is the case, La Forest J. suggested that a fiduciary duty will arise "without regard to the level of sophistication of the client, or the client's ultimate discretion to accept or reject the . . . advice" (at p. 183).

§10.55.6   Sopinka and McLachlin JJ. in dissent, however, viewed vulnerability as an all but indispensable feature of the fiduciary relationship (at p. 219):

> . . . the concepts of trust and loyalty . . . lie at the heart of the fiduciary obligation. The word "trust" connotes a state of complete reliance, of putting oneself or one's affairs in the power of the other. The correlative duty of loyalty arises from this level of trust and the complete reliance which it evidences. Where a party retains the power and ability to make his or her own decisions, the other person may be under a duty of care not to misrepresent the true state of affairs or face liability in tort or negligence. But he or she is not under a duty of loyalty. That higher duty arises only when the person has unilateral power over the other person's affairs placing the latter at the mercy of the former's discretion.

§10.55.7   The implications of this decision in the executive employment context remain unclear. The majority's finding of a fiduciary relationship in that case arguably represents a continued willingness on the part of the courts to enlarge upon the traditional categories of fiduciary relationships. If so, then the erosion of the distinction between "mere employees" and "directors and senior officers", discussed at §10.36, looks set to continue. Moreover, the shift in focus away from vulnerability as a factor may be an invitation to the courts to revisit the line of cases, discussed at §10.39 *et seq.*, which have suggested the employer's vulnerability is a factor in determining whether a particular employee is a fiduciary.

§10.56   In *Métropolitaine Compagnie d'assurance-vie v. Industrielle Compagnie d'assurance-vie*,[1] "disloyal" acts were said to have been committed by insurance agents who sold policies of one company while working for another and by agents who, having taken early retirement and while collecting a retirement allowance from one company, were encouraging the substitution of policies with another company.[2]

---

[1]   Unreported, July 25, 1983, C.S.M. 500-05-007920-828.

[2] Unreported, July 25, 1983, C.S.M. 500-05-007920-828, at 16.

§10.57 It is well established that carrying out a competing business while still employed is cause for dismissal.[1] It may, however, be cause for much more than that in certain instances. In *Terres Noires Sherrington Ltée v. Barrachina*,[2] for example, the sudden departure of a general manager to join his ex-employer's suppliers at a time calculated to cause the most damage to his ex-employer, after plotting and participating in a competing business for several months while employed, was enough to justify a condemnation of $240,000 representing the employer's lost revenue resulting from the executive's actions.

[1] *Sturton v. PPG Industries Canada Ltd.*, J.E. 84-560 (Que. S.C.); *Mison v. The Bank of Nova Scotia* (1994), 6 C.C.E.L. (2d) 159 (Ont. Ct. (Gen. Div.)).
[2] D.T.E. 88T-623 (Que. S.C.).

§10.57.1 An executive must reveal potential conflict of interest situations and failure to reveal a potential conflict may amount to cause for termination.[1]

[1] *Griffin v. Société de récupération, d'exploitation et de développement forestiers du Quebec (Rexfor)*, D.T.E. 93T-1181 (Que. S.C.).

§10.58 As early as 1881, the Quebec Court of Appeal held that a manager was properly dismissed without notice or compensation in lieu thereof for having participated in a business that was in direct competition to his employer's.[1] Another factor which may be important to consider is the fact that the new employer may also be held liable for breach. In one case,[2] the defendant employee, who was not an executive, never informed the employer at the time he accepted employment that he was already working for a competitor involved in the same line of business. In fact, the employer learned of his employee's competition only after the employment relationship ended. The court ordered the employee jointly with the competing company with which he was affiliated to pay damages to the employer on the basis that the employee had acted in bad faith by not informing the employer of the relationship that he had with a competitor.

[1] *MacDougall v. MacDougall* (1881), 11 R.L. 203.
[2] *Atlantipad Inc. v. Muratori*, D.T.E. 89T-2 (Que. S.C.).

§10.59 Similarly, a general manager was found to be in breach of his "fiduciary duty" towards his employer and of the "strict ethic" conduct which it commands when he personally made a profit that he could not have made otherwise than in the execution of his employment. The executive was ordered to account for such profits.[1]

[1]   *Brimarierre Inc. v. Laplante*, D.T.E. 84T-37 (Que. S.C.).

§10.60   In another case,[1] a computer consultant with Hydro Quebec was dismissed for having clearly placed himself in a position of conflict of interest. The employee's work required that he determine technical specifications for computer products which would be useful to Hydro Quebec in its preparation of calls for tender. The employer was able to prove that the employee had used the influence he derived from his position to convince Hydro suppliers to contract with his own computer company, in exchange for which he would make it easy for such suppliers to obtain orders from Hydro Quebec. The conventional arbitrator named to resolve the dispute decided that it did not matter whether the employee knew that he was in a conflict of interest position. The conduct of the employee in the circumstances was a manifest breach of his duty of loyalty, especially where, as in this case, and as is the case for executives, the employer placed his "entire trust" in the employee.

[1]   *Hydro-Québec v. Lesage*, D.T.E. 91T-1323 (Que. T.A.).

§10.61   Similarly, the general manager of a bus terminal was found by an arbitration tribunal to have been properly dismissed because of the conflict of interest position in which he had placed himself.[1] While working for his employer, the manager was also acting as financial consultant for a competing transportation company. He later became part owner of the competitor, while maintaining anonymity. When the manager was questioned about his interest in the competing business, he denied all participation. It was later discovered that the manager had received commissions from the competitor for issuing subcontracts to it on behalf of his employer. The conflict of interest situation having been clearly proven, the executive was dismissed for "acts of blatant disloyalty".

[1]   *Veilleux v. Clarke Transport Routier Ltée*, D.T.E. 89T-981 (Que. T.A.).

§10.62   In another case,[1] the secretary general of a college was also found to have been properly dismissed because he had tried to convince the concessions person of the college to support his efforts to topple the general manager with whom the secretary general did not get along. The tribunal found that the secretary general demonstrated disloyal conduct by trying to take advantage of his privileged position for personal gain.

¹ *Mekhael v. Collège Charles-Lemoyne de Longueuil Inc.*, D.T.E. 88T-483 (Que. T.A.).

§10.63 More recently, the case of *Datamark Inc. v. Groleau*¹ was decided along the same lines. The court held that it was disloyal for a salesman on commission to participate in a parallel and competing business to that of his employer. An interlocutory injunction was granted to prevent the salesman from participating in the competing business. Similarly, an insurance agent was found to have been properly dismissed for having sold an insurance policy emanating from an insurance company other than his employer's.²

¹ D.T.E. 90T-146 (Que. S.C.), amended on appeal on another matter D.T.E. 90T-474 (C.A.).
² *Mahoney v. Alliance, Cie mutuelle d'assurance-vie*, D.T.E. 91T-431 (Que. S.C.).

§10.64 The conduct discussed above is to be distinguished from that of the executive who, during employment, plans or simply agrees that he or she will compete with his or her employer *after* termination of employment. What is tolerated by the courts as "planning" is the administrative set-up of a potential competitor (such as incorporating a company or securing a business partner). Such conduct is permissible in itself, and does not breach any duty owed by the executive. Nor is the executive under any obligation to inform the employer of his or her intention to engage in competition after employment.¹

¹ *Grynwald v. Playfair Knitting Mills Inc.*, [1959] C.S. 200 (Que. S.C.); *Chagnon v. Magasin Coop de St-Ferdinand d'Halifax*, D.T.E. 87T-334 (Que. S.C.).

§10.65 However, using confidential information while employed to plot a sudden departure will not be tolerated. In this regard, a general manager was found to have acted disloyally when he conspired with other employees to compile useful customer information while employed.¹ This information was to be used for direct competition upon their collective resignation from the company. In this case, an interlocutory injunction was granted restricting the right of the executive and the other employees to compete.

¹ *Typoform Inc. v. Gignac*, D.T.E. 88T-622 (Que. S.C.). See also *Frank White Enterprises Inc. v. 130541 Canada Inc.*, D.T.E. 95T-683 (Que. C.A.).

§10.66 It should be noted, however, that an employer can be prohibited from alleging a conflict of interest situation when he or she has been aware of the alleged activities for a long time and, through silence or other conduct, effectively condones the practice.[1]

[1] *Gagnon v. Thetford Transport Ltée*, D.T.E. 87T-935 (Que. S.C.); *Maheu, Noiseux & associés v. Ronéo Vickers Canada Ltd.*, D.T.E. 88T-588 (Que. C.A.); *Koné Inc. v. Dugré*, J.E. 91-1392 (Que. S.C.).

§10.67 Finally, in the absence of an "exclusivity of service" clause in the employment agreement, it has generally been held that an employee is free to hold several non-conflicting positions with several employers. Although the situation is uncommon for executives, it may happen that a manager acts in one capacity for his or her employer and in another capacity either for another employer or on his or her own behalf. It is incumbent on the executive to make sure that the employers are not competitors and that no other situation exists which gives rise to a conflict of interest. In *Villeneuve v. Soutien-Gorge Vogue Inc.*,[1] the court found that a salesman's termination for having sold certain products other than his employer's constituted wrongful dismissal since the products were not competitive in nature. However, in that case, the judge nonetheless commented that the employee's conduct was reprehensible because the side products were being sold during the employee's working hours.

[1] D.T.E. 86T-739 (Que. S.C.).

§10.68 One situation which bothers many employers is the case where a key employee is intimately involved with an employee of a competitor. Does this situation amount to conflict of interest? The courts appear to be of the view that only exceptional circumstances will amount to conflict of interest justifying cause for dismissal.

§10.69 In Quebec, the *Charter of Human Rights and Freedoms*[1] specifically prohibits any form of discrimination in employment on the basis of civil status. For example, it is only where the employer is clearly able to demonstrate with sufficient evidence that a conflict of interest situation exists that a dismissal of an employee will be justified as a result of his or her spouse being employed in a competing organization.[2] In fact, circumstances are rare where an employer may interfere with an employee's off-hours personal relationships as courts have generally been reluctant to interfere with the individual's fundamental right to privacy.[3]

[1] R.S.Q., c. C-12, ss. 10 [re-en. 1982, c. 61, s. 3] and 16.
[2] *Commission des droits de la personne du Québec v. Courtier Provincial en Alimentation (1971) Inc.* (1982), 3 C.H.R.R. D/1134 (Que. S.C.).

³ *Barabe v. F. Pilon Inc.*, D.T.E. 87T-132 (Que. S.C.). *Contra*: *Canadian Imperial Bank of Commerce v. Boivert* (1986), 13 C.C.E.L. 264 (F.C.A.); *Mormina v. Ville de St-Léonard*, D.T.E. 87T-757 (Que. S.C.).

2. Whistle-Blowing

§10.70 One area of growing concern to employers is that of employees who, while employed, publicly denounce the employer and/or the conduct of its representatives ("whistle-blowing"). We can expect to see this type of behaviour, for example, in cases where the employer's activities violate environmental standards or health and safety guidelines. Some examples in American jurisprudence include complaints about radioactive contamination in nuclear production facilities,[1] allegations of political impropriety,[2] and disclosure of overcharging on government contracts.[3] In a recent American case, an employee was awarded $7.5 million for denouncing his employer in accordance with a program designed to encourage whistle-blowers to come forward with allegations of wrongdoing.[4] The employer was found guilty of having systematically overcharged on government contracts.

[1] *English v. General Electric Co.*, 4 I.E.R. Cases 395 (4th Circ., 1989).
[2] *Patkus v. Sangamon-Cass Consortium*, 1 I.E.R. Cases 1716 (7th Circ., 1985).
[3] *Markus v. McDonnell Douglas Helicopter Co.*, 5 I.E.R. Cases 1271 (Cent. Dist. Cal., 1990).
[4] *The Gazette*, Montreal, July 15, 1992.

§10.71 There are few reported cases in Canada on whistle-blowing employees, but some authors have already identified important considerations on this subject. For example, at issue are

- whether internal avenues of redress have been exhausted first;
- whether the employer is a public institution;
- whether there is a public interest in the issue;
- whether the allegations are true;
- whether the criticism is voiced in a reasonable and responsible manner.[1]

[1] S. Krashinsky and J. Sack, *Discharge and Discipline* (Toronto: Lancaster House, 1989), p. 121. See also, as it pertains to American law, J.N. Adler and M. Daniels, "Managing the Whistleblowing Employee", *The Labour Lawyer*, Vol. 8, No. 1 (1992), p. 19.

§10.72 Whistle-blowing by an employee may be held to be damaging to the employer's interests and justify dismissal. In the case of *Cooney v. St John's Metropolitan Area Bd.*,[1] an employee, following a dispute with his superior, went to the government department responsible for the regulation of the employer and complained about the internal running of the company. This was held to constitute cause for dismissal.

[1]   (1981), 35 Nfld. & P.E.I.R. 262 (Nfld. S.C.).

§10.73   Conversely, in *Colclough v. Aviation Metal Products Ltd.,*[1] it was held that an employee who had written a letter to the Minister of National Revenue complaining about irregularities in the company was improperly terminated on this ground.

[1]   Unreported, May 16, 1986 (Ont. S.C.).

§10.74   It should be noted that executives may be held to a higher standard than others. In *Barendregt v. Vancouver Game Farm Ltd.,*[1] although without discussing the obligations owed by management employees, the court described the obligations of non-management employees in these terms:

> Providing a non-managerial employee is doing the job for which he or she is hired in a satisfactory manner, then time and custom have validated the employee's immemorial right to complain about management. That is so just as long as the conduct and expression do not subvert the status, well-being, purpose and economy of the company. If it were not so, there would be very little job security in the commonwealth.

A more recent British Columbia case, however, places in question the idea that an employee, discharged for whistle-blowing, may have an action against his or her former employer. Clancy J. in *obiter* in *Campbell v. Wellfund Audio-Visual Ltd.*[2] suggested that the existence of the torts of retaliatory discharge and bad faith discharge (which would provide damages to an employee discharged in a manner contrary to public policy, such as for whistle-blowing) is in question, at least in British Columbia.

[1]   (1986), 37 A.C.W.S. (2d) 407 (B.C. Co. Ct.).
[2]   (1995), 14 C.C.E.L. (2d) 240 (B.C.S.C.), at 263.

§10.75   For the same reasons that courts have consistently made a distinction between executives and other employees, it could be argued that, in theory at least, *any* form of whistle-blowing by an executive would probably be considered disloyal and, hence, be cause for dismissal. This, however, does not seem to be the case in the present state of the law.[1]

[1]   See *Initial Services Ltd. v. Putterill,* [1968] 1 Q.B. 396 (C.A.), *per* Lord Denning, and *Fraser v. Public Service Staff Relations Board,* [1985] 2 S.C.R. 455, at 470.

3. Obligation to Report Fellow Employees' Harmful or Disloyal Conduct

§10.76 The issue of an executive's duty to report the misconduct of fellow employees has recently been considered by at least one Canadian author[1] who cites several cases where the issue has been discussed.

> [1] Howard Levitt, "The Duty to Report the Misconduct of Others — Should an Employee Report the Misconduct of Fellow Employees?" (1992), 6 *Dismissal and Employment Law Digest*, Issue 9.

§10.77 Initially, courts did not require that an employee report on the wrongdoing of another employee unless it concerned matters of extreme seriousness. This was because human nature is such that it would be impossible for two people to continue to work together when one of them feels betrayed. More recently, courts have found that the duty to report will depend on the extent to which such a duty is a component of adequate job performance.

§10.78 As early as 1936, English courts addressed the issue of an executive's duty to report. In the case of *Swain v. West (Butchers) Ltd.*,[1] a general manager of a company had contractually agreed to "do all in his power to promote, extend and develop the interests of the company". His failure to report his managing director's acts of dishonesty were found to warrant the general manager's dismissal. The court held that the general manager had a duty, flowing from the express terms of his employment contract, to act in the best interests of the company. It should be noted, however, that in this case the court relied heavily on the fact that the employee had a contract which specifically provided that he was to do *all in his power* to promote the interests of the company.

> [1] [1936] 3 All E.R. 261 (C.A.).

§10.79 In Canada, the case of *Tyrrell v. Alltrans Express Ltd.*[1] was decided in a similar manner. There, the British Columbia Supreme Court held that an employee's duty to disclose facts of which he or she is aware and which affect the employer depends largely upon the terms of the employment agreement, the position of the employee, the nature of his or her duties and the seriousness or degree of the impugned conduct.[2]

> [1] (1976), 66 D.L.R. (3d) 181 (B.C.S.C.). See also *King v. Mayne Nickless Transport Inc.* (1994), 89 B.C.L.R. (2d) 344 (C.A.).

²   (1976), 66 D.L.R. (3d) 181 (B.C.S.C), at 185.

§10.80   Since an executive's fiduciary position requires that he or she act at all times with the utmost loyalty towards the employer, the executive has an implied general duty to report any matter, including the conduct of other employees, which is not in the best interests of the company. Of course, the intensity of the duty varies with the degree of responsibility and control exercised by the executive in the course of his or her employment.

4.   Obligation to Account

§10.81   As a general rule, only those charged with fiduciary responsibilities can be forced to account for sums which they have obtained through their positions.

§10.82   Until the Civil Code of Quebec came into force in January 1944, the usual rule was that only mandataries were obligated to account in Quebec (since the concept of fiduciary duties was foreign to Civil law). In *Bank of Montreal v. Kuet Leong Ng*,¹ however, the Supreme Court of Canada held that whether the employment relationship was qualified as one of mandate or regular employment,

> . . . an employee's obligation of good faith encompasses, at a minimum, conscientious execution of his contractual obligations. However, the intensity of the employee's obligation of good faith increases with the responsibility attached to the position held by the employee.²

This is all the more true under the provisions of article 2088 of the new Civil Code which do not distinguish between "senior" and "ordinary" employees and stipulate that all employees are bound *to act faithfully and honestly* in carrying out their duties.

¹   [1989] 2 S.C.R. 429.
²   [1989] 2 S.C.R. 429, at 438.

§10.83   In an astute example of judicial reasoning, the Supreme Court, in the *Ng* case, issued a warning to all employees, even those who do not fall strictly within the definition of fiduciary or mandatary, that they will be made to account to their employer if they profit, in bad faith, from their position.

§10.84   Finally, the *Ng* case is important in another regard. The decision contained a statement by Canada's highest court which joined our two legal systems as concerns fiduciary obligations during employment:

> The fiduciary obligation recognized in these circumstances in the common law translates in the civil law into terms of good faith and loyalty of the employee to the employer and the avoidance of conflict of interest including seeking an advantage which is incompatible with the terms of employment.[1]

---

[1] [1989] 2 S.C.R. 429, at 443.

5. Fiduciary Obligations After Termination of Employment

(a) The "Canaero" Decision

§10.85 In the *Canaero* decision,[1] the Supreme Court of Canada held that once a fiduciary relationship is deemed to exist, the fiduciary obligations which ensue will subsist even after the employment relationship has ended. Otherwise, a person could avoid the duty and strict obligations that go with his or her position simply by resigning. The same solution has been reached in Quebec.

---

[1] *Canadian Aero Service Ltd. v. O'Malley*, [1974] S.C.R. 592.

§10.86 Although the question of permissible post-employment conduct has been discussed for years, new trends in business have recently brought the issue to the forefront. Recently, we have witnessed an increased movement of executives from one company to another. Indeed, the obligation of loyalty is not the sacrosanct guiding principle it once was for executives. Lifelong unquestioning devotion to the organization has been replaced by a quicker willingness to seek greener pastures when the price is right. Moreover, departing executives often succeed in convincing key employees and important clients to join them. This, in turn, has led to greater sensitivity by both departing executives and employers of their respective rights and obligations *after* the employment relationship ends.

§10.87 Where the employment agreement provides a specific clause in restraint of trade or competition, this issue usually does not arise,[1] since the parties have, in advance, regulated the scope of permissible post-employment conduct. However, where no such clause exists or where such a clause is invalidated by a court of law, the issue resurfaces.

---

[1] See Chapter 11, "The Written Employment Contract and Some Specific Provisions".

§10.88 The law in this regard seeks to balance two competing considerations.[1] On the one hand, it is the natural right of every person to earn a living and to try to better his or her situation in life. On the other hand, it is in the public interest to maintain a certain level of commercial stability, and our system of free competition requires that no one have an *unfair* advantage over another. The principles that have emerged from the jurisprudence on this matter have attempted to strike a successful balance between these two competing concerns.

[1] See *P. Brunet Assur. Inc. v. Mancuso*, unreported, Feb. 17, 1988, C.S.M. 500-05-008530-873 (Gonthier J.), at 8 of the judgment.

§10.89 Prior to beginning any analysis, a distinction must again be made between "ordinary employees" and "senior managers" or "executives". The post-employment obligations of the executive are more restrictive than those of the ordinary employee. It is appropriate to mention that since the civil law does not allow a contract to have effect after it has been terminated, until the coming into force of article 2088 of the Civil Code of Quebec, the executive's post-employment duty of loyalty resulted from a somewhat convoluted interpretation of the Civil Code of Lower Canada. Indeed, the basis for an action for damages resulting from post-employment competition was usually that the action complained of was an actionable wrong which caused damage to the former employer (*i.e.* a tort).

§10.90 Notwithstanding the fact that the civil law does not recognize fiduciary duties nor the survival of obligations beyond the termination of the contract, several cases have granted injunctions prohibiting the solicitation of clients of the ex-employer on the basis of post-employment fiduciary/loyalty obligations.[1] None of these cases, unfortunately, explained how the obligation of loyalty could continue to exist even after the employment contract had ended.

[1] *National Financial Brokerage Center Inc. v. Investors Syndicate Ltd.* (1986), 9 C.P.R. (3d) 497 (Que. C.A.); *Resfab Manufacturier de Ressort Inc. v. Archambault*, [1986] R.D.J. 32 (Que. C.A.); *Picard v. Johnson & Higgins Willis Faber Ltée*, [1988] R.J.Q. 235 (C.A.).

§10.91 Nonetheless, one thing became clear after these three Court of Appeal decisions: the ethical yardstick established by the Supreme Court in the *Canaero* decision was just as applicable to top management or senior executives in Quebec[1] as it was elsewhere in Canada. The trilogy left the lower courts in Quebec with a dual responsibility: to develop and explain the legal basis on which the post-employment obligations referred to in *Canaero* would apply in Quebec, and to inject content into and define the scope and intensity of such obligations, which resulted in a case-by-case approach by the courts, with decisions turning on the particular facts of each case.

[1] See *Excelsior compagnie d'assurance-vie v. Mutuelle du Canada*, [1992] R.J.Q. 2666 (Que. C.A.).

§10.92 In 1988,[1] Mr. Justice André Forget summarized the jurisprudence as follows:

> . . . rules of ethic, similar to those emanating from the common law as concerns managers of companies, apply in Quebec in as much as the appropriate changes are made in accordance with our Civil Code.

[1] *157079 Canada Inc. v. Ste-Croix*, [1988] R.J.Q. 2842 (Que. S.C.), at 2848 (translation); appeal settled out of court, unreported, Jan. 6, 1989, C.A.M. 500-09-001254-887.

§10.93 With the coming into force of the new Civil Code in Quebec, it is no longer necessary to extrapolate a legal basis for post-employment obligations on executives. The new Civil Code explicitly states that the obligation to act faithfully and honestly in carrying on their work continues for a reasonable period after the cessation of the contract.

(b) Post-Employment Competition

§10.94 Many judges in Quebec have spent significant time analysing the source and legal justification for prohibiting post-employment competition. Over the last decade, considerable energy has been expended in attempts to import the concept of fiduciary duties into civil law or to base similar obligations on the law of delict (tort) or the implicit duty of loyalty found at what was article 1024 of the Civil Code of Lower Canada.[1] Although this produced an interesting body of case law, it is submitted that such an exercise will no longer be necessary in view of article 2088 of the Civil Code of Quebec which expressly imposes similar obligations on employees for a reasonable period of time after the cessation of the contract. Thus, the justification is now found directly in a provision of the Civil Code. Nonetheless, it is suggested that reference to case law may still be useful to define the *extent* of the obligation. The Superior Court recently held in *Voyages Routair inc. v. Hanna* that the new Civil Code of Quebec sanctions the rules established by the courts before the Code came into force.[2]

[1] A similar provision is now found at C.C.Q., art. 1434.
[2] *Groupe Financier Assbec Ltée v. Dion*, D.T.E. 95T-70 (Que. C.A.); D.T.E. 94T-690 (Que. S.C.), in appeal.

§10.95 The type of prohibited conduct includes the obligation to refrain from soliciting the clients of the former employer. However, in absence of a restrictive covenant, the prohibited conduct will be confined to prohibiting *direct* solicitation of the former clients.[1] Advertising and accepting new business without direct solicitation is generally permissible.[2] However, where the facts are such that clients have built up a personal relationship with, and are consequently loyal to, the individual employee rather than the employer, direct solicitation post-employment may be allowed.[3]

[1]   *P. Brunet Assurance Inc. v. Mancuso*, unreported, Feb. 17, 1988, File No. C.S.M. 500-05-008530-873 (Que. S.C.); *F.C. Hume & Co. v. Actaes Inc.*, J.E. 90-1581 (Que. S.C.); *Bergeron v. Roy*, D.T.E. 95T-858 (Que. S.C.) (motion for appeal rejected 200-09-000423-951).

[2]   See *Edgar T. Alberts Ltd. v. Mountjoy* (1977), 79 D.L.R. (3d) 108 (Ont. H.C.J.).

[3]   *Anderson, Smyth & Kelly Customs Brokers Ltd. v. World Wide Customs Brokers Ltd.* (1993), 1 C.C.E.L. (2d) 57 (Alta. Q.B.), revd 20 C.C.E.L. (2d) 1 (C.A.). See discussion at §§10.40.1 *et seq.*

§10.96   In *Sure-Grip Fasteners Ltd. v. Allgrade Bolt & Chain Inc.*,[1] the Ontario Court (General Division) repeated the principle that an employee who is a fiduciary is precluded from competing with the employer by means of direct solicitation of the employer's customers for a reasonable period of time after the termination of the employment. The court analyzed the situation where two salespeople and a general manager left a company without notice and set up a competing business. The Court determined that the two salespeople had not been in a fiduciary relationship with the employer they had left, as neither of them performed management functions. However, the fact that the departing general manager, whom the sales people had joined in setting up the competing business, stood in a fiduciary position with his former employer resulted in that the sales people shared the general manager's fiduciary obligations towards the former employer. In so holding, the court applied the principle enounced in *Edgar T. Alberts Ltd. v. Mountjoy*.[2] The sales people could not be permitted to do what the general manager could not do particularly since any act on their part would *pro tanto* serve for the benefit of the general manager. Thus, it is not sufficient for an employee to merely rely on the fact that he himself is not subject to a fiduciary duty to allow him to solicit directly a former employer's customers. The employee must also see who would benefit from the solicitation and where it is found that the party who benefits is bound by a fiduciary duty not to solicit, the "ordinary" employee may consequently be bound by the same limitation on his activities.

[1]   (1993), 45 C.C.E.L. 276 (Ont. Ct. (Gen. Div.)).

[2]   (1977), 79 D.L.R. (3d) 108 (Ont. H.C.).

§10.97 In *Poirier v. Textiles Absorb-Plus Inc.*,[1] a departing vice-president of marketing was found not to be in breach of any fiduciary duty or guilty of having committed any disloyal act by simply joining a competitor following his departure. The executive had not made use of any trade secrets but had merely used his subjective ability, experience and know-how, which it was his legitimate right to use.

[1] D.T.E. 91T-329 (Que. S.C.).

§10.98 In *Fromagerie du Gourmet Inc. v. Dumas*,[1] the court found that a departing sales manager was in breach of his "fiduciary obligation of loyalty" when he began direct solicitation of clients of his ex-employer the day after his termination of employment.

[1] J.E. 91-469 (Que. S.C.).

§10.99 The decision in *Compro Communications Inc. v. Communications Promophone L.T. Inc.*[1] dealt with a case where departing directors were competing with their ex-company. The court held that they were in breach of their fiduciary duty in trying to induce clients to breach their contracts with their employer (ex-company) and in using confidential client lists in soliciting clients and in soliciting employees as well. It appears that the defendants were also involved in "passing off", which is a deceit in itself. An injunction was granted prohibiting such behaviour for 18 months.

[1] J.E. 91-1269 (Que. S.C.). See also *Frank White Enterprises Inc. v. 130541 Canada Inc.*, D.T.E. 95T-683 (Que. C.A.).

§10.100 In *Volcano Inc. v. Lavoie*,[1] the Quebec Superior Court reminds us that it is not disloyal for an employee to simply compete with his ex-employer, even if the latter suffers financial loss as a result.[2]

[1] D.T.E. 84T-871 (Que. S.C.).
[2] This was recently confirmed in *Dufresne v. Groupe Christie Ltée*, D.T.E. 92T-499 (Que. C.A.).

§10.101 Along similar lines, the Superior Court held that certain ex-employees (insurance brokers) had competed disloyally by making use of confidential client lists and other information belonging to their ex-employer after the termination of their employment.[1] An injunction was granted prohibiting them from continuing to make wrongful use of the employer's confidential information.

[1] *Assurances Leblanc & Croteau Ltée v. Assurance Danis-Corneau Inc.*, [1988] R.J.Q. 1051. See also *Arcon Canada Inc. v. Arcobec Aluminium Inc.*, [1984] C.S. 1027 (Que.)

and, more recently, *Soquelec Télécommunications Ltée v. Microvolt Électroniques Inc.*, J.E. 91-1442 (Que. S.C.).

§10.102   Also, in the case of *Mutuelle du Canada Cie d'assurance-vie v. Excelsior Cie d'assurance-vie*,[1] the Superior Court held that it would have been "disloyal competition" for departing insurance agents to systematically arrange for the transfer of insurance policies from their ex-employer to their new employer by falsely representing advantages of the various policies. Damages were awarded against both the departing agents and their new employer.

[1]   J.E. 88-969 (Que. S.C.).

§10.103   Similarly, in *Sherelco Investments v. Laflamme*,[1] an executive was found to be in "manifest bad faith" for having misappropriated his ex-employer's confidential documents for the purpose of competing disloyally by soliciting ex-customers and contracts.

[1]   J.E. 92-683 (Que. S.C.).

§10.104   In contradistinction, it was not an act of disloyal competition for an executive to compile a list of his employer's customers for his intended personal use after employment, in anticipation of a company shutdown.[1] This, the court said, was far different from the situation where an employee, while working, gathers information to be used in direct competition with his employer after he leaves.

[1]   *A. Martin & Cie v. Premier Fourrure Inc.*, J.E. 91-1296 (Que. S.C.).

§10.105   In summary, therefore, and from an analysis of the above, the following principles emerge:

(1)   As a general rule, unless restricted by contract, any employee, whether an executive, senior manager or lower-level employee, is free to take with him or her and to utilize his or her aptitudes, abilities, competence, and all other subjective elements which he or she has acquired during the course of his or her employment, with the exception of trade secrets.

(2)   Absent a non-competition clause and subject to a duty of confidentiality (discussed below), an employee is free to compete directly with his or her ex-employer, as long as it is not disloyal competition within the meaning of articles 1457 and 2088 of the Civil Code of Quebec.

(3)   Directors, senior officers and, in some circumstances, executives of a company have a "fiduciary duty", or post-employment ob-

ligation of loyalty, which varies in intensity depending on the nature of responsibilities and control exercised by the departing individual with the company.

(4) This duty imposes on them an obligation to conduct themselves in accordance with strict and rigorous rules of ethics. This means that, after employment, the individual subject to such a duty must, *inter alia*, refrain from making use of confidential information, directly soliciting ex-customers, encouraging employees of their ex-employer to join them in departing or to otherwise breach their employment obligations, or making false and misleading representations concerning their ex-employer.

H. DUTY OF CONFIDENTIALITY

§10.106 As we have seen from the *Canaero* decision, a distinction is made between a fiduciary duty and a duty of confidentiality. Unlike the fiduciary duty, which arises only from the existence of a fiduciary-type relationship, the duty of confidentiality is owed by any employee who is the recipient of information of a confidential nature related to the employer's business.[1] Ordinarily, employees obtain confidential information in particular circumstances which at least imply an obligation of confidentiality. With respect to executives, their high level of autonomy and responsibility usually renders all information belonging to the employer accessible to them; hence, in such circumstances, executives will most certainly owe a duty of confidentiality.

[1] See, generally, Richard A. Brait, "Confidentiality in the Employment Relationship" (1990), 5 Intellectual Prop. J. 187.

§10.107 Although the protection of confidential information is essentially concerned with the protection of an employer's property and proprietary rights therein,[1] the obligation of confidentiality arises in the absence of any rights under property or contract.[2] Simply stated, it is an implied obligation of every employee not to use property belonging to his or her employer or ex-employer to the latter's detriment, which property includes certain categories of information belonging to the employer that can be qualified as confidential. In theory, therefore, wrongful use of an employer's confidential information can be considered unlawful use of property at civil law, although it does not constitute property within the meaning of the theft provisions of the *Criminal Code*.[3]

[1] For a discussion of the legal methods by which confidential business information is protected in France and Quebec, see Marie Bourgeois, "Protecting Business

Confidences: A Comparative Study of Quebec and French Law" (1987), 3 Intellectual Prop. J. 259.

[2]   See Jonathan Colombo, "Confidential Information and Property Rights: A Study of Employment Contracts" (1989), 3 National Labour Review 20.

[3]   R.S.C. 1985, c. C-46, s. 322. See *R. v. Stewart*, [1988] 1 S.C.R. 963.

1. Types of Information

§10.108   With respect to types of information which can potentially be obtained by an employee during the course of his employment, courts in Quebec, and elsewhere,[1] have adopted the threefold distinction found in the British case of *Faccenda Chicken Ltd. v. Fowler*.[2] The court in that case held that information can be distinguished in three different ways:

[1]   See, e.g., *Trophy Foods Inc. v. Scott* (1995), 60 C.P.R. (3d) 231 (N.S.C.A.).

[2]   [1986] 1 All E.R. 617 (C.A.), at 623-24.

(a) Information of a Trivial Nature

§10.109   First, there is information which, because of its trivial character or its easy accessibility from public sources of information, cannot be regarded by reasonable persons or by law as confidential at all. Obviously, divulging information of this type either during or after employment cannot be seen as a breach of the executive's obligation of loyalty.[1] Thus, subject to other obligations of loyalty, an executive is at liberty to impart this kind of information belonging to his or her employer at any time and for any purpose. An example of this type of information might be a published patent specification well known to people in the industry.

[1]   See *Vulcano Inc. v. Lavoie*, D.T.E. 84T-871 (Que. S.C.) and *Ambulair Canada Inc. v. Somiper Aviation Inc.*, D.T.E. 96T-719 (Que. S.C.).

(b) Limited Confidential Information

§10.110   This is information which the executive must treat as confidential, either because he or she is expressly told that it is confidential, or because, from its character, it is obviously so. However, once this information is learned, it necessarily remains in the executive's head and becomes part of his or her own skill and knowledge applied in the course of the executive's business. As long as the employment relationship continues, the employee cannot otherwise use or disclose such information. However, when the employment relationship ends and in the absence of a clause limiting the use of confidential information, the law allows the employee to use the full skill and knowledge which he or she has acquired for his or her own benefit, even in competition with a former employer.[1] Hence, an employer wanting to protect information of this kind after the employment relationship has ended can only do so by an express contractual stipulation restraining the employee from making use of this kind of information.

[1] *Lange Co. v. Platt*, [1973] C.A. 1068 (Que.) and *Ecco Personnel Canada Inc. v. Lefebvre*, D.T.E. 96T-1112 (Que. S.C.).

§10.111 There is no exhaustive list of the types of information which would fall into the category of "limited confidential information". Anything ranging from financial statements of a private company to company marketing strategies could be considered in this category if the information is imparted to the employee in circumstances which make it clear that confidence is intended. Obviously, for the executive, virtually any information imparted to him or her would fall under this category.

(c) Trade Secrets

§10.112 The third type of information that employees can be exposed to during employment is specific trade secrets. This information is so confidential that even though it may have necessarily been memorized by the employee and even though the employee may have left the service of the company, it cannot be used for anyone's benefit other than the employer to whom it belongs.

§10.113 Trade secrets have a more industrial or commercial character and can include manufacturing processes or formulae, supplier and customer lists, marketing analyses and strategies, computer programs and other data. Although the courts have dealt with the issue of trade secrets, they have not defined them authoritatively. For example, customer lists are recognized as trade secrets, and ex-employees will be prohibited from soliciting their former employer's clients if the identity of these clients is not readily accessible[1] or if exclusive targeting of these clients takes place instead of general solicitation in the market.[2] However, even a federal-provincial working party stated that "it is probably impossible to arrive at an intrinsic definition of a trade secret."[3]

[1] See *Santé Naturelle Ltée v. Produits de Nutrition Vitaform Inc.* (1985), 5 C.P.R. (3d) 548 (Que. S.C.); *Montour Ltée v. Jolicoeur*, [1988] R.J.Q. 1323 (S.C.).

[2] See *Genesta Mfg. Ltd. v. Babey* (1984), 2 C.P.R. (3d) 32 (Ont. H.C.J.).

[3] "Trade Secrets", Institute of Law Research and Reform, Edmonton, and Federal-Provincial Working Party, Report No. 46 (July 1986).

(i) Characteristics of a Trade Secret

§10.114 Several characteristics of a trade secret have been identified:

(1) A trade secret is a plan or process, tool, mechanism or compound known only to its owner and those of the employees to whom it is necessary to confide it.

(2) A trade secret is a secret formula or process known only to certain individuals using it in compounding some articles of trade having a commercial value and does not denote the mere privacy with which an ordinary business is carried on.

(3) A trade secret may consist of any formula, pattern, device or compilation of information which is used in one's business and which gives its possessor an opportunity to obtain an advantage over competitors who do not know or use it. A trade secret is a process or device for continuous use in the operation of the business.

(4) The subject matter of a trade secret must be secret.[1]

[1] For a more complete discussion of the subject of trade secrets, see David Vaver, "Civil Liability for Taking or Using Trade Secrets in Canada" (1981), 5 Can. Bus. L.J. 253; *Hughes and Woodley on Patents* (Toronto: Butterworths, 1984), pp. 671 *et seq.*; J.A. Talpis, "Le Secret des Affaires" (1974), 5 R.G.D. 81; and in the U.S., P.J. Richey and M.J. Boosik, "Trade Secrets and Restrictive Covenants", *The Labour Lawyer*, Vol. 21 (1988).

§10.115 Although the Quebec courts have applied the *Faccenda Chicken*[1] test to determine whether information obtained in the course of employment may be used by an employee, it should be noted that article 2088 of the Civil Code of Quebec does not make this distinction. Case law will thus have to be followed closely to determine what information is protected. A strict reading of the provision leads the authors to believe that the courts may determine that the protection offered by the new Civil Code of Quebec against disclosure of confidential information following termination is more extensive than it was under the old Civil Code. Whether confidential information is to receive a broader or more restrictive definition is a matter that courts will have to determine. Information contained in clients' lists and the knowledge of an access code to the computer was considered as confidential information with regard to article 2088 of the Civil Code of Quebec.[2] However, a motion for an interlocutory injunction restraining a former employee from soliciting the petitioner's clients was rejected on the basis that the names of its clients (as opposed to a client list) do not constitute confidential information.[3]

---

[1] [1986] 1 All E.R. 617 (C.A.).

[2] *Oxygène Boucherville v. Pépin*, D.T.E. 96T-784 (Quebec Court, Civil Chamber).

[3] *Imprimerie classique limitée v. Leblanc*, D.T.E. 94T-913 (Que. S.C.); *Imprimerie d'Arthabasca Inc. v. Roux*, D.T.E. 96T-988 (Que. S.C.). See also *Panocontrôle Inc. v. Hébert*, D.T.E. 96T-1079 (Que. S.C.). But see *Gestion v. D. Bertrand et Fils inc.*, D.T.E. 94T-1228 (Que. S.C.).

2. The Springboard Theory

§10.116 A breach of confidentiality by an executive during employment clearly constitutes disloyal conduct. With respect to use of confidential information after employment, the purpose of restricting its use by ex-employees ties in to disloyal competition generally. The law intends to protect against what has come to be known as the "springboard theory". That is, departing employees should not be allowed to get a "springboard" start in competition with their ex-employer by using confidential information belonging to the latter.

§10.117 The "springboard theory" has been discussed quite frequently in common law[1] but it has only recently been considered by Quebec courts. In the case of *Positron Inc. v. Desroches*,[2] the six defendants were ex-employees of Positron Inc., a company specializing in the manufacture of equipment designed to facilitate 911 emergency calls by automatically identifying the telephone number of the caller. The ex-employees resigned together and joined an American company. The latter asked the employees to assist in the manufacture of equipment similar to that made by their ex-employer. Positron Inc. took legal action against its ex-employees, seeking to restrict their right to compete and to have them return and stop making use of confidential information belonging to it. Specifically, the court was asked to order the ex-employees to "refrain . . . from designing, developing, manufacturing, selling, promoting or otherwise dealing in" the product manufactured while with the ex-employer.

---

[1] See, e.g., *Genesta Mfg. Ltd. v. Babey* (1984), 48 O.R. (2d) 94 (H.C.J.).

[2] [1988] R.J.Q. 1636 (S.C.), appealed and settled out of court, unreported, Sept. 16, 1991, C.A.M. 500-09-000620-880.

§10.118 On the issue of the "springboard theory" in Quebec, the court referred to several decisions where it had been discussed, thus confirming that it could be applied in the appropriate circumstances (*i.e.*, where trade secrets are used by the departing employee).[1] The court, nonetheless, restrained its application within the limits of article 1053 of the Civil Code of Lower Canada.[2] However, the theory was not applied in this case because the defendants had not made use of confidential information to give them a "springboard" advantage to compete. Rather, they were simply using their "acquired knowledge with their previous employer in order to compete with him",[3] which is perfectly legal in the absence of a clause limiting the use of this type of information. Granting the plaintiff's request would be tantamount to imposing a clause restricting competition, which the parties in this case had not signed. The court did, however, order certain defendants to return to their ex-employer several confidential documents containing customer names and other information which had been wrongfully retained after employment. They were also prohibited from soliciting those customers for a limited time as a result.

---

[1] *Positron Inc. v. Desroches*, [1988] R.J.Q. 1636 (S.C.), at 1656.
[2] A similar provision exists at C.C.Q., art. 1457.
[3] *Positron Inc. v. Desroches*, [1988] R.J.Q. 1636 (S.C.), at 1659.

§10.119 The "springboard theory" was again discussed by the Superior Court of Quebec the following year in the case of *Société Pole-Lite Ltée v. Cormier*.[1] As in the *Positron* case, once the court was convinced that the departing employee did not make use of his employer's trade secrets in order to compete with him, it refused to apply the "springboard theory". Since the defendant had not made use of any information which could be qualified as confidential, the action for injunction and damages against him was dismissed. In the presence of article 2088 of the Civil Code of Quebec, it is likely that Quebec courts will be even more demanding of employees who are bound not to use *any* confidential information he or she may have obtained in carrying on or in the course of his or her work. What remains to be seen is how the courts will define confidential information. Will they still separate them into "types?" How long will the employees' obligation not to use this confidential information last? These are just some of the questions that will have to be answered by the courts.

---

[1] [1989] R.J.Q. 1584 (S.C.).

I. PATENTS AND OTHER INTELLECTUAL PROPERTY RIGHTS

§10.120 While some types of trade secrets and confidential information may be best protected by principles of private law, other types of information may benefit from statutory protection through patent, copyright or other intellectual property legislation.[1] In Canada, jurisdiction over these two subject matters is attributed to the federal government. As such, the laws on these matters are uniform across the country, but since issues such as ownership of rights may be modified by contract, which is within provincial jurisdiction, there may be peculiarities in each province in this regard.[2]

[1] See, for example, *Industrial Design Act*, R.S.C. 1985, c. I-9, and *Integrated Circuit Topography Act*, R.S.C. 1985, c. I-14.6, [S.C. 1990, c. 37], amended by S.C. 1992, c. 1; 1993, c. 15; and 1995, c. 1.

[2] See, for example, *An Act respecting the Professional Status of Artists in the Visual Arts, Arts and Crafts and Literature, and Their Contracts with Promoters*, R.S.Q., c. S-32.01, according to which a contract between an artist and a promoter which has a work of the artist as its object is subject to form and content requirements. A recognized association or group and any promoter or association of promoters may negotiate and conclude a group agreement providing minimum conditions regarding the circulation of the works of the artists. The *Act* does not apply to an artist whose services are retained by a promoter to work as an employee within the meaning of the *Labour Code*. See also *An Act respecting the Professional Status and Conditions of Engagement of Performing, Recording and Film Artists*, R.S.Q., c. S-32.1, which contains similar provisions regarding group agreements. This *Act* does not apply to a person whose services are retained for an occupation contemplated by a certification granted under the *Labour Code* or a decree passed under the *Act respecting Collective Agreement Decrees*.

§10.121 The *Patent Act*[1] provides for the protection of new inventions in Canada. The *Patent Act*, however, does not provide for any specific regime applicable to the employment relationship. The terms of an employment contract or covenant may govern issues regarding the creation, ownership and assignment of inventions between employers and employees. Where no contract or covenant exists to settle the issue between the parties, the courts have developed jurisprudential rules to deal with these situations. The determination of the rights of the patent holder, therefore, will be either fact-specific or dependent upon the terms of the contract.

[1] R.S.C. 1985, c. P-4; see also amendments enacted by R.S.C. 1985, c. 33 (3rd Supp.).

§10.122 Where the employment contract does not specify that the employer is the owner of an employee's inventions, the courts have traditionally held that an invention made by an employee, on the employer's time and using the employer's materials and equipment, is the property of the employee, who is entitled to retain a patent for that invention unless:

(1) *the employee is hired specifically to invent*; in which case, the invention belongs to the employer. Thus, for example, where a person is hired for the express purpose of developing a particular

invention, whatever new material, method or process he or she discovers belongs to the employer;[1]

(2) *the invention relates to the nature of the employment.* For example, engineers or technical personnel are under a duty to apply their inventive ingenuity to problems imposed by management; or

(3) *the individual is in a managerial capacity*, in which case, it is determined by the nature of the employment that such individual ought to apply all his or her talents to the welfare of the company.[2]

---

[1] See *Devoe-Holbein Inc. v. Yam* (1984), 2 C.I.P.R. 229 (Que. S.C.) (Dr. Y was hired by Drs. H and D, who were professors at the university, to assist and to carry out specific work in the furtherance of Drs. H and D's research; principle applied to grant injunction to Drs. H and D for non-disclosure of inventions, confidential information and know-how). See also *Comstock Canada v. Electec Ltd.* (1991), 38 C.P.R. (3d) 29 (F.C.T.D.) and *Bau-Und Forschungsgesellschaft Thermoform AG v. Paszner* (1988), 20 C.I.P.R. 234 and 25 C.I.P.R. 263 (B.C.S.C.), revd on other grounds 60 B.C.L.R. (2d) 90 (C.A.). For rights of universities and researchers with respect to inventions, see Christopher Grafflin Browning Jr., "The Souring of Sweet Acidophilus Milk: *Speck v. North Carolina Dairy Foundation* and the Rights of University Faculty to Their Inventive Ideas" (1985), 63 Intellectual Property 1248.

[2] *MacDonald and Railquip Enterprises Ltd. v. Vapor Canada Ltd.*, [1977] 2 S.C.R. 134.

§10.123 In *Comstock Canada v. Electec Ltd.*,[1] the manager of the plaintiff's electrical department had made an invention which he alleged belonged to his own company, Electec, as he was the true inventor. The work on the invention was done after hours, though on the plaintiff's premises. Inventing was not within the scope of the employment nor part of the defendant's day-to-day duties. The defendant had been open about his after-hours work for his own company (which was in a different though related business than the employing company) and the fact that he possessed a senior position in the plaintiff's company did not deprive the defendant of his rights to the invention "if that is not what he was hired to do", p. 55. In conclusion, the defendant was the inventor and the owner of the invention.

In deciding whether an employee's invention belongs to the employee or the employer, the Court set out the following factors:

(a) whether the employee was hired for the express purpose of inventing;

(b) whether the employee at the time he was hired had previously made inventions;

(c) whether an employer had incentive plans encouraging product development;

(d) whether the conduct of the employee once the invention had been created suggested ownership was held by employer;
(e) whether the invention is the product of a problem the employee was *instructed* to solve (*i.e.*, whether it was a duty to make inventions);
(f) whether the employee's invention arose following his consultation through normal company channels (*i.e.*, was help sought?);
(g) whether the employee was dealing with highly confidential information or confidential work; and
(h) whether it was a term of the servant's employment that he could not use the ideas which he developed to his own advantage.

[1] (1991), 38 C.P.R. (3d) 29 (F.C.T.D.).

§10.124 An employee's grant to an employer of a licence to use an invention will be limited by the terms of the licence. Thus, despite having a licence itself to use an employee's patent, an employer may still be found liable of inducing third party infringement. In *Dableh v. Ontario Hydro*[1] the respondent, Ontario Hydro, had a non-exclusive royalty-free licence to use a system for which the patent belonged to an Ontario Hydro employee. The licence granted use of the patented invention in Ontario Hydro's "business and undertakings". The court held that the development and improvement of the invention by the respondent in conjunction with other companies through which an exchange of technology among the companies arose did not constitute an infringement of the patent. The use of the technology, however, by other hydro companies would constitute an infringement because this was not encompassed in the respondent's "business and undertakings". The respondent's licence was no defence to an action for inducement.

[1] (1996), 68 C.P.R. (3d) 129 (F.C.A.).

1. Assignment Contracts

§10.125 Where a contract exists between an employer and employee, it will typically provide that there will be a transfer, assignment or relinquishment of all inventions by an employee in exchange for employment.[1] As in any contract, the consideration for such an exchange should be clear, concise and unambiguous.

[1] For example, in *Devoe-Holbein Inc. v. Yam* (1984), 2 C.I.P.R. 229 (Que. S.C.), a condition of Dr. Y's employment was that he sign an agreement of non-disclosure and

relinquishment of any rights to patentable data which he might encounter during the course of employment.

§10.126 Employment in and of itself has been deemed sufficient consideration by American jurisprudence if the contract is signed when employment begins or shortly thereafter. If the assignment of inventions is made after employment begins, American courts require that specific and unambiguous consideration be exchanged. Thus, in *Hewett v. Samsonite Corp.*,[1] where the purported consideration for the contract of "$1.00 and other valuable consideration" was not paid, the assignment was held to be void, and the employee accordingly continued to have the right to the discovery.

[1] 32 Colo. App. 150, 507 P. 2d 1119 (1973).

§10.127 Some assignment contracts may contain holdover clauses which specify that any discovery or invention created within a set period of time after the employment terminates will remain the property of the employer. These are used by employers to protect against the possibility that employees will not disclose discoveries or inventions during the course of employment but will attempt to use them for their personal benefit after employment terminates. Holdover clauses have been held valid to the extent that they are reasonable and protect a legitimate interest of the employer.[1]

[1] See *Dorr-Oliver Inc. v. United States*, 432 F. 2d 447, 193 Ct. Cl. 187 (1970).

§10.128 A general limitation on assignment contracts is that assigned inventions must fall within the scope of employment. However, American jurisprudence has held that an employment contract cannot be construed so broadly as to imply an assignment of all employment-related work.[1]

[1] See *Dorr-Oliver Inc. v. United States*, 432 F. 2d 447, 193 Ct. Cl. 187 (1970).

2. Validity of Inventions

§10.129 The scope of what is meant by an invention has been delimited in *Marion v. Brasserie Labatt Ltée*.[1] In that case, an observation by an employee, which after further scientific verification led to a new processing technique used by the employer, was held not to be an invention or discovery insofar as it was a mere observation that involved no creation.[2]

[1] (1987), 13 C.I.P.R. 70 (Que. S.C.); affd 33 C.P.R. (3d) 444 (C.A.).

² See also *Helbig v. Oxford Warehousing Ltd.* (1985), 9 C.C.E.L. 75 (Ont. C.A.), leave to appeal to S.C.C. refused 52 O.R. (2d) 754*n*.

J. COPYRIGHTS

§10.130 A copyright is an incorporeal right and constitutes the sole right to produce or reproduce a work or any substantial part thereof in any material form whatever, and the right to make the work public and still retain the beneficial interest therein.[1] Copyright relates only to the mode or form of expression; there is no copyright in ideas or in information conveyed *per se*. Copyright is thus distinguished from trade secrets or confidential business information. It is also important to distinguish between copyright and the physical property in which the copyright is embodied. For example, a published, copyrighted article or business plan may be used by anyone, sold or given away, but cannot be copied.

[1] R.S.C. 1985, c. C-42, s. 3.

§10.131 In Canada, the *Copyright Act*[1] permits an author or his successor to restrain others from certain acts with respect to original literary, dramatic, musical and artistic works. The *Copyright Act* grants the right to prevent the copying or reproduction of original works. Case law has extended the meaning of "original works" to cover such non-literary or non-artistic work as maps, charts, plans, tables and business correspondence.[2]

[1] R.S.C. 1985, c. C-42.
[2] See *British Oxygen Co. v. Liquid Air Ltd.*, [1925] Ch. 383.

§10.132 Under the *Copyright Act*,[1] the author of the work is generally the first owner of the copyright. Unlike the *Patent Act*,[2] the *Copyright Act* specifically provides for copyright protection within an employment relationship. Section 13(3) of the Act states that, where the author is in the employment of another person under a contract of service or apprenticeship, and the work is made during the course of employment, the employer is deemed the first owner of the copyright.[3] However, the presumption in favour of an employer may be rebutted by any agreement to the contrary.[4]

[1] R.S.C. 1985, c. C-42, s. 13(1).
[2] R.S.C. 1985, c. P-4.
[3] See *Hanis v. Teevan*, unreported, March 17, 1995 (Ont. Ct. (Gen. Div.)) where the employer, a university, was the first owner of the copyright in some communications software as its employees were the authors of the software. See also *Cartes-*

en-Ciel Inc. v. Boutique Elfe Inc. (1991), 43 C.P.R. (3d) 416 (Que. Ct.), where a company was held to be the owner of the copyright in a greeting card created by an individual who was an employee, shareholder and director of the company. This individual created the work while carrying out his functions for the benefit of the company.

[4] *Marquis v. DKL Technologies Inc.* (1989), 24 C.I.P.R. 289 (Que. S.C.). An agreement assigning the copyright to the employee must be in writing, see *Frank Brunckhorst Co. v. Gainers Inc.* (1993), 47 C.P.R. (3d) 222 (F.C.T.D.) where it had been the intention of both the employee and the employer that copyright should be vested in the employee. However, as this understanding had not been put in writing, the employer was the owner of the copyright and the claims relating to the copyright in a suit brought by the employee against a third party was therefore stricken. In *Allen v. Toronto Star Newspapers Ltd.* (1995), 63 C.P.R. (3d) 517 (Ont. Ct. (Gen. Div.)), the court considered the custom in the trade to determine copyright ownership. The custom was that, unless there was an agreement to the contrary, a photograph taken by a freelance photographer belonged to the photographer. As there was no agreement to the contrary, the photographer owned the photograph. A reproduction of a magazine cover which included the photograph was an infringement of the photographer's copyright.

§10.133   The determination of whether or not the work of the employee falls within section 13(3) of the *Copyright Act* depends on the interpretation of the phrases "contract of service", as distinguished from "contract for services", and "during the course of employment". Two tests have been used in this interpretation:

(1)   the traditional "control" test: the greater the control the employer has over an employee, the more probable it is that the employee will be found to be under a contract of service; and

(2)   the "integral part of the business" test: where a person is employed as part of the business, and the work done is an integral part of the business, then such a person is considered to be employed under a "contract of service". This is distinguished from employment under a "contract for services", where the work performed, although done for the business, is not integrated into it but is only accessory to it.[1]

The "integral part of the business" test is now used in copyright cases to determine whether the author of a work is an employee under a "contract of service",[2] thus according the employer first ownership of the work created during the course of employment.[3]

[1]   See *Stephenson, Jordan & Harrison Ltd. v. MacDonald and Evans*, [1952] 1 T.L.R. 101 (C.A.). In *Hawley v. The Queen in Right of Canada* (1990), 30 C.P.R. (3d) 534 (F.C.T.D.), the question was whether an inmate in a Kingston minimum-security establishment was the copyright owner of a painting created for the institution. Every inmate had to be "gainfully employed" and received a small salary for their work. The plaintiff had created his own work position as a painter with the consent of the institution instead of doing farm work. The purchases of materials

for the painting had been made by the institution and the motif for the painting had been chosen by common agreement between the inmate and the institution. Although some of the work on the painting might have been done in the plaintiff's spare time, the Court found that the relationship between the inmate and the institution was that of an employee/employer. The copyright, therefore, belonged to the institution. It should be noted that no distinction apparently was made between the ownership of the copyright and the ownership of the actual picture.

² See *Beloff v. Pressdram Ltd.*, [1973] R.P.C. 765 (Ch.). See also *Byrne v. Statist Co.*, [1914] 1 K.B. 622.

³ See *Hutton v. Canadian Broadcasting Corp.* (1992), 41 C.P.R. (3d) 45 (Alta. C.A.), affg (1989), 29 C.P.R. (3d) 398 (Q.B.), wherein only a contract for services was found. Hence, s. 13(3) did not apply.

§10.134 Computer programs have been recognized as work meriting statutory protection under copyright laws. In Canada, a computer program under the *Copyright Act*¹ is defined as "a set of instructions or statements expressed, fixed, embodied or stored in any manner, that is to be used directly or indirectly in a computer in order to bring about a specific result". Although the new legislation explicitly includes computer software, this technology has already been recognized by the courts as capable of being the subject of copyright; computer software has been expressly defined as a literary work,² and as such, it is protected for the life of the author plus 50 years. As with other literary works protected under the *Copyright Act*, the employer, who is not already the first owner of the copyright, may be assigned the ownership of the copyright in the computer program.

¹ R.S.C. 1985, c. C-42, s. 2 [as am. by R.S.C. 1985, c. 10 (4th Supp.), s. 1(3)].

² *Dynabec Ltée v. Société d'Informatique R.D.G. Inc.* (1985), 6 C.I.P.R. 185 (Que. C.A.).

§10.135 In *Amusements Wiltron Inc. v. Mainville*¹ the defendant K had been hired by the plaintiff company to modify its software. K provided his own workplace and was paid weekly amounts if his work was satisfactory. He was also given a company car but was responsible for its maintenance himself. After K left the plaintiff's employment he assigned the copyright of a computer poker game developed for the plaintiff to the defendant M. The two defendants subsequently marketed a game very similar to that developed for the plaintiff.

¹ (1991), 40 C.P.R. (3d) 521 (Que. S.C.).

§10.136 In determining whether K had been an employee of the plaintiff or merely an independent consultant, the Court relied on an analogy to tax and labour law evaluating the following factors: the ownership of tools, the control or direction (relationship of subordination), risk of loss and chance of profit and the integration into the business. K owned most of the tools, his work and work schedule was under no or little control by the plaintiff, K assumed the risk of loss related to his own performance and he was not integrated into the business as he did not receive orders from a superior, generally was not present at the workplace and was not accountable for how his time was spent. The Court held, that K was both the first owner and the author of the program and the plaintiff had only received a non-exclusive license to lease out the program.

§10.137 In *Dubois v. Systemes de Gestion et d'Analyse de Données Media, Media-Source Canada Inc.*[1] the Court held that the plaintiff D had developed a software program on behalf of a company to be established together with two of its officers. The software was to be improved by the plaintiff D "in the context of his functions as officer/director".[2] Due to the relationship with the respondent company (his business cards described him as "principal associate" and he was a shareholder of the respondent company), and the plaintiff's duty to that company as well as due to the fact that the respondent's name appeared in the computer program, the respondent had the appearance of right and the applicants' motion for an interlocutory injunction was dismissed. There existed no presumption that the name appearing on the copyright registration also was the name of the author, as two registrations had been issued naming different authors.

[1] (1991), 41 C.P.R. (3d) 92 (Que. S.C.).
[2] (1991), 41 C.P.R. (3d) 92 (Que. S.C.), p. 103.

§10.138 In *BBM Bureau of Measurement v. Cybernauts Ltd.*[1] the court held that the employer had a strong *prima facie* case with respect to the ownership of a computer program because when the author is under a contract of service and the work was done in the course of employment, the employer is the first owner of copyright. The court implied that the work was done in the course of employment despite the fact that the individual who created the program "[w]orked at his home, in his spare time, outside of office hours, using his own personal computer. He used a copy of a manual of the plaintiff."[2] The court did note that the author held a responsible senior position within the plaintiff's organization.

[1] (1992), 42 C.P.R. (3d) 180 (Ont. Ct. (Gen. Div.)).
[2] (1992), 42 C.P.R. (3d) 180 (Ont. Ct. (Gen. Div.)), p. 186.

§10.139 The case of *Apple Computer Inc. v. Mackintosh Computers Ltd.*[1] raises the issue of vicarious liability of corporate employers for the infringement of copyrighted computer programs by the corporation's employees. The court held that the corporate employer had not violated an order restraining copyright infringement by failing to dismiss employees who were in contempt of such an order. There had been no inducement on the part of the corporate employer to infringe on the copyright. In addition, the employer had informed the employees of the court order and had instructed the employees to act accordingly.

¹ (1988), 22 C.I.P.R. 14 (F.C.T.D.).

K. INDUSTRIAL DESIGN ACT

§10.140 The *Industrial Design Act*¹ applies to "features of shape, configuration, pattern or ornament and any combination of those features that, in a finished article, appeal to and are judged solely by the eye". Features applied to a useful article which are dictated solely by a utilitarian function do not receive protection under the *Act*.² The *Act* grants the first proprietor or his successors an exclusive right to, among others, make, import for the purpose of trade or business, sell, license or rent a registered design.³ The duration of an exclusive right expires ten years from the date of registration.

¹ R.S.C. 1985, c. I-9.
² Section 5.1.
³ It should be noted that s. 8, which was repealed by R.S.C. 1993, c. 15, s. 16, stated that "Where the author of any design has, for a good and valuable consideration, executed the same for some other person, such other person is alone entitled to register". This now follows from ss. 4(1) and (2).

§10.141 Under the *Act*, the author is generally the first proprietor of the design, unless the author has "executed the design for another person for a good and valuable consideration". In the latter case the employer is the first proprietor.

§10.142 In *Uniformes Town & Country Inc. v. Labrie*¹ a designer was the registered owner of designs for restaurant uniforms and the burden therefore rested upon the respondent company to prove that it had become the owner on the basis of section 12(1) of the *Act*. The designs had been made by the designer on request by the respondent, who was submitting the designs as a response to a call for tender by a restaurant. The Federal Court of Appeal held that the $400 given to the designer for the design of the restaurant uniforms was given to cover expenses and did not constitute "good and valuable consideration". The Trial Court had erred in not considering the fact that the appellant had retained the originals of her designs, which the respondent never requested from her. The Court did not find evidence establishing any connection between the money received and the task awaiting the appellant; it was unlikely that the appellant would have been so naive as to accept so little payment and in any circumstances such naivety was expressly protected by the *Act*.[2]

[1]   (1992), 44 C.P.R. (3d) 514 (F.C.A.).
[2]   See also *Renwal Manufacturing Co. v. Reliable Toy Co.*, [1949] Ex. C.R. 188 where it was held that the employee had received "good and valuable consideration" through his salary and that he had not incurred any expenses at all. He was therefore not the proprietor of the design and the registration of the design by him was hence invalid, *ab initio*. Reference was made to *Lazarus v. Charles* (1873), 42 L.J. Ch. 507 and *Equator Manufacturing Co., Re* (1926), 1 D.L.R. 1101 (Ont. S.C.).

L.   INTEGRATED CIRCUIT TOPOGRAPHY ACT

§10.143   The *Integrated Circuit Topography Act*[1] grants the creator of the topography[2] an exclusive right to reproduce, manufacture and import the topography, or any substantial part thereof, or an integrated circuit product incorporating the topography. The exclusive right subsists for ten years after the calendar year in which the first commercial exploitation of the topography took place or after ten years of the calendar year of the filing date of the application for registration, whichever is first in time.

[1]   C.S. 1990, c. 37, ss. 1 to 28.
[2]   "Topography" is defined as the design of the disposition of the interconnections and the elements for the making of an integrated circuit product or for the making of a customization layer (or layers) to be added to an integrated circuit product in an intermediate form.

§10.144   In the case of an employment relation, the *Act* determines that the employer, for whom the topography was created is deemed to be the creator of the topography. However, the employee and his employer may make other agreements.[1]

[1]   Section 2(4).

M.   PUBLIC SERVANTS INVENTIONS ACT

§10.145   With respect to inventions made by public servants, the *Public Servants Inventions Act*[1] establishes that all rights to an invention are vested in Her Majesty when (a) the invention is made by a public servant while acting within the scope of his duties or employment, or made by a public servant with facilities, equipment or financial aid provided by or on behalf of Her Majesty, or (b) the invention resulted from or is connected with the public servant's duties or employment (section 3). Where the appropriate minister determines that an invention is vested in Her Majesty, the minister may file an application for a patent naming the inventor. Further, the appropriate minister may authorize payment of an award to the civil servant who made the invention.

[1] R.S., c. P-31, s. 1.

§10.146 Not many cases have been decided under the *Public Servants Inventions Act*. In *Dauphinee v. The Queen*[1] the main question was whether an award given to a public servant for his inventions in accordance with section 10 of the *Act* was employment income or capital gain for taxation purposes. The invention was not within the scope of the employment and the public servant only used the facilities and equipment of the employer once the invention had been made to test it. Frequently, work on the inventions was done in his spare time. All the inventions related, however, to the employment in a general way and they therefore undisputedly came within paragraph 3(b) of the *Act*. The Court found that an award received under the *Public Servants Inventions Act* constituted "other remuneration" under the *Income Tax Act* and was therefore taxable as employment income.[2]

[1] [1980] C.T.C. 332 (F.C.T.D.).
[2] See also *Jarlan v. R.*, [1984] C.T.C. 375, which followed *Dauphinee v. The Queen*. The award received was employment income regardless of the fact that the inventor no longer was a resident of Canada.

CHAPTER 11

THE WRITTEN EMPLOYMENT CONTRACT AND SOME SPECIFIC PROVISIONS

A. INTRODUCTION

§11.1 A written employment agreement offers many advantages. One of the advantages is that it protects both the employer and the executive by reducing the risk of later misunderstandings or disputes. Indeed, exact terms of a verbal agreement often become blurred years or even months later, sometimes because those who made the verbal representations at the time are no longer around when a problem arises.

§11.2 A carefully drafted employment agreement provides a clear statement of the principal obligations and rights of the employer and the executive. This helps to reduce the uncertainty which is often at the root of litigation. Another advantage is that it provides a record for future management personnel of the conditions of employment agreed to by the parties when they entered into or modified their employment relationship. A written agreement may also enumerate in what circumstances, manner and at what costs, if any, the employment relationship may be terminated, which are issues that frequently cause parties to resort to litigation. The written agreement may list undertakings by the executive of certain obligations in favour of the employer, such as undertakings not to compete against the company or not to solicit the employer's clientele or employees after employment. Furthermore, the written agreement helps clarify the extent to which working conditions may or may not be unilaterally modified by the employer in the course of employment. Finally, it provides a sense of security to both the employer and the executive with respect to a very important part of their business and their life.

1. Common Law

§11.3 With respect to the common law, it was not until the early 1980s that courts began to affirm the validity of written employment contracts governing all aspects of the employment relationship, including notice of termination. Prior to 1980, the courts would often invoke the principles of unconscionability and inequality of bargaining power to find termination notice periods in written employment contracts void.

However, three decisions of the Ontario Court of Appeal[1] in the early 1980s upheld relatively short notice periods in the written contracts and affirmed the courts' willingness to enforce the terms of the bargain struck between the parties. In *Matthewson v. Aiton Power Ltd.*,[2] the court stated:

> The fact that [the respondent] was unemployed and needed a job, absent other factors, is not a ground for holding that there was an "inequality of bargaining power" and setting aside the contract on that ground. There is no suggestion of oppressive or unconscionable acts on the part of the appellant company in securing this contract or its terms. The notice clause, of course, equally bound the employer.

This principle was recently confirmed by the Supreme Court of Canada in *Machtinger v. Hoj Industries Ltd.*[3]

---

[1] *Wallace v. Toronto-Dominion Bank* (1983), 145 D.L.R. (3d) 431, leave to appeal dismissed (1983), 52 N.R. 157n (S.C.C.); *Jobber v. Addressograph Multigraph of Canada Ltd.* (1980), 1 C.C.E.L. 87; *Matthewson v. Aiton Power Ltd.* (1985), 8 C.C.E.L. 312.

[2] *Matthewson v. Aiton Power Ltd.* (1985), 8 C.C.E.L. 312 at 314.

[3] [1992] 1 S.C.R. 986.

§11.4 At common law, a well-drafted employment contract will be upheld by a court. However, the court will interpret the contract strictly against the party drafting the contract, which usually is the employer.

2. Civil Law

§11.5 Under Quebec law as well, a person is at liberty to enter into any type of contract and provide for any terms as long as the terms do not contravene public order and good morals. Article 9 of the Civil Code of Quebec stipulates that although, in the exercise of civil rights, derogations may be made from those rules of the code which supplement intention, no derogation is permitted from rules of public order. What constitutes public order is determined by statute[1] or by the courts.

---

[1] For example, the *Act respecting Labour Standards*, R.S.Q., c. N-1.1, is a statute of public order (see s. 93 of the Act). Employers and employees covered by this statute may not, by written contract, attempt to circumvent the minimum employment standards stipulated in the law. These minimum standards include minimum wages, overtime pay, legal holidays, annual leave with pay, rest periods, leave for family events, notice of termination, etc.

§11.6 In *Brasserie Labatt Limitée v. Villa,*[1] the Quebec Court of Appeal held that the requirement that the employee's whole family move with him to the new location following a geographical transfer was against public order.

¹ [1995] R.J.Q. 73 (Que. C.A.).

§11.6.1 In Quebec, an ambiguous clause in a contract is interpreted in favour of the person who contracted the obligation and against the person who stipulated it. But in all cases it is interpreted in favour of the employee if he or she is a party to a contract of adhesion.¹ The Civil Code defines the contract of adhesion in article 1379 as:

> a contract in which the essential stipulations were imposed or drawn up by one of the parties, on his behalf or upon his instructions, and were not negotiable.

It would be surprising for an executive's contract of employment to be an adhesion contract. More realistically, the executive's employment contract would be by mutual agreement reached through negotiation between the parties.

¹ Art. 1432 C.C.Q..

3. Illegal, Void or Unenforceable Clauses

§11.7 Should the parties include in a written employment contract a clause that is later held to be illegal, void or unenforceable, a question arises as to whether the balance of the agreement remains in force. Generally speaking, the nullity of a clause in a contract brings about the nullity of the whole agreement as it constitutes an indivisible entity. The exception to this rule is that, if the illegal, void or unenforceable clause is accessory to the whole agreement or is considered as such by the parties, it may be severed from the rest and all other provisions may remain in full force and effect. In the event the illegal, void or unenforceable clause is a principal and determinant one with regard to the entire agreement, the whole document will be void.¹ In *Ligue des Caisses d'Économie du Québec v. King*,² the entire written employment contract was declared null; many provisions, such as those concerning the length of the contract and remuneration, were in direct violation of the *Savings and Credit Unions Act*.³ As the court could not rely on the written agreement, it had to examine the issue of unlawful dismissal in the context of the general principles applicable to all employment relationships.

¹ Jean-Louis Baudouin, *Les Obligations*, 3rd ed. (Cowansville: Editions Yvon Blais, 1989), p. 220, notes 42, 43.
² D.T.E. 83T-19 (Que. S.C.).
³ R.S.Q., c. C-4 (now repealed and replaced).

(a) Severability

§11.8 To avoid the problem of having to determine whether or not the entire agreement will be void if one of its articles, paragraphs or provisions is declared illegal, a severability provision should be included in the written employment agreement. This provision generally stipulates that any illegal clause will be deemed to be severed from the remainder of the agreement. This will ensure that the entire agreement is not struck down if an individual clause is declared illegal and the valid remainder continues to apply in full force and effect.

(b) Independent Legal Advice

§11.9 It is not necessary that the employee receive independent legal advice before executing a written employment contract. However, courts have ruled that employees are not bound by the terms of a document where the company did not explain or discuss the terms with the employee, or indicate that such document was intended to be contractually binding.[1]

¹ *Carrick v. Cooper Canada Ltd.* (1983), 2 C.C.E.L. 87 (Ont. H.C.J.).

§11.10 In this chapter, we will briefly discuss provisions that are regularly incorporated in written employment agreements. Some provisions will be analyzed in greater detail than others as they are often the centrepiece of the agreement without which one or both parties would not have entered into the employment relationship.

B. DEFINING THE EXECUTIVE'S POSITION

§11.11 One of the first clauses in any written employment contract should be that which identifies the position to be held by the executive and defines his or her mandate. It sets out what general or specific type of work will be provided as well as the duties and responsibilities which are attached to this type of work. This clause is particularly useful in determining what type of work may be required to be performed by the executive. Careful drafting will prevent allegations that the employer has "constructively dismissed" the executive by assigning to him or her work which differs from that normally performed. Further, clear drafting may also allow the employer to change the nature of the executive's duties without his or her consent. The person or persons to whom the executive will report and from whom he or she will take orders is also generally specified in this clause.

C. DURATION PROVISIONS

§11.12 As discussed earlier, employment is for a fixed term or for an indeterminate period.[1] Fixed-term contracts are often used for temporary assignments and for senior-level employment. In some cases, an executive leaving stable employment for a new position may want certain guarantees including a minimum term of employment and, therefore, may require a fixed-term contract. Employers may suggest a longer term to reassure the executive of their intentions of an extended relationship, or when they want to establish costs in advance. A short-term contract may be preferred in cases where the success of the relationship is uncertain or in cases of potential corporate reorganization. If an executive is confident that within two or three years he or she will accomplish a number of achievements, a short-term contract may be favoured; this would place the executive in a stronger bargaining position for the future or provide some freedom to pursue employment with another employer.

---

[1] Refer to Chapter 6, "Provide the Work", under the heading "Duration", at §§6.42 et seq. This is also expressly stipulated at art. 2086 of the Civil Code of Quebec.

§11.13 Fixed-term contracts are often coupled with some type of renewal clause. Many employers and executives prefer to reaffirm their relationship from year to year. However, there are employment contracts whereby the term of employment is fixed but other conditions, e.g., salary, may be renewed from year to year. These generally provide that either party may sever its ties at a specific time prior to the expiry of the current term as long as written notice is provided.

D. PLACE OF WORK

§11.14 The place where the services will be provided and executed is a sensitive issue for an increasing number of people. On the one hand, the location may be particularly important if the executive has a young family or has a spouse who is also employed. On the other hand, it may be crucial to the employer to ensure that the executive is able and willing to work at many locations, allowing for a well-rounded development in view of future corporate responsibilities. Increasingly, parties to the employment relationship are stating the place of work and whether the executive is required to relocate at the unilateral request of the employer.

§11.15 Even though certain fields of employment are renowned for the fact that transfers to different locations are a regular occurrence, misunderstandings can be avoided if the parties provide for this eventuality in a written document. It may be relevant to determine at the time of hiring whether the mobility required, if any, is city-wide, province-wide, country-wide, or world-wide. In businesses involving frequent transfers, it may also be pertinent for both employer and executive to establish from the outset the probable frequency of such transfers. Failing to address this important issue may lead an employer to invest time and money in a person it believes to be a key player, only to learn that the executive is opposed to a change in location. Moreover, should the employer force the relocation, an issue of constructive dismissal may arise.

E. NON-COMPETITION

§11.16 A non-competition clause is a restrictive covenant by which the employer limits the executive's legal right to compete following the termination of the employment relationship. Employers frequently insist on these provisions when the departure of a key executive and subsequent hire by a competitor would render the employer's business vulnerable as a result of the executive's knowledge of the business and its customers or clients.

1. Civil Law

§11.17 Since non-competition clauses limit an individual's freedom to earn a living, they have been greeted by the courts with much resistance. Until recently in Quebec's civil law system, a restrictive covenant such as a non-competition provision was *prima facie* valid,[1] and thus the party who invoked the nullity of the clause had the burden of proving its invalidity.[2] The Civil Code of Quebec now provides, however, that the burden of proof that the stipulation is valid is on the employer. This view is more consistent with the view traditionally held by the common law jurisdictions, the major difference being that while at common law the restrictive covenant is *prima facie* invalid and there must be proof of its validity, at civil law the validity of the clause is recognized, it is its extent that is questioned. Although there is an absolute reversal in the burden of proof that is imposed on the party seeking to enforce the covenant in Quebec, existing case law may nonetheless be extremely valuable in so far as the same elements which were previously argued to prove its invalidity will now be used to argue its validity. Essentially, only the onus is changed. The principles remain the same.

¹ *Beneficial Finance Co. of Canada v. Ouellette*, [1967] B.R. 721 (Que. C.A.), at 728.
² C.C.L.C., art. 1203. See also *Betz Laboratories Ltée v. Massicotte*, [1980] R.P. 355 (Que. C.A.), at 370; *Toulouse v. Laiterie St-Georges Ltée*, [1978] C.A. 210 (Que.), at 211; *Elsley v. J.G. Collins Inc. Agencies*, [1978] 2 S.C.R. 916, at 928-29; *Godin v. Gary Abraham Business Consultants Inc.*, [1986] R.J.Q. 809 (S.C.), at 812; *Entreprises Ludco Ltée v. Burnac Leaseholds Ltd.*, J.E. 86-1089 (Que. S.C.).

§11.17.1 There were no express provisions in the Civil Code of Lower Canada which dealt with the existence or validity of a restrictive covenant. These covenants were, however, recognized by the courts. Article 2089 of the Civil Code of Quebec now stipulates that:

> The parties may stipulate in writing and in express terms that, even after the termination of the contract the employee may neither compete with his employer nor participate in any capacity whatsoever in an enterprise which would then compete with him.
> Such a stipulation shall be limited, however, as to time, place and type of employment, to whatever is necessary for the protection of the legitimate interests of the employer.
> The burden of proof that the stipulation is valid is on the employer.

Notwithstanding this difference, the main principle which should be retained from the Civil Code of Quebec is an express recognition of the right for the parties to agree to a restrictive covenant. It is also clear from this provision that there are limited types of restrictive covenants that are permissible. Article 2089 sets out what criteria will be examined. These criteria, which are the same as those previously recognized by the courts, are examined more fully below.

§11.17.2 One extremely important caveat regarding the enforceability of the restrictive covenant should be made, however. Under article 2095 of the new Civil Code of Quebec:

> An employer may not avail himself of a stipulation of non-competition if he has resiliated the contract without a serious reason or if he has given the employee such a reason for resiliating the contract.

This article codifies a handful of cases which had decided that the pairing of a non-competition clause and a clause allowing termination of the employee at any time without cause was invalid.[1]

---

[1] For example, *Aliments Humpty Dumpty Ltée v. Gagnon*, [1988] R.J.Q. 1840 (S.C.); *Morden et Helwig Ltée v. Perreault, Mathieu & Cie*, [1987] R.J.Q. 1572 (S.C.).

2. Common Law

§11.18   At common law, the restrictive covenant is *prima facie* invalid and, in order for it to be upheld, three questions must be answered in the affirmative:

(1) Is the restraint reasonable between the parties to the covenant in that it goes no further than protecting the employer's interests?

(2) Is the restraint reasonable in the public interest?

(3) Does the employer have an interest deserving of protection?[1]

---

[1] W.R. Gale and B.A. Grosman Q.E., "The Enforceability of Written Employment Contracts and the Termination of Probationary Employees" (1988) Institute of Continuing Legal Education.

3. Reasonableness

§11.19   With respect to reasonableness the following has been said:

> The true view at the present time, I think, is this: The public has an interest in every person's carrying on his trade freely: so has the individual. All interference with individual liberty of action in trading, and all restraints of trade of themselves, if there is nothing more, are contrary to public policy, and therefore void. That is the general rule. But there are exceptions: restraints of trade and interference with individual liberty of action may be justified by the special circumstances of a particular case. *It is a sufficient justification, and indeed it is the only justification, if the restriction is reasonable* — reasonable, that is, in reference to the interests of the parties concerned and reasonable in reference to the interests of the public, so framed and so guarded as to afford adequate protection to the party in whose favour it is imposed, while at the same time it is in no way injurious to the public.

· · · · ·

> Whatever restraint is larger than the necessary protection of the party can be of no benefit to either; it can only be oppressive, and, if oppressive, it is, in the eye of the law, unreasonable.[1]

---

[1] *Nordenfelt v. Maxim Nordenfelt Guns & Ammunition Co.*, [1894] A.C. 535 (H.L.), at 565, 549 (emphasis added). See also *Tank Lining Corp. v. Dunlop Industrial Ltd.* (1982), 40 O.R. (2d) 219 (C.A.); *Dale & Co. v. Land* (1987), 56 Alta. L.R. (2d) 107 (C.A.) and *Woodward v. Stelco Inc.* (1996), 20 C.C.E.L. (2d) 70 (Ont. Ct. (Gen. Div.)), where a non-competition clause effective indefinitely was not found to be unrea-

sonable since a lifelong retirement allowance was received in return and the employee, a senior manager, was sophisticated enough to know his contractual obligations.

§11.20 As alluded to above, the purpose of a non-competition clause must be limited to the protection of the employer's legitimate business interest.[1] This implies that the covenant should target only those executives whose knowledge of the employer's business could damage the employer's position in the market if the executive becomes a competitor with his or her former employer.[2] As one author has stated very clearly:

> ... the employer should be in a position to persuade a court that the motivating reason for the covenant is not to establish a hold upon the employee or to gain a bargaining advantage over him by inhibiting his freedom of movement but rather to protect the legitimate business interests which are the product of substantial effort or investment by the employer. Second, and closely related, the employer should be able to show that it has made every effort to keep the burden upon the employee as small as possible, consistent with reasonable protection of such interests. This involves a number of considerations: (1) The undertakings should be obtained only from those classes of employees whose positions are such that their future activities present a reasonably high probability of substantial damage. (2) When feasible, the covenant should be tailored to fit the circumstances of the individual employee; where this is not possible, reasonable classifications of employees should be devised and the covenant tailored so that the burden on each class is held to a minimum. (3) The program should be administered in a flexible manner. For example, the employer should be willing to grant waivers of the restraint in many cases. It should not be unwilling to renegotiate the terms of a covenant with an employee when conditions change if this can be done on the facts of the individual case without loss of reasonable protection and without disruption of personnel relations. (4) In some cases, the employer may even wish to consider making financial arrangements to moderate the burden on the employee.[3]

[1] *Sharpe v. Jaggs Fashions Ltd.* (1993), 50 C.P.R. (3d) 197 (Ont. Ct. (Gen. Div.)).
[2] *Elsley v. J.G. Collins Insurance Agencies Ltd.*, [1978] 2 S.C.R. 916; *Friesen v. McKague* (1992), 96 D.L.R. (4th) 341 (Man. C.A.), revg in part (1992), 42 C.C.E.L. 175 (Q.B.).
[3] H.M. Blake, "Employee Agreements Not to Compete" (1960), 73 Harv. L. Rev. 625, at 687-88.

§11.21 The question which must be asked is what employer's interests must be protected and against what?[1] In order to determine whether the criteria of reasonableness and legitimate interest are valid, the courts will examine (a) the duration of the covenant, (b) the territory it covers, and (c) the nature of the prohibited activities contained within the covenant.[2] In the absence of a legitimate proprietary interest requiring protection, a restrictive covenant is contrary to public policy and void.[3]

¹ *Herbert Morris Ltd. v. Saxelby*, [1916] 1 A.C. 688 (H.L.), at 701 (the employer did not succeed in proving that the employee could steal his clients since the employee had never had any contact with them). See also *Beneficial Finance Co. of Canada v. Ouellette*, [1967] B.R. 721 (Que. C.A.), at 728; *Nordenfelt v. Maxim Nordenfelt Guns & Ammunition Co.*, [1894] A.C. 535 (H.L.), at 565; *Canadian American Financial Corp. (Canada) Ltd. v. King* (1989), 36 B.C.L.R. (2d) 257 (C.A.).

² *Herbert Morris Ltd. v. Saxelby*, [1916] 1 A.C. 688 (H.L.); *Cameron v. Canadian Factors Corp.*, [1971] S.C.R. 148; *Moore Corp. v. Charette* (1987), 19 C.C.E.L. 277 (Que. S.C.), at 288.

³ *R.L. Crain Inc. v. Hendry* (1988), 48 D.L.R. (4th) 228 (Sask. Q.B.).

(a)   Duration

§11.22 The duration of the prohibition to compete must be limited and reasonable in respect of the employer's interests. Thus, a clause containing no such limitation will in fact prevent someone from carrying on his or her trade indefinitely and consequently be abusive, illegal and unenforceable.[1]

¹ *National Financial Brokerage Center Inc. v. Investors Syndicate Ltd.* (1986), 9 C.P.R. (3d) 497 (Que. C.A.).

§11.23 Although each case will turn on its own particular circumstances, the courts are generally more inclined to rule that a non-competition clause of less than two years' duration is reasonable. A clause exceeding two years in duration will be reasonable only in exceptional cases.[1] Indeed, many non-competition covenants that are otherwise reasonable have been invalidated because of a duration which exceeded the period necessary for protection of the employer's legitimate interests.[2] Moreover, when the duration does not specify the period by number of months or years (*e.g.*, as long as the employee holds shares in the company), it may be held invalid.[3]

¹ *Journal la Seigneurie Inc. v. Desmarteau*, [1987] R.J.Q. 2501 (S.C.) (10 years); *Toulouse v. Laiterie St-Georges Ltée*, [1978] C.A. 210 (Que.) (4-year clause valid because court aimed only at protecting the employer's interests and not at preventing the employee from working); *Nordenfelt v. Maxim Nordenfelt Guns & Ammunition Co.*, [1894] A.C. 535 (H.L.) (25-year clause valid due to limited clientele); *Hecke v. Compagnie de Gestion Maskoutaine Ltée*, [1970] C.A. 225 (Que.); *H.F. Clarke Ltd. v. Thermidaire Corp.*, [1976] 1 S.C.R. 319; *Elsley v. J.G. Collins Ins. Agencies*, [1978] 2 S.C.R. 916 (5 years); *Morin v. Société de Gestion S.S.B. Ltée*, [1982] R.P. 106 (Que. S.C.) (4 years); *Frisco Bay Industries of Canada Ltd. v. 107410 Canada Inc.*, [1984] R.L. 149 (Que. S.C.); *L.E.L. Marketing Ltée v. Otis*, D.T.E. 89T-1007 (Que. S.C.); *Shalimar Physiotherapy Ltd. v. Deans and Westwood Physiotherapy Ltd.* (1989), 68 Alta. L.R. (2d) 371 (Q.B.); *Genesis Canada Inc. v. Hill* (1994), 56 C.P.R. (3d) 419 (Ont. Ct. (Gen. Div.)); *Dale & Co. v. Land* (1987), 56 Alta. L.R. (2d) 107 (C.A.), *Béton Brunswick Ltée v. Martin*, 66 C.P.R. (3d) 320 (N.B.C.A.) (five year non-compete reasonable).

² *Maguire v. Northland Drug Co.*, [1935] S.C.R. 412 (5 years); *Standard Electric Time Co. of Canada v. Finagel*, [1965] C.S. 532 (Que.) (5 years); *Herbert Morris Ltd. v. Saxelby*, [1916] 1 A.C. 688 (H.L.) (7 years); *Dominion Blank Book Co. v. Harvey*

(1941), 79 C.S. 274 (Que.) (5 years); *Cameron v. Canadian Factors Corp.*, [1971] S.C.R.
148 (5 years); *M & M Caravane Ltée v. Gagnon*, [1973] C.S. 1020 (Que.) (3 years);
Produits V-TO v. Bolduc, [1976] C.S. 1325 (Que.) (20 years); *B.M.G. Towing v. Gee*,
[1979] R.L. 316 (Que. S.C.) (5 years); *Aliments F.B.I. Ltée v. Valade*, [1987] R.J.Q.
2600 (S.C.).
³ *Hydro-Semence Inc. v. Equilbec*, [1981] R.P. 325 (Que. S.C.).

§11.24 If the executive has intimate and special knowledge of the employer's clientele and the ways of influencing this clientele, the courts will not hesitate to recognize the validity of a non-competition clause.¹ However, in the absence of proof of such influence on the employer's clients, the courts will hesitate to recognize the validity of the clause.²

¹ *Friesen v. McKague* (1992), 96 D.L.R. (4th) 341 (Man. C.A.) at 346.
² *Aliments Humpty Dumpty Ltée v. Gagnon*, [1988] R.J.Q. 1840 (S.C.).

(b) Territory

§11.25 The territory covered by the non-competition clause must be clearly defined.¹ It must be no wider than is necessary to protect the employer's legitimate interests,² failing which it will be invalidated. Thus, if the business is localized, the territory of restraint will be fairly narrow in nature. Large urban areas may cause a problem because there are many competing businesses in the area. Blanket restrictions of the area or a part of the area may be unreasonable as the employee may be prevented from dealing with prospective clientele.³ Furthermore, the failure to stipulate a territorial limitation will cause the non-competition clause to be null.⁴ Courts are more likely to hold a geographic limitation objectionable if its enforcement would have the effect of preventing an employee from practising his or her profession.⁵

¹ *Provincial Mobile Inc. v. Lebel*, [1975] C.S. 134 (Que.), at 136. In *Mutual Life & Citizens Assur. Co. v. Picotte* (1936), 61 B.R. 390 (Que. C.A.), the court determined that a clause in which the territory was limited to the territory in which the employee had effectively exercised his duties was valid. See also *Bratton, Crews, Cumming Group Inc. v. Sinnige* (1988), 24 C.P.R. (3d) 542 (Ont. H.C.J.), where the absence of a geographical limitation did not invalidate the covenant.
² *Grossman v. Schwarz*, [1943] B.R. 145 (Que. C.A.) (the court considered that the absence of an express definition of the territory would have the effect of including the entire universe, England or Canada, which would be patently unreasonable). See also *Produits chimiques A.C.P. Chemical Inc. v. Paolitto*, D.T.E. 95T-323 (Que. S.C.); *Mutual Life Assur. Co. v. Picotte, supra*, note 1; *Beneficial Finance Co. of Canada v. Ouellette*, [1967] B.R. 721 (Que. C.A.), at 726 (the majority of the court, when examining a clause which forbade competition and solicitation in "any city or the environs or trade territory thereof in which [the employee] shall have been located or employed within one year prior to such termination", stated that the area was not "defined or described with sufficient certainty and is therefore unreason-

able and unenforceable"); *T. v. B.*, [1958] C.S. 587 (Que.), at 595 (it was decided that where no locality was mentioned, the non-competition clause was invalid since it was too indefinite); *Provincial Mobile Inc. v. Lebel*, [1975] C.S. 134 (Que.), at 136; and, more recently, *National Financial Brokerage Center Inc. v. Investors Syndicate Ltd.* (1986), 9 C.P.R. (3d) 497 (Que. S.C.), at 502.

³   *Gordon v. Ferguson* (1961), 30 D.L.R. (2d) 420 (N.S.C.A.), affd 46 M.P.R. 344 (S.C.C.).

⁴   *Cathild Inc. v. Rondeau*, D.T.E. 94T-562 (Que. C.A.); *Reed Stenhouse Ltd. v. Foster* (1989), 69 Alta. L.R. (2d) 80 (Q.B.). But see *Central Dynamics v. Tremblay*, D.T.E. 90T-1092 (Que. S.C.); *Acorn Products (Canada) Ltd. v. Adler* (1973), 10 C.P.R. (2d) 162 (Ont. H.C.J.).

⁵   *Terra Engineering v. Stewart* (1994), 56 C.P.R. (3d) 77 (B.C.S.C.); *Semiconductor Insights Inc. v. Kurjanowicz* (1995), 63 C.P.R. (3d) 532 (Ont. Ct. (Gen. Div.)), supp. reasons 65 C.P.R. (3d) 166 (Div. Ct.); *Ernst & Young v. Stuart* (1994), 92 B.C.L.R. (2d) 339 (C.A.), revg in part (1993), 46 C.C.E.L. 161 (S.C.).

§11.26 The British Columbia Court of Appeal has stated that "[t]he permissible geographic scope of a restraint is to be measured by the reasonable mutual expectations of the parties at the time of making the contract."[1]

¹   *Canadian American Financial Corp. (Canada) Ltd. v. King* (1989), 36 B.C.L.R. (2d) 257 (C.A.), at 262.

(c)   Nature of the Prohibited Activities

§11.27 The third element which will be scrutinized to determine whether the non-competition clause is reasonable and aimed at protecting the employer's legitimate interests is the nature of the prohibited activities.[1] The Supreme Court of Canada has indicated that anything more than limiting solicitation of clients of the employer may be held invalid.[2]

¹   *Godin v. Gary Abraham Business Consultants Inc.*, [1986] R.J.Q. 809 (S.C.), at 816.

²   *Elsley v. J.G. Collins Ins. Agencies*, [1978] 2 S.C.R. 916. See also *Reed Shaw Osler Ltd. v. Wilson* (1981), 17 Alta. L.R. (2d) 81 (C.A.) at 87.

§11.28 If the services offered by the executive are specialized and the efforts necessary for providing the employer's services or producing its products are great, a longer period of restraint will more likely be upheld.[1]

A restraint is not valid unless the nature of employment is such that customers will either learn to rely upon the skill or judgment of the servant or will deal with him directly and personally to the virtual exclusion of the master, with the result he will probably gain their custom if he sets up business on his own account.

¹   *Boily v. Systèmes de Formation et de Gestion Perform Inc.*, [1984] C.S. 433 (Que.).

§11.29 The courts will also hesitate to recognize the validity of a non-competition clause which aims at restricting access to potential clients who are not current clients of the employer.[1]

> [1] *Bassman v. Deloitte, Haskins & Sells of Canada* (1984), 79 C.P.R. (2d) 43 (Ont. H.C.J.); *P. Brunet Assurance Inc. v. St-Jean*, D.T.E. 90T-922 (Que. S.C.).

§11.30 Other factors which the court may examine to determine the validity of a non-competition clause include whether the clientele is limited,[1] the trade secrets which must be protected,[2] and the date of the signing of the clause. In *Société Pole-Lite Ltée v. Cormier*,[3] it was determined that a non-competition clause which was signed by an engineer who had been working for the company for over 30 years was invalid, as the employee had been encouraged to sign this document under false representation, in that he had received no true consideration in exchange for his obligations.

> [1] *Nordenfelt v. Maxim Nordenfelt Guns & Ammunition Co.*, [1894] A.C. 535 (H.L.); *Aliments Humpty Dumpty Ltée v. Gagnon*, [1988] R.J.Q. 1840 (S.C.).
> [2] *Bassman v. Deloitte, Haskins & Sells of Canada* (1984), 79 C.P.R. (2d) 43 (Ont. H.C.J.).
> [3] [1989] R.J.Q. 1584 (S.C.).

4. Reading Down the Covenant

§11.31 The onus of proving that a covenant is reasonable as between the parties falls upon the person relying on it.[1] After the employer has established the reasonableness of the restrictive covenant as between the parties, the employee has the onus of proving that it is contrary to the public interest.[2]

> [1] *Friesen v. McKague* (1992), 96 D.L.R. (4th) 341 (Man. C.A.), revg in part (1992), 42 C.C.E.L. 175 (Q.B.).
> [2] *Esso Petroleum Co. v. Harper's Garage (Stourport) Ltd.*, [1967] 1 All E.R. 699 (H.L.); *Sunsweet Fundraisers Inc. v. Moldenhauer* (1991), 40 C.P.R. (3d) 212 (Sask. Q.B.).

§11.32 If a non-competition covenant is found to be invalid, for example because its geographical scope is too wide, some parties have asked the courts to rewrite the agreement or sever the invalid portion. The British Columbia Court of Appeal has clearly stated its position on this issue:

> It is only if the covenant is not valid as it stands that a question of severance arises. The courts have always resisted rewriting a contract that the parties have made. No doubt they will continue to do so. So whether the reason for the invalidity is because the covenant as it stands is void for uncertainty or because it is unreasonable either in reference to the interests of the parties or the interests of the public, the courts will only sever the covenant and expunge a part of it if the

obligation that remains can fairly be said to be a sensible and reasonable obligation in itself and such that the parties would unquestionably have agreed to it without varying any other terms of the contract or otherwise changing the bargain. It is only if they had been told when they made the contract that they could not have what they had drafted but could have the portion that would remain after the severance and expungement, and, only if in those circumstances they would both have readily agreed to the severance and expungement without any other change in the contract, that any request for severance can succeed. It is in that context that reference is made in the cases to severing and expunging merely trivial or technical parts of an invalid covenant, which are not part of the main purport of the clause, in order to make it valid. . . . The purpose of the severance is to retain the bargain made by the parties, not to impose a new bargain on them.[1]

---

[1] *Canadian American Financial Corp. (Canada) Ltd. v. King* (1989), 36 B.C.L.R. (2d) 257 (C.A.), at 270-71. This passage has been applied in *Pembroke (City) Police Services Board v. Kidder* (1995), 22 O.R. (3d) 663 (Gen. Div.), at 674. See also *Deacon v. Stevens*, unreported March 27, 1984 (Ont. H.C.J.); *Nelson Burns & Co. v. Gratham Industries Ltd.* (1983), 74 C.P.R. (2d) 145 (Ont. H.C.J.); affd (1986), 9 C.P.R. (3d) 532 (C.A.); leave to appeal to S.C.C. refused 14 C.P.R. (3d) 446 (S.C.C.). But see *Computer Centre Personnel Ltd. v. Lagopolous* (1975), 8 O.R. (2d) 480 (H.C.J.); *Morris & MacKenzie Inc. v. Maddaugh*, unreported, Aug. 16, 1995 (Ont. Ct. (Gen. Div.)).

§11.33 At civil law, the courts interpret the clause in such a way as to apply the parties' true intent. Thus, if a distinguishable part of the clause is invalid, the courts will strike the invalid part and will maintain the rest.[1]

---

[1] *Elsley v. J.G. Collins Ins. Agencies*, [1978] 2 S.C.R. 916, at 925; *Produits V-TO Inc. v. Bolduc*, [1976] C.S. 1325 (Que. S.C.), at 1327. See also *Moore Corp. v. Charette* (1987), 19 C.C.E.L. 277 (Que. S.C.), at 291-92.

§11.34 Furthermore, some courts have recognized that a restrictive covenant which provides for alternative obligations may be valid,[1] while others have struck such clauses down.[2]

---

[1] *Produits Duvernay Ltée v. Duguay*, D.T.E. 90T-372 (Que. S.C.); *Ref-Com Commercial Inc. v. Holcomb*, D.T.E. 91T-989 (Que. S.C.); *P.A. Boutin (1986) Inc. v. Julien*, J.E. 90-1118 (Que. S.C.).
[2] *Canadian American Financial Corp. (Canada) Ltd. v. King* (1989), 36 B.C.L.R. (2d) 257 (C.A.).

F. NON-SOLICITATION OF CLIENTS

§11.35 Non-solicitation covenants of this type are aimed at preventing a former executive from soliciting the employer's clientele. The same principles as those used to determine the validity of non-competition clauses are used to determine whether a non-solicitation clause is valid. More specifically, the courts will look at the duration and the nature of the prohibited activity. However, the courts have, on several occasions, concluded that it is necessary for a non-solicitation clause to be restricted geographically.[1]

---

[1]   *Moore Corp. v. Charette* (1987), 19 C.C.E.L. 277 (Que. S.C.), at 288; *Frisco Bay Industries of Canada Ltd. v. 107410 Canada Inc.,* [1984] R.L. 149 (Que. S.C.); *Caron-Jetté Ltée v. Drapeau,* [1943] B.R. 494 (Que. C.A.). But see *W.R. Grace & Co. of Canada Ltd. v. Sare* (1980), 28 O.R. (2d) 612 (H.C.J.).

§11.36 Since a prohibition to solicit clientele is less onerous than a non-competition covenant, non-solicitation covenants are generally interpreted less strictly[1] than non-competition covenants when courts are assessing their validity and justifying their applicability:[2]

> The courts of common law attach much importance to the identification of whether the non-competition clause aims at the exercise of an occupation in general or is limited to prohibiting the solicitation of the former employer's clients. Prohibiting the exercise of an occupation to the benefit of the former employer must be limited in time and space to the immediate interests of the employer, whereas the courts will not be as demanding in the prohibition from soliciting clients of the former employer.[3]

---

[1]   *Tapis Sherbrooke Acton Ltée v. Tapis Acton Ltée,* [1976] C.S. 1123 (Que. S.C.).
[2]   *L.E.L. Marketing Ltée v. Otis,* D.T.E. 89T-1007 (Que. S.C.); *Tapis Sherbrooke Acton Ltée v. Tapis Acton Ltée,* [1976] C.S. 1123 (Que. S.C.); *Cooper Corrugated Containers v. Browning,* unreported, Feb. 8, 1988 (Ont. H.C.J.) (where the portion of a restrictive covenant preventing solicitation of customers was upheld); *Atlas Farm Services of Canada Ltd. v. Savory,* unreported, March 29, 1993 (Ont. Ct. (Gen. Div.)).
[3]   *Moore Corp. v. Charette* (1987), 19 C.C.E.L. 277 (Que. S.C.), at 287 (authors' translation).

§11.37 As with non-competition clauses, the courts will examine the nature of the executive's functions, and the nature of his or her work with the company or the company's clientele in order to assess the reasonableness of the non-solicitation covenant.[1]

---

[1]   *Elsley v. J.G. Collins Ins. Agencies,* [1978] 2 S.C.R. 916, at 924; *Aliments Humpty Dumpty Ltée v. Gagnon,* [1988] R.J.Q. 1840 (S.C.).

§11.38 Occasionally, the courts have distinguished between cases where an executive solicits the former employer's clients and cases where the executive accepts mandates from the former employer's clients. For example, in *A.B.C. Sonorisation Inc. v. Bigras,*[1] there was evidence that the defendant (the former employee) had not offered his business card but had given it to his former employer's client after she had asked for it. The court determined that if there had been any solicitation, it had been done by the former client and not the defendant and, thus, there was no breach of the non-solicitation clause.[2]

---

[1]   J.E. 88-551 (Que. Prov. Ct.), at 4 of the judgment.
[2]   This same distinction was made in *L.E.L. Marketing Ltée v. Otis*, D.T.E. 89T-1007 (Que. S.C.), where a motion for injunction was rejected for these same reasons.

§11.39 However, in *Nationwide Advertising Service Inc. v. David*,[1] the court found that there is little difference between soliciting former clients and telephoning them to advise them of one's change in employment, particularly where the new employer's business is substantially similar to the former employer's business.[2]

---

[1]   J.E. 88-1336 (Que. S.C.) (on appeal, C.A.M. 500-09-001325-885, inactive since March 1, 1989).
[2]   See also *P. Brunet Assurance Inc. v. St-Jean*, D.T.E. 90T-922 (Que. S.C.).

§11.40 With regard to the nature of the prohibited activity, it is well established that the courts will only uphold clauses that clearly define the clients with whom contact is prohibited.[1]

---

[1]   *Groupe Pétrolier Olco Inc. v. Dire*, J.E. 92-138 (Que. S.C.); *Entreprises Omnipac Inc. v. De Serres*, [1988] R.J.Q. 1951 (S.C.), citing *Lange Co. v. Platt*, [1973] C.A. 1068 (Que.), at 1071-72 (which cites *Herbert Morris Ltd. v. Saxelby*, [1916] 1 A.C. 688 (H.L.)).

G. NON-SOLICITATION OF EMPLOYEES

§11.41 The undertaking not to hire away employees following termination of employment is another clause regularly found in executive employment contracts. This prohibition aims at ensuring that employees who have special knowledge or talents are not lured away by a former executive to compete against the former employer. Again, careful drafting and proper limits are necessary for the enforceability of such a covenant. It may be argued that it is only the person who is a party to the contract who may be bound by this obligation. In the case where an employee of the executive's former employer voluntarily leaves his or her employment and solicits a position with the executive, one must wonder whether the executive is prohibited from hiring him on. Although it is unlikely that in such a case the executive could be found to breach his contractual obligations, in practice, prudence has dictated that the executive refuse to hire the employee for fear of being sued by his former employer. The Quebec Court of Appeal has ruled that even without a non-solicitation of employees covenant, ex-employees were prohibited from soliciting employees of the former employer.[1]

---

[1] *Soniplastics Inc. v. Chagnon*, D.T.E. 96T-282, J.E. 96-540 (Que. C.A.).

H. CONFIDENTIALITY PROVISIONS

§11.42 Executives are frequently made privy to highly confidential or sensitive information during the course of their employment. The extent to which such information must be kept confidential after termination of employment depends on factors such as the nature of the information and the executive's position within the hierarchy of the organization.[1] Although article 2088 of the Civil Code of Quebec states that all employees are bound not to use confidential information they may obtain in carrying on or in the course of their work and that this obligation continues for a reasonable time after cessation of the contract, confidentiality provisions are regularly included in an executive's employment contract.[2]

---

[1] See Chapter 10, "Loyalty", under the heading "Duty of Confidentiality" at §§10.106 *et seq.*

[2] The Civil Code of Lower Canada did not include such a provision. Hence, it was necessary to include it in the written employment contract so as to be binding upon the employee. In the absence of such a clause, it was necessary to attempt to include this obligation as a part of the duty of loyalty recognized at art. 1024 C.C.L.C. or prove that the confidential information was a trade secret.

§11.43 Confidentiality provisions are intended to bring to the executive's attention his or her legal duty of secrecy during and after employment. They are also used to enlarge the executive's post-employment legal duty to protect and/or maintain the employer's competitive place in the market. For example, a confidentiality provision may prevent the executive from using or divulging corporate information which the obligation of loyalty or even the fiduciary duty would not protect. The clause must be drafted clearly to allow the executive to identify with precision information which he or she is prohibited from revealing or using.

§11.44 As in the case of non-competition clauses, the courts have determined that confidentiality clauses must also meet the requirements of reasonableness and legitimate business interests, including limits with respect to duration.[1]

¹ *Davidson Hearing Aid Centre v. Stephen* (1987), 16 C.P.R. (3d) 547 (Ont. H.C.J.), at 553.

§11.45   In *Investors Syndicate Ltd. v. Vandenberg*,¹ the court granted an interlocutory injunction aimed at prohibiting the ex-employee from using client cards and from divulging to anyone confidential information relating to Investors Syndicate. In arriving at this conclusion, the court examined the nature of the work, the access Vandenberg had to the employer's confidential information and the control that he had exercised over Investors Syndicate's clients during his 20 years of employment.

¹ (1986), 10 C.C.E.L. 153 (Ont. H.C.J.). See also *Telecredit Inc. v. Lewsey*, unreported, Nov. 15, 1990 (B.C.S.C.).

H.1.   SURVIVAL OF COVENANT UPON TERMINATION OF EMPLOYMENT

§11.45.1   Case law has differed in its interpretation of the binding nature of a restrictive covenant upon termination of employment. In some cases the courts have held that if the employer terminates the employee without cause, he cannot rely upon the terms of the restrictive covenant to prohibit an employee from competing with him.¹ In other cases, this has been an irrelevant consideration.² In Quebec, article 2095 of the Civil Code of Quebec puts this issue to rest. This article provides that an employer cannot avail himself of a stipulation of non-competition if he has resiliated the contract without a serious reason or if he has himself given the employee such reason for resiliating the contract. This provision seems fair in that it prohibits the employer from preventing an employee from working after a wrongful termination. Of note, however, is the fact that this article does not make reference to the employee's duty to be loyal or not to make use of confidential information during and after the termination of employment. Thus, it would appear that these obligations are binding even if they are not expressly stipulated in the employment contract.

¹ *Gerrard v. Century 21 Armour Real Estate Inc.* (1991), 4 O.R. (3d) 191 (Gen. Div.), at 199; *Jostens Canada Ltd. v. Zbieranek* (1992), 42 C.C.E.L. 264 (Ont. Ct. (Gen. Div.)); *General Billposting Co. v. Atkinson*, [1909] A.C. 118 (H.L.).
² *Poole v. Tomenson Saunders Whitehead Ltd.* (1987), 16 B.C.L.R. (2d) 349 (C.A.).

I. REMEDIES FOR BREACH

1. Injunction

§11.46 If the executive fails to comply with the terms of any of the restrictive covenants, the employer may apply to the courts for injunctive relief. This is usually the proper recourse to take when it is difficult to assess the damages arising from the former executive's breach.[1] The injunction is also the proper recourse for a breach of the obligation of loyalty provided by C.C.Q., art. 2088.[2]

[1] *Viandes Pierre Trottier (1985) Inc. v. Trottier* (1989), 29 C.C.E.L. 305 (Que. S.C.); *Guaranteed Pure Milk Co. v. Patry*, [1957] B.R. 54 (Que. C.A.); *Manco Inc. v. Damphousse*, D.T.E. 97T-813 (Que. S.C.).

[2] *Savoie v. Tremblay*, D.T.E. 97T-118 (Que. S.C.).

2. Breach of Contract

§11.47 An employer may also initiate an action for damages for breach of contract. The disadvantage with this recourse is that it is a slow process and it may be difficult to evaluate the actual loss that an employer has suffered from the executive's breach.

3. "Liquidated Damages" Clause

§11.48 The parties may choose to incorporate a "liquidated damages" clause or, in Quebec, a penal clause which allows the parties to determine in advance the amount of damages which the executive will have to pay the employer if the executive fails to abide by the terms of the restrictive covenant.[1] The main advantage of incorporating this type of clause in the individual employment contract is the degree of certainty associated with it. In fact, article 1623 of the Civil Code of Quebec provides that a creditor who avails himself of a penal clause is entitled to the amount of the stipulated penalty without having to prove the injury he has suffered. The main disadvantage with the clause is that in cases where damages are greater than those provided for in the employment contract, such damages will not be awarded as the clause essentially places a ceiling on the amount of compensation the employer can claim from the former executive. Alternatively, some courts will refuse to enforce such clauses where the amounts agreed to are not proportionate to actual damages. Article 1623(2) of the Civil Code of Quebec allows the court to reduce the amount of the stipulated penalty if the creditor has benefitted from partial performance of the obligation or if the clause is abusive. At Common Law, these clauses are struck down as constituting a penalty and not an accurate assessment of actual damages. Moreover, article 1622(2) of the Civil Code of Quebec stipulates that although a creditor has a right to avail himself of a penal clause instead of enforcing the specific performance of the obligation, in no case may he exact both the performance and the penalty unless such penalty has been stipulated to be for mere delay in the performance of the obligation. In Ontario, however, one should be cognizant of section 99 of the *Courts of Justice Act*[2] which provides:

> A court that has jurisdiction to grant an injunction or order specific performance may award damages in addition to, or in substitution for, the injunction or specific performance.

[1] C.C.Q., arts. 1622 to 1625. See for example *133262 Canada Inc. v. Bierbrier*, D.T.E. 95T-84 (Que. C.A.). But see *Tony Murray & Associates Co. v. Law* (1991), 93 Nfld. & P.E.I.R. 292 (Nfld. T.D.).

[2] R.S.O. 1990, c. C.43.

§11.48.1 In *Zielinski v. Saskatchewan Beef Stabilization Board*,[1] the general manager's employment contract stipulated that if he was dismissed he would be compensated with a lump sum retiring allowance equal to 2.5 times his final average remuneration. The Board terminated his employment without cause or notice three and one half months after he became general manager and he sued on the basis of the clause. The court rejected the plaintiff's claim to the 2.5 years retiring allowance on the basis that it was inoperative until the employee assumed permanent status with the board one year after he commenced employment with it. Interestingly enough, the court also recalled the principle that courts will refuse to apply the express terms of a contract where the parties have, in effect, provided a penalty for breach rather than a genuine pre-estimate of damages. The court held that in this case the clause was ". . . extravagant and unconscionable in amount in comparison with the greatest loss that could conceivably be proved to have followed from the breach . . ." as "I am not aware of any life time employee in this province being awarded damages for wrongful dismissal equal to 2.5 times his yearly salary, other benefits and bonuses, let alone an employee of 5.5 months."

[1] (1992), 42 C.C.E.L. 24 (Sask. Q.B.), appeal allowed in part on other grounds [1994] 3 W.W.R. 44 (Sask. C.A.).

§11.48.2 The court also considered the fact that, under the terms of the clause, the employee would have been entitled to the same measure of damages no matter when the breach occurred, and held that this was clearly an indication that the clause was not a pre-estimate of damages, but a penalty. It was thus unenforceable. What is particularly interesting about this case is its discussion of what constitutes a penalty clause as well as the fact that it serves as a good example of a situation where an illegal clause will not be maintained even if it is drafted so as to benefit the employee.

§11.48.3 Another element which should be retained from the case is the inference which the court drew regarding the fact that the damages did not escalate in consideration of the length of service. In view of this discussion, it may be wise to ensure that all termination clauses in common law jurisdictions do not fall into this trap by ascertaining that they are drafted in such a way as to ensure that the damages reflect the length of service.

4. Rights to Relief

§11.49 The Supreme Court of Canada summarized the relative rights to relief as follows:

1. Where a fixed sum is stipulated as and for liquidated damages upon a breach, the covenantee must elect with respect to that breach between these liquidated damages and an injunction.
2. If he elects to take the liquidated damages stipulated he may recover that sum irrespective of his actual loss.
3. Where the stipulated sum is a penalty he may only recover such damages as he can prove, but the amount recoverable may not exceed the sum stipulated.
4. If he elects to take an injunction and not the liquidated sum stipulated, he may recover damages in equity for the actual loss sustained up to the date of the injunction or, if tardy, up to the date upon which he should have sought the injunction, but in either case, not exceeding the amount stipulated as payable upon a breach.
5. Where a liquidated damages sum is stipulated as payable for each and every breach, the covenantee may recover this sum in respect of distinct breaches which have occurred and he may also be granted an injunction to restrain future breaches.[1]

[1] *Elsley v. J.G. Collins Ins. Agencies*, [1978] 2 S.C.R. 916, at 938.

§11.50 It should be noted that there is a difference between a penal clause and a liquidated damages clause. In civil law, penal clauses which aim at retribution and provide for greater damages than the evaluation of the actual damages caused to the employer may be upheld; whereas at common law, a clause aimed at retribution and punishment in which the damages are significantly greater than the actual damages suffered by the employer will not be upheld.[1]

1 See Chapter 13, under the heading "Heads of Damages".

J.   REMUNERATION AND BENEFIT CLAUSES

§11.51 Remuneration clauses usually include salary, bonus, share in profits or other monetary entitlements. In each case, an amount or method of calculating the amount should be specified as well as frequency of payment. Moreover, a clause in the contract should address the issue of future salary increments. These increases may be fixed or may be based on the executive's performance during the previous fiscal or calendar year. Benefits include paid vacation, participation in insurance plans or other company benefit packages. The contract should clearly indicate the remuneration or benefits which are dependent upon the goodwill of the employer. Indeed, a frequent source of litigation is whether a bonus is an integral part of one's remuneration or is a purely discretionary payment.

§11.52 It is prudent to establish in advance whether a departing executive will be entitled to commissions on sales or a pro-rated bonus or share in the profits following his or her termination. In *Dumas v. Aeterna-Vie Cie d'Assurance*,[1] the court held that it was not against public order to stipulate in an employment contract that the employee, an insurance agent, was not entitled to commission on renewal premiums paid after his termination. The court added, however, that had it been proven that the employer had dismissed the employee to avoid paying renewal commissions, it would have considered whether that constituted an abuse of rights.

[1] J.E. 80-910 (Que. S.C.).

§11.53 It is not against public order to include in an employment contract a clause providing for the forfeiture of the right to a bonus in case of termination. A clause entitling the executive to a bonus to be calculated and paid at the end of the employer's fiscal year and providing for a *pro rata* bonus in case of discharge for cause was interpreted as also entitling the executive to a *pro rata* bonus when the contract was terminated by mutual consent before the end of the fiscal year.[1]

[1] *CJMS Radio Montréal Ltée v. Audette*, [1966] B.R. 756 (Que. C.A.).

§11.54 Written employment contracts sometimes include deferred remuneration clauses. Often referred to as "golden handcuffs", the purpose of these types of clauses is to defer the payment of part of the remuneration to a future date, provided the executive is still an employee, thereby ensuring the executive's long and loyal service. Such remuneration may consist of a bonus, stock option or supplementary pension benefit and is intended to ensure that key employees do not prematurely abandon the organization in favour of a short-term increase in salary offered by a competing or different employer.

K. NOTICE OF TERMINATION AND SEVERANCE PAYMENT

1. Scope of Contract

§11.55 Because of the multiplicity and apparent inconsistency of court decisions with respect to what misconduct or lack of performance constitutes cause and the length of the period of reasonable notice of termination in the absence of cause, it is often preferable to determine from the outset of the relationship how and in what circumstances the employment relationship will end. Such a clause may specifically envisage the advance notice which must be given to the executive in case of termination following a corporate reorganization, elimination of a position or any other reason which at law does not amount to cause for summary termination. Conduct or events which will constitute cause for termination without notice or pay in lieu thereof should also be set out in the contract. Events giving rise to immediate dismissal without notice or payment may be enlarged or restricted over those which the courts have said will justify immediate dismissal. In other words, a written contract may enumerate situations which, although not constituting cause at law (such as an at arm's length sale of the business or the executive's personal bankruptcy), will give rise to immediate termination of the employment relationship without notice or pay in lieu of notice or will allow the employer to terminate the employment relationship on short notice, provided such terms do not violate the provisions of other legislation or public policy.[1]

[1] *Wegg v. National Trust Co.* (1993), 47 C.C.E.L. 104 (Ont. Ct. (Gen. Div.)) (Where but for a contractual provision limiting notice to three months, the employee would have been entitled to a 15-month notice period).

§11.56 An employer wishing to rely upon such rights to give notice as specified in the termination clause must invoke the clause at the time of termination. Relying on the clause, once the employment relationship has ended or is before the court, may be too late since the exercise of the right to terminate under a particular clause can only arise from a valid existing contract. In that situation, the general rules of common or civil law regarding termination would apply.[1] Of course, in all circumstances it will be necessary to prove that the clause did indeed form part of the employment contract. Where, for example, the notice provisions were merely incorporated on the employment form which the employee was requested to sign on his first day of work and the provisions were not explained to him, the employee was entitled to view the form as a mere administrative document as opposed to an employment contract, the terms of which were not binding on the employee.[2]

[1] *Carr v. Fama Holdings Ltd.* (1989), 40 B.C.L.R. (2d) 125 (C.A.). See also *Nikanpour v. Fenco-Lavalin Inc.*, D.T.E. 88T-573 (Que. S.C.).
[2] *Burden v. Eastgate Ford Sales & Service (82) Co.* (1992), 44 C.C.E.L. 218 (Ont. Ct. (Gen. Div.)).

§11.56.1 Furthermore, if the employee receives a notice of termination according to the terms of his employment contract but in giving such notice the employer commits an abuse of rights, then the notice clause may be disregarded by the court. Proper notice owed to the wrongfully terminated employee will then be determined on the basis of the general rules of common or civil law regarding termination.[1]

[1] For a discussion of what constitutes an abuse of rights, see para. 14.13 *infra*. See also *Duchesne v. Produits Canadiana inc.*, D.T.E. 94T-1330 (Que. S.C.).

2. Contracting out of Notice Requirements

§11.57 Careful attention must be given to the recent Supreme Court of Canada decision, *Machtinger v. HOJ Industries Ltd.*,[1] in establishing a contractual notice period. The issue was stated as follows:

> If an employment contract stipulates a period of notice less than that required by the *Employment Standards Act*, . . . is an employee who is dismissed without cause entitled to reasonable notice of termination, or to the minimum period of notice required by the Act?[2]

The Court held that any attempt to contract out of the minimum standards in the Act is null and void; thus, the notice clause of the employment contract was also null and void. Moreover, the Court ruled that since the notice clause was null and void, it could not be used as evidence of the parties' intentions and, thus, reasonable notice at common law was required. The essence of this ruling is that notice required by the employment standards legislation must form the minimum base for notice in order to be an enforceable contractual term of the employment agreement.

[1] [1992] 1 S.C.R. 986.
[2] [1992] 1 S.C.R. 986, at 996.

§11.57.1 In Quebec, particular attention must be drawn to two new provisions in the Civil Code of Quebec:

> Art. 2091: Either party to a contract with an indeterminate term may terminate it by giving notice of termination to the other party.
> The notice of termination shall be given in reasonable time, taking into account, in particular, the nature of the employment, the special circumstances in which the work is carried on and the duration of the period of work.
> Art. 2092: The employee may not renounce his right to obtain compensation for any injury he suffers where insufficient notice of termination is given or where the manner of resiliation is abusive.

Since no decisions have yet been rendered under these provisions, one must wonder as to their repercussions. One will have to follow the decisions of the Quebec courts very closely in order to determine the impact these clauses will have on contactual notice provisions as well as on termination agreements. Will the courts interpret contractual notice provisions differently depending upon when they were entered into (pre or post new Civil Code; at the time of the drafting of the contract; during employment or at the time of termination)? What about termination agreements? Can a settlement be set aside? If so, how long after it has been concluded? Will an employee be able to reopen an agreement after he or she finds himself or herself unemployed for a period that is longer than had initially been predicted. Will the courts look at the equality of the bargaining positions when re-examining a clause? When will an employer be able to consider that the issue of reasonable notice may be set aside as a matter that is settled? The civil courts will surely be asked these and many other questions regarding the validity and binding nature of notice payments in the years to come.

§11.57.2 Another point worthy of mention is the issue that the employee, like the employer, is bound to give reasonable notice of termination (although unlike the employee, the employer is not prohibited from renouncing to his right to receive this notice).

3. Monetary Indemnity in lieu of Notice

§11.58 Some written contracts provide that dismissal for any reason other than fraud or theft will give rise to the payment to the executive of a monetary indemnity. Such termination clauses should be drafted clearly and precisely. At least one court has held that if cause for dismissal exists, the employer will not be held to the execution of its obligation to give the notice stipulated by contract.[1] Although it does not specifically mention its applicability to contactual notice periods, it is arguable that article 2094 of the Civil Code of Quebec confirms this principle. This article reads as follows:

> One of the parties may, for a serious reason, unilaterally resiliate the contract of employment without prior notice.

¹ *F. v. Erb Offset Plates*, [1955] C.S. 245 (Que.).

§11.59 In many cases, employers do not want to give the executive advance notice of his or her termination of employment because they do not want to continue furnishing the work during the notice period. Indeed, the executive who knows that his or her days are numbered will not necessarily work with the same energy or interest. Further, there may be doubts as to the executive's loyalty during this period. Hence, employers often prefer to pay the executive an amount in lieu of notice of termination.

§11.60 It is therefore useful to agree in writing as to the method to be used to calculate the amount that will be paid to the executive for that part of the notice that is not given. Litigation may be avoided if the clause specifies whether the indemnity will be calculated on the basis of the executive's base salary at the time of his termination, or whether it will include a pro-rated part of the bonus received in the preceding year. Whatever calculation is used, the notice given must be clearly set out. Furthermore, the contract should stipulate whether the amount paid in lieu of notice will be paid in one lump-sum payment following the last day of work or by equal and consecutive payments at a predetermined frequency.

4. Obligation to Mitigate Damages

§11.61 The employment contract may also refer to the executive's obligation to mitigate and provide that the payments in lieu of notice will cease upon the executive finding alternative employment. Other variations of the employer's obligations to pay may also be provided. If a mitigation clause is not included, an employee may well enjoy a windfall by being entitled to the entire liquidated amount for the balance of the term of the contract.

§11.62 In the case of *Côté v. Cie Nationale de Forage et Sondage Inc.*,¹ Côté had been hired for a two-year period with the condition that he could be dismissed upon one month's notice if his behaviour or work was unsatisfactory. He was terminated after 14 months. The court held this type of dismissal clause should be interpreted restrictively against the employer. As the court found no evidence of a reasonable and sufficient motive to terminate employment on these grounds, it ordered payment in favour of Côté of his remuneration for the balance of the term.

[1] J.E. 84-1046 (Que. S.C.).

5. Termination Payment

§11.63 Finally, if the contract stipulates that an amount will be paid to the employee upon his termination, it is advisable to specify whether the payment is in lieu of notice or whether it is a severance payment. If the payment is considered to be severance pay, the employer may be obliged to give reasonable notice of termination in addition to the severance pay. Indeed, courts have held that since notice is a legal obligation in the case of termination without cause, the payment in lieu of notice is intended to compensate the prejudice caused by the abrupt termination and must be added to any severance payment, which is a purely contractual obligation aimed at rewarding the executive for his years of loyal service. Some clauses therefore stipulate that any severance payment includes the payment in lieu of notice of termination.

§11.64 Subsection 58(7) of the Ontario *Employment Standards Act*[1] is relevant in this regard. It states:

> Severance pay under this section is payable to the employee in addition to any other payment under this Act or contract of employment without set-off or deduction, except for,

• • • • •

> (b) payments made to the employee under a contractual severance pay scheme under which payments for loss of employment based upon length of service are provided.

[1] R.S.O. 1990, c. E.14.

§11.64.1 The issue of whether the payment is a severance payment or a payment in lieu of notice is also extremely important with regard to director and officer liability. Indeed the Supreme Court of Canada[1] has confirmed that their liability is limited to those payments which arise from services rendered for the corporation.[2]

[1] In *Crabtree (Succession de) v. Barrette*, [1993] 1 S.C.R. 1027.
[2] For a discussion on directors' and officers' liability, see Chapter 20, *Duties and Liabilities of Corporate Directors*.

§11.65   To enlarge or depart from an executive's or employer's legal rights, clear and precise drafting is required. Any ambiguity may render the clause unenforceable. Furthermore, an employer's right to invoke a termination clause is not absolute. Indeed, the clause may be set aside if the executive can demonstrate that the employer abused its right to invoke it.[1]

---

[1]   See *Quaker Oats Co. of Canada v. Côté*, [1949] B.R. 389 (Que. C.A.); *Macaulay v. Imperial Life Assur. Co. of Canada*, D.T.E. 84T-395 (Que. S.C.); *Paradis v. Cie Crawley & McCracken Ltée*, D.T.E. 87T-33 (Que. Prov. Ct.); *Machtinger v. HOJ Industries Ltd.*, [1992] 1 S.C.R. 986.

§11.66   The termination clause may in some cases prevent a traumatizing termination of the employment relationship for one party or the other. It limits an employer's exposure and may prevent the making of decisions too rapidly without evaluating the financial consequences of an abrupt cessation of employment. For the executive, it constitutes a pre-negotiated agreement and a relative source of financial comfort which may permit redirection of the executive's career with a minimum negative impact.

L.   EXECUTIVE PROTECTION FROM CHANGE IN CONTROL

§11.67   Clauses which offer financial protection to an executive in case of change in control of the employer are more popularly known as "golden parachutes". Golden parachutes were introduced in the United States in response to corporate reorganizations resulting from mergers and acquisitions and by reason of the American concept of "termination at will", which enables the employer to terminate an employment relationship without notice even in cases where no cause for termination exists. Upper management are generally aware that the continuation of their employment depends on the trust the board of directors or senior-level management affords them. An acquisition, merger or any form of change in control of the corporate employer, which translates into new influential personalities appearing at the management level, threatens the stability of this trusting relationship. Indeed, new owners are often of the opinion that a change in management or in the responsibilities held by existing management is necessary to rekindle the business' success. Risk of being replaced, transferred or having working conditions changed may precipitate, slow down, or abort a tentative change in control, depending on how the executive believes this change will affect his or her continued employment with the company. Golden parachutes have thus been formulated to deal with the uncertainty that reigns in the period of turbulence caused by the tentative change in control and to ensure a smooth transition.

§11.68 Golden parachute agreements seek to compensate an executive upon a change in control of the business, usually following termination of employment or when responsibilities, remuneration or other working conditions are negatively affected, allowing for resignation for good reason and entitlement to the benefits of the parachute. Although their origins arose in the United States, golden parachutes are now an integral part of Canadian corporate culture. They are regularly incorporated into executive employment agreements. American decisions and literature, however, continue to be the main source of commentary on their parameters.

1. Elements of a Golden Parachute Agreement

§11.69 In most cases, two principal triggering events must be present to enable the beneficiary of a golden parachute to pull on his or her parachute strings and claim the monetary compensation provided.

(a) Change in Control

§11.70 The first triggering event required is a change in control of the employer. The notion of change in control is broad in scope and must therefore be defined in clear and precise terms. This is essential to permit all interested parties, including the beneficiary, to determine whether the acquisition of shares or assets or the anticipated merger or any other change in the corporate structure will result in a change in control. Change in control of the employer may be defined in many ways, including:

- the accumulation of a certain percentage of the corporation's issued and outstanding shares;
- a change in directors comprising a majority of the board;
- the replacement of the top executive or immediate superior of the beneficiary;
- the alienation of an important part of the assets of the business;
- the privatization of the business; or
- a combination of any of the above-mentioned events.

§11.71 Furthermore, certain parachute clauses are triggered only if the change in control is hostile as opposed to friendly. The employment contract must provide for this possibility; otherwise, no distinction will be made in the event of one or the other.

(b) Loss of Employment or Resignation for Good Reason

§11.72 While the change in control provision can stand alone and trigger the operation of the parachute, it is usually accompanied by the second triggering event, namely that, concurrently with the change in control, the executive loses his or her employment or resigns for good reason because of unilateral changes to his or her terms and conditions of employment. The concurrency of the first and second triggering events must be specifically provided for in the employment contract. In other words, the parachute must specify the period of time following the change in control when the termination of employment or any second triggering event must take place to permit the executive to claim the benefit of the golden parachute. Some golden parachutes are single-triggered. These single-triggered parachutes enable the executive to claim the benefits of the clause as soon as a change in control occurs whether or not employment is terminated or working terms and conditions are changed. In fact, it is these single-triggered parachute clauses that have raised the strongest indignation among shareholders and other opponents of the golden parachute clause.

§11.73 Accordingly, golden parachute agreements which require the presence of a second triggering event (either loss of employment or resignation for good reason) are more the norm today. The loss of employment generally envisaged as the second triggering event is a termination without cause. Indeed, it would be ludicrous to permit an executive terminated by reason of gross incompetence, fraud or other disloyal act to claim the benefit of the golden parachute clause for the sole reason that termination coincided with a change in control.

§11.74 More sophisticated golden parachute clauses enumerate the types of changes to the executive's terms and conditions of employment which will constitute the second triggering event. Indeed, with the elaboration of the notion of constructive dismissal, many have recognized the benefits of defining within the employment contract those events which will allow the executive to resign for good reason and claim the benefits of the golden parachute clause. These events may include:

- a reduction in salary;
- a unilateral modification in the bonus plans or share in profits that would reduce the executive's remuneration;
- a forced geographical relocation;
- a reduction in the level of responsibility of the executive, or a change in the executive's title or function;

- a modification in the corporate structure of the business that negatively affects the executive's position in the company's hierarchy.

2. Advantages and Criticism of Golden Parachute Agreements

(a) Advantages

§11.75 Proponents of golden parachute agreements argue that such clauses benefit not only the executive, but also the business and its shareholders.

§11.76 First, parachute clauses offer security to executives in situations of take-over attempts. This allows them to examine and appreciate a take-over bid or other potential change in control objectively and in the best interest of the business rather than their own, thereby maximizing the shareholders' stake. It has also been stated that such agreements allow the board of directors to rely on the executive's advice without concern for the executive's objectivity or personal interest.

§11.77 Second, golden parachutes facilitate the recruitment of key executives. The argument is that without these types of financial arrangements protecting from the risk of termination without cause in case of hostile take-overs, businesses which are the target of take-overs would have difficulty recruiting or retaining key executives.

§11.78 Third, golden parachutes provide the executive with the financial security necessary to survive the turbulent period that surrounds the take-over attempt and, if successful, the corporate reorganization that normally ensues. This ensures the continuity of key employees during periods of uncertainty. It is believed that the executive will be less likely to jump ship during troubled times in order to seek or accept employment elsewhere if a parachute is in place.

§11.79 Fourth, some proponents of golden parachutes maintain that they are a defence mechanism to hostile take-over bids. In essence, it is believed that an unwanted purchaser will be discouraged by the costs that the business will have to incur in the event the attempt becomes reality and the successor wishes to eliminate existing management.

(b) Criticism

§11.80 Opponents of golden parachutes reply that the dissuasive role afforded to golden parachutes covering one or more executives is negligible. They say that studies have shown that the compensation offered by parachute agreements constitute approximately 1% of the total cost of the transaction. The opponents use this analysis to support their argument that although it may be a factor an eventual purchaser will consider, it is improbable that the parachute standing alone would discourage a hostile take-over. Opponents also found their criticism on the excessive nature of the monetary clauses, which promotes corporate waste and overcompensates executives. They add that executives should not receive additional compensation for a pre-existing duty to be loyal and to act at all times in the best interest of the business and the shareholders. Opponents of parachute agreements caution that executives may favour take-overs that are not in the shareholders' best interest, as the thought of a lucrative exit may be more appealing than remaining with the company.

3. Golden Parachute Compensation

§11.81 Is there any limit to the benefits that can be paid to an executive who validly triggers the parachute? Are there any circumstances where shareholders or other interested parties may question the legitimacy or validity of golden parachute agreements?

(a) Business Judgment Rule

§11.82 In the United States, golden parachutes must not offend the "business judgment rule". Briefly stated, the business judgment rule stands for the proposition that there must be a valid business reason or purpose behind a golden parachute. However, since the decisions relating to amounts payable to executives are at the exclusive discretion of the board of directors, the courts will presume that a board has exercised due judgment and will not interfere in these decisions unless exceptional circumstances exist. Hence, in the absence of fraud, bad faith, gross overreaching or abuse of discretion, the courts will refrain from interfering with the exercise of business judgment by a board of directors. Because of this rule, legal action questioning these business decisions rarely succeeds.

(b) Fiduciary Duty

§11.83 In Canada, directors have a fiduciary duty (or under the Quebec *Companies Act*,[1] a mandatary duty) to act in the corporation's best interest. The controlling issue is, therefore, whether in carrying out their duties the directors have breached their fiduciary (or mandatory) duty by overcompensating the executive and are thus wasting corporate assets. One test that has been referred to as the "proper business doctrine" requires directors to exercise their powers for a proper purpose. The proper purpose test was enunciated by the British Columbia Supreme Court in *Teck Corp. v. Millar*:[2]

> The Court's jurisdiction to intervene is founded on the theory that if the directors' purpose is not to serve the interest of the company, but to serve their own interest or that of their friends or of a particular group of shareholders, they can be said to have abused their power. The impropriety lies in the directors' purpose. If their purpose is not to serve the company's interest, then it is an improper purpose. Impropriety depends upon proof that the directors were actuated by a collateral purpose, it does not depend upon the nature of any shareholders' rights that may be affected by the exercise of the directors' powers.

> • • • • •

> I think the Courts should apply the general rule in this way: The directors must act in good faith. Then there must be reasonable grounds for their belief.

[1] R.S.Q. 1977, c. C-38.
[2] (1972), 33 D.L.R. (3d) 288 (B.C.S.C.), at 312, 315.

§11.84 The test as enunciated in *Teck* was subsequently applied in *First City Financial Corp. v. Genstar Corp.*[1] and *Olympia & York Enterprises v. Hiram Walker Resources Ltd.*[2] A decision of the Nova Scotia Supreme Court suggests that *Teck* is not law in Canada. The decision, *Exco Corp. v. Nova Scotia Savings & Loan Co.*,[3] chose to follow the earlier decision of *Hogg v. Cramphorn Ltd.*,[4] in which the court proposed that the use of powers for any purpose other than the purpose for which the powers were delegated is improper, regardless of the intentions of the directors involved. *Exco* also implies that there is an onus placed on the directors to show that their motivation and actions were consistent with the best interests of the company, and inconsistent with any other interest.

[1] (1981), 33 O.R. (2d) 631 (H.C.J.).
[2] (1986), 59 O.R. (2d) 254 (Div. Ct.).
[3] (1987), 35 B.L.R. 149 (N.S.S.C.).
[4] [1966] 3 All E.R. 420 (Ch.).

§11.85 If the courts apply the two-step test enunciated in the *Teck* case, the following factors will be examined:

(1) for whose benefit the agreement was made;
(2) the time when and circumstances under which the agreement was entered into; and
(3) the method by which the golden parachute was approved by the corporation.

§11.86 If the test as formulated in *Hogg* is applied and the parachute was executed during the course of a take-over, then an argument may be made that the power of a director to determine terms of employment was not delegated for the purpose of maintaining control of the corporation.[1] If the timing of the granting of the golden parachute indicates that its purpose was defensive in order to avoid a hostile take-over, then once again the issue becomes whether a benefit has been conferred upon the corporation, and indeed is such benefit in the best interests of the corporation and its shareholders.

[1]   W.J.M. Hanson, D. MacLeod and C. Murray, "Employment Issues Following an Acquisition", *Insight* (1989), at 5.

(c) Enforceability and Validity of a Golden Parachute Clause

§11.87 Canadian cases dealing with the enforceability of golden parachute agreements have consistently found that a golden parachute agreement will not be enforceable if it has not met the requirements for its validity under the security statutes and stock exchange rules applicable to the company.[1] In the United Kingdom, the Judicial Committee of the Privy Council has addressed the validity of a golden parachute. In *Taupo Totara Timber Co. v. Rowe*,[2] the Privy Council was faced with the issue of whether a golden parachute clause was *ultra vires* the company or *ultra vires* the directors of the company. The clause contained a change in control provision whereby the employee could resign within 12 months after a person or company had acquired at least 50% of the issued capital. The termination for good reason clause was effective for a period of 12 months following the change of control and provided for the payment of a lump sum equivalent to five times the employee's gross annual salary plus other benefits in the event termination of employment occurred for any reason whatsoever. In response to the *ultra vires* argument, the Privy Council stated:

> There remains an argument based on *vires*. It was suggested that the agreement was *ultra vires* the company or *ultra vires* the directors of the company. Their Lordships cannot accept either of these contentions. There can be no doubt as to the general power of the company to engage servants and to enter into service agreements with them. There is no question as to the *bona fides* of the directors in entering into this particular agreement. *It was shown that similar agreements had been entered into with other employees and that to do so had been the company's policy for several years.* The view that inclusion of a provision giving protection in the event of a take-over was in the interest of the company, was clearly one that reasonable and honest directors might take. *In its absence, the staff might be likely to go elsewhere.* In the case of the respondent, as has been noted, *an agreement in substantially similar form had been entered into in 1969 and there could be nothing suspicious, or open to criticism, in replacing that agreement in 1971* when he became managing director. As had been pointed out, there is explicit power in the articles to appoint a

managing director on such terms as the directors, acting of course *bona fide*, think fit. These points therefore fail.[3]

Clearly the Privy Council was persuaded by the timing of the implementation of the agreement. As well, the Privy Council implicitly recognized the "retention of management" justification. Whether Canadian courts will follow this line of reasoning remains to be seen.

[1] *Hamelin v. Seven Mile High Group Inc.* (1994), 89 B.C.L.R. (2d) 298 (C.A.) and *Rajani v. Davis Wire Industries Ltd.* (1995) 15 C.C.E.L. (2d) 262 (B.C.S.C.).
[2] [1977] 3 All E.R. 123 (P.C.).
[3] [1977] 3 All E.R. 123 (P.C.) at 128 (emphasis added).

(d) Taxing Provisions

(i) In the United States

§11.88 Mention must be made of the taxing provisions that have been enacted in the United States to deal with the compensation afforded to an executive under a golden parachute. Specific golden parachute rules were enacted in the U.S. in 1984 in response to the increasing trend towards their use. None prohibit the corporation from entering into a golden parachute agreement. However, they operate in an attempt to limit excessive payments under golden parachutes by denying certain deductions to the employer and taxing the recipient on excessive parachute payments.

§11.89 Unfortunately, these taxing provisions have, in some cases, removed the parachutes from court scrutiny if they fall within the exempting limits. Two court decisions in Ohio expressly relied on the fact that the severance payments fell within the "three times" limit, to support their decisions that the payments were reasonable.[1]

[1] See *Buckhorn Inc. v. Ropak Corp.*, 656 F. Supp. 209 (S.D. Ohio, 1987), affd 815 F. 2d 76 (6th Circ., 1987); *Worth v. Huntington Bancshares Inc.*, [1987] WL 25694 (Ohio App., Nov. 25, 1987) (No. S2861), affd on this point by (1989), 540 N.E. 2d 249 (Ohio S.C.).

(ii) In Canada

§11.90 Canadian taxing authorities have not taken similar action pursuant to our tax statutes. One can only speculate whether Revenue Canada will contemplate similar enactments. Perhaps the lack of response to date is due to the lack of Canadian jurisprudence pronouncing on the validity of golden parachutes.

(e) Surviving Judicial Scrutiny

§11.91 Employers who wish to implement golden parachute agreements as part of their compensation plan should take into account the following considerations to increase the chances that the agreement survives judicial scrutiny.

(i) Timing

§11.92 The timing of the conclusion of a golden parachute (at the beginning of employment, during employment, or on the eve of a take-over) may be relevant in the determination of whether the agreement was concluded for reasons of self-interest or in the shareholders' interest. If the parachute is executed on the eve of or during a take-over, it will be more difficult to allege many of the above-mentioned justifications cited in support of its use.

(ii) Origin of Proposal

§11.93 The golden parachute should, where possible, be proposed by a disinterested majority of the board of directors, and most certainly adopted by a disinterested majority.

(iii) Relationship to the Services Performed

§11.94 The parachute benefits should bear some reasonable relationship to the services performed or offered by the executive. When the value of those services is non-existent or inadequate, it is equivalent to a gift and may be invalid. Indeed, payments of amounts which would constitute a waste of the business' assets will not be justified. The amount which constitutes a waste of the business' assets depends on the reasonable value which the business receives in return for the promise of payment. The question is, therefore, whether in the long run the parachute agreement will profit the business. The compensation payable to the executive must be proportional to his or her abilities, responsibilities, years of loyal service, as well as to the business' profits and any other relevant element or circumstance. Hence, only those clauses which allow the legitimate objectives of the business to progress will survive judicial scrutiny.

(iv) Employee Obligation to Search for Alternative Employment

§11.95 Another issue that should be addressed in a parachute agreement is whether the executive has an obligation to search for alternative employment to be eligible for payment of the parachute indemnity and whether the indemnity payments will cease when the executive finds adequate or similar employment or commences self-employment. In this respect, the parties may wish to define the nature of adequate or similar employment. Should the parachute agreement be silent regarding these issues, then the employer may be obliged to pay the full fixed amount even if the executive finds employment immediately following his or her termination of employment or fails altogether to search for employment during the period of indemnity. The Alberta Court of Appeal[1] has found that if the employment contract contains a clause which provides for the payment of a stipulated amount upon termination rather than notice of termination, then the rules of mitigation do not apply. The employee is entitled to claim the full fixed amount rather than damages for failure to receive notice. A claim in damages brings about the corresponding obligation to mitigate one's damages.

[1] *Mills v. R. in right of Alberta*, [1986] 5 W.W.R. 567.

(v) Summary

§11.96 Obviously, there are many considerations which must be taken into account before undertaking the preparation of a golden parachute agreement. Both the content of the compensation undertaking and the procedural mechanism used to put it in place will be scrutinized. Documentation in support of the decision to execute a parachute should be recorded in the corporate records. Moreover, one must be prepared to show that the agreement is indeed in the best interest of the shareholders.

M. ARBITRATION PROVISIONS

§11.97 Essentially, an arbitration clause provides that the parties agree to submit the resolution of a present or future dispute to binding third party arbitration to the exclusion of the courts normally competent to hear such matters.[1] In the context of an employment contract, an arbitration provision prevents the employer and employee from exercising their right to seek the assistance of the courts in case of disagreement. In Ontario, the *Arbitration Act, 1991*[2] governs these matters. The Act provides that the court will only interfere

1. To assist the conducting of arbitrations.
2. To ensure that arbitrations are conducted in accordance with arbitration agreements.
3. To prevent unequal or unfair treatment of parties to arbitration agreements.

4. To enforce awards.[3]

The validity of such clauses was recognized by the Supreme Court of Canada in *Zodiak International Products v. Poland*.[4]

[1] In Quebec, see C.C.Q., art. 2638-2643 (previously C.C.L.C., art. 1926.1).
[2] S.O. 1991, c. 17.
[3] S.O. 1991, c. 17, s. 6.
[4] [1983] 1 S.C.R. 529.

§11.98 A general arbitration clause binding the employer and the executive would include, but not be limited to, any disputes pertaining to remuneration, vacation entitlement or the employer's right to unilaterally amend certain responsibilities of the executive as well as the determination of whether an event constituting cause for termination or otherwise has occurred.

§11.99 Arbitration requires that the adjudicator render a decision on the respective rights of the parties involved once they have had the opportunity to tender evidence and make submissions. The *Arbitration Act, 1991* states that an arbitral tribunal shall decide a dispute in accordance with the law, including equity, and may order specific performance, injunctive and other equitable remedies.[1]

[1] *Arbitration Act, 1991*, S.O. 1991, c. 17, s. 31.

§11.100 In contrast to decisions of administrative tribunals (such as an arbitrator appointed under labour relations legislation) which are subject to judicial review by the courts, decisions rendered under an arbitration agreement are binding on the parties and recourse by way of appeal to a court to set aside any such award is limited under section 46 of the *Arbitration Act*[1] (in Ontario) or by application for annulment as strictly regulated by article 947 of the *Code of Civil Procedure*[2] (in Quebec). The reasons for an appeal or for nullity are limited to those enumerated and generally include:

(1) one of the parties was not qualified to enter into the arbitration agreement (*i.e.*, not legally capacitated);
(2) the arbitration agreement is invalid;
(3) the party against whom the award is invoked was not given proper notice of the appointment of an arbitrator or of the arbitration proceedings or was otherwise unable to present its case;
(4) the award deals with a dispute not contemplated by or not falling within the terms of the arbitration agreement, or it contains decisions on matters beyond the scope of the agreement, in

which case the only provision annulled is the irregular one if it can be disassociated from the rest;

(5) the mode of appointment of arbitrators or the applicable arbitration procedure was not observed.

¹ S.O. 1991, c. 17.
² R.S.Q., c. C-25 [as am. 1986, c. 73, s. 2].

§11.101 Arbitration or alternative dispute resolution is becoming relatively popular and offers certain advantages over court litigation:

(1) the rapidity of the process (avoidance of procedural delays, backlog of the courts, etc.);
(2) limited rights of appeal;
(3) costs and fees are generally less;
(4) confidentiality and discretion (the hearing is not public);
(5) particular competence of the arbitrator, since people with particular experience or knowledge in similar matters or in a particular industry may be chosen as arbitrators.

§11.102 There are very few elements required for the validity of an arbitration agreement. In Quebec, the agreement must be in writing,¹ although this is not the case in Ontario. Secondly, the clause must clearly indicate that the employer and executive have agreed to defer to arbitration. An obligation to use arbitration is necessary; an option to use it is not sufficient. There must be recognition by the parties that the arbitrator's decision will be final and binding. Indeed, the Quebec Court of Appeal decided, in *Industrial Development & Renovation Organization of Iran v. Bertrand*,² that the absence of this third element rendered the arbitration agreement incomplete and therefore not obligatory.

¹ C.C.Q., art. 2640 (it is deemed to be evidenced in writing if it is contained in an exchange of communications which attest to its existence or in an exchange of proceedings in which its existence is alleged by one party and is not contested by the other party).
² [1984] R.D.J. 15. This decision was rendered before the current provisions came into force. It is no longer clear whether the recognition that the decision is binding is necessary (see *Gestion Claude Hébert v. Jacques Vinet Electrix*, unreported, April 18, 1988, File Nos. C.A.M. 500-09-00123-877, C.A.P. 88C-191, although prudence would dictate that such a provision be included.

§11.103 An arbitration provision affords greater freedom to the parties, allowing them to tailor the recourse to fit their particular needs. Indeed, the parties may determine the number of arbitrators who will be nominated to settle the dispute as well as the way in which they will be chosen. The parties may choose the law, local or foreign, that the arbitrator will apply, or exclude altogether the application of a certain statute. In addition, the parties may determine the procedure which will apply to the hearing as well as any delays which must be respected. Their choice is limited only by any mandatory provisions of the law, which are provisions of public order aimed at guaranteeing litigants the same measure of justice as that provided by the courts in terms of impartiality of the arbitrator and rules of fundamental justice. Where the parties have not provided any special procedural requirements, the procedure will be that provided by the *Code of Civil Procedure* or the *Arbitration Act*. The Code and Act become supplementary sources of law only in those areas where the parties have failed to stipulate particular rules.

§11.104   An arbitration provision may determine the language of the proceedings (written or verbal) and the location of the arbitration hearing. It may also be advisable to determine in advance how the fees and costs of the arbitrators will be shared by the parties.

§11.105   An arbitration provision is worth considering in any employment contract. It is a faster and less expensive way for the employer and executive to have their disputes settled. The parties may tailor the procedure to their needs and personalize it to the particular business within which their employment relationship exists.

PART III
TERMINATION OF THE EMPLOYMENT RELATIONSHIP

CHAPTER 12

TERMINATION OF EMPLOYMENT

A. INTRODUCTION

§12.1 The right of the employer or the executive to terminate the employment relationship and the consequences which flow from a termination are of central importance in the field of employment law. In general, an employment contract may be terminated upon the occurrence of a certain event or it may be repudiated by one of the parties to the contract. In addition, it may be terminated, at any time, by mutual agreement of the employer and the executive.[1] The parties may also agree to suspend, rather than sever, the employment relationship.[2]

---

[1] *Lees v. Arthur Greaves Ltd.*, [1974] I.C.R. 501 (C.A.). See C.C.Q., art. 2090.

[2] *Morin v. Honeywell Ltée*, D.T.E. 90T-529 (Que. S.C.), appeal abandoned July 3, 1990, C.A.M. 500-09-000517-904. See *Oleynick v. Jefferson Securities Inc.*, unreported, Sept. 16, 1991, Vancouver Doc. C901055 (B.C.S.C.), where the plaintiff/employee failed to show that his employer had acquiesced to his proposed temporary suspension of the employment contract.

B. TERMINATION UPON THE OCCURRENCE OF AN EVENT

1. Expiry of Term

§12.2 As noted in Chapter 6, "Provide the Work", employment contracts may be concluded for a fixed or indeterminate period.[1] Contracts concluded for a fixed period will automatically come to an end at the expiry of the term.[2] At that time, neither notice nor reasons for termination need to be given by either party since there is no dismissal or resignation involved.[3]

---

[1] See C.C.Q., art. 2086.

[2] *Groulx v. Commission Municipale du Québec*, D.T.E. 90T-739 (Que. S.C.); *Tinker-Labrecque v. Corp. de l'Hôpital d'Youville de Sherbrooke*, [1986] R.J.Q. 1283 (C.A.); *United Talmud Torahs of Montreal Inc. v. Dulude*, D.T.E. 84T-41 (Que. S.C.); *Dombrowski v. Dalhousie University* (1974), 55 D.L.R. (3d) 268 (N.S.S.C.), affd 79 D.L.R. (3d) 355 (C.A.); *MacLeod v. Bd. of School Commrs. of the Town of Dominion* (1958), 16 D.L.R. (2d) 587 (N.S.S.C.).

[3] *Lemay v. Boileau & associés Inc.*, D.T.E. 88T-618 (Que. S.C.); *Bélair v. Communications Radiomutuel Inc.*, D.T.E. 88T-268 (Que. S.C.).

2. Frustration/Impossibility of Performance

§12.3 When one of the parties to the employment contract, through no personal fault, becomes unable to perform his or her obligations, the contract of employment is severed and both parties are released from their respective obligations.[1] In this situation, the contract is said to be frustrated.

> [1] See C.C.Q., art. 1693 (previously C.C.L.C., art. 1202), and C.C.Q., art. 2093 (previously C.C.L.C., art. 1668).

(a) Illness

§12.4 The executive's inability to perform his or her work due to illness must be of a permanent or significant duration to justify severing the employment relationship.[1] It is difficult, however, to determine exactly how long an executive's involuntary absence may extend before the employer is entitled to treat the contract as rescinded. Among other things, this will depend on the nature and expected length of the illness, the prospect for recovery, the importance of the executive's duties and responsibilities, and the nature of the business. Consideration should also be given to human rights legislation, which generally prohibits discrimination based on disability or handicap.

> [1] *White v. Woolworth Canada Inc.* (1996), 139 Nfld. & P.E.I.R. 324 (Nfld. C.A.), application for leave to appeal dismissed (without reasons) [1996] S.C.C.A. No. 319; *MacLellan v. H.B. Contracting Ltd.* (1990), 32 C.C.E.L. 103 (B.C.S.C.); *Bolduc v. Tremblay*, J.E. 80-531 (Que. S.C.); *Bruneau v. Caverhill* (1909), 37 C.S. 271 (Que. Ct. of Rev.); *Dartmouth Ferry Commn. v. Marks* (1903), 34 S.C.R. 366; but see *Bohun v. Similco Mines Ltd.*, [1995] 6 W.W.R. 552 (B.C.C.A.) where the British Columbia Court of Appeal questioned the application of the *Dartmouth* case to modern-day employment relationships containing short-term and long-term disability provisions.

(b) Fortuitous Event and Financial Difficulties

§12.5 The situation may also arise when the employer is unable to perform its obligations. In order for the employer to be completely exonerated, its inability to perform must result from a fortuitous event. Examples of such events would include a fire, flood, earthquake, or any other natural disaster beyond the employer's control.[1] Moreover, the employer's inability to perform its obligations must not be temporary. It is only when the fortuitous event produces a lasting effect that the contract will be severed.

> [1] *Polyco Window Manufacturers Ltd. v. Saskatchewan (Director of Labour Standards)* (1994), 3 C.C.E.L. (2d) 101 (Sask. C.A.).

§12.6 Despite the arguments raised by some employers, courts have held that financial difficulties,[1] economic depression,[2] and non-renewal by a third party of a contract[3] do not qualify as fortuitous events.[4] The fact that the contract becomes less profitable than expected does not result in an impossibility to perform. It can be concluded, then, that dismissal for one of the above reasons is a dismissal without cause and the employer is required to give prior notice or payment in lieu of notice.

[1] *St. John v. TNT Canada Inc.* (1991), 56 B.C.L.R. (2d) 311 (S.C.); *Selick v. 149244 Canada Inc.* (1991), 39 C.C.E.L. 23 (Que. S.C.) (on appeal); *Burgess v. Central Trust Co.* (1988), 19 C.C.E.L. 193 (N.B.Q.B.); *Bordeleau v. Union Carbide of Canada Ltd.* (1984), 6 C.C.E.L. 88 (Que. S.C.); *Bergeron v. Emballages Purity Ltée*, J.E. 84-811 (Que. S.C.); *Leduc v. Union Carbide du Canada Ltée*, J.E. 84-783 (Que. S.C.); *Harkans v. Hercules Canada Ltée*, D.T.E. 84T-635 (Que. S.C.); *Luchuk v. Sport B.C.* (1984), 3 C.C.E.L. 117 (B.C.S.C.); *McNair and Guy v. J.D. Bremner & Son Ltd.* (1983), 58 N.S.R. (2d) 222 (S.C.); *Benson v. Brown Boveri Canada Ltd.*, [1983] C.S. 229 (Que. S.C.); *Lefebvre v. Westmount Life Ins. Co.*, J.E. 81-122 (Que. S.C.); *Smith v. Tamblyn (Alberta) Ltd.* (1979), 9 Alta. L.R. (2d) 274 (S.C.); *Maritime National Fish Ltd. v. Ocean Trawlers Ltd.*, [1935] 3 D.L.R. 12 (P.C.). See to the contrary *Commission des normes du travail v. Poudres Métalliques du Québec Ltée*, unreported, Jan. 13, 1984, 765-02-000101-83 (Que. Prov. Ct.); *Greenberg v. Gresca Co.* (1918), 55 C.S. 263 (Que. S.C.).

[2] *Thomas v. Surveyer, Nenniger & Chênevert Inc.*, D.T.E. 85T-192 (Que. S.C.), confirmed on appeal D.T.E. 89T-640 (C.A.); *Auger v. Albert Dyotte Inc.*, D.T.E. 85T-2 (Que. S.C.); *Labelle v. Experts-Conseils Shawinigan Inc.*, D.T.E. 84T-547 (Que. S.C.), appeal settled out of court Mar. 26, 1985, C.A.M. 500-09-000846-840; *Ferland v. Lachute (Cité)*, J.E. 82-920 (Que. Prov. Ct.); *Corriveau v. Larose* (1903), 24 C.S. 44 (Que. Circ. Ct.).

[3] *Cadorette v. O.G.I.S. Inc.*, D.T.E. 88T-575 (Que. S.C.); *Martin v. Okanagan Helicopters Ltd.*, unreported, May 24, 1985, 650-05-000100-843 (Que. S.C.).

[4] *Cadorette v. O.G.I.S. Inc.*, D.T.E. 88T-575 (Que. S.C.); *Misovic v. Acres Davy McKee Ltd.* (1985), 7 C.C.E.L. 163 (Ont. C.A.), varg 22 A.C.W.S. (2d) 50 (Co. Ct.); *Holloway v. Marystown (No. 2)* (1985), 58 Nfld. & P.E.I.R. 214 (Nfld. Dist. Ct.); *Martin v. Okanagan Helicopters Ltd.*, unreported, May 24, 1985, 650-05-000100-843 (Que. S.C.); *Oxford v. Advocate Mines Ltd.* (1983), 56 Nfld. & P.E.I.R. 296 (Nfld. Dist. Ct.).

§12.7 Financial difficulty on the part of the executive does not allow the employer to unilaterally terminate the employment contract nor does it constitute cause for dismissal.[1]

[1] *Leblond v. Québec (Procureur général)*, D.T.E. 89T-554 (Que. C.A.).

(c) Change of Employer

§12.8 The effect of a change of employer on the employment relationship will differ depending upon whether the employment contract is governed by civil law or common law. For this reason, it is extremely important when negotiating the sale of the assets of a business to determine the law which governs the employment relationship between the vendor and its employees. The effect of a sale of shares, however, will be the same in both legal systems, as the employer remains the same person and the employment relationship continues. At common law, in the event of a sale of assets of a business, the employer's liability under existing employment contracts does not automatically end, nor does it automatically pass on to the purchaser. By selling the business and ceasing to furnish the work agreed upon, the employer will have unilaterally terminated such contracts.[1]

[1] *Mercer v. Kits Cameras Ltd.* (1989), T.L.W. 911-002 (B.C.S.C.); *Addison v. M. Loeb Ltd.* (1986), 25 D.L.R. (4th) 151 (Ont. C.A.); *McKeough v. H.B. Nickerson & Sons Ltd.* (1985), 71 N.S.R. (2d) 134 (S.C.), affd 74 N.S.R. (2d) 84 (C.A.); *Re Foster Clark Ltd.'s Indenture Trusts*, [1966] 1 All E.R. 43 (Ch.); *Sloan v. Union Oil Co. of Canada*, [1955] 4 D.L.R. 664 (B.C.S.C.); *Collier v. Sunday Referee Publishing Co.*, [1940] K.B. 647.

§12.8.1 In Quebec, since the coming into force of the new Civil Code of Quebec, the effects are remarkably different. Article 2097 of the Civil Code of Quebec now provides that:

> A contract of employment is not terminated by alienation of the enterprise or any change in its legal structure by way of amalgamation or otherwise.
> The contract is binding on the representative or successor of the employer.

Unlike in common law jurisdictions, a change in employer will not affect the continuity of the employment contract.[1] The impact of this new provision should not be underestimated and must be carefully considered in drafting all employment contracts as well as when negotiating business transactions. The effect of this provision is to override the principle that a person who is not a party to a contract may not be bound by it. Thus, unless the employee is terminated with notice or payment in lieu thereof by the vendor-employer prior to the sale, the purchaser will be bound by the terms of the employment contract, and if he wishes to terminate the employee, to provide him or her with reasonable notice of termination, taking into account, in particular, the nature of the employment, the special circumstances in which it is carried on and the duration of the period of work, as if there had been no change in employer. One must also consider that this provision may have some consequences upon the new employer's right to unilaterally change the working conditions of the employees, as the new employer is said to be bound by its predecessor's contract. The issue may also arise, for example, with regard to purchaser employer's right to alter the pension plan, etc. The exact extent of this provision on the employment contract cannot yet be defined but the case law will have to be followed very closely in the months and years to come to determine the extent of the parties' rights.

[1] Similar provisions exist regarding labour standards (see R.S.Q., c. N-1.1, s. 96 and 97) and collective agreements (see R.S.Q., c. C-27, s. 45). The provision in the Civil

Code of Quebec is unique, however, in that its application is not limited to a particular group of employees. It applies to all employment relationships.

§12.8.2 One alternative to consider in order to avoid the consequences of the application of article 2097 of the Civil Code of Quebec may be to include a jurisdiction clause on the employment contract stipulating that the contract will be governed by the laws of another jurisdiction. However, article 3118 of the Civil Code of Quebec stipulates that:

> The designation by the parties of the law applicable to a contract of employment does not result in depriving the worker of the protection to which he is entitled under the mandatory provisions of the law of the country where the worker habitually carries on his work, even if he is on temporary assignment in another country or, if the worker does not habitually carry on his work in any one country, the mandatory provisions of the law of the country where his employer has his domicile or establishment.

The employer may not be able to rely on such a clause to prove that the governing law should not be the civil law if the courts determine that article 2097 of the new Civil Code is of public order. A similar result may occur in the case where an employment contract expressly stipulates that the employment contract will terminate upon the sale of an undertaking. Even in absence of case law on the subject to date, the authors are of the view that reference may be made to case law decided on similar provisions in other legislation including section 45 of the Quebec Labour Code[1] and sections 96 and 97 of the *Act Respecting Labour Standards*[2] provision. Indeed, it may well be that, like its counterparts, article 2097 is a provision of public order which the employee may not contract out of with the consequence that even in the presence of such a clause, the employment contract will be binding upon the representative or successor of the employer.

[1] R.S.Q., c. C-27.
[2] R.S.Q., c. N-1.1.

§12.9 At common law, the employment relationship would not be transferred and an issue of constructive dismissal could occur if such a sale materially altered the nature of the executive's work.

§12.10 However, if the executive is offered continued employment with the new employer under the same working conditions, the executive will not be successful in claiming damages for breach of contract against his or her former employer, since the executive will have suffered no damages as a result of his or her former employer's breach of contract.[1] Moreover, if the executive refuses continued employment under the new employer, the executive will have failed to mitigate his or her damages.[2]

[1] This assumes that the terms of the executive's employment with the former employer did not provide for severance pay upon termination of employment without imposing a corresponding obligation to mitigate damages.

[2] *McKeough v. H.B. Nickerson & Sons Ltd.* (1985), 71 N.S.R. (2d) 134 (S.C.), affd 74 N.S.R. (2d) 84 (C.A.); *Sawarin v. Canadian Acceptance Corp.* (1983), 34 Sask. R. 234 (C.A.), revg 34 Sask. R. 235 (Q.B.).

(d) Death

§12.11 The death of the executive terminates the employment relationship.[1] Moreover, the deceased executive's estate may not be held liable for any damages caused to the employer by the executive's inability to perform his or her obligations under the contract.

[1] *Hall v. Wright* (1859), El. Bl. & El. 765, 120 E.R. 695, in which Pollock C.B. makes the comment *in obiter* that executors of an employee would not be liable in damages if the employee was prevented from performing his or her obligations by death. See also C.C.Q., art. 2093 (previously C.C.L.C., art. 1668).

§12.12 In the common law provinces, where the employment relationship is especially personal in nature, the employment contract will be terminated[1] upon the death of the employer. In Quebec the same result will sometimes occur.[2] This is an exception to the general principle that upon the death of one of the parties, the rights and obligations arising from a contract pass to its heirs, if the nature of the contract permits it.[3]

[1] *Graves v. Cohen* (1929), 46 T.L.R. 121 (K.B.).
[2] C.C.Q., art. 2093(2).
[3] C.C.Q., art. 1441.

C. REPUDIATION BY THE EXECUTIVE

1. Resignation

§12.13 Under a fixed-term contract, an executive cannot cease to perform his or her obligations until the term has expired. However, in the case of a contract of indeterminate duration, an executive may unilaterally terminate the employment relationship upon providing his or her employer with reasonable notice or the notice agreed upon by the parties.[1] An executive who fails to give sufficient notice of resignation may be held liable for wrongful breach of contract and have to compensate the employer for the resulting damages.[2]

[1] C.C.Q., art. 2091(1); either party to a contract with an indeterminate term may terminate it by giving notice of termination to the other party.

[2] *Terres Noires Sherrington Ltée v. Barrachina*, D.T.E. 88T-623 (Que. S.C.); *Canadian Aero Service Ltd. v. O'Malley*, [1974] S.C.R. 592; *Payzu Ltd. v. Hannaford*, [1918] 2 K.B. 348. See also Chapter 16, "Other Issues Concerning Wrongful Termination and Damage Awards".

§12.14 The length of notice which must be given by an executive can only be determined on the merits of each case. The factors which the court will consider include the normal time and difficulty for the employer to find a suitable replacement, the geographic location, the type of work involved and the specific skills required.[1]

[1] Provincial employment standards legislation contains explicit statements as to the length of notice which must be given. See, *e.g.*, the Manitoba *Employment Standards Act*, R.S.M. 1987, c. E110, s. 39(5), (6); Nova Scotia *Labour Standards Code*, R.S.N.S. 1989, c. 246, s. 72(1); Prince Edward Island *Labour Act*, R.S.P.E.I. 1988, c. L-1, s. 93(1). The Manitoba statute also prescribes penalties for failure to provide adequate notice; see subss. 39(11) *et seq*; see also C.C.Q., art. 2091(2).

§12.15 The requirement that a suitable period of notice be given is most understandable when an employer's business activity is concentrated within a few weeks or months during the year. In this situation, an abrupt resignation of a key executive during the peak period could seriously harm the company. In *Terres Noires Sherrington Ltée v. Barrachina*,[1] the plaintiff was a company which imported fresh produce into Canada. The defendant was hired in Canada to act as the plaintiff's managing director in Spain. During the months of August, September, and October of each year, the plaintiff engaged in negotiations for the purchase of fresh produce from Spain. On August 8, the defendant informed a Spanish representative of the plaintiff of his resignation. On August 20, the defendant sent his resignation letter to Canada, which was retroactive to August 2. In its judgment, the court held that the notice provided by the executive was insufficient. The executive could not ignore the fact that August was the most inappropriate month in which to resign.

[1] D.T.E. 88T-623 (Que. S.C.).

§12.16 If an executive has cause to terminate the employment relationship, no prior notice of resignation is owed to the employer.[1] An executive will be found to have cause if the employer fails to fulfil its obligations under the contract of employment. For example, if the employer fails to pay the agreed wages or materially alters the powers and duties of the executive, the executive may be justified in abruptly terminating his or her employment agreement.[2] The failure of the employer to fulfil its obligations under the contract is discussed later in this chapter under the heading "Constructive Dismissal".[3]

---

[1] C.C.Q., art. 2094; *Grenier v. Radiodiffusion mutuelle Canada Ltée* (1987), 18 C.C.E.L. 256 (Que. S.C.); *Sarfati v. Bendwell & associés Ltée*, J.E. 79-1031 (Que. S.C.), affd on appeal May 16, 1980, C.A.M. 500-09-001373-794.

[2] *Nerada v. Hobart Canada Inc.* (1982), 1 C.C.E.L. 116 (B.C.S.C.); *Sarfati v. Bendwell & associés Ltée.*, J.E. 79-1031 (Que. S.C.), affd on appeal May 16, 1980, C.A.M. 500-09-001373-794; *Brown v. Canada Biscuit Co.*, [1935] S.C.R. 212; *Abramoff v. Podratz*, [1920] 2 W.W.R. 6 (Sask. C.A.); *Montreal Public Service Co. v. Champagne* (1916), 33 D.L.R. 49 (P.C.).

[3] See §§12.70 *et seq.*

§12.17   In order for a resignation to be valid, it must be voluntary. In determining whether a resignation was voluntary, the courts will consider the substance of the termination, not just its form.[1] If it is found that a resignation resulted from coercion or fear, or was obtained under the threat of dismissal, the resignation will not be valid. A forced resignation amounts to dismissal and the law regarding wrongful dismissal will apply.[2] The burden of proof is on the employee to show that he did not voluntarily resign but was, in fact, dismissed.[3]

---

[1] *McIlvaney v. Estee Lauder Cosmetics Ltd.*, unreported, Nov. 20, 1991, New Westminster Doc. C900859 (B.C.S.C.); *Assouline v. Ogivar Inc.* (1991), 39 C.C.E.L. 100 (B.C.S.C.); *Bouffard v. Canico Hydraulique Inc.*, D.T.E. 89T-717 (Que. S.C.). *Bélair v. Communications Radiomutuel Inc.*, D.T.E. 88T-268 (Que. S.C.); *Carrick v. Cooper Canada Ltd.* (1983), 2 C.C.E.L. 87 (Ont. H.C.J.); *Robson v. General Motors of Canada Ltd.* (1982), 37 O.R. (2d) 229 (Co. Ct.).

[2] *Côté v. Placements M & A Brown Inc.*, D.T.E. 87T-956 (Que. Prov. Ct.); *Ewasiuk v. Estevan Area Home Care District 9 Inc.* (1985), 9 C.C.E.L. 267 (Sask. Q.B.); *Buchanan v. Continental Bank of Canada* (1984), 58 N.B.R. (2d) 333 (Q.B.); *Landry v. Comterm Inc.*, J.E. 84-451 (Que. S.C.); *Re Gillingham and Metropolitan Toronto Bd. of Commrs. of Police* (1979), 26 O.R. (2d) 77 (Div. Ct.); *Johnson, Drake & Piper Int. Corp. v. Robert*, [1958] B.R. 378 (Que. C.A.); *Smith v. Campbellford Bd. of Education* (1917), 39 O.L.R. 323 (C.A.).

[3] *Walker v. International Tele-Film Enterprises Ltd.* (1994), 4 C.C.E.L. (2d) 147 (B.C.S.C.).

§12.18   The executive must also be competent at the time of the resignation for it to be valid. Thus, if the executive was mentally incompetent at the time of his or her resignation, it will be void.[1] Likewise, executive error may result in the resignation being set aside.[2] Employers should guard against acting on a resignation given in the heat of the moment, for example in the course of heated argument. In *Cox v. Victoria Plywood Co-operative Assn.*, the court held that a reasonable board of directors had acted hastily in accepting the plaintiff's resignation.[3] It should have waited until tempers cooled and then heard what the plaintiff had to say. The plaintiff was in fact dismissed. Lack of judgment, however, even when it is due to intoxication, is not sufficient reason for a resignation to be rendered void.[4]

[1] *Hooper v. Wellington County Bd. of Education* (1983), 43 O.R. (2d) 108 (H.C.J.); revd on other grounds 46 O.R. (2d) 680 (Div. Ct.).

[2] *Grenier v. Radiodiffusion Mutuelle Canada Ltée*, (1987), 18 C.C.E.L. 256 (Que. S.C.); *Dufresne v. Dorion*, D.T.E. 86T-223 (Que. Prov. Ct.); *Robitaille v. Québec (Procureur général)*, J.E. 85-22 (Que. S.C.).

[3] (1994), 2 C.C.E.L. (2d) 78 (B.C.S.C.).

[4] *Ross v. Hawker Siddeley Canada Inc.*, D.T.E. 88T-589 (Que. C.A.); *Boulay v. Stelco Inc.*, D.T.E. 88T-620 (Que. S.C.); *Tardif v. Ville de Montréal*, D.T.E. 87T-320 (Que. S.C.), affd D.T.E. 90T-530 (C.A.).

2. Constructive Resignation

§12.19   There are situations which will give rise to a finding that the executive has constructively resigned. In general, these situations involve conduct on the part of the executive which indicates an abandonment of his or her employment. For example, if an executive fails to return to work without explanation or works for another employer, it can be concluded that the executive has effectively resigned.[1] Similarly, when an executive's words are tantamount to inviting dismissal or if an executive threatens to resign if his or her demands are not met, the employer may be entitled to conclude that the executive has resigned.[2] In *Farrugia v. Ashland Oil Canada Ltd.*,[3] the executive failed to give adequate notice of his intention to take time off. He returned the company keys and credit cards, and removed his personal effects from the office. In *Marleau v. Overnite Express (1980) Inc.*,[4] the executive did not respond to the president's offer of another position. Instead, he left temporarily for health reasons, and later returned to empty his office of all personal belongings. In *Gagné v. Algoma Builders Supply Ltd.*,[5] the executive asked for all money owed to him, including "holdback pay", before leaving for vacation. In all three cases, the court held that the employer was entitled to conclude that the executive had resigned.

[1] *Wood Gundy Inc. v. Giroux-Garneau*, D.T.E. 94T-1251 (Que. S.C.) on appeal.

[2] *Jacques v. 96955 Saskatchewan Ltd. (The Drapery Shoppe)* (1984), 31 Sask. R. 96 (Q.B.); *Tall v. Deconinck* (1983), 51 N.B.R. (2d) 62 (Q.B.), vard 51 N.B.R. (2d) 55 (C.A.).

[3] (1986), 75 A.R. 11 (Q.B.).

[4] D.T.E. 87T-754 (Que. C.A.).

[5] (1987), 18 C.C.E.L. 66 (Ont. Dist. Ct.).

§12.20   Finally, the fact that an employee searches for alternative employment or signs an employment agreement with someone else does not in itself amount to resignation.[1]

[1] *McCallion v. Zephyr Ford Truck Centre Ltd.* (1992), 41 C.C.E.L. 91 (B.C.S.C.).

D. REPUDIATION BY THE EMPLOYER

1. Dismissal

§12.21 The employer has a right to unilaterally terminate the executive's employment, regardless of whether the employment relationship is for a fixed or indeterminate duration. Moreover, the right to terminate the employment relationship is unaffected by the concept of "just cause". However, the consequences flowing from the presence or absence of just cause are quite different.

(a) Dismissal for Cause

§12.22 When an employer has just cause for dismissal, the employment contract can be terminated without notice or payment in lieu of notice.[1] An employer has cause for termination when an executive fails to fulfil his or her obligations under the employment contract. In general, conduct which is inconsistent with the express or implied terms of employment will justify dismissal.[2] An often-cited definition of the causes for dismissal is:

> If an employee has been guilty of serious misconduct, habitual neglect of duty, incompetence, or conduct incompatible with his duties, or prejudicial to the employer's business, or if he has been guilty of wilful disobedience to the employer's orders in a matter of substance, the law recognizes the employer's right summarily to dismiss the delinquent employee.[3]

[1] C.C.Q., art. 2094; *Daigle v. Caisse populaire Les Etchemins*, D.T.E. 90T-442 (Que. S.C.); *Gobeil v. C.L.S.C. Saguenay-Nord*, J.E. 82-524 (Que. S.C.). It should be noted that the Civil Code of Quebec uses the words "for a serious reason." Although some authors are of the view that these words may grant a wider discretion than "just cause" which is frequently found in other statutes, the better view seems to be that "a serious reason" in art. 2094 of the Civil Code of Quebec should be interpreted to mean "just cause."

[2] *Commission scolaire de Sept-Iles v. Club de ski Gallix*, D.T.E. 91T-653 (Que. S.C.); *Bilodeau v. Bata Industries Ltd.*, [1986] R.J.Q. 531 (C.A.); *Charlton v. B.C. Sugar Refining Co.*, [1925] 1 W.W.R. 546 (B.C.C.A.), affd, unreported (S.C.C.); *Denham v. Patrick* (1910), 20 O.L.R. 347 (C.A.); *Smith v. Kamloops & District Elizabeth Fry Society* (1996), 20 C.C.E.L. (2d) 303 (B.C.C.A.).

[3] *R. v. Arthurs, ex p. Port Arthur Shipbuilding Co.* (1967), 62 D.L.R. (2d) 342 (Ont. C.A.), at 348; revd on other grounds [1969] S.C.R. 85.

§12.23 The courts have held that the executive's misconduct must be of a serious nature for cause to exist.[1] The Ontario Court of Appeal decision in *McIntyre v. Hockin*[2] states:

> The causes which are sufficient to justify dismissal must vary with the nature

of the employment and the circumstances of each case. Dismissal is an extreme measure, and not to be resorted to for trifling causes. The fault must be something which a reasonable man could not be expected to overlook, regard being had to the nature and circumstances of the employment . . .

[1] *Campbell v. J.I. Case Canada* (1990), 75 Alta. L.R. (2d) 292 (Q.B.); *Jolicoeur v. Lithographie Montréal Ltée*, [1982] C.S. 230 (Que.), appeal dismissed, unreported, April 15, 1987, C.A.M. 500-09-000314-823; *MacDonald v. Richardson Greenshields of Canada Ltd.* (1985), 69 B.C.L.R. 58 (S.C.); *Thorneloe v. C.S.R. Eastern Townships*, D.T.E. 84T-870 (Que. S.C.).

[2] (1889), 16 O.A.R. 498 (C.A.), at 501.

§12.24 As noted in the above quotation, a court will examine the circumstances of each case to determine whether cause exists.[1] The factors which a court will consider include the length of the executive's service, the past conduct of the executive, and the executive's duties and responsibilities within the organization.[2] With regard to this last factor, the greater the trust placed upon an executive in relation to particular matters, the less tolerant a court will be.[3]

[1] *Dupré Quarries Ltd. v. Dupré*, [1934] S.C.R. 528.

[2] *Gagnair Consultants Ltée v. Dupras*, D.T.E. 90T-869 (Que. C.A.); *Durand v. Quaker Oats Co. of Canada Ltd.* (1990), 45 B.C.L.R. (2d) 354 (C.A.), revg 20 C.C.E.L. 223 (S.C.); *Brown v. OK Builders Supplies Ltd.* (1985), 11 C.C.E.L. 243 (B.C.S.C.), affd 14 C.C.E.L. xxxi (C.A.); *Risi v. Benson & Hedges (Canada) Inc.*, unreported, 1986 (Ont. Dist. Ct.).

[3] *Valcourt v. Maison L'Intervalle*, D.T.E. 95T-322 (Que. S.C.).

§12.25 Only in exceptional circumstances will a single act of misconduct be regarded as sufficient cause for dismissal. For cause to exist, the act must trigger a complete breakdown of trust in the executive and fundamentally undermine the employment contract. It must be wilful, deliberate, and show gross incompetence in order to justify dismissal without prior warning.[1] However, the high level of authority and autonomy of an executive allows the employer to be more demanding of him or her and therefore, a court will be more critical of the executive's shortcoming than it is with regards less senior employees.[2]

[1] *Paulin v. Computer-Tech Consultants Ltd.* (1994), 90 B.C.L.R. (2d) 69 (C.A.); *Murphy v. Sealand Helicopters Ltd.* (1988), 72 Nfld. & P.E.I.R. 9 (Nfld. S.C.).

[2] *Valcourt v. Maison L'Intervalle*, D.T.E. 95T-322 (Que. S.C.).

§12.26 An accumulation of minor acts of misconduct may also justify dismissal when such acts cause a serious deterioration in the business relationship of the parties or inhibit the parties' ability to perform their obligations.[1] Moreover, if there is a series of minor acts or a gradual deterioration of performance, an employer may have a duty to warn the executive before dismissing him or her.[2]

<hr />

[1]   *Perham v. Canada Trust Co.* (1988), 23 C.C.E.L. 277 (B.C.S.C.); *Scott v. Domtar Sonoco Containers Inc.* (1987), 20 C.C.E.L. 290 (Ont. Dist. Ct.); *Nossal v. Better Business Bureau of Metropolitan Toronto Inc.* (1985), 51 O.R. (2d) 279 (C.A.); *Doyle v. London Life Ins. Co.* (1985), 23 D.L.R. (4th) 443 (B.C.C.A.), leave to appeal to S.C.C. refused 64 N.R. 318n; *Fonceca v. McDonnell Douglas Canada Ltd.* (1983), 1 C.C.E.L. 51 (Ont. H.C.J.); *Atkinson v. Boyd, Phillips & Co.* (1979), 9 B.C.L.R. 255 (C.A.); *Ross v. Willards Chocolates Ltd.*, [1927] 2 D.L.R. 461 (Man. K.B.).

[2]   *Kakoske v. Carter Motors Ltd.* (1984), 6 C.C.E.L. 184 (Man. Q.B.); *Robson v. General Motors of Canada Ltd.* (1982), 37 O.R. (2d) 229 (Co. Ct.); *Dewitt v. A. & B. Sound Ltd.* (1978), 85 D.L.R. (3d) 604 (B.C.S.C.). In *Laramée v. Poly-Actions Inc.*, D.T.E. 90T-923 (Que. S.C.), the court said that management-level employees should be able to amend unsatisfactory conduct and their failure to do so may justify termination without the necessity of progressive discipline.

§12.27   The employer has the burden of proving that cause for dismissal exists.[1] In establishing cause for dismissal, courts in common law provinces have held that an employer may rely on conduct of which it was not aware at the time the executive was fired,[2] as long as the misconduct existed at the time of the dismissal.[3] In Quebec, the courts have expressed conflicting views on this issue.[4] Furthermore, some courts have held that the employer need not explain the cause for dismissal so long as cause exists.[5]

<hr />

[1]   *Gignac v. Trust Général du Canada*, D.T.E. 91T-231 (Que. S.C.); *Briant v. Gerber (Canada) Inc.* (1989), T.L.W. 925-027 (Ont. S.C.); *Fonceca v. McDonnell Douglas Canada Ltd.* (1983), 1 C.C.E.L. 51 (Ont. H.C.J.); *Jolicoeur v. Lithographie Montréal Ltée*, [1982] C.S. 230 (Que. S.C.), affd Apr. 15, 1987, C.A.M. 500-09-000314-823; *Lucking v. Thomas* (1919), 50 D.L.R. 724 (Sask. C.A.).

[2]   *Carr v. Fama Holdings Ltd.* (1989), 40 B.C.L.R. (2d) 125 (C.A.); *Lake Ontario Portland Cement Co. v. Groner*, [1961] S.C.R. 553; *King v. Mayne Nickless Transport Inc.* (1994), 89 B.C.L.R. (2d) 344 (C.A.).

[3]   *Tracey v. Swansea Construction Co.*, [1965] 1 O.R. 203 (H.C.J.), affd [1965] 2 O.R. 182n (C.A.).

[4]   *Caron v. Yaccarini*, J.E. 83-447 (Que. S.C.); contra: *Mahoney v. Alliance, Cie mutuelle d'assurance-vie*, D.T.E. 91T-431 (Que. S.C.); *Racine v. Services Bio-Contrôle Inc.*, D.T.E. 95T-1322 (Que. S.C.).

[5]   *Thorn v. RGO Office Products Ltd.* (1993), 15 Alta. L.R. (3d) 346 (Q.B.) at 364; *Carr v. Ireco Canada II Inc.* (1991), 80 Alta. L.R. (2d) 154 (Q.B.).

§12.27.1   Generally speaking, once a contract of employment has been terminated, the subsequent conduct of the former employee may not be relied upon to justify the termination. However, where the employer gives notice of termination which effectively terminates the employee's contract of employment only at the expiration of the notice period, the employer may rely on the employee's conduct during the notice period to terminate the contract immediately without notice, if the employee's conduct amounts to a breach of the employment contract. In *Aasgaard v. Harlequin Enterprises Ltd.*[1] the employer decided to shut down his business, instructed the plaintiff employee to start shutting down the operations and offered the plaintiff a severance payment equivalent to nine months salary as well as the possibility of an additional payment if he had not found employment at the expiration of the nine months. While shutting down the business, the plaintiff/employee started up his own business and began transferring the employer's inventory to his business without informing the employer. When the employer discovered the employee's conduct, he immediately terminated the employee's contract without further notice and without making any of the payments discussed in the termination package. The employee's action was dismissed as the court found that the employer's intention had been to retain the employee during the entire notice period and consequently the employee was bound to respect his employment obligations. It was the employee's conduct which amounted to a repudiation of the employment contract, not the employer's.

[1] (1993), 48 C.C.E.L. 192 (Ont. Ct. (Gen. Div.)), affd [1997] O.J. No. 1112, No. C16138 (C.A.).

§12.28 Common examples of the types of conduct which have been held to constitute cause for dismissal include theft, fraud, insubordination, absenteeism or lateness, intoxication, breach of company rules or policies, incompetence, and disloyalty.

(i) Theft, Fraud or Dishonesty

§12.29 If theft is alleged by an employer, it must be proven on a balance of probabilities.[1] As a result, it may be possible to establish theft as cause even if an executive is acquitted in criminal proceedings.[2]

[1] *Forshaw v. Aluminex Extrusions Ltd.* (1988), 24 C.C.E.L. 92 (B.C.S.C.), affd 27 C.C.E.L. 208 (C.A.); *Delorme v. Banque Royale du Canada* (1987), 19 C.C.E.L. 298 (Que. S.C.); *Johnson v. Able-Atlantic Taxi Ltd.* (1987), 17 C.C.E.L. 239 (Ont. Dist. Ct.); *Jivrag v. City of Calgary* (1986), 45 Alta. L.R. (2d) 343 (Q.B.), revd in part 18 C.C.E.L. xxx (C.A.); *Hanes v. Wawanesa Mutual Ins. Co.*, [1963] S.C.R. 154.
[2] *Hughes v. R.T. Holman Ltd.* (1982), 40 Nfld. & P.E.I.R. 190 (P.E.I.S.C.); *Hayes v. Alliance Québec*, D.T.E. 96T-248 (Que. S.C.).

§12.30 Dishonest or fraudulent conduct which is prejudicial to the interests of the employer or is incompatible with the discharge of the executive's duties may be cause for dismissal.[1] Central to this ground of cause is the breach of the relationship of trust between an employer and executive. Moreover, courts have held that dishonest behaviour of managerial executives outside the workplace may be cause for dismissal on the basis that employers must be able to trust their senior managers to act on their behalf.

[1]   *Beyea v. Irving Oil Ltd.* (1985), 8 C.C.E.L. 128 (N.B.Q.B.), affd 14 C.C.E.L. 67 (C.A.); *Roy v. Maple Creek Credit Union Ltd. and Saskatchewan Co-operative Credit Society Ltd.* (1983), 24 Sask. R. 43 (Q.B.); *Hughes v. R.T. Holman Ltd.* (1982), 40 Nfld. & P.E.I.R. 190 (P.E.I.S.C.); *Jewitt v. Prism Resources Ltd.* (1980), 110 D.L.R. (3d) 713 (B.C.S.C.), affd 127 D.L.R. (3d) 190 (C.A.); *Aspinall v. Mid-West Collieries Ltd.*, [1926] 3 D.L.R. 362 (Alta. C.A.); *Hayes v. Alliance Québec*, D.T.E. 96T-248 (Que. S.C.). See also *O'Leary v. Wal-Mart Canada Inc.* (1996), 147 Sask. R. 79 (Q.B.), where it is stated that a finding of dishonesty requires proof of a dishonest act and intent to commit a dishonest act.

[2]   *McMahon v. Caisse populaire de St-Marc-sur-Richelieu*, D.T.E. 96T-1047 (Que. S.C.).

§12.31 In general, the honesty of senior executives is subject to more rigorous scrutiny than that of lower-level employees.

(ii) Insubordination

§12.32 If an executive refuses to obey a reasonable request of the employer, and this refusal is incompatible with the executive's obligation to faithfully carry out his or her duties, the employer will have cause for dismissal. However, in order for insubordination to be established, the executive must not have been provoked by the employer.[1] The employer's request must relate to a matter of substance;[2] the request must be within the scope of the employment contract;[3] and the employer's instructions must be clear and unambiguous.[4] Finally, just cause will not be found if there is a reasonable excuse for the executive's disobedience.[5]

[1]   *Paitich v. Clarke Institute of Psychiatry* (1988), 19 C.C.E.L. 105 (Ont. H.C.J.), affd 30 C.C.E.L. 235 (C.A.); *Latta v. Acme Cheese Co.* (1923), 25 O.W.N. 195 (C.A.), revg 23 O.W.N. 611 (H.C.).

[2]   *English v. NBI Canada Inc.* (1989), 24 C.C.E.L. 21 (Alta. Q.B.); *Mullen v. Neon Products Ltd.* (1981), 33 A.R. 51 (Q.B.).

[3]   *Beal v. Grant* (1984), 52 N.B.R. (2d) 163 (C.A.); *Lewis v. Associated Laboratories Ltd.* (1981), 44 N.S.R. (2d) 567 (S.C.); *Smith v. Mills* (1913), 10 D.L.R. 589 (Sask. C.A.).

[4]   *Bolen v. MacMillan Bloedel* (1988), T.L.W. 737-017 (B.C. Co. Ct.); *Schiavetto v. Don District Training Programme Inc.* (1982), 15 A.C.W.S. (2d) 40 (Ont. Co. Ct.); *Heyes v. First City Trust Co.* (1981), 12 A.C.W.S. (2d) 104 (B.C.S.C.).

[5]   *Kozak v. Aliments Krispy Kernels Inc.* (1988), 22 C.C.E.L. 1 (Ont. Dist. Ct.); *Doyle v. London Life Ins. Co.* (1985), 23 D.L.R. (4th) 443 (B.C.C.A.), leave to appeal to S.C.C. refused 64 N.R. 318n; *Carnaghan v. Bernard Freedman Ins. Ltd.* (1982), 16 A.C.W.S. (2d) 32 (N.S.S.C.); *MacDonald v. White Rock Waterworks Co.* (1973), 38 D.L.R. (3d) 763 (B.C.S.C.); *Goldbold v. Puritan Laundry Co.* (1917), 12 O.W.N. 343 (H.C.).

(iii) Intoxication

§12.33 Intoxication can constitute cause for dismissal if it prevents the executive from adequately performing his or her duties effectively and efficiently. Generally, the executive must have received warnings regarding the possible consequences of the reproached behaviour.[1] Also, if the intoxication is due to the executive's alcoholism, the employer cannot terminate the executive's employment without first attempting to accommodate the illness, since such illness may constitute a handicap under provincial human rights legislation.[2]

[1] *Hayes v. Eastman Oil Well Survey Co.*, [1976] W.W.D. 104 (Alta. S.C.); *MacDonald v. Azar*, [1948] 1 D.L.R. 854 (N.S.S.C.).
[2] *Human Rights Code*, R.S.O. 1990, c. H.19, s. 5(1) prohibits discrimination in employment on the grounds of, *inter alia*, handicap. Alcoholism or alcohol dependency has been held to constitute a handicap or disability for the purposes of provincial human rights legislation in several cases: see, *e.g.*, *Entrop v. Imperial Oil Ltd.* (1995), 24 C.C.E.L. (2d) 87 (Ont. Bd. of Inquiry); *Entrop v. Imperial Oil Ltd.* (1996), 24 C.C.E.L. (2d) 122 (Ont. Bd. of Inquiry) and see discussion of these decisions at §9.61.4 *et seq.*; *Handfield v. School District No. 26* (1995), 95 C.L.L.C. 230-015 (B.C. Human Rts. Council).

(iv) Breach of Company Rules or Policies

§12.34 If breach of a company rule or policy is alleged, the employer must establish that the rule was known, clear and unambiguous,[1] and that the rule applied to the executive.[2] The executive must also have been warned that breach of the rule would lead to immediate dismissal.[3] In addition, the rule must be reasonable, and it must have been consistently enforced by the company. The implications of breach must be sufficient to justify termination, and no reasonable excuse must exist for the executive's breach.[4]

[1] *Bodor v. B.C. Lottery Corp.* (1988), 24 C.C.E.L. 172 (B.C. Co. Ct.); *Ennis v. Textron Canada Ltd.* (1987), 82 A.R. 260 (Q.B.).
[2] *Jivrag v. City of Calgary* (1986), 45 Alta. L.R. (2d) 343 (Q.B.), revd in part 18 C.C.E.L. xxx (C.A.) and *Bergeron v. Banque nationale du Canada*, D.T.E. 96T-337 (Que. S.C.).
[3] *Forshaw v. Aluminex Extrusions Ltd.* (1988), 24 C.C.E.L. 92 (B.C.S.C.), affd 27 C.C.E.L. 208 (C.A.).
[4] *Newlands v. Sanwa McCarthy Securities Ltd.*, unreported, October 7, 1996 (Ont. Gen. Div.).
[5] *Skene v. Dearborn Motors Ltd.* (1988), 14 A.C.W.S. (3d) 193 (B.C. Co. Ct.), vard 29 C.C.E.L. 107 (C.A.); *Hancock v. Sobey's Stores Ltd.* (1988), 70 Nfld. & P.E.I.R. 338 (Nfld. S.C.).

(v) Incompetence

§12.35 Executive incompetence is not established on the basis of employer dissatisfaction with an executive's performance.[1] Rather, the approach of the courts is to apply an objective standard in determining whether an executive has been incompetent in the performance of his or her duties.[2] In addition, the courts will consider whether the employer established reasonable objectives for performance and informed the executive of these objectives,[3] whether the executive was warned that his or her position was in jeopardy,[4] and whether he or she was afforded a reasonable period of time to correct the situation.[5]

[1] *Woodward v. Sound Insight Ltd.* (1986), 73 N.S.R. (2d) 396 (S.C.); *Coyes v. Ocelot Industries Ltd.* (1984), 33 Alta. L.R. (2d) 102 (Q.B.); *Carveth v. Railway Asbestos Packing Co.* (1913), 24 O.W.R. 151 (H.C.); *Jeykal v. Nova Scotia Glass Co.* (1888), 20 N.S.R. 388 (C.A.).

[2] *Cheetham v. Barton* (1990), T.L.W. 947-001 (Ont. Dist. Ct.); *Longpré v. Carrière & Lefebvre (1978) Inc.* (1989), 28 C.C.E.L. 277 (Que. S.C.); *Stevens v. Electrolux Canada* (1985), 6 C.C.E.L. 254 (N.B.Q.B.); *Matheson v. Matheson International Trucks Ltd.* (1984), 4 C.C.E.L. 271 (Ont. H.C.J.).

[3] *Rogers v. Canadian Acceptance Corp.* (1982), 50 N.S.R. (2d) 537 (S.C.); *Gorman v. Westfair Foods Ltd.*, unreported, November 5, 1996 (Man. Q.B.).

[4] *Scholler v. Samario Construction* (1984), 25 A.C.W.S. (2d) 86 (Ont. Co. Ct.); *Robson v. General Motors of Canada Ltd.* (1982), 37 O.R. (2d) 229 (Co. Ct.); *Coventry v. Nipawin & District Nursing Home* (1981), 12 Sask. R. 40 (Q.B.); *Hansen v. Viking Sprinkler Co.* (1981), 7 A.C.W.S. (2d) 508 (B.C.S.C.), affd 14 A.C.W.S. (2d) 333 (C.A.).

[5] *Frankcom v. Tandy Electronics Ltd.* (1984), 4 C.C.E.L. 40 (Ont. H.C.J.); *Hemmingway v. South Huron & District Assn. for the Mentally Handicapped Inc.* (1982), 17 A.C.W.S. (2d) 242 (Ont. Co. Ct.); *Robson v. General Motors of Canada Ltd.* (1982), 37 O.R. (2d) 229 (Co. Ct.); *Ferguson v. Spalding Co-operative Assn.* (1980), 9 Sask. R. 303 (Q.B.); *Manning v. Surrey Memorial Hospital Society* (1975), 54 D.L.R. (3d) 312 (B.C.S.C.).

(vi) Disloyalty

§12.36 An executive must be faithful and honest in his or her dealings with the employer. In addition, an executive also has a duty not to divulge information which is obtained during the course of employment for his or her own purposes and contrary to the employer's interests. Furthermore, an executive is required to avoid conflicts of interest with his or her employer. This duty is rigorously enforced by the courts. Often, a single violation of conflict of interest rules will justify immediate dismissal. Common examples of breaches of conflict of interest include: establishing a business which competes with the employer, becoming involved with the employer's competitors, disclosing confidential information, and concealing facts which should be disclosed from the employer.[1]

[1] *Chisamore v. Molson Brewery of Canada Ltd.*, unreported, Dec. 11, 1991, Vancouver Doc. C893090 (B.C.S.C.); *Monarch Messenger Services Ltd. v. Houlding* (1984), 5 C.C.E.L. 219 (Alta. Q.B.); *Sheather v. Associates Financial Services Ltd.* (1979), 15 B.C.L.R. 265 (S.C.); *Fabian v. Arm Industries Inc.* (1982), 16 Man. R. (2d) 91 (Q.B.); *Bee Chemical Co. v. Plastic Paint & Finish Specialties Ltd.* (1978), 41 C.P.R. (2d) 175 (Ont. H.C.J.), affd 47 C.P.R. (2d) 133 (C.A.); *Crawley v. Trans-Power Construction Ltd.* (1996), 23 C.C.E.L. (2d) 34 (B.C.S.C.). See Chapter 10, "Loyalty".

§12.37 The duty is most rigorously applied to senior or managerial executives. In *Ma v. Columbia Trust Co.*,[1] the Vice-President of Finance of a trust company was dismissed when he deposited his mother's money into a high interest rate term deposit which had been set up as a benefit for executives and their spouses only. The court held that this behaviour was serious enough to constitute cause for dismissal. According to the court, the executive had breached the duty of fidelity since "the highest propriety of conduct is demanded of an executive and particularly a financial executive when dealing with his field of finances."[2]

[1] (1985), 9 C.C.E.L. 300 (B.C.S.C.).
[2] (1985), 9 C.C.E.L. 300 (B.C.S.C.), at 311.

(vii) Other Causes

§12.38 Redundancy, economic difficulties, or company reorganization will not constitute cause for dismissal.[1] A refusal to accept a geographical transfer imposed by the employer will not constitute just cause unless the employer can establish an express or implied contractual term that the executive comply with all reasonable requests for transfers.[2] The refusal by a third party, such as a client or a business partner, to work with or be served by a particular executive does not amount to cause for the executive's dismissal.[3] Finally, the fact that an executive searches for alternative employment will not constitute cause for discharge.[4]

[1] *Vanderzander v. Mattabi Mines Ltd.* (1984), W.D.P.M. 217-023-3 (Ont. H.C.J.); *Young v. Okanagan College Bd.* (1984), 5 C.C.E.L. 60 (B.C.S.C.); *Baker v. United Grain Growers Ltd.*, [1978] 5 W.W.R. 370 (Alta. S.C.); *Sublett v. Facit-Addo Canada Ltd.* (1977), 16 O.R. (2d) 791 (H.C.J.); *Burton v. MacMillan Bloedel Ltd.*, [1976] 4 W.W.R. 267 (B.C.S.C.); *Gillespie v. Bulkley Valley Forest Industries Ltd.* (1974), 50 D.L.R. (3d) 316 (B.C.C.A.), affg. 39 D.L.R. (3d) 586 (S.C.); *Paterson v. Robin Hood Flour Mills Ltd.* (1969), 68 W.W.R. 446 (B.C.S.C.).
[2] *Rose v. Shell Canada Ltd.* (1985), 7 C.C.E.L. 234 (B.C.S.C.); *Page v. Jim Pattison Industries Ltd.*, [1984] 4 W.W.R. 481 (Sask. C.A.); *Canadian Bechtel Ltd. v. Mollenkopf* (1978), 1 C.C.E.L. 95 (Ont. C.A.).
[3] *Shawinigan Lavalin Inc. v. Espinosa*, D.T.E. 90T-261 (Que. C.A.).
[4] *Robb v. Green*, [1895] 2 Q.B. 1.

(viii) Condonation

§12.39 An employer who condones an executive's misconduct which would have constituted just cause for dismissal may be prevented from terminating the executive for that misconduct.[1] Condonation can only occur, however, if the employer is fully aware of the executive's misconduct.

> [1]   *McIntyre v. Hockin* (1889), 16 O.A.R. 498 (C.A.).

§12.40   A determination of whether condonation has occurred will depend on the facts of each case. In general, however, an employer is entitled to a reasonable period of time to decide on an appropriate course of action, including time to complete an investigation.[1]

> [1]   *Duguay v. Maritime Welding & Rentals Ltd.* (1989), 28 C.C.E.L. 126 (N.B.Q.B.); *Tracey v. Swansea Construction Co.*, [1965] 1 O.R. 203 (H.C.J.), affd. [1965] 2 O.R. 182n (C.A.); *Caven v. C.P.R.*, [1925] 1 D.L.R. 122 (Alta. C.A.), affd. [1925] 3 D.L.R. 841 (P.C.).

(b)   Dismissal Without Cause

(i)   Fixed-Term Contract

§12.41   An employer who unilaterally and without cause terminates a contract concluded for a fixed term prior to its expiration, or terminates a contract for a specific undertaking prior to its completion, is liable for payment of the executive's entire remuneration for the balance of the term.[1] Damages awarded for an employer's breach of a fixed-term contract are discussed in detail in Chapter 13, "Damages Awarded for Wrongful Dismissal".

> [1]   *Mainville v. Brasserie Michel Desjardins Ltée*, D.T.E. 88T-292 (Que. S.C.), appeal abandoned Sept. 16, 1988, C.A.M. 500-09-000185-884; *Paddon v. Phillips Barratt Kaiser Engineering Ltd.* (1987), 18 B.C.L.R. (2d) 170 (S.C.); *Hawkins v. Ontario* (1985), 8 C.C.E.L. 183 (Ont. H.C.J.); *Landry v. Radio du Pontiac Inc.*, D.T.E. 83T-200 (Que. S.C.); *O'Callahan v. Transair Ltd.* (1975), 58 D.L.R. (3d) 80 (Man. C.A.); *Walker v. Copp Clark Publishing Co.*, [1962] O.R. 622 (H.C.J.).

(ii)   Contract of Indeterminate Duration

§12.42   In relation to contracts of indeterminate duration, there is an implied term that an executive is entitled to reasonable notice of dismissal without cause.[1] In Quebec, this is expressly provided for at article 2091 of the Civil Code of Quebec. Failure to provide notice of termination is a breach of the employer's contractual obligations which entitles the executive to claim the remuneration that would have been earned had he or she continued working through the notice period.[2] The issue of damages which can be awarded when no notice or insufficient notice is given is also discussed in Chapter 13.

[1] *Soupes Campbell Ltée v. Cantin*, D.T.E. 91T-741 (Que. C.A.); *Carter v. Bell & Sons (Canada) Ltd.*, [1936] O.R. 290 (C.A.).

[2] *Surveyer, Nenniger & Chênevert Inc. v. Thomas*, D.T.E. 89T-640 (Que. C.A.); *Perron v. Cie Minière Québec Cartier*, D.T.E. 89T-290 (Que. S.C.); *Gardner v. Rockwell Int. of Canada Ltd.* (1975), 9 O.R. (2d) 105 (H.C.J.).

(iii) Establishing Reasonable Notice of Termination

§12.43 Although every Canadian jurisdiction has employment standards legislation which provides a minimum notice period with respect to the termination of employment, reasonable notice of termination for an executive is much longer than statutory notice.

§12.44 In general, the purpose of reasonable notice is to provide the executive with sufficient time to find comparable employment. The courts focus on a number of factors in determining the length of the notice period, including the circumstances of the hiring, the nature and importance of the position held at the time of dismissal, the length of service with the employer, and the age of the executive.[1] Additional factors include the presence or absence of inducement to leave previous stable employment, the intentions of the contracting parties at the time of the formation of the contract, and the difficulty the executive may have in finding an equivalent position.[2] This is the "Bardal" approach. Iacobucci J. in *Machtinger v. HOJ Industries Ltd.*[3] noted that it is the most frequently cited approach to assessing reasonable notice. It has recently been applied by the Ontario Court of Appeal in *Cronk v. Canadian General Insurance Co.*[4] and by the New Brunswick Court of Appeal in *Dey v. Valley Forest Products Ltd.*[5] However, there is case law which suggests that the "Bardal" approach may not be the correct approach for determining reasonable notice in at least Saskatchewan. In *Bartlam v. Saskatchewan Crop Insurance Corp.*[6] the Saskatchewan Queen's Bench held that the appropriate test for determining reasonable notice is what the employer and employee would have decided on if they had addressed the question at the time of hiring.

[1] See, for example, *Arcand v. Denharco Inc.*, D.T.E. 96T-840 (Que. S.C.).

[2] *Bardal v. Globe & Mail Ltd.* (1960), 24 D.L.R. (2d) 140 (Ont. H.C.J.); *PCL Construction Management Inc. v. Holmes* (1994), 8 C.C.E.L. 192 (Alta. C.A.); *Wiebe v. Central Transport Refrigeration*, [1994] 6 W.W.R. 305 (Man. C.A.); see also C.C.Q., art. 2091.

[3] [1992] 1 S.C.R. 986.

[4] (1995), 25 O.R. (3d) 505 (C.A.).

[5] (1995), 162 N.B.R. (2d) 207 (C.A.).

[6] [1993] 8 W.W.R. 671 (Sask. Q.B.).

§12.45 In the common law provinces, some courts have stated that there is no minimum or maximum period of reasonable notice.[1] Other courts have cited a range of 18 to 24 months as a maximum unless exceptional circumstances exist.[2] However, a recent New Brunswick Court of Appeal decision states that there should be no specific limit on notice periods.[3] In Quebec, the courts have awarded notices of up to 12 months.[4] However, very recently the Court of Appeal, although stressing the exceptionality of this case, has broken the 12-month barrier and awarded 18 months' notice to a wrongfully terminated employee.[5]

[1] *Birney v. B.C. Automobile Assn.* (1988), T.L.W. 748-010 (B.C.S.C.), affd 40 B.C.L.R. (2d) 76 (C.A.); *Suttie v. Metro Transit Operating Co.* (1985), 9 C.C.E.L. 19 (B.C.C.A.), affg 1 C.C.E.L. 123 (S.C.); *Ball v. GTE Sylvania Canada Ltd.* (1984), T.L.W. 411-029 (Ont. Co. Ct.); *Lamberton v. Vancouver Temperance Hotel Co.* (1904), 11 B.C.R. 67 (C.A.).

[2] *Webster v. B.C. Hydro & Power Authority* (1992), 42 C.C.E.L. 105 (B.C.C.A.); *Sorel v. Tomenson Saunders Whitehead Ltd.* (1987), 16 C.C.E.L. 223 (B.C.C.A.); *Locke v. Avco Financial Services Canada Ltd.* (1987), 85 N.B.R. (2d) 93 (Q.B.); *Ansari v. B.C. Hydro & Power Authority* (1986), 2 B.C.L.R. (2d) 33 (S.C.), affd 55 B.C.L.R. (2d) xxxiii (C.A.); *Donnelly v. B.C. Hydro & Power Authority* (1986), T.L.W. 636-036 (B.C.S.C.).

[3] *Dey v. Valley Forest Products Ltd.* (1995), 162 N.B.R. (2d) 207 (C.A.).

[4] *Standard Broadcasting Corp. v. Stewart*, [1994] R.J.Q. 1751 (C.A.); *White v. E.D. Eastern Ltd.*, D.T.E. 89T-141 (Que. S.C.).

[5] *Hippodrome Blue Bonnets Inc. v. Jolicoeur*, D.T.E. 95T-185 (Que. C.A.).

§12.45.1 It has been found by the Nova Scotia Supreme Court that the employer's reorganization, downsizing, restructuring, financial mismanagement and redundancy are not factors to be taken into account in diminishing the appropriate period of reasonable notice.[1]

[1] *Swinamer v. Unitel Communications Inc.* (1996), 17 C.C.E.L. (2d) 59 (N.S.S.C.).

(1) Position

§12.46 To determine the length of reasonable notice for a particular executive, the courts often look beyond his or her title to determine the character of the employment,[1] since the actual responsibilities and duties which the executive exercised more accurately determine his or her position in the employer's organization. However, a few courts have stated that the parties should be held to their characterization of the job.[2]

[1] *Magnusson v. Laing Property Corp.* (1991), 35 C.C.E.L. 248 (B.C.S.C.); *Landry v. Canadian Forest Products Ltd.* (1991), 34 C.C.E.L. 37 (B.C.S.C.), revd on other grounds 42 C.C.E.L. 59 (C.A.); *Findlay v. Kershaw Mfg. Canada Ltd.* (1989), 29 C.C.E.L. 10 (Ont. H.C.J.); *Rose v. Herman Miller of Canada Ltd.* (1989), 30 C.C.E.L. 33 (Ont. Dist. Ct.); *Imprimeries Stellac Inc. v. Plante*, D.T.E. 89T-116 (Que. C.A.); *Plummer v. W. Carsen Co.* (1985), 10 C.C.E.L. 19 (Ont. Dist. Ct.); *George v. Muller Sales & Services Ltd.*

(1984), 31 Sask. R. 201 (Q.B.). See also *White v. E.D. Eastern Ltd.*, D.T.E. 89T-141 (Que. S.C.).

² *Robertson v. B.F. Goodrich Canada Inc.* (1986), T.L.W. 636-034 (Ont. H.C.J.); *Sullivan v. Mack Maritime Ltd.* (1982), 39 N.B.R. (2d) 298 (Q.B.).

§12.47 In general, a senior, upper-level management executive, or one in a highly skilled, technically demanding position, is entitled to a longer period of notice than a junior or semi-skilled executive.[1] The Ontario Court of Appeal reaffirmed that this is the law in Ontario in *Cronk v. Canadian General Insurance Company.*[2]

¹ *Birney v. B.C. Automobile Assn.* (1989), 40 B.C.L.R. (2d) 76 (C.A.); *McKay v. Eaton Yale Ltd.* (1996), 31 O.R. (3d) 216 (Gen. Div.); *Johnston v. Algoma Steel Corp.* (1989), 24 C.C.E.L. 1 (Ont. H.C.J.); *Heinz v. Cana Construction Co.* (1987), 55 Alta. L.R. (2d) 382 (Q.B.); *De Freitas v. Canadian Express & Transportation Ltd.* (1986), 16 C.C.E.L. 160 (Ont. H.C.J.), affd 18 C.C.E.L. xxx (C.A.); *Bohemier v. Storwal Int. Inc.* (1983), 44 O.R. (2d) 361 (C.A.), revg in part 40 O.R. (2d) 264 (H.C.J.); *Cringle v. Northern Union Ins. Co.* (1981), 124 D.L.R. (3d) 22 (B.C.S.C.); *Chrétien v. Explosifs Austin Ltée.*, D.T.E. 96T-66 (Que. S.C.), on appeal; but see *Wilks v. Moore Dry Kiln Co. of Canada* (1981), 32 B.C.L.R. 149 (S.C.).

² (1995), 25 O.R. (3d) 505 (C.A.).

(2) Age

§12.48 In general, an older executive is entitled to a longer notice period since it is assumed that he or she will have greater difficulty finding subsequent employment. Some courts have held that unless the executive is 50 or older, his or her age will not affect the determination of the notice period which should be given.[1] Other courts have extended special treatment to executives over the age of 40 on the basis that these executives have a more difficult time changing jobs than younger executives.[2] Finally, it should be noted that if an older executive is employed for a relatively short period, his or her age will be of less significance in determining the notice period.[3]

¹ *McKee v. NCR Canada Ltd.* (1986), 10 C.C.E.L. 128 (Ont. H.C.J.); *Sorel v. Tomenson Saunders Whitehead Ltd.* (1985), 9 C.C.E.L. 226 (B.C.S.C.), vard 16 C.C.E.L. 223 (C.A.); *MacDonald v. White Rock Waterworks Co.* (1973), 38 D.L.R. (3d) 763 (B.C.S.C.); *Johnston v. Northwood Pulp Ltd.*, [1968] 2 O.R. 521 (H.C.J.).

² *McGraw v. Canadian Forest Products Ltd.* (1989), 17 A.C.W.S. (3d) 542 (B.C.S.C.); *Kelly v. Monenco Consultants Ltd.* (1987), T.L.W. 713-030 (Ont. H.C.J.).

³ *Wark v. Richards Melling Ltd.* (1989), T.L.W. 906-029 (B.C.S.C.); *Findlay v. Kershaw Mfg. Canada Ltd.* (1989), 29 C.C.E.L. 10 (Ont. H.C.J.); *Habitations Populaires Desjardins de Lanaudière Inc. v. Boyer*, D.T.E. 88T-550 (Que. C.A.).

§12.48.1 Employees terminated at or after pensionable age have a right to notice if the termination is without cause.[1]

¹ *Schulz v. NRS Block Bros. Realty Ltd.* (1994), 97 B.C.L.R. (2d) 114 (S.C.), vard (1996), 26 B.C.L.R. (3d) 114 (B.C.C.A.) (award of 18 months reduced to eight weeks pursuant to contractual notice provision). See also *Wilding v. Qwest Foods Ltd.* (1994), 4 C.C.E.L. (2d) 141 (B.C.C.A.); *Heslop v. Cooper's Crane Rental Ltd.* (1994), 6 C.C.E.L. (2d) 252 (Ont. Ct. (Gen. Div.)).

(3) Induced to Leave Stable Employment

§12.49 If an employer induced an executive to leave previous stable employment, a court may award a longer notice period[1] because the courts assume that the executive would not have left his or her former job unless there had been an implied term of reasonable job security with the new employer.[2] This factor is especially influential if the executive was employed for a short duration before being dismissed.[3]

¹ *Gignac v. Trust Général du Canada,* D.T.E. 91T-231 (Que. S.C.); *Choquette v. F.O.I.S.I. Forces Immobilières & Stratégies d'Investissements Inc.,* D.T.E. 91T-1187 (Que. S.C.); *Saint John Shipbuilding Ltd. v. Perkins* (1989), 24 C.C.E.L. 106 (N.B.C.A.); *Carignan v. Infasco Division Ivaco Inc.,* D.T.E. 89T-118 (Que. S.C.); *Gerontakos v. Deli-Briskets Inc.,* D.T.E. 89T-117 (Que. S.C.), appeal settled out of court Jan. 27, 1989, C.A.M. 500-09-001504-885; *Reynolds v. First City Trust Co.* (1989), 27 C.C.E.L. 194 (B.C.S.C.); *Jackson v. Makeup Lab Inc.* (1989), 27 C.C.E.L. 317 (Ont. H.C.J.); *Longpré v. Carrière & Lefebvre (1978) Inc.* (1989), 28 C.C.E.L. 277 (Que. S.C.); *St-Germain v. Pro Optic Inc.,* D.T.E. 88T-293 (Que. S.C.); *Société Hotelière Canadien Pacifique v. Hoeckner,* D.T.E. 88T-548 (Que. C.A.); *Lefrançois v. Crane Canada Inc.,* D.T.E. 88T-574 (Que. S.C.); *Chang v. Simplex Textiles Ltd.* (1985), 6 C.C.E.L. 247 (Ont. C.A.); *Brisbois v. Casteel Inc.* (1983), 2 C.C.E.L. 35 (Ont. H.C.J.); *Cringle v. Northern Union Ins. Co.* (1981), 124 D.L.R. (3d) 22 (B.C.S.C.); *Cathcart v. Longines Wittnauer Watch Co.* (1980), 1 C.C.E.L. 287 (Ont. H.C.J.); *Jones v. Sky Rentals Ltd.* (1970), 70 C.L.L.C. 14,024 (Ont. S.C.); *Larivière V.O.E. inc. compagnie canadienne d'équipement de bureau,* D.T.E. 97T-155 (Que. S.C.).

² *Gignac v. Trust Général du Canada,* D.T.E. 91T-231 (Que. S.C.); *Choquette v. F.O.I.S.I. Forces Immobilières & Stratégies d'Investissements Inc.,* D.T.E. 91T-1187 (Que. S.C.); *Saint John Shipbuilding Ltd. v. Perkins* (1989), 24 C.C.E.L. 106 (N.B.C.A.); *Carignan v. Infasco Division Ivaco Inc.,* D.T.E. 89T-118 (Que. S.C.); *Gerontakos v. Deli-Briskets Inc.,* D.T.E. 89T-117 (Que. S.C.), appeal settled out of court Jan. 27, 1989, C.A.M. 500-09-001504-885; *St-Germain v. Pro Optic Inc.,* D.T.E. 88T-293 (Que. S.C.); *Société Hotelière Canadien Pacifique v. Hoeckner,* D.T.E. 88T-548 (Que. C.A.). See also *Lefrançois v. Crane Canada Inc.,* D.T.E. 88T-574 (Que. S.C.).

³ *Kennedy v. Gescan Ltd.* (1991), 41 C.C.E.L. 134 (B.C.S.C.); *Ansari v. B.C. Hydro & Power Authority* (1986), 2 B.C.L.R. (2d) 33 (S.C.), affd 55 B.C.L.R. (2d) xxxiii (C.A.); *A Contrario, Farrugia v. Selecta Générale, Compagnie d'assurances Inc.,* D.T.E. 95T-682 (Que. S.C.).

§12.50 In order for the court to find that enticement or inducement occurred, something beyond mere persuasion must be shown.[1] Similarly, if the executive initiated the discussions or was searching for employment at the time, a longer notice period will not be ordered.[2] Factors which have been focused on by the courts include moving to accept a job and the fact that a spouse has had to give up a secure job.[3]

[1] *Surveyer, Nenniger & Chênevert Inc. v. Short*, D.T.E. 88T-60 (Que. C.A.); *Desseroit v. Delta Hotels Ltd.* (1985), T.L.W. 422-018 (Ont. H.C.J.); *Dickinson v. Northern Telecom Canada Ltd.* (1985), 7 C.C.E.L. 139 (Ont. Co. Ct.).
[2] *McCaw v. Dresser Canada Inc.* (1983), 2 C.C.E.L. 51 (Ont. H.C.J.).
[3] *Wilson v. Northwinds Northern Inc.* (1988), 22 C.C.E.L. 146 (Man. Q.B.); *Adamson v. Watts & Henderson (Atlantic) Ltd.* (1987), 16 C.C.E.L. 74 (Ont. H.C.J.); *Helbig v. Oxford Warehousing Ltd.* (1985), 9 C.C.E.L. 75 (Ont. C.A.), leave to appeal to S.C.C. refused 52 O.R. (2d) 754n; *Ellis v. Whitepass Transportation Ltd.* (1983), 42 B.C.L.R. 351 (C.A.). But see *Surveyer, Nenniger & Chênevert Inc. v. Short*, D.T.E. 88T-60 (Que. C.A.).

§12.51 Inducing someone to leave stable employment is not limited to acts of direct solicitation by upper-level management personnel. Approaches made by less senior executives with a view to causing a person to resign from his or her employment and join another organization may also be taken into account.[1]

[1] *Toupin v. Ventes Mercury des Laurentides Inc.*, D.T.E. 89T-445 (Que. C.A.).

(4) Finding Similar Employment

§12.52 If an executive is expected to have difficulty finding similar employment, a longer notice period is required. Among the factors which may affect an executive's ability to find similar employment are job characteristics, personal characteristics, geographic location, economic climate, manner of dismissal, training, qualifications and experience. Courts have occasionally said that in determining reasonable notice, the time an individual takes to find other employment should be considered.[1]

[1] *A Contrario, Farrugia v. Selecta Générale, Compagnie d'assurances Inc.*, D.T.E. 95T-682 (Que. S.C.); *Meyer v. Jim Pattison Industries Ltd.* (1991), 38 C.C.E.L. 101 (B.C.S.C.); *Ostick v. Novacorp Int. Consulting Inc.* (1989), 27 C.C.E.L. 286 (B.C.S.C.); *Imprimeries Stellac Inc. v. Plante*, D.T.E. 89T-116 (Que. C.A.); *Surveyer, Nenniger & Chênevert Inc. v. Jackson*, D.T.E. 88T-667 (Que. C.A.), leave to appeal to S.C.C. refused Mar. 2, 1989; *Ma v. Columbia Trust Co.* (1985), 9 C.C.E.L. 300 (B.C.S.C.); *Bordeleau v. Union Carbide of Canada Ltd.* (1984), 6 C.C.E.L. 88 (Que. S.C.); *Chrétien v. Explosifs Austin Ltée.*, D.T.E. 96T-66 (Que. S.C.), on appeal; *Mazzella v. Compagnie Christie Brown, une division de Nabisco Brands Ltée*, D.T.E. 96T-312 (Que. S.C.).

§12.53 Education or training can negatively affect an executive's ability to find similar employment if the executive has a low level of education relative to the job status achieved.[1] Similarly, if an executive has general training in an area and his or her skills have grown rusty, increased notice will be required.[2] However, if an executive has training and experience which is in demand, less notice may be required.[3] This is especially the case when an executive's experience is quite broad and not specialized.[4]

---

[1]   *Smith v. Pacific National Exhibition* (1991), 34 C.C.E.L. 64 (B.C.S.C.); *Lutley v. Exact Weight Scale Inc.* (1991), T.L.W. 1040-009 (Ont. Ct. (Gen. Div.)); *Wilson v. Sandwell & Co.* (1986), T.L.W. 640-018 (B.C.S.C.).

[2]   *Douglas v. Sandwell & Co.* (1977), 81 D.L.R. (3d) 508 (B.C.S.C.).

[3]   *Speck v. Greater Niagara General Hospital* (1983), 43 O.R. (2d) 611 (H.C.J.), affd 51 O.R. (2d) 192 (C.A.).

[4]   *Hanoski v. Dominion Life Assurance Co.* (1987), T.L.W. 710-032 (B.C.S.C.); *Russello v. Jannock Ltd.* (1985), T.L.W. 514-015 (Ont. H.C.J.), revd in part on other grounds 15 C.C.E.L. 209 (Div. Ct.).

---

§12.54   In general, if the executive occupied a unique or very specialized, or high-level position in a limited industry, he or she may also be entitled to greater notice, since the number of similar positions available to the executive would be very limited.[1] If an executive is married or has dependent children, this may prolong the notice required since it could affect the executive's ability to relocate.[2] Increased notice may also be required if the executive is pregnant, disabled or suffering from poor health.[3] However, some courts have held that poor health or disability may not be proper considerations.[4]

---

[1]   *Hasler v. Spagnol's Wine & Beer Supplies Ltd.*, unreported, Oct. 24, 1991, Vancouver Doc. C907448 (B.C.S.C.); *Smith v. Pacific National Exhibition* (1991), 34 C.C.E.L. 64 (B.C.S.C.); *Hippodrome Blue Bonnets v. Jolicoeur*, D.T.E. 95T-185 (Que. C.A.); *Stewart v. Standard Broadcasting Corp.* (1989), 29 C.C.E.L. 290 (Que. S.C.); *Cornil v. Mondia Distribution Inc.*, D.T.E. 88T-584 (Que. S.C.).

[2]   *Longpré v. Carrière & Lefebvre (1978) Inc.* (1989), 28 C.C.E.L. 277 (Que. S.C.); *Rupchan v. Simpson Timber Co. (Sask.) Ltd.* (1988), 24 C.C.E.L. 47 (Sask. Q.B.).

[3]   *Smith v. Pacific National Exhibition* (1991), 34 C.C.E.L. 64 (B.C.S.C.); *Maycock v. MDI Mobile Data Int. Inc.* (1988), T.L.W. 833-003 (B.C.S.C.); *Tremblett v. Aardvark Pest Control Ltd.* (1987), 16 C.C.E.L. 306 (Ont. Dist. Ct.); *Bohemier v. Storwal Int. Inc.* (1983), 44 O.R. (2d) 361 (C.A.), leave to appeal to S.C.C. refused 3 C.C.E.L. 79n.

[4]   *Landry v. Canadian Forest Products Ltd.* (1991), 34 C.C.E.L. 37 (B.C.S.C.), revd on other grounds 42 C.C.E.L. 59 (C.A.); *Toffolo v. I.U.O.E. Local No. 115* (1987), T.L.W. 705-035 (B.C.S.C.); *Dixon v. Merland Explorations Ltd.* (1984), 30 Alta. L.R. (2d) 310 (Q.B.); *Nicholls v. Richmond* (1984), 52 B.C.L.R. 302 (S.C.).

---

§12.55   The geographic location of the executive can increase the length of notice which he or she is entitled to receive if the executive has special training and is dismissed by the only possible employer in the area.[1] If the executive has to relocate, this will also be considered by the court because of the extra time this will involve and the disruption to the executive's life.[2]

¹ *Jervis v. Raytheon Canada Ltd.* (1990), 35 C.C.E.L. 73 (Ont. Ct. (Gen. Div.)); *Johnston v. Algoma Steel Corp.* (1989), 24 C.C.E.L. 1 (Ont. H.C.J.); *Kadash v. Kipling Credit Union Ltd.* (1987), 56 Sask. R. 295 (C.A.).
² *Mackin v. Kings Regional Rehabilitation Centre* (1990), 95 N.S.R. (2d) 238 (S.C.); *McIntosh v. Saskatchewan Water Corp.* (1989), 26 C.C.E.L. 196 (Sask. C.A.).

§12.55.1 In *Lehan v. Gulf Canada Corporation*[1] the court held that employee transfers, especially when they are paid by the Company, may create expectations of prolonged employment and increase the amount of notice an employee is entitled to receive upon being dismissed.

¹ (1993), 10 Alta. L.R. (3d) 75 (Q.B.).

§12.56 Being dismissed during high unemployment in general or within the executive's industry will usually entitle the executive to special consideration.[1] However, some courts have expressed little sympathy for executives who insist on staying where there are no jobs.[2]

¹ *Rupchan v. Simpson Timber Co. (Sask.) Ltd.* (1988), 24 C.C.E.L. 47 (Sask. Q.B.); *Grant v. MacMillan Bloedel Industries Ltd.* (1982), 83 C.L.L.C. 14,002 (Ont. H.C.J.); *Ellis v. Whitepass Transportation Ltd.* (1983), 42 B.C.L.R. 351 (C.A.).
² *Danyluk v. Simpson Timber Co. (Sask.)* (1989), 27 C.C.E.L. 132 (Sask. Q.B.); *Harris v. Eastern Provincial Airways (1963) Ltd.* (1981), 35 Nfld. & P.E.I.R. 152 (Nfld. S.C.).

§12.57 Some courts have extended the notice required when the general economic climate is poor.[1] This is especially the case when an entire industry is depressed or there is a particularly poor market in relation to the executive's occupation.[2] However, other courts have downplayed the importance of economic climate, or denied that it is a proper consideration. Generally, this is justified either on the basis that a poor economy will have hurt both parties equally[3] or that it cannot be implied that the parties had agreed at the time of hiring that a greater notice period would be owed in the event of recession.[4]

¹ *Schwann v. Husky Oil Operations Ltd.* (1989), 27 C.C.E.L. 103 (Sask. C.A.); *Hunter v. Northwood Pulp & Timber Ltd.* (1985), 7 C.C.E.L. 260 (B.C.C.A.); *Labelle v. Experts-Conseils Shawinigan Inc.*, D.T.E. 84T-547 (Que. S.C.), appeal settled out of court Mar. 26, 1985, C.A.M. 500-09-000846-840; *Farrugia v. Wabco-Standard Inc. c.o.b. American-Standard* (1984), 4 C.C.E.L. 329 (Ont. H.C.J.); *Carrick v. Cooper Canada Ltd.* (1983), 2 C.C.E.L. 87 (Ont. H.C.J.); *Blackburn v. Coyle Motors Ltd.* (1983), 3 C.C.E.L. 1 (Ont. H.C.J.); *Olson v. Sprung Instant Greenhouses Ltd.* (1985), 12 C.C.E.L. 8 (Alta. Q.B.); *Garcia v. Crestbrook Forest Industries Ltd.* (1993), 86 B.C.L.R. (2d) 394 (C.A.).
² *Garcia v. Crestbrook Forest Industries Ltd.* (1993), 2 C.C.E.L. (2d) 48 (B.C.C.A.); *Anstey v. Fednav Offshore Inc.* (1990), 34 F.T.R. 192; *Mann v. Andres Wines Ltd.* (1988), 19 C.C.E.L. 1 (Ont. Div. Ct.), varg 9 C.C.E.L. 63 (Dist. Ct.); *Sawko v. Foseco Canada Ltd.* (1987), 15 C.C.E.L. 309 (Ont. Dist. Ct.); *Mifsud v. MacMillan Bathurst Inc.* (1987), 60 O.R. (2d) 58 (H.C.J.), revd on other grounds 28 C.C.E.L. 228 (C.A.), leave

to appeal to S.C.C. refused 39 O.A.C. 153; *Hunter v. Northwood Pulp & Timber Ltd.* (1985), 7 C.C.E.L. 260 (B.C.C.A.); *Johnston v. Canada Cement Lafarge Ltd.* (1984), 12 C.C.E.L. 108 (Alta. C.A.); *Thomson v. Bechtel Canada Ltd.* (1983), 3 C.C.E.L. 16 (Ont. H.C.J), affd 30 A.C.W.S. (2d) 354 (C.A.); *Trudeau-Linley v. Plummer Memorial Public Hospital* (1993), 1 C.C.E.L. (2d) 114 (Ont. Gen. Div.).

[3] *Adamson v. Watts & Henderson (Atlantic) Ltd.* (1987), 16 C.C.E.L. 74 (Ont. H.C.J.); *Patterson v. SNC Group* (1986), T.L.W. 612-033 (Ont. H.C.J.); *Bordeleau v. Union Carbide of Canada Ltd.* (1984), 6 C.C.E.L. 88 (Que. S.C.); *Breeze v. Federal Business Development Bank*, J.E. 84-963 (Que. S.C.); *Russello v. Jannock Ltd.* (1985), T.L.W. 514-015 (Ont. H.C.J.), revd in part on other grounds 15 C.C.E.L. 209 (Ont. Div. Ct.); *Rossato v. Pitney Bowes of Canada Ltd.* (1983), 2 C.C.E.L. 154 (Ont. Co. Ct.).

[4] *Nicholls v. Richmond* (1984), 52 B.C.L.R. 302 (S.C.); *French v. Pike's Transport Ltd.* (1984), 48 Nfld. & P.E.I.R. 119 (Nfld. Dist. Ct.).

§12.57.1 In *Garvin v. Rockwell International of Canada Ltd.*[1] the court found that there is no rule that the notice period should shrink in adverse economic times. Economic circumstances are merely one factor to be considered in determining the reasonable notice. In making such a finding, Mr. Justice Ferguson analyzed the earlier decision rendered in *Bohemier v. Storwal International Inc.*[2] and held that the *Bohemier* decision did not stand for the principle that the notice period should shrink in adverse economic times but merely that such conditions are a factor to be considered in assessing reasonable notice.[3] Conversely, in a recent Ontario decision[4] the court held that poor prospects of employment at the time of the dismissal of the plaintiff, due to a high rate of unemployment, lengthened the notice period owed to him.

[1] (1993), 50 C.C.E.L. 296 (Ont. Ct. (Gen. Div.)); for a discussion on the rule in Alberta see *Russell v. Winnifred Stewart Assn. for the Mentally Handicapped* (1993), 49 C.C.E.L. 176 (Alta. Q.B.).

[2] (1982), 40 O.R. (2d) 264 (H.C.).

[3] See also *Garcia v. Crestbrook Forest Industries Ltd.* (1993), 86 B.C.L.R. (2d) 394 (C.A.).

[4] *Ashton v. Perle Systems Inc.* (1994), 2 C.C.E.L. (2d) 243 (Ont. Ct. (Gen. Div.)).

§12.57.2 In a wrongful dismissal action, the possibility that the plaintiff will be out of work longer than for the period of reasonable notice is not a factor which can be weighed against the employer whose liability is limited by the period of reasonable notice.[1]

[1] *Crang et al. v. Delta Catalytic Constructors Ltd.*, unreported, Jan. 24, 1994, File No. C932993 (B.C.S.C.).

§12.58 If the manner in which an executive was dismissed was harsh and unfair, the notice period may be lengthened.[1] In the event of unsubstantiated allegations of misconduct, allegations of poor job performance, a failure to warn, or threats made against the executive, the notice period may also be lengthened.[2] It should also be noted that the

Civil Code of Quebec provides that an employee may not renounce his right to obtain compensation for any injury he suffers where the manner of resiliation is abusive.[3]

[1] *Société Hôtelière Canadien Pacifique v. Hoeckner*, D.T.E. 88T-548 (Que. C.A.); *Hiscox v. A.E. LePage Real Estate Services Ltd.* (1986), T.L.W. 618-032 (Ont. H.C.J.); *Marks v. Cresson Investments* (1986), T.L.W. 619-019 (Ont. H.C.J.); *Eyers v. City Buick Pontiac Cadillac Ltd.* (1984), 6 C.C.E.L. 234 (Ont. H.C.J.), revd in part 13 O.A.C. 66 (C.A.).

[2] *Marks v. Cresson Investments* (1986), T.L.W. 619-019 (Ont. H.C.J.); *Dauphinée v. Bank of Montreal* (1985), 10 C.C.E.L. 36 (B.C.S.C.); *Rahemtulla v. Vanfed Credit Union* (1984), 4 C.C.E.L. 170 (B.C.S.C.); *Cadenhead v. Unicorn Abrasives of Canada Ltd.* (1984), 5 C.C.E.L. 241 (Ont. H.C.J.).

[3] C.C.Q., art. 2092.

(5) Length of Service

§12.59 In general, the length of reasonable notice increases in proportion to the length of the executive's continuous service.[1] Courts tend to believe that an executive who has been in one job or with one employer for a number of years will have received narrower experience and will be less employable.[2]

[1] *Chotani v. Westinghouse Canada Inc.*, D.T.E. 91T-328 (Que. S.C.); *Habitations Populaires Desjardins de Lanaudière Inc. v. Boyer*, D.T.E. 88T-550 (Que. C.A.); *Roscoe v. McGavin Foods Ltd.* (1983), 2 C.C.E.L. 287 (B.C.S.C.). See *Addison v. M. Loeb Ltd.* (1986), 25 D.L.R. (4th) 151 (Ont. C.A.), regarding the recognition given to the period of employment with the predecessor employer when an employee has been employed by the purchaser of a business after having been employed by the vendor.

[2] *Cook v. Royal Trust* (1990), 31 C.C.E.L. 6 (B.C.S.C.); *Durrant v. B.C. Hydro & Power Authority* (1988), T.L.W. 748-009 and T.L.W. 806-013 (B.C.S.C.), revd in part on other grounds 49 B.C.L.R. (2d) 263 (C.A.); *Bohemier v. Storwal Int. Inc.* (1982), 40 O.R. (2d) 264 (H.C.J.), revd in part 44 O.R. (2d) 361 (C.A.), leave to appeal to S.C.C. refused 3 C.C.E.L. 79n; *Turner v. Canadian Admiral Corp.* (1980), 1 C.C.E.L. 130 (Ont. H.C.J.).

§12.60 It is not unusual for an executive to work for different corporate entities within the same group of related companies. Corporate reorganizations for fiscal or other business reasons, or even an executive's normal career path within a multinational organization, often yield this result. In these circumstances, the number of years of service spent within the corporate group will be the basis of the court's determination of the notice to which an executive is entitled in the event of his or her dismissal without cause.[1]

[1] *Castagna v. Design Hydraulics Inc.*, D.T.E. 88T-1006 (Que. S.C.); *Olson v. Sprung Instant Greenhouses Ltd.* (1985), 12 C.C.E.L. 8 (Alta. Q.B.); *Holmes v. British Steel Canada Inc.* (1984), 25 A.C.W.S. (2d) 19 (B.C.S.C.); *Matheson v. Matheson Int. Trucks Ltd.*

(1984), 4 C.C.E.L. 271 (Ont. H.C.J.); *Taggart v. Kwikasair Express Ltd.* (1980), 26 B.C.L.R. 352 (C.A.); *Bagby v. Gustavson Int. Drilling Co.* (1980), 24 A.R. 181 (C.A.).

(6)   Other Factors

§12.61   Whether an employer who is experiencing economic difficulty is entitled to give a shorter notice period is an issue upon which the courts have conflicting views. Some courts have held that requiring an employer to give normal periods of notice when it is experiencing economic difficulty is unduly harsh, and could drive the employer into bankruptcy or receivership.[1] Many of these courts cite the principle that notice must be reasonable for both the executive and the employer as the basis for their decision. This principle was first expressed by the Ontario Court of Appeal in *Bohemier v. Storwal Int. Inc.*[2] Other courts have attempted to limit the principle expressed in *Bohemier* or deny it altogether.[3] In general, these courts have expressed the opinion that the concept that notice should be reasonable for both the executive and the employer undermines the fundamental rationale of reasonable notice, which is to provide the executive with enough time to find new employment.[4]

---

[1]   *Orke v. Quintette Coal Ltd.* (1991), 39 C.C.E.L. 146 (B.C.S.C.); *Gagnon v. Thetford Transport Ltée*, D.T.E. 87T-935 (Que. S.C.); *Palchinski v. Sperry Inc.* (1986), 48 Sask. R. 281 (Q.B.); *McBride v. W.P. London & Associates Ltd.* (1984), 5 C.C.E.L. 314 (Ont. H.C.J.); *Henry v. Shawinigan Energy Consultants Ltd.* (1983), 2 C.C.E.L. 160 (Ont. H.C.J.); *Rossato v. Pitney Bowes of Canada Ltd.* (1983), 2 C.C.E.L. 154 (Ont. Co. Ct.); *Frost v. Montreal Engineering Co.* (1983), 3 C.C.E.L. 86 (Alta. Q.B.); *MacDonald v. Empire Theatres Ltd.* (1983), 51 N.B.R. (2d) 243 (Q.B.).

[2]   (1983), 44 O.R. (2d) 361 (C.A.).

[3]   *Jeffrey v. Plant Forest Products Corp.* (1990), 32 C.C.E.L. 237 (Sask. Q.B.); *Farquhar v. Butler Brothers Supplies Ltd.* (1988), 23 B.C.L.R. (2d) 89 (C.A.); *Anderson v. Haakon Industries (Canada) Ltd.* (1987), 48 D.L.R. (4th) 235 (B.C.C.A.); *Ansari v. B.C. Hydro & Power Authority* (1986), 2 B.C.L.R. (2d) 33 (S.C.), affd 55 B.C.L.R. (2d) xxxiii (C.A.); *Moore v. Zurich Ins. Co.* (1984), 4 C.C.E.L. 188 (Ont. Co. Ct.).

[4]   *Jeffrey v. Plant Forest Products Corp.* (1990), 32 C.C.E.L. 237 (Sask. Q.B.); *Misovic v. Acres Davy McKee Ltd.* (1985), 7 C.C.E.L. 163 (Ont. C.A.), varg 22 A.C.W.S. (2d) 50 (Co. Ct.).

---

§12.62   Non-profit organizations should not be treated differently from any other employer in terms of the length of notice they must give to their employees in case of termination without cause.[1]

---

[1]   *Ballard v. Alberni Valley Chamber of Commerce* (1992), 39 C.C.E.L. 225 (B.C.S.C.); *River T.V. Assn.*, unreported, May 16, 1983, Campbell River No. 107/82 (B.C.S.C.).

---

§12.63   In some cases, the custom of an industry is taken into consideration in establishing reasonable notice. However, the executive must be aware of the custom in order for it to be a factor. But it was stated in one decision that custom is not binding on the court.[1]

> [1] *Grant v. Cooper Market Ltd.* (1979), 13 B.C.L.R. 100 (Co. Ct.).

§12.64 Some courts have considered the precariousness of the executive's job security as a factor in determining the notice period. These courts take the position that if the executive is aware of the precariousness of his or her job security well in advance of the termination of the employment contract, the notice period should be short. An executive's job security has been held to be precarious if the executive was the last one to be kept pending the sale of the business, the employer was in receivership, the executive's position was experimental, or the employer had lost its major contract.[1]

> [1] *Porter v. Highmont Operating Corp.* (1990), 29 C.C.E.L. 164 (B.C.S.C.), vard 36 C.C.E.L. 1 (C.A.); *Luchuk v. Sport B.C.* (1984), 3 C.C.E.L. 117 (B.C.S.C.); *Engel v. Clarkson Co.*, [1983] 1 W.W.R. 657 (Sask. Q.B.); *Quigley v. Gulton Industries (Canada) Ltd.* (1983), T.L.W. 222-031 (Ont. Co. Ct.). See also *Ahmad v. Procter & Gamble* (1987), 18 C.C.E.L. 124 (Ont. H.C.J.), affd 34 C.C.E.L. 1 (C.A.).

§12.65 Some courts have increased the notice period when the executive received assurances of job security prior to termination.[1] Similarly, notice is increased if the employer leads its executives to believe there is no chance of dismissal or if a receiver undertakes major restructuring and renovations, which leads executives to believe the business has a promising future.[2]

> [1] *Brause v. Microtel Ltd.* (1989), 27 C.C.E.L. 260 (B.C.S.C.); *Keighan v. Kool-Fire Ltd.* (1984), 6 C.C.E.L. 196 (Ont. H.C.J.), affd 9 C.C.E.L. xxxiv (C.A.); *Gardner v. Rockwell Int. of Canada Ltd.* (1975), 9 O.R. (2d) 105 (H.C.J.).
> [2] *Gresmak v. Yellowhead Town & Country Inn* (1989), 30 C.C.E.L. 85 (B.C. Co. Ct.); *Mutch v. Norman Wade Co.* (1987), 17 B.C.L.R. (2d) 185 (S.C.); *Johnston v. Canada Cement Lafarge Ltd.* (1984), 12 C.C.E.L. 108 (Alta. C.A.).

§12.66 In exceptional circumstances, courts have also considered such factors as the mistaken belief of being bound by a term contract, and the executive's particular personal situation.[1]

> [1] *Boudreault v. Centre Hospitalier St-Vincent de Paul*, D.T.E. 90T-771 (Que. S.C.); *Castagna v. Design Hydraulics Inc.*, D.T.E. 88T-1006 (Que. S.C.).

§12.67 Dismissal shortly before an executive reaches pensionable age causing the loss of a substantial pension benefit does not entitle the executive to a more extensive period of notice or notice to retirement age.[1] However, some courts have said that one can extend reasonable notice to the day a benefit vests so long as this only involves an extension by a few days of a notice which is otherwise reasonable.[2] Moreover, availability of early retirement is not a factor which should be taken into account in fixing the period of reasonable notice.[3] In *Gaudrey v. Woodward's Ltd.*,[4] the British Columbia Court of Appeal quoted an earlier decision,[5] and held that:

> [T]he law seems to place a cap of reasonableness upon the notice period and does not compensate an employee to retirement age, whatever that may be, even though there is little or no likelihood of alternative equivalent employment. I believe this because:
>
> (a) such a law would amount to a guarantee of lifetime income;
> (b) it would fix the employer with all responsibility for the lack of employment opportunities; and
> (c) the law presumes that no employer would accept such an onerous responsibility at the time of engagement.

[1] *Webster v. B.C. Hydro & Power Authority* (1992), 42 C.C.E.L. 105 (B.C.C.A.), appeal dismissed 2 B.C.L.R. (3d) 1 (S.C.C.); *Tedford v. Woodward Stores Ltd.* (1990), 31 C.C.E.L. 1 (B.C.C.A.); *Ansari v. B.C. Hydro & Power Authority* (1986), 2 B.C.L.R. (2d) 33 (S.C.), affd 55 B.C.L.R. (2d) xxxiii (C.A.).

[2] *Athwal v. The City of Edmonton* (1986), 72 A.R. 316 (C.A.); *PCL Construction Management Inc. v. Holmes* (1994), 8 C.C.E.L. (2d) 192 (C.A.).

[3] *Regan v. Commercial Union Assurance Co.*, (1993), 48 C.C.E.L. 208 (B.C.S.C.).

[4] 40 A.C.W.S. (3d) 289 (B.C.C.A.).

[5] *Ansari v. British Columbia Hydro and Power Authority* (1986), 2 B.C.L.R. (2d) 33 (S.C.), affd 55 B.C.L.R. (2d) xxxiii (C.A.).

(7) "Ball Park" Doctrine

§12.68   The "ball park" doctrine places the onus on the executive to show that the notice period provided by the employer was unreasonable. A court which adopts the "ball park" doctrine will not make an independent determination of what constitutes reasonable notice. Instead, the court will examine the reasonableness of the notice provided by the employer in a deferential manner. Only if the notice provided by the employer is grossly inadequate will the court make its own determination of the notice period.[1]

[1] *De Freitas v. Canadian Express & Transportation Ltd.* (1986), 16 C.C.E.L. 160 (Ont. H.C.J.), affd 18 C.C.E.L. xxx (C.A.).

§12.69   The "ball park" doctrine has not been consistently applied in Canadian case law. While some courts have applied the doctrine,[1] others have expressed doubt concerning the application of the doctrine and others have denied it altogether.[2] The Alberta Court of Appeal rejected this approach in *Rahmath v. Louisiana Land & Exploration Co.*[3] No other Court of Appeal has definitively ruled on the issue. In British Columbia, although some courts have applied the doctrine (albeit with reservations),[4] the recent case of *Spooner v. Ridley Terminals Inc.*[5] utterly rejected the ball park doctrine, saying that it would be an abdication of the court's responsibility in a wrongful dismissal case. Courts in Quebec have not applied this doctrine. An extensive analysis of the "ballpark" doctrine and its inapplicability in Ontario was set out in *Garvin v. Rockwell International of Canada Ltd.*[6] The Court held that the threshold or "ballpark" approach to the determination of reasonable notice, whereby the court refuses to interfere if the notice or pay in lieu of notice given by the employer falls within the range of what is reasonable, is inappropriate in Ontario. The court's role is to make an objective determination in accordance with established factors as to what the length of the notice should be. It is not appropriate for the court to express its views in terms of a range. Moreover, the threshold approach is unfair in allocating risk between the employer and the employee. The threshold approach is not consistent with the role of a trial court in an adversary system. Recently, similar rulings were made in *Slater v. Sandwell Inc.*,[7] *Morris v. Rockwell International of Canada*[8] and *Monk v. Coca-Cola Bottling Ltd.*[9]

[1] *Allen v. Assaly Holdings Ltd.* (1991), 34 C.C.E.L. 81 (Ont. Ct. (Gen. Div.)); *Erskine v. Viking Helicopter Ltd.* (1990), 35 C.C.E.L. 322 (Ont. Ct. (Gen. Div.)); *McKee v. NCR Canada Ltd.* (1986), 10 C.C.E.L. 128 (Ont. H.C.J.); *Rivers v. Gulf Canada Ltd.* (1986), 13 C.C.E.L. 131 (Ont. H.C.J.); *Donnelly v. B.C. Hydro & Power Authority* (1986), T.L.W. 636-036; *Perry v. Gulf Minerals Canada Ltd.* (1985), T.L.W. 513-025 (Ont. H.C.J.); *Schmidt v. Saskatchewan Oil & Gas Corp.* (1993), 38 A.C.W.S. (3d) 311 (Sask. Q.B.); *Kemp v. Saskatchewan Oil & Gas* (1992), 42 C.C.E.L. 6 (Sask. Q.B.).

[2] *Battaja v. Canada Tungsten Mining Corp.*, [1990] 2 W.W.R. 72 (N.W.T.S.C.); *Rahmath v. Louisiana Land & Exploration Co.* (1989), 59 D.L.R. (4th) 606 (Alta. C.A.); *De Freitas v. Canadian Express & Transportation Ltd.* (1986), 16 C.C.E.L. 160 (Ont. H.C.J.), affd 18 C.C.E.L. xxx (C.A.); *Miller v. Petro Canada* (1993), 36 A.C.W.S. (3d) 403 (Sask. Q.B.); *McCrea v. Conference Board of Canada* (1993), 45 C.C.E.L. 29 (Ont. Ct. (Gen. Div.)).

[3] (1989), 59 D.L.R. (4th) 606 (Alta. C.A.).

[4] *Koren v. White Spot Ltd.* (1988), 29 B.C.L.R. (2d) 121 (S.C.); *Michalchuk v. B.C. Hydro & Power Authority*, unreported, Apr. 22, 1987, Vancouver Doc. C861041 (B.C.S.C.).

[5] (1991), 62 B.C.L.R. (2d) 132 (S.C.). See also *Ward v. Royal Trust Corp. of Canada* (1993), 1 C.C.E.L. (2d) 153 (B.C.S.C.); *Ellchuk v. Int. Stage Lines Inc.* (1989), 28 C.C.E.L. 309 (B.C. Co. Ct.); *Araki v. Balco Industries Ltd.*, [1988] B.C.W.L.D. 650 (S.C.); *Ward v. Royal Trust Corp. of Canada* (1993), 39 A.C.W.S. (3d) 117 (B.C.S.C.).

[6] (1993), 50 C.C.E.L. 296 (Ont. Ct. (Gen. Div.)).

[7] (1994), 5 C.C.E.L. (2d) 308 (Ont. Ct. (Gen. Div.)).

[8] (1993), 47 C.C.E.L. 183 (Ont. Ct. (Gen. Div.)).

[9] (1996), 20 C.C.E.L. (2d) 280 (N.S.S.C.).

(iv) Statutory Limitations on the Right to Dismiss Without Cause

§12.69.1 Although generally at common law an employer has an unfettered right to terminate the executive's employment, subject only to the obligation to provide the executive with reasonable notice in the case where an employee is terminated without cause, in some cases statutory provisions will prevent such an exercise of the employer's discretion. For example, in Quebec, the *Act Respecting Labour Standards*[1] prevents the employer from terminating the employment of an employee who is pregnant or has reached the age of retirement. Another statute prevents the employer from terminating an employee because he/she is disabled because of a work-related injury. Similar provisions exist under the *Canada Labour Code* and other statutes. The employer must review the applicable legislation in each province to know the rights and restrictions which may apply to the right to terminate employment. Some of the statutory prohibitions provide for the reinstatement of the employee if it is found that the employee was terminated on a proscribed ground. The employee may have the option of filing a claim for breach of contract and/or a statutory recourse and will have to evaluate the advantages and disadvantages of each recourse. It should be noted, however, that even though the employee may not be prohibited from filing more than one claim, *issue estoppel* may be available to prevent the litigant from having the second claim heard once the issue has already been decided in another forum.[2]

---

[1] R.S.Q. c. N-1.1, ss. 122, 122.1, and 124.

[2] *Rasanen v. Rosemount Instruments Ltd.* (1994), 17 O.R. (3d) 267 (C.A.), leave to appeal refused 19 O.R. (3d) xvi (S.C.C.); *Fayant v. Campbell's Maple Village Ltd.*, [1994] 3 W.W.R. 171 (Alta. Q.B.).

2. Constructive Dismissal

§12.70 Constructive dismissal of an executive occurs when an employer abruptly and unilaterally alters a fundamental condition of employment.[1] If the executive does not accept the abrupt change and resigns, he or she will be entitled to damages for wrongful dismissal.[2]

---

[1] *Farber v. Royal Trust Co.*, [1997] 1 S.C.R. 846; *Roy v. Caisse Populaire de Thetford Mines*, [1991] R.J.Q. 2693 (S.C.); *Henderson v. Westfair Foods Ltd.* (1990), 32 C.C.E.L. 152 (Man. Q.B.), revd on other grounds 40 C.C.E.L. 81 (C.A.); *Poole v. Tomenson Saunders Whitehead Ltd.* (1987), 18 C.C.E.L. 238 (B.C.C.A.); *Moore v. University of Western Ontario* (1985), 8 C.C.E.L. 157 (Ont. H.C.J.); *Reber v. Lloyds Bank Int. Canada* (1985), 61 B.C.L.R. 361 (C.A.); *Orth v. Macdonald Dettwiler & Associates Ltd.* (1986), 16 C.C.E.L. 41 (B.C.C.A.); *Kalker v. Brother International Corp.*, D.T.E. 95T-1323 (Que. S.C.), on appeal.

² Contra: *Lancup v. Société canadienne internationale d'informatique ltée.*, D.T.E. 97T-228 (S.C.).

§12.70.1 The Supreme Court of Canada[1] set the parameters defining the difficult concept of constructive dismissal, by putting together a list of all the factors that must be taken into account while deciding if an employee has been constructively dismissed and, in doing so, it did not depart from principles which were previously enunciated by lower courts. It ruled that in order to determine if an individual has been constructively dismissed, one must refer to the test of how a reasonable person would have considered the offer made by the employer. The court must determine whether, at the time the offer was made, a reasonable person in the same situation as the employee would have felt that the essential terms of the employment contract were being substantially modified. The determination as to whether or not a change in position constitutes a constructive dismissal also involves the objective comparison of the different components of the position previously held by the employee and the position offered to him. These components or attributes include the remuneration, status, prestige and responsibilities of these positions. In *Farber v. Royal Trust Co.*, the Supreme Court of Canada concluded that such changes as the loss of a guaranteed base salary were sufficient to constitute constructive dismissal.

¹ *Farber v. Royal Trust Co.*, [1997] 1 S.C.R. 846.

§12.71 The courts generally allow employers a certain degree of flexibility to vary some terms of employment. This stems from a recognition of the fact that employment relationships are not stagnant, but are constantly evolving. Moreover, it is understood that some leeway is necessary to reflect the changing nature of the business and to allow employers to reorganize and restructure their businesses. The Quebec Court of Appeal, in *Owens Illinois Canada Inc. v. Boivin*,[1] proposed the following tests:

> For there to be a disguised dismissal in the present case, one must conclude that the circumstances were fabricated by the appellants [the employer] so as to leave the respondent [the executive] little choice but to refuse the assignment. Alternatively, one must conclude that the proposed assignment involved such a disparity in status, advantages, duties and modalities as to constitute substantially new conditions of employment.

Indeed, the British Columbia Court of Appeal has held[2] that the subjective views on how a transfer might have been effected differently are not legally significant. The question is whether the proposed change is objectively a fundamental breach of the employment contract.

¹ (1988), 23 C.C.E.L. 255, at 260. See also *Gravino v. Gulf Canada Ltée*, D.T.E. 91T-1059 (Que. S.C.), appeal abandoned Sept. 25, 1991, C.A.M. 500-09-001184-910; *Bélair v. Communications Radiomutuel Inc.*, D.T.E. 88T-268 (Que. S.C.).
² *Cayen v. Woodwards Stores Ltd.* (1993), 45 C.C.E.L. 264 (B.C.C.A.), at 273.

§12.72 In determining which conditions are the essential elements of the employment contract and whether the changes made by an employer affect the essence of the contract, the circumstances of each case must be considered. In addition, it is the executive who has the burden of proving that the changes violate the essential elements of the employment contract.[1] In this regard, the executive's perception of the employer's conduct is not sufficient to warrant the conclusion that the employer has breached the contract.[2]

¹ *Ratté v. Pavillon Lincoln Mercury Inc.*, D.T.E. 97T-990 (Que. S.C.).
² *Barrett v. Sutherland Motors Ltd.* (1989), 28 C.C.E.L. 239 (N.B.Q.B.); *Snyders v. Saint John Shipbuilding Ltd.* (1989), 29 C.C.E.L. 26 (N.B.C.A.), leave to appeal to S.C.C. refused 103 N.B.R. (2d) 89n; *Smith v. Viking Helicopter Ltd.* (1989), 24 C.C.E.L. 113 (Ont. C.A.); *Lesiuk v. B.C. Forest Products Ltd.* (1986), 15 C.C.E.L. 91 (B.C.C.A.), affg 56 B.C.L.R. 216 (S.C.); *Orth v. Macdonald Dettwiler & Associates Ltd.* (1986), 16 C.C.E.L. 41 (B.C.C.A.); *Wermenlinger v. Gestion financière Talvest Inc.*, D.T.E. 97T-917 (Que. S.C.).

§12.73 Obviously, an express or implicit agreement to any modification of the employment contract, even touching upon an essential element of the contract, will prevent the executive from alleging constructive dismissal. Consequently, it is crucial that the executive react as soon as he or she becomes aware of the employer's unilateral changes to the conditions of employment or the executive may be deemed to have implicitly accepted the new conditions.[1] However, in one case the Court of Appeal upheld the employee's claim of constructive dismissal, even though he resigned 18 months after the unilateral and fundamental changes to his job.[2] The Court said that the employee's constant opposition and complaints about his demotion coupled with the employer's reassurances that the situation was only temporary in that he would be transferred to a job that did not amount to a demotion and that his salary and benefits would be preserved, indicated that the employee could not be deemed to have accepted the new working conditions. The employee had explained that he resigned when he realized that the employer had no intention of finding him another assignment.

¹ *Roy v. Caisse Populaire de Thetford Mines*, [1991] R.J.Q. 2693 (S.C.); *Gilbert v. Hôpital*

Général de Lachine, D.T.E. 89T-666 (Que. S.C.). See also *Hrycyk v. Ayerst McKenna*, unreported, June 21, 1990, C.S.M. 500-05-011282-884 (S.C.).

[2] *Groupe Commerce (Le), compagnie d'assurances v. Chouinard*, D.T.E. 95T-269 (Que. C.A.).

(a) Remuneration and Benefits

§12.74 Courts have held that a unilateral reduction in salary, failure to pay commissions earned, or failure to provide advances to which the executive is entitled, constitutes constructive dismissal.[1] Constructive dismissal may also be found if the employer changes the formula which prescribes the method by which salary is to be calculated, even if it is alleged that the level of compensation would remain the same.[2] Similarly, the reduction or modification of the territory for which an executive is responsible, thereby reducing his or her potential to earn commissions or bonuses, may constitute constructive dismissal.[3]

[1] *Farquhar v. Butler Brothers Supplies Ltd.* (1988), 23 B.C.L.R. (2d) 89 (C.A.); *Rémi Carrier Inc. v. Nolan*, D.T.E. 86T-370 (Que. C.A.); *Olson v. Sprung Instant Greenhouses Ltd.* (1985), 12 C.C.E.L. 8 (Alta. Q.B.); *Pearl v. Pacific Enercon Inc.* (1985), 7 C.C.E.L. 252 (B.C.C.A.); *Hill v. Peter Gorman Ltd.* (1957), 9 D.L.R. (2d) 124 (Ont. C.A.); *Evans v. Fisher Motor Co.* (1915), 8 O.W.N. 19 (H.C.). For more details on the effect of changing remuneration, see Chapter 7, "Provide Remuneration".

[2] *Nyveen v. Russell Food Equipment Ltd.*, D.T.E. 88T-294 (Que. S.C.); *Roberts v. Versatile Farm Equipment Co.* (1987), 16 C.C.E.L. 9 (Sask. Q.B.); *Pearl v. Pacific Enercon Inc.* (1985), 7 C.C.E.L. 252 (B.C.C.A.); *Bishop v. Vachon Inc.* (1979), 22 Nfld. & P.E.I.R. 148 (Nfld. S.C.); *Farber v. Royal Trust Co.*, unreported, Aug. 11, 1989, C.S.M. 500-05-004698-856 (Que. S.C.) (on appeal, C.A.M. 500-09-001201-896).

[3] *Vassallo v. Crosbie Enterprises Ltd.* (1981), 9 A.C.W.S. (2d) 335 (Nfld. S.C.). Not constructive dismissal: *Snelling v. Tenneco Canada Inc.* (1992), 40 C.C.E.L. 122 (B.C.S.C.).

§12.75 In *Lavigne v. Sidbec-Dosco Inc.*,[1] the court found that the loss of an anticipated salary increase, in conjunction with other factors, amounted to constructive dismissal. It has also been held that the elimination of a fringe benefit such as an "expatriation allowance" or the use of the company vehicle may constitute constructive dismissal where the benefit is of significant value to the executive.[2]

[1] D.T.E. 85T-4 (Que. S.C.); affd, unreported, May 4, 1988, C.A.M. 500-09-001556-844.

[2] *Schwann v. Husky Oil Operations Ltd.* (1989), 27 C.C.E.L. 103 (Sask. C.A.); *Bell v. Trail-Mate Products of Canada Ltd.* (1986), 15 C.C.E.L. 39 (Ont. Dist. Ct.); *Allison v. Amoco Production Co.*, [1975] 5 W.W.R. 501 (Alta. S.C.); *Nerada v. Hobart Canada Inc.* (1982), 1 C.C.E.L. 116 (B.C.S.C.).

§12.76 However, some courts have held that a minor change in pay or benefits would not constitute a fundamental change in some circumstances.[1] In *Poole v. Tomenson Saunders Whitehead Ltd.*,[2] the plaintiff accepted a senior position with the defendant company. He was to be paid a salary plus an annual bonus of not less than 15% of his salary, contingent on satisfactory service. In late 1981, the defendant company experienced serious financial difficulties, and undertook a reorganization of upper-level management. As a result of this reorganization, the plaintiff's salary was frozen, and his bonus was reduced. The court held that the refusal to pay the full bonus was not a fundamental breach because the difference in pay was $4,500 out of the total compensation of $100,000.

1   *Barrett v. Sutherland Motors Ltd.* (1989), 28 C.C.E.L. 239 (N.B.Q.B.); *Purdy v. Vancouver Island Helicopters Ltd.* (1988), W.D.P.M. 747-034-3 (B.C.S.C.); *Pathak v. Jannock Steel Fabricating Co.* (1996), 21 C.C.E.L. (2d) 12 (Alta. Q.B.).
2   (1987), 18 C.C.E.L. 238 (B.C.C.A.).

(b)   Duties and Responsibilities

§12.77   A demotion or other unilateral change in an executive's functions and duties, or a change in the nature of the work, may also amount to constructive dismissal.[1] Similarly, a mandatory promotion can constitute constructive dismissal.[2] In general, an employer is not permitted to alter an executive's terms of employment to the degree that the executive is obliged to perform an entirely different job.[3]

1   *Garreau v. Ile-Perrot (Ville de l')*, D.T.E. 95T-1106 (Que. Q.C.); *Wilding v. Qwest Foods Ltd.* (1994), 93 B.C.L.R. (2d) 295 (C.A.); *Courchesne v. Restaurant & Charcuterie Bens Inc.*, J.E. 90-236 (Que. C.A.), leave to appeal to S.C.C. refused June 14, 1990; *Chouinard v. Groupe Commerce Cie d'assurances*, D.T.E. 95T-269 (Que. C.A.); *Désormeaux v. Banque de Montréal*, D.T.E. 87T-210 (Que. S.C.); *Welsh v. Robertson Motors (1972) Ltd.* (1983), 22 A.C.W.S. (2d) 242 (Ont. Co. Ct.); *Fredin v. Village of Granisle* (1983), 23 A.C.W.S. (2d) 386 (B.C.S.C.); *Baker v. Burns Foods Ltd.* (1977), 74 D.L.R. (3d) 762 (Man. C.A.); *O'Grady v. Insurance Corp. of British Columbia* (1975), 63 D.L.R. (3d) 370 (B.C.S.C.). In *Reber v. Lloyds Bank Int. Canada* (1985), 61 B.C.L.R. 361 (C.A.), the court held that a transfer involving a loss of prestige and position does not automatically imply that the person has been demoted.
2   *Noonan v. Northwest Community College*, [1991] B.C.D. Civ. 1302-03.
3   *Elderfield v. Aetna Life Insurance Co. of Canada* (1996), 22 C.C.E.L. (2d) 159 (B.C.C.A.).

§12.78   However, it has been held that an executive's duties are not totally frozen when a job description is prepared. An employer must be allowed reasonable leeway to alter duties, especially if changes are necessary for the company's economic survival and there is no change of authority.[1] Moreover, some courts have held that executives have expressly or implicitly agreed to job reassignments at the employer's discretion,[2] especially if there is a history of accepting reassignment, or if the employer merges with another company, or if the employer is in financial difficulty.[3]

[1] *Henderson v. Westfair Foods Ltd.* (1990), 32 C.C.E.L. 152 (Man. Q.B.), revd on other grounds 40 C.C.E.L. 81 (C.A.); *Farber v. Royal Trust Co.*, unreported, Aug. 11, 1989, C.S.M. 500-05-004698-856 (Que. S.C.) (on appeal, C.A.M. 500-09-001201-896); *Giuliani v. Ontario (Ombudsman)* (1989), 27 C.C.E.L. 13 (Ont. H.C.J.); *Tymrick v. Viking Helicopters Ltd.* (1985), 6 C.C.E.L. 225 (Ont. H.C.J.); *Lesiuk v. B.C. Forest Products Ltd.* (1984), 56 B.C.L.R. 216 (S.C.), affd 15 C.C.E.L. 91 (C.A.); *Cadenhead v. Unicorn Abrasives of Canada Ltd.* (1984), 5 C.C.E.L. 241 (Ont. H.C.J.); *Tetrault v. Burns Fry Ltd.*, unreported, March 9, 1981, No. 500-05-011640-784 (Que. S.C.).

[2] *Charbonnier v. Air Canada Touram*, D.T.E. 90T-407 (Que. C.A.); *Ruel v. Banque Provinciale du Canada*, [1971] C.A. 343 (Que.).

[3] *Jervis v. Raytheon Canada Ltd.* (1990), 35 C.C.E.L. 73 (Ont. Ct. (Gen. Div.)); *Guilbeault v. Centre d'Intégration Socio-Professionnel de Laval* (1989), 30 C.C.E.L. 149 (Que. C.A.); *Morgan v. Northern Telecom Ltd.* (1985), T.L.W. 422-015 (Ont. H.C.J.); *Rose v. Shell Canada Ltd.* (1985), 7 C.C.E.L. 234 (B.C.S.C.).

§12.79 An example in which a demotion was held to constitute constructive dismissal is *Cox v. Royal Trust Corp. of Canada*.[1] Here, the plaintiff had been working for the defendant since 1965 and, in 1977, became a department manager with 23 staff members reporting to him. In January 1984, the plaintiff's managerial skills were criticized, and he was told that significant improvement was required. In March 1984, the plaintiff was offered the choice of leaving the company or accepting a transfer to a position as "Senior Trust Officer, Consultant". Since the plaintiff would lose all his management functions and responsibilities and would have to revert to his old position, the court found that there had been a demotion. It was therefore held that the plaintiff had been constructively dismissed.

[1] (1989), 26 C.C.E.L. 203 (Ont. C.A.), leave to appeal to S.C.C. refused 33 C.C.E.L. 224n. See also *Board v. Shawinigan Energy Consultants Ltd.* (1985), W.P.D.M. 523-025-3 (Ont. H.C.J.); *Rogerson v. A.E. MacLennan Ltd.* (1976), 12 Nfld. & P.E.I.R. 48 (P.E.I.S.C.).

§12.80 The same decision was reached in *Saint John Shipbuilding Ltd. v. Perkins*,[1] in which the duties and responsibilities of a 55-year-old senior management executive changed after a company reorganization. Instead of supervising 40 to 45 people, he found himself supervising two people. In addition, his salary was frozen for a period of time. In view of these changes, the court held that the executive had been constructively dismissed.

[1] (1989), 24 C.C.E.L. 106 (N.B.C.A.).

§12.81 However, job reassignment was held not to constitute constructive dismissal due to economic factors in *Pullen v. John C. Preston Ltd.*[1] In this case, the plaintiff was hired by the defendant as a regional marketing and sales manager. During a period of severe economic difficulties, the plaintiff was required to take a cut in salary and receive a commission on sales rather than a share of the profits. The plaintiff also received a new job description which required him to report to an executive whom he had previously hired. In rendering its decision, the court was influenced by the fact that the defendant was experiencing financial difficulty. According to the court, the reduction of the plaintiff's managerial functions was not deliberate, but dictated by financial necessity. The court also noted the fact that not all of the plaintiff's managerial functions had been eliminated. As a result, it was held that the plaintiff had not been constructively dismissed.

[1]   (1985), 7 C.C.E.L. 91 (Ont. H.C.J.), affd 16 C.C.E.L. xxiii (C.A.).

§12.82   Failure to promote is not equivalent to a demotion and therefore does not constitute constructive dismissal.[1] One court has said that if, at the time of any promotion within an organization, no specific agreement is reached to the contrary, the parties will have tacitly agreed that, if the employee does not function adequately in the new position, the employer may, without committing a fundamental breach, return the employee, within a reasonable time, to a position similar to the one vacated.[2] In other words, a reasonable period of probation in case of promotion is an implied term of the employment contract. In *Cayen v. Woodwards Stores Ltd.*[3] the British Columbia Court of Appeal held that the trial judge had erred in concluding that it was reasonable to imply a term into the employee's contract that she would be transferred to a position of increased responsibility, stature and remuneration. In addition, in absence of specific contractual provision, the right of an employer to demote an employee depends entirely upon the circumstances of the case.

[1]   *Gravino v. Gulf Canada Ltée*, D.T.E. 91T-1059 (Que. S.C.), appeal abandoned Sept. 25, 1991, C.A.M. 500-09-001184-910.
[2]   *Mifsud v. MacMillan Bathurst Inc.* (1990), 28 C.C.E.L. 228 (Ont. C.A.), leave to appeal to S.C.C. refused 39 O.A.C. 153.
[3]   (1993), 45 C.C.E.L. 264 (B.C.C.A.).

§12.83   In determining whether a demotion has occurred, the court may consider whether there has been a change in the working conditions of the employee, including a change in working hours.[1] However, where such change in working conditions is an implied term of the employee's contract of employment, courts have found that a demotion did not occur.[2]

[1] *Dorion v. Stewart, Weir Land Data Inc.*, unreported, October 29, 1996 (Alta. Q.B.).

[2] *Mifsud v. MacMillan Bathurst* (1989), 28 C.C.E.L. 228 (Ont. C.A.), leave to appeal to S.C.C. refused 39 O.A.C. 153.

(c) Status

§12.83.1 The status and prestige associated with a particular position within an organization often represent important aspects of the employment relationship.[1] In these particular areas, a change in the status of an executive within the organization is constructive dismissal.[2] Often, a change in status results from an employer's alteration of the chain of command.[3]

[1] In *Jervis v. Raytheon Canada Ltd.* (1990), 35 C.C.E.L. 73 (Ont. Ct. (Gen. Div.)), the court recognized that in certain situations, there is more status and prestige in an employee's position on a certain project than in the overall hierarchy of the company.

[2] *Stea v. Kulhawy* (1996), 18 C.C.E.L. (2d) 246 (Alta. Q.B.).

[3] *Snyders v. Saint John Shipbuilding Ltd.* (1989), 29 C.C.E.L. 26 (N.B.C.A.), leave to appeal to S.C.C. refused 103 N.B.R. (2d) 89n.

§12.84 In *Reilly v. Hotels of Distinction (Canada) Inc., Hotel Le Grand/Grand Hotel*,[1] the executive, who was the director of sales with the defendant company, was informed that she had to give up her office, use of the company car, and part of her responsibilities in favour of her newly hired immediate superior. The court found that the employer had altered the chain of command and demoted her, and therefore it held that this amounted to constructive dismissal.

[1] D.T.E. 87T-645 (Que. S.C.). See also *Zocchi v. Wang Canada Ltée*, D.T.E. 87T-646 (Que. S.C.) and *Leroux v. Société Générale du Cinéma*, D.T.E. 85T-85 (Que. T.A.).

(d) Geographical Transfer

§12.85 Another factor which would support an action for constructive dismissal is forced geographical transfer. A request to consider a transfer to another location will not allow an executive to claim that he or she has been constructively dismissed.[1] In general, the court will examine the reasonableness of the forced transfer in the circumstances of the case to determine whether constructive dismissal exists.[2]

[1] *Marleau v. Overnite Express (1980) Inc.*, D.T.E. 87T-754 (Que. C.A.).

[2] *Page v. Jim Pattison Industries Ltd.*, [1984] 4 W.W.R. 481 (Sask. C.A.), revg [1982] 5 W.W.R. 97 (Q.B.); *Muhlenfeld v. Northern Alberta Rapeseed Producers' Co-op. Ltd.* (1980), 13 Alta. L.R. (2d) 105 (Q.B.); *Hunt v. Cimco Ltd.* (1976), 2 A.R. 514 (S.C.).

§12.86 In several recent cases, courts have been sensitive to the business needs of the multi-location employer.[1] The courts in these cases have found an implied term in the employment contract that an executive will accept reasonable transfers which do not involve a demotion or undue hardship. Factors which have been considered in determining whether such an implied term exists include the size and number of branches, the importance of transfers within the employer's business structure, and the level at which the executive is employed. Other factors include the job history of the executive, including acquiescence to previous transfers, the absence of undue hardship, and the existence of good faith on the part of the employer.

[1] *Stewart v. Computalog Gearhart Ltd.* (1986), 45 Alta. L.R. (2d) 396 (Q.B.); *Rose v. Shell Canada Ltd.* (1985), 7 C.C.E.L. 234 (B.C.S.C.); *Page v. Jim Pattison Industries Ltd.*, [1984] 4 W.W.R. 481 (Sask. C.A.), revg [1982] 5 W.W.R. 97 (Q.B.); *Durrant v. Westeel-Rosco Ltd.* (1978), 7 B.C.L.R. 14 (S.C.); *Canadian Bechtel Ltd. v. Mollenkopf* (1978), 1 C.C.E.L. 95 (Ont. C.A.).

§12.87 In *Owens Illinois Canada Inc. v. Boivin*,[1] the executive was hired in 1978 as a salesman in Canada. In 1981, at the invitation of the parent company, he was transferred to Toledo, Ohio, to act as "Export Products Manager". This position required extensive travel. In July 1983, the executive was informed that business conditions prevented his continued employment in the office of export manager. As a result, he was offered a six-month assignment to a subsidiary in England at the same salary, including relocation expenses. It was understood that this assignment was the only available employment at the time, and he would be guaranteed continued employment upon the expiry of the six months. It was also understood that if the assignment was refused, the executive would be considered to have resigned. The executive declined the assignment. In its decision, the court held that there was no constructive dismissal. According to the court, the requirements of the job in the international operations of a temporarily depressed manufacturing company included the type of assignment which was offered to the executive. Moreover, given the considerable amount of travelling involved in his job, the relocation to London could not be considered unduly harsh.

[1] (1988), 23 C.C.E.L. 255 (Que. C.A.).

§12.88 In *Holgate v. Bank of Nova Scotia*,[1] the plaintiff's position as comptroller in Saskatoon with the defendant bank was eliminated after a reorganization. As a result, the plaintiff started training as an "Assistant Manager – Credit", and the defendant offered the plaintiff this position in Prince Albert. However, the plaintiff refused because his wife was employed in Saskatoon, and he regarded the offer to be a demotion. The court found that the offer constituted, at most, a slight and temporary demotion which involved no loss of salary. Consequently, it was held that there was no constructive dismissal.

[1] (1989), 27 C.C.E.L. 201 (Sask. Q.B.).

§12.89 In *Gravino v. Gulf Canada Ltée*,[1] the court held that an employer's management rights allowed it to transfer a senior executive to positions which might involve new functions and responsibilities, as long as the lateral transfer did not in any way reduce the executive's salary or status.

[1] D.T.E. 91T-1059 (Que. S.C.) (appeal abandoned Sept. 25, 1991, C.A.M. 500-09-001184-910).

§12.90 An opposite result was reached in *Morris v. International Harvester Canada Ltd.*[1] Here, the plaintiff had worked for the defendant company for 21 years in London, Ontario. The plaintiff's position was eliminated as a result of an economic downturn, and he was offered a lateral transfer from London to Toronto as a fleet accounts executive. The court held that the executive had been constructively dismissed. In reaching its decision, the court stated that, while an executive must normally accept a geographic move if the salary and position remain unchanged, this was not the case in relation to the plaintiff since he had been employed for a substantial period in one location, and the nature of his position made knowledge of the area an important qualification for the job.

[1] (1984), 7 C.C.E.L. 300 (Ont. H.C.J.).

(e) Employer Conduct

§12.91 Conduct by the employer which undermines an executive's authority or is otherwise humiliating or damaging to morale may constitute constructive dismissal if it is not condoned by the executive.[1] However, an executive's responsibilities and authority are not diminished by the employer providing more input or closer supervision.[2] In addition, if an employer allows a hostile work environment to develop and makes the employment relationship impossible, the executive may be entitled to claim that he or she has been constructively dismissed.[3]

[1] *Stewart v. Computalog Gearhart Ltd.* (1986), 45 Alta. L.R. (2d) 396 (Q.B.); *Rose v. Shell Canada Ltd.* (1985), 7 C.C.E.L. 234 (B.C.S.C.); *Canadian Bechtel Ltd. v. Mollenkopf* (1978), 1 C.C.E.L. 95 (Ont. C.A.).

[2] *Colasurdo v. CTG Inc.* (1988), 18 C.C.E.L. 264 (Ont. H.C.J.); *Roberts v. Versatile Farm*

Equipment Co. (1987), 16 C.C.E.L. 9 (Sask. Q.B.); *Dudziak v. Boots Drug Stores (Canada) Ltd.* (1983), 3 C.C.E.L. 130 (Ont. S.C.).

³ *Roy v. Caisse Populaire de Thetford Mines*, [1991] R.J.Q. 2693 (S.C.); *Paitich v. Clarke Institute of Psychiatry* (1988), 19 C.C.E.L. 105 (Ont. H.C.J.), affd 30 C.C.E.L. 235 (C.A.); *Henderson v. Westfair Foods Ltd.* (1990), 32 C.C.E.L. 152 (Man. Q.B.), revd on other grounds 40 C.C.E.L. 81 (C.A.); *Walker v. Canadian Newspapers Co. c.o.b. Lethbridge Herald* (1985), 6 C.C.E.L. 209 (Alta. Q.B.); *Frankcom v. Tandy Electronics Ltd.* (1984), 4 C.C.E.L. 40 (Ont. H.C.J.).

CHAPTER 13

DAMAGES AWARDED FOR WRONGFUL DISMISSAL

A. INTRODUCTION

§13.1 An executive is wrongfully dismissed when his or her employment is terminated without legal cause and without advance notice. A wrongfully terminated executive cannot seek to be reinstated in his or her job unless specific legislation grants the executive this right (some labour standards legislation and human rights legislation allow reinstatement in certain circumstances). Despite this rule of non-reinstatement, some courts have granted interlocutory injunctions calling for the reinstatement of a wrongfully terminated employee. One of these cases involves an executive and secretary who owned 34% of the employer company.[1] The Court found that having regard to the very particular circumstances of the case—the employee, an officer and director, was really a partner owning a large block of shares and he had been dealt with improperly—the long standing doctrine that reinstatement is not an option in wrongful termination cases did not apply. The Court felt that the ousted executive would suffer serious and irremediable prejudice if he did not maintain his status as an officer and employee, and that the balance of convenience was in his favour. Monetary compensation made available at some future time was not adequate relief. The executive needed to be present to protect his interests on a day-to-day basis as one of the two major shareholders, and as an officer and top management level employee. In this chapter we will review the notice periods for which damages may be claimed by the wrongfully dismissed executive and the heads of damages under which compensation may be awarded.

[1] *Zucker v. Computertime Network Corp.*, D.T.E. 94T-454 (Que. S.C.).

B. LENGTH OF NOTICE PERIOD

§13.2 The first step in determining the damages a wrongfully dismissed executive is entitled to is to establish what constitutes reasonable notice of termination. The notice period generally reflects the time period that it should take for the executive to obtain new employment. Courts have also looked at the notice period as being a period equal to the advance notice that the employer should have provided to the executive if both parties had already agreed upon a specific notice period.[1] The length of the notice period will also depend on whether the employment contract is for a fixed term or one of indeterminate duration.

[1] *Choquette v. F.O.I.S.I. Forces Immobilières & Stratégies d'Investissement Inc.*, D.T.E. 91T-1187 (Que. S.C.); *Lazarowicz v. Orenda Engines Ltd.*, [1961] O.R. 141 (C.A.); *Wiebe v. Central Transport Refrigeration (Man.) Ltd.*, [1994] 6 W.W.R. 305 (Man. C.A.).

§13.3 On the issue of notice, reference is frequently made to *Bardal v. Globe & Mail Ltd.*,[1] where the Ontario High Court stated:

> There can be no catalogue laid down as to what is reasonable notice in particular classes of cases. The reasonableness of the notice must be decided with reference to each particular case, having regard to the character of the employment, the length of service of the servant, the age of the servant and the availability of similar employment, having regard to the experience, training and qualifications of the servant.[2]

[1] (1960), 24 D.L.R. (2d) 140 (Ont. H.C.J.).
[2] (1960), 24 D.L.R. (2d) 140 (Ont. H.C.J.), at 145; In Quebec, see also C.C.Q., art. 2091(2): "The notice of termination shall be given in reasonable time, taking into account, in particular, the nature of the employment, the special circumstances in which the work is carried on and the duration of the period of work."

§13.3.1 The Supreme Court of Canada reiterated in *Wallace v. United Grain Growers Limited*,[1] that the factors to be considered when determining reasonable notice, mentioned in *Bardal v. Globe & Mail Ltd.*[2] were not exhaustive. Mr. Justice Frank Iacobucci who wrote the decision for the majority of the Court stated:

> This Court adopted the foregoing list of factors in *Machtinger v. HOJ Industries Ltd.*[3] Applying these factors in the instant case, I concur with the trial judge's finding that in light of the appellant's advanced age, his 14-year tenure as the company's top salesman and his limited prospects for reemployment, a lengthy period of notice is warranted. I note, however, that *Bardal*[4] does not state, nor has it been interpreted to imply, that the factors it enumerated were exhaustive: see *e.g., Gillepsie v. Bulkley Valley Forest Industries Ltd.*,[5] *Corbin v. Standard Life Assurance Co.*,[6] *Bishop v. Carleton Co-operative Ltd.*[7] Canadian courts have added several additional factors to the *Bardal* list. The application of these factors to the assessment of a dismissed employee's notice period will depend upon the particular circumstances of the case.
>
> One such factor that has often been considered is whether the dismissed employee had been induced to leave previous secure employment: see *e.g., Jackson v. Makeup Lab Inc.*,[8] *Murphy v. Rolland Inc.*,[9] *Craig v. Interland Window Mfg. Ltd.*[10] According to one authority, many courts have sought to compensate the reliance and expectation interests of terminated employees by increasing the period of reasonable notice where the employer has induced the employee to
>> "quit a secure, well-paying job ... on the strength of promises of career advancement and greater responsibility, security and compensation with the new organization." (I. Christie et al.[11])

Several cases have specifically examined the presence of a promise of job security: see *e.g.*, *Makhija v. Lakefield Research*,[12] affirmed by the Ontario Court of Appeal,[13] *Mutch v. Norman Wade Co.*[14] In particular, I note that the British Columbia Court of Appeal recently adopted this approach in *Robertson v. Weavexx Corp.*[15] The facts of this case were very similar to those currently before this Court. Writing for the court, Goldie J.A. stated at pp. 271-72:

> Also part of the inducement to the respondent in making the move he did was, no doubt, the discussion as to long term employment ... As I have concluded, those discussions lacked contractual force in terms of the respondent's assertion of a fixed term contract but nevertheless, they were and are, in my opinion, significant on the issue of reasonable notice.

In my opinion, such inducements are properly included among the considerations which tend to lengthen the amount of notice required. I concur with the comments of Christie et al.,[16] and recognize that there is a need to safeguard the employee's reliance and expectation interests in inducement situations. I note, however, that not all inducements will carry equal weight when determining the appropriate period of notice. The significance of the inducement in question will vary with the circumstances of the particular case and its effect, if any, on the notice period is a matter best left to the discretion of the trial judge.

---

[1] Unreported, Oct. 13, 1997, file no. 24986 (S.C.C.).
[2] (1960), 24 D.L.R. (2d) 140 (Ont. H.C.J.).
[3] [1992] 1 S.C.R. 986, at 998.
[4] (1960), 24 D.L.R. (2d) 140 (Ont. H.C.J.).
[5] [1975] 1 W.W.R. 607 (B.C.C.A.).
[6] (1995), 15 C.C.E.L. (2d) 71 (N.B.C.A.).
[7] (1996), 21 C.C.E.L. (2d) 1 (N.B.C.A.).
[8] (1989), 27 C.C.E.L. 317 (Ont. H.C.J.).
[9] (1991), 39 C.C.E.L. 86 (Ont. Ct. (Gen. Div.)).
[10] (1993), 47 C.C.E.L. 57 (B.C.S.C.).
[11] *Employment Law in Canada*, 2nd ed. (1993), pp. 749-750; R.B. Schai, "Aggravated Damages and the Employment Contract" (1991), 55 Sask. L. Rev. 345, at 355; J. Swan, "Extended Damages and Vorvis v. Insurance Corporation of British Columbia" (1990), 16 Can. Bus. L. at 213.
[12] (1983), 14 C.C.E.L. 131 (Ont. H.C.J.).
[13] (1986), 14 C.C.E.L. xxxi (Ont. C.A.).
[14] (1987), 17 B.C.L.R. (2d) 185 (S.C.).
[15] (1997), 25 C.C.E.L. (2d) 264 (B.C.C.A.).
[16] *Employment Law in Canada*, 2nd ed. (1993).

1. The Fixed-Term Employment Contract

§13.4 If an employer prematurely terminates the executive's fixed-term contract without just cause, the executive is entitled to claim all remuneration and benefits he or she would have received for the unexpired term.[1] However, even in such cases, the executive's entitlement is subject to the obligation to mitigate his or her damages.[2] The duty to mitigate will be discussed in greater detail in Chapter 16, "Other Issues Concerning Wrongful Termination and Damages Awarded".

---

[1] *Wollock v. Sochaczeski*, D.T.E. 95T-1187 (Que. S.C.), leave to appeal; *Occhionero v.*

Roy, D.T.E. 92T-632 (Que. S.C.); *Laporte v. Sofati Ltée*, D.T.E. 90T-228 (Que. S.C.); *Bouffard v. Canico Hydraulique Inc.*, D.T.E. 89T-717 (Que. S.C.); *Gardner v. Stan-Canada Inc.* (1989), 13 A.C.W.S. (3d) 411 (Ont. H.C.J.); *Leinwather v. Construction Loriot Inc.*, D.T.E. 88T-572 (Que. S.C.); *Mainville v. Brasserie Michel Desjardins Ltée*, D.T.E. 88T-292 (Que. S.C.), appeal abandoned Sept. 11, 1988, C.A.M. 500-09-000185-884; *Paddon v. Phillips Barratt Kaiser Engineering Ltd.* (1987), 18 B.C.L.R. (2d) 170 (S.C.); *Shaw v. Ecole E.C.S. Inc.*, J.E. 85T-560 (Que. S.C.); *Hawkins v. Ontario* (1985), 8 C.C.E.L. 183 (Ont. H.C.J.); *Mailhot v. Société de Radiodiffusion Audiogramme CKLM Ltée*, J.E. 84-1047 (Que. S.C.); *Côté v. Cie Nationale de Forage et Sondage Inc.*, J.E. 84-1046 (Que. S.C.); *Landry v. Radio du Pontiac*, D.T.E. 83T-200 (Que. S.C.); *Savoie v. Roy*, [1983] C.A. 513 (Que.); *Desrochers v. Centre de Langues Feuilles d'Érables Ltée*, J.E. 80-635 (Que. S.C.), appeal abandoned Aug. 25, 1981, C.A.M. 500-09-000892-802; *Dynacast Ltd. v. Pearson*, [1972] C.A. 339 (Que.); *Lafayette Glass Co. v. Laplante*, [1967] B.R. 757 (Que. C.A.).

² *Red Deer College v. Michaels*, [1976] 2 S.C.R. 324; *Lafayette Glass Co. v. Laplante*, [1967] B.R. 757 (Que. C.A.).

§13.5   An issue arises in the case where an executive is bound to the employer by a fixed-term contract which provides for automatic renewal. The Quebec Court of Appeal recently addressed this issue in *Québec (Procureur général) v. Corriveau*.[1] The relevant contractual provision read as follows:

> The general manager is hired for a four year period, starting July 3, 1978. His appointment shall be renewed for the same period as long as the board of directors does not advise the general manager of its intention to end the contract upon at least 90 days written notice prior to the expiration of the term in course.[2]

The Court of Appeal overturned the Superior Court's decision which had awarded compensation for the balance of the initial four-year term and 50% of the renewed term. The Court of Appeal ordered that compensation should be paid for the balance of the initial term only. The court held:

> Although non-renewal of the contract could result from a unilateral act of one of the parties, renewal forcibly requires the express or tacit agreement of minds. To foresee what could have been the situation and the position of the parties had Mr. Corriveau continued his employment at the C.L.S.C. up to the summer of 1982, suggests, in my mind, at least, a problematic and conjectural problem.[3]

¹ [1989] R.J.Q. 1 (C.A.).
² [1989] R.J.Q. 1 (C.A.), at 5 (authors' translation).
³ [1989] R.J.Q. 1 (C.A.), at 7 (authors' translation). See also *Gardner v. Stan-Canada Inc.* (1989), 13 A.C.W.S. (3d) 411 (Ont. H.C.J.).

2. The Indeterminate Employment Contract

§13.6   Termination by the employer of an indeterminate term contract entitles the executive to reasonable notice of such dismissal. In the absence of such notice, the executive is entitled to damages in lieu of the remuneration payable during the notice period.[1] Generally only salary and benefits that would have accrued during the notice period can be awarded as damages.[2] Damages generally accrue from the date of termination to the end of the notice period. In this regard, the date of termination must be established in every case.

[1] *Olson v. Sprung Instant Greenhouses Ltd.* (1985), 12 C.C.E.L. 8 (Alta. Q.B.); *Lang v. Modern Garment Co.*, [1950] R.L. 296 (Que. S.C.); *Mongeau & Robert & Cie Ltée v. Raby* (1933), 55 B.R. 243 (Que. C.A.).

[2] *Turner v. Canadian Admiral Corp.* (1980), 1 C.C.E.L. 130 (Ont. H.C.J.); *Canadian Bechtel Ltd. v. Mollenkopf* (1978), 1 C.C.E.L. 95 (Ont. C.A.).

§13.7 The British Columbia Court of Appeal has restated the purpose of the damages award as follows:

> . . . a damage award for wrongful dismissal is not a fund of money to make the plaintiff feel better or to compensate him for his injured feelings or disappointment but is merely to compensate him for a breach of contract. Every expense incurred by a dismissed employee would not be recoverable, but where the loss flows, as I have said, from the employment, then it is my view that it is properly recoverable as damages consequent upon the breach.[1]

[1] *Husson v. Alumet Mfg.* (1991), 37 C.C.E.L. 252 (B.C.C.A.), at 254.

§13.7.1 In some cases even the probationary employee may be entitled to receive reasonable notice which may be greater than statutory notice if the employee is terminated during the probationary period. In *Newman v. Stokes Inc.*[1] the Quebec Superior Court held that "an employee who is on probation clearly has less job security that (sic) one who enjoys the status of a permanent employee. But failure to treat the probationer fairly renders the employer liable to indemnify the employee."[2]

The court then added that, at the end of a probation period, an employer who is not satisfied is not obliged to retain the services of a probationary employee, but, if the employer dismisses the probationary employee before the expiry of the probation period, he must either show cause for dismissal or pay the employee the salary he would have received until the probation period is expired.[3]

[1] D.T.E. 93T-553 (Que. S.C.).

[2] D.T.E. 93T-553 (Que. S.C.), at 7; the Court also refers to previous decisions in *Serapiglia v. Eastern Provincial Airways (1963) Ltd.*, J.E. 79-242 (Que. S.C.) and *Stewart v. Standard Broadcasting Corp.*, J.E. 90-75 (Que. S.C.).

[3] D.T.E. 93T-553 (Que. S.C.), at 8 and 9.

C. HEADS OF DAMAGES

§13.8 In evaluating an executive's damages, the courts consider all salary and benefits, including use of company automobiles, club fees, bonuses, profit sharing, pension rights and vacation pay, that the employee would have received had he or she continued working during the notice period. The court will award damages for those payments or benefits which the executive would normally have received during the course of his or her employment.[1]

---

[1] *Sylvester v. British Columbia* (1997), 146 D.L.R. (4th) 207 (S.C.C.).

§13.9 Hence, whether an "extra" was provided because it was necessary for the work involved or whether it was granted as a "perk" or fringe benefit is an important issue in deciding which damages should be claimed. The court will consider:

> . . . not what the plaintiff would have been paid if he had not been dismissed, but what he would have been paid during the period in which reasonable notice was running . . .[1]

---

[1] *Sandelson v. Int. Vintners Ltd.* (1987), 18 B.C.L.R. (2d) 86 (S.C.), at 90.

§13.10 The executive bears the onus of proving his or her entitlement to benefits in excess of the base salary, as well as the value of those benefits.[1] In the absence of evidence indicating the value of a benefit, the particular claim may be denied. Similarly, where no pecuniary loss is proven, compensation will be denied.[2] The executive must also be capable of establishing that the damages are an immediate result of the failure to receive notice.[3]

---

[1] *Jolicoeur v. Lithographie Montréal Ltée*, [1982] C.S. 230 (Que. S.C.), affd, unreported, April 15, 1987, C.A.M. 500-09-000314-823; *Red Deer College v. Michaels*, [1976] 2 S.C.R. 324.

[2] *McGraw v. Canadian Forest Products Ltd.* (1989), 17 A.C.W.S. (3d) 542 (B.C.S.C.).

[3] *Nikanpour v. Fenco-Lavalin Inc.*, D.T.E. 88T-573 (Que. S.C.); *Charlebois v. Bigelow Canada Ltée*, J.E. 80-437 (Que. S.C.); *Auberge Le Martinet Inc. v. Arial*, [1972] C.A. 704 (Que.).

§13.11 While the headings that we will review are by no means exhaustive, they are indicative of those damages which have been awarded by the courts.

1. Salary

§13.12 An award in damages includes an amount which represents the gross salary the employee would have earned during the notice period.[1] Hence, where an executive is entitled to a one-year notice of dismissal, the executive can claim the salary he or she would have received during this one-year period.

[1] *Dixon v. Merland Explorations Ltd.* (1984), 30 Alta. L.R. (2d) 310 (Q.B.); *Lyonde v. Canadian Acceptance Corp.* (1983), 3 C.C.E.L. 220 (Ont. H.C.J.); *Cathcart v. Longines Wittnauer Watch Co.* (1980), 1 C.C.E.L. 287 (Ont. H.C.J.); *Turner v. Canadian Admiral Corp.* (1980), 1 C.C.E.L. 130 (Ont. H.C.J.).

§13.13 Clearly, in many executive employment relationships, salary alone is a substantial component of remuneration. However, as the law of employment evolves, more complex methods of providing remuneration are being developed, and it is becoming increasingly common that an executive's remuneration will be composed of elements not found in a base salary.

2. Increase in Salary

§13.14 Whether a wrongfully dismissed executive is entitled to a salary increase as part of an award of damages depends on the interpretation of the employment contract or the employer's past practice in this regard.

§13.15 An employer generally has no obligation to grant annual or periodic increases in salary. Salary increases are discretionary unless the parties to the employment contract intend such increases to form part of the conditions of employment.[1] In the absence of a company policy or written agreement providing for fixed salary increases, courts generally deny an executive's claim to an increase in salary that he or she alleges would have been received had proper notice of dismissal been given.[2]

[1] *Brock v. Matthews Group Ltd.* (1988), 20 C.C.E.L. 110 (Ont. H.C.J.), vard 34 C.C.E.L. 50 (C.A.); *Herbison v. Intercontinental Packers Ltd.* (1983), 29 Sask. R. 296 (C.A.); *Rooney v. Reed Ltd.* (1978), 20 O.R. (2d) 665 (H.C.J.); *Koor v. Metropolitain Trust Co. of Canada* (1993), 48 C.C.E.L. 216 (Ont. Ct. (Gen. Div.)); *Pathak v. Jannock Steel Fabricating Co.* (1996), 21 C.C.E.L. (2d) 12 (Alta. Q.B.).
[2] *Lachapelle v. Bourse de Montréal*, D.T.E. 92T-218 (Que. S.C.); *Chouinard v. Groupe Commerce, Cie d'Assurances*, D.T.E. 90T-528 (Que. S.C.), affd D.T.E. 95T-269 (C.A.); *Mainville v. Brasserie Michel Desjardins Ltée*, D.T.E. 88T-292 (Que. S.C.), appeal abandoned Sept. 16, 1988, C.A.M. 500-09-000185-884; *Steinberg's Ltd. v. Lecompte*, [1985] C.A. 223 (Que.).

§13.16 However, if there is evidence that increases in salary were granted automatically, they may properly be awarded as damages.[1] In

Turner v. Canadian Admiral Corp.,[2] the court accepted the claim for increase in salary on the basis that the increases were forthcoming every year and had become part of the employee's salary structure. In such cases, the employer's past practice will be the determinative factor. In addition, one Ontario case suggests the need for evidence of the amount of the increase before such shall be awarded.[3]

[1]   *Langlois v. Farr Inc.* (1988), 26 C.C.E.L. 249 (Que. C.A.); *Dixon v. Merland Explorations Ltd.* (1984), 30 Alta. L.R. (2d) 310 (Q.B.); *Turner v. Canadian Admiral Corp.* (1980), 1 C.C.E.L. 130 (Ont. H.C.J.).

[2]   (1980), 1 C.C.E.L. 130 (Ont. H.C.J.). See also *Langlois v. Farr Inc.*, D.T.E. 88T-1005 (Que. C.A.); *Rooney v. Reid Ltd.* (1978), 20 O.R. (2d) 665 (H.C.J.).

[3]   *Brock v. Matthews Group Ltd.* (1988), 20 C.C.E.L. 110 (Ont. H.C.J.), vard 34 C.C.E.L. 50 (C.A.).

3. Commissions

§13.17   An executive's damages may be particularly difficult to evaluate when his or her remuneration consists, in whole or in part, of commissions. Generally, commissions that would have accrued during the notice period will be allowed when awarding damages,[1] unless the terms of the employment contract expressly stipulate that commission payments will be limited after termination.[2]

[1]   *Valentini v. Monarch Broadcasting Ltd.* (1992), 41 C.C.E.L. 243 (B.C.S.C.); *Roberts v. Versatile Farm Equipment Co.* (1987), 16 C.C.E.L. 9 (Sask. Q.B.); *MacDonald v. Richardson Greenshields of Canada Ltd.* (1985), 69 B.C.L.R. 58 (S.C.); *Prozak v. Bell Telephone Co. of Canada* (1984), 46 O.R. (2d) 385 (C.A.); *Thomas Cook Overseas Ltd. v. McKee*, D.T.E. 83T-572 (Que. C.A.); *Larsen v. A & B Sound Ltd.* (1996), 18 C.C.E.L. (2d) 237 (B.C.S.C.); *Watson v. Moore Corp.* (1996), 20 C.C.E.L. (2d) 21 (B.C.C.A.).

[2]   *Dumas v. Aeterna-Vie Cie d'Assurance*, J.E. 80-910 (Que. S.C.); *Confederation Life Assn. v. Berry*, [1927] S.C.R. 595.

§13.18   Courts will require sufficient evidence to allow them to calculate what commissions would have been earned during the notice period.[1] The courts have used a number of tests to determine appropriate damages, including averages of previous months' or years' commissions,[2] projections based on company-wide sales,[3] and what a replacement employee earned.[4]

[1]   *Robertson v. Equivest Securities Ltd.* (1980), 19 B.C.L.R. 274 (S.C.); *Cathcart v. Longines Wittnauer Watch Co.* (1980), 1 C.C.E.L. 287 (Ont. H.C.J.).

[2]   *Farmer v. Foxridge Homes Ltd.* (1994), 18 Alta. L.R. (3d) 182 (C.A.); *Valentini v. Monarch Broadcasting Ltd.* (1992), 41 C.C.E.L. 243 (B.C.S.C.); *Springer v. Merrill Lynch, Royal Securities Ltd.* (1984), 4 C.C.E.L. 81 (Ont. H.C.J.).

[3]   *Shulman v. Xerox Canada Inc.* (1986), 75 N.S.R. (2d) 7 (S.C.).

[4]   *Vassallo v. Crosbie Enterprises Ltd.* (1981), 9 A.C.W.S. (2d) 335 (Nfld. S.C.).

§13.19   The executive's previous earnings are usually held to be a reliable measure of projected commissions.[1] However, the award will be reduced if there is evidence of reduced sales or of economic trends in the industry that in all probability would have resulted in the executive's decreased ability to generate commissions.[2] Similarly, evidence may be adduced to show that the executive would have been entitled to greater commissions during the notice period. In *Vigeant v. Canadian Thermos Products Ltd.*,[3] where the elimination of an important competitor combined with a generally favourable economic climate would in all probability have increased earnings, the loss of commissions was assessed to be approximately 25% higher than the average commissions earned during the previous four years.

[1] See *Gilligan v. Les Immeubles Leopold Ltée*, unreported, Nov. 22, 1990, C.S.M. 500-05-012553-846 (Que. S.C.), where the court ordered payment of commissions normally forfeited upon termination of employment because the employee had been constructively dismissed; *Nyveen v. Russell Food Equipment Ltd.*, D.T.E. 88T-294 (Que. S.C.); *Douglas v. Fabrigear Ltd.*, D.T.E. 85T-412 (Que. S.C.); *Goldberg v. Western Approaches Ltd.* (1985), 7 C.C.E.L. 127 (B.C.S.C.); *Grossman v. Rosemount Knitting Inc.*, J.E. 81-123 (Que. S.C.) (appeal abandoned Apr. 13, 1981).

[2] *Rémi Carrier Inc. v. Nolan*, D.T.E. 86T-370 (Que. C.A.). See, generally, *Bragg v. London Life Ins. Co.* (1983), 60 N.S.R. (2d) 1 (S.C.); *Desnoyers v. Mitchell Industries Ltd.*, J.E. 81-43 (Que. S.C.); *Charlebois v. Bigelow Canada Ltée*, J.E. 80-437 (Que. S.C.); *Perina v. Versailles Ford Sales Ltée*, [1974] R.D.T. 590 (Que. Prov. Ct.); *Montel Inc. v. De Blois*, [1971] C.A. 316 (Que.).

[3] D.T.E. 88T-295 (Que. S.C.).

4. Bonuses and Profit Sharing

§13.20   When a bonus incentive plan or profit sharing plan is in place, the issue is whether the employee has a contractual right to the bonus which would have been exercisable during the notice period. If no contractual right exists, generally no bonus is due and payable to the executive.[1]

[1] *Brock v. Matthews Group Ltd.* (1988), 20 C.C.E.L. 110 (Ont. H.C.J.), vard 34 C.C.E.L. 50 (C.A.); *Koor v. Metropolitan Trust Co. of Canada* (1993), 48 C.C.E.L. 216 (Ont. Ct. (Gen. Div.)).

§13.21   One Ontario court has stated:

If bonuses and salary increases for employees are discretionary on the part of the employer then it follows that an employee who has been given proper notice of termination of his employment cannot insist on bonuses or pay increases between the date of the notice and the termination of his employment. In my view an employee who has been given proper notice of termination can only demand bonuses and pay increases given to other employees during the term of the notice if he could have demanded such bonuses and pay increases if he had not been discharged. In other words he must show he has a contractual right to such bonuses and pay increases.[1]

Hence, damages may be awarded for the loss of a bonus or the loss of a share in the profits which would have been paid during the notice period or balance of the term when there is evidence that the benefit formed an integral part of the executive's remuneration.[2] To form an integral part of the remuneration, the benefit must be one the executive anticipated he or she would have received had he or she not been prematurely terminated.[3]

[1] *Brock v. Matthews Group Ltd.* (1988), 20 C.C.E.L. 110 (Ont. H.C.J.), at 119-20, vard 34 C.C.E.L. 50 (C.A.).

[2] *Hasler v. Spagnol's Wine & Beer Supplies Ltd.*, unreported, Oct. 24, 1991, Vancouver Doc. C907448 (B.C.S.C.); *Prins v. Lakeview Development of Canada Ltd.* (1990), 33 C.C.E.L. 155 (Ont. Ct. (Gen. Div.)); *Dixon v. Merland Explorations Ltd.* (1984), 30 Alta. L.R. (2d) 310 (Q.B.); *Koor v. Metropolitain Trust Co. of Canada* (1993), 48 C.C.E.L. 216 (Ont. Ct. (Gen. Div.)).

[3] *Lachapelle v. Bourse de Montréal*, D.T.E. 92T-218 (Que. S.C.); *Stevens v. Globe & Mail* (1992), 7 O.R. (3d) 520 (Ont. Ct. (Gen. Div.)); *Prins v. Lakeview Development of Canada Ltd.* (1990), 33 C.C.E.L. 155 (Ont. Ct. (Gen. Div.)); *Speight v. Uniroyal Goodrich Canada Inc.* (1989), 97 N.B.R. (2d) 216 (Q.B.); *Jasmin v. Jean-Luc Surprenant Inc.*, J.E. 83-683 (Que. S.C.); *Longchamps v. Denis Pépin Automobiles Ltée*, J.E. 83-495 (Que. S.C.), affd D.T.E. 88T-852 (C.A.).

§13.22   The anticipated benefit is one that has been paid with regularity in the past and is readily determinable (by formula, for example) or fairly predictable. To resolve the issue of entitlement, the courts usually refer to a written contract, company policy or plan, or evidence of past practice.[1] With respect to the quantum of damages to be awarded, the factors weighed include amounts paid to other executives,[2] amounts the executive would expect based on prior communication by the employer,[3] past practice,[4] or what is a reasonable amount.[5]

[1] *Stewart v. Standard Broadcasting Corp.* (1989), 29 C.C.E.L. 290 (Que. S.C.); *Bouffard v. Canico Hydraulique Inc.*, D.T.E. 89T-717 (Que. S.C.); *Couture v. Volcano Inc.*, J.E. 84-496 (Que. S.C.); *CJMS Radio Montréal Ltée v. Audette*, [1966] B.R. 756 (Que. C.A.).

[2] *Brock v. Matthews Group Ltd.* (1988), 20 C.C.E.L. 110 (Ont. H.C.J.), vard 34 C.C.E.L. 50 (C.A.).

[3] *Cardwell v. Young Manufacturer Inc.* (1988), 20 C.C.E.L. 272 (Ont. Dist. Ct.).

[4] *Findlay v. Kershaw Mfg. Canada Ltd.* (1989), 29 C.C.E.L. 10 (Ont. H.C.J.).

[5] *Hillhouse v. Alexander Consulting Group Ltd.* (1989), 28 C.C.E.L. 73 (Ont. H.C.J.); *Arnot v. General Wire & Cable Co.* (1982), 2 C.C.E.L. 208 (Ont. H.C.J.).

§13.23   When the employer theoretically has the discretion to pay a bonus or to grant a share of the profits, but has systematically exercised this discretion in favour of the executive, then such payment may be deemed to be an integral part of the executive's remuneration and it may follow that the executive is entitled to receive a bonus or share of profits.[1]

> [1] *Reynolds v. First City Trust Co.* (1989), 27 C.C.E.L. 194 (B.C.S.C.); *Sandelson v. International Vintners Ltd.* (1987), 18 B.C.L.R. (2d) 86 (S.C.); *Turner v. Canadian Admiral Corp.* (1980), 1 C.C.E.L. 130 (Ont. H.C.J.).

§13.24 Payment of a bonus will not be ordered if the employer can successfully prove that, given the company's financial difficulties or policies, the executive would not have received any bonus even if he or she had worked until the end of the fixed term or during the notice period.[1]

> [1] *Bouffard v. Mediacom Inc.*, D.T.E. 88T-353 (Que. Prov. Ct.); *Tétrault Shoe Ltd. v. Baillargeon*, [1964] R.D.T. 193 (Que. Lab. Bd.).

§13.25 The employment contract may provide that the executive forfeits his or her right to a bonus or share of profits in the case of termination. In *Brock v. Matthews Group Ltd.*,[1] under the terms of the company share option plan, a person could not exercise any options after he "ceased to be an employee" of the defendant. The Ontario Court of Appeal held that Brock ceased to be an employee as soon as his active employment came to an end, despite the fact that his dismissal was wrongful. In coming to this conclusion, the Court of Appeal apparently rejected the view expressed by other courts[2] that this type of plan is subject to an implied term that the termination will not be wrongful. In other words, if the termination is without cause, reasonable notice of termination will be given. In another case,[3] the Ontario Court of Appeal has ruled that an employer cannot disentitle an employee from damages for a bonus that would otherwise be payable by claiming that a term of employment or a term of the bonus plan is that bonuses are never paid after termination.

> [1] (1991), 34 C.C.E.L. 50 (Ont. C.A.).
> [2] *Prince v. T. Eaton Co.* (1992), 41 C.C.E.L. 72 (B.C.C.A.), leave to appeal refused, [1993] 2 S.C.R. xi; *Burns v. Oxford Development Group Inc.* (1992), 32 A.C.W.S. (3d) 422 (Alta. Q.B.).
> [3] *Furuheim v. Bechtel Canada Ltd.* (1990), 30 C.C.E.L. 146 (Ont. C.A.).

5. Pension

§13.26 The value of the employee's lost pension benefits is another important factor to be considered in awarding damages for wrongful dismissal. The reduction of pension benefits will be taken into account in assessing damages.[1] When confronted with a defined benefit pension plan, the courts are divided with respect to the method that should be used to assess this head of damages, which aims at compensating the executive for the reasonable expectation that, had the executive not been prematurely dismissed, he or she would have been entitled to greater pension benefits.

---

[1]   *Boylan v. Canadian Broadcasting Corporation* (1994), 3 C.C.E.L. (2d) 64 (Alta. Q.B.); *Cook v. Royal Trust* (1990), 31 C.C.E.L. 6 (B.C.S.C.); *Durrant v. B.C. Hydro & Power Authority* (1990), 49 B.C.L.R. (2d) 263 (C.A.); *Mainville v. Brasserie Michel Desjardins Ltée*, D.T.E. 88T-292 (Que. S.C.), appeal abandoned Sept. 16, 1988, C.A.M. 500-09-000185-884; *Steinberg's Ltd. v. Lecompte*, [1985] C.A. 223 (Que.); *Lemyre v. J.B. Williams (Canada)*, D.T.E. 84T-752 (Que. S.C.); *Labelle v. Experts-Conseils Shawinigan Inc.*, D.T.E. 84T-547 (Que. S.C.), appeal settled out of court Mar. 26, 1985, C.A.M. 500-09-000846-840; *Plamondon v. Commission Hydro-Electrique de Québec*, [1976] C.S. 105 (Que. S.C.); *Bardal v. Globe & Mail Ltd.* (1960), 24 D.L.R. (2d) 140 (Ont. H.C.J.). However, some Quebec courts have refused to compensate the employee for pension plan benefits that would have been received had he or she remained in his or her employment through the notice period. These courts concluded that the pension plan is an expectancy, not a right: *Pascal Internoscia v. Ville de Montréal*, unreported, Feb. 28, 1980, No. 05-12-56-766 (Que. S.C.).

§13.27   A first school of thought is to the effect that the executive is entitled to an amount representing the contributions his or her employer would have made to the pension plan during the period with respect to which compensation is owed.[1]

---

[1]   *Surveyer, Nenniger & Chênevert Inc. v. Thomas*, D.T.E. 89T-640 (Que. C.A.); *Imprimeries Stellac Inc. v. Plante*, D.T.E. 89T-116 (Que. C.A.); *Vigeant v. Canadian Thermos Products Ltd.*, D.T.E. 88T-295 (Que. S.C.); *Gagnon v. Thetford Transport Ltée*, D.T.E. 87T-935 (Que. S.C.); *Labelle v. Experts-Conseils Shawinigan Inc.*, D.T.E. 84T-547 (Que. S.C.), appeal settled out of court Mar. 26, 1985, C.A.M. 500-09-000846-840; *McKilligan v. Pacific Vocational Institute* (1979), 14 B.C.L.R. 109 (S.C.), vard 28 B.C.L.R. 324 (C.A.); *Fleming v. Safety Kleen Canada Inc.* (1996), 20 C.C.E.L. (2d) 140 (Ont. Ct. (Gen. Div.)); *Buerman v. Canada (Attorney General)* (1996), 19 C.C.E.L. (2d) 127 (Ont. Ct. (Gen. Div.)). Quebec courts appear to espouse the first school of thought.

§13.28   A second school is to the effect that the executive must be compensated for the actual loss incurred in terms of benefits. In other words, the executive will receive an amount reflecting the difference between the pension benefits he or she will actually receive upon retirement and those he or she would have received had employment continued for the full term or through the notice period with regular contributions having been maintained.[1]

---

[1]   *Ansari v. B.C. Hydro & Power Authority* (1986), 2 B.C.L.R. (2d) 33 (S.C.), affd on a different point 55 B.C.L.R. (2d) xxxiii (C.A.); *Doyle v. London Life Ins. Co.* (1985), 23 D.L.R. (4th) 443 (B.C.C.A.), leave to appeal to S.C.C. refused 64 N.R. 318*n*; *Turner v. Canadian Admiral Corp.* (1980), 1 C.C.E.L. 130 (Ont. H.C.J.). This approach is somewhat less common in Quebec although it has in some instances been fol-

lowed; see *Padveen v. London Life Cie d'Assurance-Vie*, D.T.E. 84T-421 (Que. Arb. Bd.); *Desfosses v. Les Services Financiers Avco Ltée*, S.A. 124-87-017.

§13.29 Courts in the common law provinces, when quantifying damages, have also considered whether entitlement to an employer's contributions or to early retirement would have vested during the notice period.[1] The question of the vesting of retirement benefits may prove to be particularly important for the executive employee. In *Vorvis v. Insurance Corp. of British Columbia*,[2] the Supreme Court of Canada refused to grant to the employee the right to be a member of the company's pension plan but instead ordered payment of his contributions. The reason given was that, even if proper notice had been given to Vorvis, he would not have acquired a vested interest in the pension plan during the notice period.

[1]   *Burns v. Oxford Development Group Inc.* (1992), 32 A.C.W.S. (3d) 422 (Alta. Q.B.); *Durrant v. B.C. Hydro & Power Authority* (1990), 49 B.C.L.R. (2d) 263 (C.A.); *Reber v. Lloyds Bank Int. Canada* (1985), 61 B.C.L.R. 361 (C.A.), revg 52 B.C.L.R. 90 (S.C.); *Sturrock v. Xerox of Canada Ltd.*, [1977] 1 A.C.W.S. 203 (B.C.S.C.).

[2]   [1989] 1 S.C.R. 1085.

§13.30 It is important when assessing damages under a pension plan to consult the appropriate specialists. There is considerable variety in the format of pension plans and they differ widely in the amount of benefits payable thereunder. An actuarial analysis of the loss suffered enables the courts to better evaluate the amount of damages to be awarded.

6. Insurance and Medical Plans and Other Marginal Benefits

§13.31 Damages for the loss of insurance and medical plans are properly included in an award of damages for wrongful dismissal.[1]

[1]   See *Barrette v. Wabasso Inc.*, J.E. 88-416 (Que. S.C.), where the court required proof that the employee effectively took out insurance similar to that he had with his previous employer; *Leduc v. Union Carbide du Canada*, J.E. 84-783 (Que. S.C.); *Carey v. F. Drexel Co.*, [1974] 4 W.W.R. 492 (B.C.S.C.); *Nevin v. British Columbia Hazardous Waste Management Corp.* (1995), 129 D.L.R. (4th) 569 (B.C.C.A.).

§13.32 However, the courts disagree on the appropriate remedy for the loss. Some court decisions have evaluated the loss based on the cost to the employee to purchase similar coverage.[1] This is the favoured approach of the British Columbia courts:

Mr. Wilks also claims damages for the loss of fringe benefits, including medical, dental and group life insurance, as well as contributions to the Canada Pension Plan, Unemployment Insurance Commission, Workers' Compensation Board and company pension plan. The defendant admittedly expended $4,335.19 in the last year of Mr. Wilks' employment in providing these benefits to him, and Mr. Wilks claims he is entitled to a proportionate amount of that sum for the period of notice to which this court finds he was entitled. The defendant, on the other hand, argues that he can claim only those amounts which he has expended in making other provision for these services during this period. I accept the defendant's contention. The question is not what the defendant has gained by the dismissal, but what the plaintiff has lost. This loss must be established on the evidence. If the plaintiff fails to show that he has paid out or lost money or has otherwise suffered by reason of the absence of fringe benefits, his claim cannot succeed: *McKilligan v. Pac. Vocational Institute* (1981), 28 B.C.L.R. 324 at 340, per Macdonald J.A., Seaton J.A. concurring. *The only loss demonstrated on the evidence in this case is payments for medical insurance.* Mr. Wilks is entitled to these for the ten months following his dismissal.[2]

[1]   *Cooper v. MacMillan Bloedel Ltd.* (1991), 56 B.C.L.R. (2d) 341 (S.C.); *Vigeant v. Canadian Thermos Products Ltd.*, D.T.E. 88T-295 (Que. S.C.); *Sorel v. Tomenson Saunders Whitehead Ltd.* (1985), 9 C.C.E.L. 226 (B.C.S.C.), vard 16 C.C.E.L. 223 (C.A.); *Addison v. M. Loeb Ltd.* (1986), 25 D.L.R. (4th) 151 (Ont. C.A.), revg 45 O.R. (2d) 399 (H.C.J.); *Douglas v. Sandwell & Co.* (1977), 81 D.L.R. (3d) 508 (B.C.S.C.); *Nevin v. British Columbia Hazardous Waste Management Corp.* (1995), 129 D.L.R. (4th) 569 (B.C.C.A.).

[2]   *Wilks v. Moore Dry Kiln Co. of Canada* (1981), 32 B.C.L.R. 149 (S.C.), at 152-53 (emphasis added).

§13.33 Some courts judged that an executive should not be awarded compensation for benefits which were not "lost" in practice, *i.e.* not replaced by the executive or which, since they had not previously been really "enjoyed", were not really "lost".[1]

[1]   *Prince v. T. Eaton Co.* (1992), 41 C.C.E.L. 72 (B.C.C.A.), leave to appeal refused, [1993] 2 S.C.R. xi; *Wilson v. Bentall Group Ltd.* (1990), T.L.W. 1008-010 (B.C.S.C.); *Sorel v. Tomenson Saunders Whitehead Ltd.* (1987), 16 C.C.E.L. 223 (B.C.C.A.); *Wilks v. Moore Dry Kiln Co. of Canada* (1981), 32 B.C.L.R. 149 (S.C.); *Nevin v. British Columbia Hazardous Waste Management Corp.* (1995), 129 D.L.R. (4th) 569 (B.C.C.A.).

§13.33.1 However, this line of cases has been expressly rejected by the Ontario Court of Appeal:[1]

Allelix cross-appealed against the award of damages for loss of benefits proposed by the trial judge relying on a line of British Columbia decisions. They held that the loss of benefits from termination of employment is limited to losses or expenses actually incurred, the sum of $6,052.97 referred to above for which Dr. Davidson was entitled to be compensated under the benefit coverage: see *Sorel v. Tomenson Saunders Whitehead Ltd.* (1987), 16 C.C.E.L. 223, 39 D.L.R. (4th) 460 (B.C.C.A.); *Wilks v. Moore Dry Kiln Co. of Canada* (1981), 32 B.C.L.R. 149 (S.C.); and *McKilligan v. Pacific Vocational Institute* (1981), 28 B.C.L.R. 324 (C.A.).

Counsel for Allelix candidly acknowledged that there was conflicting jurisprudence on this point. In my opinion the British Columbia decisions do not apply in Ontario where the law is settled that a wrongfully dismissed employee may claim, in addition to lost salary, the pecuniary value of lost benefits flowing from such dismissal.

The plaintiff in that case was compensated for the value of the medical plan, rather than for the expenses actually incurred.

[1]   *Davidson v. Allelix Inc.* (1991), 7 O.R. (3d) 581 at 589.

§13.33.2   *Allelix* was followed in *Alpert v. Carreaux Ramca Ltée,*[1] where the plaintiff was held to be entitled to damages for loss of coverage under the employee medical plan calculated by reference to the cost to the defendant of maintaining the plan in favour of the plaintiff.

[1]   (1992), 9 O.R. (3d) 207 (Ont. Ct. (Gen. Div.)).

§13.33.3   However, *Alpert* was distinguished in *Neely v. State Group Ltd.,*[1] and the plaintiff in that case was found not to be entitled to payment during the notice period for dental and prescription benefits, which were paid to the employee only when the employee used such services, then made a claim for reimbursement. The grounds for distinction were that the medical plan in *Alpert* was funded by a third-party insurer, whereas the defendant's dental and drug plans in *Neely* were self-funded. In other words, whereas the employer in *Alpert* had a fixed cost in maintaining the medical plan, whether or not the employee used it, in *Neely* the defendant only paid when the employee made a claim.

[1]   (1995), 12 C.C.E.L. (2d) 242 (Ont. Ct. (Gen. Div.)), affd [1997] O.J. No. 1549, Doc. No. CA C22433 (C.A.).

§13.34   Earlier cases from the common law provinces and the Quebec courts chose to quantify employer contributions to these plans as the proper measure of damages.[1] In *Prince v. T. Eaton Co. Ltd.,*[2] Prince was fired without notice. During the period which would have constituted reasonable notice, he became disabled. The British Columbia Court of Appeal held that had Prince received proper notice of termination, he would have been eligible for disability benefits. Therefore, the court ordered that he be compensated for the full value of the disability benefits he would have received. In *Card Estate v. John A. Robertson Mechanical Contractors (1985) Ltd.,*[3] the defendant was liable for lost life insurance proceeds.

[1]   *Lemyre v. J.B. Williams (Canada)*, D.T.E. 84T-752 (Que. S.C.) (medical insurance); *Carey v. F. Drexel Co.*, [1974] 4 W.W.R. 492 (B.C.S.C.).
[2]   (1992), 41 C.C.E.L. 72 (B.C.C.A.).

[3] (1989), 26 C.C.E.L. 294 (Ont. H.C.J.). But see *Thom v. Goodhost Foods Ltd.* (1987), 17 C.C.E.L. 89 (Ont. H.C.J.).

§13.35 Executives will be awarded damages to compensate them for the replacement value with respect to government-sponsored medical plans.[1]

[1] *Heffernan v. Barry Cullen Chevrolet Oldsmobile Ltd.* (1986), T.L.W. 634-020 (Ont. H.C.J.).

7. Club Membership Fees, Company Car or Car Allowance

§13.36 Club dues may be claimed by the executive if they were paid by the employer for the personal enjoyment of the executive.[1] However, if their primary purpose was to assist the executive in furthering the employer's business interests through entertaining at such facilities, damages will not be awarded.[2] Recent decisions also prohibit an award of damages when the executive does not renew membership at the club.[3]

[1] *Dixon v. Merland Explorations Ltd.* (1984), 30 Alta. L.R. (2d) 310 (Q.B.).
[2] *Gagnon v. Thetford Transport Ltée*, D.T.E. 87T-935 (Que. S.C.); *Domaine de l'Isle aux Oyes Inc. v. D'Aragon*, J.E. 84-499 (Que. C.A.); *Dauphinée v. Bank of Montreal* (1985), 10 C.C.E.L. 36 (B.C.S.C.).
[3] *Spooner v. Ridley Terminals Inc.* (1991), 62 B.C.L.R. (2d) 132 (S.C.); *Roscoe v. McGavin Foods Ltd.* (1983), 2 C.C.E.L. 287 (B.C.S.C.).

§13.37 Similarly, if a car was provided to the executive for his personal enjoyment or an allowance was given as a prerequisite of employment, the allowance or an amount representing the loss of private use of the vehicle for the notice period will usually be awarded.[1] However, if the vehicle was furnished for the performance of the executive's duties, courts have refused to award compensation.[2]

[1] *Stevens v. Globe & Mail* (1992), 7 O.R. (3d) 520 (Ont. Ct. (Gen. Div.)); *Bruce-Vaughan v. Dalmys (Canada) Ltd.* (1992), 40 C.C.E.L. 112 (B.C.S.C.); *Brown v. Black Clawson-Kennedy Ltd.* (1989), 29 C.C.E.L. 92 (Ont. Dist. Ct.); *Carle v. Comité Paritaire du Vêtement pour Dames* (1987), 22 C.C.E.L. 281 (Que. S.C.); *Taskos v. 104880 Canada Inc.*, [1987] R.J.Q. 2574 (S.C.); *Turcot v. Conso Graber Inc.*, D.T.E. 87T-668 (Que. S.C.); *Wood v. Brown Boveri Canada Inc.* (1986), 15 C.C.E.L. 178 (B.C.C.A.); *Douglas v. Fabrigear Ltd.*, D.T.E. 85T-412 (Que. S.C.); *Dixon v. Merland Explorations Ltd.* (1984), 30 Alta. L.R. (2d) 310 (Q.B.); *Blackburn v. Coyle Motors Ltd.* (1983), 3 C.C.E.L. 1 (Ont. H.C.J.); *Lefebvre v. Beaver Road Builders Ltd.* (1993), 49 C.C.E.L. 207 (Ont. Ct. (Gen. Div.)).
[2] *Webster v. B.C. Hydro & Power Authority* (1990), 31 C.C.E.L. 224 (B.C.S.C.), vard 42 C.C.E.L. 105 (C.A.), affd on other grounds, [1994] 3 S.C.R. 549; *Laporte v. Sofati Ltée*, D.T.E. 90T-228 (Que. S.C.); *Cornil v. Mondia Distribution Inc.*, D.T.E. 88T-584 (Que. S.C.); *Gagnon v. Thetford Transport Ltée*, D.T.E. 87T-935 (Que. S.C.); *Landry v.*

Comterm Inc., J.E. 84-451 (Que. S.C.); *Kokonis v. Shaw Pipe Industries* (1983), 19 A.C.W.S. (2d) 84 (Alta. Q.B.). See also *McGraw v. Canadian Forest Products Ltd.* (1989), 17 A.C.W.S. (3d) 542 (B.C.S.C.), where compensation was denied because no pecuniary loss was proven.

§13.38 In *Bouffard v. Canico Hydraulique Inc.*,[1] the employee had weekend use of the vehicle notwithstanding the fact that his contract stipulated that it was furnished only to facilitate his business travel. The Quebec Superior Court ordered compensation representing two-sevenths of the value of using the vehicle for the period which deserved compensation, which in this case was the balance of Mr. Bouffard's fixed-term contract.[2] The same rationale would probably be applicable to the use of company boats, private cars or trains, and company airplanes. Miscellaneous costs in relation to the car, such as repairs,[3] parking[4] and insurance costs[5] may also be compensable.

[1] D.T.E. 89T-717 (Que. S.C.).
[2] See also *Bédard v. Les Aliments Krispy Kernels Inc.*, unreported, Sept. 21, 1990, 200-05-001114-888 (Que. S.C.).
[3] *Findlay v. Kershaw Mfg. Canada Ltd.* (1989), 29 C.C.E.L. 10 (Ont. H.C.J.).
[4] *Wilson v. Bentall Group Ltd.* (1990), T.L.W. 1008-010 (B.C.S.C.).
[5] *Backman v. Hyundai Auto Canada Inc.* (1990), 100 N.S.R. (2d) 24 (S.C.).

8. Moving Expenses and Other Expenses Incurred in Searching for Alternative Employment

§13.39 The courts have taken different views on whether costs incurred in searching for alternative employment may be recovered as damages for wrongful dismissal.[1] Some courts have held that since the executive has the duty to mitigate his or her damages, costs incurred in carrying out the search are generally compensable. However, there are common law decisions that have limited damages to those expenses incurred during the notice period.[2]

[1] *Vigeant v. Canadian Thermos Products Ltd.*, D.T.E. 88T-295 (Que. S.C.); *Morency v. Swecan Int. Ltée*, D.T.E. 86T-582 (Que. Prov. Ct.); *Sarton v. Fluor Canada Ltd.* (1986), 73 A.R. 241 (C.A.); *Breeze v. Federal Business Development Bank*, J.E. 84-963 (Que. S.C.) (relocation counselling); *Thomas Cook Overseas Ltd. v. McKee*, D.T.E. 83T-572 (Que. C.A.). The court awarded compensation for moving expenses and for hotel, telephone, advertising and car rental expenses incurred while searching for employment: *Charlebois v. Bigelow Canada Ltée*, J.E. 80-437 (Que. S.C.); *Robson v. General Motors of Canada Ltd.* (1982), 37 O.R. (2d) 229 (Co. Ct.).
[2] *Pelliccia v. Pink Pages Advertising Ltd.* (1989), 28 C.C.E.L. 261 (B.C.S.C.); *Rahmath v. Louisiana Land & Exploration Co.* (1989), 59 D.L.R. (4th) 606 (Alta. C.A.); *Gagné v. Algoma Builders Supply Ltd.* (1987), 18 C.C.E.L. 66 (Ont. Dist. Ct.).

§13.40 Whether moving expenses are recoverable is also a subject of debate. Some court decisions have ruled that moving expenses are compensable as damages if the relocation and expenses associated with the move are reasonable and necessary or if their payment was an implied term of the employment contract.[1] Other courts, which have held that an employer does not have to compensate a former employee for moving expenses, have maintained this position on the basis that moving expenses are not the result of the fact that the termination of employment is wrongful.[2] These expenses are the result of the termination itself and arguably would still have been incurred even if reasonable notice had been given or the fixed term had expired.

[1]   *Bruce v. Region of Waterloo Swim Club* (1990), 73 O.R. (2d) 709 (H.C.J.); *Roberts v. Dresser Industries Canada Ltd.* (1987), T.L.W. 732-013 (Ont. Dist. Ct.), affd 28 C.C.E.L. 221 (C.A.); *Klapperbein v. Kamco Music & Sound Systems Ltd.* (1986), 49 Alta. L.R. (2d) 376 (C.A.).

[2]   *MacWilliam v. Rudy's Petroleum Services Ltd.* (1990), 32 C.C.E.L. 310 (B.C.S.C.); *Vézina v. Fairmont Granite Ltd.*, J.E. 81-1068 (Que. S.C.).

§13.41 If an executive is invited or induced to move to a new city in order to accept a position, from which he or she is fired shortly thereafter, courts have held that the executive may claim some of the expenses incurred in moving to the new location and moving back to the previous location.[1] Indeed, the executive's argument is that he or she would not have moved unless there was some certainty of continued employment. However, damages have been refused where there was no agreement whereby the employer would reimburse the employee for relocation expenses.[2]

[1]   *Biorex Groupe Conseil Inc. v. Closset*, D.T.E. 90T-305 (Que. S.C.), appeal settled out of court May 15, 1990; *Saint John Shipbuilding Ltd. v. Perkins* (1989), 24 C.C.E.L. 106 (N.B.C.A.), where damages were given to compensate for the costs incurred to return to the original location; *Campbell v. Pringle & Booth Ltd.* (1988), 30 C.C.E.L. 156 (Ont. H.C.J.); *Castagna v. Design Hydraulics Inc.*, D.T.E. 88T-1006 (Que. S.C.); *Reber v. Lloyds Bank Int. Canada* (1984), 52 B.C.L.R. 90 (S.C.), revd on other grounds 61 B.C.L.R. 361 (C.A.); *Landry v. Radio du Pontiac Inc.*, D.T.E. 83T-200 (Que. S.C.) (the Superior Court considered it normal that relocation expenses be awarded to a plaintiff who had been invited by his employer to set up residence in the United States for five years).

[2]   *Baumgart v. Convergent Technologies Canada Ltd.* (1989), 28 C.C.E.L. 250 (B.C.S.C.).

§13.42 In Quebec, the type of employment from which the executive is terminated may be an important factor in determining whether moving expenses will be compensated in the damage award.[1]

[1]   *Gignac v. Trust Général du Canada*, D.T.E. 91T-231 (Que. S.C.); *Jolicoeur v. Hippodrome Blue Bonnets Inc.*, D.T.E. 90T-306 (Que. S.C.), D.T.E. 95T-185 (C.A.).

§13.43 A further issue arising in this area is the treatment of any gain or loss on the sale of the executive's home if relocation is necessary. Generally, the courts have disallowed the executive's claim for losses on resale.[1] However, real estate agency fees and legal fees for the purposes of relocation have been both allowed[2] and denied[3] under varying circumstances.

[1] *Saint John Shipbuilding Ltd. v. Perkins* (1989), 24 C.C.E.L. 106 (N.B.C.A.); *Brisbois v. Casteel Inc.* (1983), 2 C.C.E.L. 35 (Ont. H.C.J.).

[2] *Hennessey v. La France Textiles Canada Ltd.* (1981), 12 A.C.W.S. (2d) 233 (Ont. H.C.J.); *Earl v. Northern Purification Services (Eastern) Ltd.* (1980), 1 C.C.E.L. 267 (Ont. H.C.J.), affd, unreported, Dec. 3, 1981 (C.A.); leave to appeal to S.C.C. refused 1 C.C.E.L. 267n.

[3] *Rajakaruna v. Regional Municipality of Peel* (1981), 10 A.C.W.S. (2d) 522 (Ont. Co. Ct.); *Tanel v. Rose Beverages (1964) Ltd.* (1987), 57 Sask. R. 214 (C.A.).

9. Vacation Pay

§13.44 Another area of disparity concerns the awarding of vacation pay that would have been earned during the notice period had the executive not been wrongfully dismissed. At common law, some courts have disallowed entitlement to vacation pay which would have accrued during the notice period.[1] This is based on the theory that a pattern has been established and it is reasonable to infer that the executive would have taken the actual earned vacation during the notice period. However, the general approach has been to compensate executives for vacation pay lost during the notice period.[2] Appellate courts in both British Columbia and Ontario have held that where an employee shows no specific evidence of loss, expense or damage resulting from his or her inability to take a vacation during the notice period, awarding lost vacation pay would amount to a "double indemnity".[3] Some courts in Quebec have refused to award damages under this heading, since vacation pay is only due on salary that has been earned through work.[4] Other Quebec courts have awarded, without explanation, vacation pay corresponding to the notice period or the balance of the fixed term.[5]

[1] *Stander v. B.C. Hydro & Power Authority* (1988), 25 B.C.L.R. (2d) 40 (C.A.), where the court awarded damages for loss of enjoyment of earned vacation time; *Herbison v. Intercontinental Packers Ltd.* (1983), 29 Sask R. 296 (C.A.); *Taggart v. Kwikasair Express Ltd.* (1980), 26 B.C.L.R. 352 (C.A.).

[2] *Card Estate v. John A. Robertson Mechanical Contractors (1985) Ltd.* (1989), 26 C.C.E.L. 294 (Ont. H.C.J.); *Brown v. Black Clawson-Kennedy Ltd.* (1989), 29 C.C.E.L. 92 (Ont. Dist. Ct.); *Mandell v. Apple Canada Inc.* (1990), 34 C.C.E.L. 319 (B.C.S.C.); *Cook v. Royal Trust* (1990), 31 C.C.E.L. 6 (B.C.S.C.); *Stander v. B.C. Hydro & Power Authority* (1988), 25 B.C.L.R. (2d) 40 (C.A.); *Lefebvre v. Beaver Road Builders Ltd.*

(1993), 49 C.C.E.L. 207 (Ont. Ct. (Gen. Div.)); *Koor v. Metropolitain Trust Co. of Canada* (1993), 48 C.C.E.L. 216 (Ont. Ct. (Gen. Div.)).

3   *Scott v. Lillooet School District No. 29* (1991), 60 B.C.L.R. (2d) 273 (C.A.); *Cronk v. Canadian General Insurance Co.* (1995), 25 O.R. (3d) 505 (C.A.).

4   *Plante v. Télévision St-François Inc.*, [1984] C.S. 450 (Que. S.C.).

5   *Laporte v. Sofati Ltée*, D.T.E. 90T-228 (Que. S.C.); *Nikanpour v. Fenco-Lavalin Inc.*, D.T.E. 88T-573 (Que. S.C.); *Vigeant v. Canadian Thermos Products Ltd.*, D.T.E. 88T-295 (Que. S.C.); *Groupe Promodor Inc. v. Jean*, D.T.E. 88T-189 (Que. C.A.); *Carle v. Comité Paritaire du Vêtement pour Dames* (1987), 22 C.C.E.L. 281 (Que. S.C.); *Turcot v. Conso Graber Inc.*, D.T.E. 87T-668 (Que. S.C.); *Landry v. Comterm Inc.*, J.E. 84-451 (Que. S.C.); *Plante v. Télévision St-François Inc.*, [1984] C.S. 450 (Que.); *Jolicoeur v. Lithographie Montréal Ltée*, [1982] C.S. 230 (Que.), confirmed on appeal Apr. 15, 1987, C.A.M. 500-09-000314-823.

10. Expense Accounts

§13.45 Courts may award damages for the loss of sums provided to an employee as a clothing allowance or to cover other personal expenses, if such expenses were not considered a business expense.[1] One court awarded half the amount the employee claimed as a personal expense account for the reason that the other half "would have actually been spent" had the employee remained at work.[2] Whether such amounts are damages is a question of fact and depends on the particular circumstances of each arrangement and whether they can be considered a personal benefit to the executive.

1   *Brown v. Waterloo Regional Bd. of Commrs. of Police (No. 2)* (1985), 52 O.R. (2d) 300 (Div. Ct.).

2   See *Bergeron v. Emballages Purity Ltée*, J.E. 84-811 (Que. S.C.).

11. Severance Pay/Termination Pay

§13.46 Employment contracts and company policies may include severance pay and/or termination pay provisions. Severance pay and termination pay are predetermined or determinable amounts, calculated in relation to the length of service, payable to the executive upon termination or retirement, and usually only when the termination is without cause.

§13.47 In Ontario (and other common law provinces), severance pay and termination pay are provided for by statute.[1] However, if the legislation does not apply to the executive or the severance/termination scheme in an employment contract provides for a greater benefit than that required by statute, the contract will govern.

1   *Employment Standards Act*, R.S.O. 1990, c. E.14. Severance pay is provided for in s. 58 and termination pay is provided for in s. 57.

§13.48 It is important to distinguish between a severance payment or termination payment and pay in lieu of notice of termination. A severance or termination payment is an allowance paid in recognition of past services and is, generally, a statutorily required payment upon termination of employment. Pay in lieu of notice is a damage award payable only if notice of termination is absent or insufficient, or if employment is terminated before the expiry of a fixed term.

§13.49 What also differentiates these two concepts is that generally the executive does not have to mitigate his or her damages in order to validly claim the statutory severance or termination payment. However, in Ontario, termination and severance payments, payable in accordance with the *Employment Standards Act*[1], are deductible from the damages awarded for wrongful dismissal at common law.[2] There are no statutory severance provisions in Quebec.

[1] R.S.O. 1990, c. E.14, ss. 57 and 58; *Stevens v. Globe & Mail* (1996), 28 O.R. (3d) 481 (C.A.).

[2] *Brown v. Black Clawson-Kennedy Ltd.* (1989), 29 C.C.E.L. 92 (Ont. Dist. Ct.); *Lefebvre v. Beaver Road Builders Ltd.* (1993), 49 C.C.E.L. 207 (Ont. Ct. (Gen. Div.)).

§13.50 Because of the different ramifications which may result depending upon the classification of the award, it is extremely important to properly assess whether a promised payment is notice or severance.[1] The courts will generally order that an employer pay to his employee the promised contractual amount representing severance pay[2] and will certainly enforce the statutory requirements. However, in the case of *Rondeau v. Lamarre Valois Int. Ltée*,[3] the court refused to give effect to the severence pay provision in the employment contract. Applying the abuse of rights theory to the contractual context on the basis of article 1024 of the Civil Code of Lower Canada, it found that the employee had displayed such bad faith in the execution of his job that the whole contract was annulled and therefore no severence was owed to the employee.

[1] For example, directors and officers may be personally liable for the payment of severance provisions when the debt arises of services rendered. This is not the case for notice payments. For a more complete discussion, see Chapter 20, "Duties and Liabilities of Corporate Officers" and the recent Supreme Court of Canada decision *Crabtree [succession de] v. Barrette*, [1993] 1 S.C.R. 1027.

[2] *Beaulieu v. Services Financiers Avco Canada Ltée*, J.E. 85-78 (Que. S.C.).

[3] [1975] C.S. 805 (Que. S.C.); revd, unreported, Sept. 26, 1978, C.A.M. 500-09-000834-754.

12. Share Option Plans and Share Purchase Plans

§13.51 Common law courts have decided that when a share option plan calls for the termination of the option upon termination of employment, it is intended to mean that it shall end upon the lawful cessation of employment, since the employer may not, by breaching its contract, prematurely terminate an executive's entitlement to these benefits. Hence, if termination is without cause, then the option will lapse only at the end of the appropriate period of notice or expiry of the term.[1] The difference between the option price and the market value of the shares on the date on which the plaintiff could first have exercised his or her option has been held to be the appropriate measure of damages.[2] In the event this information is not available, one may use the mean difference between the highest and lowest market value of the shares during the relevant notice period or balance of the term. There are other plans that may be in place, each resulting in a different calculation with respect to damages.

[1] *McGraw v. Canadian Forest Products Ltd.* (1989), 17 A.C.W.S. (3d) 542 (B.C.S.C.); *McDonald v. LAC Minerals Ltd.* (1987), 8 A.C.W.S. (3d) 70 (Ont. H.C.J.); *Hardie v. Trans-Canada Resources Ltd.* (1976), 2 A.R. 289 (C.A.); *Carey v. F. Drexel Co.*, [1974] 4 W.W.R. 492 (B.C.S.C.).

[2] *Colasurdo v. CTG Inc.* (1988), 18 C.C.E.L. 264 (Ont. H.C.J.); *Hardie v. Trans-Canada Resources Ltd.* (1976), 2 A.R. 289 (C.A.).

§13.52 Similarly, the executive may be compensated for the opportunity to participate in a stock purchase plan which was lost because of the wrongful termination. In some cases, the executive has been allowed to pay any amount outstanding to receive the stock.[1] In *Brause v. Microtel Ltd.*,[2] although it offered no reasons for its decision, the court awarded the wrongfully dismissed employee the stock option benefit which was provided during employment during the whole of the notice period. In *Marshall v. Rae*,[3] after concluding that the employees had been wrongfully dismissed, the B.C. Court of Appeal held that they were entitled to purchase their shares after valuation.

[1] *Villa v. John Labatt Ltée*, [1990] R.J.Q. 2247 (S.C.); revd in part on another issue *La Brasserie Labatt Limitée v. Villa*, [1995] R.J.Q. 73 (C.A.); *Mandell v. Apple Canada Inc.* (1990), 34 C.C.E.L. 319 (B.C.S.C.).

[2] (1989), 27 C.C.E.L. 260 (B.C.S.C.).

[3] (1990), 20 A.C.W.S. (3d) 371 (Ont. H.C.J.).

§13.53 If the contract requires the executive to sell back any shares upon termination, the difference between the value at termination and at the end of the notice period may be claimed.[1]

[1] *Rooney v. Reed Ltd.* (1978), 20 O.R. (2d) 665 (H.C.J.); *Carey v. F. Drexel Co.*, [1974] 4 W.W.R. 492 (B.C.S.C.).

13. Director's Fees

§13.54 If the executive was also a director of the employer, no loss in respect of director's fees may be claimed[1] as these fees do not arise from the employment relationship.

[1] *Dixon v. Merland Explorations Ltd.* (1984), 30 Alta. L.R. (2d) 310 (Q.B.).

14. Income Tax Deduction Benefits

§13.55 Some executives benefit from special income tax deductions because of the particular characteristics of their employment. They may lose these benefits by reason of a premature termination of employment.[1] Recently, courts have compensated employees for the monetary loss resulting from an abrupt loss of tax benefits. In *Vigeant v. Canadian Thermos Products Ltd.*,[2] the Quebec Superior Court ordered that an amount of $567 be paid to the plaintiff. This amount represented the benefit that the plaintiff enjoyed by reason of a tax deduction for maintaining an office in his home.

[1] See *Biorex Groupe Conseil Inc. v. Closset*, D.T.E. 90T-305 (Que. S.C.), where the claim was disallowed because a termination with proper notice would have brought about the same tax losses.
[2] D.T.E. 88T-295 (Que. S.C.).

15. Other Claims

§13.56 The damages that may be claimed will depend upon the remuneration and benefits provided to the executive. The benefits that an executive may be entitled to are numerous; accordingly, the types of damages are wide in scope.

§13.57 Executives may recover damages for a preferential rate of interest on a loan.[1] However, interest on a loan taken out to meet expenses such as life, mortgage and automobile insurance premiums, the cost of an apartment, alimony payments and other personal expenses, following an executive's wrongful termination, may not be compensable.[2] Similarly, a claim for the value of a foreign service premium was not allowed where it was intended to compensate the employee for the added cost of working in another country.[3]

[1] *Tedford v. Woodward Stores Ltd.* (1990), 31 C.C.E.L. 1 (B.C.C.A.).
[2] *Charlebois v. Bigelow Canada Ltée*, J.E. 80-437 (Que. S.C.).

³ *Paddon v. Phillips Barratt Kaiser Engineering Ltd.* (1987), 18 B.C.L.R. (2d) 170 (S.C.); *Côté v. Cie Nationale de Forage et Sondage Inc.*, J.E. 84-1046 (Que. S.C.).

§13.58 A claim for compensation on the basis that the employee had to work harder at his new employment than he did when employed by his former employer was unsuccessful. The court held that the value of such additional effort could not be measured in monetary terms.[1] The value of occasional trips to resorts in Florida, which were paid for on a totally discretionary basis by the employer and which also depended on company profits, was refused.[2] However, an employee on the verge of receiving a promotion was awarded damages for the loss of such an advantage when he was wrongfully dismissed.[3]

¹ *Vigeant v. Canadian Thermos Products Ltd.*, D.T.E. 88T-295 (Que. S.C.).
² *Gagnon v. Thetford Transport Ltée*, D.T.E. 87T-935 (Que. S.C.).
³ *L'Heureux v. Québec (Procureur général)*, D.T.E. 86T-374 (Que. S.C.).

§13.59 Loss of an employee's discount on employer products has also been compensated.[1] One court has said that the loss of an employee's discount is compensable provided there is sufficient evidence of its past use to enable the court to conclude that it would have been exercised during the notice period had prior notice been given.[2]

¹ *Macdonald v. Woodward Stores Ltd.* (1991), 39 C.C.E.L. 58 (B.C.S.C.).
² *Bruce-Vaughan v. Dalmys (Canada) Ltd.* (1992), 40 C.C.E.L. 112 (B.C.S.C.).

§13.60 An employer may in certain cases be liable towards a former employee for lost unemployment insurance benefits. In *Loiselle v. Brunet Lasalle Corp.*,[1] the employer, in addition to paying an amount representing six months' notice in compensation for Loiselle's wrongful dismissal, was liable for $4,500 in lost unemployment benefits. This sum represented the unemployment insurance benefits Loiselle had not been able to collect from the appropriate authorities because of the employer's unusual system of pay. In this case, the employer had not regularly deducted unemployment insurance premiums from Loiselle's pay cheques and the employee thus had been disqualified from receiving benefits. In addition, it should be noted that the employer is not permitted to attempt to reduce the notice he must provide by deducting the amount the employee has received or will receive from the Canada Employment Insurance Commission. Instead, the *Employment Insurance Act* forces the employer to reimburse the Commission, on the employee's behalf, for the amounts paid to the employee up to the date the notice is finally paid by the employer.

¹ D.T.E. 87T-983 (Que. S.C.); affd Nov. 30, 1988, C.A.M. 500-09-001165-877.

§13.61 Where one of the benefits of the employment contract contemplated by the parties is the maintenance and potential increase of the employee's exposure to the public, for example through the television medium, that publicity has an intrinsic value. Hence the lost publicity brought about by the wrongful termination of the employment contract may lead to additional damages payable to the employee. In one case, the lost publicity was worth $20,000.[1]

[1] *Cranston v. C.B.C.* (1994), 2 C.C.E.L. (2d) 301 (Ont. Ct. (Gen. Div.)).

D. CONCLUSION

§13.62 The damages suffered by a wrongfully terminated executive may run much deeper than mere loss of salary. The various heads of damages must be carefully considered to ensure full compensation or even in reaching an adequate termination agreement.

The next chapter discusses compensation which may be sought for damages of a less tangible nature: moral damages due to the termination of employment.

CHAPTER 14

AGGRAVATED/MORAL AND PUNITIVE/EXEMPLARY DAMAGES

A. INTRODUCTION

§14.1 As discussed in Chapter 13, "Damages Awarded for Wrongful Dismissal", a wrongfully dismissed executive may recover compensation for damages flowing from the premature breach of his or her employment contract. In addition, the employer may be held liable for damages of a less tangible nature if, in the process of termination, further injury befalls the executive. Such claims are categorized by the common law courts as claims for either aggravated damages, under which damages for mental distress are usually sought, or punitive damages.

§14.2 Aggravated damages, unlike punitive damages, are compensatory in nature. Punitive damages are designed to punish conduct of a harsh, vindictive, reprehensible and malicious nature. Although punitive damages are very rare in contract cases, they have been awarded in appropriate cases where the conduct of the employer was so egregious as to be deserving of special censure.[1] Waddams, in *The Law of Damages*, clearly distinguishes between aggravated damages and punitive damages:

> An exception exists to the general rule that damages are compensatory. This is the case of an award made for the purpose not of compensating the plaintiff but of punishing the defendant. Such awards have been called exemplary, vindictive, penal, punitive, aggravated, and retributory, but the expressions in common modern use to describe damages going beyond compensatory are exemplary and punitive damages. . . . The expression "aggravated damages", though it has sometimes been used interchangeably with punitive or exemplary damages, has more frequently in recent times been contrasted with exemplary damages. In this contrasting sense, aggravated damages describes an award that aims at compensation but takes full account of the intangible injuries, such as distress and humiliation, that may have been caused by the defendant's insulting behaviour. The expressions vindictive, penal and retributory have dropped out of common use.[2]

---

[1] *Vorvis v. Insurance Corp. of British Columbia*, [1989] 1 S.C.R. 1085; *Newlands v. Sanwa McCarthy Securities Ltd.* (1996), 12 O.T.C. 81 (Ont. Ct. (Gen. Div.)).

> [2]   S.M. Waddams, *The Law of Damages*, 2nd ed. (Aurora: Canada Law Book Inc., 1991), p. 11-1.

§14.3 Intangible elements such as pain, anguish, grief, humiliation, wounded pride, damaged self-confidence or self-esteem, loss of faith in friends or colleagues, and similar matters that are caused by the conduct of the defendant have all been categorized as aggravated damages.[1]

> [1]   *Huff v. Price* (1990), 51 B.C.L.R. (2d) 282 (C.A.), at 294, leave to appeal refused, [1991] 1 S.C.R. *vii.*

§14.4 Quebec courts have compensated executives under the heading of "moral damages" for mental distress, anxiety, humiliation and loss of reputation.[1] However, they have usually refused to grant compensation for the pain and suffering which "normally" flows from or is inherent in the loss of employment.[2] The term "moral damages" is unique to Quebec.

> [1]   Whereas in most cases, a distinct amount will be awarded for moral damages, some courts instead will increase the reasonable notice period of termination; see *Société Hôtelière Canadien Pacifique v. Hoeckner*, D.T.E. 88T-548 (Que. C.A.).
> [2]   *Fournier v. Tout-Rôti Ltée*, D.T.E. 90T-131 (Que. S.C.); *Langlois v. Farr Inc.* (1988), 26 C.C.E.L. 249 (Que. C.A.); *Société Hôtelière Canadien Pacifique v. Hoeckner*, D.T.E. 88T-548 (Que. C.A.). In *Vigeant v. Canadian Thermos Products Ltd.*, D.T.E. 88T-295 (Que. S.C.), at 17 of the judgment, the court said: "disregard for the sensibilities and welfare of a long time and loyal employee is not in itself wrongful conduct, giving rise to a claim for damages".

§14.5 Punitive damages and exemplary damages will be discussed in detail later in this chapter.

B.   LEGAL BASIS OF THE AWARD

§14.6 In what circumstance will the courts award aggravated or moral damages as compensation to a person who has been terminated?

§14.7 The Supreme Court of Canada's decision in *Vorvis v. Insurance Corp. of British Columbia*[1] limited the circumstances under which aggravated damages and punitive damages may be awarded. In *Vorvis*, the appellant, a 54-year-old solicitor, was terminated by the respondent, ICBC, after being employed for approximately eight years. In his statement of claim, Vorvis advanced a claim for "mental distress, anxiety, vexation and frustration suffered by the plaintiff as a result of the termination of his contract of employment by the defendant".[2] Vorvis based his claim on the offensive and unjustifiable conduct of a superior officer for whom he worked. The officer had become frustrated and critical with respect to the pace at which Vorvis worked and had subjected him to harassment and inquisitions during meetings.

¹ [1989] 1 S.C.R. 1085.
² [1989] 1 S.C.R. 1085 at 1097.

§14.8 The issue that was before the Court was whether or not aggravated damages could be awarded in an action for breach of contract, based on the wrongful dismissal of an employee. The Court considered the cases of *Addis v. Gramophone Co.*¹ and *Peso Silver Mines Ltd. v. Cropper.*² The Court noted that the *Peso Silver Mines* decision disclosed a clear application of the *Addis* principle which suggests that:

> . . . in a case of wrongful dismissal damages are limited to the earnings lost during the period of notice to which the employee is entitled and cannot include damages for the manner of dismissal, for injured feelings, or for loss sustained from the fact that the dismissal makes it more difficult for the plaintiff to obtain other employment.³

The Court, in *Vorvis*, then concluded that:

> The rule long established in the *Addis* and *Peso Silver Mines* cases has generally been applied to deny such damages [aggravated damages], and the employer/employee relationship . . . has always been one where either party could terminate the contract of employment by due notice, and therefore the only damage which could arise would result from a failure to give such notice.
> I would not wish to be taken as saying that aggravated damages could never be awarded in a case of wrongful dismissal, particularly where the acts complained of were also independently actionable, a factor not present here.⁴

And finally:

> Furthermore, while the conduct complained of, that of Reid, was offensive and unjustified, any injury it may have caused the appellant cannot be said to have arisen out of the dismissal itself. The conduct complained of preceded the wrongful dismissal and therefore cannot be said to have aggravated the damage incurred as a result of the dismissal. Accordingly, I would refuse any claim for aggravated damages in respect of the wrongful dismissal.⁵

¹ [1909] A.C. 488 (H.L.).
² [1966] S.C.R. 673.
³ *Vorvis v. I.C.B.C.*, [1989] 1 S.C.R. 1085 at 1100-1101.
⁴ *Vorvis v. I.C.B.C.*, [1989] 1 S.C.R. 1085 at 1103.
⁵ *Vorvis v. I.C.B.C.*, [1989] 1 S.C.R. 1085 at 1104.

§14.9 The Supreme Court of Canada has therefore clarified the law in two respects. First, no claim for aggravated damages may be based on conduct leading up to the dismissal. Aggravated damages will only be awarded based on the harsh manner in which the termination is effected, or based on subsequent conduct. Second, aggravated damages will not likely be awarded unless the conduct complained of amounts to a separate actionable wrong. Recent lower court cases have put more emphasis on the former of these factors than on the latter. In *Rock v. The Canadian Red Cross Society*, the court awarded $25,000 for aggravated damages because the plaintiff, the former medical director of the Canadian Red Cross transfusion centre in Ottawa, was treated by the executives of the Canadian Red Cross as a common criminal at the time of the termination of her employment.[1] The court felt there was no need to change the locks as the Red Cross had all of the documentation required to carry out their internal audit to complete their investigation. The seizure of her personal files and manuscripts as well as instructing employees not to communicate with her was found by the court to be demeaning.

[1] (1994), 5 C.C.E.L. (2d) 231 (Ont. Ct. (Gen. Div.)).

§14.10 Also, the Ontario courts have awarded aggravated damages in circumstances where the defendants acted in an improper, insensitive, and high-handed manner in terminating the plaintiff's employment. In *Hughes v. Gemini Food Corp.*,[1] the Court awarded $75,000 in aggravated damages where the plaintiff, who had served as president and chief executive officer of a well known company was terminated in a very public manner (there was an announcement in the provincial legislature that he had been fired because of an alleged conflict of interest in respect of his duties as C.E.O. of a publicly owned corporation) and the effect was public humiliation, particularly in view of the fact that the allegations were unfounded.

[1] (1992), 45 C.C.E.L. 113 (Ont. Ct. (Gen. Div.)), affd (1997), 97 O.A.C. 147 (C.A.).

§14.11 The Supreme Court of Canada, in a case originating in Manitoba, clarified the awarding of damages due to the manner in which employees are terminated in *Wallace v. United Grain Growers Limited*.[1] The court decided that when an employee was dismissed, he was entitled to be treated in a candid, reasonable, honest and forthright fashion and he could not be dealt with on an untruthful, misleading or insensitive basis. While the court did not recognize that this claim for damages was a separate actionable ground, it did confirm that the factors enunciated in determining reasonable notice could include the manner in which the termination was carried out. Canada's highest court stated that when the employee was humiliated after being abruptly and insensitively fired, the damages in lieu of providing reasonable notice could be increased. The employee Wallace, a salesman, 59 years old, with 14 years of service, had been induced to leave a previous position he held for 25 years and promised security at the time he was hired by United Grain Growers. In this particular case, the court awarded 24 months notice to a salesman, reversing the Court of Appeal of Manitoba which reduced the notice to 15 months.

[1] Unreported, Oct. 13, 1997, file no. 24986 (S.C.C.).

§14.12 In *Dixon v. British Columbia Transit*,[1] the British Columbia Supreme Court found that dismissal without a satisfactory explanation not only led to unnecessary frustration, but also hampered the executive's search for new employment. While this does not constitute an actionable wrong, it was the basis for an award of aggravated damages.

[1] (1995), 9 B.C.L.R. (3d) 108 (S.C.). See also discussion at §10.11.1.

§14.13 In Quebec, courts have said that since good faith is an implicit obligation in all contractual relationships[1] (and consequently in all employment relationships[2]), the employer must exercise its rights in the "prudent and diligent manner of a reasonable individual and within the confines of fair play".[3] The Civil Code of Quebec now expressly states that parties to a contract must conduct themselves in good faith.[4] Hence, failure to act in good faith in terminating an employee is an abuse of rights. An abuse of rights also exists when the employer terminates a person's employment maliciously or unreasonably.[4] An abuse of rights may give rise to contractual liability for moral damages.[5] To terminate without cause and without notice does not in itself constitute an abuse of rights.[6]

[1] *National Bank of Canada v. Houle*, [1990] 3 S.C.R. 122; *National Bank of Canada v. Soucisse*, [1981] 2 S.C.R. 339.
[2] *Drouin v. Electrolux Canada Ltée Division de Les Produits C.F.C. Ltée*, D.T.E. 88T-329 (Que. C.A.); *Macaulay v. Imperial Life Assur. Co. of Canada*, D.T.E. 84T-395 (Que. S.C.); *Marcotte v. Assomption Cie Mutuelle d'Assurance-Vie*, [1981] C.S. 1102 (Que.).
[3] *National Bank of Canada v. Houle*, [1990] 3 S.C.R. 122.
[4] Article 1375 C.C.Q. provides: "The parties shall conduct themselves in good faith both at the time the obligation is created and at the time it is performed or extinguished". See also articles 6 and 7 C.C.Q.. In addition, article 2092 C.C.Q. recognizes the right to compensation in case of an abusive termination of employment.
[5] *Standard Broadcasting Corp. v. Stewart*, D.T.E. 94T-815 (Que. C.A.); *Langlois v. Farr*, [1988] C.A. 2682 (Que.); *Procureur général du Québec v. Corriveau*, [1989] R.J.Q. 1 (C.A.); *Domtar v. St-Germain*, [1991] R.J.Q. 1271 (C.A.); *Sofati v. Laporte*, [1992] R.J.Q. 321 (C.A.).

⁶ *Groupe Commerce (Le), compagnie d'assurances v. Chouinard*, D.T.E. 95T-269 (Que.
C.A.). See also *Standard Broadcasting Corp. v. Stewart*, D.T.E. 94T-815 (Que. C.A.).

§14.14   Moral damages may also be delictual in nature, when they are
the result of a fault committed by the employer at the time of the termination events.[1]

The Quebec Court of Appeal recently held as follows:

> The bases in law which may justify the payment of moral damages are twofold:
> the termination was accompanied by conduct which was vexatious, malicious, in
> bad faith or simply abusive, or subsequently to the termination, management
> made malicious, vexatious or abusive statements of a libellous or defamatory
> character which could injure the reputation or credibility of the employee.[2] (trans-
> lation)

[1]   See article 1457 C.C.Q..

[2]   *Taxis Coop Québec, 525-5191 v. Proulx*, [1994] R.J.Q. 603 (C.A.) at p. 605; see also
Banque Nationale du Canada v. Gignac, D.T.E. 96T-31 (Que. C.A.).

§14.15   Misleading executives on the true reasons for their termination
and depriving them of a chance to apply for a more prestigious and
higher-paying job may constitute an abuse of right.[1] An abnormal,
tactless or incorrect exercise of the right to terminate has led several
courts to award moral damages.[2] Further, courts have determined that
false accusations made by an employer to cover up an irrational, arbi-
trary and unjust decision to terminate employment, which accusations
then spread within the executive's particular field of business, may result in a damage award.[3]

[1]   *Mailloux v. Association Montréalaise d'Action Récréative et Culturelle, Pavillon du Canada*, unreported, Sept. 11, 1990, No. 500-05-009452-887 (Que. S.C.).

[2]   *Compagnie canadienne d'équipment de bureau v. Blouin*, D.T.E. 94T-563 (Que. C.A.);
Gignac v. Trust Général du Canada, D.T.E. 91T-231 (Que. S.C.); *Bernardini v. Alitalia
Air Lines*, D.T.E. 93T-519 (Que. S.C.); *Lefrançois v. Crane Canada Inc.*, D.T.E. 88T-574
(Que. S.C.); *Lefrançois v. Hydro-Québec*, D.T.E. 88T-551 (Que. S.C.); *Lazure v. Cor-
riveau*, unreported, Oct. 27, 1988, No. 200-09-000406-865 (Que. C.A.).

[3]   See *Groupe Commerce (Le), compagnie d'assurances v. Chouinard*, D.T.E. 95T-269
(Que. C.A.) for other examples given by the court. See also *DeMoor v. Harvey*
(1989), 24 C.C.E.L. 293 (B.C.S.C.); *Rahemtulla v. Vanfed Credit Union* (1984), 4
C.C.E.L. 170 (B.C.S.C.). See also *Compagnie canadienne d'équipment de bureau v.
Blouvin*, D.T.E. 94T-563 (Que. C.A.).

§14.16   Courts have acknowledged that allocating an amount of
money in an attempt to soothe pain and suffering is not an easy task.
Indeed, Mr. Justice Lamer of the Supreme Court of Canada stated:

> The amount awarded is necessarily arbitrary, in view of the difficulty of measur-

ing objectively such loss in pecuniary terms, especially when it concerns someone else's reputation.[1]

[1] *Snyder v. Montreal Gazette Ltd.*, [1988] 1 S.C.R. 494, at 505.

§14.17 Some courts had ordered additional compensation when the abrupt manner in which the employment was terminated, without cause, effectively ended the executive's career in that particular field. The employer was held liable even in the absence of malice or bad faith, the court being of the view that the failure to give notice constitutes in itself a fault or an abuse of rights giving rise to damages.[1] The Quebec Court of Appeal, in the case of *Standard Broadcasting Corp. v. Stewart*,[2] has recently rejected this line of reasoning.

[1] *Thomas Cook Overseas Ltd. v. McKee*, D.T.E. 83T-572 (Que. C.A.); *Gignac v. Trust Général du Canada*, D.T.E. 91T-231 (Que. S.C.).

[2] D.T.E. 94T-815 (Que. C.A.). See also *Omicron International Translation Systems Inc. v. Boyer*, (October 14, 1994) Montreal 500-09-000722-926 (Que. C.A.).

§14.18 In that case, Stewart was the vice-president and general manager of a radio station. After nine years of employment, Stewart was abruptly fired without cause but was offered an indemnity in lieu of notice. Stewart was unable to re-establish himself in the radio industry. The Superior court had ordered compensation of $75,000 in moral damages, being of the view that failure to give notice was in itself a fault worthy of damages due to the particularly sensitive nature of Stewart's job. The Court of Appeal overturned the Superior court's decision on this issue for the following reasons:

> I believe that it is incorrect in law to equate a termination without cause to an abuse of right. As was said by R. Breton, "L'indemnité de congédiement en droit commun", (1990) 31 C. de D. 3 p. 62: unmoderated reference to abuse of right these last few years has probably resulted in creating a very convenient catch all concept, which however contributes greatly to the state of confusion that exists in regards to the termination of an employment contract of indeterminate duration.
> There can only be abuse of rights if the employer exceeds the normal exercise of his right to fire by paying a reasonable indemnity, in other words, to use the expression employed by Mr. Justice Hannan of the Superior Court in *Lavigne v. Sidbec-Dosco*, [1985] C.S. 26, if the employer "... acts in a quasi-delictual manner...". To fire someone is not a fault; to fire someone in a humiliating, degrading, hurtful or mortifying manner, can be a fault. (p. 16) (translation)

The Court of Appeal adds that this rule does not mean that it will never order additional compensation based on the abuse of rights theory. Compensation in addition to the indemnity in lieu of notice may be warranted where injury to the employee results from the employer's bad faith and negligence. The Court of Appeal issues a notice of great prudence to all courts regarding the award of additional damages in the absence of bad faith or intentional fault since in general the prejudice suffered may already have been compensated by the indemnity in lieu of notice.

§14.19   The executive bears the burden of proving both the employer's abuse of right or other faulty conduct and his or her suffering.[1] In addition, claims for damages should be specifically pleaded.[2]

> [1]   *Mainville v. Brasserie Michel Desjardins Ltée*, D.T.E. 88T-292 (Que. S.C.), appeal abandoned Sept. 16, 1988, C.A.M. 500-09-000185-884; *Nyveen v. Russell Food Equipment Ltd.*, D.T.E. 88T-294 (Que. S.C.); *Vigeant v. Canadian Thermos Products Ltd.*, D.T.E. 88T-295 (Que. S.C.); *Bérubé v. Marcel E. Savard Inc.*, D.T.E. 88T-15 (Que. Prov. Ct.); *Lavigne v. Sidbec-Dosco Inc.*, D.T.E. 85T-4 (Que. S.C.), affd May 4, 1988, C.A.M. 500-09-001556-844; *Beaulieu v. Services Financiers Avco Canada Ltée*, J.E. 85-78 (Que. S.C.); *Thomas Cook Overseas Ltd. v. McKee*, D.T.E. 83T-572 (Que. C.A.).
>
> [2]   *Lobrutto v. University of St. Jerome's College* (1989), 44 C.P.C. (2d) 104 (Ont. H.C.J.); *Thom v. Goodhost Foods Ltd.* (1987), 17 C.C.E.L. 89 (Ont. H.C.J.), where damages for mental distress were not allowed as they were not specifically pleaded.

§14.20   Unfortunately, some courts have awarded damages for humiliation, mental anguish and other inconveniences without identifying the employer's faulty conduct and sometimes without even mentioning whether there was any fault or abuse of right.[1]

> [1]   *Leinwather v. Construction Loriot Inc.*, D.T.E. 88T-572 (Que. S.C.); *Delorme v. Banque Royale du Canada* (1987), 19 C.C.E.L. 298 (Que. S.C.), where the court awarded $10,000 for the reason that "it is not easy for a bank manager, wrongfully fired for corruption and dishonesty, to meet his former colleagues and approach other banks with that kind of reference"; *Jean v. Groupe Promodor Inc.*, D.T.E. 85T-64 (Que. S.C.); *Landry v. Comterm Inc.*, J.E. 84-451 (Que. S.C.); *Freeme de Wallens v. Visirecords Systems Canada Ltd.*, J.E. 81-548 (Que. S.C.).

C.   HUMILIATION

§14.21   Outside of Quebec, damages for humiliation are usually encompassed in a claim for damages for mental distress rather than as an independent claim. In Quebec, it is well established that damages for humiliation may be claimed only where there is proof that the employer acted in bad faith or was abusive in discharging its employee.[1]

> [1]   *Larkin v. Lauremat Inc.*, D.T.E. 91T-1024 (Que. S.C.); but see *Jean v. Groupe Promodor Inc.*, D.T.E. 85T-64 (Que. S.C.), vard D.T.E. 88T-189 (C.A.).

§14.22   Employers must handle a termination situation not only with discretion but also with respect. They must be careful not to place the executive in a situation in which he or she will be humiliated or embarrassed. The case of *Champagne v. Club de Golf Lévis Inc.*[1] illustrates this point. At the end of the golfing season, the employer invited the administrative comptroller of the club to say a few words to the other employees. The comptroller said that she was looking forward to seeing them next season. However, this took place in the presence of the employer's representatives who knew she was about to be terminated and that her replacement had already been hired. After learning of her termination, the comptroller felt humiliated about having addressed the audience the way she had. The court held that the employer should have told her before the meeting that her employment would be terminated or should not have had her address the other employees. Damages were evaluated at $3000.[2]

[1] D.T.E. 87T-548 (Que. Prov. Ct.). See also *Carle v. Comité Paritaire du Vêtement pour Dames* (1987), 22 C.C.E.L. 281 (Que. S.C.); *Wuorinen v. Workers' Compensation Bd.* (1983), 1 C.C.E.L. 29 (B.C.S.C.).
[2] See also *Lefrançois v. Crane Canada Inc.*, D.T.E. 88T-574 (Que. S.C.) ($3,000); *Barabe v. F. Pilon Inc.*, D.T.E. 87T-132 (Que. S.C.); *Clément v. Simpsons Sears Ltée*, J.E. 83-844 (Que. S.C.).

§14.23 In *Maheu v. Catalytic Enterprises Ltd.*,[1] the court held that although Maheu felt humiliated when he heard his three subordinates tell his superior that they did not want to work under Maheu's orders, no malice was involved, and consequently no damages were awarded. In *Lavigne v. Sidbec-Dosco Inc.*,[2] the court felt that notwithstanding the humiliation which the employee personally felt on being advised of the extent of his demotion (which amounted to a constructive dismissal), evidence did not disclose that the employer used any tactic to exacerbate the employee's natural distress at being rejected.

[1] D.T.E. 84T-636 (Que. S.C.).
[2] D.T.E. 85T-4 (Que. S.C.), affd May 4, 1988, C.A.M. 500-09-001556-844.

D. ANXIETY AND MENTAL DISTRESS

§14.24 The Ontario Court of Appeal, in *Brown v. Waterloo Regional Bd. of Commrs. of Police*,[1] stated the following:

> There is sufficient authority to justify the statement that damages will be awarded for mental suffering caused by the wanton or reckless breach of a contract to render a performance of such a character that the promisor had reason to know when the contract was made that a breach would cause such suffering for reasons other than pecuniary loss.[2]

This case has been followed by numerous courts.[3]

[1] (1983), 43 O.R. (2d) 113 (C.A.).

[2] (1983), 43 O.R. (2d) 113 (C.A.), at 120.

[3] *Ribeiro v. Canadian Imperial Bank of Commerce* (1989), 24 C.C.E.L. 225 (Ont. H.C.J.) appeal allowed (1992), 44 C.C.E.L. 165 (Ont. C.A.) (punitive damages and damages for mental distress increased to $50,000 and $20,000 respectively); *Moran v. Atlantic Co-operative Publishers* (1988), 23 C.C.E.L. 205 (N.S.S.C.); *Russello v. Jannock Ltd.* (1987), 15 C.C.E.L. 209 (Ont. Div. Ct.); *Rivers v. Gulf Canada Ltd.* (1986), 13 C.C.E.L. 131 (Ont. H.C.J.); *Jackson v. SNC Inc.* (1985), 8 C.C.E.L. 274 (Ont. H.C.J.); *Misovic v. Acres Davy McKee Ltd.* (1985), 7 C.C.E.L. 163 (Ont. C.A.); *Sheehy v. Wolf* (1984), 6 C.C.E.L. 101 (Ont. Co. Ct.); *Pilato v. Hamilton Place Convention Centre Inc.* (1984), 45 O.R. (2d) 652 (H.C.J.); *Luchuk v. Sport B.C.* (1984), 3 C.C.E.L. 117 (B.C.S.C.); *Carrick v. Cooper Canada Ltd.* (1983), 2 C.C.E.L. 87 (Ont. H.C.J.); *Bohemier v. Storwal International Inc.* (1982), 40 O.R. (2d) 264 (H.C.J.), upheld on appeal 44 O.R. (2d) 361 (C.A.), leave to appeal to S.C.C. refused 3 C.C.E.L. 79n.

§14.25   As in the case of aggravated damages, however, the *Vorvis* decision[1] has altered the scope of when damages for mental distress may be awarded.

> The plaintiff makes a claim for mental distress, anxiety, vexation and frustration suffered by the plaintiff as a result of the termination of his contract of employment by the defendant.[2]

The appellant based his claim on the offensive and unjustifiable conduct of Reid, his superior. Reid had become frustrated and critical with respect to the pace at which the appellant worked and had subjected him to many inquisitions during meetings and much harassment in this respect. The Court looked at the conflicting case law where on the one hand damages were awarded when it was shown that the parties had contemplated at the time the contract was entered into that a breach in certain circumstances would cause a plaintiff mental distress,[3] versus the older case law[4] which suggested damages for mental distress ought not to be awarded in any breach of contract claims. The Supreme Court of Canada ruled that the harassment and pressure complained of were not independently actionable and, because they preceded the wrongful dismissal, they could not be said to have aggravated the damage incurred as a result of the dismissal. Thus, damages were not awarded.

[1] *Vorvis v. Insurance Corp. of British Columbia*, [1989] 1 S.C.R. 1085.

[2] *Vorvis v. Insurance Corp. of British Columbia*, [1989] 1 S.C.R. 1085, at 1097.

[3] *Brown v. Waterloo Regional Bd. of Commrs. of Police* (1983), 43 O.R. (2d) 113, where the Ontario Court of Appeal ruled that damages for mental distress can be awarded where the manner of termination was wanton or reckless and the parties had reason to know at the time the employment contract was made that mental distress would result from a termination in such manner. Lack of notice is the compensable part. See also cases mentioned, *supra*, §14.24, at note 3.

[4] *Peso Silver Mines Ltd. v. Cropper*, [1966] S.C.R. 673; *Addis v. Gramophone Co.*, [1909] A.C. 488 (H.L.).

§14.26 In *Wankling v. Saskatchewan Urban Municipalities Assn.*,[1] the Saskatchewan Court of Queen's Bench applied *Vorvis* so as to deny a claim for damages for mental distress and stated:

> The manner of the dismissal is the basis of Mr. Wankling's claim for damages for mental distress. He described the afternoon of July 28, 1987 as "brutal . . . an unpleasant situation . . . a blow to my ego . . . which caused loss of confidence". He conceded that he was not humiliated by the fact that staff members were upstairs during the meeting. While he was required to clean out his office that day he was allowed to return later to retrieve personal papers stored in a filing room. His description of his mental state then and thereafter appears to me to be the reasonable and natural reaction of a senior executive who has been advised that an organization to which he has devoted many years no longer requires or desires his services. This would be so whether or not he was given reasonable notice.[2]

What is most relevant is that the court implicitly suggested that the normal termination procedure that one might expect will not warrant damages for mental distress in light of the *Vorvis* decision.

[1] (1989), 27 C.C.E.L. 31 (Sask. Q.B.). See also *McHugh v. City Motors (Newfoundland) Ltd.* (1989), 26 C.C.E.L. 57 (Nfld. C.A.) and *Girling v. Finning Ltd.* (1996), 23 C.C.E.L. (2d) 216 (Alta. Q.B.).

[2] *Wankling* (1989), 27 C.C.E.L. 31 (Sask. Q.B.), at 44-45.

§14.27 Damages for anxiety, psychological shock and mental distress have been awarded by the Quebec courts when they have been proven to result from abusive or malicious termination.[1]

[1] *Bédard v. Capitale (La), Maître courtier inc.*, D.T.E. 94T-814 (Que. C.A.) on appeal; see for example, *Occhionero v. Roy*, D.T.E. 92T-632 (Que. S.C.).

§14.27.1 In *Bernardini v. Alitalia Air Lines*[1] the court held that

> the omission to act so as to minimize the trauma caused to an employee forced into premature retirement may also constitute blameworthy behaviour equivalent to fault. Whatever the standards might have been in the past, it is no longer acceptable for a large corporation to abruptly dismiss a senior, long-time employee, who has done nothing to warrant his dismissal, without trying to some extent to help him or her overcome the traumatic effect of the loss of employment. At a minimum, the employer should be required to announce the bad news in a kind and sympathetic manner. It should offer the employee assistance and cooperation in seeking new employment, and, if there are positions open for which he or she is qualified and would like to apply, it should allow the employee to seek new employment within its own organization. It should offer and pay promptly to the discharged employee a reasonable indemnity so as to spare him or her unnecessary economic hardship; financial anxiety tends to handicap a person who is out

of work, and may affect his or her ability to search for a new beginning. An employer who neglects to fulfil these elementary methods of softening the blow to the dismissed employee exposes himself to a claim based on article 1053 C.C.[2] for the injury caused to the self esteem and sensibilities of the victim and for the delay which such injury causes in the employee's rehabilitation in the workplace.

The Court awarded moral damages equivalent to six months salary, on the basis that Defendant's omissions resulted in a delay in Plaintiff's reinstatement into the job market for that duration, if not more. This amount was in addition to the twelve month notice period which was awarded to the employee. This case is interesting in that it seems to impose a positive duty on the employer to try to minimize the trauma which may result from the termination of employment. It is no longer sufficient to avoid positive harmful actions. Omissions may also result in employer liability. In view of the similarities between the law of tort and delictual liability in Quebec, this case may likely be referred to at common law.

[1]   D.T.E. 93T-519 (Que. S.C.), at 10-11; affd, unreported, Ct. No. 500-09-000748-939 (Que. C.A.).
[2]   As it was then. A similar provision is now found at art. 1457 of the Civil Code of Quebec.

§14.28   In *Charest v. Institut Val du Lac Inc.*,[1] the employee's claim for $5,000 in compensation for embarrassment, loss of self-confidence and moral damage was denied. The court concluded that there was absence of bad faith or abuse of rights. Similarly, claims for libel and insult,[2] verbal prejudice,[3] anxiety[4] and inconvenience[5] failed because there was no evidence of malice or abuse of rights on the part of the employer. Again, the principle of abuse of rights plays a key role in determining liability.

[1]   J.E. 81-797 (Que. S.C.).
[2]   *Vézina v. Fairmont Granite Ltd.*, J.E. 81-1068 (Que. S.C.).
[3]   *Rajotte v. P.H. McCarthy Transport Inc.*, J.E. 82-487 (Que. S.C.), revd in part on other grounds J.E. 85-421 (C.A.).
[4]   *Nikanpour v. Fenco-Lavalin Inc.*, D.T.E. 88T-573 (Que. S.C.); *Benson v. Brown Boveri Canada Ltd.*, [1983] C.S. 229 (Que. S.C.).
[5]   *Thorneloe v. C.S.R. Eastern Townships*, D.T.E. 84T-870 (Que. S.C.).

E.   LOSS OF REPUTATION

§14.29   The common law cases show some difficulty categorizing loss of reputation as a particular heading of damage separate and apart from damages for mental distress.[1] However, there is authority for the proposition that damages for loss of reputation are independently compensable. In this regard, reference is made to the Ontario Supreme Court's decision in *Ribeiro v. Canadian Imperial Bank of Commerce*.[2] Although this case did not deal with an executive, it may be argued that the statement made by the court is equally applicable to executives. The court stated:

> In my opinion then if the circumstances are available I can see no reason why damages for loss of reputation, as with damages for mental distress, cannot be allowed in a breach of contract case, and specifically that involving an employment agreement. It is not difficult in my mind to conclude that there are cases in which it can be found that it was in the reasonable contemplation of the parties at the time they entered into a contract that a wrongful breach thereof and wanton and reckless conduct in relation thereto could cause a loss of reputation. But unlike the claim for damages for mental distress, there is a further problem when dealing with such a claim. If in reality the claim represents one for defamation, then in my opinion it must be advanced as such.[3]

The last part is noteworthy and in fact, in *Foley v. Signtech Inc.*,[4] the Ontario High Court reclassified two-thirds of a claim for loss of reputation as a claim for defamation.

[1] *Semenoff v. Saskatoon Drug & Stationery Co.* (1988), 49 D.L.R. (4th) 102 (Sask. Q.B.); *Desloges v. Radio-Television Representatives Ltd.* (1987), 62 O.R. (2d) 633 (H.C.J.), at 636, where the court stated: "I have no doubt that in a wrongful dismissal action, damages are not available for loss of reputation which results from the fact or the manner of termination"; *Wright v. 308489 Ontario Inc.* (1984), 45 C.P.C. 45 (Ont. S.C.). See also *Frost v. Montreal Engineering Co.* (1983), 3 C.C.E.L. 86 (Alta. Q.B.).

[2] (1989), 24 C.C.E.L. 225 (Ont. H.C.J.); appeal allowed and damages for each head increased significantly at (1992), 44 C.C.E.L. 165 (Ont. C.A.).

[3] (1989), 24 C.C.E.L. 225 (Ont. H.C.J.), at 286.

[4] (1988), 66 O.R. (2d) 729 (H.C.J.).

§14.30 Harris has accurately stated that because *Ribeiro* was decided prior to *Vorvis*, it must be read in light of *Vorvis*.[1] Harris suggests that "[i]n the event a claim for loss of reputation from a contractual breach is indeed actionable, it is to be presumed that the same test for a claim for aggravated damages and punitive damages is to be met to support the action."[2] In any event, in the recent case of *Rock v. The Canadian Red Cross Society*, the court refused to grant damages for loss of reputation to a medical director of the defendant's transfusion centre in Ottawa for the reason that these types of awards are restricted to a group of people that have a very distinct and unique classification, such as artists, entertainers or professional athletes.[3] The court saw no justification to extend the classification to include scientists.

[1] D. Harris, *Wrongful Dismissal* (Don Mills: Richard De Boo, 1984).

[2] D. Harris, *Wrongful Dismissal* (Don Mills: Richard De Boo, 1984), at 4-178.

[3] (1994), 5 C.C.E.L. (2d) 231 (Ont. Ct. (Gen. Div.).

§14.30.1 In British Columbia, in a case involving a very public dismissal, the employer failed to provide a satisfactory explanation to the public as to why the executive had been terminated. In fact, the employer had made public insinuations which indicated that the executive had been terminated with cause, when this was clearly not true. The Court awarded aggravated damages because this conduct on the part of the employer interfered with the executive's search for employment by reason of damage to his reputation. It was further found that the employer's action, in providing misleading information to the media about the employee's dismissal and other vindictive and malicious actions, entitled the employee to punitive damages. (See discussion of punitive damages at the end of this chapter.)[1]

---

[1] *Dixon v. British Columbia Transit* (1995), 9 B.C.L.R. (3d) 108 (S.C.).

§14.31 In Quebec, liability will ensue if the employer's wrongful actions had a definite prejudicial effect on the individual's reputation.[1] An executive's testimony alone will rarely suffice to establish to the court's satisfaction that his or her reputation was damaged. Since the executive is an interested party, corroborating testimony is almost essential to a successful claim. Mr. Justice Deschênes, in *Mainville v. Brasserie Michel Desjardins Ltée*,[2] held that although the employee's version of the facts was plausible with respect to damage to his reputation, in the absence of any corroborating evidence, his claim should be denied.[3]

---

[1] *Villa v. John Labatt Ltée*, [1990] R.J.Q. 2247 (S.C.); revd in part on another issue *La Brasserie Labatt Limitée v. Villa*, [1995] R.J.Q. 73 (C.A.). No such damage was proven in the cases of *Fournier v. Tout-Rôti Ltée*, D.T.E. 90T-131 (Que. S.C.) and *Carle v. Comité Paritaire du Vêtement pour Dames* (1987), 22 C.C.E.L. 281 (Que. S.C.).

[2] D.T.E. 88T-292 (Que. S.C.), appeal abandoned Sept. 16, 1988, C.A.M. 500-09-000185-884.

[3] Other cases where the former employee failed to show that his or her reputation had suffered by reason of the employer's wrongdoing include: *Villeneuve v. Soutien-Gorge Vogue Inc.*, D.T.E. 86T-739 (Que. S.C.); *Mailhot v. Société de Radiodiffusion Audiogramme CKLM Ltée*, J.E. 84-1047 (Que. S.C.); *Lemyre v. J.B. Williams (Canada)*, D.T.E. 84T-752 (Que. S.C.); *Goulet v. Equipement de Bureau Astro-Tech Ltée*, J.E. 84-364 (Que. S.C.); *Banville v. Procureur général du Québec*, D.T.E. 84T-172 (Que. S.C.).

§14.32 The case of *Dumas v. Aeterna-Vie Cie d'Assurance*[1] illustrates how an employer may damage its employee's reputation. Following the dismissal of the insurance agent Dumas, the employer sent Dumas' clients a note telling them that Dumas was no longer employed by the insurance company. The note was written in such a way that it could lead a reader to infer that Dumas had been dismissed because of theft or dishonesty, which was not the case. Dumas was consequently entitled to compensation.[2]

¹ J.E. 80-910 (Que. S.C.).

² See also *Miron Inc. v. Des Cheneaux*, D.T.E. 88T-14 (Que. C.A.); Faule v. Sun Life du Canada, J.E. 84-363 (Que. S.C.); *Talbot v. Caisse d'Établissement Bellerive*, J.E. 83-62 (Que. S.C.).

§14.33 When the employee continues to enjoy an excellent reputation even after dismissal, there is no valid claim for damages under this heading.¹

> ¹ *Landry v. Comterm Inc.*, J.E. 84-451 (Que. S.C.). See also *Murray v. Jets Hockey Ventures* (1996), 21 C.C.E.L. (2d) 183 (Man. Q.B.) where damages for loss of reputation were denied due to the lack of job security in a particular career field, namely professional coaching.

§14.34 Rumours and speculation as to the cause of a dismissal are often the result of normal curiosity that surrounds the loss of employment of a co-employee or a high-profile figure in the community. Where the publicity is not proven to be directly attributable to or provoked by the employer, the employer will generally not be held responsible for any damages the employee may suffer as a result of this publicity.¹

> ¹ *Standard Broadcasting Corp. v. Stewart*, D.T.E. 94T-815 (Que. C.A.); *Bazinet v. Radiodiffusion Mutuelle Ltée*, D.T.E. 85T-640 (Que. S.C.), as amended by D.T.E. 89T-1081 (Que. C.A.); *Landry v. Radio du Pontiac Inc.* D.T.E. 83T-200 (Que. C.A.); *Clément v. Simpsons Sears Ltée*, J.E. 83-844 (Que. S.C.); *Jolicoeur v. Lithographie Montréal Ltée*, [1982] C.S. 230 (Que.), affd Apr. 15, 1987, C.A.M. 500-09-000314-823; *Hydro-Québec v. Arsenault*, unreported, 1979, No. 09-000446-73 (Que. C.A.); *Levasseur v. Allard 5-10-15 Ltée*, [1972] C.S. 658 (Que.); *Ruel v. Banque Provinciale du Canada*, [1971] C.A. 343 (Que.).

F. REFERENCES AND OTHER VERBAL OR WRITTEN COMMUNICATIONS REGARDING A TERMINATED EMPLOYEE

§14.35 Employers should avoid causing unnecessary harm to an executive when third parties call upon them for references. Offering information that is not relevant or that is misleading or incorrect may allow a former executive to recover additional damages. In *Langlois v. Farr Inc.*,¹ a representative of Farr Inc. had informed a potential employer who sought references on Langlois that Langlois had been fired for cause and was in the process of suing Farr Inc. for damages. The Court of Appeal held that at the time of Langlois' dismissal, the president of Farr Inc. knew there was no cause to dismiss Langlois. The Court of Appeal awarded Langlois $5,000 for the prejudice suffered by Langlois in his search for new employment.²

¹ (1988), 26 C.C.E.L. 249 (Que. C.A.).
² *Contra*: *Vézina v. Fairmont Granite Ltd.*, J.E. 81-1068 (Que. S.C.), where the employee's claim for damages failed.

§14.36 Employers must also exercise caution in the manner in which they inform their other employees, customers, suppliers or any other persons they deal with, of the departure of an executive. The courts will scrutinize the written or verbal communication for wrongdoing.¹ The courts acknowledge that in some cases an employer is required to inform other persons of the departure of an executive employee. Good business reasons are often the justification for informing a third party of an executive's termination. For example, it may be a way of introducing the executive's replacement. The courts will not find any wrongdoing if the interested parties are given factual information.² An employer should generally abstain from acting in such a way that doubt is cast on a person's honesty or professionalism.

¹ *Duquette v. Location de Voitures Compactes (Canada) Ltée*, D.T.E. 90T-343 (Ct. of Que.). See also *Girouard v. Les Coopérants, Société-Mutuelle d'Assurance-Vie*, unreported, April 5, 1990, 450-05-000350-849 (Que. S.C.), where damages were awarded partly because of unnecessary prejudicial comments on the employee's record of employment; and *Dumas v. Aeterna-Vie, Cie d'Assurance*, J.E. 80-910 (Que. S.C.).
² *Habitations Populaires Desjardins de Lanaudière Inc. v. Boyer*, D.T.E. 88T-550 (Que. C.A.).

G. PUNITIVE AND EXEMPLARY DAMAGES

§14.37 At common law, punitive damages, the purpose of which is to punish and deter, are rarely awarded in cases of wrongful dismissal.¹

¹ Where punitive damages were not awarded: *Colasurdo v. CTG Inc.* (1988), 18 C.C.E.L. 264 (Ont. H.C.J.); *Pierce v. Canada Trust Realtor, Division of Canada Trust Realty Inc.* (1986), 11 C.C.E.L. 64 (Ont. H.C.J.). Where punitive damages were awarded: *Makarchuk v. Midtransportation Services Ltd.* (1985), 6 C.C.E.L. 169 (Ont. H.C.J.); *Thom v. Goodhost Foods Ltd.* (1987), 17 C.C.E.L. 89 (Ont. H.C.J.).

§14.38 The Supreme Court of Canada canvassed the issue of punitive damages in *Vorvis v. Insurance Corp. of British Columbia*,¹ and restricted the circumstances in which they can be awarded. The Court held:

> Turning to the case at bar, it is clear from the judgments below that the appellant's superior, Reid, treated him in a most offensive manner. As has been noted, the trial judge would have awarded punitive damages had he been of the view that it was open to him to do so. The question before us now is whether the trial judge was right in concluding that it was not open to him to award the punitive damages. In my view, while it may be very unusual to do so, punitive damages

may be awarded in cases of breach of contract. It would seem to me, however, that it will be rare to find a contractual breach which would be appropriate for such an award.[2]

Further, the Court stated:

> Moreover, punitive damages may only be awarded in respect of conduct which is of such nature as to be deserving of punishment because of its harsh, vindictive and malicious nature. I do not suggest that I have exhausted the adjectives which could describe the conduct capable of characterizing a punitive award, but in any case where such an award is made the conduct must be extreme in its nature and such that by any reasonable standard it is deserving of full condemnation and punishment.[3]

On the facts, the Court ruled that the conduct of Reid "was not considered sufficiently offensive, standing alone, to constitute actionable wrong".[4] Therefore, Vorvis was denied punitive damages.

---

[1] [1989] 1 S.C.R. 1085.
[2] [1989] 1 S.C.R. 1085, at 1107.
[3] [1989] 1 S.C.R. 1085, at 1107-8.
[4] [1989] 1 S.C.R. 1085, at 1110.

§14.39 The *Vorvis* decision was applied in *Bell v. Canada Development Investment Corp.*[1] In the *Bell* decision, the plaintiff was induced to leave his employment as senior vice-president and executive vice-president of Petro-Canada to commence a five-year appointment as president and chief executive officer of the defendant, a federal Crown corporation. The plaintiff's employment was summarily terminated without cause three years prior to the expiry of the fixed term of employment. The court, in its assessment of a punitive damage award, applied *Vorvis* and stated:

> Mr. Justice McIntyre pointed out that punitive damages are designed to punish, and that an award should always receive the most careful consideration, and the discretion to award punitive damages should be most cautiously exercised. Mr. Justice McIntyre suggested that punitive damages could be awarded in respect of conduct . . . "of such nature as to be deserving of punishment because of its harsh, vindictive, reprehensible and malicious nature."
>
> I strongly disapprove of the conduct of CDIC in this case. There is no doubt that Mr. Bell was shabbily treated. However, I do not think that the conduct of CDIC quite meets the test set out in *Vorvis*, and it is with regret that I have decided that no award of punitive damages should be made.[2]

---

[1] (1990), 32 C.C.E.L. 16 (Ont H.C.J.). *See also Squires v. Corner Brook Pulp and Paper Ltd.* (1994), 5 C.C.E.L. (2d) 206 (Nfld. S.C.).
[2] (1990), 32 C.C.E.L. 16 (Ont H.C.J.), at 41-42.

§14.40   The Ontario Court of Appeal in *Francis v. Canadian Imperial Bank of Commerce* awarded punitive damages where the employer had, without conducting a full investigation, flagrantly made serious allegations against the plaintiff amounting to fraud or moral turpitude, without providing the plaintiff with an opportunity to answer the allegations.[1]

---

[1]   (1994), 21 O.R. (3d) 75 (C.A.). See also *Moffatt v. Canso Pharmacy Ltd.* (1990), 30 C.C.E.L. 22 (N.S.S.C.); *Ballard v. Alberni Valley Chamber of Commerce* (1992), 39 C.C.E.L. 225 (B.C.S.C.), where exemplary damages were awarded.

§14.41   The Nova Scotia Court of Appeal has explained and confirmed the *Vorvis* decision in determining that, where there was indeed an actionable wrong, the employer could be held liable to pay punitive damages. In *Conrad v. Household Financial Corp.*,[1] the Court held that, where an employer had dismissed an employee without cause under cloud of criminal investigation one day before she was to be transferred to another province and after she had made arrangements to move, the employer went beyond the confines of the employment contract and breached its duty of care not to injure her. It is liable upon its actionable wrong to pay her damages to make her whole. It is liable because its conduct was reprehensible, to be punished by way of punitive or exemplary damages (in addition to reasonable notice). The circumstances call for punitive damages as a warning to other employers not to abuse their relatively advantageous positions over their employees.

---

[1]   (1992), C.C.E.L. 81 (N.S.S.C. (Appeal Div.)).

§14.42   In *Dixon v. British Columbia Transit*,[1] the Court had cause to discuss the law regarding punitive damages in wrongful dismissal cases in detail. Subsequent to terminating Mr. Dixon, the defendant Crown corporation had made public statements which the Court found to amount to the torts of deceit and defamation. The Court based its award of punitive damages on the commission of actionable wrongs by the defendant and on the public policy rationale that such conduct should be discouraged, especially when committed by a Crown corporation.

---

[1]   (1995), 9 B.C.L.R. (3d) 108 (S.C.).

§14.43   Traditionally, Quebec courts have not awarded punitive damages.[1] However, the new Civil Code of Quebec at article 1621 now recognizes some specific cases where such awards may be granted.[2]

Generally, in Quebec, exemplary damages may be ordered if the defendant has violated a particular statute giving rise to this type of award. The *Charter of Human Rights and Freedoms*,[3] for example, provides for an award of exemplary damages if a person intentionally and unlawfully interferes with a right or freedom protected by the Charter.

[1] *Chouinard v. Groupe Commerce, Cie d'Assurances*, D.T.E. 90T-528 (Que. S.C.), affd D.T.E. 95T-269 (Que. C.A.); *Cournoyer v. Institut National de la Recherche Scientifique*, [1989] R.J.Q. 251 (C.A.); *Delorme v. Banque Royale du Canada* (1987), 19 C.C.E.L. 298 (Que. S.C.).

[2] Arts. 1899, 1902 and 1968 C.C.Q.

[3] R.S.Q. 1977, c. C-12, s. 49.

§14.44 In *Delorme v. Banque Royale du Canada*,[1] Delorme had been unjustly fired for reasons of corruption and dishonesty. Since there was no proof that the employer had intentionally violated the employee's fundamental Charter right to respect of his honour and reputation, the court refused to award exemplary damages.

[1] (1987), 19 C.C.E.L. 298 (Que. S.C.).

§14.45 The Quebec Court of Appeal, in *West Island Teachers' Assn. v. Nantel*,[1] analyzed the meaning of an "intentional" violation under the Charter. The court held:

> The unlawful interference with one of the rights recognized by the Charter is a delict. To be intentional it must be committed in circumstances that indicate a determined will to cause the damage resulting from the violation. This will can be manifested in many ways. It is susceptible to appear upon the finding that the fault committed is serious or gross to the point that one cannot imagine that the person who has committed the fault could not realize from the beginning that it would produce the prejudicial consequences that followed. The fault is equally intentional if it comes from a disturbed and reckless carelessness for another person's right to respect, in full knowledge of the immediate and natural or at least extremely probable consequences that the conduct will cause to the victim.[2]

This passage has been applied as the test for the finding of intention, which triggers liability under the Quebec Charter.[3]

[1] [1988] R.J.Q. 1569 (C.A.).

[2] [1988] R.J.Q. 1569 (C.A.), at 1574 (authors' translation).

[3] *Occhionero v. Roy*, D.T.E. 92T-632 (Que. S.C.); *Gignac v. Trust Général du Canada*, D.T.E. 91T-231 (Que. S.C.).

§14.46 In evaluating the amount of exemplary damages, the court has a broad discretion. It will generally consider the following factors: the preventive or punitive aspect of the award, the conduct of the wrongdoer, the prejudice suffered, the capacity to pay and the quantum of damages awarded for the actual prejudice suffered.[1]

---

[1] *West Island Association v. Nantel*, [1988] R.J.Q. 1569 (C.A.) and see Pierre E. Audet, "Évaluation des dommages-intérêts exemplaires", (1981-1982) F.B. du B. 255; *Tardif v. Hydro-Québec*, D.T.E. 97T-867 (S.C.).

---

§14.47 Punitive damages must not exceed what is sufficient to fulfil their preventive purpose. Article 1621 of the Civil Code of Quebec states that they are to be assessed "in the light of all the appropriate circumstances, in particular the gravity of the debtor's fault, his patrimonial situation, the extent of the reparation for which he is already liable to the creditor and, where such is the case, the fact that the payment of the damages is wholly or partly assumed by a third person".

H.   CONCLUSION

§14.48 The employer must take care in the way an executive's employment is terminated, even where notice or an indemnity in lieu of notice is given. The courts are increasingly less tolerant of those who act in bad faith or in disrespect of other's rights.

Furthermore, in Quebec, article 2092 C.C.Q. provides that an employee cannot renounce his right to obtain compensation for any injury he suffers where insufficient notice of termination is given or where the manner of termination is abusive. We believe this article means that an employee cannot renounce a right to compensation in advance, for example, at hiring or upon conclusion of a written employment contract. However, the renunciation obtained at the time of termination or thereafter, in a release and discharge document or a severance agreement for example, is valid. Interpreting this article to mean that all renunciations are invalid, irrespective of the time they are given, would mean that an employee could at any time repudiate any agreement regarding the monetary terms of his termination of employment.

§14.49 In addition, article 1609 C.C.Q. stipulates in essence that an acquittance (release), transaction or statement obtained in connection with a bodily or *moral* injury within thirty days of the act which caused the injury is without effect, for example, an abusive termination of employment. This article prevents an employer, in certain circumstances, from relying on an otherwise valid release signed by the executive.

§14.50 In the next chapter, we discuss some recourses open to employers in case of violation by the executive of his or her obligations of employment.

CHAPTER 15

EMPLOYER RECOURSES FOR BREACH OF CONTRACT BY EXECUTIVES

A. INTRODUCTION

§15.1 An employer may commence legal proceedings against an executive for damages suffered by reason of the breach of the executive's employment obligations. In practice, relatively few employers commence such actions because the time, energy and cost commanded by a lawsuit is often greater than the damages directly imputable to the employee. Regardless of the probability of a lawsuit being launched by an employer, an executive should carefully evaluate the timeliness of a resignation and the advance notice which should be given in this respect. Similarly, the executive should be aware of the possible consequences of failing to provide the services he or she has agreed to render, or using company property or his or her position in an inappropriate manner.

§15.2 The following sections briefly outline the recourse employers may have against their executive employees by reason of the breach of particular obligations senior employees owe to their employers.

B. DAMAGES FOR AN EXECUTIVE'S PREMATURE RESIGNATION

§15.3 As mentioned in a previous chapter,[1] executives, like other employees bound by an indeterminate employment contract, must give their employers prior reasonable notice of their intention to resign.[2] Those bound to a fixed-term contract generally cannot resign before the term expires or before providing the specific notice period that is set out in the employment contract. Failure to provide notice, or resigning before the expiry of the fixed term, will render the executive liable for damages incurred by his or her employer which are the immediate and direct result of the premature resignation.[3] Indeed, just as an employer is liable for damages caused by a premature and wrongful termination, so too can an executive be found liable for any damages caused by his or her failure to provide sufficient notice of resignation. The Supreme Court of Canada, in *Asbestos Corp. Ltd. v. Cook*,[4] referred to French authority on this point:

It follows that he who wishes to end the agreement must manifest his will by giving notice to the other, and the notice implies a certain delay in the interest of the one to whom it is given; if the delay is not sufficient, there is room for damages.[5]

[1] See Chapter 12, "Termination of Employment".

[2] Article 2091 of the Civil Code of Quebec provides that *either party* to a contract with an indeterminate term may terminate it by giving notice. For further discussion, see "Repudiation by the Executive" in Chapter 12.

[3] *Lazarowicz v. Orenda Engines Ltd.*, [1961] O.R. 141 (C.A.); *Engineered Sound Systems Ltd. v. Klampfer* (1994), 3 C.C.E.L. (2d) 105 (Ont. Ct. (Gen. Div.)).

[4] [1933] S.C.R. 86, at 94 (authors' translation).

[5] *Principes de droit civil*, 4th ed. (Paris: Librairie A. Marescq, 1887), vol. 25, no. 513.

§15.4 As with an employer, if the executive has good reason to terminate the relationship, he or she will be exonerated from liability.[1] Whether the executive has good reason must be examined in light of the employer's conduct and actions. Generally, those factors that constitute a claim for constructive dismissal will support a claim of resignation for good reason.

[1] See C.C.Q., art. 2094.

§15.5 In 1987, Mr. Justice Henri LaRue of the Quebec Superior Court awarded $10,000 to an employer for damages suffered as a result of the employee's failure to provide appropriate notice of resignation.[1] In awarding damages, the court placed emphasis on the confusion and chaos which followed the employee's abrupt departure and the resulting resignation of other employees.

[1] *Grenier v. Radiodiffusion Mutuelle Canada Ltée* (1987), 18 C.C.E.L. 256 (Que. S.C.).

§15.6 The employer is entitled to claim the damages incurred by it during the notice period found to be appropriate in the circumstances.[1] The main purpose of requiring the executive to provide reasonable notice is to allow the employer reasonable time to recruit and hire a replacement. The damages may include lost profits or extraordinary expenses incurred in an effort to compensate the negative impact of the sudden departure of the executive. Any salary that is owed to the executive at the time of his or her resignation may be set off against the damage claim, subject to applicable employment standards legislation.

[1] In *Sure-Grip Fasteners Ltd. v. Allgrade Bolt & Chain Inc.* (1993), 45 C.C.E.L. 276 (Ont. Ct. (Gen. Div.)), the Court held when a general manager and two salespeople resigned from a small company without notice, the defendants breached their employment contract with the plaintiff and in particular the implied term to give reasonable notice which would have been one and a quarter months in the case of the salespeople and six months in the case of the general manager.

§15.7 The employer bears the burden of proving the loss incurred as a result of the executive's wrongful resignation. Failure to prove its damages will cause a court to reject an employer's claim.[1]

> [1] *Godbout v. Théroux*, D.T.E. 92T-174 (Ct. of Que.).

§15.8 The employer is under an obligation to mitigate the losses which result from the premature resignation. The employer must use honest, reasonable and expeditious efforts to replace the departed employee. Often the damages are relatively insignificant as a result of the employer's ability to replace the departed employee with a temporary employee until a permanent solution is found, either in the form of a new hire or a reorganization of the duties between existing employees. However, this may not be the case with executives as they may not necessarily be easily replaced and their value to the employer may be significant.

§15.9 The executive who alleges that the employer has failed to mitigate its losses bears the burden of proving that the employer acted unreasonably in recruiting a replacement or arranging to have his or her duties and responsibilities fulfilled by others and that the damages alleged are not the direct and immediate result of the failure to give reasonable or appropriate notice of resignation.

§15.10 In the recent case of *Terres Noires Sherrington Ltée v. Barrachina*,[1] an executive who abruptly resigned at the most inappropriate time of the year was held liable for the profits the company lost in the financial year following his resignation, and for extraordinary expenses and costs incurred by the employer in an effort to mitigate its losses. The employer, Terres Noires, operated a fruit import and export business in Canada. In 1982, it incorporated a company in Spain and hired the executive, Barrachina, to act as general manager of the Spanish subsidiary. On August 20, 1985, Barrachina mailed his letter of resignation dated August 2, 1985, from Spain. In fact, on August 2, 1985, he had commenced acting as the representative for the Spanish fruit suppliers who normally did business with Terres Noires but who had since decided to sell their products directly to the Canadian market. The Spanish suppliers gave Terres Noires only a few days' notice that they would cease business relations with Terres Noires.

> [1] D.T.E. 88T-623 (Que. S.C.).

§15.11 Terres Noires spent more than $20,000 travelling to Spain in an effort to mitigate its anticipated losses in seeking new suppliers. The

Quebec Superior Court emphasized the fact that August, September and October were the months in which negotiations of purchase agreements for Spanish products took place. Transportation and shipping of the products to Canada then ran from November to February. Barrachina resigned at the most crucial period of the 1985-86 import industry year. The Superior Court held that Barrachina's notice of resignation was clearly insufficient. It also ruled that Barrachina's participation in the suppliers' reorganization of their businesses demonstrated his lack of loyalty towards his ex-employer.

§15.12   Terres Noires suffered a loss in revenues of almost $3,000,000 for the year 1985-86. The Superior Court held that Terres Noires was entitled to $240,000 as damages for loss of net profits. Barrachina and his new employer were held jointly liable for the damages. Barrachina's liability appears to have been founded both in contract (for failure to give reasonable notice of resignation) and in tort (disloyalty and unfair competition).

§15.13   In *Systems Engineering & Automation Ltd. v. Power*,[1] the Newfoundland Supreme Court found two technicians liable for their failure to provide appropriate notice of resignation. Because of their key role in the business, their abrupt departure caused hardship and losses to their former employer. The court ruled that the technicians could have foreseen these losses. Under Newfoundland's labour standards legislation,[2] the employees should have given their employer one to two weeks' notice of resignation. The court therefore held the technicians liable for some $10,000 lost profits during the notice period and expenses in completing projects in which the technicians were involved.

---

[1]   (1989), 78 Nfld. & P.E.I.R. 65 (Nfld. S.C.), vard 92 Nfld. & P.E.I.R. 235 (S.C.). See also *Henderson v. Westfair Foods Ltd.* (1990), 32 C.C.E.L. 152 (Man. Q.B.), revd on this point (for lack of evidence) 40 C.C.E.L. 81 (C.A.).

[2]   *Labour Standards Act*, S.N. 1977, c. 52, s. 51 [now R.S.N. 1990, c. L-2, s. 55]. Other provinces also have legislation governing employee notice periods. See, *e.g.*, *Employment Standards Code*, S.A. 1988, c. E-10.2, s. 59; *Employment Standards Act*, R.S.M. 1987, c. E110, s. 39(5), (6); *Labour Standards Code*, R.S.N.S. 1989, c. 246, s. 73(1); *Labour Act*, R.S.P.E.I. 1988, c. L-1, s. 93(1)(*b*).

§15.13.1   In one case, a court granted an injunction preventing a former employee from working for a competitor during the period that should have been given as notice of resignation. An announcer on a popular morning radio show in Montreal resigned less than one hour before he was scheduled to go on the air even though his written contract stipulated he was obliged to provide three months' notice of his resignation. The Court upheld the ex-employer's request that the morning man be prevented from working for the competing station during a three-month period following his date of resignation because he had acted with the utmost bad faith. In this case, although a recourse in damages was available to the ex-employer, it did not prevent him from obtaining an injunction against the ex-employee.[1]

[1] *Metro Media CMR Inc. v. Tétrault*, D.T.E. 94T-359 (Que. S.C.).

§15.14   One final point should be noted with respect to the resignation of an executive. The Ontario Court of Appeal[1] has ruled that if a letter of resignation is not accepted as offered, then the employee's employment is not terminated. Moreover, the effect of an alternative offer of reasonable notice of termination of employment or pay in lieu thereof by the employer in response to the notice of resignation may result in the wrongful dismissal of the executive if reasonable notice is not given by the employer.

[1] *Oxman v. Dustbane Enterprises Ltd.* (1988), 23 C.C.E.L. 157.

C. NULLITY OF THE EMPLOYMENT CONTRACT

§15.15   If an executive breaches the terms of an employment contract, the employer may accept the breach and treat the contract as having been repudiated. The contractual liability between the parties and the obligations owing are no different than those obligations arising under any other type of contract. Therefore, if there is a breach of a fundamental term or a term going to the root of the contract, the innocent party may accept the breach and treat the contract as having been repudiated, thereby bringing to an end the future performance by the parties.

§15.16   In *Rondeau v. Lamarre Valois Int. Ltée*,[1] the Quebec Court of Appeal annulled the written employment contract and confirmed the Superior Court's decision that called for Rondeau to pay $4,376 to his former employer. This amount represented the cost of airplane tickets for the employee and his spouse, transportation costs for the move of their personal effects, and all salary and advances the employee had received.

[1] Unreported, Sept. 26, 1978, C.A.M. 500-09-000834-754 (Que. C.A.).

D. EXECUTIVE LIABILITY IN TORT

§15.17   Can an employer sue an executive for the negligent performance or non-performance of his or her duty? The Ontario District Court considered this issue in *Dominion Manufacturers Ltd. v. O'Gorman*.[1] The employee was an experienced accountant, hired by the plaintiff employer as its comptroller. There was no written employment contract governing the parties' relationship. The court found that the defendant was hired on the express understanding that he was capable of performing all the functions for which he was hired. The defendant in carrying out his duties had failed to make payments to various government agencies resulting in the employer incurring penalties in the amount of $13,654. The court stated:

> Without doubt the employer-employee relationship is a contractual one but the decided cases seem to indicate that the parties may owe one another for the duties arising from relationships which co-exist between them. Thus, the employee may also owe the employer a duty in tort.[2]

[1]   (1989), 24 C.C.E.L. 218 (Ont. Dist. Ct.). See also *Ferguson v. Allstate Ins. Co. of Canada* (1991), 35 C.C.E.L. 257 (Ont. Ct. (Gen. Div.)).
[2]   *Dominion Manufacturers Ltd. v. Gorman* (1989), 24 C.C.E.L. 218 (Ont. Dist. Ct.), at 222.

§15.18   The court looked to the dissenting judgment of the British Columbia Court of Appeal in *D.H. Overmyer Co. of Canada v. Wallace Transfer Ltd.*[1] in establishing the test for liability. The relevant portion of that dissenting judgment is as follows:

> If an employee, by lack of care, causes loss to his employer, I do not think that it should be presumed that the employee will be liable, and I do not think that we should look at decisions on other employment contracts for the answer. We should look at the hiring to see what was said and at the circumstances to see what might properly be implied. It follows that this employment and this error must be looked at to see what terms were in the contract and whether they were breached.[2]

[1]   (1975), 65 D.L.R. (3d) 717 (B.C.C.A.).
[2]   (1975), 65 D.L.R. (3d) 717 (B.C.C.A.), at 724-25.

§15.19   Following this, the court in *Dominion Manufacturers* found that there was an implied term of the oral contract at hiring that the employer would be indemnified for the losses caused by the act or non-acts of the employee, and awarded damages accordingly.

§15.19.1   In *Thorn v. RGO Office Products Ltd.*,[1] the court held that the employer could validly sue an employee he had dismissed for breach of trust when the employer was able to show that the employee's conduct had resulted in loss of goodwill and future business potential with respect to a client who refused to do business with the employer because of the employee's conduct. In this case, the employee had asked a client/supplier for a personal commission for introducing the supplier to a particular customer and threatened to damage the supplier's reputation in the business if he was not paid.

In Quebec, article 2088 of the Civil Code of Quebec states that the employee is bound to carry on his work with prudence and diligence. We will have to examine the case law which will be decided under this provision to determine whether or not it can be relied upon as the basis for a claim for damages.

[1] (1993), 15 Alta. L.R. (3d) 346 at 364 (Q.B.).

E. PROFITS AND EXPENSES WRONGFULLY ACQUIRED

§15.20 If the executive uses the company's property or takes advantage of his or her position to engage in transactions for his or her personal benefit, without the authorization or knowledge of the employer, the executive may be liable to account to the employer for any profits made.[1] If the executive carries out actions for which he or she did not receive proper authorization, the employer may under certain conditions claim reimbursement for any expenses incurred.[2]

[1]   *Jones v. Linde British Refrigeration Co.* (1901), 2 O.L.R. 428 (C.A.).
[2]   See *Poulin v. Chez Nous des Artistes Inc.*, D.T.E. 89T-739 (Que. S.C.), where the court denied the employer's claim because the employee had acted within his authority in ordering certain works.

§15.21 In *Bank of Montreal v. Kuet Leong Ng*,[1] a foreign currency exchange specialist, in the course of his activities, carried out transactions in some of the bank's client accounts which enabled him to realize large profits. He also engaged in transactions for two of the bank's clients on the secret condition that he receive one-half of any trading profits. Although the bank did not suffer any losses attributable to the acts of Kuet Leong Ng, it instituted an action to recover the profits. The Supreme Court of Canada awarded the full amount of profits to the bank, which totalled more than $600,000. The Court ruled that a senior employee such as Kuet Leong Ng is accountable for the consequences of the funds he controls because of his position. The Court also held that to allow Kuet Leong Ng to retain the profits would violate the principle that no one should profit from the breach of his or her duty of good faith and loyalty.

§15.21.1 In *Produits chimiques A.C.P. Chemical Inc. v. Paolitto*,[2] the defendant was made to disgorge profits he had illegally made while in the employ of the plaintiff. The defendant, also a shareholder of the plaintiff, had signed an agreement which provided that so long as he was a shareholder, he was to devote his full time efforts and attention to the business of the plaintiff and act at all times to the best advantage of the plaintiff. During his employment, the defendant was commercially involved with one of the plaintiff's clients and performed services which were normally rendered by the plaintiff or that could have been. The court held that the defendant had breached his obligation of loyalty and was to pay to the plaintiff damages for lost profits. The court ordered the same with respect to similar services which were performed for the client in question, but following the defendant's resignation from his employment with the plaintiff for the reason that it was the continuation of a commercial relationship which had been illegally commenced.

[1] [1989] 2 S.C.R. 429.
[2] D.T.E. 95T-323 (Que. S.C.).

CHAPTER 16

OTHER ISSUES CONCERNING WRONGFUL TERMINATION AND DAMAGE AWARDS

A. NEAR CAUSE/CONTRIBUTORY FAULT

§16.1 In certain circumstances, the terminated executive may commit an act of misconduct which, although inappropriate and an instrumental factor in the decision to terminate, is not sufficient on its own to justify termination for cause. Such misconduct has been characterized as "near cause" in the common law provinces and "contributory fault" in Quebec. Whether or not near cause or contributory fault can serve to reduce the notice period and consequently moderate the damages awarded for wrongful dismissal has been the subject of great debate in many provinces and by many courts.

§16.2 In some earlier decisions in Quebec, courts shortened the notice period where an employee was partly to blame for his or her dismissal,[1] or reduced the amount of damages for wrongful termination in consideration of the employee's faulty conduct.[2] However, the Quebec Court of Appeal has recently ended this practice.[3] The court held that in cases of alleged wrongful termination, the sole issue to be determined is whether or not the employee's unsatisfactory conduct or performance was sufficient to constitute cause for dismissal. If not, it cannot serve to reduce the notice or damages in lieu of notice owed.

[1] *Dupuis v. Datagram Inc.*, D.T.E. 87T-936 (Que. S.C.).
[2] *Sperano v. Héritiers de M. André St-Pierre*, D.T.E. 84T-174 (Que. Prov. Ct.).
[3] *Maheu, Noiseux & Associés v. Ronéo Vickers Canada Ltd.*, D.T.E. 88T-558 (Que. C.A.).

§16.3 This view has been supported by the appellate courts of Saskatchewan, New Brunswick, British Columbia, Newfoundland and Manitoba.[1] The position of these courts is well summarized by the Saskatchewan Court of Appeal as follows:

> In my opinion, the "third alternative" or "almost cause" or "near cause" has no place in cases involving the alleged wrongful dismissal of an employee or cases involving breaches of a contract of employment, whether written or oral or breaches of express or implied terms of a contract of employment. If the employer

dismisses an employee for cause and it is subsequently discovered that there is no cause, the employee is entitled to compensation in lieu of notice . . .

• • • • •

There is no middle ground. The employer either has cause or he does not.[2]

---

[1]   *Beyea v. Irving Oil Ltd.* (1986), 14 C.C.E.L. 67 (N.B.C.A.); *Marystown Shipyard Ltd. v. Rose* (1985), 6 C.C.E.L. 220 (Nfld. C.A.); *Page v. Jim Pattison Industries Ltd.*, [1984] 4 W.W.R. 481 (Sask. C.A.); *Steinicke v. Manning Press Ltd.* (1984), 4 C.C.E.L. 294 (B.C.C.A.); *Courchaine v. Metal-Pac Mfg. Ltd.* (1984), 27 Man. R. (2d) 151 (C.A.).

[2]   *Page v. Jim Pattison Industries Ltd.*, [1984] 4 W.W.R. 481 (Sask. C.A.) at 489, 490.

§16.4   In Nova Scotia, however, the ruling in *Connor v. Canada Life Assur. Co.*[1] runs counter to the above-mentioned position. The Nova Scotia Supreme Court ruled that although the former employee's misconduct (destroying a note in her personnel file) was not so serious as to constitute cause for immediate dismissal, her absence of good judgment justified a reduction of one month's salary in the damage award for wrongful dismissal. The Nova Scotia Court of Appeal has endorsed this approach. In *Babcock v. C. & R. Weickert Enterprises Ltd.*,[2] the general manager of a retail store was dismissed for incompetence without notice. The trial judge dismissed the plaintiff's action for wrongful dismissal. The Court of Appeal overturned the decision and determined that, although the general manager was incompetent, the employer did not grant him reasonable time to correct his deficiencies and therefore, there was not just cause to dismiss the general manager without notice. In setting the appropriate period of notice at five months, the court took into account the ample evidence before the trial judge that established the general manager's incompetence and therefore, it invoked a "near cause" or "moderated damages" principle in determining the appropriate period of notice.

---

[1]   (1991), 108 N.S.R. (2d) 361 (S.C.).

[2]   (1993), 50 C.C.E.L. 1 (N.S.C.A.). The applicability of the "near cause" or "moderated damages" principle was affirmed by this same court in *Dowling v. Halifax (City)* (1996), 136 D.L.R. (4th) 352, at 358 (N.S.C.A.), notice of appeal filed February 27, 1997, [1996] S.C.C.A. No. 405.

§16.5   In Alberta, the issue does not appear to be settled.[1]

---

[1]   Rejecting near cause: *English v. NBI Canada Inc.* (1989), 24 C.C.E.L. 21 (Alta. Q.B.); accepting near cause: *Beaudoin v. Canadian Corporate News Inc.* (1989), 32 C.C.E.L. 84 (Alta. Q.B.).

§16.6   The Ontario Court of Appeal has recently held, in *Queensbury Enterprises Inc. v. J.R. Corporate Planning Associates Inc.*,[1] that:

... we are not prepared to hold as a matter of law that a defendant [the employer] may never claim a reduction in the damages for wrongful dismissal for conduct short of that justifying dismissal, but we are satisfied that there can be no reduction in the circumstances of this case.

Some of the decisions of the Ontario courts which uphold the "near cause" principle do not label their actions as such; rather, the misconduct of the employee is considered a factor in assessing the appropriate notice period.[2]

[1] (1989), 27 C.C.E.L. 56, at 57. See also *Housepian v. Work Wear Corp. of Canada* (1981), 33 O.R. (2d) 575 (Co. Ct.); *Chantler v. Applied Power* (1982), 1 C.C.E.L. 141 (Ont. H.C.J.).

[2] *Rock v. The Canadian Red Cross Society* (1994), 5 C.C.E.L. (2d) 231 (Ont. Ct. (Gen. Div.)).

§16.6.1 Other recent Ontario decisions have refused to apply the principle[1] or have questioned whether the doctrine is recognized in law.[2]

[1] *TSE v. Trow Consulting Engineers Ltd.* (1995), 14 C.C.E.L. (2d) 132 (Ont. Ct. (Gen. Div.)).

[2] *Judge v. Pelham (Town)* (1995), 9 C.C.E.L. (2d) 134 (Ont. Ct. (Gen. Div.)).

B. BUSINESS EXPENSES PERSONALLY INCURRED IN EARNING REMUNERATION

§16.7 Some executives personally incur business expenses in order to generate income. For example, a director of sales paid wholly or partly on the basis of the performance of his or her sales force may personally have to incur promotional expenses, travel expenses or other costs in an effort to stimulate the workforce to increase sales and, hence, generate more income for himself or herself. In such cases, the issue raised is whether such expenses will be taken into account in the award for wrongful dismissal.

§16.8 Some courts have held that the executive is to be compensated on the basis of his or her net income (remuneration paid by the employer less business expenses normally incurred by the employee to generate his or her income) as stated in his or her income tax return.[1] The reasoning behind these decisions is that the monetary award is intended to place the employee in the same position he or she would have been in had he or she been given reasonable notice of termination and been allowed to remain in the employer's employ during such period. The award is not intended to place the terminated employee in a more advantageous position because of the termination.[2]

¹ *Heuman v. Spartan Agencies Ltd.* (1987), 5 A.C.W.S. (3d) 24 (B.C.S.C.); *Nokes v. A. Lambert Int. Inc.*, unreported, June 4, 1990, C.S.M. 500-05-009685-874 (Que. S.C.); *Jaremko v. A.E. LePage Real Estate Services Ltd.* (1989), 60 D.L.R. (4th) 762 (Ont. C.A.); *Drouin v. Electrolux Canada Ltée, Division de Les Produits C.F.C. Ltée*, D.T.E. 88T-329 (Que. C.A.); *Bell v. Trail-Mate Products of Canada Ltd.* (1986), 15 C.C.E.L. 39 (Ont. Dist. Ct.); *Wilden v. Stationers Warehousing Ltd.* (1984), 26 A.C.W.S. (2d) 432 (Ont. H.C.J.); *George C. Sweet Agencies Ltd. v. Sklar-Peppler Furniture Corp.* (1995), 138 N.S.R. (2d) 101 (C.A.). See also *Nyveen v. Russell Food Equipment Ltd.*, D.T.E. 88T-294 (Que. S.C.).

² See *D.H. Howden & Co. v. Sparling*, [1970] S.C.R. 883.

§16.8.1   Business expenses that would have been incurred by the employee whose income is earned by commissions ought to be taken into account in fixing the amount of his damages to the extent that the employee has not incurred them while trying to mitigate his damages.¹

¹ *Johnston v. Ecolab Ltd./Ecolab Ltée* (1994), 6 C.C.E.L. (2d) 293 (B.C.S.C.); *Kinsey v. SPX Canada Inc.* (1994), 2 C.C.E.L. (2d) 66 (B.C.S.C.).

C.   MITIGATION

1.   Nature of the Obligation

§16.9   A wrongfully terminated executive has the obligation to attempt to mitigate the damages flowing from the loss of his or her employment.¹ Thus, the executive must make an honest and reasonable effort to find comparable employment and he or she must act in a prudent and diligent manner in his or her attempts at mitigation.² The executive must not refuse job offers which are reasonable given the circumstances.³ The rules of mitigation apply whether the employment relationship was governed by a fixed-term employment contract or one of indeterminate duration,⁴ unless the contract specifies to the contrary.

¹ *Bouffard v. Canico Hydraulique Inc.*, D.T.E. 89T-717 (Que. S.C.); *Mifsud v. MacMillan Bathurst Inc.* (1989), 28 C.C.E.L. 228 (Ont. C.A.), leave to appeal to S.C.C. refused 39 O.A.C. 153; *Deis v. S.N.C. Inc.*, D.T.E. 88T-527 (Que. S.C.); *Shiels v. Saskatchewan Government Insurance* (1988), 20 C.C.E.L. 55 (Sask. Q.B.); *Mailly v. Commissaires d'Écoles de la Cité de Hull* (1937), 62 B.R. 278 (Que. C.A.).

² *Fournier v. Tout-Rôti Ltée*, D.T.E. 90T-131 (Que. S.C.), where the court said that the employer is not liable for damages resulting from the employee's carelessness or indolence.

³ *Standard Radio Inc. v. Doudeau*, [1994] R.J.Q. 1782 (Que. C.A.). See also *Logiciels Suivitel Inc. v. Coupal*, [1995] R.J.Q. 375 (Que. C.A.); *Chan v. IBM Canada Ltd.* (1996), 25 C.C.E.L. (2d) 58 (Ont. Ct. (Gen. Div.)).

⁴ *Carr v. Fama Holdings Ltd.* (1989), 40 B.C.L.R. (2d) 125 (C.A.); *Mainville v. Brasserie Michel Desjardins Ltée*, D.T.E. 88T-292 (Que. S.C.), appeal abandoned Sept. 16, 1988, C.A.M. 500-09-000185-884; *Neilson v. Vancouver Hockey Club Ltd.* (1988), 20

C.C.E.L. 155 (B.C.C.A.), leave to appeal to S.C.C. refused (1988), 29 B.C.L.R. (2d) xxxii; *Desrochers v. Centre de Langues Feuilles d'Érables Ltée*, J.E. 80-635 (Que. S.C.), appeal abandoned Aug. 25, 1981, C.A.M. 500-09-000892-802; *Sinclair v. Canadian Ice Machine Co.*, [1955] S.C.R. 777; *Little v. Laing*, [1932] 1 W.W.R. 210 (Sask. C.A.). The New Brunswick Court of Appeal in *Hanley v. C.E.P.U., Local 601N* (1995), 14 C.C.E.L. (2d) 78, determined that under a contract for a fixed term there is an obligation to mitigate, although perhaps not to the same extent as in a contract for an indeterminate period. However, some courts have held that there is no duty to mitigate if the employee had a fixed-term contract.

§16.10 Since the courts attempt to place the executive in the same financial position (but not better) as he or she would have been in but for the wrongful breach of contract, the damage award will be reduced by any income earned during the notice period.[1] This is the first aspect of the principle of mitigation.

[1] *Lachapelle v. Bourse de Montréal*, D.T.E. 92T-218 (Que. S.C.); *Renaud v. Desmarais*, D.T.E. 92T-149 (Que. S.C.); *Brunelle v. Ballets Jazz de Montréal Inc.*, D.T.E. 88T-619 (Que. S.C.); *Lefrançois v. Crane Canada Inc.*, D.T.E. 88T-574 (Que. S.C.); *Ellis v. Whitepass Transportation Ltd.* (1983), 42 B.C.L.R. 351, supp. reasons at 43 B.C.L.R. 103 (C.A.).

§16.11 The second aspect of the obligation to mitigate is that, if the executive fails to search honestly and reasonably for comparable employment, his or her damages will be reduced accordingly.[1] The employer is liable only for those losses that flow from the wrongful or premature termination of the employment contract.[2] The courts will not order an employer to compensate its former executive for losses that could have been avoided had the latter properly mitigated his or her losses. The Supreme Court of Canada has said that:

> . . . the defendant cannot be called upon to pay for avoidable losses which would result in an increase in the quantum of damages payable to the plaintiff.[3]

[1] *Rivard v. Hitachi (H.S.C.) Canada Inc.* (1990), 30 C.C.E.L. 15 (Man. Q.B.); *Queensbury Enterprises Inc. v. J.R. Corporate Planning Associates Inc.* (1989), 27 C.C.E.L. 56 (Ont. C.A.).

[2] *Queensbury Enterprises Inc. v. J.R. Corporate Planning Associates Inc.* (1989), 27 C.C.E.L. 56 (Ont. C.A.); *Mainville v. Brasserie Michel Desjardins Ltée*, D.T.E. 88T-292 (Que. S.C.), appeal abandoned Sept. 16, 1988, C.A.M. 500-09-000185-884; *Jolicoeur v. Lithographie Montréal Ltée*, [1982] C.S. 230 (Que. S.C.), affd Apr. 15, 1987, C.A.M. 500-09-000314-823.

[3] *Red Deer College v. Michaels*, [1976] 2 S.C.R. 324, at 330.

§16.12 Whether an executive has fulfilled the duty to mitigate is a question of fact and each case will be judged on its merits, taking into account all of the relevant circumstances.[1] The employer has the burden of proving that the executive could have reasonably avoided all or part of the losses claimed.[2] Evidence must be adduced which, on a balance of probabilities, shows that no honest and reasonable efforts were made to find comparable employment.

[1] *Logiciels Suivitel Inc. v. Coupal*, [1995] R.J.Q. 375 (Que. C.A.); *Boccia v. Bata Industries Ltd.* (1989), 4 D.E.L.D. 10 (Ont. H.C.J.).

[2] *Red Deer College v. Michaels*, [1976] 2 S.C.R. 324.

§16.13　In order to substantiate such a claim, the employer must establish that comparable employment was available at the relevant time and that the executive failed to make reasonable efforts to secure it.[1] Expert testimony on the probability of finding employment and copies of job advertisements may be helpful in proving that jobs were available in a former executive's field of work. The employer may also show that the executive unreasonably refused a job offer.[2]

[1] *Starr v. Woodward Stores Ltd.* (1991), 37 C.C.E.L. 316 (B.C.S.C); *Cook v. Royal Trust* (1990), 31 C.C.E.L. 6 (B.C.S.C.); *Richer v. Le Droit Ltée* (1983), 23 A.C.W.S. (2d) 484 (Ont. Co. Ct.); *Jorgenson v. Jack Cewe Ltd.* (1978), 9 B.C.L.R. 292 (C.A.), affd [1980] 1 S.C.R. 812.

[2] *McIntosh v. Saskatchewan Water Corp.* (1989), 26 C.C.E.L. 196 (Sask. C.A.); *Richer v. Le Droit Ltée* (1983), 23 A.C.W.S. (2d) 484 (Ont. Co. Ct.).

§16.13.1　The Quebec Court of Appeal[1] has again recently reiterated the terminated employee's obligation to search for work in his same area of expertise and to accept reasonable job offers. The extent of this obligation depends on the circumstances of each case, for example on the economic climate:

> During a period of recession, when job offers are scarce and less interesting financially, one can expect, firstly, tighter job hunting and, secondly, more flexibility in accepting job offers which, although they do not correspond entirely to the job lost, remain interesting because the job offered is in the same sphere of activity or presents comparable benefits.

[1] *Standard Radio inc. v. Doudeau*, D.T.E. 94T-843 (Que. C.A.).

§16.14　The Federal Court has ruled that simply to deliver one's resume to a prospective employer and not follow up with further inquiry may not constitute a reasonable effort to obtain the position.[1]

[1] *Gelfand v. R.*, unreported, Oct. 12, 1988, No. T-2133-86 (F.C.T.D.), revd in part on another question [1994] R.J.Q. 1751 (Que. C.A.).

§16.15　If the court finds that the executive would not have found a similar position even if he or she had actively searched for one, the damage award will not be reduced. For example, in *Stewart v. Standard*

Broadcasting Corp.,[1] the vice-president and general manager of two important radio stations in Montreal was wrongfully dismissed. Evidence demonstrated that no similar employment with similar pay and employment conditions was available in Montreal. In all of Canada, less than a dozen such jobs existed, and they rarely became available. Mr. Stewart searched for employment for approximately two months and, following that period, joined his father in the family business. Notwithstanding the short period of search, the court ordered full compensation for a period of 12 months for the following reasons:

> The proof established that due to the unique character of the broadcasting business in Canada, the scarcity of positions more or less equivalent to that held by the plaintiff, and the infrequency of their availability, the plaintiff by the end of August 1987 had exhausted all possibilities of finding appropriate employment in the radio field and was forced by financial considerations to accept his father's offer of a job.[2]

[1] (1989), 29 C.C.E.L. 290 (Que. S.C.).
[2] (1989), 29 C.C.E.L. 290 (Que. S.C.) at 301.

§16.16 In *Auger v. Albert Dyotte Inc.*,[1] the court held that the plaintiff should have received three months' notice of termination. However, it ordered the payment of only two months' salary as damages for wrongful termination because the plaintiff had failed to mitigate his damages. The plaintiff had waited five months before searching for employment and the defendant proved that the plaintiff's current employer would have hired him within two months of his termination.

[1] D.T.E. 85T-2 (Que. S.C.).

§16.17 In *Pongs v. Dales Canada Inc.*,[1] the court held that a middle management employee, aged 55, dismissed after more than ten years' service, and earning almost $50,000 annually, was entitled to no more than four months' remuneration because he had failed to search promptly and actively for comparable employment. It was found that the employee had refused to send his resume to his former employer and had indicated to his former employer that he intended to renovate his home. He had also indicated to a representative of one of the placement agencies that he was going on vacation and would call upon his return. He never called.

[1] D.T.E. 91T-1288 (Que. S.C.).

§16.18 In *Reynolds v. First City Trust Co.*,[1] the British Columbia Supreme Court found that a former senior officer and vice-president was not diligent in his search for employment and, accordingly, reduced the notice period. Evidence showed that the plaintiff had responded to seven advertisements found in the *Vancouver Sun* and the *Toronto Globe & Mail* National Edition. He did not look at the Calgary newspapers, even though he had roots and connections there, or at the newspapers from other cities. The plaintiff had not availed himself of executive search firms or relocation counsellors. He did not seek help from the owners of the defendant who might have extended help. He did not ask for letters of reference from either of the presidents for whom he had worked nor contact his long-time former employer, connections in the Toronto financial community, nor had he searched for employment in Toronto. In addition, the defendant's counsel had submitted as evidence advertisements in both the *Vancouver Sun* and the *Globe & Mail* to which the plaintiff had not responded even though the job specifications had similarities to those to which he had responded.

[1]   (1989), 27 C.C.E.L. 194 (B.C.S.C.).

§16.19   In *Sotnick v. Lyphomed Inc.*,[1] the president and general manager of the defendant, a subsidiary of a U.S. company, was offered the position of general manager of the Canadian portion of a joint-venture partnership that had been formed. The position would have reported to a committee composed of both the Canadian company and another company rather than merely two representatives of the U.S. parent. The court held that technically the employee was terminated from his prior employment without reasonable notice. The employee's action in damages for wrongful termination was dismissed, however, because the court found that he had failed to mitigate his damages. Although the employee had no obligation to accept the position offered, he had an obligation to seek employment to otherwise mitigate his damages. The court held that the employee should have accepted the general manager position to mitigate his damages. The fact that he would have suffered a loss of approximately $6,000 per annum in remuneration ($68,000 base salary plus $8,000 bonus) was not significant enough to enable him to turn down the job since the salary offer was substantially the same, the working conditions would not be substantially different, and there was no evidence that the work was demeaning. Furthermore, there were no acrimonious personal relationships.

[1]   [1991] O.J. No. 146, No. 22101/87 (Ont. H.C.J.). See also *Sawarin v. Canadian Acceptance Corp.* (1983), 34 Sask. R. 234 (C.A.).

2.   Alternative Employment

§16.20   An issue of obvious practical importance is the nature of the position of employment the courts will consider reasonable for the executive to seek, accept or even refuse in mitigation. The executive is required to make honest and reasonable efforts to find and to accept, if available, comparable employment. Generally, an executive is not obliged to accept work of a different nature or at a lower-level position within the hierarchy of an employer's organization even if the remuneration offered is the same. However, this may not be the case if the executive had little experience in the field, industry or employment from which he was terminated. Moreover, if he or she had equal or greater experience in another field or industry, then the executive may be in breach of the duty to mitigate for failure to search for employment in that area in the event the search to replace his or her former job with a similar one proved unsuccessful.

§16.21 The recent case of *Stevens v. Globe & Mail*[1] provides an excellent example of the obligations and rights of a senior employee in searching for comparable employment. The plaintiff, Stevens, was appointed managing editor of the defendant newspaper in 1983. His employment was terminated following the appointment of a new editor-in-chief. After his termination, he looked for management jobs in the newspaper and other related businesses, particularly the *Toronto Star*, *Southam Press*, *MacLean's*, the *Fifth Estate* and several publishing corporations. There was a writing job available in London, England through *Southam Press* which Stevens declined to accept in the belief that he would not ultimately obtain a management position. He eventually obtained a one-year appointment as a university lecturer, and accepted a position as a freelance columnist at the *Vancouver Sun* and as a consultant with T.V. Ontario. In determining whether Mr. Stevens had fulfilled his mitigation obligation, the court stated:

> I am of the view that Stevens, having been in the management stream since 1981, managing editor since 1983, and a member of the *Globe and Mail* management team since 1985, did not act unreasonably in seeking management positions in the period following his removal as managing editor and, in particular, for not accepting the Southam London writing position on the basis of there being a reasonable prospect of his obtaining management positions in Canada which would, in all probability, be lessened if he accepted the position in London and thus would not be on the scene.
>
> No evidence was adduced on behalf of the *Globe and Mail* that any other suitable employment positions (management or otherwise) were available to the plaintiff in 1989 or 1990.
>
> Therefore, for the foregoing reasons, I find that the defendants have failed to demonstrate, on a balance of probabilities, that Stevens has failed to properly mitigate his damages . . .[2]

---

[1] (1992), 7 O.R. (3d) 520 (Ont. Ct. (Gen. Div.)), appealed on separate grounds (1996), 28 O.R. (3d) 481 (C.A.).

[2] (1992), 7 O.R. (3d) 520 (Ont. Ct. (Gen. Div.)) at 528.

§16.22   The British Columbia Court of Appeal has held:

> That "duty" — to take reasonable steps to obtain equivalent employment else-where and to accept such employment if available — is not an obligation owed by the dismissed employee to the former employer to act in the employer's interests....
>
> The duty to "act reasonably", in seeking and accepting alternate employment, cannot be a duty to take such steps as will reduce the claim against the defaulting former employer, but must be a duty to take such steps as a reasonable person in the dismissed employee's position would take *in his own interests* — to maintain his income and his position in his industry, trade or profession. The question whether or not the employee has acted reasonably must be judged in relation to his own position, and not in relation to that of the employer who has wrongfully dismissed him. The former employer cannot have any right to expect that the former employee will accept lower paying alternate employment with doubtful prospects, and then sue for the difference between what he makes in that work and what he would have made had he received the notice to which he was entitled.[1]

[1]   *Forshaw v. Aluminex Extrusions Ltd.* (1989), 27 C.C.E.L. 208, at 212-13 (emphasis added). See also *Nevin v. British Columbia Hazardous Waste Management Corp.* (1995), 129 D.L.R. (4th) 569 (B.C.C.A.).

§16.23   In *Torrebadell v. Dave Buck Ford Sales Ltd.*,[1] the plaintiff's award for wrongful dismissal was reduced by $20,000 even though the plaintiff had earned only $15,000 during the notice period. The court ruled that work was available in the plaintiff's area of expertise which would have allowed him to earn $20,000 during the notice period. Thus, the former employer did not have to bear the cost of the plaintiff's choice of a new career:

> The plaintiff has a duty to mitigate. The evidence establishes that he could have earned $20,000 over an eight month period in the position of a sales manager in the car industry. However, he chose to seek out a different career and during that period of time he was able to earn something less, amounting to $15,491. The defendant is entitled to have damages reduced to the extent of the plaintiff's failure to mitigate.[2]

[1]   (1987), 4 A.C.W.S. (3d) 273 (B.C.S.C.).
[2]   (1987), 4 A.C.W.S. (3d) 273 (B.C.S.C.), at 9 of the judgment.

§16.24   Can the duty to mitigate require that a person take an alternate offered position with the employer responsible for the wrongful dismissal? It would appear that in certain circumstances, an executive ought to accept the position, at least on a temporary basis, while continuing to search for other employment. If the employer offers the same kind of work or similar work which a reasonable person would accept, the executive must accept such work, failing which a court will reduce his or her claim accordingly.[1] The Ontario Court of Appeal[2] dealt with this issue where the plaintiff had been transferred to a different position within the same organization, which he viewed as an act amounting to constructive dismissal. The court stated:

> The fact that the transfer to a new position may constitute in law a constructive dismissal does not eliminate the obligation of the employee to look at the new position offered and evaluate it as a means of mitigating damages. . . . Where the salary offered is the same, where the working conditions are not substantially different or the work demeaning, and where the personal relationships involved are not acrimonious (as in this case), it is reasonable to expect the employee to accept the position offered in mitigation of damages during a reasonable notice period, or until he finds acceptable employment elsewhere.[3]

[1] *Larochelle v. Kindersley Transport Ltd.* (1990), 33 C.C.E.L. 236 (Sask. Q.B.); *Entreprises de Pipe-Line Universel Ltée v. Prévost*, D.T.E. 88T-549 (Que. C.A.). See also *Buchanan v. Canada Valve Inc.* (1987), 59 O.R. (2d) 681 (Ont. H.C.J.), where the employer had been taken over by another company. The court ruled that the employee should have accepted the new position in carrying out his duty to mitigate.

[2] *Mifsud v. MacMillan Bathurst Inc.* (1989), 28 C.C.E.L. 228 (Ont. C.A.), leave to appeal to S.C.C. refused 39 O.A.C. 153. But, see also *Davidson v. Allelix Inc.* (1991), 7 O.R. (3d) 581 where the Ontario Court of Appeal found that it would be unreasonable to expect the plaintiff to accept the alternate position offered by the employer since such position lacked the characteristics of the managerial position which had attracted the plaintiff.

[3] *Mifsud v. MacMillan Bathurst Inc.* (1989), 28 C.C.E.L. 228 at 238.

§16.25 In *Deis v. S.N.C. Inc.*,[1] the Quebec Superior Court reduced the executive's losses by the amount he would have earned had he accepted his former employer's offer of part-time work for a five-month period. The court ruled that working part-time would have allowed Deis sufficient time to search for alternative permanent employment.

[1] D.T.E. 88T-527 (Que. S.C.).

§16.26 However, the executive is not expected to accept a position with his or her former employer if that would involve working in an atmosphere of hostility, embarrassment or humiliation.[1]

[1] *Cayen v. Woodward Stores Ltd.* (1991), 34 C.C.E.L. 95 (B.C.S.C.), revd on other grounds (1993), 75 B.C.L.R. (2d) 110 (C.A.); *Larochelle v. Kindersley Transport Ltd.* (1990), 33 C.C.E.L. 236 (Sask. Q.B.); *Misfud v. MacMillan Bathurst Inc.* (1990), 28 C.C.E.L. 228 (Ont. C.A.), leave to appeal to S.C.C. refused 39 O.A.C. 153; *Pelliccia v. Pink Pages Advertising Ltd.* (1989), 28 C.C.E.L. 261 (B.C.S.C.); *Farquhar v. Butler Brothers Supplies Ltd.* (1988), 23 B.C.L.R. (2d) 89 (C.A.); *Park v. Parsons Brown & Co.*, unreported, 1988, Vancouver Doc. C875177 (B.C.S.C.), vard (1989), 27 C.C.E.L. 224 (C.A.); *Lesiuk v. B.C. Forest Products Ltd.* (1984), 56 B.C.L.R. 216 (S.C.), affd (1986), 15 C.C.E.L. 91 (C.A.).

§16.27   Some courts have ruled that an executive who is offered an inferior position at a lesser salary may be entitled to refuse such offer.[1] Similarly, the obligation to mitigate one's damages does not oblige a person to accept a job offered by the former employer when the executive has no qualification for this job and the former job is still available.[2]

---

[1]   *Cook v. Royal Trust* (1990), 31 C.C.E.L. 6 (B.C.S.C.); *Vigeant v. Canadian Thermos Products Ltd.*, D.T.E. 88T-295 (Que. S.C.); *Tymrick v. Viking Helicopters Ltd.* (1985), 6 C.C.E.L. 225 (Ont. H.C.J.); *Eyers v. City Buick Pontiac Cadillac Ltd.* (1984), 6 C.C.E.L. 234 (Ont. H.C.J.), vard. 13 O.A.C. 66 (C.A.); *Duplessis v. Irving Pulp & Paper Ltd.* (1982), 39 N.B.R. (2d) 584 (Q.B.), vard (1983), 1 C.C.E.L. 196 (C.A.).

[2]   *Desrosiers v. Association Iris Inc.*, D.T.E. 89T-665 (Ct. of Que.).

§16.28   Not only is failing to search for similar employment or for employment for which one is qualified failure to mitigate, but seeking employment of a different character may also contravene one's duty to mitigate. Generally, courts have held that the former employer does not have to support the costs of the executive's career change.

§16.29   In *Priestman v. Swift Sure Courier Services Ltd.*,[1] the plaintiff, a sales representative for a courier company, was terminated. He had been in the courier business for nine years. Instead of seeking similar employment, Priestman decided to begin a new career in the field of insurance. Priestman studied and passed the necessary exams but was unable to earn more than $2,000 in the first year following his termination. The British Columbia Supreme Court held that Priestman had failed in his obligation to mitigate his damages and ordered payment of two weeks' salary which, according to the court, corresponded to the time it would have taken Priestman to find employment similar to that from which he had been terminated. Indeed, a representative of the defendant company had testified to the effect that at the time of Priestman's termination, there was a strong demand for experienced sales representatives. The court stated:

> In the final analysis, the question is one of fact and not of law. The issue is: did the plaintiff "act reasonably in the adoption of remedial measures"?
>
> In my view, while the plaintiff was perfectly entitled to pursue whatever career opportunities he wished, the realistic ramifications of his choice are not for the defendant's account. The plaintiff could not reasonably expect to enjoy gainful employment in the life insurance industry. Given his age, his lack of any contacts, and his extended absence from the industry, his choice did indeed amount to a choice to adopt a new life-style based on lesser earnings.
>
> Even if the plaintiff's new career choice was a reasonable one, the question of the appropriate amount of notice is dictated to some extent by the degree of difficulty, if any, which the plaintiff could have been expected to experience in finding similar alternate employment. The plaintiff admits that he did not look for any

work in the courier business. There appears to be no dispute that an equivalent position as a commissioned salesman was readily available. Indeed, Cahill testified that this was particularly so in the case of an experienced salesman such as Mr. Priestman. In these circumstances, I find the two week period of notice was reasonable. To the extent that this period of notice was not adequate, in my view any additional period of notice (and thus any additional damages) are offset by the plaintiff's own failure to take reasonable steps to mitigate his loss.[2]

[1]   (1989), 14 A.C.W.S. (3d) 251 (B.C.S.C.).
[2]   (1989), 14 A.C.W.S. (3d) 251 (B.C.S.C.) at 8 of the judgment.

3. Geographic Area of Search

§16.30   The geographic area within which a person must search for employment in order to satisfy the duty to mitigate and whether one should be forced to relocate to another city or province has led to much debate. Although many courts have held, for a variety of reasons, that failure to relocate or restricting one's area of search to the town where the employee had been employed is not unreasonable,[1] other courts have come to the opposite conclusion. From these decisions, it would appear that generally a person is not required to relocate or travel great distances in order to mitigate his or her loss. However, the nature of the position, custom in the industry, poor prospects of employment in a particular area and a variety of other factors have been relied upon by the courts to conclude in certain cases that refusing to relocate was unreasonable.[2]

[1]   *Allen v. CP Express & Transport Ltd.* (1989), 29 C.C.E.L. 279 (B.C.S.C.); *Suttie v. Metro Transit Operating Co.* (1983), 1 C.C.E.L. 123 (B.C.S.C.), affd (1985), 9 C.C.E.L. 19 (C.A.); *David v. Eastend Union Hospital Bd.* (1979), 99 D.L.R. (3d) 73 (Sask. Q.B.).
[2]   *Kozak v. Hallmark Engineering Ltd.* (1983), 1 C.C.E.L. 113 (B.C.S.C.); *Stefanovic v. SNC Inc.* (1988), 22 C.C.E.L. 82 (Ont. H.C.J.).

§16.31   In *Shiels v. Saskatchewan Government Insurance*,[1] after having been dismissed, the plaintiff looked for work in Saskatchewan and Manitoba without success. He was contacted about two possible opportunities in Ottawa but did not apply for either, in large part due to the fact that he was not prepared to move the distance from Saskatchewan to Ottawa. The court stated:

> There was no duty upon the plaintiff to move across the country, possibly at his own expense, simply to lessen the damages to which he was otherwise entitled.[2]

Unfortunately, the court did not discuss the reasons for this conclusion.

[1]   (1988), 20 C.C.E.L. 55 (Sask. Q.B.).

²   (1988), 20 C.C.E.L. 55 (Sask. Q.B.) at 67.

§16.32   Evidence that comparable employment was available in an area where a reasonable person would have searched and that the plaintiff failed to carry out that search should suffice to prove failure to mitigate. Indeed, it may be reasonable in the beginning to restrict one's search to the area of former employment. However, as time passes and alternative employment cannot be found, the reasonable person test will probably require the executive to enlarge the area of search.

§16.33   In *Chouinard v. Groupe Commerce, Cie d'Assurance*,[1] the plaintiff had restricted his search for employment to the St-Hyacinthe area. The Quebec Superior Court ruled that it would uphold a finding of failure to mitigate if the employer proved that his former employee had refused a job offer which required him to leave this area.[2] The plaintiff had been without employment for four years.

¹   D.T.E. 90T-528 (Que. S.C.).
²   The authors disagree with the court's reported reasoning, on the basis that failure to mitigate should not necessarily require proof of refusal of a job offer.

§16.34   In *Thomas Cook Overseas Ltd. v. McKee*,[1] McKee, a unilingual anglophone employee, held employment in Quebec. The Court of Appeal was of the view that McKee's decision to search for employment outside Quebec was reasonable. The court ruled it would have been unreasonable to require that he retrain in another field of work within Quebec, rather than move, given his age and knowledge of the English language only.

¹   D.T.E. 83T-572 (Que. C.A.).

§16.35   In the case of *Smith v. Viking Helicopter Ltd.*,[1] the Ontario Court of Appeal placed significant emphasis on the employer's reason for a change of location and its consequent impact upon the employee in question. The court stated:

> In my opinion a damage action for constructive dismissal must be founded on conduct by the employer and not simply on the perception of that conduct by the employee. The employer must be responsible for some objective conduct which constitutes a fundamental change in employment or a unilateral change of a significant term of that employment. A decision to change its manner of conducting its business or a move to another place of business does not necessarily result in such a fundamental breach of its contract with its employees as to constitute a constructive dismissal.[2]

In this case, the employer, for economic reasons, had moved its operation from Ottawa to a location within the province of Quebec. The plaintiff employee was offered a position of continuing employment at the Quebec location as well as his moving expenses and costs. The employee sued for constructive dismissal. Although the employee was successful at trial, the Ontario Court of Appeal unanimously overturned the trial judge's decision and held that he had not been constructively dismissed. It should be noted that not only was the employee requested to move from one province to another, the move also would have resulted in a change from a common law environment to a civil law environment. It would appear that this case will serve as the guide by which future issues of constructive dismissal by reason of geographic location will be assessed within the province of Ontario.

[1] (1989), 24 C.C.E.L. 113 (Ont. C.A.).
[2] (1989), 24 C.C.E.L. 113 (Ont. C.A.) at 116-17.

4. Starting a Business (Self-Employment)

§16.36 Whether embarking upon a career by starting one's own business or embarking upon self-employment fulfils the obligation to mitigate is a question which has frequently been raised. The courts have found that starting a business or commencing self-employment may satisfy the duty to mitigate. In this respect, some of the courts have required the former employee to have attempted, even though unsuccessfully, to replace the lost employment by similar or comparable employment and show that the failure to search was reasonable given the circumstances of the case.[1] One court found that it was reasonable for the plaintiff, a man who had worked for 26 years in a large institution in the financial services market, to determine that he could no longer depend on a large corporation for job security and to go into business for himself, given his age and his experience.[2] He intended to open a wine kit processing business in a mall.

[1] *Cook v. Royal Trust* (1990), 31 C.C.E.L. 6 (B.C.S.C.); *Forshaw v. Aluminex Extrusions Ltd.* (1989), 27 C.C.E.L. 208 (B.C.C.A.); *Mainville v. Brasserie Michel Desjardins Ltée*, D.T.E. 88T-292 (Que. S.C.), appeal abandoned Sept. 16, 1988, C.A.M. 500-09-000185-884; *Shiels v. Saskatchewan Government Insurance* (1988), 20 C.C.E.L. 55 (Sask. Q.B.).
[2] *Ward v. Royal Trust Corp.* (1993), 1 C.C.E.L. (2d) 153 (B.C.S.C.). See also *Nevin v. British Columbia Hazardous Waste Management Corp.* (1995), 129 D.L.R. (4th) 569 (B.C.C.A.).

§16.37 In *Christakos v. Chantex Fashions Inc.*,[1] the Ontario Supreme Court limited the damage award for wrongful dismissal because it was shown that had the employee sought similar employment rather than start a business, he could reasonably have found employment. The court stated:

> In any event, I am satisfied that Christakos did not make reasonable efforts to mitigate his loss. I am of the view that after selling shares in Charan, and after payment of commission, that left him with approximately $1,351,000, he quickly decided he was not going to work for someone else but would open up his own business with Dubrow. Their new business was incorporated on January 14, 1988. In my view, Christakos made no genuine effort to find another job comparable to the one he had lost. If he had made such an effort, I am satisfied he could have replaced his job within six months.[2]

Accordingly, the notice period was set at six months.

[1]   (1989), 15 A.C.W.S. (3d) 429 (Ont. H.C.J.).
[2]   (1989), 15 A.C.W.S. (3d) 429 (Ont. H.C.J.) at 6 of the judgment.

§16.38 Conversely, in the case of *Hillhouse v. Alexander Consulting Group Ltd.*,[1] the employee, an actuary and pension consultant, contacted 13 firms, followed up with three or four of them, and made further attempts following his dismissal. Only one month after having been dismissed, the employee set up his own consulting firm but continued to search for alternative employment for another two months. Without reasons, the court found that there was no lack of mitigation on the part of the employee.

[1]   (1989), 28 C.C.E.L. 73 (Ont. H.C.J.).

§16.39 In another case, *Shiels v. Saskatchewan Government Insurance*,[1] the court stated:

> . . . the plaintiff's area of expertise is very narrow, and his employment opportunities were correspondingly few. There simply is not a ready employment market for his skills. His decision to establish his own business certainly appears to have been the right one.

[1]   (1988), 20 C.C.E.L. 55 (Sask. Q.B.), at 67.

§16.40 The courts appear to require the plaintiff to demonstrate that, having followed all reasonable steps to find suitable employment, he or she had no other reasonable choice but to start a business. Alternatively, it must be shown that the prospects of starting a successful business were greater than those of finding similar employment.

§16.41 In *Oxman v. Dustbane Enterprises Ltd.*,[1] the Ontario Court of Appeal rejected the defendant company's allegation that Mr. Oxman had failed in his obligation to mitigate his damages because he had started his own business. At the time of his dismissal, Mr. Oxman held the position of vice-president and earned more than $100,000 annually. The court, with little discussion, concluded that, on the evidence submitted at first instance, the employee should not be penalized for starting his own business. It is suggested that the court was influenced by the fact that the notice period was only six months, as it stated:

> . . . it is difficult to expect a senior executive making $100,000 per year to re-establish himself in a similar position in the area of his limited expertise within that time.[2]

[1] (1988), 23 C.C.E.L. 157 (Ont. C.A.). See also *Gignac v. Trust Général du Canada*, D.T.E. 91T-231 (Que. S.C.).

[2] *Oxman v. Dustbane Enterprises*, (1988), 23 C.C.E.L. 157 (Ont. C.A.) at 160-61.

§16.42 Income earned from self-employment during the notice period will be deducted from the damages award.[1] However, business start-up costs may be allowed if incurred during the notice period.[2] In addition, the increase in equity of the business during this same period may also be applied in the reduction of the damages award.[3]

[1] *P.C.L. Construction Inc. v. Holmes* (1994), 8 C.C.E.L. 192 (Alta. C.A.).

[2] *Shiels v. Saskatchewan Government Insurance* (1988), 20 C.C.E.L. 55 (Sask. Q.B.).

[3] In *Shiels v. Saskatchewan Government Insurance*, *ibid.*, the court was asked to value in mitigation the long-term value of the new business. The court did not discount this but ruled that it had no evidence of value and, therefore, it would be speculative to do so.

§16.43 The Alberta Court of Queen's Bench, in *Henze v. Kamor Furniture Ltd.*,[1] reduced the employee's damages to three months because in the year following his dismissal the plaintiff had played an important role in the planning and production of his spouse's business. The court was of the opinion that during this time the plaintiff could have earned income equivalent to that which he had earned from his former employer, even though his wife's company showed a deficit. The court stated:

> I am satisfied that Klaval Design was under way by October or November of 1982 and that the plaintiff played a significant role in its planning and production. I am satisfied that by 1st April 1983, the plaintiff was devoting almost his total time to the affairs of this company. . . . [F]rom 1st April 1983 on, and notwithstanding the alleged loss of Klaval Design for 1983, the plaintiff was earning or was entitled to earn from Klaval Design at least as much as his monthly salary and benefits from the defendant.[2]

[1] (1985), 39 Alta. L.R. (2d) 343 (Q.B.).

[2] (1985), 39 Alta. L.R. (2d) 343 (Q.B.), at 349.

5. Termination Provision

§16.44 If an employment contract or a termination agreement contains a provision which provides expressly for the payment of a fixed amount upon termination of employment, the executive is entitled to the amount fixed by the contract and nothing more. Consequently, it has been held that the executive is under no obligation to mitigate and the employer may not claim a reduction for sums earned by the executive during the notice period where the contract expressly provides for all of the obligations of the employer upon termination.[1]

> [1] *Bédard v. Capitale (la) maître courtier inc.*, D.T.E. 94T-814 (Que. C.A.) on appeal; *Hamel v. Centre d'accueil de Wotton*, D.T.E. 92T-151 (Que. S.C.) (on appeal); *Paquin v. Gainers Inc.* (1991), 37 C.C.E.L. 113 (Alta. C.A.); *Wilkinson v. Kwantlen College* (1991), 38 C.C.E.L. 303 (B.C.S.C.); *Mills v. R. in right of Alberta*, [1986] 5 W.W.R. 567 (Alta. C.A.); *Bazinet v. Radiodiffusion Mutuelle Ltée*, D.T.E. 85T-640 (Que. S.C.), vard D.T.E. 89T-1081 (C.A.); *Emery v. Royal Oak Mines Inc.* (1995), 24 O.R. (3d) 302 (Gen. Div.), supp. reasons 26 O.R. (3d) 216 (Gen. Div.).

§16.44.1 In *Desrochers v. Emballages Novotel Inc.*,[1] the Quebec Superior Court held that the employer may not rely on a notice provision that is stipulated in an employment contract when the employer acts in bad faith.

> [1] D.T.E. 93T-1182 (Que. S.C.).

6. Anticipated Mitigation

§16.44.2 When the notice period payable to a wrongfully terminated executive, as determined by a court, extends beyond the date of the court's decision, should the court deduct from the award in damages a sum representing what the executive may earn between the date of the decision and the expiry of the notice period, in recognition of his duty to mitigate? The same question arises in the case of a prematurely terminated fixed term contract when the term extends past the date of the court's decision. Surely, if the executive has a job at the time of the hearing and there is nothing to indicate that the situation will change during the remaining portion of the notice period which his former employer should have given him, then those future earnings should be deducted from the pay in lieu of notice for the corresponding period. In addition, some courts have reduced the award of damages by taking into account the possibility that the plaintiff may find a job after the trial and before expiry of the employment contract period[1] or the notice period.[2] One court has recently held however, that if there is nothing in the evidence to demonstrate that the plaintiff will earn some revenue in that coming period, then no amount should be deducted as anticipated mitigation.[3] Other courts have refused to discount the damages award where evidence showed that it was unlikely that the plaintiff would find employment during the balance of the notice period or the term.[4]

---

[1] *Vondette v. Vancouver Port Corp.* (1987), 21 B.C.L.R. (2d) 209 (S.C.).

[2] *Smith v. Pacific National Exhibition* (1987), 34 C.C.E.L. 64 (B.C.S.C.); *Carlson v. Ideal Cement Co.* (1987), 18 B.C.L.R. (2d) 24 (S.C.); *Boyd v. Whistler Mountain Ski Corp.*, [1990] B.C.J. No. 821 (S.C.);

[3] *Ward v. Royal Trust Corp.* (1993), 1 C.C.E.L. (2d) 153 (B.C.S.C.).

[4] *Kinsey v. SPX Canada Inc.* (1994), 2 C.C.E.L. (2d) 66 (B.C.S.C.); *Tokawa v. Canadianoxy Industrial Chemicals Ltd.* (1993), 49 C.C.E.L. 247 (B.C.S.C.).

D. PENSION, DISABILITY OR UNEMPLOYMENT BENEFITS RECEIVED DURING THE NOTICE PERIOD

1. Pension Benefits

§16.45 Are pension payments received by an employee who elects to take retirement after his dismissal deductible from the award a court would grant in lieu of reasonable notice? Some courts have deducted from the damages payable to the employee any pension payments the employee received during the notice period.[1] Other courts have taken the opposite view and have held that pension payments should not be deducted.[2] In *Cohnstaedt v. University of Regina*,[3] Sherstobitoff, J.A., in dissent, calculated the appellant's damages to be an amount equivalent to his gross salary during the period in question, without regard to pension contributions and without regard to pension benefits actually received or that he would have received had he worked. On appeal, the Supreme Court allowed the appeal (based on other grounds) "substantially for the reasons of the dissenting judge, Mr. Justice Sherstobitoff, in the Court of Appeal",[4] with no mention of this particular calculation.

---

[1] *Taylor v. C.B.C.*, unreported, Nov. 7, 1984, File No. 15243/82 (Ont. H.C.J.); *Laakso v. R.* (1986), 15 C.C.E.L. 139 (F.C.T.D.); *Rivers v. Gulf Canada Ltd.* (1986), 13 C.C.E.L. 131 (Ont. H.C.J.); *Perry v. Gulf Minerals Canada Ltd.* (1985), T.L.W. 513-025 (Ont. H.C.J.).

[2] *Edwards v. Royal Alexandra Hospitals* (1994), 5 C.C.E.L. (2d) 196 (Alta. Q.B.); *Heinz v. Cana Construction Co.* (1987), 55 Alta. L.R. (2d) 382 (Q.B.); *Horodynski v. Electrohome Ltd.*, [1990] O.J. No. 2088 (Ont. Ct. (Gen Div.)) (for the reason that early retirement benefits were offset by the fact that the employee's later entitlement would be reduced); *Girling v. Crown Cork & Seal Canada Inc.* (1994), 92 B.C.L.R. (2d) 181 (S.C.), affd (1995), 9 B.C.L.R. (3d) 1 (C.A.); *Chandler v. Ball Packaging Products Canada Ltd.* (1992), 2 C.C.P.B. 99 (Ont. Ct. (Gen. Div.)), affd (1993), 2 C.C.P.B. 99 (Div. Ct.); *Wright v. Kimberly-Clark Canada Inc.* (1995), 11 C.C.E.L. (2d) 34 (Ont. Ct. (Gen. Div.)); *Emery v. Royal Oak Mines Inc.* (1995), 24 O.R. (3d) 302 (Gen. Div.), supp. reasons 26 O.R. (3d) 216 (Gen. Div.).

³ [1994] 5 W.W.R. 154 (Sask. C.A.).
⁴ [1996] 1 W.W.R. 153 (S.C.C.), at 153.

§16.45.1 One court has said that although the general rule in wrongful dismissal cases is that pension benefits are not to be deducted from damages in lieu of notice, *enhanced* early retirement benefits made available to employees for the express purpose of compensating the loss of employment resulting from a reorganization are to be deducted. If the enhanced benefits are linked to an employee's severance of employment, a portion of the actuarial value of these benefits constitutes payment in lieu of or towards reasonable notice.[1] The result is the same as if the value of the benefit was deducted from the damages award.

¹ *Regan v. Commercial Union Assurance Co.* (1993), 48 C.C.E.L. 208 (B.C.S.C.).

§16.46 Interestingly, none of these cases mentioned the Supreme Court of Canada decision of *Guy v. Trizec Equities Ltd.*,[1] in which Guy was injured when a piece of plywood fell from the roof of an office building owned and occupied by Trizec. At the time, Guy was vice-president and general manager of Nova Scotia Savings & Loans. He suffered physical injury which forced him to retire. Upon retirement he was entitled to a yearly pension of $14,000 plus other compensation for his service as a director.

¹ [1979] 2 S.C.R. 756.

§16.47 Guy sued Trizec for the loss of future earnings from employment as a result of his injuries. He was awarded $250,000 against Trizec at trial. The Court of Appeal not only reduced this amount but deducted from it the pension benefits Guy received from Nova Scotia Savings & Loans' pension plan. The Supreme Court held that the pension benefits were not to be deducted from the award, as they were derived from a contributory pension plan contracted with Guy's employer, and that the payments made pursuant to that plan were akin to payments under an insurance policy.

§16.48 The Supreme Court approved the House of Lords' decision in *Parry v. Cleaver*,[1] which had held that a claim for lost employment earnings due to injuries should not be affected by the pension payments the plaintiff was receiving. The House of Lords held that moneys received under a contract of insurance are not to be taken into account in assessing damages, since it would be unjust that money spent by an injured man on premiums should enure to the benefit of a tortfeasor and that a pension is a form of insurance. Lord Pearce said regarding pension payments that:

> . . . they are intended by payer and payee to benefit the workman and not to be a subvention for wrongdoers who will cause him [the employee] damage.[2]

However, it would seem that Lord Pearce recognized that the court was deciding this issue within the particular context of personal injury where the payments come from a relationship to which the wrongdoer is not a party. Indeed, Lord Pearce acknowledged that had the situation involved an employer-employee relationship, a different approach to the deductibility of pension payments may have been warranted:

> . . . there might be some difference of approach where it is the employer himself who is the defendant tortfeasor, and the pension rights in question come from an insurance arrangement which he himself has made with the plaintiff as his employee.[3]

[1] [1970] A.C. 1.
[2] [1970] A.C. 1 at 37.
[3] [1970] A.C. 1.

§16.49 *Guy v. Trizec Equities Ltd.* has been applied on numerous occasions since 1980.[1] However, like *Guy*, these cases have been decided outside the employment or wrongful dismissal context. As well, none of these cases make reference to the possibility or need for a different approach in situations where the employer, rather than a third-party wrongdoer, is the defendant.

[1] See, *e.g.*, *Poole v. Morgan* (1987), 50 Alta. L.R. (2d) 120 (Q.B.); *Crew Estate v. Nicholson* (1989), 68 O.R. (2d) 232 (C.A.).

§16.50 More recently, again in the personal injury context, the Supreme Court of Canada in *Ratych v. Bloomer*[1] acknowledged the earlier Supreme Court decisions and approved the principles enunciated in *Parry* that benefits in the nature of proceeds of insurance should not be deducted from a plaintiff's damages. However, the Court did stress the fundamental rule that the measure of damages should be the plaintiff's actual loss and overruled decisions which had failed to deduct from a claim for lost earnings wage benefits paid while a plaintiff is unable to work, except where the employer or fund which paid the wage benefits is entitled to be reimbursed for them on the principle of subrogation (such as workers' compensation). As the *Ratych* case only involved the issue of the deductibility of wage benefits, the Court did not discuss or confirm the reasoning of earlier decisions which held that pension benefits are akin to insurance and said that its comments regarding the deductibility of wage benefits

> . . . should not be taken as extending to types of collateral benefits other than lost earnings, such as insurance paid for by the plaintiff and gratuitous payments made by third parties. Those issues are not before the Court and must be left for another day.[2]

¹ [1990] 1 S.C.R. 940.
² [1990] 1 S.C.R. 940, at 983.

§**16.51** The cases above which held that pension payments were akin to insurance analyzed contributory pension plans. A question arises whether non-contributory pension payments would also be held to be akin to insurance. Although it would appear that no court has dealt directly with this issue, two courts have suggested, *in obiter*, that the fact that a pension plan is non-contributory would not change its characterization.[1]

¹ *Melnychuk v. Moore*, [1989] 6 W.W.R. 367 (Man. C.A.), at 383; *Parry v. Cleaver*, [1970] A.C. 1 (H.L.), at 37. See also the decision of the Supreme Court in *Cunningham v. Wheeler*, [1994] 1 S.C.R. 359, revg in part (1991), 95 D.L.R. (4th) 655 (B.C.C.A.), where, in the context of an insurance disability claim, the court determined that non-contributory disability benefits will be viewed akin to insurance where there is some evidence that some type of consideration was given by the employee in return for the payments.

2. Disability Benefits

§**16.52** Do workers' compensation benefits, disability benefits or sick pay received during the notice period reduce the damage award? Prior to the decision of the Supreme Court of Canada in *Sylvester*,[1] discussed below, the law was unsettled and the answer would vary depending upon the jurisdiction in which the claim was brought. For example, the Quebec Court of Appeal, in *Industries de Caoutchouc Mondo (Canada) Ltée v. Leblanc*,[2] had held that any workers' compensation benefits received during the notice period could not serve to reduce the damages for wrongful dismissal. This same reasoning had also been applied by the Ontario courts.[3] However, other courts, including the Alberta Court of Appeal, had found these benefits to be properly deductible. The Alberta court stated:

> If the money came from earnings from a complete stranger, the appellant would have the advantage of it in mitigation of the loss. As a matter of policy, I am quite unable to see why it ought not to be deducted where it is paid from a fund contributed to by the employer by force of law, particularly where the pay-

ment is in lieu of earnings and to compensate for their loss while unable to work because of injury sustained during the course of the respondent's employment.[4]

[1] *Sylvester v. British Columbia* (1997), 146 D.L.R. (4th) 207.
[2] D.T.E. 87T-394.
[3] *Veerdonk v. Dustbane Enterprises Ltd.*, [1978] 3 A.C.W.S. 229 (Ont. Dist. Ct.).
[4] *Salmi v. Greyfriar Developments Ltd.* (1985), 7 C.C.E.L. 80 (Alta. C.A.), at 84. It should be noted that this decision was based on the fact that the employee made no contribution under the Workmen's Compensation scheme. Where the employer and employee have contributed equal payments under plans of disability insurance, the Alberta Court of Appeal has not deducted such benefits. See *Nanji v. Mercs* (1993), 7 Alta. L.R. (3d) 435 (C.A.), leave to appeal refused, [1994] 1 S.C.R. ix. See also *Zelisko v. "99" Truck Parts & Equipment Ltd.* (1985), 8 C.C.E.L. 201 (B.C.S.C.).

§16.53 The case of *Prince v. T. Eaton Co.*,[1] a decision of the British Columbia Court of Appeal, reaffirmed the principle that the damages to which an employee is entitled in the event of wrongful dismissal will be determined on the basis of putting the employee in the same position he or she would have been in had the dismissal not been wrongful and the employer provided reasonable notice of termination. In this case, the plaintiff employee was given 8 weeks' notice of termination and 34 weeks of severance pay. He did not accept these arrangements in full satisfaction of his entitlement and commenced an action for damages for wrongful dismissal. Approximately six months after his termination, the plaintiff was totally disabled in a motor vehicle accident and asserted an additional claim for entitlement to long-term disability benefits. At trial and on appeal, the plaintiff was successful in asserting his claim, the court essentially holding that long-term disability benefits would be available to the employee and would not otherwise reduce his entitlement under the head of damages for wrongful breach of his employment contract.

[1] (1992), 41 C.C.E.L. 72 (B.C.C.A.), leave to appeal to S.C.C. refused (1993), 78 B.C.L.R. (2d) xxxiv; on the other hand, in *McGarry v. Bosco Homes Edmonton* (1992), 42 C.C.E.L. 198 (Alta. Q.B.), it was decided that unless the employee could prove that she personally had contributed to the scheme under which she received benefits, the long-term disability benefits could be deducted from the damage award. See also *Cunningham v. Wheeler*, [1994] 1 S.C.R. 359, revg in part (1991), 95 D.L.R. (4th) 655 (B.C.C.A.), where, in the context of an insurance disability claim, the court determined that non-contributory disability benefits will not be deducted from an award where some consideration was given by the employee in return for the payments; *Nanji v. Mercs* (1993), 7 Alta. L.R. (3d) 435 (C.A.), leave to appeal refused, [1994] 1 S.C.R. ix.

§16.53.1 In *Datardina v. Royal Trust Corp. of Canada*,[1] the court held that an employee who was wrongfully terminated while on long-term disability was entitled to receive both the amounts that she would have received while on long-term disability *and* an indemnity equivalent to reasonable notice on the principle that there was no double recovery since there were two different losses: loss of the ability to work at an existing job because of injury, and the loss of the opportunity to search for and find new employment. In making this decision, the court distinguished *Ratych v. Bloomer*[2] which stands for the proposition that there are limits on the right of the plaintiff to be awarded double recovery, and held that the *Ratych* case referred to compensation from two different sources for the same loss.[3] The court also found that the employer was responsible for any damage which resulted from its acceptance at face value of its consulting firm's recommendations which were erroneous.

---

[1] [1994] 2 W.W.R. 176 (B.C.S.C.), affd (1995), 6 B.C.L.R. (3d) 1 (C.A.). See also *Bohun v. Similco Mines Ltd.* (1995), 6 B.C.L.R. (3d) 22 (C.A.).

[2] [1990] 1 S.C.R. 940.

[3] See also *McKay v. Camco Inc.* (1986), 53 O.R. (2d) 257 (C.A.); *Dunlop v. British Columbia Hydro & Power Authority* (1988), 32 B.C.L.R. (2d) 334 (C.A.).

§16.53.2 However, in light of the decision of the Supreme Court of Canada in *Sylvester v. British Columbia*,[1] the decisions discussed above may no longer be good law, at least in so far as they address the issue of whether workers' compensation, disability and sickness benefits are deductible from an award of damages for wrongful dismissal. The issue in this appeal was whether disability payments received by the employee during the notice period from a plan established solely by the employer should have been deducted from the damages payable to the employee following the employee's dismissal without notice. Major J. for the court held that the answer in such cases will depend on the intention of the parties, and the intention demonstrated in this particular case was that the parties did not intend the employee to have received both amounts. As a result, it was appropriate to deduct the disability payments from the award of damages.

---

[1] (1997), 146 D.L.R. (4th) 207 (S.C.C.). See also commentary at §9.55.1.

§16.53.3 The facts were as follows. Sylvester was employed by the appellant provincial government as the Director of Private Training Institutions in its Ministry of Advanced Education, Training and Technology pursuant to an oral contract of employment. In June 1992 he became ill and started receiving short-term disability payments, consisting of 75% of his salary, pursuant to the employer's Short Term Illness and Injury Plan (STIIP). The STIIP provided benefits for up to seven months to an employee who was unable to work due to illness or injury. If an employee remained disabled after the seven month

STIIP period, the employee would become eligible to receive benefits under the employer's Long Term Disability Plan (LTDP). Both the STIIP and the LTDP were funded entirely by the employer. The employee did not make any direct or indirect contributions to the plan. In July 1992, a month after he had started receiving short-term disability benefits, Sylvester was advised that his employment would be terminated because of a reorganization. The employer offered Sylvester 12.5 months' notice commencing August 31, 1992 and indicated it would "top up" any payments received under the STIIP or the LTDP during the notice period to 100% of his salary. Sylvester rejected the offer and sued for wrongful dismissal, claiming damages in lieu of 24 months' notice, with such damages to be in addition to benefits received under the STIIP and LTDP. At trial the plaintiff was awarded 15 months' notice, less the STIIP benefits received. On appeal, the Court of Appeal increased the notice period to 20 months commencing July 23, 1992 and held that Sylvester was entitled to STIIP and LTDP benefits in addition to such damages. In other words, the Court of Appeal held that the disability benefits should not be deducted from the damages for wrongful dismissal.

§16.53.4   The issue on the appeal to the Supreme Court of Canada was restricted to the deductibility or non-deductibility of the disability benefits. Major J. made reference to the *Salmi v. Greyfriar Developments Ltd.*,[1] *White v. Woolworth Canada Inc.*,[2] and *Industries de Caoutchouc Mondo (Canada) Ltée v. Leblanc*[3] cases, discussed above, but held that these cases were unhelpful in that they involved workers' compensation benefits, which are statutory, in contrast to disability benefits, which are contractual. Several cases involving unemployment insurance benefits (see next section, below) were similarly distinguished.

[1]   (1985), 7 C.C.E.L. 80 (Alta. C.A.).
[2]   (1996), 139 Nfld. & P.E.I.R. 324 (Nfld. C.A.).
[3]   D.T.E. 87T-394.

§16.53.5   Major J. held that the STIIP and LTDP plans should not be considered contracts distinct from the employment contract but rather should be considered integral components of it. The terms of the STIIP and LTDP were intended to be a substitute for the employee's regular salary. An employee who receives disability benefits under either plan does not receive a salary, and benefits are reduced by other benefits or income received by the employee. Secondly, the simultaneous payment of disability benefits and damages for wrongful dismissal is inconsistent with the terms of the employment contract. The contractual right to damages for wrongful dismissal and the right to disability benefits are based on opposite assumptions about the employee's ability to work and it is incompatible with the employment contract for the employee to receive both amounts. The damages are based on the premise that he would have worked during the notice period. The disability payments are only payable because he could not work. This conclusion was reinforced by the fact that, had the employer provided adequate notice and not breached the contract, the employee would not have received both disability benefits and salary during the notice period. If disability benefits are paid in addition to damages for wrongful dismissal, the employee collecting such benefits would be in a better position than the employee who is dismissed while working. Major J. concluded that such a result would be a deterrent to employers to setting up disability plans. The court did leave open the question of the deductibility of benefits where the employee has contributed to the plan. The court recognized that there may be cases where such a plan would be akin to a private insurance plan. However, as that question was not before the court, it declined to rule on the issue.

§16.53.6 Although the *Sylvester* decision by its own terms distinguishes contractual disability benefits from statutory workers' compensation and employment insurance benefits, the Ontario Court of Appeal has since extended the deductibility principle to workers' compensation benefits. In *Dowsley Estate v. Viceroy Fluid Power International Inc.*,[1] the Court of Appeal followed the conclusion in the *Salmi v. Greyfriar Developments Ltd.*[2] and *White v. Woolworth Canada Inc.*[3] cases, and rejected its own earlier suggestion to the contrary from *McKay v. Camco Inc.* The Court of Appeal accordingly allowed the appeal to the extent that the damages awarded at trial were to be reduced by the amount of the workers' compensation benefits received by the employee during the period of reasonable notice.

[1] 34 O.R. (3d) 57 (C.A.).
[2] (1985), 7 C.C.E.L. 80 (Alta. C.A.).
[3] (1996), 139 Nfld. & P.E.I.R. 324 (Nfld. C.A.).

3. Employment Insurance

§16.54 In some early decisions, courts deducted from damages for wrongful termination any unemployment insurance benefits (employment insurance benefits as of June 30, 1996) received during the notice period, and ordered that the employee remit these amounts to the Unemployment Insurance Commission.[1] These courts considered that unemployment insurance benefits were earnings from other sources during the notice period and should, therefore, be deducted from the employee's damage award. Other courts have declared that the *Unem-*

ployment Insurance Act, now repealed and replaced by the *Employment Insurance Act,*[2] has no bearing on the award of damages and, therefore, have not taken into account any benefits received by the employee thereunder during the notice period.[3]

---

[1]   *Charlebois v. Bigelow Canada Ltée,* J.E. 80-437 (Que. S.C.); *Burton v. MacMillan Bloedel Ltd.,* [1976] 4 W.W.R. 267 (B.C.S.C.).

[2]   R.S.C. 1985, c. U-1, repealed and replaced S.C. 1996, c. 23.

[3]   *Olson v. Motor Coach Industries Ltd.,* [1977] 4 W.W.R. 634 (Man. Q.B.), affd [1978] 1 W.W.R. 726 (C.A.); *Gordie's Auto Sales Ltd. v. Pitre* (1976), 73 D.L.R. (3d) 559 (N.B.C.A.).

§16.55 The Supreme Court of Canada finally ended the controversy in the case of *Jack Cewe Ltd. v. Jorgenson.*[1] The Court held that unemployment insurance benefits should not be deducted from the damages owed to the employee in compensation for the wrongful termination. The employer's liability for wrongful dismissal would not be altered because the employee had chosen to claim unemployment insurance benefits.[2]

---

[1]   [1980] 1 S.C.R. 812.

[2]   This same reasoning has been applied in *Deschênes v. Centre Local de Services Communautaires Seigneurie de Beauharnois,* D.T.E. 85T-900 (Que. S.C.); *Paquet v. Laurier Auto Inc.,* D.T.E. 85T-16 (Que. S.C.), revd on other grounds [1987] R.J.Q. 804 (C.A.); *Freeme de Wallens v. Visirecords Systems Canada Ltd.,* J.E. 81-548 (Que. S.C.); *Grossman v. Rosemount Knitting Inc.,* J.E. 81-123 (Que. S.C.), appeal abandoned Apr. 13, 1981; *Careau v. Sogemec Inc.,* [1981] C.S. 862 (Que. S.C.); *Girardeau v. Nadeau,* [1980] C.A. 258 (Que.); *McKay v. Camco Inc.* (1986), 53 O.R. (2d) 257 (C.A.); *Jalbert v. Commission Touristique de Port-Joli Inc.,* J.E. 81-777 (Que. Prov. Ct.); *Peck v. Levesque Plywood Ltd.* (1979), 27 O.R. (2d) 108 (C.A.).

§16.56 However, in order to avoid double compensation during the notice period, the *Employment Insurance Act*[1] stipulates that if the employee receives both benefits and remuneration from the employer for all or part of the reasonable notice period, the employee must reimburse the Receiver General in an amount equal to the benefits received during such notice period. Furthermore, if the employer has reason to believe that the employee has received benefits, it must ascertain whether the amount referred to is repayable by the employee and, if so, withhold this amount from any monies paid to the employee and remit it to the Receiver General.[2]

---

[1]   S.C. 1996, c. 23, s. 45.

[2]   S.C. 1996, c. 23, s. 46.

§16.57 The Ontario Court of Appeal[1] concluded that the predecessor versions of the aforementioned provisions were relevant when the employer became liable for "remuneration" to the employee. The court concluded that an award of damages for wrongful dismissal does not fall within the term "remuneration". Other court cases, however, do not agree with this view.

[1] *Peck v. Levesque Plywood Ltd.* (1979), 27 O.R. (2d) 108 (C.A.).

E. TERMINATION PACKAGES AND RELEASE AND DISCHARGE TRANSACTIONS

§16.58 In an effort to avoid litigation and/or provide for an orderly, amicable and professional conclusion to the employment relationship, written agreements outlining the terms or conditions that will govern upon termination of employment are frequently executed by the parties. These are often referred to as termination or severance packages. Such agreements may simply provide for the payment of a lump sum or periodic payments over a defined period. Alternatively, they may be more elaborate and provide for, among other things, continuance of benefits for a fixed period, relocation counselling, pension bridging, reference letters, non-disclosure of confidential information, return of employer property, payment of a fixed amount for financial services, as well as any number of other terms or conditions.

§16.59 In consideration of the satisfaction of the termination arrangements, many employers will require the executive to release them from any and all present and future claims with respect to their employment and the termination thereof. This document is commonly referred to as a "Release and Discharge".

§16.60 The question of whether the wrongfully dismissed employee is entitled to unreduced early retirement benefits and pay in lieu of notice for the same time period was also discussed in *Girling v. Crown Cork & Seal Canada Inc.*[1] In this case it was determined that the test to be applied to determine whether the pension benefits are a collateral benefit, which should not be deducted, or whether they are benefits received by the plaintiff that should be treated as any other income of the plaintiff was: *would the benefits have been received "but for" the dismissal?* Where the receipt of early benefits did not prevent the wrongfully dismissed employee from earning income from another employer which would be deducted on a mitigation accounting of the damages and did not consume any of the employee's time freed by the cessation of his employment, the unreduced early retirement benefit under the pension plan was not income which the court should deduct from the ordinary damages awarded to the employee.[2]

[1] (1994), 92 B.C.L.R. (2d) 181 (S.C.), affd (1995), 9 B.C.L.R. (3d) 1 (C.A.).
[2] For a similar analysis, see *Chandler v. Ball Packaging Products Canada Ltd.* (1992), 2 C.C.P.B. 99 (Ont. Ct. (Gen. Div.)), affd on appeal (1993), 2 C.C.P.B. 99 (Div. Ct.).

§16.61 In Quebec, termination agreements are generally called "Transactions". Article 2631 of the Civil Code of Quebec defines a transaction as follows:

> Transaction is a contract by which the parties prevent a future contestation, put an end to a lawsuit or settle difficulties arising in the execution of a judgment by way of mutual concessions or reservations.

A transaction must involve some reciprocal undertakings or concessions by the parties.[1] Most often in consideration of a settlement, the terminated employee releases the employer of all present and future claims arising from the termination of the employment. The reciprocal undertakings or concessions need not be of equal weight.[2]

[1] *Renaud v. Desmarais*, D.T.E. 92T-149 (Que. S.C.).
[2] P.B. Mignault, *Le droit civil canadien*, vol. 8 (Montréal: Wilson & Lafleur, 1909), pp. 302-303.

§16.62 Some employees have attempted to challenge the enforceability of the termination agreement and seek greater monetary compensation than is provided for in the contract. The circumstances surrounding the conclusion and acceptance of the termination agreement and the execution of the release will determine whether the release is valid and binding.

§16.63 The executive will be held to the terms of the termination agreement and release provided its terms are clear and they represent the agreement of the parties. Generally, the agreement will be binding unless there is evidence of duress, undue influence, intimidation or misrepresentation, which may successfully lead to the invalidation of the agreement.[1] Duress, undue influence or intimidation will not be found to have occurred in cases where the parties were allowed adequate time to review the agreement or to seek independent legal advice. This is particularly applicable to executives who are looked upon as being sophisticated parties to any such agreements and capable of understanding the ramifications of entering into a contract. In this regard, reference is made to the Ontario Court of Appeal's decision in *Matthewson v. Aiton Power Ltd.*,[2] where the court stated:

> The respondent was experienced in business and dealt daily with complicated contracts. There is no issue that he knew what he was signing. The fact that he was unemployed and needed a job, absent other factors, is not a ground for hold-

ing that there was an "inequality of bargaining power" and setting aside the contract on that ground.

¹ *Ewasiuk v. Estevan Area Home Care District 9 Inc.* (1985), 9 C.C.E.L. 267 (Sask. Q.B.), where the court ruled that the termination clause in a corollary document was not valid. See also *Waterman v. Frisby Tire Co. (1974) Ltd.* (1995), 13 C.C.E.L. (2d) 184 (Ont. Ct. (Gen. Div.)).

² (1985), 8 C.C.E.L. 312 (Ont. C.A.), at 314. See also *Henderson v. Advantage Marketing & Advertising Inc.* (1991), 35 C.C.E.L. 200 (B.C.S.C.); *Stacey v. Consolidated Foods Corp. of Canada* (1987), 15 C.C.E.L. 113 (N.S.S.C.).

§16.63.1 However, the new provision in the Civil Code of Quebec which states that an employee may not renounce his right to obtain compensation for any injury he suffers where insufficient notice of termination is given where the manner of resiliation is abusive[1] begs the question of whether a renunciation or release in a transaction is valid or whether the transaction may be reviewed by the court to determine if the notice is sufficient. In other words, when, if ever, can an employee validly release the employer?

¹ C.C.Q., art. 2092.

§16.64 Furthermore, evidence of the executive successfully negotiating more favourable terms before signing the document in question may demonstrate that the terms were freely entered into, thereby preventing the transaction from being invalidated.[1]

¹ *Middleton v. Bristol Myers Canada Inc.* (1988), 8 A.C.W.S. (3d) 419 (B.C.S.C.); *Sapieha v. Intercontinental Packers Ltd.* (1985), 10 C.C.E.L. 87 (Sask. Q.B.); *Goddard v. Blackwood Hodge Equipment Ltd.* (1983), 2 C.C.E.L. 299 (Sask. Q.B.).

§16.65 In *Williams v. Domfab Ltd.*,[1] the sales director was advised after three months of employment that his services were no longer required. Upon termination, he accepted one month's pay as settlement. The employee later asked the court to invalidate the agreement and order that the employer pay an amount corresponding to reasonable notice. The court refused this request and held that, although the amount agreed upon was not generous, it had been accepted by the employee. The employee's precarious financial situation at the time he entered into the contract did not invalidate the agreement, as there was no evidence of duress or threat by the employer.

¹ J.E. 83-477 (Que. S.C.). See also *Bibeau v. Centre Local des Services Communautaires du Marigot*, D.T.E. 86T-2 (Que. S.C.).

§16.66 The act of cashing a cheque on which the employer had written "payment in full" or "settlement in full" has prevented employees from making any further claims such as seeking additional payment in lieu of notice of termination.[1] In other cases, courts must draw the appropriate inference as to the existence of any agreement between the parties by analyzing all the circumstances including whether the employee deposited monies offered by the employer in his or her account, representations made at that time, subsequent negotiations, etc.[2]

> [1] *Lemieux v. Puits du Québec Inc.*, J.E. 81-1119 (Que. C.A.); *QIT Fer & Titane Inc. v. Barron*, J.E. 81-1120 (Que. Prov. Ct.).
> [2] *Gregov v. Canocean Resources Ltd.*, unreported, Feb. 17, 1989, Vancouver Doc. CA008249 (B.C.C.A.).

§16.67 An agreement to pay a certain amount in lieu of notice of dismissal was not repudiated by the employer when it deducted from that amount monies due for income tax.[1]

> [1] *Fieguth v. Acklands Ltd.* (1989), 37 B.C.L.R. (2d) 62 (C.A.).

§16.68 Discovering reprehensible conduct after the parties have reached a termination agreement does not allow the employer to call the deal off. The Quebec Superior Court has held that an employee has no duty to disclose such conduct and it is not sufficient to constitute an error going to the root of the agreement.[1]

> [1] *Séguin v. Dale-Parizeau Inc.*, D.T.E. 91T-579 (Que. S.C.).

F. PERSONAL LIABILITY OF THE PERSON WHO TERMINATES

§16.69 The individual responsible for dismissing another from his or her employment must have the necessary authority to do so and must act within the scope of his or her authority. If a specific procedure exists, it must be followed. A person who terminates an executive without the necessary authority may be acting outside his or her mandate or responsibilities and may be held personally responsible for any damages inflicted upon the wrongfully terminated executive.[1]

> [1] *Weber v. 685367 Ontario Ltd.* (1989), 17 A.C.W.S. (3d) 282 (Ont. Dist. Ct.).

§16.70 For example, in *Lavigne v. Sabex Internationale Ltée*,[1] company regulations provided for a specific procedure to be followed in the event of termination of an officer's employment. The company president failed to follow the procedure, which required a majority vote of the board of directors, and fired two vice-presidents without cause.

The court found that the president had abused his position, thereby committing a fault for which he was liable.[2] The court ordered the president and the company (because it had failed to invalidate the president's action) to pay 12 months' salary to each vice-president.

---

[1] J.E. 80-887 (Que. S.C.), appeal settled out of court May 7, 1984.

[2] C.C.L.C., art. 1053 as it then was. A similar liability may now be found under arts. 1457 and 1458 of the Civil Code of Quebec.

PART IV
OTHER EXECUTIVE
EMPLOYMENT-RELATED STATUTES

CHAPTER 17

IMMIGRATION AND EMPLOYMENT

A. INTRODUCTION

§17.1 Canada, like the United States, Australia and New Zealand, is a country developed primarily through immigration. Immigration law and policy are viewed as critical areas for research and policy affecting a variety of domestic issues, including federal-provincial relations, employment levels, and demographic planning. This chapter will focus on immigration law as it affects the employment in Canada of executives and professionals, primarily from the perspective of the Canadian employer seeking to retain the services of a foreign national.

§17.2 The *Immigration Act*[1] (the "Act") sets out the basic requirements, policies and principles of Canadian immigration law. Canada's immigration program is administered by Human Resource Development Canada ("HRDC").

[1] R.S.C. 1985, c. I-2 as amended.

§17.3 Most of the practical information required by prospective immigrants or visitors is contained in regulations, operations memoranda, and guidelines, which are frequently amended and revised. It is virtually impossible to determine how Canadian immigration law operates by examining the Act alone.[1] For businesses and individuals seeking to relocate key personnel to Canada, to identify Canadian investment opportunities, or to obtain access to the Canadian market, a working knowledge of Canadian immigration law confers a significant advantage.

[1] The actual workings of the Act are best understood through its regulations, which are in turn supplemented by manuals by regular operations memoranda and by other interpretive guides. In Quebec, a separate, parallel, legislative scheme is enforced by a provincial Ministry with concurrent jurisdiction.

§17.4 In an effort to attract educated, trained immigrants and visitors, as well as those who are able to invest in the Canadian economy, Canada has sought to favour business travel and business immigration. This can be attributed in part to the demands of the international business community and the creation of "free market" economies.[1] Concurrently, there has been a liberalization of temporary entry and permanent residence procedures for certain business persons who are able to purchase, maintain or invest in Canadian business and of temporary entry procedures for visitors who are U.S. and Mexican citizens as a direct result of the North American Free Trade Agreement ("NAFTA").[2] Despite the increasingly complex and rigid administration of the immigration program, persons coming to Canada for business reasons or for investment in businesses are given favourable treatment.

[1] The Business Immigration Program was introduced in 1986. The North American Free Trade Agreement ("NAFTA") between Canada, the United States and Mexico came into force on June 23, 1993 (replacing the 1989 Canada-U.S. Free Trade Agreement).

[2] See Chapter 16 of NAFTA.

§17.4.1 In addition, Annex 1B of the Agreement Establishing the World Trade Organization, known as the General Agreement on Trade in Services (GATS) involving 126 Member Nations, came into force on January 1, 1995. GATS deals with trade in services and temporary entry of persons involved in designated service sectors. Under the terms of GATS, Canada has agreed to allow citizens of Member Nations who work in those service sectors to access our domestic market through the establishment of a business in Canada, and to facilitate the temporary entry of certain categories of business persons who work in those service sectors.

B. RESPONSIBILITIES OF THE CANADIAN EMPLOYER

§17.5 Anyone who is neither a permanent resident nor a Canadian citizen, may not work in Canada unless prior authorization is obtained.

§17.6 Before any foreign national can work in Canada, the Canadian employer must either seek approval from a local Human Resource Development Center, or prepare the appropriate offer of temporary employment letter for the candidate, pursuant to the appropriate exemption category.

§17.7 In the event that HRDC determines that there are qualified Canadian citizens or permanent residents available for the position, the application may be refused. In addition, a person may be inadmissible to Canada for reasons related to health, because of a criminal record or, more rarely, because the person poses a security risk. In such cases, the individual may be refused entry to Canada for reasons completely unrelated to the offer of employment.

§17.8 Accordingly, no employer in Canada should make an unconditional offer of employment without expressly reserving the right to withdraw it in the event that Human Resource Development Canada ("HRDC") approval is withheld or the visa is otherwise refused. Alternatively, an offer of employment could be stipulated to be conditional upon obtaining the necessary immigration documentation. Even with these precautions, a contract of employment may contain an implied term to the effect that the employer will use best efforts to obtain approval of the offer of temporary employment. Failure to use best efforts may expose the employer to contractual liability for breach of contract.[1]

[1] *Bruce v. Region of Waterloo Swim Club* (1990), 73 O.R. (2d) 709 (H.C.J.).

§17.9 Canadian employers who fail to comply with the Act are subject to strict penalties and fines. The Act creates offences punishable on summary conviction and indictment, including knowingly making a misleading statement in connection with the admission to Canada of any person, knowingly making a false promise of employment or representation which induces a person to seek admission to Canada, and knowingly attempting to induce, aid or abet any person to contravene the Act or regulations.[1] Punishment ranges from fines to imprisonment, or both.[2]

[1] *Immigration Act*, ss. 94(1)(*h*) 94(1)(*i*) and 94(1)(*j*).
[2] *Immigration Act*, s. 94(2).

C. COMING TO CANADA

§17.10 Only two classes of persons have the right to enter into and remain in Canada: Canadian citizens and permanent residents.[1] Everyone else who wishes to come to Canada is subject to the conditions and restrictions in the Act which govern admissibility and entry to Canada.[2]

[1] *Immigration Act*, ss. 4(1) and 4(2). Unlike citizens, permanent residents' rights are qualified by the restrictions set out in s. 27 of the Act. Convention refugees have a right to remain in Canada pursuant to s. 4(2.1) of the Act.
[2] *Immigration Act*, ss. 5(1)-5(3).

§17.11 All persons seeking to enter Canada who are neither citizens nor permanent residents are divided into two streams, namely persons seeking temporary entry or "visitors", and persons seeking permanent residence or "immigrants".[1]

<hr>

[1] The term "immigrant" has a technical meaning in the Act and should not be confused with "permanent resident". An immigrant is a person who seeks landing, that is, who seeks to establish permanent residence in Canada but has not yet become a permanent resident. See *Immigration Act*, s. 2(1).

1. Visitor or Immigrant?

§17.12 There are two types of visas: visitor visas and permanent residence visas. Visitors include tourists, persons seeking to engage in employment, and students. Unless otherwise authorized, a visitor may not remain in Canada for a period in excess of six months from the date of entry.[1] On the other hand, a permanent resident may stay in Canada indefinitely, provided that permanent residence is not abandoned or that the permanent resident is not found to be "described" under section 27(1) of the Act, which ultimately leads to inquiry and removal from Canada.

<hr>

[1] *Immigration Act*, R.S.C. 1985, c. I-2, s. 26(2).

§17.13 The distinction between visitors and immigrants is critical. Every person seeking to enter Canada is presumed to be an immigrant. This statutory presumption places the burden of proof on visitors to show that they have no intention of residing permanently in Canada and are therefore genuine visitors. Alternatively, immigrants are required to have met all the conditions of the Act and regulations, and to have sought and obtained an immigrant visa prior to presenting themselves at a port of entry.[1] An individual seeking temporary entry to Canada is subject to the statutory regime governing visitors, whereas the applicant seeking to obtain permanent residence is treated as an immigrant and must conform to completely different application procedures. For most practical purposes, the two regimes are mutually exclusive.

<hr>

[1] See *Immigration Act*, R.S.C. 1985, c. I-2, ss. 8(2), 9(1), 9(1.1) and 9(1.2).

§17.14 Canadian employers seeking to employ a foreign national, may offer employment on either a temporary or permanent basis. Where advance planning is possible and the foreign worker is expected to take up employment for a lengthy period of time of unforeseen duration, permanent residence may be more appropriate. However, it should be borne in mind that permanent residence applications presently may take between 12 and 18 months to process.

§17.15 Positions that need to be filled on an urgent basis can usually be processed through either HRDC or an exemption category.

2. Visa Requirements

§17.16 As a rule, both immigrants and visitors must apply for and obtain a visa before appearing at a Canadian port of entry.[1] The applicant is in fact assessed twice: once when a visa officer overseas determines whether the applicant meets the requirements of the Act and regulations in order to issue the visa, and secondly by the immigration officer at the port of entry.[2]

---

[1] See *Immigration Act*, s. 9(1).

[2] See *Grewal v. Canada (Minister of Employment & Immigration)*, [1990] 1 F.C. 192 (C.A.).

§17.17 As discussed above, there are two types of visas: visitor visas and immigrant visas. The requirement of obtaining a visa prior to seeking entry to Canada applies almost universally to persons seeking permanent residence who must apply for and obtain their visas from a visa office outside Canada before arriving in Canada to take up permanent residence.[1] The rule as it applies to immigrants is that no immigrant may seek admission to Canada at a port of entry without having obtained an immigrant visa first.[2]

---

[1] There are exceptions for spouses of Canadian citizens or permanent residents and refugees who may apply for landing within Canada. See *Immigration Act*, ss. 114(2) and 46.04(1).

[2] *Immigration Act*, ss. 114(2) and 46.04(1). Spouses who seek landing at a point of entry or in Canada may be processed for landing in Canada on public policy grounds. As of the time of writing, the Minister had not yet announced whether spouses will constitute a class under the new s. 6(5).

§17.18 Unlike immigrants, visitors are not always required to obtain visas prior to presenting themselves at a Canadian port of entry. Nationals of prescribed countries are exempt, notably nationals of the United States, most western European countries, Australia, New Zealand and Japan, to name a few.[1] Although nationals of these countries do not require a visa before travelling to Canada, they must still apply at a port of entry to enter Canada, and they remain subject to the admissibility requirements discussed below. All visitors intending to work or study temporarily in Canada must also comply with authorization requirements for employment and study in Canada. Obtaining authorization to work or study is a condition precedent to engaging in either of those activities in Canada.

¹   See *Immigration Regulations, 1978,* SOR/78-172, s. 13 and Schedule II.

3. Admissibility

§17.19 Admissibility to Canada depends on a number of factors, the most important of which relate to the medical, security and criminal records of the person seeking to enter Canada.

§17.20 All immigrants must undergo medical and security checks which form part of the permanent residence application process. In fact, these checks take up a significant portion of the usual delays for processing a permanent residence application (roughly 12 to 18 months).

§17.21 Visitors, on the other hand, may or may not be subject to these checks, depending on the circumstances. Medical examinations, for example, may be required if the applicant has resided in a country posing health risks or if the individual seeks employment in a health-related field.[1]

¹   Immigrants, refugees and visitors may be required to undergo medical examinations: *Immigration Act,* ss. 11(1), 11(1.1) and 11(2).

4. Passport Requirements

§17.22 Like most countries, Canada requires that persons seeking admission to Canada have a valid travel document such as a passport to establish identity and admissibility.[1] This rule has a number of important exceptions, including exceptions for U.S. citizens and permanent residents.[2] As a rule, however, obtaining a valid passport is recommended prior to embarking on any immigration-related application process, regardless of the foreign national's citizenship.

¹   See, *e.g., Immigration Regulations,* s. 14.
²   See, *Immigration Regulations,* s. 14(4).

D. EMPLOYMENT

§17.23 Sections 6(1) and 6(2) of the *Canadian Charter of Rights and Freedoms* guarantee mobility rights in Canada for Canadian citizens and permanent residents (the rights of permanent residents are less absolute, however). The mobility rights enshrined in section 6 of the Charter do not subsume the right to work in Canada as an express right for foreign nationals, and there is no constitutionally protected "right to work" as a matter of entitlement between nation states until a foreign national satisfies domestic requirements.[1] In Canada, a critical feature of that requirement is the employment authorization.

[1] See *Black v. Law Society of Alberta*, [1989] 1 S.C.R. 591, at 612; *Law Society of Upper Canada v. Skapinker*, [1984] 1 S.C.R. 357.

1. What is "Employment"?

§17.24 "Employment" is defined in the Act as any activity for which the person performing it receives or might reasonably expect to receive valuable consideration.[1] What constitutes "employment" for the purposes of the Act will depend upon the nature and circumstances relating to the work.[2]

[1] *Immigration Act*, s. 2(1).
[2] See *Georgas v. Minister of Employment & Immigration*, [1979] 1 F.C. 349 (C.A.).

§17.25 Like all domestic legislation, the Act does not have extra-territorial effect; that is, it has no reach outside Canadian boundaries. Consequently, the Act does not prevent a foreign national from performing services for a Canadian company outside Canada. Conversely, the definition of "employment" might include services rendered in Canada for a non-Canadian company, even if the individual were paid outside Canada. For example, a foreign national performing management consultancy services in Canada under contract for a French firm will be "employed" in Canada for the purposes of the Act.[1]

[1] Consultancy services are subject to the general requirement of an employment authorization. There is a limited exception for U.S. and Mexican management consultants on business visits to Canada under NAFTA.

§17.26 This highlights an important distinction between employment law and immigration law. Many services which do not fall within the framework of an employment relationship as that term is understood in employment law do nevertheless constitute "employment" for the purposes of determining whether an employment authorization must be obtained under the Act. Employers who seek advice as to whether a particular position requires an employment authorization should contact their local Human Resource Development Canada.

2. The Employment Authorization Requirement

§17.27 No person other than a Canadian citizen or permanent resident may seek to engage in employment in Canada without first receiving authorization.[1] This type of authorization is called an "employment authorization". It is issued by visa offices outside Canada or by immigration officers at Canadian ports of entry. It is a separate and distinct requirement from the visa requirement discussed above, and must be obtained before any foreign national takes up employment in Canada.

[1]   Section 10 of the Act provides:

> Except in such cases as are prescribed, every person, other than a Canadian citizen or a permanent resident, who seeks to come into Canada for the purpose of
>
> • • • • •
>
> (c) engaging in employment
>
> shall make an application to a visa officer for and obtain authorization to come into Canada for that purpose before the person appears at a port of entry.

§17.28 The holder of an employment authorization is only permitted to work in Canada for the employer and in the position designated on the employment authorization for the time period specified. The authorization extends only to the type of employment or activity described on it.

§17.29 Citizens of treaty countries (NAFTA, GATS) or workers seeking employment authorization under exemption categories may apply upon arrival at the port of entry to Canada, although prior approval is sometimes requested at a Consulate or Embassy abroad. The Consulate will issue an approval letter which the worker must present at the port of entry in addition to the letter from the Canadian employer.

3. Selected Exceptions to the Employment Authorization Requirement

§17.30 There are a number of exceptions to the employment authorization requirement.[1]

[1]   Section 19 of the *Immigration Regulations* provides a list of exempt activities for which an employment authorization is not required.

§17.31 An important exception exists for visitors who are travelling for business reasons. Business visits to Canada do not, as a rule, constitute "employment" within the meaning of the Act. A visa officer may permit a visitor temporary entry to Canada for up to 90 days without the need for an employment authorization if the visitor is a permanent and continuing employee of a foreign business and the purpose of the visit is for consultations or inspection in concert with other employees in Canada who are in the same company framework,[1] or for the purpose of selling goods other than to the general public.[2]

[1] *Immigration Regulations*, s. 19(1)(*i*).
[2] *Immigration Regulations*, s. 19(1)(*h*).

§17.32 For lengthier stays, a "visitor record" is available to *bona fide* business persons carrying on activities for a business outside Canada. The visa may be issued for a period of 12 months, and may be endorsed as multiple-entry.[1] This type of document is not available at present to U.S. citizens and permanent residents, although these persons are routinely admitted to Canada for temporary entry as business persons under NAFTA, GATS (General Agreement on Trade in Services) or otherwise.[2]

[1] Employment & Immigration Canada, *Immigration Manual: Selection and Control*, vol. 1, p. 11-2.
[2] See, *e.g.*, *Immigration Regulations*, s. 19(1)(*v*).

§17.33 Under NAFTA, U.S. citizens may be granted temporary entry as business persons for periods of up to one year in order to engage in a restricted range of activities and professions, including research and design, marketing and sales, and professions such as law, accounting and management consultancy. In addition, many categories of professionals who are not receiving remuneration in Canada may be admissible as business persons under NAFTA or GATS.

4. The Validation Requirement

§17.34 If an employment authorization is required, the offer of employment must be approved by Human Resource Development Canada ("HRDC") before it can be offered to a person who is not a Canadian citizen or permanent resident. There are exceptions to this general rule, but this approval is usually the first step in the process of obtaining an employment authorization.

§17.35 The employment authorization and the prior approval requirement have been held to be a legitimate exercise of legislative competence, *intra vires* Parliament, and not to infringe the *Canadian Bill of Rights*.[1] Concern for unemployment levels and labour market conditions are among the policy considerations that underlie the requirement for validation. Unless the employment sought is exempt from validation, visa officers must consider the opinion of National Employment Services in Canada as to whether a Canadian may be found to do the job.[2]

¹ See, *e.g.*, *Doran v. R.*, [1977] 1 F.C. 3 (T.D.), at 9; *Immigration Regulations*, s. 20, referring to labour market considerations and job validation procedures. See also *Saravia v. 101482 Canada Inc.*, [1987] R.J.Q. 2658 (Prov. Ct.).

² *Immigration Regulations*, ss. 20(1)(*a*), 20(3) and 20(4).

§17.36 As a rule, the validation process is initiated by the Canadian employer in Canada. The employer is required to contact a local HRDC office. Once approval is obtained, the file is sent to the designated visa office (usually in the country of residence of the foreign executive) to request the issuance of the employment authorization. Depending on the type of employment and the location of the visa office overseas, the validation and processing of the employment authorization may take several weeks.

§17.37 In Quebec, the approval of the provincial government is also required in the validation approval process of offers of temporary employment.

5. Selected Exceptions to the Validation Requirement

§17.38 Although there are a number of exceptions to the validation requirement, the two that shall be dealt with in this section are intra-company transferees and the professional category.

(a) Intra-Company Transferees

§17.39 There are two types of intra-company transferees. One is only available to U.S. and Mexican citizens under NAFTA, or to citizens of Member Nations under GATS, and the other is available to persons of any national origin (often referred to as Code E15).

§17.40 Under either category, persons may be transferred to an affiliate, subsidiary or parent company.[1] Since these employment authorizations are exempt from the requirement of prior approval from HRDC, they may be obtained at a Canadian port of entry by persons who are nationals of countries listed in Schedule II of the *Immigration Regulations* without the necessity of applying at a visa office first. General documentary requirements for intra-company transferees include a letter from the Canadian employer setting out the person's current job description, the title, position description and salary of the employment in Canada, and the organizational structure of the company, focusing on a clear and comprehensive description of the relationship between the Canadian and foreign corporate entities.

[1] Joint ventures are also permitted in the NAFTA category under certain conditions which deal primarily with ownership and control by the parent corporations. See Employment & Immigration Canada, "Operations Memorandum IS 406", p. 29.

(i) The Intra-Company Transferee under NAFTA and GATS

§17.41 To qualify under NAFTA, a U.S. or Mexican citizen must have been employed by the U.S. or Mexican parent, subsidiary or affiliate for a period of one continuous year during the three-year period immediately preceding the date of the application and must be seeking employment in a capacity that is managerial, executive or involves specialized knowledge. The initial employment authorization is available for one year, and is renewable thereafter under NAFTA, up to a maximum of five years for executives and managers, and five years for persons with specialized knowledge, and under GATS, up to a maximum of three years. Under GATS, a citizen of a Member Nation must have been employed for the 12 months immediately preceding the transfer.

§17.42 Under NAFTA and GATS, "managerial" means that the person is responsible and accountable for directing the organization or unit of the organization by supervising and controlling the work of other supervisory, professional or managerial employees. Authority to hire and dismiss or to recommend these actions, as well as authority to authorize other personnel activities, must be part of the incumbent's responsibilities. There must also be direct authority over day-to-day operations.[1]

[1] Employment & Immigration Canada, "Operations Memorandum IS 406", p. 30.

§17.43 "Executive" means that the individual is responsible and accountable for the organization or for a major component of the organization. Duties must include establishing goals and policies of the organization and exercising decision-making powers. The executive normally reports directly to the board of directors or shareholders. If reporting to another level, the executive must receive only general supervision.[1]

[1] Employment & Immigration Canada, "Operations Memorandum IS 406", p. 30.

§17.44 "Specialized knowledge" means that the individual has a level of expertise and proprietary knowledge of the organization's products, services, research, equipment, techniques, etc. The purpose of entry must be demonstrably related to the use of the specialized knowledge.

(ii) Code E15

§17.45 An executive transfer may also be made pursuant to s. (20)(5)(*e*)(i) (Code E15) of the *Immigration Regulations*, and applies only to senior managerial and executive employees. The principle underlying this category is similar to the NAFTA and GATS categories, although there is no specialized knowledge classification.

§17.46 Persons of any citizenship, including U.S. and Mexican citizens, are eligible to apply pursuant to Code E15. In this category, senior management means general manager or more senior. "Executive" is not defined in the guidelines, but many visa offices will only process persons who are vice-presidents or more senior.

§17.47 At present, there is no requirement for a Code E15 applicant have been employed by the corporate affiliate for any particular length of time prior to applying for the employment authorization. The employment authorization may be issued for a period of up to three years and may be renewed thereafter, although exceptional circumstances are usually required after five years.

(b) Professional Category

§17.48 U.S. and Mexican citizens seeking temporary entry into Canada to engage in employment at a professional level and who otherwise meet the existing requirements for entry under the Act may be granted entry to Canada under the professional categories of NAFTA or GATS. The employment authorization is issued pursuant to section 20(5)(*b*)(i) of the *Immigration Regulations*. The professions which are recognized under NAFTA are set out in the Agreement itself, and include accountants, scientists, engineers, architects, lawyers and management consultants, to name a few. The professions recognized under GATS are limited to six.

§17.49 Provided the foregoing requirements are met, the employment authorization can be obtained at a point of entry (such as at an airport or border crossing) or at a Canadian consulate. The applicant should have proof of professional qualifications (such as the original of a diploma or university transcript showing that a university degree has been obtained), proof of citizenship (either a passport, birth certificate or naturalization certificate), the prescribed fee, and a letter from the Canadian employer affirming the professional activity for which the applicant is seeking entry and setting out the anticipated length of stay and arrangements for remuneration. Since certain professions have licensing requirements which vary from province to province, compliance with an exemption from local licensing requirements should always be verified.

§17.50 An employment authorization issued pursuant to the professional category is usually issued for one year and is renewable.

E. PERMANENT RESIDENCE IN CANADA

1. An Overview

§17.51 Application for permanent residence must be submitted to a Canadian Mission outside of Canada except those applications by spouses of Canadians and refugees, who are entitled to remain in Canada during the application process subject to approval by the Minister.

§17.52 The *Immigration Act* provides for a number of ways in which a person may apply for permanent residence in Canada. Canadian citizens or permanent residents may sponsor their relatives who are members of the "family class" (a category corresponding roughly to members of the immediate family). Persons in this category are independent applicants, but they need only meet a lower point threshold instead of the usual 70 points. This section will focus on the category of independent applicants, which includes entrepreneurs, investors and persons with an arranged offer of employment from a Canadian employer.

§17.53 A distinctive feature of Canadian immigration law is that independent applicants are usually assessed on the basis of a "point system" which assigns numerical values to a range of factors including education, language ability, specific vocational preparation and experience. Unless otherwise specified, independent applicants require 70 points. In addition, immigration officers evaluate admissibility criteria and determine whether the applicant is likely to become successfully established in Canada.

§17.54 The early stages of the procedures may involve the completion of an optional pre-application questionnaire ("PAQ") which may be used for a preliminary assessment of the applicant's eligibility.[1] The applicant then completes an application for permanent residence, which is usually submitted to a visa officer at a Canadian visa office outside of Canada along with supporting documentation.

¹ The PAQ is a service offered by External Affairs used to pre-screen applicants by visa offices overseas. However, an applicant is entitled to request the formal application form without having to fill out the questionnaire beforehand: See *Choi v. Canada (Minister of Employment & Immigration)*, [1992] 1 F.C. 763 (C.A.).

§17.55 All applicants and their dependants must undergo a medical examination by a designated physician, and medical assessments are the responsibility of Health Canada. Each applicant is also required to submit to a security investigation, which typically takes several months to complete. Both the medical and security checks are the responsibility of the federal authorities regardless of the province of destination.

2. The Province of Quebec

§17.56 In Canada, legislative power over immigration law is shared between the provinces and the federal government. Only the Province of Quebec has exercised its jurisdiction and enacted comprehensive legislation. Pursuant to an agreement entered into between the federal government and the Province of Quebec, Quebec is solely responsible for selecting its permanent residents.

§17.57 Applicants destined for the Province of Quebec must first be approved or "selected" by the Ministère des Relations avec les Citoyens et de l'Immigration ("MRCI"). An Application for a Certificate of Selection of Quebec is submitted to a Quebec delegation abroad for approval before the application for permanent residence can be forwarded to Canadian immigration authorities for processing.[1]

¹ *An Act respecting the Ministère des Communautés culturelles et de l'Immigration*, R.S.Q., c. M-23.1.

3. Family Class

§17.58 Canadian immigration law facilitates family reunification by means of "relaxed" selection criteria for immigrants who are members of the family class. To qualify, the family class immigrant is sponsored by an eligible Canadian citizen or permanent resident 19 years of age or over, who is a resident of Canada. The family class is defined by reference to the sponsoring Canadian resident and includes the sponsor's spouse, unmarried children under 19 years of age, parents, and under certain circumstances, orphaned brothers and sisters.[1]

¹ *Immigration Regulations*, s. 4(1).

§17.59 An application to sponsor is processed and approved in Canada. The applicant must then complete permanent resident application forms which are sent to the visa office overseas located nearest to the applicant's residence following receipt of the file from Canada. Family class members are not subject to the points system referred to above, and are processed on a priority basis.[1]

[1] Spouses and dependent children receive priority processing, that is, within six months from the time that the sponsorship is approved.

4. Independent Applicants

§17.60 Independent applicants include assisted relatives, entrepreneurs, investors, persons with arranged employment and skilled workers.

§17.61 The single most important feature of the selection process is the point system which awards points to immigrants on the basis of factors set out in Schedule I of the *Immigration Regulations*. Unless otherwise specified, 70 points are the minimum required to succeed. The factors include education, specific vocational preparation, experience, occupational demand, arranged employment or designated occupation, demographic factor, age, knowledge of French and English, personal suitability, and the presence of relatives in Canada.[1]

[1] *Immigration Regulations*, Schedule I.

§17.62 To qualify as a permanent resident of Canada, an applicant must obtain the necessary number of points prescribed for the category for which he or she is applying. Immigration officers have the discretion to admit borderline candidates who may fall just short of the necessary point allocation but who, for reasons such as exceptional ability, initiative or suitability, may nevertheless be granted landing.[1]

[1] See *Immigration Regulations*, s. 11.

(a) Entrepreneurs

§17.63 An entrepreneur is an immigrant who establishes, purchases or makes a substantial investment in a business or commercial venture in Canada.[1] While no minimum investment is provided by regulation, the investment must be "substantial" and sufficient to capitalize the type of business proposed in Canada. Entrepreneurs are assessed under a modified version of the points system, the success or failure of which will depend largely upon the viability of a business proposal in which the applicant describes the nature of the proposed investment.

[1]   See *Immigration Regulations*, s. 23.1(1).

§17.64   The business or commercial venture must make a significant contribution to the economy whereby employment opportunities are created or continued for one or more Canadian citizens or permanent residents other than the entrepreneur and his or her dependants. It is also a condition of this class that the entrepreneur participate actively in the management of the business or the commercial venture on an ongoing basis.[1]

[1]   *Immigration Regulations*, s. 23.1(1).

§17.65   The applicant is required to set up the business within a stipulated time period. Monitoring and follow-up are achieved by placing a condition on the immigrant visa. This condition will require the entrepreneur to demonstrate that he or she has successfully established the business in Canada within a certain period of time (two years) following the landing of the permanent resident in Canada. Once this is done, immigration officials will remove the condition.

(b) Investors

§17.66   The Immigrant Investor Program was established pursuant to Canada's Business Immigration Program in 1986 to provide a means for admitting to Canada immigrants with business skills and experience who are prepared to invest in a Canadian business. To qualify, an immigrant investor must be at least 19 years of age, must have business experience and must also have accumulated a prescribed net worth.[1]

[1]   *Immigration Regulations*, s. 2(1).

§17.66.1   Under the current interim investor program, a minimum investment of $250,000 is required on offerings which were approved by the federal government before December 31, 1994, and on new provincially-administered venture capital funds. Under proposed regulations, the investor program will provide for a minimum investment of $350,000 in Newfoundland, New Brunswick, Prince Edward Island, Saskatchewan and the Northwest Territories, and $450,000 in Quebec, Ontario, British Columbia and Alberta.

§17.67 The Immigrant Investor Program differs from the Entrepreneur Program in several respects. First, there is a minimum level of investment prescribed by regulation. Second, the investor does not need to be actively involved in the business, although there is no restriction on becoming involved. Third, the invested funds are "locked in" for a prescribed period of time. If both the business and the immigrant qualify under the Immigrant Investor Program and the investor is otherwise admissible to Canada, the permanent residence application will be processed on a priority basis.

§17.68 To qualify, the investor makes an irrevocable investment for a minimum period of five years in provincially-approved funds.

§17.69 The Act provides that investors may invest in businesses or funds which are approved. "Fund" means:

> . . . a privately administered investment syndicate . . . or a government-administered venture capital fund.[1]

[1] *Immigration Regulations*, s. 2(1).

(i) Privately Administered Investment Syndicate

§17.70 Provided it is acceptable to the province of investment and the Minister, the main purpose of the privately administered investment syndicate is to provide equity to establish, purchase, expand or maintain two or more eligible businesses of significant economic benefit to the province of destination.

(ii) Government-Administered Venture Capital Fund

§17.71 The main purpose of this investment is to provide equity or loan capital to establish, purchase or maintain an eligible business or commercial venture.

(iii) Quebec

§17.72 Special criteria apply to the Province of Quebec, where immigrants are selected pursuant to an agreement entered into between the federal government and the provincial government. The Quebec Immigrant Investor Program requires that the minimum investment be placed in the hands of an authorized dealer registered under Quebec

securities legislation.[1] The onus for ensuring that the investment qualifies under the Quebec regulations lies on the authorized dealer.

[1] *Securities Act*, R.S.Q., c. V-1.1.

(c) Persons with Arranged Employment in Canada

§17.73 Independent applicants may apply to Canada on the strength
of a permanent job offer which is initiated by a Canadian employer.
An application is made by the Canadian employer to Canada Citizenship and Immigration in order to approve the position in the context of
a permanent residence application. The application procedure usually
requires that the Canadian employer be in a position to demonstrate
that a Canadian cannot be found for the position, although these requirements may vary from position to position.

§17.74 Following the approval of the job offer, the Canadian government will then forward the approved job offer to a visa office overseas,
which will then forward to the applicant the applications for permanent residence. Job offer approval for immigrants to the province of
Québec is obtained from the MRCI.

§17.75 This category is advantageous in that it provides 15 points to
the applicant who may not otherwise succeed in attaining the minimum 70 points required for most of the independent applicant categories.[1]

[1] See *Immigration Regulations*, Schedule I.

F. MAINTAINING PERMANENT RESIDENCE IN CANADA

§17.76 Once an immigrant lands, permanent resident status may only
be maintained if that individual physically resides in Canada and intends to maintain Canada as his or her principal place of permanent
residence.

§17.77 Under Canadian immigration law, a person who leaves Canada with the intention of abandoning Canada will be deemed to have
abandoned permanent resident status in Canada. In addition, an absence from Canada of 183 days in any one-year period will trigger a

provision of the Act whereby the person will be deemed to have abandoned permanent resident status in Canada.[1]

[1] *Immigration Act*, R.S.C. 1985, c. I-2, s. 24.

§17.78 In the event that any prolonged absence is envisaged, the Act provides that a permanent resident may apply for a returning resident permit.[1] This permit may be obtained in Canada or overseas, and is issued for one or two years. It is available under a range of circumstances, including a transfer of a permanent resident by a Canadian employer to a position outside Canada. Dependent family members are also entitled to the permit where the principal applicant is eligible. The legal impact of this permit is that, in the absence of evidence to the contrary, possession of a returning resident permit will be proof that the person did not intend to abandon Canadian permanent resident status.

[1] *Immigration Act*, R.S.C. 1985, c. I-2, s. 25(1) and 25(2).

§17.79 Although new legislation[1] eliminated the returning resident permit, this permit continued to be issued as at the time this section was last updated. When the returning resident permit is effectively abolished, the same criteria will apply to determine whether a permanent resident has lost such status.

[1] Bill C-86.

G. CONCLUSION

§17.80 Businesses seeking to relocate executives or other key personnel to Canada must be fully aware of Canadian immigration laws and regulations to understand which entry status should be sought so as to fully meet any needs in terms of duration of stay and delay in obtaining any necessary visa.

The next chapter deals with tax planning for executives.

CHAPTER 18

TAX CONSIDERATIONS

A. TAX PLANNING AND THE EMPLOYMENT CONTRACT

§18.1 The determination and the method of payment of an executive's remuneration is a fundamental part of the employment contract. And, given that the objective of this is to make the executive better off financially, the tax implications of his or her remuneration should carry considerable weight.

§18.2 Although the payment of a salary to an executive will create a tax liability, there may be significant differences in the taxation of other forms of compensation. Generally, employee compensation results in an income deduction for the employer and a corresponding income inclusion for the employee. But, between alternative forms of compensation, there are distinctions to be made having regard to the amount that is subject to tax and the timing of both the deduction for the employer and the income inclusion for the employee.

§18.3 Considering this potential for differences, the question of what factors one should consider logically arises. There is no all-encompassing list, but a checklist of items to consider should usually include the following:

- As a matter of tax law, is the executive an employee or an independent contractor, and what contractual provisions are consistent with the status of the executive?
- Do the parties wish the services to be rendered by a corporation?
- Is the executive a resident of Canada for income tax purposes? If so, does the executive intend to depart from Canada before, during, or after the course of his or her employment and, if so, what are the consequences of this?
- If the executive is a non-resident of Canada for income tax purposes, does entering into the employment contract bring the executive and his or her family within the Canadian tax net? In particular, do the financial, family and social decisions taken by the executive as a result of the move have any impact on his or

her exposure to Canadian taxes? If so, is this something that the executive would wish to avoid? Should the executive seek compensation from his or her employer for unforeseen or additional taxes and, in turn, what would the consequences of this be?

- How does the application of any income tax treaty between Canada and the country either from which the executive originates or to which the executive is going affect the outcome of the tax analysis?

- What is the appropriate mix between salary, benefits and other forms of compensation? Are certain benefits, such as options to acquire shares, bonuses or sabbatical leaves, more desirable from a tax point of view?

- Does the executive wish to share in the profits of his or her employer?

- Is some form of deferred compensation desirable?

- Does the employer have any preferences between compensation alternatives in terms of cash flow and deductibility?

- How will the employer's obligation to make source deductions affect the executive's cash flow?

- Is the employer a public or private corporation, and how does this affect the potential for offering shares to the executive?

- If some form of share participation plan is desired, how should it be structured?

- Where the employer does not wish to make the executive a shareholder but the executive wishes to participate in the employer's growth, should other alternatives, such as phantom stock plans, be considered?

- What are the tax implications of a parachute clause in the event of a change in control?

- Do any of the tax incentives for working in remote regions of Canada or outside Canada apply?

- How do provincial taxes come into play?

- Are there international agreements for social security taxes and benefits?

- What importance does the employer's residence have for income tax purposes under either domestic legislation or applicable international tax treaties?

- What are the tax consequences of other types of payments, such as payments in respect of insurance, death benefits or payments in respect of loss of employment or retirement?

- Does the executive wish his or her salary escrowed in advance with a third party in the event that the employer is in financial difficulty?

- Does the place of residence of the trustee or custodian have any importance if any portion of the employee's remuneration is to be entrusted with a trustee or custodian?

The above checklist of items to consider is by no means exhaustive. Instead, the points noted serve merely to begin delineating an area that is vast.

§18.4 The object of this chapter is to review summarily the taxation of executive compensation. The rules in this regard flow principally from the provisions of the federal *Income Tax Act*[1] and also from administrative policy and case law. Given that the text has been written principally for the benefit of the executive rather than to satisfy the tax specialist, many details are intentionally omitted. Moreover, the discussion leaves out many distinctions that an in-depth review would make.

[1] S.C. 1970-71-72, c. 63 as amended (hereafter "ITA" or "the Act").

B. THE TAXPAYER

§18.5 Where services are rendered by an individual, the character of the income affects the computation of the individual's taxes. Indeed, the rules of the Act turn on whether the individual's income is employment income or business income. The former is earned by an employee, the latter by an independent contractor. A fundamental issue, then, is to ascertain whether an individual who renders services is doing so as an employee or as an independent contractor.

§18.6 Where personal services are rendered by a corporation, the income of the corporation is usually taxed as business income. There are, however, rules to counter abuses in the use of a corporation to earn what is basically employment income.

1. Employee or Independent Contractor?

§18.7 The Act does not clearly distinguish the employee from the independent contractor. Under the Act, "employee" includes "officer".[1] There is, however, no definition of either term. Nor is there a definition of the expression "independent contractor". The word "employed" is defined as meaning performing the duties of an office or employment,[2] while "employment" means the position of an individual in the service of some other person.[3] The Act defines "office" as being:

... the position of an individual entitling him to a fixed or ascertainable stipend or remuneration and includes a judicial office, the office of a minister of the Crown, the office of a member of the Senate or House of Commons of Canada, a member of a legislative assembly or a member of a legislative or executive council and any other office, the incumbent of which is elected by popular vote or is elected or appointed in a representative capacity and also includes the position of a corporation director ...[4]

---

[1] ITA, s. 248(1).
[2] ITA, s. 248(1).
[3] ITA, s. 248(1).
[4] ITA, s. 248(1).

§18.8 Where a person's services are rendered through a corporation, there is usually no characterization issue. There is no employment contract between the beneficiary of the services and the individual who physically renders the services. Instead, the individual's employment relationship, if any, is with the corporation, and it is with the corporation that the beneficiary contracts to obtain the services in question.

§18.9 Where an individual renders services directly, rather than through a corporation, difficult characterization problems frequently arise. It is often the case that an individual wishes to render "employment type" services and yet, for tax purposes, desires to be considered an independent contractor. In other cases, an employer will suggest that, in order to avoid source deductions or social security payments, an individual who would otherwise be an employee be considered as an independent contractor. The executive may be motivated to seek treatment as an independent contractor so as to be entitled to additional deductions for expenses. While an executive's right to tax deductions is quite restricted,[1] an independent contractor has greater latitude as most of its expenses can be deducted to the extent that they are incurred for the purpose of gaining or producing income.[2] Important restrictions on deductibility may still apply, however, to the independent contractor, including limitations imposed on deductions for club dues,[3] entertainment expenses,[4] conventions[5] and home office expenses,[6] to name but a few.

---

[1] See Interpretation Bulletin IT-352R2: "Employee's Expenses, Including Work Space in Home Expenses".
[2] ITA, s. 18(1)(*a*).
[3] ITA, s. 18(1)(*l*). See also Interpretation Bulletin IT-148R3: "Recreational Properties and Club Dues".
[4] ITA, s. 67.1(1). See also Interpretation Bulletin IT-518: "Food, Beverages and Entertainment Expenses".
[5] ITA, s. 67.1(3). See also Interpretation Bulletin IT-131R2: "Convention Expenses".

⁶ ITA, s. 18(12). See also Interpretation Bulletin IT-514: "Work Space in Home Expenses".

§18.10 Tax law makes a distinction between a contract *of* service (an employment contract) and a contract *for* services (a contract with an independent contractor). While the Act is relatively silent as to the nature of the distinction, Canadian tax court decisions have provided some guidelines to distinguish an employee from an independent contractor. These decisions generally turn on principles akin to those considered by labour tribunals. However, because labour laws generally have social objectives, the precedents from the labour tribunals may not always be applicable. The laws of the province governing the contract must all be considered. Although the principles are very similar both in common law jurisdictions and in Quebec and the precedents of the common law have had a definite influence in Quebec, the common law principles are not applicable in Quebec. A determination in Quebec has to be made using the civil law principles.

(a) Common Law Jurisdictions

§18.11 In *Wiebe Door Services Ltd. v. M.N.R.*,[1] the Federal Court of Appeal reviewed the various common law criteria which are instrumental to the characterization of a person as either an employee or an independent contractor. In *Wiebe*, the appellant was in the business of installing and repairing overhead doors. At issue was whether unemployment insurance premiums and Canada Pension Plan contributions had been properly made. The Tax Court of Canada held that the door installers and repairmen who rendered services to the appellant were employees of Wiebe Door Services Ltd. rather than independent contractors. In support of its conclusion, the court relied on such factors as control over the individuals, ownership of tools, chance of profit and risk of loss, and integration within the company's operation.

[1] [1986] 5 W.W.R. 450 (F.C.A.).

§18.12 On appeal, the Federal Court of Appeal disagreed with the Tax Court's analysis. It concluded that, for the purpose of its decision, there is no magic formula which may be stated to apply. Rather, all the circumstances must be examined and it is not simply a matter of questioning the degree to which one person is integrated within the business of another person. The court noted that, in *Market Investigations Ltd. v. Minister of Social Security*,[1] Mr. Justice Cooke offered the best synthesis of the correct approach:

The observations of Lord Wright, of Denning L.J., and of the judges of the Supreme Court in the U.S.A. suggest that the fundamental test to be applied is this: "Is the person who has engaged himself to perform these services performing them as a person in business on his own account?" If the answer to that question is "yes", then the contract is a contract for services. If the answer is "no", then the contract is a contract of service. No exhaustive list has been compiled and perhaps no exhaustive list can be compiled of considerations which are relevant in determining that question, nor can strict rules be laid down as to the relative weight which the various considerations should carry in particular cases. The most that can be said is that control will no doubt always have to be considered, although it can no longer be regarded as the sole determining factor; and that factors which may be of importance are such matters as whether the man performing the services provides his own equipment, whether he hires his own helpers, what degree of financial risk he takes, what degree of responsibility for investment and management he has, and whether and how far he has an opportunity of profiting from sound management in the performance of his task. The application of the general test may be easier in a case where the person who engages himself to perform the services does so in the course of an already established business of his own; but this factor is not decisive, and a person who engages himself to perform services for another may well be an independent contractor even though he has not entered into the contract in the course of an existing business carried on by him.

¹   [1968] 3 All E.R. 732 (Q.B.), at 737-38.

(b) Quebec

§18.13 Quebec tax courts have taken a narrower view of the applicable criteria and have thus relied less on the four criteria generally applied in common law jurisdictions, namely control, ownership of tools, chance of profit or risk of loss, and integration. The principal criteria that are considered in Quebec tax courts are those of control and the subordination of the worker to his or her employer.¹ The other traditional common law criteria have less importance.

¹   *Dennis Sports Imports Ltée v. Québec (Deputy Minister of Revenue)*, [1987] R.D.F.Q. Plan-Doc. 3 (Prov. Ct.). See also *Québec (Deputy Minister of Revenue) v. Petroles Veltra (1979) Ltée*, J.E. 91-595 (Que. C.A.); *Beiss v. Québec (Deputy Minister of Revenue)*, [1981] R.D.F.Q. 48 (Prov. Ct.).

(c) Contractual Implications

§18.14 Whether common law principles or those of the Province of Quebec are applied, Canadian tax courts continue to struggle with the difficult issue of distinguishing employees from independent contractors. The determination is highly subjective and, consequently, no general rules exist. Moreover, one finds at times that Canadian tax courts are not necessarily consolidated with labour law principles, perhaps due to the fact that underlying social principles which embody provincial labour laws may differ from those of taxation laws. Hence, law reports are replete with cases involving the employee/independent contractor distinction.

§18.15 It is apparent, therefore, that in negotiating a contract with an executive, it is essential to first address the basis upon which the services of the executive are to be rendered. Where the parties agree that the executive is an employee, there should be no uncertainty as to the tax consequences, given that tax authorities will not likely dispute this position. Where the executive is to be treated as an independent contractor, however, potential exposure to a tax reassessment increases for both contracting parties. In these cases, it is incumbent upon the parties to verify whether the common or civil law, as the case may be, will support their contention, and close attention must be paid to the terms of the contract.

2. Personal Services Corporations

§18.16 Under Canadian income tax laws, a corporation that earns active business income enjoys a rate of tax that is more favourable than that which is applicable to high-income employees earning a salary. In fact, the Act currently reduces the tax on the first $200,000 of a Canadian-controlled private corporation's taxable income from an active business.[1] Through a tax credit known as the "small business deduction", this first $200,000 of taxable income is subject to a federal rate of 13.12% (including a 4% surtax)[2] and to provincial tax rates which vary between approximately 5% and 10% (rounded). This compares favourably with combined federal-provincial marginal tax rates for individuals which can exceed 50% (including surtaxes). These differentials in tax rates explain why an executive may well prefer to render his or her services through a corporation, thereby profiting from the lower rate of tax with regard to the first $200,000 of taxable income.

[1] ITA, s. 125(1).
[2] The 1995 Federal Budget increased the corporate surtax from 3% to 4% for taxation years ending after February 27, 1995. For taxation years that include February 27, 1995, the surtax increase is protected.

§18.17 Governments have traditionally frowned upon the executive's use of a corporation to gain access to preferential tax rates. Prior to the introduction of specific legislative provisions, Revenue Canada addressed the issue by ignoring the existence of many such corporations on the basis that they were shams. However, most of the early court decisions were unfavourable to Revenue Canada.

§18.18   One of the most frequently cited cases involved the head coach of the Hamilton Tiger Cat football team, Ralph Sazio.[1] Mr. Sazio, on the advice of his lawyer, incorporated a private corporation under the name of Ralph J. Sazio Ltd., undertaking to make his coaching services available exclusively to the corporation which in turn had a contract with the football team. The fees paid to the corporation were identical to the salary paid to Mr. Sazio prior to the creation of his company. According to Mr. Sazio's agreement with the company, however, his salary was limited to $6,000 per year.

[1]   *Sazio v. M.N.R.*, [1968] C.T.C. 579 (Ex.).

§18.19   The Minister of National Revenue sought to deny the existence of the corporation, arguing that Ralph Sazio was in reality an employee of the football club and that the payments made to the company represented remuneration for Mr. Sazio's personal services. The Minister thus sought to assess Mr. Sazio for the full amounts paid to the company rather than just his $6,000 salary.

§18.20   The Exchequer Court of Canada, however, did not concur with Revenue Canada's views, refusing to find that the company was a "mere sham, simulacrum or cloak". Rather, Cattanach J. concluded:

> There is no doubt whatsoever that the Company is a properly constituted legal entity and that the Company could legitimately carry on the objects for which it was incorporated. Any person rendering services may incorporate a company to render those services provided there is no prohibition of those services being performed by a corporation rather than a natural person.[1]

Mr. Justice Cattanach's comments in this case became one of the accepted standards against which many similar personal services corporation cases were measured.

[1]   *Sazio v. M.N.R.*, [1968] C.T.C. 579, at 587.

§18.21   In the early 1980s, the government amended the Act in an effort to eliminate, to a large extent, the tax benefit that had previously been enjoyed from the use of personal service corporations. Because the personal services corporation had been recognized as a legitimate tax planning vehicle as a matter of law, the government of the day chose to tackle the issue by addressing the tax benefit specifically and amended the law so as to deny the small business deduction regarding a corporation's income generated from a "personal services business".

§18.22   The Act defines a "personal services business" as a business of providing services, where the individual who actually performs these services on behalf of the corporation owns 10% or more of the shares of any class of the corporation and who would, but for the existence of the corporation, reasonably be regarded as an officer or an employee of the person or entity to whom the services are rendered.[1] Whether or not a business is a "personal services business" rests on a factual determination, but the essence of the exercise is to ask whether it can reasonably be considered that the individual rendering the services is really just an employee of the person to whom the services are rendered. There is, however, an important exception to the personal services business rule. A corporation will not be held to engage in a personal services business where the corporation employs, throughout the year, more than five full-time employees.[2] According to case law, "more than five full-time employees" means six or more, not five and a part-time employee.[3]

[1] ITA, s. 125(7), "personal services business".
[2] ITA, s. 125(7), "personal services business", para. (c).
[3] The Queen v. Hughes & Co. Holdings Ltd., [1994] 2 C.T.C. 170 (F.C.T.D.).

§18.23 Corporations engaged in a personal services business are also limited in the types of deductions to which they are entitled. In computing its income, a corporation that is engaged in a personal services business will not be entitled to deductions for expenses other than:

(1) the salary, wages or other remuneration paid in the year to the individual who is performing the services on behalf of the corporation;

(2) the cost to the corporation of any benefit or allowance provided to the individual;

(3) any amount expended by the corporation in connection with the sale of property or the negotiating of contracts; and

(4) any amount paid for legal expenses incurred in collecting amounts owing to it on account of services rendered.[1]

The effect of the above rule is basically to restrict allowable deductions to those that would ordinarily be available to the executive if he or she had not interposed the corporation.

[1] ITA, s. 18(1)(p).

§18.24 The advantage of using a personal services corporation for the individual is mainly to defer taxes, rather than a permanent tax saving. Where the corporation pays less tax on its income than the executive would pay on a salary received directly, the difference in tax between what is actually paid by the corporation and the taxes that would otherwise be paid by the employee may be recovered at the time that the corporation distributes its income to the individual through the payment of a dividend. The precise amount of tax payable on the dividend will depend, *inter alia*, on the amount of the dividend, the individual's other income and the province of residence. However, as a general rule, if the individual requires the earnings of the corporation for personal or living expenses, there will be no material advantage to using a personal services corporation to the extent that the tax differential will be recovered on the dividend distributions.

C. SITUS OF EMPLOYMENT

§18.25 A resident of Canada is subject to income tax on his or her worldwide income.[1] Thus, where an individual is a resident of Canada, his or her income, wherever earned, is taxable in Canada, and the situs of his or her employment is of no particular importance. The individual may, however, be entitled to a limited tax credit in respect of certain prescribed forms of employment outside Canada.[2]

---

[1] ITA, s. 2(1).
[2] ITA, s. 122.3. See Interpretation Bulletin IT-497R3: "Overseas Employment Tax Credit".

§18.26 Where an individual is not a resident of Canada, the individual is taxable in Canada on what is referred to as his or her "taxable income earned in Canada for the year".[1] This concept includes income from the duties of offices and employments performed in Canada.[2]

---

[1] ITA, s. 2(3). See Interpretation Bulletin IT-171R2: "Non-Resident Individuals — Computation of Taxable Income Earned in Canada and Non-refundable Tax Credits".
[2] ITA, s. 115(1).

§18.27 Revenue Canada considers a non-resident individual to be employed in Canada if the individual performs any part of his or her duties of employment in Canada.[1] It is not necessary that the individual be present in Canada on a permanent basis. Rather, it is merely necessary that the non-resident individual be physically present in Canada at some time and that he or she exercise the duties of an office or an employment in order to be considered employed in Canada. In addition, the individual's employer need not be a Canadian resident. Thus, a non-resident individual who is present in Canada for the purpose of executing any part of his or her employment duties for a non-resident employer may also be deemed to be employed in Canada. In the latter case, however, the employee may be entitled to relief under an international tax treaty.

[1] See Interpretation Bulletin IT-420R3: "Non-Residents — Income Earned in Canada".

§18.28 The Canadian employment income of a non-resident person will include, among other things, salary, benefits, signing bonuses, and any remuneration for services and for covenants not to compete. In this regard, the non-resident individual may again be entitled to relief from Canadian taxation by virtue of an international tax treaty.

D. PLACE OF RESIDENCE

§18.29 In view of the charging provisions of the Act, the determination of the executive's place of residence is fundamental. Where an executive is a resident in Canada for a full taxation year, he or she is subject to tax on his or her worldwide income.[1] Where, instead, the executive is a resident of Canada for only part of a year, the executive is still subject to tax on his worldwide income but only for that part of the year in which he or she was resident in Canada.[2]

[1] ITA, s. 2(1).

[2] ITA, s. 114. See Interpretation Bulletin (Special Release) IT-193 SR: "Taxable Income of Individuals Resident in Canada during Part of a Year". Note that the individual must not be employed in Canada or carrying on a business in Canada. See [1984] *Canadian Tax Foundation Conference Report*, Revenue Canada Round Table, Question 35, p. 807. See also Interpretation Bulletin IT-262R2: "Losses of Non-Residents and Part-Year Residents", Part II.

§18.30 Where the executive is not a resident of Canada for the whole year or any part thereof, the executive will still be subject to tax in Canada on his or her Canadian employment income for the year or the part of the year unless he or she is entitled to relief under an international tax treaty.[1] The executive will, however, escape Canadian tax on other income unless such income, because of its Canadian nexus, is subject to tax by virtue of another provision of the Act and is not relieved from tax by an international tax treaty.

[1] ITA, s. 2(3). See Interpretation Bulletin IT-420R3: "Non-Residents — Income Earned in Canada".

§18.31 It is important to note that the Act contains a statutory "sojourner" rule.[1] Under this rule, a non-resident person will be deemed to have been a resident in Canada throughout a taxation year if he or she sojourned in Canada for 183 days or more during the taxation year. As a consequence, the otherwise non-resident taxpayer may become liable to Canadian tax on his or her worldwide income for the entire year. It will be particularly important to consider the possible application of this rule where a non-resident individual is asked by his or her employer to spend time in Canada for any purpose. Once again, an international treaty may offer relief.

¹   ITA, s. 250(1).

§18.32   It is clear that the residence rules will be of interest where a non-resident individual contemplates Canadian employment. Before accepting either full-time or part-time employment in Canada, the executive will wish to consider whether, by virtue of his or her presence in Canada, he or she will become a resident of Canada or will be deemed to have become a resident in Canada for taxation purposes.

§18.33   The residence rules will also be of interest in situations where an executive leaves Canada either as a result of his or her employment or because of his or her retirement. In such cases, the executive will wish to consider whether, from the standpoint of the Act, he or she shall be deemed to have terminated his or her Canadian residence, and whether this has an impact on his or her exposure to Canadian taxes.

1.   The Domestic Rules of Residency

§18.34   Under Canadian tax law, residency is distinct from domicile or citizenship. There is no tax imposed by Canada on a person merely because that person is domiciled in, or is a citizen of, Canada. A person may be held to have more than one residence. This is a principle which the Exchequer Court of Canada held in *Thomson v. M.N.R.*¹ to be well established. In this case, the court concluded that an individual may be ordinarily resident in more than one country if his or her stay in each is substantial and habitual in the ordinary course of the routine of living. This conclusion was subsequently upheld by the Supreme Court of Canada when it rejected the Minister of National Revenue's appeal.² It is in such cases of multiple residences that one commonly invokes international tax treaties so as to avoid double taxation.

¹   [1945] C.T.C. 63.
²   [1946] S.C.R. 209.

§18.35   Determining the residence of an individual for Canadian income tax purposes is a subjective matter. It involves weighing of a number of factors. While rules are difficult to formulate, a number of broad principles do exist. First, the intent of an individual is not determinative. While change of domicile depends on the individual's intention, change of residence is a question of fact. The individual's desires are generally not a consideration. Second, there are a number of indicia which Revenue Canada considers relevant.[1] Some of the more influential factors to consider were set out by the Exchequer Court of Canada in *Schujahn v. M.N.R.*[2] These include length of stay in Canada, presence of the individual's family, location of personal assets including the family home, bank accounts and credit cards, regularity and length of visits to Canada by the individual, the individual's social ties, and the permanence and purpose of any stay abroad.

[1] See Interpretation Bulletin IT-221R2: "Determination of an Individual's Residence Status".

[2] [1962] C.T.C. 364.

§18.36 The issue of residence will also be of concern when a resident individual departs from Canada. From Revenue Canada's perspective, in order for an individual to become a non-resident of Canada, there must be a degree of permanence to the stay abroad. Revenue Canada's position is that where a Canadian resident is absent from Canada for whatever reason for less than two years, the individual will be presumed to have retained his or her Canadian residence status while abroad, unless he or she can clearly establish that positive actions have been taken to sever all residential connections with Canada.[1]

[1] See Interpretation Bulletin IT-221R2: "Determination of an Individual's Residence Status". See also *Erickson v. M.N.R.*, [1980] C.T.C. 2117 (T.R.B.).

§18.37 Other elements which militate against the severance of ties to Canada include maintaining provincial hospitalization and medical insurance coverage, having a seasonal residence in Canada, keeping professional memberships in Canada, and receiving family allowance payments. These factors, among others, may be invoked by Revenue Canada in holding that an individual has remained a resident of Canada. Furthermore, if there is evidence that the individual's return to Canada was foreseen at the time of his or her departure (for example, if he or she has a contract for employment upon his or her return to Canada), Revenue Canada will presume that the individual did not sever all residential ties upon leaving Canada.[1] On the other hand, where the individual is absent from Canada for two or more years, he or she will be presumed to have become a non-resident of Canada, provided that, on an examination of the facts, he or she may be considered to have severed his ties to Canada.[2]

[1] See Interpretation Bulletin IT-221R2: "Determination of an Individual's Residence Status". See also *Erickson v. M.N.R.*, [1980] C.T.C. 2117 (T.R.B.).

[2] *Ibid.*

§18.38   Consistent with Revenue Canada's policies, the courts will give weight to an individual's centre of vital interests. In *Shpak v. M.N.R.*,[1] a husband and wife bought a house in, and moved to Point Roberts, Washington, because the market value of comfortable housing there was one-quarter of the price being paid for comparable homes in Vancouver. The Shpaks had no relatives in the United States. They commuted daily to Vancouver for work. Most of their social life was centred around Canadian friends and most of their banking was done in Canada. In light of these facts, the Tax Review Board concluded that, as their "customary mode of living" included spending a considerable portion of their time socializing and engaging in economic activities in Canada, the Shpaks continued to be taxable as residents of Canada notwithstanding that they had taken up domicile in the U.S. There was almost no evidence that they had taken any steps, much less sufficient steps, to sever their residential ties with Canada.

[1]   [1981] C.T.C. 2429 (T.R.B.).

2. International Tax Treaties

§18.39   Canada has an important network of reciprocal international tax agreements. Broadly speaking, the objective of these treaties is to provide relief from double taxation where a person may otherwise be subject to tax on his or her income in more than one country. With regard to the issue of residence, the treaties provide rules to determine in which state an individual will be held to reside where the individual may, under the laws of both signing countries to any such treaty, have a dual residence. These are generally known as "tie-breaker" rules.

§18.40   The treaties also establish the extent to which the country of which the individual is not a resident may tax the individual's employment income from services performed in that country. In this respect, the treaties contain relieving provisions which generally turn on the amount of employment income earned in the said country, the number of days present in the country,[1] and whether the employer has a permanent establishment or fixed base in the country.

[1]   See Interpretation Bulletin IT-298: "Canada-U.S. Tax Convention — Number of Days 'Present' in Canada".

§18.41   Where, notwithstanding the relieving provisions, both countries are entitled to tax the individual's income, the treaties provide rules to give relief from foreign taxes in the individual's country of residence. There are also rules which address other areas, such as the taxation of other types of income including, for instance, income from dividends, interest, royalties, capital gains and pensions.

E. THE TAXATION OF EMPLOYMENT INCOME

§18.42 This section reviews the taxation of the principal forms of employment income other than stock or quasi-stock benefits, which are reviewed in the next section.

1. Salary, Wages and Other Remuneration

(a) The Basic Inclusion Rules

§18.43 An individual must include as income from an office or employment the "salary, wages and other remuneration", including gratuities, received in the year.[1] The terms "salary and wages" are defined by the Act, but not for the purpose of determining employment income. "Remuneration" is not defined in the Act at all.[2] Consequently, it is necessary to rely on case law for an understanding of these terms.

---

[1] ITA, s. 5(1).

[2] In *Lin (R.K.) v. Canada*, [1995] 2 C.T.C. 2971D #2 (T.C.C.), Bauman, J.T.C.C. referred to the definition of "remuneration" in s. 100 of the Regulations. Although, as he mentioned, a regulation cannot be used to interpret a statute, he examined the system comprising both the Act and the Regulation in rendering his decision.

§18.44 Tax courts have a long tradition of defining "salary, wages and remuneration" in the broadest of terms. Generally, their approach may be described as favouring the inclusion as income of any amount which one may objectively look to as having been received directly, or indirectly, as a result of the individual's employment.[1] The case books are rife with examples.

---

[1] This is consistent with the administrative approach. See, *e.g.*, Interpretation Bulletin IT-389R: "Vacation Pay Trusts Established under Collective Agreements".

§18.45 Because the terms "salary, wages and remuneration" imply a connection to an employment, the Act contains rules to discourage attempts at treating amounts as having been received other than in respect of employment remuneration. Were it not for these rules, an individual could arrange for the payment of amounts either prior to or after a period of employment, and argue that the said amounts do not represent employment income.

§18.46 To clarify the tax treatment in such situations, there are specific deeming provisions in the Act.[1] First, any amount received by a person during a period in which he or she is an officer of or in the employment of another person is deemed to be remuneration. Second, any amount received on account or in lieu of payment of or in satisfaction of an obligation arising out of an agreement made immediately prior to, during, or immediately after a period that the payee was an officer of or in the employment of the payor is similarly deemed to be employment remuneration. These deeming provisions are, however, subject to important limitations and only apply to the extent that:

- the amount received is consideration or partial consideration for accepting the office or entering into the contract of employment (a signing bonus, for example);
- the amount received is remuneration or partial remuneration for the services as an officer or under a contract of employment; or
- the amount received is consideration for or partial consideration for a covenant with reference to what the officer or employee is or is not to do before or after the termination of the employment (a non-competition covenant, for example).

[1]   ITA, s. 6(3). See Interpretation Bulletin IT-196R2: "Payments by Employer to Employee".

(b)   Timing of Income Inclusion

§18.47   Before 1986, salary, wages or other remuneration were generally taxed only on a "received" basis and accrued employment income was generally not taxed until it was received. The Exchequer Court of Canada, in *M.N.R. v. Rousseau*,[1] concluded that amounts which had been placed to the taxpayer's credit on the books of the company had not been received by the taxpayer. There have, however, been several attempts to tax employment amounts as having been "constructively" received by the employee in similar circumstances.

[1]   [1960] C.T.C. 336.

§18.48   Because the taxation of employee remuneration was essentially on a "received" basis (except where amounts could be held to have been constructively received), it was a popular tax planning technique prior to 1986 to defer the receipt of employment income beyond the end of the calendar year. Ideally, the employer would claim a deduction in the current taxation year on the basis that liability had been incurred (although not yet paid) and that the employee would hopefully only pay tax in a later calendar year, that is, at the time of receipt.

§18.49 In 1986, the Act was amended to introduce the "salary deferral arrangement" rules.[1] By reason of these rules, an executive must generally include in his or her income for a taxation year any amount he or she is entitled to receive in the said year in respect of salary, wages or other remuneration. Although the salary deferral arrangement rules are complex and are subject to many exceptions, their thrust is generally to include as income any amount of salary which an executive is entitled to receive, in circumstances where the actions of the parties indicate an intent to defer tax. The salary deferral arrangement rules contain many exceptions, however. For example, a noteworthy exception to these rules is the ability to defer tax on a bonus for a period extending up to three years following the end of the taxation year in which the services giving rise to the bonus are rendered. Although this exception may at first glance be appealing, its scope is limited by the meaning which the courts have given to a "bonus".

[1] ITA, s. 56(1)(w). See Interpretation Bulletin IT-109R2: "Unpaid Amounts".

(c) Indirect Payments

§18.50 An executive may not avoid tax by directing his or her employer to pay to some other person amounts which would otherwise accrue to the executive. Where, for example, an executive instructs his or her employer to deposit his or her pay cheque in his or her spouse's bank account, the executive will nevertheless be personally subject to tax on the amount deposited. Here, there is no ambiguity in the Act. The "indirect payments"[1] rule provides that a payment or transfer of property made pursuant to the direction of, or with the concurrence of, a taxpayer to some other person for the benefit of the taxpayer must be included in computing the taxpayer's income to the extent that it would be so included if the payment or transfer had been made directly to the taxpayer. This is equally the case when the payment or transfer is made to some other person because the taxpayer wishes to have a benefit conferred on that person.

[1] ITA, s. 56(2). See Interpretation Bulletin IT-335R: "Indirect Payments".

2. Employment Benefits

§18.51 Where an amount does not constitute salary, wages or other remuneration, the amount is nevertheless subject to tax if it falls within the employment benefit rules of the Act. The Act provides that the income of a person from an office or employment must include the value of board, lodging and other benefits of any kind whatsoever, received or enjoyed by the person in the year in respect of, in the course of, or by virtue of an office or employment.[1] The underlying policy in this area appears to be that amounts that result in some form of benefit to an employee by reason of his or her employment, whether or not the employee receives a cash payment, should be taxed. The measure of the benefit is at times controversial, however. Case law is to the effect that, in determining the value of a benefit, one may take its cost to the employer into consideration. However, its fair market value will also frequently be considered.[2]

[1] ITA, s. 6(1)(*a*).
[2] *Youngman v. R.*, [1990] 2 C.T.C. 10 (F.C.A.).

§18.52 Rules defining employment benefit are also broad. As Mr. Justice Cullen noted in deciding *Splane v. Canada:*[1]

> [T]he legislators deliberately chose to make this section very broad in order to ensure that "perks" or "fringe benefits" received from an employer are swept into the computation of an employee's income.

[1] [1990] 2 C.T.C. 199 (F.C.T.D.), at 200-201, affd 92 DTC 6021 (F.C.A.).

§18.53 The Act does not, however, define "benefit". It simply states that employment income includes a benefit of any kind whatsoever, received or enjoyed by a person in the year in respect of, in the course of, or by virtue of an office or employment.[1] In *R. v. Poynton,*[2] Mr. Justice Evans characterized the essence of a taxable benefit by stating:

> I do not believe the language to be restricted to benefits that are related to the office or employment in the sense that they represent a form of remuneration for services rendered. If it is a material acquisition which confers an economic benefit on the taxpayer and does not constitute an exemption, eg loan or gift, then it is within the all-embracing definition of section 3 [now section 6(1)(*a*) of the Act, relating to taxable benefits].

[1] ITA, s. 6(1)(*a*).
[2] [1972] C.T.C. 411 (Ont. S.C.), at 420.

§18.54 Mr. Justice Evans' view was specifically adopted by the Supreme Court of Canada in *R. v. Savage*[1] and has become one of the principal standards against which taxable benefit issues are measured.

[1] [1983] C.T.C. 393.

§18.55 Revenue Canada provides the following examples of taxable benefits:[1] board and lodging, rent-free and low-rent housing, travel benefits, the personal use of an employer's motor vehicle, holiday trips, prizes and incentive awards, frequent flyer benefits, travelling expenses for the employee's spouse, premiums under provincial hospitalization and medical care insurance programs, financial counselling other than as a result of loss of employment, and income tax return preparation. Revenue Canada has also ruled that a discount on automobile insurance given to an employee gives rise to a taxable benefit.[2] This list is by no means exhaustive.

[1] See Interpretation Bulletin IT-470R: "Employees' Fringe Benefits".
[2] RevCan Views, January 1991-103: "Employee Discounts — Automobile Insurance Premiums".

§18.56 As may be expected, however, there are exceptions which may be categorized as either legislative, administrative or judicial. As will be discussed in more detail later, the exceptions stem primarily from social policy, such as in the area of pension and health benefits, or from the desire of the administration and the courts to tax only amounts which result in some form of enrichment to the employee personally. It follows that amounts paid in order to allow an individual to execute duties of employment, such as business travel reimbursements, are generally not subject to tax.

§18.57 Some of the more common employment benefits and their tax treatment are reviewed below.

(a) Automobiles

§18.58 Where an employer supplies an automobile to an employee for personal use, the Act subjects the employee to two tax incidences. The employee is deemed to have received a taxable benefit equal to the portion of the operating expenses of the automobile paid by the employer which is attributable to the employee's personal use and to have received a "reasonable standby charge", the object of which is to tax the employee annually on a specified portion of the acquisition or rental cost of an employer-supplied automobile.[1] It should also be noted that the issue of free parking has also been considered by Revenue Canada.[2]

[1] See Interpretation Bulletin IT-63R5: "Benefits, Including Standby Charge for an Automobile, from the Personal Use of a Motor Vehicle Supplied by an Employer-After 1992".
[2] RevCan Views, 9234405: "Parking and benefits".

§18.59 The calculation of the personal-use portion of employer-paid operating expenses is relatively straightforward[1] and involves allocating the operating expenses between personal and business use. An employee who wishes to establish a specific portion of business use will, however, generally be required to produce detailed records.

[1] See Interpretation Bulletin IT-522R: "Vehicle, Travel and Sales Expenses of Employees".

§18.60   For its part, the standby charge is calculated pursuant to a formula.[1] Where the employer purchases the automobile, the standby charge to be included in income is an amount equal to 2% per month of the cost of the automobile to the employer, or 24% per year, prorated on the basis of the number of kilometres driven for personal use. Where, instead, the automobile is leased by the employer, the employee must include in income what amounts to the personal-use portion of two-thirds of the lease payments made by the employer.

[1] See Interpretation Bulletin IT-63R5: "Benefits, Including Standby Charge for an Automobile, from the Personal Use of a Motor Vehicle Supplied by an Employer-After 1992".

§18.61   The Act contains special relieving provisions for the computation of the standby charge and the deemed benefit for employees engaged principally in selling or leasing automobiles. Another relieving rule which is elective also exists. Instead of including the actual personal-use portion of employer-paid operating expenses, an employee may elect to include in income one-half of the standby charge, less operating costs reimbursed by the employee to the employer. The principal advantage of this latter approach is that it obviates the need to keep records.

§18.62   An executive who requires an automobile for the performance of his or her employment will have several options. Indeed, the executive may ask that the employer purchase or lease an automobile to be made available to the executive. In this case, the rules discussed above may apply. On the other hand, the executive may wish to use his or her personal automobile and be reimbursed on an allowance basis for any costs relating to the business use of the automobile. In this area, there are no hard and fast rules as the relative merits of each option depend on both the employer's and the employee's tax situations.

(b) Aircraft

§18.63   Personal use of an employer-supplied aircraft is treated in much the same manner as the use of an employer's automobile. When the executive pays less than a reasonable charge for such use, Revenue Canada considers the executive to have derived a taxable benefit therefrom. That benefit is valued at the cost that the executive would have incurred had he or she chartered a comparable aircraft at the current commercial rate for the time of personal use.[1] In determining the equivalent charter cost, any flat fee plus all related costs which would normally be associated must be included. Where more than one passenger is on the flight, the costs are prorated on a per employee basis.

[1] See Interpretation Bulletin IT-160R3: "Personal Use of Aircraft". See also Interpretation Bulletin IT-522: "Vehicle and Other Travelling Expenses — Employees", para. 11.

(c) Club Memberships

§18.64 The payment by an employer of an executive's club dues will constitute a taxable benefit if it is in the nature of a fringe benefit with little or no advantage to the employer's business. However, if it is established that it was clearly to the employer's advantage for the executive to be a member of the club, the executive will not be considered to have received a taxable benefit.[1]

[1] Interpretation Bulletin IT-148R3: "Recreational Properties and Club Dues".

§18.65 The employer, however, will not be entitled to a deduction for club dues.[1] For this reason, if the executive is entitled to a taxable benefit, the employer may wish to consider paying additional salary to the executive (grossed-up for taxes) to cover the club dues.

[1] ITA, s. 18(1)(*l*).

(d) Legal Services Plans

§18.66 The employer may wish to give assistance to the executive in respect of personal legal costs. If the plan is insured, that is, if the employer pays premiums to secure a commitment to the effect that legal services will be rendered to the executive, he or she should realize a benefit equal to the portion of the premiums attributable to him or her in the year that the premiums are paid. Payments out of the plan will not be taxable however.[1] If the employer self-insures the plan, payments to the executive by the employer in respect of the executive's legal expenses will be taxable. A recurring issue in this regard is whether the reimbursement of legal expenses to the executive constitutes a benefit to him or her, particularly if the legal action can be tied directly or indirectly to the executive's functions.[2]

[1] RevCan Views, June 1991-201: "Taxation of legal services plan".
[2] *Clemiss v. M.N.R.*, [1987] 2 C.T.C. 2275 (T.C.C.).

(e) Child Care

§18.67 The executive's child care expenses, when paid by the employer, will be treated as a taxable benefit received by the executive. This might be the case, for example, when the employer provides day care services for the young children of its executives. This, again, raises some valuation issues where the employer provides the services directly (rather than merely reimbursing or subsidizing expenses incurred by the executive). Revenue Canada has taken the position that no taxable benefit accrues to an employee who uses "in-house child care facilities", defined as facilities managed directly by the employer.[1] However, where the employer subsidizes a facility operated by a third party or where the employer makes the facilities available at higher rates to non-employees, this subsidy must be included in the employee's income. The amount of this benefit will be considered as an amount paid on account of child care for the purpose of the section 63 deduction for child care expenses.

[1] RevCan Views, 96107/25: "Taxable benefit from employer provided child care".

(f) Employer-Paid Vacations

§18.68 Revenue Canada considers that the payment of a trip or vacation by the employer for the executive or his or her immediate family amounts to a taxable benefit arising from employment.[1] The basis on which the benefit will be valued is the fair market value of that benefit. This is clearly the case when, for instance, the vacation or trip is entirely for personal/immediate family enjoyment. However, when the executive's trip involves some business, the taxable portion of the benefit may be reduced.

[1] See Interpretation Bulletin IT-470R: "Employees' Fringe Benefits".

§18.69 A taxable benefit also arises where the employer funds, in whole or in part, the travel costs of the executive's spouse. In many such cases, the issue becomes whether the presence of the spouse was necessary for business.[1]

[1] See *Hale v. M.N.R.*, [1968] C.T.C. 477 (Ex.).

(g) Sickness or Accident Benefits and Disability Income Benefits

§18.70 Employer contributions to group sickness or accident plans will not constitute a taxable benefit to the executive.[1] This will include disability and income maintenance plans.[2] To qualify, a plan must be based on insurance. Benefits received by an individual from the plan will, however, be taxable to the extent of their excess over the executive's contributions.[3] Where an employer contributes to a non-group plan, the result will be the opposite: the employer contributions will give rise to a taxable benefit, and the payments out of the plan will not be taxable.[4] If an employer makes a voluntary payment to the executive due to his or her sickness or accident, that payment will be taxed as an employment benefit.[5]

[1] ITA, s. 6(1)(*a*)(i).
[2] Interpretation Bulletin IT-85R2: "Health and Welfare Trusts for Employees".
[3] ITA, s. 6(1)(*f*). See Interpretation Bulletin IT-428: "Wage Loss Replacement Plans". An issue that arises frequently is whether the plan constitutes an "employee-pay-all plan" so that the benefits received are not taxable to the employee. See also *Dagenais v. Canada*, [1995] 2 C.T.C. 100 (F.C.T.D.).
[4] ITA, s. 6(1)(*a*).
[5] See *Ouimet v. M.N.R.*, [1979] C.T.C. 2172 (T.R.B.).

(h) Insurance Premiums

§18.71 An executive will be subject to a taxable benefit equal to the product of the level of the insurance times the average annual cost of insurance for the premium category, minus the amount paid by the executive, if any.[1] It appears that a group policy which provides for automatic coverage of dependants will not qualify. However, a policy with optional dependants coverage paid for by the executive will qualify.[2] Where the coverage exceeds $25,000, the executive must include the value of those premiums paid by the employer which relate to this excess coverage. However, any payment by the insurer to the beneficiary of the policy as a result of the death or disability of the insured is not taxable.

[1] ITA, s. 6(4).
[2] RevCan Views, November 1991-26: "Definition of 'group term life insurance policy' in subsection 248(1)".

§18.72 Where an employer pays life insurance premiums on a non-group policy, the premium paid will be taxable as a benefit received by the executive.[1]

[1] ITA, s. 6(1)(*a*).

(i)   Sales for Less than Fair Market Value

§18.73   In cases where an employer sells property or services to an employee at a price that is less than the usual arm's length value of such goods or services, the employee may be subject to a taxable benefit. There are, however, exceptions. If the employer's usual practice is to sell merchandise to its employees at a discount (rather than an extraordinary arrangement with an employee or a select group of employees), Revenue Canada's stated policy is that the benefits enjoyed by employees in exercising such a privilege are not normally considered as taxable benefits.[1] In addition, Revenue Canada appears to disregard reciprocal arrangements between two or more employers under which employees of one employer may exercise their privileges with another person with whom they are not employed.[2]

[1]   See Interpretation Bulletin IT-470R: "Employees' Fringe Benefits".
[2]   Interpretation Bulletin IT-470R: "Employees' Fringe Benefits".

(j)   Loans and Advances

§18.74   Where an employer makes a loan to an employee, two principal issues must be considered.[1]

[1]   Note that Revenue Canada distinguishes between a loan and an advance: see Interpretation Bulletin IT-222R: "Advances to Employees".

§18.75   First, to the extent that the loan was made at an interest rate which is less than the "prescribed" rate required by Revenue Canada, the employee will be required to include the difference between the prescribed rate and the contractual rate of interest on the loan as income.[1] The prescribed rate is a rate specified by regulation, and varies from time to time. However, for home purchase and home relocation loans, there are relieving rules. For these types of loans, the Act fixes the prescribed rate at the beginning of the loan and every five years thereafter.[2] In addition, for home relocation loans, the employee may claim a deduction for the amount of the prescribed rate of interest applying to the lesser of the loan amount of $25,000 and the amount of the imputed benefit on the relocation loan.[3]

[1]   ITA, s. 80.4(1). Note that if the term of the loan exceeds 5 years, s. 80.4(6) deems a new loan to be received every 5 years.
[2]   ITA, s. 80.4(4).
[3]   ITA, s. 110(1)(j).

§18.76   The second issue relates to the forgiveness of the employee's loan. Where an employee's loan is settled by the employer without any payment by the employee, or by a payment by the employee lesser than that of the outstanding loan at that time, the employee is deemed to have received a taxable benefit equal to the amount by which the balance of the loan exceeds the amount reimbursed by the employee.[1] Therefore, where a loan is entirely extinguished, the employee will be deemed to have received a taxable benefit equal to the amount of the loan. Conversely, where the employer continues to require repayment but not of the full amount of the loan, that amount which the employee is not required to repay will be included in the calculation of the employee's employment income.[2]

---

[1] ITA, s. 6(15).
[2] Concerning the forgiveness of employee loans, see *McArdle v. M.N.R.*, [1984] C.T.C. 2277 (T.C.C.); *Cousins v. M.N.R.*, [1972] C.T.C. 2017 (T.R.B.).

§18.77 Taxable benefit issues may arise even where the employee's loan is not made directly by the employer. If, for example, an employer undertakes with a third-party lender to pay or guarantee any amount in respect of a loan to its employee, the loan may arguably be deemed to have been made by virtue of the employee's employment, with the result that the employee may be viewed as having received a taxable benefit in respect of the loan and the guarantee. This does, however, raise certain timing and valuation problems.

§18.78 It should be noted that, if the employee is also a shareholder of the employer, it will be necessary to assess whether he or she has received the loan as an employee or as a shareholder. The Act contains specific provisions directed at loans to shareholders.[1]

---

[1] See ITA, s. 15(2). See Interpretation Bulletin IT-421R2: "Benefits to Individuals, Corporations and Shareholders from Loans or Debt".

(k) Retirement Plans

§18.79 The area of retirement benefits is vast, and the applicable rules are complex. Generally speaking, pension plans may be registered or non-registered, and may be funded or unfunded. Plans known as deferred profit sharing plans also form part of the recognized retirement vehicles. Retirement plan permutations are extremely varied. Employer contributions to a registered pension plan do not give rise to a taxable benefit. This area is examined more fully below in Chapter 19, "Retirement Income Provisions".

(l) Private Health Services Plans

§18.80 An employer's contribution to a "private health services plan" does not result in a taxable benefit to employees.[1] Unlike group sickness or accident insurance plans, benefits out of the plan are not taxable. A "private health services plan" is defined to include both a contract of insurance in respect of hospital expenses, medical expenses or any combination of such expenses, as well as a medical care insurance plan or hospital care insurance plan or any combination thereof.[2] Revenue Canada's policy is that contracts or plans in respect of dental care also fall within the definition of a "private health services plan".[3]

---

[1] ITA, s. 6(1)(*a*).
[2] ITA, s. 248(1).
[3] See Interpretation Bulletin IT-339R2: "Meaning of 'Private Health Services Plan' ". Regarding a proposed plan, see Advance Tax Ruling ATR-23.

§18.81 For a plan to qualify as a private health services plan, Revenue Canada requires that the plan satisfy the following basic conditions:

- it must be an undertaking of one person;
- it must be established to indemnify another person;
- there must be an agreed consideration;
- it must provide coverage for a loss or liability in respect of an event the happening of which is uncertain; and
- the coverage provided by the plan must be based on some method of computation involving actuarial or similar studies.[1]

---

[1] Interpretation Bulletin IT-339R2: "Meaning of 'Private Health Services Plan' ". IT-339R2 is currently being revised to incorporate changes discussed in §18.82.

§18.82 Notwithstanding the requirement that the plan benefits be actuarially based, there is some administrative leeway. For example, a "cost plus" plan may qualify as a private health services plan. Under such a plan, the employer contracts with a trustee or insurance company for the indemnification of employees' claims on defined risks. The employer promises the trustee or insurer to reimburse it for the cost of claims, and to pay an administration fee. Similarly, a plan under which an employer reimburses employees directly for medical or hospital care expenses may qualify as a "private health services plan" provided that the employer is obliged under the employment contract to reimburse the employees for such expenses as are incurred by them or their dependants. As a result of a 1996 decision of the Canadian Human Rights Commission, Revenue Canada has reviewed its position regarding the definition of a "private health services plan". Accordingly, plans that provide coverage for the same sex partner of an employee can be regarded as a "private health services plan".[1]

[1] RevCan Views, 9710558: "Private health services plan coverage for same sex life partner of an employee". See also Revcan Views, Technical Interpretation 9638755.

(m) Supplementary Unemployment Benefit Plans

§18.83 A "supplementary unemployment benefit plan", often known as a guaranteed wages plan, is defined by the Act as an arrangement under which payments are made by an employer to a trustee to be held in trust exclusively for payment to employees who are or may be laid off for a temporary or indefinite period.[1] Not included in this definition are arrangements in the nature of pension funds and employee profit sharing plans. Provided the requirements for registration of a guaranteed wages plan are met,[2] the contributions made to the trustee by the employer can be deducted in calculating the employer's income[3] and the income earned by the trust is exempt from tax while in the trustee's possession and control.[4] While the amounts actually paid to an employee do constitute income and will, therefore, be subject to tax upon receipt, a contribution to such a plan for the benefit of employees does not itself give rise to a taxable benefit.

[1] ITA, s. 145(1), "supplementary unemployment benefit plan".
[2] ITA, s. 145(1), "registered supplementary unemployment benefit plan".
[3] ITA, s. 145(5).
[4] ITA, s. 145(2).

(n) Health and Welfare Trusts

§18.84 Revenue Canada recognizes that there are various hybrid forms of employee health and welfare plans. Indeed, health and welfare benefits for employees may be provided through a master trust arrangement, incorporating or combining benefit programs from an individual group sickness or accident plan, a private health services plan, and a group term life insurance policy. Where such an omnibus plan meets Revenue Canada's conditions, it will be designated as a health and welfare trust by Revenue Canada,[1] and employer contributions to the plan will not constitute taxable benefits. Furthermore, any employee covered by the plan will be deemed to have received a taxable benefit only to the extent that the employee would have received such a benefit had the plan been structured individually as an individual group sickness or accident insurance plan, a private health services plan or a group term life insurance policy, assuming that these are the only components of the plan.

[1]   See Interpretation Bulletin IT-85R2: "Health and Welfare Trusts for Employees".

§18.85   Where employees have personally funded disability insurance policies and assign their policies to a health and welfare trust established by their employer which then pays the premiums, Revenue Canada takes the position that the plan is not a group plan. Therefore, the employer-paid premiums give rise to a taxable benefit.[1] To avoid this, it appears that expenses must be paid directly by the employer.

[1]   RevCan Views, March 1991-27: "Health and Welfare trusts — disability insurance".

§18.86   Where contributions to a health and welfare plan are made on a shared basis by the employer and its employees, Revenue Canada will assume that each benefit under the plan is paid as a result of both employer and employee contributions unless the plan clearly establishes that the trustee must use the employee contributions to pay all or some part of the cost of a specific benefit.[1] Generally, the proportion of the benefits received by employees that is traceable to employee contributions will be non-taxable. The taxable benefits received which are attributable to the employer's contributions will, however, be included in the employee's income and will, accordingly, be subject to tax.

[1]   RevCan Views, March 1991-27: "Health and Welfare trusts — disability insurance".

(o) Flexible Benefit Plans

§18.87   Recently, there has been growing interest on the part of both employers and employees in flexible employee benefit arrangements, commonly referred to as "cafeteria plans". Such plans reflect the reality that the individual needs or preferences of employees differ. The rules that govern flexible benefit arrangements are not contained in the Act but, rather, flow from administrative policy statements of Revenue Canada.[1]

[1]   See RevCan Views, 9606655: "Mandatory conversion of salary to flex".

§18.88   The essence of a flexible benefit plan is to provide employees with a choice of options regarding employment benefits. Thus, for example, an employer may institute a plan which offers employees the flexibility to select among a menu of benefits which include the reimbursement of medical expenses, the payment of premiums for a wage loss replacement plan, term life insurance, accidental death and dismemberment insurance, retirement planning advice, employee counselling services, and loans at a favourable rate of interest. Regardless of the exact menu offered, such plans typically function similarly. The employer credits an amount to the benefit of each employee, with the employee then allocating the credit among his or her benefit choices. The benefit choices are usually made at the beginning of each benefit program year. The employee may elect to receive a portion of the credits in the form of benefits and the balance in cash.

§18.89 In designing a flexible benefit plan, structure is crucial. The plan credits should not be construed as disguised salary. Where an employer offers an employee the opportunity to convert amounts that the employee would otherwise receive as salary, bonuses or other employment benefits into flexible benefit plan credits, these credits will be taxed at the time that they are made.[1] Moreover, Revenue Canada's position is that, where the plan permits employees to change their coverage during the year and thereby request a cash refund of any excess cash in the plan, all credits made to the plan in the year that are capable of being withdrawn in cash will be taxable, regardless of whether they are actually withdrawn. It follows that, in order to avoid tax, an irrevocable designation regarding the utilization of the plan credits should be made at the beginning of the benefit program year.

[1] RevCan Views, 9531035: "Trading vacation or bonus for health care".

§18.90 The tax consequences that attach to flexible benefit plans depend on the underlying components of each plan. Flexible benefit plans are essentially umbrella arrangements which regroup a number of employment benefits. Where a flexible benefit plan includes a plan which, on its own, would qualify as a private health services plan, the employee should not be taxed on the contributions that may be earmarked as being in respect of the private health services plan. However, if the plan has a low or no interest mortgage feature, each employee who benefits from the feature will be subject to a taxable benefit in relation to this component. One must, therefore, look to the components of each flexible benefit plan to determine whether taxable benefits will arise.

(p) Counselling Services

§18.91 The Act provides that benefits derived from counselling services in respect of the mental or physical health of an employee or a person related to the employee are not taxable. This also extends to counselling services in respect of the re-employment or retirement of the employee.

§18.92 Revenue Canada has indicated that services such as tobacco, drug or alcohol counselling, stress management counselling, and job placement and retirement counselling will be considered to be not taxable.[1] Revenue Canada has made a distinction, however, between the "treatment" of a disorder and "counselling". Thus, treatment for addiction, though it involves counselling, is not exempt under subparagraph 6(1)(*a*)(iv) of the Act.[2] In another position, Revenue Canada attempted to distinguish between retirement planning which is not taxable and financial planning which is taxable.[3]

[1] See Interpretation Bulletin IT-470R: "Employees' Fringe Benefits", para. 46.
[2] RevCan Views, 9431825: "Employee benefit of a treatment addiction".
[3] RevCan Views, August 1991-52: "Whether financial counselling is an exempt benefit for employees".

(q) Relocation Expenses

§18.93 The taxability of payments by an employer arising from an employee's moving or relocating expenses has been the subject of much litigation. Usually, the issue concerns payments made to the employee as compensation for losses incurred on the sale of the employee's house, or compensation for added expenses due to higher house prices or higher housing costs, generally.

§18.94 In *Splane v. Canada*,[1] the Federal Court of Canada, Trial Division, had occasion to consider whether mortgage interest differential payments received by the employee-plaintiff from his employer constituted remuneration to be included in employment income as being a benefit received therefrom. In this case, the plaintiff was employed by the Canadian government as a Senior Court Registrar for the Federal Court of Canada in Ottawa when he was asked to relocate to the registry office in Edmonton. The plaintiff purchased a new home near Edmonton which he financed with a mortgage loan bearing an interest rate of 14.25%, 1.75% higher than the 12.50% he had been paying on his Ontario mortgage. The Canadian government, following its policy of compensating employees who were relocated, paid Mr. Splane certain amounts to reimburse him for these higher interest charges. Revenue Canada included the said amounts in its calculation of Mr. Splane's income.

¹ [1990] 2 C.T.C. 199 (F.C.T.D.).

§18.95 In deciding in favour of the plaintiff, Mr. Justice Cullen (whose judgment was subsequently confirmed by the Federal Court of Appeal) summarized much of the existing case law and stated which test is to be applied when determining whether a payment constitutes a taxable benefit. He concluded that the mortgage interest differential payment did not constitute taxable benefits under the relevant provisions of the Act because:

> No economic benefit of any significant value was conferred upon this plaintiff. The plaintiff moved at the request of his employer, incurred certain expenses in the move, and suffered a loss. The reimbursement of these expenses cannot be considered as conferring a benefit within the terms of the Act. The plaintiff was simply restored to the economic situation he was in before he undertook to assist his employer by relocating to the Edmonton office.¹

¹ [1990] 2 C.T.C. 199, at 203.

§18.96 This statement of Cullen J. opened the debate whether for a taxable benefit to have been conferred, the employee must have gained some economic advantage from the payment received.

§18.96.1 In *Phillips v. M.N.R.*¹ the Federal Court of Appeal held that a taxpayer who had received the sum of $10,000 to assist him in the purchase of a new home following a company-requested relocation had received a taxable benefit as only an amount paid by the employer to compensate an actual loss to the employee is a non-taxable benefit. Where the amount is paid in consideration of the increased housing costs on the purchase of a replacement property, this was a taxable benefit as it increased the net worth of the employee.

¹ [1994] 1 C.T.C. 383 (F.C.A.).

§18.96.2 Since the Federal Court of Appeal decision in *Phillips*, there have been a spate of cases decided by the Tax Court of Canada under its Informal Procedure which have revisited the scope of *Splane* and *Phillips*. Five cases, *Hoefele v. The Queen*,¹ *Zaugg v. The Queen*,² *Mikkelsen v. The Queen*,³ *Krall v. The Queen*⁴ and *Krull v. The Queen*⁵ dealt directly with the issue whether a subsidy for additional interest payments due entirely to an increase in mortgage principal was taxable. Each of these cases involved mortgage interest differential payments to a relocated employee, which Robertson, J.A. had characterized in *Phillips* as an expense incurred in the new work location. In each case, the amount of the payments were determined by establishing a market differential between the old work and new work locations. When the employee's home in the old location was sold, the proceeds of disposition were multiplied by the differential rate to establish the maximum cost of comparable housing in the new location for which the employee relocation plan would provide assistance. The program subsidized the increased interest charges on the difference in principle values, on a declining balance, with 100% being subsidized in the first year until the tenth year when no further assistance would be available.

¹ [1995] 1 C.T.C. 2177 (T.C.C.), affd [1996] 1 C.T.C. 131 (F.C.A.).
² [1994] 2 C.T.C. 2425 (T.C.C.), affd [1996] 1 C.T.C. 131 (F.C.A.).
³ [1995] 2 C.T.C. 2940D (T.C.C.), affd [1996] 1 C.T.C. 131 (F.C.A.).
⁴ [1995] 1 C.T.C. 2570 (T.C.C.), affd [1996] 1 C.T.C. 131 (F.C.A.).
⁵ [1995] 2 C.T.C. 2204 (T.C.C.), revd [1996] 1 C.T.C. 131 (F.C.A.).

§18.96.3 Sobier, O'Connor, McArthur and Mogan, T.C.JJ. all held in *Hoefele, Zaugg, Mikkelsen* and *Krall*, respectively, that the payments fell within the tax-free parameters of *Splane*. Each of these Tax Court judges found that no economic advantage flowed to the employee as a result of the interest subsidy by the employer, notwithstanding that the new house had a greater value than the old house. In the fifth of these cases, *Krull*, Taylor, T.C.J. parted ranks with his colleagues. Without referring to their decisions in *Hoefele, Zaugg, Mikkelsen,* and *Krall*, Taylor, T.C.J. applied the "strict boundaries" placed on *Ransom* and *Splane* by Robertson, J.A. in *Phillips* to conclude that the mortgage interest subsidy was taxable.

§18.96.4 On appeal to the Federal Court of Appeal in *Canada (Attorney General) v. Hoefele,*[1] a majority of the Court allowed the taxpayer's appeal in *Krull* and dismissed the Crown's appeal in *Hoefele, Zaugg, Mikkelsen,* and *Krall*. Linden, J.A. (MacGuigan, J.A., concurring) restates the issue in the following terms:

> ... the question to be decided in each of these instances is whether the taxpayer is restored or enriched. Though any number of terms may be used to express this effect — for example, reimbursement, restitution, indemnification, compensation, make whole, save the pocket — the underlying principle remains the same. *If, on the whole of a transaction, an employee's economic position is not improved, that is, if the transaction is a zero-sum situation when viewed in its entirety, a receipt is not a benefit and, therefore, is not taxable under paragraph 6(1)(a). It does not make any difference whether the expense is incurred to cover costs of doing the job, of travel associated with work or of a move to a new work location, as long as the employer is not paying for the ordinary, every day expenses of the employee.* [Emphasis added.][2]

¹   95 DTC 5602 (F.C.A.).
²   95 DTC 5602 (F.C.A.), at 5605.

§18.96.5 After cursorily reviewing the mobility rights of taxpayers and reasserting the need to determine tax issues on a case-by-case basis in accordance with the general principles established in the case law, Linden, J.A. concludes, as did four of the five Tax Court Judges, that the mortgage interest subsidy was not a taxable benefit:

> ... the mortgage interest subsidy scheme established in these cases did not increase the mortgagor's equity in their homes. No economic gain accrued to any of the taxpayers as a result of the subsidy. Their net worth was not increased. Thus, a fundamental requirement of paragraph 6(1)(a) was unfulfilled. *Where no economic gain is present, a receipt is not to be taxed.* ... [Emphasis added.][1]

[1] 95 DTC 5602 (F.C.A.), at 5606.

§18.96.6 Robertson, J.A. dissented, largely over the concern that the majority decision would lead to the extension of the principle in *Ransom* to other types of expenses incurred by a relocating employee in the new work location:

> ... the majority position paves the way for other tax-free benefits intended to redress variations in the cost of living from one region of Canada to another. For the astute tax planner, today's decision represents a window of opportunity. ...[1]

[1] 95 DTC 5602 (F.C.A.), at 5613.

§18.96.7 However, in *Gernhart v. Canada*,[1] the Tax Court of Canada refused to extend the principle that there is no taxable benefit unless there is an economic advantage to tax equalization payments. In that case, the Tax Court of Canada ruled that a payment received by an employee as a reimbursement of the amount by which Canadian income taxes exceeded the United States income taxes which would have applied if the employee had remained in the United States was *taxable as a benefit* from employment.

[1] 96 DTC 1672 (T.C.C.).

(r) Reimbursement of Employment-Related Costs

§18.97 Concerning the taxability of employment benefits, the Act is rather laconic. Although it does state that employment benefits are taxable, it offers little guidance on how to determine whether any specific amount constitutes a benefit. This is largely left to Revenue Canada and the courts.

§18.98 The essence of the benefit test applied by the courts is that tax should arise in connection with amounts which, personal in nature or stated otherwise, enrich the individual.[1] The flip side of this proposition is that the reimbursement of expenses incurred strictly for employment purposes should not amount to a taxable benefit.[2] Clearly though, the scope of this latter principle is being continuously stretched by taxpayers.

[1] *Splane v. Canada*, [1990] 2 C.T.C. 199 (F.C.T.D.).
[2] *Ransom v. M.N.R.*, [1967] C.T.C. 346 (Ex.). See also *R. v. Poynton*, [1972] C.T.C. 411 (Ont. S.C.).

§18.98.1 In *Guay*,[1] a taxpayer who was employed in rotational duty in Ottawa and abroad as a foreign service officer, received a reimbursement of tuition fees for his children when he enrolled them in the French lycée system to ensure continuity in their education. The Tax Court of Canada examined whether there was a sufficiently direct relationship between the expense incurred or loss suffered by the taxpayer and his employment. It found that the relationship was close, but not close enough. The Tax Court of Canada held, therefore, that the reimbursement was a taxable benefit.

[1] *Guay v. Canada*, [1996] 3 C.T.C. 2384 (T.C.C.).

§18.98.2 The Federal Court of Appeal, however, overturned the decision of the Tax Court of Canada, and held that the only realistic option the taxpayer had to ensure that his children received French language instruction, that was recognized around the world, was to enroll the child in a private school. This decision was imposed on the employee by the permeability of his occupation. There was a sufficient link between the expenses incurred by the taxpayer and his employment. As a result, the moneys received by the taxpayer fell outside the scope of section 6(1)(*a*) since the reimbursement the taxpayer received for the school fees did not result in the taxpayer incurring a benefit, but rather placed the taxpayer in the same position he would have been in if he had not accepted the foreign service position with the employer.[1]

[1] *Guay v. Canada*, 97 DTC 5267 (F.C.A.).

§18.99 The issue of the reimbursement of clothing costs has been considered by the Federal Court. In *Huffman v. R.*,[1] the taxpayer was a plainclothes police officer required by the police force to wear ordinary clothing consisting of a conservative style suit, blazer or sports jacket with coordinating shirt, tie and trousers. The officer's collective agreement stipulated that he would be reimbursed for costs of up to $500 worth of such clothing per year. However, in the year in question, the Minister of National Revenue added this amount in the calculation of the taxpayer's income.

¹ [1989] 1 C.T.C. 32 (F.C.T.D.), affd [1990] 2 C.T.C. 132 (F.C.A.).

§18.100 The evidence clearly demonstrated that the actual clothing purchased by the officer was of such a type and style that he would not, and indeed did not, wear the clothes other than on the job. In light of this evidence and other case law dealing with employment benefits, Jerome A.C.J. of the Federal Court, Trial Division, stated:

> . . . I am unable to conclude in these circumstances that the plaintiff received a benefit. The plaintiff was required, in order to carry out his duties as a plain-clothes officer and receive a salary as such, to incur certain expenses regarding his clothing, and reimbursement of these expenses should not be considered as conferring a benefit under paragraph 6(1)(a) of the Act. . . . The taxpayer was simply being restored to the economic situation he was in before his employer ordered him to incur the expenses.¹

¹ [1989] 1 C.T.C. 32 (F.C.T.D.), at 37.

§18.101 On the strength of *Huffman*, there may be scope to embrace other "benefits" within the non-taxable category.

3. Allowances

§18.102 In addition to its provisions regarding employment benefits, the Act contains rules pertaining to payments made to an employee in the form of allowances. The Act specifies that, save for certain exceptions provided for in the Act, a taxpayer must include in income any amount received as an allowance for personal or living expenses or as an allowance for any other purpose.¹ The language requiring that an allowance "for any other purpose" also be included in income creates a very broad scope of application for the charging provision. The broad policy underlying the allowance provisions is to ensure that amounts which in reality constitute disguised remuneration are taxed as such. But, to be taxable, any such amount must constitute an allowance, as defined by the courts,² and not a non-taxable reimbursement of expenses.³

¹ ITA, s. 6(1)(b).
² *R. v. Pascoe*, [1975] C.T.C. 656 (F.C.A.); *Gagnon v. R.*, [1986] 1 C.T.C. 410 (S.C.C.).
³ See discussion on reimbursement of employment-related costs, *supra*, at §§18.97 *et seq.*

§18.103 The Act contains a number of exceptions to the general inclusionary rule governing allowances.[1] For example, a reasonable allowance for travelling expenses or for the use of a motor vehicle will not be taxable if the allowance is measured on the basis of kilometres driven and if the expenses incurred are not reimbursed separately.[2] Revenue Canada has also recently taken the position that allowances paid to an employee for the purpose of purchasing protective clothing and safety accessories are under certain circumstances non-taxable reimbursements of expenses.[3]

---

[1] ITA, s. 6(1)(b).
[2] ITA, s. 6(1)(b). See Interpretation Bulletin IT-522R: "Vehicle, Travel and Sales Expenses of Employees".
[3] RevCan Views, 9335877: "Taxable benefits — clothing allowance".

4. Directors' Fees

§18.104 Because corporate directors hold "office" as defined by the Act, directors' fees are treated as employment income. Consequently, fees received by an individual in consideration for having acted as a director of a corporation are taxable on the same basis as salary, wages and other remuneration.

5. Employees' Profit Sharing Plans

§18.105 Where an employer wishes to share its business profits with employees, the employer may structure an employee's profit sharing plan ("EPSP"). The Act defines an EPSP as an arrangement under which payments, computed by reference to (or paid out of) the employer's profits from its business, are made by an employer to a trustee in trust for the benefit of officers or employees of the employer or of a corporation with whom the employer does not deal at arm's length.[1]

---

[1] ITA, s. 144(1). See also Interpretation Bulletin (Special Release) IT-280R: "Employees Profit Sharing Plans — Payments Computed by Reference to Profits".

§18.106 There are no registration requirements for an EPSP. There are, however, rules that ensure that payments into an EPSP are taxed on a current basis. The trustee must allocate annually to participating individual officers or employees, either contingently or absolutely, all amounts received from the employer and most profits on property held in trust.[1] Any employee participating in the plan is thus taxed on any amount allocated to him or her by the trustee. This is true whether actual payments have in fact been made out of the trust to the employee. The employee is not, however, taxed again on payments received out of the plan.

[1] See Interpretation Bulletin IT-379: "Employees Profit Sharing Plans — Allocations to Beneficiaries".

§18.107 In view of the applicable rules just described, an EPSP is not a tax deferral mechanism. Its purpose is to provide a structure to facilitate some form of profit sharing between employers and employees, not to defer tax. In fact, since allocations are taxed in the taxation year in which they are made to employees' accounts by the trustee, the rules do induce participants to demand that allocations, plus earned income on the allocation or a portion thereof, be distributed annually by the plan.

6. Deferred Compensation

§18.108 Deferring the payment or receipt of compensation is often in the interest of both the employer and the employee. For the employer, the interest lies in maximizing available cash. For the employee, the concern is primarily to reduce or defer taxes. Successful planning in this area lies in reconciling the preferences of the employer and of the employee concerned, while not running afoul of the rules of the Act.

§18.109 Aggressive tax planning in this area has led to the introduction in the Act of a substantial number of provisions that are more in the nature of anti-avoidance measures than deferred compensation rules.

§18.110 There are the salary deferral arrangement rules which operate to tax employees on amounts of remuneration to which they are entitled but which are objectively seen as having been delayed with a view to deferring taxes. Where the salary deferral arrangement rules apply, the employer is entitled to a deduction for amounts paid or payable, but the employee faces immediate tax whether or not the amounts at issue have been paid.

§18.111 There are rules designed to achieve matching of deductions by employers and income inclusions by employees. Thus, where an employer contributes an amount to a third party for the benefit of an employee, the employer will generally only be entitled in the year to a deduction for the contribution to the extent that the amount is taxed in the employee's hands in the same taxation year. Where the employee is not subject to tax in the year that the amounts are contributed, the employer is denied a deduction until the year in which the employee is subject to tax. This latter result may occur where, for example, the salary deferral arrangement rules do not apply. The employer may then be construed to have paid amounts into an employee benefit plan.[1]

---

[1] ITA, s. 248(1). See also Interpretation Bulletin IT-502: "Employee Benefit Plans and Employee Trusts".

§18.112 "Retirement compensation arrangement" rules also exist. They are reviewed below in Chapter 19, "Retirement Income Provisions".

§18.113 In view of the applicable rules, structuring any deferred compensation arrangement is a delicate procedure. Indeed, it requires the parties to weave through a myriad of tax provisions in order to assess whether the proposed plan has any pitfalls. Nevertheless, a deferred compensation plan may at times achieve interesting results from either the employer's or the executive's perspective, depending on the circumstances. Perhaps the employer is not in a taxable position and thus does not care much for a tax deduction. It may also be that the proposed plan is not a salary deferral arrangement.

§18.114 Although the rules just referred to are restrictive, the Act does allow some latitude. Of importance is the provision that the salary deferral arrangement rules do not apply to a plan or arrangement under which an employee has a right to receive a bonus, in respect of services rendered by him or her in a taxation year, that is to be paid within three years following the end of the year. In addition, the salary deferral arrangement rules do not apply to "sabbatical leave plans" under which an employee may be permitted to defer a maximum of one third of his or her salary for the purpose of a leave of absence,[1] or to certain plans or arrangements (commonly referred to as phantom stock plans or stock appreciation rights), under which an employee or his or her estate is entitled to receive certain rights, such as notional shares of the employer, or amounts which reflect the increase in value of the employer's shares. These plans are reviewed in more detail later.

---

[1] See Advance Tax Ruling ATR-39.

F. THE EMPLOYEE AS A SHAREHOLDER OR QUASI-SHAREHOLDER

§18.115 Permitting an employee to participate in the growth of his or her employer through equity ownership or through rights that have such equivalents is a popular means of providing additional compensation, particularly in situations where cash flow is reduced and an employee wishes to benefit from the increase in value of his or her employer's shares. Stock option structures may assume any number of forms and the tax consequences vary depending on the chosen structure. The employer may facilitate the acquisition of stock by loaning money to participating employees, in which case the rules reviewed previously regarding loans and advances will apply.

§18.116 An employer may offer employees the opportunity to acquire shares out of its treasury. Under such a structure, commonly referred to as a stock option plan, employees may be granted options to purchase shares of the employer or of an affiliate, often at a price which is lower than the fair market value of the shares. There may be a "vesting period" during which the employee's rights are restricted, usually in respect of the right to vote, to receive dividends, or to have his or her shares repurchased. Depending on the structure, there may be an issue as to whether shares have been acquired.[1]

[1] *Wargacki v. R.*, [1992] 1 C.T.C. 269 (F.C.T.D.).

§18.117 Employees may also, under a stock purchase plan, be offered the opportunity to acquire their employer's shares or those of an affiliate. Stock purchase plans are more common to situations where a corporation wishes to provide stock incentives to a broad base of employees, rather than to a select group of executives. Under a stock purchase plan, the use of a third party trust is prevalent, and the plan may be wholly or partially employer-funded. Where a trust is used, the employee's shares are purchased by the trust, out of funds which originate from the employer, the employee, or both parties. The trust acquires the shares on the open market or from the company's treasury.

§18.118 Employees may also receive "quasi-stock" rights. In these cases, the employees are not issued actual shares. Rather, the employer issues share-equivalent rights. These rights enable participating employees to benefit from the growth of the company, without having the status of actual shareholders of the company. The value of their rights increases with that of the employer's shares. Employees may also be entitled to amounts equal to the dividends which they would have received had they owned the shares. These rights may represent an acceptable compromise between an executive's desire to benefit from the success of his or her employer and the employer's reluctance to issue shares to the executive. The plan may be designed so as to give employees credit only for the increase in the value of the employer's shares after the plan is implemented; such a plan is commonly referred to as a share appreciation right. Employees may also be offered a payout equal to the full value of the stock on the day on which the entitlement is calculated; this is usually referred to as a phantom stock plan. It should be noted however that, in either case, receipts out of the plan are taxed as ordinary income, rather than as capital gains. The employee is therefore not entitled to benefit from the capital gains exemption.

§18.119   Each of the forms of stock or quasi-stock incentives just discussed has particular tax characteristics. For example, a current issue in relation to stock option or stock purchase plans is whether it is appropriate to offer downside protection to an employee where the employee is subject to a taxable benefit in respect of the plan. The difficulty in this regard arises for the employee where he or she is subject to a fully taxable employment benefit (based on the value of the shares at the time of acquisition) but may only be entitled to claim a capital loss (deductible only against capital gains) for any subsequent decline in value. It has been suggested that the judicious use of convertible preferred shares may solve this problem. This illustrates that to implement any one of those plans, one must contend with a host of technical tax provisions.

1. Stock Options Plans

§18.120   The provisions of the Act which address stock option plans distinguish on the basis of whether or not the employer is a Canadian-controlled private corporation.[1] In general terms, the Act defines a Canadian-controlled private corporation as a private corporation that is not controlled, directly or indirectly in any manner whatever, by non-resident persons or by public corporations.[2]

---

[1]   ITA, s. 7.
[2]   ITA, s. 125(7), "Canadian-controlled private corporation".

§18.121   Where the employer is not a Canadian-controlled private corporation and one of its employees acquires shares by exercising a stock option, the employee is deemed to have received an employment benefit equal to the amount by which the value of the shares at the time they were acquired exceeds the amount he or she has paid or will pay the corporation.[1] This deemed benefit is added not only to the employee's income in the taxation year of acquisition,[2] but also to the cost to the employee of the shares.[3] If, for example, the exercise price of the option is six dollars at a time when the fair market value of the shares is ten dollars, the employee is deemed to have received a four dollar benefit, and this benefit is fully taxable. However, for the purposes of computing a gain on any subsequent disposition of the shares, the cost to him of the shares will be ten dollars. Thus, if the employee eventually disposes of the share for thirteen dollars, his capital gain will be three dollars, and three-quarters of this gain will be subject to tax.[4]

[1] ITA, s. 7(1). See also Interpretation Bulletin IT-113R4: "Benefits to Employees — Stock Options"; Advance Tax Ruling ATR-15.
[2] ITA, ss. 7(1) and 6(1)(a).
[3] ITA, s. 53(1)(j).
[4] ITA, ss. 3, 38, 39 and 40.

§18.122 Where an employee of a corporation that is not a Canadian-controlled private corporation is held to have received an employment benefit because of the exercise of a stock option, the employee is entitled to deduct from his or her taxable income an amount equal to one-quarter of the benefit if:

- the share is a "prescribed share" (basically a common share) at the time of its sale or issue;
- the amount payable by the employee to acquire the share is not less than the fair market value of the share at the time the stock option agreement was made; and
- at the time immediately after the stock option agreement was made, the employee was dealing at arm's length with the corporation.[1]

Where these conditions are met, the net inclusion rate of the benefit is three-quarters, which corresponds to that applying to capital gains.

[1] ITA, s. 110(1)(d).

§18.123 Where the corporation that confers the option is a Canadian-controlled private corporation, the rules are somewhat different. Upon the exercise of the option, the employee is deemed to have received a taxable benefit equal to the difference between the value of the shares at the time he or she exercised the option and the exercise price of the option. However, the taxable benefit is not included in the employee's income until the taxation year in which the employee subsequently disposes of the shares.[1] There is thus a deferral of tax on the benefit. Second, the rules governing the ability to claim a deduction equal to one-quarter of the benefit are less stringent than those which apply to other corporations. The principal condition for the deduction is that

the employee not dispose of the shares (otherwise than as a consequence of his or her death) within two years after the date on which he
or she acquired them.[2]

---

[1]   ITA, s. 7(1.1).
[2]   ITA, s. 110(1)(*d*.1).

§18.124 Note that even where the individual has ceased to be an employee at the time he or she exercises the stock option, the individual is
nevertheless subject to the aforementioned rules.[1]

---

[1]   See Interpretation Bulletin IT-113R4: "Benefits to Employees — Stock Options".

2. Stock Purchase Plans

§18.125 As previously noted, an employer may offer employees the
opportunity to purchase shares of the company or of an affiliate
thereof. Where the shares are offered to employees at a discount, the
rule just discussed regarding the computation of an employment benefit will apply. Where there is no *prima facie* discount (because the
shares are purchased by the trust at fair market value) but the employer funds a portion of the purchase price indirectly by payments
into the trust, the employees will be subject to tax on the amounts contributed to the trust by the employer. But this may raise a characterization issue, as the employer's contribution may be attributed to
employees either as a stock option benefit or as additional remuneration.[1] Technically, the interest of the distinction lies in establishing
whether the employer is entitled to a deduction for the contribution,
thus circumventing a prohibition of the Act,[2] and in determining
whether the employee has access to the stock option rules, including
the deduction equal to one-quarter of the amount that is to be included
in his or her income. It thus becomes evident that, in designing a stock
purchase plan, structure is crucial.

---

[1]   See *Placer Dome Inc. v. R.*, [1991] 1 C.T.C. 453 (F.C.T.D.), revd [1992] 2 C.T.C. 99
(F.C.A.). Note also that the arrangement may be characterized as an employee
benefit plan; see Advance Tax Ruling ATR-17.
[2]   See ITA, s. 7(3).

3. Phantom Stock Plans

§18.126 As previously noted, an employee who is a participant in a
phantom stock plan will usually be attributed a number of notional
shares with a value equivalent to the same number of issued shares of
the employer. The plan is structured to allow the employee, via his or

her notional shares, to benefit from the increase in value of the employer's issued shares.

§18.127 The design of a phantom stock plan is a contractual matter, given that such plans are not creatures of corporate law. Thus, the rules to be applied are subject to negotiation between the employer and the employee. Even the method of valuing the units is subject to a mutual agreement. Given that an essential purpose of the plan is to benefit employees based on the increase in the value of the company, discussions regarding the correct method of computing the company's income will figure prominently in the negotiations. An important issue will concern the extent to which the corporation may distribute property to shareholders of the corporation.

§18.128 Although corporate law does not regulate phantom stock plans, there are important tax rules to address. A fundamental issue is whether the plan will be held to be a salary deferral arrangement. Should the plan constitute such an arrangement, participating employees may be taxed on the value of their units or the annual increase in such value, even though they do not actually receive any amount out of the plan. The deferral advantage of a phantom stock plan would then be lost.

§18.129 The salary deferral arrangement rules exempt a phantom stock plan from their application if certain conditions are met.[1] But these conditions are restrictive. They may generally be paraphrased as follows:

- the plan must be between a corporation and an employee of the corporation or a corporation related thereto;
- the benefits under the plan must be reasonably attributable to the employee's duties;
- all amounts that may be received under the plan must be so received on or before the end of the first calendar year after the employee's death or retirement; and
- the amounts which the employee may be entitled to receive pursuant to the plan must be based on the fair market value of the shares of the capital stock of the corporation (or the corporation related thereto).

[1] See ITA, s. 248(1), "salary deferral arrangement", para. (*l*), and *Income Tax Regulations* ("ITR"), C.R.C. 1978, c. 945 as amended, s. 6801(*d*).

§18.130 The rules governing phantom stock plans are quite technical, and many of the facets of these rules are not presently reviewed. For example, a plan will not qualify if it contains certain forms of stop-loss arrangements. Thus, a guarantee to reduce the impact of any reduction in the fair market value of the shares of the corporation may disqualify the plan. If the plan does not qualify, the employee will annually be subject to tax on the amount by which his or her units of participation increase in value. In addition to the basic components of the plan and the contractual definitions, matters which will require specific attention will include the employer's entitlement to a tax deduction, the time at which the employee will be subject to tax, and the employer's obligation to make withholdings at source and remittances to federal or provincial governments.

4. Share Appreciation Rights

§18.131   A plan which does not meet the rules described above may nevertheless not be a salary deferral arrangement if it meets Revenue Canada's administrative policies in relation to "share appreciation rights" (SARs). Revenue Canada considers that where, on a specified date, the employee is entitled to receive only the increase in value of the underlying phantom share, the plan may not be considered to be a salary deferral arrangement.[1] However, if the plan is not exempted from the salary deferral arrangement rules (either by virtue of the Act or the administrative policy applying to SARs), the deferral arrangement will be lost. This will occur, for example, in instances where the employee is entitled as a minimum to the value of the shares at the time the plan is implemented, notwithstanding that such value may fluctuate.

---

[1]   [1988] *Canadian Tax Foundation Conference Report*, Revenue Canada Round Table, Question 26, p. 53:44. See also Advance Tax Ruling, ATR-45.

G. TERMINATING EMPLOYMENT

§18.132   Where an executive's employment ceases, either voluntarily or because his or her employment is terminated, the executive will often receive payments from his or her former employer after the effective date of the termination of employment. These payments may, for example, be for unpaid salary or benefits, or they may be in respect of severance, which is usually granted in consideration of the length of service of the employee, or represents damages for the termination by the employer of the employment contract. The severance payment may be triggered as a result of a change of control, in which case it is usually referred to as a "parachute". In such cases, the executive may also be entitled to exercise any unexercised stock options.

§18.133 Where a former executive receives salary or benefits after his or her employment ceases, the executive will be subject to tax on any such amounts on the basis that the amounts constitute employment income.[1] This has already been reviewed. Where the former employee is entitled to exercise stock option rights, any benefit derived therefrom will similarly be characterized as employment income.

[1] ITA, ss. 6(3) and 115(1).

§18.134 With regard to severance payments, the Act requires that the "retiring allowance"[1] be included as income. The retiring allowance is defined to include, *inter alia*, all payments in respect of long service, so-called parachutes, and damages for wrongful dismissal. There is, however, authority to the effect that a retiring allowance does not include damages that do not relate strictly to the termination of the employment, but are rather damages in respect of torts of another kind, such as damages for injury to the employee's reputation.[2] There is also authority to the effect that a retiring allowance does not include payments in respect of the termination of employment that has not yet begun. In *Schwartz v. Canada*,[3] the taxpayer had accepted an offer of employment but was informed that his services were no longer required before his employment had actually commenced. The Supreme Court of Canada held that the payment which the taxpayer received in respect of the termination was not a retiring allowance and, thus, was not taxable.

[1] ITA, s. 248(1), "retiring allowance".
[2] *Bédard v. M.N.R.*, [1991] 1 C.T.C. 2323 (T.C.C.).
[3] 96 DTC 6103 (S.C.C.).

§18.135 Where a retiring allowance must be included in the executive's income, he or she may be entitled to transfer all or a portion of any such amount to a registered retirement savings plan.[1] The employee thus obtains a deduction for the amount so transferred in computing his or her income. The allowable deduction, simply stated, is equal to $2,000 per year of service, plus $1,500 per year of service before 1989 in respect of which employer contributions to a pension plan or deferred profit sharing plan had not vested in the employee. The employee should, however, be wary of minimum tax implications.[2]

[1] ITA, s. 60(*j*.1)
[2] ITA, Division E.1.

H. DEPARTING FROM CANADA

§18.136 When an executive departs from Canada, because of a job relocation or because of retirement, it is important to review the tax consequences of his or her departure.

§18.137 A fundamental issue to be addressed is whether the executive has severed his or her residential ties with Canada so as to become a non-resident of Canada for income tax purposes. As previously noted,[1] the determination of the place or residence of an individual is a question of fact. Moreover, Revenue Canada may require evidence of a departure from Canada for a period in excess of two years before it is prepared to concede that an individual has become a non-resident of Canada.[2] If the individual continues to be a resident of Canada for income tax purposes, the individual will be subject to Canadian income taxes on his or her worldwide income, subject to foreign tax credits and the effect of international tax treaties.

---

[1] See, *supra*, §§18.29 *et seq.*

[2] See Interpretation Bulletin IT-221R2: "Determination of an Individual's Residence Status".

§18.138 Second, assuming that the individual has become a non-resident of Canada at the time of his or her departure, there may nevertheless be tax consequences attaching to payments to the executive that originate from Canada. Where the executive is to be paid money that is consideration for having accepted his or her former employment in Canada or that is remuneration for services performed in Canada or for an agreement not to compete, the payment may be subject to Canadian tax.[1] Similarly, payments to a non-resident in respect of a retiring allowance, or in respect of interest, royalties or dividends will usually attract a withholding tax at either 25%[2] or at a reduced rate provided in an applicable international tax treaty. Other income earned in Canada by the individual, whether of a business nature or not, may similarly be subject to some form of Canadian tax.

---

[1] ITA, s. 115(2)(*c*.1).

[2] See, ITA, Part XIII.

§18.138.1 The meaning of the words "retiring allowance" was analyzed in the case of *R. v. Albino*.[1] In that case, the former President and Chief Executive Officer of Rio Algom Mines Limited had received, following his dismissal, a sum of $603,753.90 pursuant to an Incentive Performance Plan in which he participated from 1973 to 1987 as an employee of Rio Algom. The former C.E.O. treated the sum as a "retiring allowance", which because he was a non-resident for tax purposes afforded him a tax treatment of 25%. This tax rate was more advantageous than his full marginal tax rate, which would have applied if the sum was treated as "remuneration" under the Income Tax Act. The Minister of National Revenue reassessed the C.E.O.'s income tax report, being of the view that the sum was remuneration and that the full marginal rate applied.

The stated objectives of the Plan were to provide an incentive to employees who made major contributions to the success of Rio Algom and to incite them to continue to devote their energies to achieving its continued growth. Different vesting provisions encouraged long term employment. Payments under the plan would only take place upon a participant ceasing to be an employee. These provisions permitted the Court to conclude that the scheme of the Plan was to encourage employees to remain with Rio Algom and that the amount to be paid to employees would reflect their long service with Rio Algom. The fact that the Plan, in addition to encouraging lengthy service, encouraged contribution to the growth of Rio Algom did not disqualify the payment from constituting a retiring allowance, since the objective of long service was not merely an incidental one.

[1] [1994] 1 C.T.C. 205 (F.C.T.D.).

§18.139 Third, any individual who becomes a non-resident of Canada will wish to assess the impact of Canada's "departure" tax. Under the Act, any individual who ceases to be a resident of Canada is deemed to have disposed of his or her property, except in the case of a class of property known as "taxable Canadian property", at its fair market value at the time of departure.[1] There are, however, basic planning issues which must be considered. For example, while taxable Canadian property is not deemed to be disposed of at its fair market value at the time of the individual's departure, the individual may elect that such a disposition take place — this may be of interest to the individual if he or she has not fully claimed his or her $100,000 capital gains lifetime deduction or if the individual has unused capital losses. A second planning issue may arise as a result of the fact that while property other than taxable Canadian property[2] is deemed be disposed of at fair market value, the individual may elect that the property not be deemed to be so disposed of.[3] A requirement of the latter election is that the individual furnish acceptable security.[4]

[1] ITA, s. 128.1(4).
[2] ITA, s. 115(1)(b). See also Interpretation Bulletin IT-176R2: "Taxable Canadian Property — Interests in and Options on Real Property and Shares".
[3] ITA, s. 128.1(4)(b)(iv).

[4]   ITA, s. 128.1(4)(*b*)(iv).

§18.140   There will obviously be a host of other considerations to be reviewed at the time of departure from Canada. These will include the impact on stock options, health care, pensions,[1] social security arrangements,[2] liability to foreign taxes, and the interaction between such taxes and Canadian taxes. An individual who relocates to another country for employment reasons may seek to be compensated for additional costs incurred. Moving costs will assuredly be a factor.

[1]   See Interpretation Bulletin IT-76R2: "Exempt Portion of Pension When Employee has been a Non-Resident".
[2]   See Information Circular 84-6.

I. ENTERING CANADA

§18.141   Similarly to the individual who departs from Canada, the individual who enters Canada for the purpose of exercising employment duties in Canada must consider whether his or her presence in Canada will be such as to render him or her a resident of Canada for income tax purposes. As previously noted, the place of residence of an individual is determined principally in accordance with principles established by case law. Under these rules and those of the Act, an individual may be held to have become a resident of Canada for the whole of a taxation year or part of such year.[1] In addition, Canada deems an individual to be a resident of Canada throughout a taxation year if he or she sojourned in Canada for a period of 183 days or more in the taxation year.[2] Where an individual is held to be a resident of more than one country under the domestic taxation laws of such countries, international tax treaties may apply to provide "tie-breaker rules".

[1]   ITA, s. 114.
[2]   See, *supra*, §18.31.

§18.142   Where an individual becomes a resident of Canada for income tax purposes, he or she is deemed to have acquired at that time, at fair market value, all of his or her property except property that constitutes "taxable Canadian property" or property with regard to which, on a previous date on which he or she ceased to be a resident of Canada, he or she made an election to defer taxation at the time of his or her departure.[1] The practical effect of the deemed acquisition at fair market value is that any gain realized by the individual as a result of the disposition of his or her property after he or she becomes a resident of Canada is measured with reference to a cost that corresponds to the fair market value of the property at the time the individual became a resident of Canada. Thus, any increase in value of the property before the time at which the individual became a resident of Canada is not subject to Canadian tax.

[1] ITA, s. 128.1(1)(b)(iv).

§18.143 Given that the assumption of Canadian residency for income tax purposes entails Canadian taxation on worldwide income, this move should be carefully planned. For example, it may at times be advisable for an individual to dispose of property before the time at which the individual becomes a Canadian resident. At the very least, assets should be appraised upon entering Canada. An important issue will often be the consequences of the receipt in Canada of amounts from foreign sources, for example, from foreign pension plans or from former employers. In addition, an individual with substantial assets may make use in certain circumstances of a non-resident trust to shelter certain forms of income from Canadian tax for a period of up to five years.[1] This latter type of planning is, however, complex and requires considerable precautions.

[1] ITA, s. 94.

J. WITHHOLDING AND CONTRIBUTION OBLIGATIONS

§18.144 The payment of a salary by an employer obliges it to deduct amounts at source on account of the employee's income taxes.[1] Non-resident employees may, however, be exempt from withholdings.[2] Based on the employee's income, the estimated allowable tax deductions for the year, and tax withholding tables, the employer is required to withhold taxes at source and remit the said amounts to the tax authorities. There is an obligation to withhold in this manner in respect of both federal and provincial income taxes. At the time when the individual files his or her income tax return for the year, the individual then calculates his or her income taxes payable for the year and reconciles the amount payable with the amounts withheld at source. Any positive or negative difference may then result in an amount of taxes payable or refundable.

[1] ITA, s. 153(1)(a); ITR, ss. 100-108.
[2] See Interpretation Bulletin IT-161R3: "Non-Residents — Exemption from Tax Deductions at Source on Employment Income".

§18.145 Canadian laws also impose certain contribution obligations on the employer, the employee, or both. Both the employer and the employee are required to contribute an equal amount to the Canada or Quebec Pension Plan, as the case may be, and to make unemployment insurance contributions. Employers may also be required to contribute for other purposes, such as for workers' compensation or payroll taxes. The employer's specific obligations in this regard will depend on the province in which it carries on business.

CHAPTER 19

RETIREMENT INCOME PROVISIONS

A. INTRODUCTION

§19.1 The form and level of retirement income are ordinarily critical considerations for both parties to the executive employment contract. The executive seeks to ensure that his or her post-retirement income will be substantial and secure, and that it will enjoy optimal tax treatment. The employer will wish to satisfy the executive's requirements in this regard while minimizing its costs and administrative burden and maximizing its own tax position. Either or both parties may also be interested in the provision of retirement counselling services and/or post-retirement insurance coverage to the executive.

§19.2 Post-retirement income can be furnished through one or more of the following: registered retirement savings plans ("RRSPs"), registered pension plans, deferred profit sharing plans ("DPSPs"), and various supplementary retirement income programs. Generally speaking, the first three vehicles benefit from the most favourable tax treatment, but there are strict limits on the amounts that can be contributed into or received out of these types of plans. Conversely, the various types of supplementary programs ordinarily enjoy much less favourable tax treatment, but are advantageous in that the payout from such programs is limited only by the employer's generosity and, in certain cases, the tax authorities' views on reasonableness. This chapter will highlight some of the key design, cost and tax considerations to bear in mind when negotiating the retirement provisions of an executive employment contract.

B. TAX-SHELTERED RETIREMENT SAVINGS VEHICLES

§19.3 From a tax viewpoint, both the executive and the employer have an incentive to maximize the use of the three favoured retirement savings vehicles: the registered pension plan, the RRSP and the DPSP. Because contributions to all three plans are tax-deductible and plan income is in each case tax-sheltered, these three types of plans are the most cost-efficient. The limits on contributions to and/or payouts out of the three, though, are such that the executive will not likely be able to count on much more than $60,000 to $70,000 per year in retirement income from these favoured vehicles.

§19.4 This estimate assumes that the executive accumulates retirement income for approximately 35 years, throughout which period the system of comprehensive limits on retirement savings enacted in 1990 remains in force, and accepts the basic accuracy of the actuarial conversion assumptions on which that system is founded. It also ignores the post-2005 indexation built into the system. Obviously, it can be expected that, since pay rates vary widely over different time periods, the $60,000-$70,000 estimate will prove too high or too low in most cases. Nonetheless, it is a useful point of departure for determining whether consideration should be given to establishing a supplementary program.

§19.5 If one adopts the rule of thumb that post-retirement income (other than Old Age Security and Canada/Quebec Pension Plan benefits) should be no less than 70% of pre-retirement earnings, then any executive whose annual salary significantly exceeds $85,000 to $100,000 should consider negotiating a supplementary retirement income package as part of his or her employment arrangement.

§19.6 This section will canvass the principal alternatives available under the three tax-sheltered formats. A discussion of various supplementary programs can be found in the following section.

1.   Registered Retirement Savings Plan

(a)   Individual RRSP

§19.7 Where the executive wishes to assume primary responsibility for providing his or her own retirement income, he or she may be content to stay out of his or her employer's pension plan and instead maximize his or her annual RRSP contributions. The maximum deductible RRSP contribution is $13,500 for each year from 1997 through 2003, $14,500 for 2004, and $15,500 for 2005.[1] Thereafter the annual limit will be indexed to changes in the average industrial wage.[2] By virtue of the carryover rules in the *Income Tax Act*, unused RRSP contribution room in one year may be carried forward to future years. Certain restrictions on the carryforward period and amount which had originally been imposed were removed in the March 6, 1996 budget.[3]

---

[1] *Income Tax Act* ("ITA"), R.S.C. 1985, 5th Supp., c. 1 as amended, ss. 146 and 147.1.

More precisely, the maximum deductible contribution equals the lesser of 18% of the previous year's earned income and the particular dollar amount.

² ITA, ss. 146 and 147.1.

³ ITA, s. 146(1).

§19.8 In addition to deductible contributions, it is possible to contribute as much as $2,000 (on a cumulative as opposed to annual basis) that will not be deductible but the income on which will be tax-sheltered.[1]

¹ ITA, s. 204.2.

§19.9 As a technical matter, RRSP contributions may only be made by an individual, not a corporation.[1] This is not to say, however, that the executive and the employer are prevented from contracting to have the employer increase the executive's salary by the annual RRSP contribution limit for the year and directing that increase to the RRSP designated by the executive on the executive's behalf. The employer may direct the executive's RRSP contributions in this manner by payroll deduction without having to deduct taxes from those contributions at source.[2] If this procedure is followed, the time value of the executive's contribution money will be maximized.

¹ ITA, s. 146 *in fine.*

² *Income Tax Regulations* ("ITR"), C.R.C. 1978, c. 945 as amended, s. 100(3)(*c*).

(b) Group RRSP

§19.10 Due to the increased regulatory burden on pension plan administrators, many employers have replaced their registered pension plans with much simpler group RRSPs. Unless and until pension benefits regulators decide to bring group RRSPs under their purview, as has been recommended by some[1] and rumoured by many, this trend can be expected to continue.

¹ See Government of Ontario, *Report of the Task Force on Inflation Protection for Employment Pension Plans* (1988), pp. 269-71.

§19.11 A group RRSP is essentially a collection of individual RRSPs, whose costs and administration are borne by the employer. Since the investment options in a group RRSP are usually fairly limited, many executives may choose not to enrol in such a plan but to contribute to their own individual RRSPs where they have more control over the investment of the fund. An executive might be especially wary of joining a group RRSP which ties the fate of his or her retirement income to his or her employer's fortunes, as would be the case where the group

RRSP purchased, for instance, employer company shares. It should be underscored that such shares may only be held by RRSPs in certain circumstances, such as when they are publicly traded.[1] RRSPs may only hold private company shares where those shares meet a series of legal conditions.[2]

---

[1] ITA, s. 146(1).
[2] ITR, s. 4900(6) *et seq.*

§19.12 An RRSP as such may generally be collapsed at any time before maturity. While some employers who sponsor group RRSPs have attempted to lock in contributions until retirement, in the absence of any statutory basis for requiring such locking-in, it is conceivable that a member of such a group RRSP could insist on collapsing his or her account in the plan prior to retirement.

(c) Creditor Protection

§19.13 In and of itself, an RRSP is not exempt from seizure by the holder's creditors.[1] However, in certain circumstances and depending upon the province in which the executive resides, specific RRSP vehicles can be rendered exempt from seizure to a limited degree by the proper designation of beneficiaries.[2] This possibility is ordinarily limited to insurance company annuity contracts. In Quebec, however, creditor protection can also be enjoyed by certain RRSPs issued by trust companies.[3] The executive may wish to take advantage of this creditor protection and the flexibility of a self-directed RRSP offered by trust companies in Quebec either through their own networks or through investment dealers.

---

[1] See, *e.g.*, *Re Gero*, [1979] C.T.C. 309 (F.C.T.D.).
[2] See, *e.g.*, Alberta *Insurance Act*, R.S.A. 1980, c. I-5, s. 265; *Saskatchewan Insurance Act*, R.S.S. 1978, c. S-26, s. 158.
[3] *Act respecting Trust Companies and Savings Companies*, R.S.Q. c. S-29.01, s. 178.

§19.14 However, even this limited creditor protection may not be available in all circumstances. The Supreme Court of Canada has laid to rest certain concerns in this regard under the *Bankruptcy and Insolvency Act*.[1] The protection may be overridden in certain circumstances, though, by family law, fraudulent preferences, or other legislation.

---

[1] R.S.C. 1985, c. B-3, s. 91. See *Ramgotra v. North American Life Assur. Co.* (1996), 10 C.C.P.B. 113.

2. Registered Pension Plan

§19.15 Other than the individual RRSP, probably the most common approach is to have the executive enrol in a registered pension plan sponsored by the employer. Such a plan is registered both with the relevant pension benefits regulators (either at the federal or the provincial level, depending on the industry) and with the federal tax authorities. Contributions to the plan by the employer and, where the plan is contributory, by the executive are deductible within certain limits, and the income earned by the plan is tax-sheltered.

§19.16 Where a pension plan operates on a defined contribution (*i.e.*, money purchase) basis, the executive's eventual pension will depend on the performance of the pension fund up until the date of retirement. Thus, the risk of poor investment performance rests with the executive, just like in an RRSP. Where, on the other hand, the pension plan operates on a defined benefit basis, the employer essentially promises the executive a certain level of pension, such that the risk of poor investment performance rests with the employer. The trade-off to the high-paid executive for the greater security of a defined benefit plan is that the pension to which he or she will eventually become entitled is subject to a maximum annual amount, imposed under the *Income Tax Act* so as to avoid excessive tax-sheltering inside pension plans. That maximum is equal to $1,722 multiplied by the executive's years of pensionable service, as augmented by an indexing factor after 2004; thus, in the case of an executive who has accrued 35 years of service, the maximum annual pension would be $60,270 (before indexing).

§19.17 In most cases, the newly hired executive will enrol in an existing company pension plan, whether that plan be for all employees, all salaried employees, or a defined class of executives. In some cases, however, it may be more advantageous to the executive to have the company establish an individual pension plan for that executive alone. Below, we will examine briefly some of the considerations to bear in mind under both scenarios, *i.e.*, the standard pension plan scenario and the individual pension plan scenario.

(a) Standard Plan

(i) Contribution Limits

§19.18 In a defined contribution plan, the maximum permissible contribution per year is the so-called money purchase limit, as defined in the *Income Tax Act*. This limit is frozen at $13,500 until 2002; it will rise to $14,500 in 2003 and to $15,500 in 2004.[1] Thereafter, the money purchase limit will be indexed to the average industrial wage index, rising only in tandem with the latest Statistics Canada measurement.

[1] More precisely, the maximum permissible contribution equals the lesser of 18% of the year's compensation and the money purchase limit: ITA, ss. 147.1 and 147.1(8).

§19.19 Every dollar contributed to a defined contribution pension plan by either the employer or the executive reduces the executive's maximum permissible RRSP contribution the following year by an equivalent amount. Even where the maximum permissible pension contribution is made, however, the executive is still free to contribute up to $1,000 to his or her RRSP in the following year.[1]

[1] Pursuant to the February 27, 1995 and March 6, 1996 budget proposals, this has temporarily ceased to be true.

§19.20 The maximum permissible contribution to a defined benefit pension plan can be arrived at only after performing certain complex actuarial calculations. In order to ensure a rough equivalence between defined benefit and defined contribution plan payouts, the *Income Tax Regulations* set out a formula for the determination of such contributions. This formula is a function of certain assumptions as to plan design and likely return on money purchase plan contributions. Where the plan stands in surplus, the employer may be required to reduce its contribution or to eliminate such contribution altogether.[1]

[1] ITA, s. 147.2(2)(*d*).

§19.21 Defined benefit pension contributions also reduce permissible RRSP contributions, though not in quite the same dollar-for-dollar manner as is the case for defined contribution plans. Here, too, no matter how much is put into the pension plan one year, the executive may still put at least $1,000 into his or her RRSP the next year.[1]

[1] Pursuant to the February 1995 and March 1996 budget proposals, this has temporarily ceased to be true.

(ii) Enrolment

§19.22 Pension benefits statutes generally require that all employees in the same class be entitled to enrol in the pension plan operated for employees of that class.[1] Depending upon the jurisdiction, the company can require that a newly hired employee not be entitled to enrol in the plan for a certain number of years after beginning employment, although this requirement will rarely exceed one or two years.[2] Many pension plans, though, contain provisions allowing the company to waive any mandatory delay in enrolment, and an undertaking by the employer to invoke such a waiver clause forms a legitimate matter for inclusion in most executive employment contracts. This will be of particular interest to the executive in the case of a non-contributory plan, that is, a pension plan to which members do not themselves contribute. However, it should be noted that such a waiver in any particular case may require that the employer waive the plan provision for all similarly situated employees.

[1] See, *e.g.*, Quebec *Supplemental Pension Plans Act* ("QSPPA"), R.S.Q., c. R-15.1, s. 34; Ontario *Pension Benefits Act* ("OPBA"), R.S.O. 1990, c. P.8, s. 31.

[2] See, *e.g.*, QSPPA, s. 34; OPBA, s. 31.

(iii) Vesting and Locking-in

§19.23 Most pension plans provide that the employer contribution to an employee's pension does not vest in the employee, *i.e.*, the employee does not gain an irrevocable right to the benefit of such a contribution until a minimum number of years of participation have elapsed. Under current legislation, vesting cannot be delayed for any longer than five years of membership in certain provinces[1] and two years of membership in the others.[2] As a general rule, the parties to the executive employment contract cannot stipulate an accelerated vesting schedule unless the employer is willing to amend the plan to provide accelerated vesting for all other members as well.

[1] See, *e.g.*, Alberta *Employment Pension Plans Act*, S.A. 1986, c. E-10.05, s. 23.

[2] See, *e.g.*, QSPPA, s. 69; OPBA, s. 37.

§19.24 The flip side of the vesting coin is the rule on locking-in of benefits. Once a member is vested, his or her pension credits ordinarily are also locked in; that is to say, they may not be withdrawn by the member but may only be used to purchase a deferred annuity or transferred to another locked-in vehicle. While there are certain minor exceptions to this rule,[1] this paternalism serves essentially to prevent plan members from yielding to temptation and cashing in their pension entitlement to satisfy their immediate needs. It also contrasts with the rule governing RRSPs, which are generally collapsible at any time prior to retirement.

[1] See, *e.g.*, QSPPA, s. 93(5); OPBA, s. 50.

(iv)   Portability

§19.25   All pension legislation requires that pensions be "portable". In other words, should a plan member leave the employment of a company prior to retirement, he or she is entitled to request (subject to certain restrictions based on age and other criteria) that his or her vested pension credits be transferred from his or her former pension plan to any new pension plan in which he or she enrols which permits such transfers or to a locked-in registered retirement savings plan or locked-in retirement account. An executive who is not subject to portability restrictions should compare the benefits provided under any previous pension plan to which he or she belonged with those provided under the new employer's plan and, if the latter are more generous and the new employer's plan so allows, transfer his or her accrued pension credits to the new employer's plan.

(v)   Residual Surplus Entitlement upon Termination

§19.26   Where a defined benefit pension plan is terminated at a time when the assets in the pension fund exceed the sum required to satisfy all plan liabilities, the allocation of such surplus assets as between the employer and the plan participants will depend on the terms of the plan, the plan funding agreement and related documents, as well as the terms of the applicable pension legislation. In many cases, the documentation does not clearly attribute entitlement to either the employer or the participants, thus leading to disputes which are resolved either by negotiations between the parties or by litigation.[1]

---

[1]   See, *e.g.*, *Schmidt v. Air Products of Canada Ltd.* (1994), 3 C.C.P.B. 1 (S.C.C.).

§19.27   Surplus assets paid out to participants upon plan termination in the form of cash must be included in the calculation of income in the year of distribution and tax must be paid on that income accordingly in that year. Alternatively, however, where a pension plan has not previously provided for the maximum pension benefits allowable for tax purposes, the employer may amend the plan prior to termination so as to use some or all of the surplus to enhance those benefits,[1] and such benefits will be eligible (within limits) for tax-free rollover to another pension plan, to certain RRSPs, or to certain registered retirement income funds.[2] This latter course of action requires the active cooperation of the employer prior to plan termination, cooperation which may be more easily obtained in the case of a plan for a relatively restricted group of executives than for a plan covering a broader range of employees.

[1] Some pension benefits authorities may restrict the scope of such pre-termination amendments.

[2] ITA, s. 147.3.

(b) Individual Plan

§19.28 As a result of the addition of a series of new provisions to the *Income Tax Regulations* in 1992,[1] it was thought that the individual pension plan might become a popular alternative in certain circumstances. Strictly speaking, the expression "individual pension plan" is a misnomer, since the regulations in question refer to "designated plans", which often have only one member but can in fact have more than one member if the membership is composed primarily of very highly paid executives or shareholders of the employer. Thus, the rules described below may apply not only to single-member pension plans but also to certain executive pension plans.

[1] ITR, s. 8515.

§19.29 Generally speaking, it may be advantageous to the executive to have his or her employer establish a defined benefit pension plan for the executive alone where the employer's standard plan (if any) is not especially generous and where the amount that could be contributed to such an individual plan exceeds the RRSP contribution limit for that year by a significant amount. As a basic rule of thumb, this will more likely prove to be the case where the executive is close to retirement age, since the actuary who determines the allowable contributions will be able to recommend larger annual contributions when fewer years remain to build up the assets necessary to generate the maximum pension. Again, this estimate is based on a number of broad assumptions, as set out above. It should also be noted that the regulations contain an anti-avoidance rule designed essentially to prevent funding through a pension plan of pre-1990 past service in lieu of a payment or other benefit to which the executive would otherwise be entitled.[1]

[1] ITR, s. 8503(15).

§19.30 Since a pension plan must ordinarily be registered with the pension benefits authorities, who require that an initial plan text be prepared, an information return be submitted every year and an actuarial evaluation be submitted every three years, the differential between the permissible RRSP and pension contributions must be sufficiently large to cover these compliance costs and still allow greater capital accumulation in the pension plan format. Consideration must also be given to any additional conditions or restrictions which the pension benefits authorities may place on individual plans. Generally speaking, it is unlikely that an individual pension plan will be of particular interest to anyone much below 45 years of age. Even for an executive above that age, the actuarial assumptions prescribed in the Income Tax Regulations for designated plans to prevent perceived "abuses" have had the effect of rendering the individual pension plan much less attractive in most cases.

§19.31 Other considerations to be taken into account in choosing between an RRSP and an individual pension plan include the differing investment rules and capacity for creditor protection. A pension plan is usually required to limit its holdings in any one investment to no more than 10% of its portfolio,[1] while an RRSP has no such restriction. On the other hand, a pension plan generally enjoys greater protection from the participant's creditors than does an RRSP;[2] as described above, the creditor protection available under an RRSP depends on the type of vehicle selected and certain other factors.[3]

---

[1] See, *e.g.*, QSPPA, s. 172; OPBA Reg., R.R.O. 1990, Reg. 909, s. 70(1).
[2] See, *e.g.*, QSPPA, s. 264; OPBA, s. 66.
[3] See §§19.13 *et seq.*

§19.32 Should the employer and executive agree to establish an individual pension plan, the employment contract should specify which party will bear the costs of the plan (*i.e.*, preparation and registration of the plan text, preparation of annual information returns and triennial actuarial valuations, preparation of the plan termination report, and consultants' fees for these and other incidental administrative or interpretative matters). The contract should also specify a reputable professional firm whose services will be retained to draft the plan and the actuary who will be responsible for preparing the triennial valuations.

3. Deferred Profit Sharing Plan

§19.33 The third, and least frequently encountered, of the three tax-sheltered retirement savings vehicles is the DPSP. Contributions to a DPSP may be made only by the employer, not the executive,[1] and may not exceed one-half the money purchase limit for the year.[2] Every dollar contributed to a DPSP in respect of the executive reduces by that same dollar the amount the executive may place in his or her RRSP the following year.

¹   ITA, s. 147(2)(*a*.1).
²   ITA, s. 147(5.1). The annual money purchase limits are set out in §19.18 above.

§19.34 Like the group RRSP, the DPSP imposes relatively little administrative burden on the employer. It has the additional advantage to the employer of allowing contributions to be made only in profitable years, though this feature and the relative lack of individual control over investments may lead the executive to prefer an individual RRSP to DPSP membership. Just as with the group RRSP, the executive might also be wary of joining a DPSP which ties the fate of his or her retirement income too closely to his or her employer's fortunes through, for instance, investment in employer company shares. Such shares may only be held by DPSPs in certain circumstances, such as when they are publicly traded or the company meets specified historical "legal for life" earnings or dividend tests.[1]

¹   ITA, s. 204. See also §19.11 above.

C. SUPPLEMENTARY EXECUTIVE RETIREMENT PLANS

§19.35 As noted above, the three tax-sheltered retirement savings vehicles together are unlikely to generate much more than $60,000 to $70,000 per annum of retirement income, which will replace only $85,000 to $100,000 per year of salary. It should be remembered that these are very rough estimates based on a large number of assumptions, and consequently, they ignore the post-2004 indexing built into the tax system. Nonetheless, when the executive's annual salary exceeds that range by a significant amount, consideration should be given to providing for a supplementary executive retirement plan in the employment contract. This is especially so given that maximum benefits payable out of a registered pension plan have been essentially frozen since 1976, and the indexing promised on such ceiling has been repeatedly postponed.

§19.36 The fundamental question which must be resolved in structuring a supplementary arrangement is whether or not that arrangement should be pre-funded, *i.e.*, whether monies should be set aside in trust prior to retirement to guarantee eventual payment. If such monies are set aside, the executive's interests will be secured but the tax consequences can be quite harsh. On the other hand, if no funds are set aside in trust, the tax position should be more favourable but the executive is at risk.

§19.37 This section will analyze some of the principal funded and unfunded alternatives. The decision as to which alternative to select is probably the most critical decision the employer and high-paid executive will make in negotiating the retirement provisions of their contract.

1. Retirement Compensation Arrangement

§19.38 A retirement compensation arrangement ("RCA") is a funded supplementary program under which monies are deposited with a third party custodian or set aside by the employer to be held in trust for the executive.[1] From the executive's point of view, this type of arrangement is ideal, since the assets out of which his or her supplementary retirement income is to be paid are segregated from the employer's assets, such that the fate of that income is not tied to the employer's financial health.

[1] ITA, s. 248(1).

§19.39 The hitch is that the custodian or employer must pay a tax equal to 50% of all contributions to the RCA and 50% of all income earned on the assets held in the RCA.[1] The tax is refundable, but only as retirement benefits are paid out and without interest, so that the cost in terms of time value of money can be substantial.

[1] ITA, s. 207.7.

§19.40 Where an instrument such as a letter of credit is used to secure a pension promise, Revenue Canada takes the position that the 50% tax is payable only on the letter of credit fee.[1] Revenue Canada has also stated that a personal guarantee by a shareholder of the employer to an employee will not in itself constitute an RCA.[2]

[1] [1992] *Canadian Tax Foundation Conference Report*, Round Table Question 48.
[2] [1990] *Canadian Tax Foundation Conference Report*, Round Table Question 6.

§19.41 Where the employer chooses to acquire a life insurance policy to fund post-retirement benefits for the executive, the RCA rules will apply to require payment of the 50% tax.[1] The use of life insurance to fund or secure supplementary executive retirement plans has recently received new attention by planners.

[1] ITA, s. 207.6(2).

2. Secular Trust

§19.42 Some commentators have argued that it is more tax-efficient to fund a supplementary pension through a "secular trust" than through an RCA.[1] Under a secular trust, the amounts needed to finance the supplementary pension would be paid by the employer to the executive and placed in trust, with the trust assets funding the supplementary pension.

[1] See, e.g., (1991), 2 Pension Tax Reports 67.

§19.43 This alternative is only viable in provinces where the top combined federal and provincial marginal tax rate is below 50%. The tax efficiency of the secular trust varies directly with the length of time the assets remain in the trust. Like an RRSP, a secular trust may be collapsed by the executive at any time before retirement.

3. Unfunded Retirement Income Arrangement

§19.44 The secular trust aside, the main alternative to the funded RCA is the unfunded retirement income arrangement. If properly structured, an unfunded arrangement should not attract any tax until actually paid upon retirement, and payments under such arrangement should be deductible by the employer. However, the absence of prefunding means that a supplementary retirement income promise of this sort is simply that — a promise. Should the employer run into financial difficulty prior to the executive's retirement, the executive will have to stand at the end of the line with the company's other unsecured creditors to collect on his or her promise.[1]

[1] For example, see *Canada (Attorney General) v. Confederation Life Insurance Co.*, (1997) 145 D.L.R. (4th) 747.

§19.45 In many cases, the unfunded arrangement will amount to a contractual retiring allowance, *i.e.*, an amount paid in recognition of the executive's "long service".[1] This means that some or all of the amount paid out may qualify for a tax-free rollover by the executive to his RRSP. The amount that qualifies for such rollover is $2,000 for each calendar year of service before 1996 with the employer or a related person.[2] If the executive does not have a vested right to the employer's or related person's contribution to a registered pension plan or DPSP, an additional $1,500 may be rolled over for each calendar year of service before 1989.[3]

[1] ITA, s. 248(1).

§19.46 Typically, an unfunded retirement income arrangement is structured as a defined benefit pension. Often, the pension will be equal to the difference between the pension the executive would have received under the registered pension plan if not for Revenue Canada's maximum pension rules and such maximum pension. As long as this amount is reasonable in the circumstances, it will be deductible to the employer as it is paid out.[1] Benefits can be paid on a periodic basis or in a lump sum.

[1]   See Revenue Canada Interpretation Bulletin IT-337R2, para. 8, for guidelines on the deductibility of retiring allowances.

§19.47 Some employers have attempted to structure unfunded arrangements according to a defined contribution formula, with notional contributions being made to a fictional account, the balance in which is augmented each year by a notional return. Caution should be exercised in employing such formulae, however, since Revenue Canada has sometimes indicated that such notional return is subject to immediate taxation under the "interest accrual" rules in the *Income Tax Act*.[1] Those are the rules which tax, for example, accrued interest on compound interest Canada Savings Bonds on an annual basis prior to receipt.

[1]   ITA, s. 12(4). See *Window on Canadian Tax Newsletter* (July 1991), p. 15, para. 1138.

§19.48 In some cases, it might be argued that unfunded pension arrangements should be subject to pension benefits legislation, requiring registration, pre-funding, and compliance with a host of other rules. This is clearly not the case in some provinces where the arrangement supplements a registered plan under which the maximum pension is being provided, since there is an explicit legislative exception for such cases.[1] In other jurisdictions, there is no such exception, though in practice the pension benefits authorities have generally turned a blind eye to these arrangements.

[1]   See, *e.g.*, QSPPA, s. 2(2), OPBA Regulations, R.R.O. 1990, Reg. 909, s. 47(3).

§19.49 Caution should also be taken to ensure that the supplementary retirement income is not promised in lieu of a portion of current salary that would otherwise be payable to the executive. If such were the case, the arrangement could be characterized as a "salary deferral arrangement" under the *Income Tax Act*, which would lead to taxation of the executive on amounts not yet received.[1]

[1] ITA, s. 6(1)(*a*)(v).

D. RETIREMENT COUNSELLING SERVICES

§19.50 Retirement after a long career can dramatically affect any or all of the executive's lifestyle, financial status, and emotional well-being. Numerous counselling services exist to help the executive with this transition. Where such counselling services are paid for by the employer, they will not be considered a taxable benefit to the executive.[1]

[1] ITA, s. 6(1)(*a*)(iv).

E. POST-RETIREMENT INSURANCE COVERAGE

§19.51 A topic of increasing concern to retiring executives is the extent of their employer-funded insurance benefits following retirement. This is especially true of medical benefits, with the progressive scaling back of provincial Medicare coverage,[1] but the same concern applies to life and other coverage, as well.

[1] See, *e.g.*, Quebec *Act respecting prescription drug insurance* (S.Q. 1996, c. 32).

§19.52 The executive may accordingly wish to include in the employment contract a firm commitment by the employer to fund such coverage following retirement. Where the commitment is stated in sufficiently absolute terms, the executive's entitlement should accordingly vest, or crystallize, at the moment of retirement.[1]

[1] See, *e.g.*, *Dayco (Canada) Ltd. v. National Automobile, Aerospace & Agricultural Implement Workers Union*, [1993] 2 S.C.R. 230; *Kennedy v. Canadian Saltfish Corp.* (1995), 11 C.C.P.B. 103 (Nfld. T.D.).

CHAPTER 20

DUTIES AND LIABILITIES OF CORPORATE DIRECTORS AND OFFICERS

GENERAL PRINCIPLES

A. INTRODUCTION

§20.1 The purpose of this chapter is to outline for individuals who are employed as executives and act as directors and/or officers some of the basic duties and liabilities of directors and officers with regard to employment issues under federal and certain provincial laws in Canada. Other areas will also be canvassed insofar as they raise questions related to liabilities incurred by employees, particularly officers of a corporation.

§20.2 A corporation acting as an employer has obligations towards its employees, some of which are founded in contract, such as the payment of wages, while others are statutory, such as the remittance of payroll deductions to the Minister of Revenue as required by tax laws. Employment law provides in various cases for the personal liability of directors and officers of a corporation in order to ensure that employees receive wages or other benefits to which they are entitled. In other areas, such as the environment, law makers have concluded that public policy objectives are important enough to justify holding directors, officers or employees liable when the corporation violates the law. In the result, penal sanctions may also be imposed on the directors or officers of a corporation which does not comply with statutory requirements.

§20.3 The general rule to be observed by directors and officers is, in principle, fairly simple: they should ensure that the corporation they serve complies with its duties as an employer and as a corporate citizen. As the standards expected of directors and officers in fulfilling their duties become increasingly more rigorous it is essential that they understand the requirements, obligations and potential liabilities and risks that their position entails. Failure to do so may result in substantial fines, imprisonment and other sanctions.

§20.4 It should be noted that only selected aspects of the duties and liabilities of directors and officers will be examined. Numerous other issues may arise under the rubric of directors' and officers' duties and liabilities in a broader sense. Here, however, the focus is directed towards matters specifically related to employment law. We shall first review the liability of directors and officers towards the corporation's employees. A summary of some statutory liabilities towards other parties, including the Crown, will follow, and finally, measures that directors or officers may take to limit such liabilities will be canvassed briefly, to be explored in greater depth in Chapter 22.

§20.5 A preliminary distinction must be made between the types of liability described in this chapter. There are several types of liability: (1) a personal obligation to pay employees or third parties amounts which the corporation has failed to pay; and (2) exposure to penal sanctions and damage awards relating to a failure to fulfil a personal statutory obligation or an acquiescence or participation in the corporation's failure.

§20.6 It should be noted that the provisions governing directors' and officers' liability may vary depending on the jurisdiction of incorporation of the corporation as well as where it carries on its business. Federal and provincial governments have each enacted legislation providing for the incorporation and regulation of corporations. Although the policy behind the requirements of each statute is essentially the same, there are more or less subtle differences between them and the considerations involved in electing to incorporate under the federal or a provincial statute are beyond the scope of this work.

§20.7 In addition to these general statutes of incorporation, numerous federal and provincial statutes provide for the creation of specific types of corporations. Insurance companies, banks, cooperatives and credit unions, to cite only a few examples, are creatures of such Acts and the liability of the directors and officers of such entities will be governed by those statutes. This chapter focuses on the legislation governing business corporations under federal, Quebec, Ontario and British Columbia law.

§20.8 Regardless of whether a corporation is created under a federal or provincial statute or whether it carries on business in Quebec or elsewhere in Canada, it must conform to all applicable statutes, whether federal or provincial. With regard to taxes and employee deductions, for instance, both federally incorporated and provincially incorporated corporations are liable to pay applicable federal as well as provincial taxes, and directors' and officers' liability can arise under both federal and provincial statutes.[1]

§20.9 The diversity of duties and liabilities emanating from different provinces is particularly apparent in Quebec. For historical reasons, Quebec has retained a civil law system, while the other provinces and territories of Canada are common law jurisdictions. This inevitably has some bearing on the status of directors and officers. For example, the relationship between directors or officers and the corporation in Quebec is regulated in part by the provisions of the Civil Code, which has no exact equivalent in the other jurisdictions. Although the Supreme Court of Canada has stated that the principles of civil law differ little from those of the common law with regard to directors' and officers' duties and liabilities, not all recent Quebec decisions are in agreement with this.[1] Some writers have argued that the Civil Code has taken a step closer to the common law in this area, and that common law principles will likely be used to interpret directors' liability under the CCQ which, in some cases, uses language similar to the common law statutes.[2] The new provisions of the Civil Code respecting directors have not yet been the subject of enough judicial decisions to determine whether Quebec courts will use them to depart from common law principles previously cited frequently.

[1] *Bank of Montreal v. Kuet Leong Ng*, [1989] 2 S.C.R. 429.
[2] See, for instance, Maurice Martel and Paul Martel, *La compagnie au Québec: Les aspects juridiques* (Montréal: Wilson & Lafleur, Martel Ltée, 1995), pp. 582 ff.

§20.10 It has been necessary from time to time throughout this chapter to distinguish among various types of corporations and jurisdictions of incorporation, as well as between the law in Quebec and the rest of Canada. It should be noted, however, that although directors' and officers' liability may vary according to the jurisdiction of incorporation and where a given corporation carries on business, in recent years there has been a significant move towards standardization of liability rules so that, notwithstanding legislative diversity, this chapter will provide a useful overview for directors and officers of all types of corporations.

B. DIRECTORS AND OFFICERS

1. Directors

(a) The Concept

§20.11 A distinction is made in corporate and employment-related legislation between "directors" and "officers". It is important to be aware of this distinction, as the rules governing the respective liabilities of directors and officers differ. For example, officers will not necessarily be liable for all acts of commission or omission that result in directors' liability. One must look to the wording of the statute.

§20.12 Federal and provincial statutes require shareholders to elect or appoint directors and allow directors to designate officers of the corporation. The board of directors exercises all corporate powers and is required to manage or supervise the business and affairs of the corporation. Except in the few matters where the various statutes reserve final responsibility to the shareholders, the law assumes that directors ultimately wield all power related to the corporation's activities. This legal structure does not always coincide with reality however. In many corporations, directors do not actually conduct the day-to-day management of the corporation, which is instead entrusted to the corporation's executive officers. A director's role is often supervisory only.

§20.13 Furthermore, whether a person should be considered to be a director of a corporation at any given moment may be a rather complicated matter. While directors are normally elected or appointed by the shareholders, they may also, in some cases, be appointed by the board of directors. The law also recognizes that a person will occasionally assume the duties and responsibilities of a director without having been officially elected or appointed. A person who takes part in an obvious fashion in the management of the corporation and conducts himself or herself as a director by, for example, attending meetings, signing the minutes or representing himself or herself as a director could be considered a *de facto* director[1] and could be held liable to the same extent as a properly elected or appointed director.[2] In the case of *Standard Trust Co. (Liquidator of) v. Cattanach*,[3] the directors were held to be mere puppets and the shareholders were held to be *de facto* directors with the same duties and responsibilities as directors. A person who has been officially elected or appointed need not be actively involved in the corporation's business and management in order to be considered a director.[4]

[1] J.M. Wainberg and Mark I. Wainberg, *Duties and Responsibilities of Directors in Canada*, 6th ed. (Don Mills: CCH, 1987), p. 8.

[2] *Re Owen Sound Lumber Co.* (1917), 38 O.L.R. 414 (C.A.).

[3] (1995), 24 O.R. (3d) 492 (Gen. Div.).

[4] *Amiri v. Champagne*, J.E. 94-836 (Que. C.A.).

§20.14 A person who has been properly elected or appointed is deemed to be a director until the corporation receives an official and effective resignation.[1] In order to be effective, a resignation must usually fulfil various statutory requirements, such as being in writing and filed with the appropriate authorities.[2] A recent Quebec case held that even though a director had resigned, such resignation was not opposable to employees suing for lost wages, because the requisite filings had not been made with the government to remove the director's name from the register kept under the *Legal Publicity Act*.[3] Furthermore, despite having resigned, a director may be deemed to continue to hold this position if he or she subsequently conducts himself or herself as a director. Under the OBCA, a director named in the articles of the corporation (that is, a founding director) or a sole director cannot resign without having a successor.[4] Certain authors claim that the same result occurs in Quebec even though the law is less explicit.[5] In *Brown v. Shearer*, [1995] 6 W.W.R. 68 (Man. C.A.), the court held that nothing in the CBCA prevented the directors from resigning even if the corporation would be left with no directors. It must also be emphasized that the bankruptcy of a corporation does not automatically terminate a director's functions.[6] Certain statutes, however, such as the B.C.C.A. provide that, upon the appointment of a receiver-manager (such as pursuant to a security agreement) a director's functions in respect of that part of a company's operations, cease.[7]

[1] *Andrews v. Wait*, J.E. 92-174 (Ct. of Que.).

[2] See *Canada Business Corporations Act* ("CBCA"), R.S.C. 1985, c. C-44, s. 108(2); Ontario *Business Corporations Act* ("OBCA"), R.S.O. 1990, c. B.16, s. 121(2); British Columbia *Company Act* ("BCCA"), R.S.B.C. 1996, c. 62, s. 130(2); Quebec *Companies Act* ("QCA"), R.S.Q., c. C-38, s. 123.76(2) [re-en. 1980, c. 28, s. 14].

[3] *Commission de la construction du Québec v. Beaurivage*, J.E. 96T-103 (C.Q.) and *An Act respecting the legal publicity of sole proprietorships, partnerships and legal persons*, R.S.Q., c. P-45 (the "Legal Publicity Act").

[4] OBCA, s. 119(2). See *Zwierschke v. M.N.R.*, [1991] 2 C.T.C. 2783 (T.C.C.).

[5] Martel, Maurice and Paul Martel, *La compagnie au Québec: Les aspects juridiques* (Montréal: Wilson & Lafleur, Martel, Ltée, 1995), pp. 471 ff. *Contra:* See *Aikens v. St.-Pierre*, J.E. 97-1827 (C.Q.).

[6] *Banque Provinciale du Canada v. Ross*, [1955] C.S. 292 (Que. S.C.), at 295; *Kalef v. Canada*, 96 DTC 6132 (F.C.A.). See also *Hartnell v. Canada*, (1996) T.C.J. No. 1635, Oct. 29, 1996. (T.C.C.)

[7] R.S.B.C. 1996, c. 113, s. 95.

§20.15 While directors may not manage themselves, they must supervise, for it is they who are ultimately answerable for the corporation's affairs before the shareholders and, increasingly, before third parties, including the Crown. As stated above, the law on directors' liability often does not take into account current management practices, however, making directors liable even in cases where they are far removed from the decisions taken by the corporation. Although this may appear unfair, the public policy rationale is that liability must rest with persons who are fairly easily identifiable in order to ensure compliance with the law.[1]

[1] *Commission de la construction du Québec v. Couture*, J.E. 93-1180. For discussion of the gulf between theory and practice in the matter of directors' powers and responsibilities, see Bruce L. Welling, *Corporate Law in Canada: The Governing Principles*, 2nd ed. (Toronto: Butterworths, 1991), pp. 297-304.

§20.16 It should be noted that directors are not *per se* usually considered to be employees of the corporation; they are not necessarily paid for their services as directors.[1] Of course, an employee may also be a director, but his or her duties and liabilities as a director must be clearly distinguished and analyzed separately from his or her duties and liabilities as an employee. A director who is also an officer has been considered to be an employee.[2]

[1] See, for example, *Wright v. Rider Resources Inc.* (1994), 21 Alta. L.R. (3d) 149 (Q.B.); *Roray v. Howe Sound Mills & Logging Co.* (1915), 22 D.L.R. 855 (B.C.C.A.); *Fortier v. Québec*, J.E. 96-914 (Que. C.A.); *Québec (Commission de la santé et de la sécurité de travail) et Distribution Raymond Martineau Inc.*, J.E. 96T-692 (Que. C.A.L.P.).

[2] *Oger v. Chiefscope Inc.* (1996), 29 O.R. (3d) 215 (Gen. Div.).

(b) Independent Directors and Liability

§20.17 A further important distinction in the analysis of directors' responsibilities should be noted. Corporate and securities law in Canada requires that a certain proportion of the directors of a corporation which has distributed securities to the public, or which intends to do so, be persons who are not officers or employees of the corporation or of any of its affiliates. Such persons are variously called "outside" or "independent" directors. The purpose of this requirement is to protect the shareholders' interest by ensuring that the board of directors will be in a position to objectively assess the performance of officers and employees of the corporation. This means necessarily that some directors will be more removed from the corporation's management and less informed about its business than "inside" directors. Nevertheless, corporate and employment law in Canada usually does not distinguish between inside and outside directors with regard to duties and liabilities.[1] For instance, similar policies and provisions (or lack thereof) apply under tax laws concerning employees' deductions;[2] the fact that a director is "outside" will not in itself be sufficient to absolve him or her from the responsibility of ensuring that tax is deducted and remitted to Revenue Canada.[3] "Due diligence", as will be discussed below, is a possible defence to such actions.

[1]   J.M. Wainberg and Mark I. Wainberg, *Duties and Responsibilities of Directors in Canada*, 6th ed. (Don Mills: CCH, 1987), pp. 7 and 23.
[2]   See, *e.g.*, *Income Tax Act*, S.C. 1970-71-72, c. 63, s. 227.1 and §20.139ff.
[3]   T.S. Wach, "Directors' Liability for Taxes" (1989), 6 Business & the Law 1.

§20.18 It must be noted that although directors' liabilities are normally assessed by objective standards, with little reference to background, experience or level of participation in the corporation's affairs, facts related to the level of attention directors bring to the corporation's business may be weighed differently according to the degree of reliance such directors could legitimately put on the officers of the corporation or other responsible persons. The liability of directors in such matters is determined on a case-by-case basis and outside directors may, in some cases, be able to show more easily than inside directors that they acted with the required degree of diligence and prudence in relying on persons with greater knowledge of the corporation's affairs.

§20.19 It remains true, however, that an outside director's position may be more vulnerable in that he or she is not "on site". Notwithstanding a relative lack of involvement in the corporation, he or she is theoretically just as liable as a director who is personally involved in the management of the corporation and is intimately acquainted with its business and problems.[1] Outside directors should therefore use their best efforts to keep themselves informed about the corporation's affairs on an ongoing basis.

[1]   J.M. Wainberg and Mark I. Wainberg, *Duties and Responsibilities of Directors in Canada*, 6th ed. (Don Mills: CCH, 1987), p. 8.

2. Officers

§20.20 Generally, directors will entrust part or all of the corporation's activities to persons who receive wages for conducting or overseeing such activities, that is, employees. Some employees will be managers and may hold a high degree of responsibility.

§20.21 Officers of a corporation are a hybrid category. Usually some are directors (such as the chairperson of the board), while others will be managers only, who nevertheless bear important responsibilities within the corporation. Some legislation specifies that certain officers must be chosen from among the directors but the by-laws may provide otherwise. Section 121 of the CBCA refers to "officers" as persons to whom the powers to manage the business and internal affairs of the corporation have been delegated. They are the persons whom the directors have chosen to run the corporation. Officers commonly occupy positions such as chairperson, president, secretary, treasurer or general manager, but may also hold any other position designated by resolution of the directors or under the by-laws of the corporation.

§20.22   The existence of a title is not determinative of whether a given individual is an "officer" of a corporation. The degree of control that a person exercises within the corporation, the degree of control exercised in a given transaction, the power to give instructions and orders, as well as his or her supervisory powers, may all be taken into account in distinguishing an officer from a person who merely executes orders. These criteria will vary with the corporation's structure and division and allocation of powers. Temporary limited control exercised by a person in one transaction may suffice to qualify that person as an officer for the purposes of such transaction. In any given situation, a person may be deemed an officer if he or she qualifies as the "directing mind and will of the corporation".

§20.23   Officers of corporations are subject to many of the same fiduciary obligations, due diligence requirements and minimum standard of care as directors. As with directors, the Civil Code of Québec ("CCQ") and the QCA deems officers to be "mandataries" of their corporation "mandator." As will be discussed below, mandataries owe specific duties of loyalty and good faith to their mandators. In *Bank of Montreal v. Kuet Leong Ng*,[1] the Supreme Court of Canada recently stated that the duty of good faith of officers and other trusted employees under article 1024 of the *Civil Code of Lower Canada* increases in accordance with their rank and functions. The same principle holds true in other jurisdictions.[2]

---

[1] [1989] 2 S.C.R. 429; art. 1024 of the Civil Code of Lower Canada has been repealed and replaced by art. 1434 of the Civil Code of Quebec. If the director or officer is also an employee, he or she may be bound to respect C.C.L.C., art. 2088 as well, which imposes obligations of loyalty, prudence, diligence and honesty on employees towards their employer.

[2] *Canadian Aero Service Ltd. v. O'Malley*, [1974] S.C.R. 592.

§20.24   Officers' liability is, nevertheless, generally slightly less onerous than directors' liability. Although an officer owes a form of fiduciary duty to the corporation and will also be liable for damages caused to an employee through his or her personal fault, as opposed to through the execution of corporate functions, officers often escape the extraordinary statutory liability towards employees which is imposed on directors. Certain statutes do, however, impose liability on both directors and officers. Officers may also incur penal liability for offences committed by the corporation with their knowledge, consent or acquiescence and, since they often determine and implement the day-to-day policy of the corporation, may be more easily held liable in matters such as failure to make income tax remittances or other corporate offences. As previously stated, the reader should take care to note distinctions between the liabilities of directors and the liabilities of officers discussed in this chapter.

C. LEGAL DUTIES OF DIRECTORS AND OFFICERS

1. Framework

§20.25   The general principle is that directors and officers of a corporation should always act honestly and in good faith with a view to the best interests of the corporation and should exercise the care, diligence and skill that a reasonably prudent person would bring to the task in comparable circumstances.[1] An officer or director who meets this standard will normally be shielded from personal liability.

---

[1]   This wording is borrowed from s. 122(1) of the CBCA. Although there may be important technical variations in the wording of this duty in other federal and provincial statutes and between the status of directors and officers, the same basic principles would apply in a general fashion to directors or officers of companies created under other statutes. It may be noted in passing that many (but not all) of the comments in this summary apply equally to directors of a non-profit corporation.

§20.26   Officers and directors owe a primary duty to the corporation, which can sue them if they are remiss. Outside claimants will usually first address their grievances to the corporation, but shareholders may, in some circumstances, especially the insolvency of the corporation, bring an action directly against the directors. Under most corporate statutes, shareholders also have the right to bring an action against directors in the name of the corporation itself, with leave of the court (the "derivative" action). It should also be noted that, in most jurisdictions, where a corporation or its directors act in an oppressive manner or unfairly disregard the interests of any of their constituency, including creditors (such as an employee seeking unpaid wages), a court may order that the corporation or director rectify the matter complained of.[1]

In some cases, courts have gone so far as to find a shareholder and/or director jointly liable with the corporation towards the latter's creditor.[2]

[1]   This statutory *oppression remedy* exists under the CBCA and most comparable provincial Acts. The QCA, however, is conspicuous in not providing any such remedy.

[2]   *Canadian Opera Co. v. Euro-American Motor Cars* (1990), 75 O.R. (2d) 720 (Div. Ct.); *Great Lake Brick and Stone Ltd. v. 837004 Ontario Ltd.* (1993), 8 C.L.R. (2d) 104 (Ont. Ct. (Gen. Div.)).

§20.27 Directors and officers also cannot circumvent their statutory responsibilities. Section 122(3) of the CBCA provides, for instance, that no provision in a contract, or in the articles, by-laws or resolutions of the corporation, may relieve a director or officer from the duty to act in accordance with the CBCA and its regulations, or relieve him or her from liability for breach thereof. This prohibition on avoidance of statutory duties has only one exception: unanimous shareholder agreements may limit a director's liability when what would normally be a director's power (and the concomitant responsibility) is transferred to the shareholders.[1] A unanimous shareholder agreement would therefore relieve the director of his or her duties and liabilities under the CBCA to the extent that the management powers of that director have been restricted by the unanimous shareholder agreement.[2] Pursuant to s. 247 of the CBCA, a complainant or a creditor may apply for an order requiring any "director, officer", among others to comply with the CBCA, the corporation's constituting documents and/or any unanimous shareholder agreement. Article 321 of the Civil Code of Quebec stipulates that a director is a mandatary of the corporation who shall, in the performance of his duties, conform to the obligations imposed on him by law, the constituting act or the by-laws, and that he shall act within the limits of the powers conferred on him.

[1]   Section 146(5) of the CBCA reads as follows:

> A shareholder who is a party to a unanimous shareholder agreement has all the rights, powers and duties of a director of the corporation to which the agreement relates to the extent that the agreement restricts the powers of the directors to manage the business and affairs of the corporation, and the directors are thereby relieved of their duties and liabilities, including any liabilities under section 119, to the same extent.

See *Canada Corporations Law Reporter*, CCH Canadian, vol. 1, ¶7240, p. 2016.

[2]   Similar provisions are found in the QCA (s. 123.92) and in the OBCA (s. 108(5)). The extent of the transfer of responsibilities is, however, often far from clear.

§20.28 The following is a brief description of the duties generally imposed on directors and officers and how courts have interpreted these general duties. The law governing officers is not as well defined, since courts have been more concerned with directors' liability during the last century. It appears likely, however, that similar rules would usually be applied to officers. Although their scope and application may vary according to the jurisdiction of incorporation, these general principles are likely to be used, directly or indirectly, to judge the acts of all directors and officers. These general obligations are supplemented by specific statutory duties and liabilities, which will be discussed later in this chapter.[1]

[1]   See §§20.50 *et seq.*

2.   Duty to Exercise Care, Diligence and Skill

(a)   General Nature

§20.29 The statutory performance standard under the OBCA, CBCA and CCQ basically requires directors and officers to do the best that they can with their own skills and business judgment, but to act reasonably diligently in seeking qualified assistance to make up for their own shortcomings.

§20.30 Under the OBCA and CBCA, a director or officer, in exercising powers and discharging duties, is to exercise the care, diligence and skill that a reasonably prudent person would exercise in comparable circumstances.[1] A similar provision exists in the BCCA, but applies to directors only.[2] This statutory obligation is based on a similar, but not identical, common law test (which is still the law applied in several Canadian jurisdictions). The test derives from the early judgment of the English Court of Appeal in *Re City Equitable Fire Ins. Co.*,[3] where it was held, in considering directors' duties, that:

(1)   directors need not exhibit a greater degree of skill than may reasonably be expected from persons with their knowledge and experience;

(2)   directors are not liable for errors in business judgment, as their primary function is to use their own particular talents in advocating corporate risk-taking; and

(3)   directors are not bound to give continuous attention to the affairs of the corporation and, "in the absence of grounds for suspicion", they can trust corporate officials to be honest.

In other words, with the common law test there is no high objective standard generally expected of directors and the courts will not question the business judgment of the directors. The statutory test, although framed more objectively in its reference to a "reasonably prudent person" standard, also contains an extensive subjective element, inherent in the phrase "in comparable circumstances". The skills and knowledge of the particular director or officer are relevant. There is no one objective standard of the reasonably skilled and knowledgeable director or officer. Similarly, the Quebec Civil Code states at article 322 that a director must act with prudence and diligence. Although no reference is made to officers, as a mandatary, an officer is charged with the same duties of prudence and diligence and responsibilities.

¹ OBCA, s. 134(1)(b); CBCA, s. 122(1)(*b*).
² BCCA, s. 118.
³ [1925] 1 Ch. 407.

(b) Standards of Care, Diligence and Skill

§20.31 Early common law cases considering the degree of attention directors were to give to their task imposed almost no objective standard of diligence and evidenced a somewhat relaxed attitude towards compliance with this duty. Later cases attempted to raise this standard somewhat and the statutory test attempts to impose some objective standard of prudence. Sections 135(4) of the OBCA and 123(4) of the CBCA expressly encourage reliance on the advice of various professionals for those situations in which the director does not have the requisite skill. Section 123.84 of the QCA is typical, stating that a director is presumed to have acted with the appropriate skill and prudence if he relies on the opinion or report of an expert. The duty to be diligent could consequently require that the director seek out professional assistance in certain circumstances. Of note, however, is the fact that while directors can shelter under the provisions of sections such as 135(4) of the OBCA and 123(4) of the CBCA, officers may not be able to do so.

§20.32 Attendance at most board meetings by directors would also seem to be required. Even in those jurisdictions where the somewhat lax common law test still applies, the courts will probably now upgrade the expected standard to bring it more in line with the statutory modifications in other jurisdictions. Sections 135(1) of the OBCA and 123(1) of the CBCA encourage attendance by providing that directors are deemed to consent to resolutions passed at a meeting, whether they attended or not, unless they file a dissent to the resolution within seven days of becoming aware that a resolution has been passed.

§20.33 Directors and officers must be informed of the policies, business and affairs of the corporation and should not rely blindly on other persons, be they experienced officers or well-known directors. Undue reliance on another person coupled with a failure to exercise a reasonable level of supervision will attract directors' or officers' liability if the person to whom a task has been delegated proves negligent or incompetent. What constitutes a reasonable level of supervision will vary according to factors such as the officer's functions, the size of the corporation and the importance of the tasks delegated.

§20.34 It should be emphasized that serious or repeated breaches of duty by employees or by the corporation, even without the knowledge of a particular director or officer, could indicate a lack of diligence on the part of such director or officer. If the director or officer could have found out about the wrongdoing through reasonable efforts, he or she may be liable for such failure.

§20.35 Unlike the OBCA and the CBCA, the QCA contains no explicit provision defining the degree of skill that directors should bring to their duties. As mentioned, article 322 imposes the general duty of "prudence and diligence" on the director and any mandatary, such as an officer, is bound, by article 2138 of the CCQ to act with prudence and diligence in performing the mandate.[1] Although no objective standard is set out, Quebec courts are likely to require of Quebec directors a similar standard of skill and diligence as the common law cases have established. The subject of what a director's duty of diligence and care should be, is discussed in detail in Chapter 23 on corporate governance.

---

[1] General provisions relating to mandate begin at art. 2130, the first paragraph of which reads as follows:

> Mandate is a contract by which a person, called the mandator, empowers another person, the mandatary, to represent him in the performance of a judicial act with a third person, and the mandatary, by his acceptance, binds himself to exercise the power who by his acceptance obliges himself to perform it.

3. Duty of Fairness to Shareholders, Creditors and Others

§20.36 The CBCA and OBCA both contain a provision which is commonly referred to as the "oppression remedy" section. These provisions apply, in part, to the actions of directors. The oppression remedy basically provides that directors shall not exercise or threaten to exercise their powers in a manner that is oppressive or unfairly prejudicial to or that unfairly disregards the interests of any security holder, creditor, director or officer of the corporation.[1] An Alberta case considering a similar provision in the Alberta statute summarized the remedy as imposing an obligation of "fairness" on the corporation and the directors.[2] Oppression remedy cases have consistently supported this proposition.[3] Further, courts have consistently stated that the fairness obligation under the oppression remedy provision is specific to the factual context.[4] The court is given the power to order any remedy it sees fit to rectify the matter, including an order restraining the conduct, an order removing the directors, and a compensation order.

[1] CBCA, s. 241(2); OBCA, s. 248(2).
[2] *Westfair Foods Ltd. v. Watt* (1990), 73 Alta. L.R. (2d) 326 (Q.B.); affd 79 Alta. L.R. (2d) 363 (C.A.).
[3] *Keho Holdings Ltd. v. Noble* (1987), 38 D.L.R. (4th) 368 (Alta. C.A.), at 372; *Elder v. Elder & Watson Ltd.*, [1952] C.S. 49 (Que.), at 55.
[4] *Westfair Foods Ltd. v. Watt* (1990), 73 Alta. L.R. (2d) 326 (Q.B.); affd 79 Alta. L.R. (2d) 363 (C.A.); *First Edmonton Place Ltd. v. 315888 Alberta Ltd.* (1988), 60 Alta. L.R. (2d) 122 (Q.B.), at 140, appeal adjourned 71 Alta. L.R. (2d) 61 (C.A.); *Re Ferguson and Imax Systems Corp.* (1983), 150 D.L.R. (3d) 718 (Ont. C.A.), at 727, leave to appeal to S.C.C. refused 52 N.R. 317n.

§20.37 The type of conduct which may be alleged to be "unfair" is limited only by the imagination of the complainant. To the extent that directors are acting in the best interests of the corporation and with the required degree of care, diligence and skill, they should be protected. However, this may not always be the case. Although the business judgment rule may protect the directors from challenges to the substantive decisions which they make, the court may nevertheless find that the interests of the complainant have been unfairly disregarded. The caselaw has made it clear that even a decision objectively in the best interests of the corporation may be, in some way, oppressive to the interests of certain groups. Further, no evidence of bad faith on the part of directors is required for a finding of oppression.[1]

[1] *Brant Investments Ltd. v. Keeprite Inc.* (1991), 3 O.R. (3d) 289 (C.A.).

§20.38 Directors should be sensitive to their fairness obligations any time action is to be taken which can affect shareholder expectations or values. It should be noted that the oppression remedy and general obligations of fairness have been applied by courts to directors of public corporations as well as private corporations taking it beyond its original intent to remedy the procedural difficulties that existed for Canadian shareholders of small corporations in bringing suits against corporations and directors. Although the section provides a remedy for persons other than shareholders of the corporation, courts have most often considered the remedy in the context of shareholders' rights. However, a number of cases have given judgment to creditors under the oppression remedy. Although neither the *Quebec Companies Act*[1] nor the *Civil Code of Quebec*[2] specifically provide an "oppression" remedy for shareholders or other prejudiced parties, some authors and cases have suggested that section 33 of the *Code of Civil Procedure*[3] (the "CCP") and the provincial *Winding-Up Act*[4] could possibly be used to obtain liquidation of the company or a personal judgment against a director who had unfairly used his or her power to the detriment of a complainant. However, to date, Quebec courts have been reluctant to use these provisions in the manner suggested and, outside of requiring directors to comply with statutory duties such as the holding of meetings, access to books, etc., there are few Quebec cases providing relief to prejudiced parties in the same manner as an oppression remedy.[5] If actual fraud can be proved, new article 316 of the CCQ provides that an "interested person" can obtain damages against a founder, director, senior officer or member of the corporation if such person has participated in the fraudulent act or personally profited from it.[6]

[1] R.S.Q. 1977, c. C-38.
[2] S.Q. 1991, c. 64.
[3] R.S.Q., c. C-25.
[4] R.S.Q. 1977, c. L-4.
[5] See *Placements Eloy Inc. v. Laurin*, J.E. 93-100 which states s. 33 is a last resort and *Développements urbains Candiac v. Combest Corp.*, [1993] R.J.Q. 1321 (C.A.), where the court upheld the winding up of the company, opining that Quebec law did not provide other remedies in situations of abuse.
[6] Martel, Maurice and Paul Martel, *La compagnie au Québec: Les aspects juridiques* (Montréal: Wilson & Lafleur, Martel, Ltée, 1995), pp. 540.4.1, 583, 766.1, 770.1, 770.2.

4. Fiduciary Duties of Directors and Senior Officers

§20.39 Under common law jurisprudence, a director or officer has an obligation to act honestly and in good faith with a view to the best interests of the corporation. This has been codified in the CBCA and the OBCA, as well as in the CCQ.[1] Both common law statutes contain specific references to officers' obligations. One reaches the same result in Quebec through the concept of mandate, since officers are mandataries of the corporation.

[1] CBCA, s. 122(1)(*a*); OBCA, s. 134(1)(a); C.C.Q., arts. 322, 2138.

§20.40 At article 2138, the new CCQ codifies the jurisprudential rule to the effect that directors and officers owe duties of good faith and loyalty very similar to those at common law. A civil law mandatary is bound to "act honestly and faithfully in the best interests of the mandator", and avoid placing himself in a position that puts his own interests in conflict with that of his mandator. These duties were found to be implicit to a high level employee's contractual obligations even before the new Civil Code.[1] The duties of directors and officers under the QCA and the Civil Code are therefore substantially the same as those under the CBCA and other corporate statutes.

---

[1]   *National Bank of Canada v. Houle*, [1990] 3 S.C.R. 122. See also *Bank of Montreal v. Kuet Leong Ng*, [1989] 2 S.C.R. 429, at 443.

§20.41   The "corporation" for the purpose of the common law test includes the shareholder body "as a whole" and not any particular shareholder constituency.[1] The board and officers may also consider the interests of future shareholders. Some courts have suggested that the board should also consider the interests of creditors, employees and other interested parties (indeed, the oppression remedy provision discussed above would appear to mandate some such consideration of their interests).[2] Legislation in the United Kingdom also reflects this trend.[3] This duty towards the stakeholders is slowly becoming the subject of judicial comment. A lower court Quebec case held, in *obiter*, that directors of a financially troubled corporation did not, solely on the ground that they knew of the financial troubles, become liable for the debts of the corporation, in the absence of fraud on their part.[4] The court refused to "lift the corporate veil" to find the directors liable for debts of the corporation. However, in *Aprikian v. Tesam Consultants Inc.*[5] the Court of Quebec held a director liable for a bankrupt corporation's debt because he had assured the creditor he would be paid. Also in *Baltimore Aircoil of Canada Inc. v. Process Cooling Systems Inc.*,[6] the Ontario Court of Appeal permitted a case to go to trial which alleged fraudulent misrepresentation by a director as to the financial condition of a company. There is a growing line of cases in the United States and Australia which indicates that directors of insolvent corporations or corporations operating "in the vicinity of insolvency" do owe very specific duties towards creditors.

---

[1]   *820099 Ontario Inc. v. Harold E. Ballard Ltd.* (1991), 3 B.L.R. (2d) 123 (Ont. Ct. (Gen. Div.)); affd (1991), 3 B.L.R. (2d) 113 (Ont. Div. Ct.); *PWA Corporation v. Gemini Group Automated Distribution Systems* (1993), 101 D.L.R. (4th) 15 (Ont. Ct. (Gen. Div.)), affd (1993), 103 D.L.R. (4th) 609, leave to appeal refused, [1993] 3 S.C.R. vi. See also *Calmont Leasing Ltd. v. Kredl*, [1995] 8 W.W.R. 179 (Alta. C.A.); *ASI Holdings Inc., Re* (1996), 28 B.L.R. (2d) 74 (Nfld. S.C.).

[2]   M. Lizée, "Le principe du meilleur intérêt de la société commerciale en droits anglais et comparé" (1989), 34 McGill L.J. 653, at 668 *et seq.* The author refers, *inter alia*, to L.C.B. Gower's seminal treatise, *The Principles of Modern Company Law*, 4th ed. (London: Stevens & Sons, 1979). See also Bruce L. Welling, *Corporate Law in Canada: The Governing Principles*, 2nd ed. (Toronto: Butterworths, 1991), pp. 342-56, and cases and authors cited therein.

[3] See the *Companies Act, 1985* (U.K.), c. 6, s. 309(1).

[4] *Beaudry v. Clark*, J.E. 96-384 (C.Q.).

[5] J.E. 93-695 (C.Q.).

[6] (1996), 30 O.R. (3d) 159.

§20.42 The primary obligations, which overlap, to some extent, the general duty to act in the best interests of the corporation are (a) a duty to avoid or disclose conflicts of duty and interest; and (b) a duty not to usurp opportunities properly belonging to the corporation.

(a) Conflicts of Duty and Interest

§20.43 Early judicial decisions considering the fiduciary duty of a director or senior officer to avoid conflicts of duty and interest precluded such person from entering into arrangements with the corporation by which he or she would obtain a personal benefit. Subsequent case law alleviated the harsh effect of this judicial rule by exempting transactions where shareholder ratification of the arrangement was obtained.

§20.44 The CBCA, OBCA and BCCA have adopted "safe harbour" provisions which extend when a director and officer may enter into such arrangements. In the case of directors, generally, if the nature of the director's interest is fully disclosed to the other directors, if the director does not vote on the resolution approving the transaction and if the transaction is reasonable and fair to the corporation, the director will not be liable to account for any profit or gain and the transaction will not be void or voidable by reason only of the relationship. The director can still be included in the determination of the quorum despite his or her inability to vote. Furthermore, subsequent approval of a fair and reasonable transaction by the shareholders (by a two-thirds vote in the case of an OBCA corporation) will shield a director or officer, provided the disclosure requirements of the Act were complied with. Where an officer is involved, he or she should disclose the interest forthwith after he or she becomes aware that the transaction is to be considered or has been considered at a meeting of directors.

§20.45 If the director or officer fails to comply with the provisions in the CBCA or the OBCA, shareholders and the corporation itself may apply to the court to set aside the transaction. In addition, where the corporation involved is an "offering corporation", the Ontario Securities Commission may apply to the court to set aside the transaction and order the director or officer to account to the corporation.

§20.45.1 The position of a Quebec director under the CCQ is similar. He must avoid placing himself in positions of conflict of interest and declare to the corporation any interest he has in an enterprise or association which may place him in a situation of conflict (article 324). Further, he must declare any interest he may have in any property under his administration or in a contract with the corporation. The director's interest is to be recorded and he is to abstain from discussion or voting on the question (article 325). Failure to comply with this section may lead to an action to annul the impugned act or to require the director to account to the corporation for any profit or benefit resulting from the property interest or contract. Mandataries, such as officers, are also bound generally to avoid placing themselves in positions of conflicts of interest (article 2138), and are bound to account to the mandator (the corporation) for the use of any information or property received pursuant to their administration, unless the corporation authorizes the use of the property or the information (article 2146).

§20.46   Many matters are left unregulated by these statutes. There are no statutory criteria for what constitutes a "material contract" or when a transaction is "fair and reasonable". Nor is there any requirement to establish an independent committee to review such contracts (although this is often done to provide some evidence of the fairness of the transaction).

(b)   Misappropriating Corporate Opportunities

§20.47   It is a generally recognized principle of Canadian corporate law that as part of his or her fiduciary obligations a director or senior officer must not take personal advantage of opportunities that come his or her way by virtue of such position, particularly where those opportunities might be exploited by the corporation. The leading Canadian case on what has become known as the "corporate opportunity doctrine" is the 1973 decision of the Supreme Court of Canada in *Canadian Aero Service Ltd. v. O'Malley* (*"Canaero"*).[1] The Court held that a director or senior officer is precluded from obtaining for himself or herself, either secretly or without the approval of the corporation (after full disclosure), any property or business advantage either belonging to the corporation or for which it has been negotiating, especially where the director or officer is a participant in the negotiations. It was further held that there was no precise test to determine when a director or senior officer would be entitled to make use of an opportunity that came his or her way by virtue of his or her position with the corporation. However, a number of factors to assist in determining this question were enumerated by the Court in the following passage from the judgment:

> The general standards of loyalty, good faith and avoidance of a conflict of duty and self-interest to which the conduct of a director or senior officer must conform must be tested in each case by many factors which it would be reckless to attempt to enumerate exhaustively. Among them are the factor of position or office held, the nature of the corporate opportunity, its ripeness, its specificness [sic] and the director's or managerial officer's relation to it, the amount of knowledge possessed, the circumstances in which it was obtained and whether it was special or, indeed, even private . . .[2]

In *Canaero*, the senior officers were held liable notwithstanding that they had left the corporation at the time that they bid on the project which the corporation was also bidding on.

[1] [1974] S.C.R. 592.
[2] [1974] S.C.R. 592, at 620.

§20.48 In a B.C. case, *Roper v. Murdoch and Northstar Productions Inc.*,[1] former officers were held liable for usurping a maturing business opportunity which the corporation had been actively pursuing, notwithstanding that the corporation was on the verge of going, and had subsequently gone, bankrupt. In other words, the standard is a relatively high one not necessarily dependent on whether the corporation would actually have been able to profit from the opportunity. This rule with respect to opportunities that come the director's or officer's way by reason of his or her position applies to potential, as well as actual, conflicts of interest.

[1] (1987), 14 B.C.L.R. (2d) 385 (S.C.).

§20.49 The concept of a director acquiring an opportunity "by reason of" his or her position as such is widely construed. For example, a director on the negotiating team for a lucrative contract for the corporation would breach his or her fiduciary duty to the corporation even if he or she was approached by the other party to bid on the contract himself or herself because of his or her excellent reputation in the industry.[1]

[1] See also *Balaban v. Bryndon Ventures Ltd.* (1993), 13 Alta. L.R. (3d) 171, (Q.B.) where a director who misappropriated a business opportunity that the company was pursuing was ordered to turn over to the company the interest he had acquired upon payment of his acquisition costs. See also *Hanson v. Clifford* (1994), 21 B.L.R. (2d) 108 (B.C.S.C.).

§20.49.1 Quebec directors are bound to the same duties of loyalty, good faith and avoidance of conflicts of interest although the term "fiduciary" is seldom used in civil law. The Quebec Civil law uses the rules of mandate to require that a director or an officer not misappropriate corporate opportunities, directors and officers being mandataries of the corporation. A mandatary is forbidden, even through an intermediary, to become a party to an act which he has agreed to perform for the corporation, unless the corporation authorizes it or is aware of his quality as a contracting party.[1] The corporation can ask for the transaction to be declared null and presumably sue for damages as well as for breach of the director's or officer's duty. Article 2146 forbids a mandatary from using for his benefit any information he obtains by reason of his mandate or any property he is charged with administering unless the mandator consents to such use. Further, article 316 is also a possible avenue for suing for misappropriation of corporate opportunities since it provides a remedy in damages for a director or officer who has "derived profit" from any act of "fraud with respect to the [corporation]".[2] The Supreme Court of Canada case of *Bank of Montreal v. Kuet Leong*[3] offers an in-depth analysis of how mandataries, in this case an employee, and middle-level staff owe particular duties of loyalty which forbid them to use their positions in bad faith to derive personal profit.

[1]   Art. 2147, CcQ.
[2]   See Martel, Maurice and Paul Martel, *La compagnie au Québec: Les aspects juridiques* (Montréal: Wilson & Lafleur, Martel, Ltée, 1995), pp. 532, 767 ff.
[3]   [1989] 2 S.C.R. 429.

CIVIL LIABILITY RELATED TO EMPLOYMENT LAW

A.   INTRODUCTION

§20.50   The civil liability of directors and officers with regard to employees and other matters will now be discussed, with an emphasis on employment law. Directors and officers will, for example, occasionally be compelled to pay the corporation's creditors for monies owed, in addition to being held accountable for their personal transgressions of the law. A description of the extent of such liabilities must always be read having regard to the analysis of the general duties of honesty, care and skill provided in the previous section. However, even honest, skilful and dedicated directors (and, less frequently, officers) may be found liable for the repayment of sums due by the corporation they have served, even where they can show their utmost good faith; employment law extends their liability beyond the generally applicable rules.

B. LIABILITY TOWARDS EMPLOYEES

1. Directors' Liability for Wages

§20.51 Under most incorporation statutes, the directors of a corporation are jointly and severally liable to the corporation's employees for all debts not exceeding six months' wages for services performed for the corporation by the employees which become payable during the period in which they acted as directors.[1] Any director may therefore be sued by all the company's employees for the total of such unpaid wages. This is one of the most common incidents of director liability, and one of the costliest, especially if the corporation has numerous employees. As well, the employment standards statutes of various jurisdictions impose similar or slightly different liability. Reference must always be made to the actual statute imposing liability as there can be important differences such as in the definitions of what are wages and who is responsible for the payments.

> [1] See CBCA, s. 119(1); OBCA, s. 131(1); and QCA, s. 96(1), the wording of which differs slightly in French and in English. See Ontario *Employment Standards Act*, R.S.O. 1990, c. E.14, s. 58.20(7) [en. 1991, Vol. 2, c. 16, s. 6]. Specific provisions also apply in areas such as the construction industry in Quebec.

§20.52 However, a director's liability for wages thereunder may be restricted or mitigated in various ways. For instance, directors are usually only secondary debtors to employees, who must first attempt to recover their wages from the corporation. Liability may be further restricted by statutory deadlines for filing suit, which is discussed in greater detail below.

(a) The Debtor

§20.53 Only the directors of a company are statutorily liable for unpaid wages under incorporation statutes. More accurately, the directors at risk are those who held office during the period in which the services for which wages are claimed were performed, regardless of whether they were actively involved in the management of the corporation. In other words, outside directors are as liable in such situations as inside directors. A director is not liable for debt related to services rendered to the corporation before his or her election to the board or after he or she has effectively resigned. On the other hand, a person who has not been elected or appointed to the board may nonetheless be held liable if that person has acted as a director during the relevant time period. Further, the issue of whether a resignation is, in fact, effective may be problematic if a director's successor has not been appointed.

§20.54 Both directors and officers are liable for wages owed to employees in British Columbia and in Ontario, under their employment standards legislation.[1] Directors and officers of corporations incorporated under provincial statute in British Columbia are liable for up to the equivalent of two months' wages only, rather than the six months provided for in other jurisdictions. Federally, under the *Canada Labour Code*, directors only are liable for six-months' wages to the extent the entitlement arose during the director's incumbency and the amount is impossible or unlikely to be recovered from the corporation.[2]

[1] *Employment Standards Act*, R.S.B.C. 1996, c. 113, s. 96; R.S.O. 1990, c. E.14, as amended.
[2] Section 251.17.

§20.54.1 In Ontario, both directors and officers may be liable for unpaid wages to the Employee Wage Protection Program. Following amendments to the *Employment Standards Act*,[1] the program, which is managed by a program administrator, was established to compensate employees for unpaid wages and other debts that they could not recover from their own employer for certain stated reasons. Once the program compensates an employee, it is subrogated to all of his or her rights against the employer or against its directors. For all practical purposes, the administrator steps into the employee's shoes and can claim from the directors any amount that the employee could have claimed on account of unpaid wages and vacation pay. The liability is for a maximum of six months' pay and 12 months' vacation pay[2] and remains in effect for six months after a person ceases to be a director or officer.[3] Although one cannot contract out of this liability, a corporation is allowed to indemnify the officer or director if he or she was acting in good faith and believed his or her conduct to be lawful.

[1] R.S.O. 1990, c. E.14, Pt. XIV.1 and XIV.2.
[2] *Employment Standards Act*, R.S.O. 1990, c. E.14, s. 58.20(7).
[3] *Business Corporations Act*, R.S.O. 1990, c. B.16, s. 131(2).

§20.54.2 With reference to these amendments to Ontario law, it should also be noted that, if a director against whom a claim for unpaid wages has been assessed by an employment standards officer, fails to comply with the latter's order to pay, that director is guilty of an offence under the Act and may be liable, on conviction, to a fine not exceeding $50,000, in addition to the payment of the unpaid wages to employees.[1] The *Canada Labour Code* is also particularly severe as it provides that an inspector who finds that an employer has not paid an employee wages to which the employee is entitled under Part III of the Code can issue a written payment order to the employer or a director, and the director cannot appeal the inspector's decision unless he or she pays to the Minister the amount indicated or the maximum amount of the director's liability under the Code.

[1] See *Employment Standards Act*, s. 58.27.

§20.55 Resignation will not enable a director to avoid liability for wage debts incurred while he or she was in office, but will limit the period during which such liability accrues to the extent that such resignation is effective, as discussed above.[1] A person who continues to act as a director despite having tendered his or her resignation may still be considered a director and held liable to employees.

[1] See, *e.g.*, CBCA, s. 108(2); OBCA, ss. 119(2) and 121(2); QCA, s. 123.76(2) [re-en. 1980, c. 28, s. 14]. See also *Zwierschke v. M.N.R.*, [1991] 2 C.T.C. 2783 (T.C.C.); *Brown v. Shearer*, [1994] 96 Man. R. (2d) 34 (Q.B.), vard (1995), 102 Man. R. (2d) 76 (C.A.); *R. v. Lark Manufacturing*, unreported, December 18, 1995 (Ont. C.A.).

§20.56 A director who resigns or whose term has expired should ensure that the corporation sends the appropriate statutory notice regarding a change of directors, as the government certificate attesting to the composition of the board of directors may be held to be conclusive proof in a court that such person is still a director, notwithstanding his or her resignation.[1]

[1] See, *e.g.*, CBCA, ss. 113(1) and 256(2); *Andrews v. Wait*, J.E. 92-174 (Ct. of Que.).

§20.57 It should also be noted that, in certain circumstances, resignation may not be in the best interests of a corporation and might conceivably constitute a breach of the general duties of a director, thus exposing the resigning director to different or additional liabilities towards the corporation or its shareholders. Before jumping from a sinking ship, a director would be well advised to weigh carefully his or her liabilities against his or her duties.

§20.58 The bankruptcy of a corporation does not automatically put an end to a director's appointment, even when the corporation's property is turned over to a trustee.[1] Directors continue to be responsible for matters related to internal management, such as registration of stock transfers or the calling of shareholder meetings.[2] However, as noted above, the appointment of a receiver-manager under a security agreement may be taken to terminate a director's duties in certain respects.

[1] *Bankruptcy and Insolvency Act*, R.S.C. 1985, c. B-3, s. 16(3) [re-en. R.S.C. 1985, c. 31 (1st Supp.), s. 3]. The director's personal bankruptcy, however, terminates his or her office: CBCA, ss. 108(1) and 105(1); OBCA, ss. 121(1) and 118(1); QCA, s. 123.73(4); BCCA, s. 114.

[2] It may be noted that failure to call a shareholders' meeting within statutory time requirements is an offence.

§20.59 Where a director is kept away from a company's affairs due to a conflict between shareholders or directors, for instance, that person may still be held liable to employees for matters he or she knows nothing about and could not in any practical way influence.

§20.59.1 A brief mention should be made of the fact that certain employment statutes such as the B.C. *Employment Standards Act*,[1] appear to "pierce the corporate veil". Section 95 of this Act allows the Employment Standards Branch to deem corporations which are under common control to be considered "one employer". Thus the directors of one company could be held liable for the unpaid wages of another company if the companies were deemed to be "one employer".

[1] R.S.B.C. 1996, c. 115, s. 95.

(b) The Creditors

§20.60 Directors are liable to *employees*. Contractors or other autonomous providers of services cannot claim payment of their fees from directors. Senior managers will, however, usually be considered employees of the company. Directors who are employees may also be covered.[1]

[1] *Breton v. Breton Precast and Block Ltd.* (1995), 13 C.C.E.L. (2d) 136 (Ont. Ct. (Gen. Div.)).

§20.61 Determining who is, in fact, an employee may be a difficult question and no precise rule can be enunciated in this regard. The general trend of corporate law and other statutes affecting directors' duties is to increase the exposure and liabilities of directors. This is demonstrated by the evolution and multiplication of provisions governing their obligations in federal and provincial statutes in the past 20 years,[1] and is particularly apparent in the area of liability for unpaid wages. In the case of *Mills-Hughes v. Raynor*,[2] Justice Blair, who had to sort out the rights of mid-level management executives, stated:

> It is obvious that the intent of Parliament in changing the section was to extend its protection to all employees and not merely the limited group of employees formerly covered.[3]

[1] J.M. Wainberg and Mark I. Wainberg, *Duties and Responsibilities of Directors in Canada*, 6th ed. (Don Mills: CCH, 1987), p. 12.

[2] (1988), 19 C.C.E.L. 6 (Ont. C.A.).

[3] (1988), 19 C.C.E.L. 6 (Ont. C.A.).

§20.62 Courts have usually considered a relationship of control over a person's work to be the most telling factor in deciding who is an employee. Where the corporation directs most aspects of a person's work, that person is likely to be an employee. On the other hand, where the corporation merely establishes an objective to be reached, but leaves the choice of means and methods to another person, that person is not likely to be deemed an employee. A professional on a retainer would therefore not be an employee.

§20.63 Other factors may also be considered in order to determine the parties' intentions when they established a relationship. Regular remuneration may tend to indicate employment, as will income tax deductions related to employment or contributions towards pension plans or unemployment insurance. The latter obligations are required only where a person is an employee and would therefore tend to indicate that the parties intended to create such a relationship. Where, for instance, a person's compensation was strictly a draw on sales earned, where he had no office, worked at home, was not supervised, was not to be found in the company's employee files and where the company had made none of the aforementioned contributions, that person was held not to be an employee. Similarly, the exclusive manager of a medical clinic who had complete independence from the corporation was held not to be an employee, as payments from the corporation to the manager were considered to be professional fees only.[1]

[1] See *Kornblum v. Dye* (1986), 59 C.B.R. (N.S.) 219 (Ont. Dist. Ct.). See also *Greenstone v. Geffin*, J.E. 78-6 (Que. Prov. Ct.) and *Asselin v. Jolicoeur*, J.E. 81-56 (Que. Prov. Ct.).

§20.64 The duration of the relationship is not in itself determinative of whether an employee/employer relationship exists. A person may well be an employee although the period of employment is short or predetermined in a contract. A person hired as a temporary replacement for an employee would most likely also be an employee. Furthermore, the mere statement in a contract that the hired party is not an employee of the company would not bind the court in the presence of facts indicating that the relationship was indeed one of employment, although it may serve as some evidence of how to classify such a relationship.

§20.65 In a fairly unusual case, where unemployed persons were hired by an employer in the framework of a federal employment development program, and their income took the form of increased unemployment insurance benefits, the Supreme Court of Canada went so far as to hold those persons to be employees with regard to the application of employment laws because their activities were controlled by their "employer".[1] Although this case was not concerned with directors' liability for unpaid wages, it does demonstrate that judicial interpretations of who is an "employee" may not always be consistent with the commonly accepted understanding of the word.

[1] *YMHA Jewish Community Centre of Winnipeg v. Brown*, [1989] 1 S.C.R. 1532.

§20.66 In summary, it may be stated that each case will be decided on its particular facts, with no single factor being necessarily determinative. However, the existence of a relationship in which the corporation controls and directs the means and methods of the hired person's work and activities would be a very strong indicator of an employee/employer relationship.

(c) The Nature of the Debts

(i) What Can Be Claimed

§20.67 Directors are liable for *debts* the company owes to employees for services performed, not exceeding six months' wages. *Debts* is a broad term and may include all types of remuneration and is not restricted to wages or salary in the strictest sense.[1] In contrast to the employment statutes, the corporate statutes do not define what exactly composes "wages" or "debts" which is left to interpretation by the courts. A recent case indicates that gross wages can be claimed, rather than simply the net amount.[2] The phrase "six months' wages" in section 119 of the CBCA, section 131 of the OBCA[3] and section 96 of the QCA refers to the monetary equivalent of six months' wages, rather than to actual time worked.[4] In *Filion v. Ayers*,[5] where an employee worked less than six months, but was also entitled to payment of vacation, sick days and other advantages, such that the total sum due equalled six months of salary or more, the employee was able to claim an amount equalling six months' salary. Furthermore, directors are usually liable for vacation pay.[6]

[1] *Schwartz v. Scott*, [1985] C.A. 713 (Que.).
[2] *Land v. Alberta (Umpire under Employment Standards Code)* (1992), 3 Alta. L.R. (3d) 354 (Q.B.).

3   Which must be read in conjunction with s. 58.20 of the *Employment Standards Act*, [as am. 1991, Vol. 2, c. 16, s. 6] which includes officers.
4   *Filion v. Ayers*, [1990] R.J.Q. 610 (Ct. of Que.).
5   [1990] R.J.Q. 610 (Ct. of Que.).
6   *Mills-Hughes v. Raynor* (1988), 19 C.C.E.L. 6 (Ont. C.A.). See also *Edward v. Reinblatt*, J.T. 95-1375 (C.Q.) to the same effect. See B. Manarin, "Directors' Liability to Employees When the Company Fails" (1989-90), 11 Advocates' Q. 43.

§20.68   Although "debts" is broader than "wages", the latter term itself includes diverse items.[1] In Ontario, the term "wages" is defined under the *Employment Standards Act*[2] as including any monetary remuneration payable by an employer to an employee or any payment to be made by an employer to an employee under the Act, which would include holiday pay, overtime pay and other premiums provided to employees for services rendered.[3]

1   Maurice Martel and Paul Martel, *La compagnie au Québec: Les aspects juridiques* (Montréal: Éditions Wilson & Lafleur, Martel Ltée, 1995), p. 548.
2   R.S.O. 1990, c. E.14, s. 1.
3   In *I.B.E.W., Local 2345 v. Callahan*, unreported, June 16, 1995 (Ont. C.A.), it was held that the employee's right to recover vacation pay against a director was absolute and unfettered by any factors which might affect a claim against a guarantor but the director can claim in the bankruptcy in the employee's place and for contribution by co-directors.

§20.69   Directors may be liable for benefits due to an employee under a collective agreement[1] and, according to case law, for marginal or fringe benefits,[2] for union dues,[3] which are considered to be an integral part of remuneration. It is not clear whether the contributions which a corporation may be required to make to a supplemental pension plan regulated federally[4] are included as part of the employee's "wages" for which a director will be held responsible. Certain cases in Quebec suggest that such pension contributions will be included within the term "wages" as they are part of the fringe benefits which an employee is receiving as part of his or her salary.[5]

1   See, for example, OBCA, s. 131, *Employment Standards Act*, R.S.O. 1990, c. E.14, s. 28; R.S.Q. c. N-1.1, ss. 66-77. J.M. Wainberg and Mark I. Wainberg, *Duties and Responsibilities of Directors in Canada* (Don Mills: CCH, 1987), p. 44.
2   *Bresner v. Goldin*, [1979] C.S. 1022 (Que. S.C.). See also *Whittington v. Patry*, J.E. 82-1086 (Que. S.C.), appeal settled out of court Mar. 21, 1986, C.A.Q. 200-09-000737-822 and *Commission de la construction du Québec v. Bouchard* (1990), R.J.Q. 1451 (C.Q.).
3   *Union internationale des ouvriers et ouvrières du vêtement pour dames (Conseil conjoint québécois) v. Sobel*, J.E. 93-1038.
4   Most provincial pension statutes such as the Quebec Supplemental Pension Plans Act expressly provide for director's liability for employer pension contributions.
5   See *Bresner v. Goldin*, [1979] C.S. 1022 (Que. S.C.). See also *Alias Raymond, Chabot*

Inc., [1995] R.J.Q. 1122 (C.S.) which held an employer's pension contributions to be part of wages in the context of a liquidation.

§20.70   Accrued interest on unpaid wages or salaries may be claimed, as well as costs incurred by an employee in bringing his or her action against the corporation for judgment.[1] In Quebec, an additional interest indemnity may also be sought under the CCQ.[2]

> [1]   *Lagueux v. Landry*, [1984] C.P. 147 (Que. Prov. Ct.).
> [2]   C.C.Q., art. 1619. See also *Filion v. Ayers*, [1990] R.J.Q. 610 (Ct. of Que.).

§20.71   Where, on the basis of all the relevant facts, a person paid on a commission basis is considered to be an employee rather than an independent agent, unpaid commissions may be found to be debts for the purposes of provisions governing directors' liability, as they are by nature a type of remuneration akin to wages in many cases.[1] In *Lagueux v. Landry*,[2] it was held that:

> It is trite to say that, in an economy based on free enterprise, remuneration . . . is not necessarily fixed but may be based on production . . . Sometimes remuneration combines a fixed base amount with remuneration varying . . . according to sales.[3]

> [1]   *E.g., Zavitz v. Brock* (1974), 46 D.L.R. (3d) 203 (Ont. C.A.).
> [2]   [1984] C.P. 147 (Que. Prov. Ct.).
> [3]   [1984] C.P. 147 (Que. Prov. Ct.) at 150 (authors' translation). See also *Greenstone v. Geffin*, J.E. 78-6 (Que. Prov. Ct.), where the person involved was found not to be an employee.

§20.72   As stated earlier, claims that may be made against directors are not limited to salary or its equivalent. Vacation pay can potentially be a significant part of "debts" due and thus represent an onerous liability for directors. In one case, more than $47,000 was claimed against several directors for unpaid vacation pay which had become due.[1] Under Ontario law, for instance, directors' liability for vacation pay accrued for a period of not more than 12 months is explicitly provided for in section 131 of the OBCA as well as pursuant to the provisions of the *Employment Standards Act*. Courts have held vacation pay to be a part of wages that can be claimed from directors under the federal and Quebec corporate statutes.[2] An employer is obliged to accrue and segregate vacation pay as it is earned and to hold it in trust for employees to be paid when vacations are taken or upon termination of employment, at which time vacation pay is considered a "debt" due to employees for services performed for the corporation.[3] However, directors may not be liable for holiday pay, accrued but not yet payable.[4]

1   *Schwartz v. Scott*, [1985] C.A. 713 (Que.).
2   See, *e.g.*, *Schwartz v. Scott*, [1981] C.S. 735 (Que. S.C.), revd in part [1985] C.A. 713; *Brown v. Shearer*, [1994] 96 Man. R. (2d) 34 (Q.B.), vard (1995), 102 Man. R. (2d) 76 (C.A.). See also J.M. Wainberg and Mark I. Wainberg, *Duties and Responsibilities of Directors in Canada* (Don Mills: CCH, 1987), p. 44.
3   *Mills-Hughes v. Raynor* (1988), 19 C.C.E.L. 6 (Ont. C.A.), at 11. See also *Fréchette v. Patenaude*, J.E. 90-1707 (Ct. of Que.).
4   *Re Westar Mining Ltd.* (1996), 41 C.B.R. (3d) 145 (B.C.C.A.).

§20.73 Likewise, directors may have ultimate responsibility for unpaid benefits of various types. For example, directors have been held liable for the wages which correspond to statutory or public holiday entitlements (such as Christmas) or other forms of statutory leave such as sick days,[1] floating holidays,[2] or leave for family events where applicable.[3] In Ontario, explicit mention is made of the right to benefits under collective agreements.[4] Where an employment contract or a collective agreement grants employees benefits which are more generous or greater than those provided by statute, directors may be liable for the value of such augmented benefits.[5]

1   *Thiboutot v. Kantor*, J.E. 94-798 (Qué. C.Q.); *Whittington v. Patry*, J.E. 82-1086 (Que. S.C.), appeal settled out of court Mar. 21, 1986, C.A.Q. 200-09-000737-822; *Nadeau v. Boisvert*, J.E. 84-488 (Que. C.A.). In *Filion v. Ayers*, [1990] R.J.Q. 610 (Ct. of Que.), it was held that sick leaves could not constitute salary unless the conditions by which they could be called into play (such as sickness of the employee prior to the bankruptcy of the company) were fulfilled.
2   *Filion v. Ayers*, [1990] R.J.Q. 610 (Ct. of Que.).
3   In Quebec, see *Filion v. Ayers*, [1990] R.J.Q. 610 (Ct. of Que.); *Nadeau v. Boisvert*, J.E. 84-488 (Que. C.A.). In Ontario, see s. 58.20 of the *Employment Standards Act* [as am. 1991, Vol. 2, c. 16, s. 6].
4   OBCA, s. 131. See also in Ontario, the *Employment Standards Act*, R.S.O. 1990, c. E.14, ss. 28 *et seq.* and, in Quebec, the *Act respecting Labour Standards*, R.S.Q., c. N-1.1, ss. 66-77 [am. 1990, c. 73, ss. 22-28].
5   For example, collective insurance, see *Masson v. Thompson*, J.E. 97-434 (Que. C.S.).

§20.74 Directors will also be liable for the payment of guaranteed bonuses, which are treated as constituting an additional increment in salary. They will not be personally liable, however, for bonuses payable under a condition that has not been fulfilled, such as a requirement that a certain level of profits be achieved.[1]

1   *Mills-Hughes v. Raynor* (1988), 19 C.C.E.L. 6 (Ont. C.A.). Whether directors would be liable for the payment of a conditional bonus where the condition has been realized has not been determined by the courts; the condition had not been met when the company went bankrupt in *Mills-Hughes*.

§20.75 Whether an amount such as a bonus will be characterized as a debt under the relevant statutory provisions must be decided by interpreting the text of the employment contract or having resorted to the parties' intentions. However, the parties' intentions may be difficult to determine. In *Hurtubise v. Berthiaume*,[1] for example, the court interpreted the words requiring indemnification of the employee "according to the corporation's means" in an indemnification agreement between the corporation and the employee as an enforceable term of the contract rather than as a condition of payment, thus making the corporation liable notwithstanding the provision. A similar ambiguity surrounds the status of stock option plans and other non-monetary forms of remuneration. Where these could be considered as part of an executive's "wages", albeit in a somewhat different form, directors may be liable.

[1]   [1987] R.J.Q. 678 (Prov. Ct.).

§20.76 This raises another issue in relation to executive employment contracts: How is the value of "six months' wages", for which directors are liable, to be determined where remuneration takes a variety of forms other than a weekly pay cheque? Canadian courts have not yet considered this matter in depth. It may well be that a broad construction would be given to provisions governing directors' liability, so that all amounts paid or distributed for services performed over six months would be deemed to be wages.

(ii)   What Cannot Be Claimed

§20.77 As discussed in Chapter 13, an employee must receive prior notice of termination or pay in lieu of notice from the employer if he or she is terminated without legal cause. Termination and severance payments, outside the situation discussed in the next paragraph, are usually not treated as debts giving rise to directors' liability, as they are not sums due as compensation for services rendered to the corporation by the employee.[1] They are, rather, damages for breach of the employment contract.[2] In *Barrette v. Crabtree Estate*, the Supreme Court of Canada upheld the decision of the Quebec Court of Appeal refusing to hold directors of an insolvent corporation liable for severance pay, stating that, "An amount payable in lieu of notice does not flow from services performed for the corporation, but rather from the damage arising from non-performance of a contractual obligation to give sufficient notice".[3]

[1]   *Mills-Hughes v. Raynor* (1988), 19 C.C.E.L. 6 (Ont. C.A.). Although not, of course, binding in Canada, it is interesting to note that the House of Lords, England's highest court, also distinguishes between wages and payment in lieu of notice, the latter being damages: *Delaney v. Staples*, [1992] 1 All E.R. 944 (H.L.). See also

Aubé v. Astell, [1988] R.J.Q. 845 (Prov. Ct.); *Vopni v. Groenewald* (1993), 10 C.B.R. (3d) 292 (Ont. H.C.J.).

[2] *Mills-Hughes v. Raynor* (1988), 19 C.C.E.L. 6 (Ont. C.A.), at 14; contra, *Meyers v. Walters Cycle Co.* (1990), 71 D.L.R. (4th) 190 (Sask. C.A.), commented on by J. Fleisher, "Directors' Liabilities on the Increase in Saskatchewan" (1991), 8 Business & the Law 17.

[3] [1993] 1 S.C.R. 1027, at 1048-1049.

§20.78 Before *Barrette v. Crabtree*,[1] it was not certain whether the situation would be different where a contract or agreement between the corporation and employees specifically provides for a payment upon termination of employment. In *Schwartz v. Scott*,[2] the Quebec Court of Appeal construed such an agreement as forming part of the employees' remuneration, thus creating a "debt" for which the directors could be held personally liable.[3] One commentator[4] expressed the opinion that, even under employment contracts lacking such a provision, a court could in certain circumstances hold severance pay to be compensation for past services. Following *Schwartz*, in *Faure v. Sauvé*,[5] where an employee was fired without notice and the contract between the corporation and the employee contained a clause stipulating that six months' notice would be given prior to terminating employment, the court held that the whole employment contract fell within the protection given to employees' wages under the QCA and, therefore, the directors were liable for pay in lieu of the notice period. However, a recent Quebec case has followed the *Barrette v. Crabtree* line of reasoning in a pursuit by employees for, among others, two weeks' pay in lieu of notice on termination of their employment, as set out in their collective agreement. The court held that this did not constitute a debt for services rendered to the corporation but rather a compensatory indemnity and thus it was not possible to recover this amount against the directors.[6] In *Ng v. Audia*,[7] the Alberta Court of Appeal held that directors were not liable for a termination indemnity because these were intended to cover "inconveniences and relocation expenses" which could not be classified as being "for services performed for the corporation" as set out in s. 114(1) of the *Alberta Business Corporations Act*, S.A. 1981, c. B-15.[8]

[1] [1993] 1 S.C.R. 1027.

[2] [1985] C.A. 713 (Que.).

[3] An appeal was launched from the decision in *Schwartz*, but was abandoned. The Supreme Court of Canada in *Barrette v. Crabtree* referred to *Schwartz*, but refused to comment on the correctness of the decision.

[4] B. Manarin, "Directors' Liability to Employees When the Company Fails" (1989-90), 11 Advocates' Q. 43.

[5] D.T.E. 89T-1008 (Que. S.C.).

[6] *Edward v. Reinblatt*, J.T. 95-1375 (C.Q.). See also *Lafrenière v. Wise*, J.E. 95-1444 (C.S.).

[7]   (1993), 9 Alta. L.R. (3d) 134 (C.A.).

[8]   See generally the following articles and case law which they refer to: Weisz, Steven J. "Liability of former directors for claims by terminated employees: When do their obligations cease?" (March 1992), v. 1, no. 12, Employment and Labour Law Reporter 137-140; Palamar, Jeffrey J., "Liability of Corporate Directors for severance pay" (March 1993), v. 2, no. 12, Employment and Labour Law Reporter 136-138; [Case comment on *Ng v. Audia*], The Editors, (July 1993), v. 2, no. 4, Employment and Labour Law Reporter 45-47.

(iii)   A Special Case: Executive Termination and "Golden Parachutes"

§20.79   Executive severance pay often raises specific questions in those situations where executives are provided with exceptional advantages on termination through explicit contractual provisions. It is often asked whether such "golden parachutes" are enforceable in Canada and whether directors may be held personally liable for payment of such amounts to terminated executives if the corporation is unable to fulfil its contractual obligations.[1]

[1]   Questions related to liability of directors who have granted unreasonably generous compensation to executives, be it through "parachutes" or otherwise, are examined, *infra*, at §§20.115 *et seq.*, where the "business judgment rule" is also considered in more detail.

§20.80   Although there is as yet no developed case law on the subject in Canada, it is likely that a "golden parachute" in an executive's employment contract would be treated as entitlements arising on termination and would therefore not give rise to a director's personal liability. However, the prudent approach for a corporation would be to explicitly describe such compensation in the agreement as constituting damages on account of termination of employment. This obviously raises a paradox: A "golden parachute" will be reasonable and enforceable insofar as it is related to the value of an executive's services to the corporation, but, in order to protect a director, it should be drafted in such a way that it is not a form of recognition for services rendered; that is, it should not appear to be "wages", but merely damages flowing from termination. How our courts will judge attempts at reconciling these requirements remains to be seen.

§20.81   Given the lack of Canadian jurisprudence on golden parachutes it is not unlikely that our courts will look to the American caselaw which is far more developed in this area.[1] Therefore, the following will canvas some of the U.S. caselaw in this area.

[1]   The disclosure requirements introduced in 1993 in Ontario for reporting compa-

nies respecting executive compensation specifically includes the disclosure of "golden parachutes".

§20.82 Golden parachutes have been described in passing by the United States Supreme Court as agreements

> ... between a corporation and its top officers which guarantee those officers continued employment, payment of a lump sum, or other benefits in the event of a change of corporate ownership.[1]

> [1] *Schreiber v. Burlington Northern Inc.*, 472 U.S. 1 (1985), at 3, note 2.

§20.83 Golden parachutes developed in a context where aggressive corporate take-over bids seemed to be the norm and where compensation apparently knew no limits. To assuage anxieties expressed by key executives and to attract others, contracts were developed so as to provide an individual who was dismissed or whose responsibilities were reduced (amounting to constructive dismissal) the right to receive a significant sum of money and other benefits. Such golden parachute agreements would often provide for payments of salary ranging from a year to ten years or more after termination.[1] Other benefits would also be extended for a similar period. In certain cases, compensation was to be paid to an executive after a change in control of the corporation, regardless of whether the employee left employment or remained with the company.[2]

> [1] P.L. Coffey, "Golden Parachutes: A Perk That Boards Should Scrutinize Carefully" (1984), 67 Marquette L. Rev. 293, at 297. A study done in 1995 stated that 47% of all companies studied and 75% of those which used a multiple for the parachute package used 2.99 or 3 for the CEO. Gail McGowan, editor, *Change of Control: Triggers & Parachutes*, Executive Compensation Reports, Monograph Series (Fairfax Station, Virginia: DP Publications, 1995). Parachutes worth $4 million and more are not unheard of: Coffey, p. 303, citing the case of the president of Thiokol who left in 1982 after a takeover.
> [2] In 1982, Bendix Corp.'s chief executive officer was promised payments of $805,000 per year for five years following a takeover, regardless of his continuing employment or departure from the company.

§20.84 Some parachute agreements have even dispensed with the laying down of specific criteria triggering the opening of the parachute permitting the executive to elect to leave for any reason. Needless to say, such understandings have raised controversy.[1] At the very least, such a contract ought normally to stipulate that the employee will get no benefit at all where the termination occurs as a result of fraud or embezzlement by the employee or in the case of death, so that directors could not be found to be manifestly depleting the corporation's assets.

[1] P.L. Coffey, "Golden Parachutes: A Perk That Boards Should Scrutinize Carefully" (1984), 67 Marquette L. Rev. 293, at 298. Perhaps the most blatant case of apparent abuse occurred at Burnup & Sims, where the chief executive officer left, exercising a $4 million parachute, and later returned to the company as chief executive officer. Litigation ensued.

§20.85 Arguments in favour of and against the provision of golden parachute agreements have been exchanged in various forums. The proponents claim that parachutes provide security in case of change of control (or presumably, in case of other circumstances threatening the viability of the enterprise), that they are a required incentive in order to recruit good executives[1] (particularly where a corporation's prospects are unsure) and that they are a deterrent against hostile takeovers.[2] It has also been argued that they are in fact an efficient risk allocation method which, if suppressed, would have to be replaced by some equivalent device.[3] Opponents, on the other hand, contend that there is no reason for a corporation to pay a ransom to ensure exclusive loyalty that ought already to have been guaranteed by the employee by reason of the employment contract. Other harmful effects are often also cited.

[1] That aspect is heightened by the fact that an executive will be reluctant to consider new employment unless his or her compensation is increased; if the executive benefits already from the promise of a generous parachute or some other golden handcuffs, only more generous offers would entice him or her: P.L. Coffey, "Golden Parachutes: A Perk That Boards Should Scrutinize Carefully" (1984), 67 Marquette L. Rev. 293, at 299, note 36, who mentions the case of John Sculley, who hesitated before leaving the presidency of Pepsi-Cola for that of Apple Computer, though Apple promised him a $1 million parachute. See also *Freedman v. Barrow*, 427 F. Supp. 1129 (S.D.N.Y., 1976).

[2] A case in point is *Allen v. Gulf Resources & Chemical Corp.*, unreported, No. 82-27756 (Tex. Dist. Ct.), cited in Coffey, *supra*, at 307. In that case, stockholders who had gained control of the company refused to pay a $13 million collection of parachutes; the company had lost close to $78 million during the previous year. An agreement favouring the company was apparently reached in 1984.

[3] Coffey, *supra*, at 293; K. Johnsen, "Golden Parachutes and the Business Judgment Rule: Toward a Proper Standard of Review" (1985), 94 Yale L.J. 909. Numerous other studies regarding golden parachutes were published in the '80s in the United States.

§20.86 In 1985, the Supreme Court of Wisconsin ruled on the validity and enforceability of golden parachute agreements. In *Koenings v. Joseph Schlitz Brewing Co.*,[1] the court considered the "parachute" clauses to be reasonable stipulated damages under the circumstances and thus upheld the agreement between Schlitz and its former employees whereby key employees were to receive their salary and fringe benefits for the two-year duration of the agreement, whether they resigned or not. The court concluded that such an arrangement could be in the best interests of the corporation, that the damages were reasonable (taking into consideration damages suffered by the employee, including certain damages which were difficult to determine, and the relationship between the injury suffered and the amount of damages) and, incidentally, that the business judgment rule protected Schlitz's directors in agreeing to provide such controls.

---

[1]   377 N.W. 2d 593.

§20.87 In addition, attempts to restructure golden parachutes as compensation or deferred compensation plans will probably not escape review.[1] In a 1987 decision, various advantages conferred on executives ancillary to such agreements were found to be illegal. In *Buckhorn Inc. v. Ropak Corp.*,[2] Buckhorn's board and its chief executive officer had commenced the renegotiation of the CEO's compensation package. A take-over bid for the corporation proved to be a decisive incentive for the board to grant more advantages to that officer (including a ten-year contract) as well as to other key managers. Other defensive measures were also implemented against the attacking corporation. The U.S. District Court of Ohio found that the board had attempted to entrench the current management team and that such a tactic was not proper. It also found that the vesting of stock options and the granting of new stock options to executives were not reasonable actions in relation to the threat posed by their departure where those employees had already been given other significant guarantees. If such defensive measures had been taken before a tender offer and for demonstrably reasonable business purposes, they might well have been upheld. Other measures (including golden parachutes) taken by the directors at the same time were deemed reasonable in relation to the threat and were allowed to stand.

---

[1]   *Balch John v. Commissioner*, 100 T.C. No. 21 (1933).
[2]   656 F. Supp. 209 (S.D. Ohio, 1987), affd 815 F. 2d 76 (6th Circ., 1987).

§20.88 The Court of Appeal of Georgia took a more tolerant view of the "freedom to contract" in *Royal Crown Companies Inc. v. McMahon*,[1] where the golden parachute agreement "freely negotiated between the president of a wholly-owned subsidiary and the parent corporation" was upheld. The agreement provided for one year's salary and other benefits if the employee resigned or was fired within a given period of time following the parent's take-over. To quote the court:

> The express purpose of the agreement was to protect the interests of the company and its shareholders by reinforcing and encouraging the continued attention and dedication of key management to their assigned duties . . .[2]

The decision goes further than that in the *Koenings* case, mentioned earlier, in that the court did not attempt to apply a reasonableness test to the amounts to be paid to the employee who had elected to quit. The court refused to "interfere with the parties' freedom to contract", particularly in light of the efforts of one of the parties to avoid being bound to an agreement it had freely signed.

[1]   359 S.E. 2d 379 (1987).
[2]   359 S.E. 2d 379 (1987), at 380.

§20.89 The case of *Worth v. Huntington Bancshares Inc.*[1] presents a slightly different situation. In this case, the court found that the employee could not claim the benefit of his parachute, as he was attempting to exercise it for improper motives. Although his employer had been taken over, the employee had suffered no material loss of responsibility but merely wanted to quit the banking industry and the state where he lived to start a new venture. His actions were viewed as an attempt to gain a windfall by exercising his parachute a short time prior to its expiry. It was held that "golden parachutes" are "most certainly not void as against public policy", are "within the sound discretion of the corporation's board of directors"[2] and, if neither excessive nor tainted by self-interest, are protected by the business judgment rule.

[1]   540 N.E. 2d 249 (Ohio S.C., 1989).
[2]   540 N.E. 2d 249 (Ohio S.C., 1989), at 255.

§20.90 Unless the United States Supreme Court thinks fit to overrule the trend established by these authorities, it would seem fair to believe that golden parachutes or other forms of executive compensation will be upheld in the United States provided that they are not excessive to the point of unreasonableness. It is likely that a similar policy would be followed by Canadian courts and that such forms of compensation would therefore, at least in principle, be held to be valid and enforceable against a corporation.

§20.91 Care must be exercised, however, in the conception and structure of compensation packages in order to ensure that the costs which the corporation incurs can reasonably be expected to be offset by the benefits gained.[1] There may well be limits to contractual freedom, as was recognized in the United States in the *Royal Crown* case,[2] and plans that are excessively generous, or that can be triggered in situations where the executive is in no way threatened, might be struck down by the courts. Insofar as possible, provisions providing for golden parachute benefits should be included in the executive's employment contract at the outset, so as to simplify the establishment of the reasonableness of the relationship between employment and corresponding compensation.

¹ *Buckhorn Inc. v. Ropak Corp.*, 656 F. Supp. 209 (S.D. Ohio, 1987), affd 815 F. 2d 76 (6th Circ., 1987); K. Johnsen, "Golden Parachutes and the Business Judgment Rule: Toward a Proper Standard of Review" (1985), 94 Yale L.J. 909, at 921-25.
² See §20.88.

§20.92 The question of whether a "parachute" is reasonable often turns on the nature of the services provided by the employee and the importance of his or her contribution to the business enterprise; the value and structure of compensation offered in relation to the size of the enterprise; and, generally, the advantages accruing to the corporation by reason of the compensation offered. The benefit must be real and lasting.

(iv) Alternate Liability

§20.93 It is important to remember that a director's liability is alternate to that of the corporation employer. Under relevant statutory provisions, a director may be held liable to the corporation's employees for the equivalent of up to six months' wages where the employees have first attempted to claim such amounts against the corporation and where the corporation has not fulfilled its obligations for payment of wages to the employees. The corporation will be deemed to have failed to fulfil its obligations when:

(1) an employee was unable, wholly or in part, to have a judgment against the company executed;
(2) liquidation or dissolution proceedings have been launched; or
(3) the corporation becomes bankrupt within the meaning of the *Bankruptcy and Insolvency Act*.¹

Where a portion of an employee's wage or vacation pay claim has been satisfied by the company, a director will be liable only for the unsatisfied balance. The director's liability in cases of liquidation or bankruptcy is also predicated on the employee having duly proved a claim which has not been satisfied. In Quebec, a recent case reiterated the point that the directors could not be sued for wages until the corporation had been subject to a judgment or execution and the directors were only liable for the shortfall after the execution of such a judgment.

¹ R.S.C. 1985, c. B-3.

§20.94   Under the Ontario *Employment Standards Act*, as noted above, employees may, in various circumstances, be compensated under a statutory program. The administrator of such program is then subrogated to the rights of the compensated employee and may therefore commence an action against the directors and officers to recover the compensation paid to the employee.

(v)   Joint and Several Liability

§20.95   Directors' (and sometimes officers') liability in this area is both joint and several. Any employee may therefore sue any director individually for his or her wage claim and such director may be ordered to fully reimburse the employee. An employee may also elect to sue some or all of the directors rather than one individual director. All of the director's property and assets are potentially subject to seizure by unpaid creditors such as employees, except such property or assets as are specifically declared by law to be exempt from seizure or specifically pledged to a creditor. A director who appears to employees to have greater assets than the others might therefore be sued for more than his or her share and would have to commence an action against fellow directors for their share of the liability.

(vi)   Statutory Limitation Periods

§20.96   Employees have a limited period of time in which to bring a suit against a director for unpaid debts. As a director is subject only to alternate or secondary liability, an employee must usually first file a claim against the corporation itself, which must be done within a specified (and fairly short) period. Should such an approach prove unsuccessful, employees who wish to sue directors will usually be required to do so before another statutory limitation period expires.

§20.97   Under the CBCA,[1] a suit must be brought against the corporation or a claim must be proven (in cases of liquidation, dissolution or bankruptcy) within six months after the debt becomes due. Should the corporation be unable to pay, employees will be precluded from suing a former director who has left the board more than two years before. In such cases, the only persons who would be liable are those who still sit on the board and those who ceased to be directors less than two years before a suit is instituted against them.

[1]   Ss. 119(1) and (2) [am. 1992, c. 27, s. 90(1)(*h*)].

§20.98   Under section 96 of the QCA, in order for a creditor to be liable for wages owing to employees, one of two conditions must be met. A suit against the corporation must be brought within one year after the debt becomes due and a writ of execution must have been returned unsatisfied wholly or in part, or the employer must have, within one year from the date the debt became due, filed a claim in bankruptcy or winding-up of the company. No special limitation period exists for an employee's suit against a director after the foregoing requirements have been met, therefore the employee's claim would be subject to the general rules regarding limitation periods which provide that such a claim is barred after three years.[1] Any person who was a director at the time the claimed wages were earned may therefore be liable. Any director who left the board more than three years before the suit was instituted should be able to oppose this limitation period.

[1] Art. 2925, C.C.Q.

§20.99 The OBCA establishes a slightly different procedure. Whatever the cause of the corporation's failure to pay its debts to employees, both the corporation and the director must be sued together within six months from the time the debt becomes payable in order for a director's liability to arise.

2. Liability for Wrongful Dismissal

§20.100 A common action brought against corporations and, more recently, directors is one for damages for wrongful dismissal. Damages for wrongful dismissal are not considered a debt for services performed for the corporation and directors are therefore *usually* not liable to former employees for such damages under the provisions of the corporate and employment statutes we have just been considering.[1]

[1] *Mesheau v. Campbell* (1982), 39 O.R. (2d) 702 (C.A.); *Schouls v. Canadian Meat Processing Corp.* (1983), 41 O.R. (2d) 600 (H.C.J.); *Bouffard v. Canico Hydraulique Inc.*, D.T.E. 89T-717 (Que. S.C.); *Hudon v. Frishling*, J.E. 96-176 (Que. C.A.). See Jordan, Donald J., "Directors Liability under the *Canada Business Corporations Act*: Are Directors personally liable for wrongful dismissal awards?", (Sept. 1993), v. 3, no. 6, Employment and Labour Law Reporter 69-71.

§20.101 However, employees suing directors on the basis of wrongful dismissal sometimes attempt, usually unsuccessfully, to found the directors' personal liability on general contract principles. It has been written that:

> Courts hearing suits against directors or officers responsible for contentious dismissals usually turn down such claims because a dismissal, however reprehensible or unjustified, and even if it stems from a personal conflict between whoever

ordered the dismissal and its victim, is made in the name of the company, so that only it can be sued for breach of contract.[1]

In *Schouls v. Canadian Meat Processing Corp.*,[2] for example, a director was deemed to have acted on behalf of the corporation and not to have assumed any personal liability in the contractual relationship between the corporation and the complainant. The action for damages for wrongful dismissal against the director was therefore rejected. The court did hold both the corporation and the director responsible for costs and legal fees, however, because the director's behaviour was unacceptable and he was, in fact, responsible for the problematic situation.

[1] Maurice Martel and Paul Martel, *La compagnie au Québec: Les aspects juridiques* (Montréal: Wilson & Lafleur, Martel Ltée, 1995), p. 587 (authors' translation).

[2] (1983), 41 O.R. (2d) 600 (H.C.J.).

§20.102   This does not mean, however, that all claims against directors for damages for wrongful dismissal will be rejected. Some claims not based on contractual principles have been more successful. In *PCM Construction Control Consultants Ltd. v. Heeger*,[1] an employee fired without notice and without just cause was found to be entitled to damages for wrongful dismissal against the directors. The directors had stripped the corporation of its assets following the employee's departure so that judgment against the corporation alone would have been ineffective. The directors were held to be jointly and severally liable for nine months' salary, as they were found to have acted in an oppressive and prejudicial manner. In the same vein, directors were held liable for damages for wrongful dismissal and "dommages moraux" in *Taskos v. 104880 Canada Inc.*[2] after having fraudulently encouraged an employee to act contrary to his personal interests. The new tort of inducement to breach a contract, discussed below, can also be used to ground a claim for wrongful dismissal.

[1] (1989), 67 Alta. L.R. (2d) 302 (Q.B.).

[2] [1987] R.J.Q. 2574 (S.C.).

3. Liability for Inducement to Breach a Contract

§20.103   The basic principle respecting a director's liability for inducing breach of contract was enunciated in the case of *Imperial Oil Ltd. v. C & G Holdings Ltd.*[1] In this case, the Newfoundland Court of Appeal held, on the issue of interference with contractual relations, that a director of a corporation is not liable for inducing breach of contract between the corporation and a third party if the director acted in good faith, within the scope of his or her authority and in the best interests of the corporation, and if his or her primary concern was not to deprive the third party of the benefits of the contract.[2] On the other hand, the corporation itself may remain insulated from the legal consequences of such an act if the director or officer acted outside the scope of his or her authority.[3] A director or officer who has acted fraudulently cannot, of course, be said to have acted in the best interests of the corporation and would be held personally liable for the full amount of resulting damages.[4]

[1] (1989), 62 D.L.R. (4th) 261 (Nfld. C.A.).
[2] These matters have been reviewed in legal literature under both contract and tort liability.
[3] *McFadden v. 481782 Ontario Ltd.* (1984), 47 O.R. (2d) 134 (H.C.J.).
[4] *Kepic v. Tecumseh Road Builders* (1985), 29 B.L.R. 85 (Ont. H.C.J.), affd 18 C.C.E.L. 218 (C.A.).

§20.104 In *Jackson v. Trimac Industries Ltd.*[1] the plaintiff was claiming damages for inducing breach of contract against the president of Trimac. The court recognized the possibility of directors, officers and employees having a defence to a claim for inducing breach where torts were committed in the course of carrying out the legitimate aims of the company. However, where a servant takes advantage of his employment to commit a tort for his own ends, such a defence is not available.

[1] [1994] 8 W.W.R. 237 (Alta. C.A.).

§20.105 Thus, a director or officer who is instrumental in having the corporation breach a contract could be held personally liable if he or she fails to prove that he or she acted *bona fide* within the scope of his or her authority and in the best interests of the corporation. It should be noted that liability for inducement to breach a contract has been primarily developed in common law jurisdiction, although civil law principles governing extra-contractual responsibility could presumably lead to a similar result.

4. New Legislation

§20.106 As has been mentioned, in Quebec, the new CCQ,[1] contains some general provisions regarding directors' liability which are intended to complete the special corporate statutes. There is, as yet, little interpretation of these new provisions. Directors and officers may be held liable by a court for a fraud committed by the corporation if they participate in the fraudulent act or if they gain personal profit from it.[2]

[1] *Civil Code of Québec*, S.Q. 1991, c. 64.
[2] C.C.Q., art. 316. Article 358 provides for liability on liquidation but is not applicable to most corporations.

§20.107 Under the new legislation, a court may also forbid anyone from becoming or continuing to be a director if that person has acted fraudulently or dishonestly in a corporate matter or has repeatedly failed to comply either with applicable corporate law or his or her obligations as a director. This sanction can remain in effect for up to five years.[1]

[1] C.C.Q., arts. 329 and 330.

C. LIABILITY TO OTHER CONSTITUENCIES

§20.108 Directors and officers may be liable to many other constituencies under general principles of law or specific statutes. Liability to shareholders for lack of exercise of reasonable skill and care is the most obvious example. It is beyond the scope of this chapter to discuss all such liabilities, but a broad outline can be provided. As well, a few words will be said on an employment-related matter, namely, liability towards shareholders where unduly generous remuneration has been paid to a corporation's executives.

1. General Rules

§20.109 In accordance with the principles set out in wrongful dismissal cases against directors, civil liability based on an employment contract should normally not be placed upon directors or officers, as they are not parties to the contracts between the corporation and its employees. However, where directors or officers are bound personally by a contract or where an employee may in good faith have believed that directors or officers were parties to a contract, they may in some cases be held liable. Accordingly, directors and officers should take care to be explicit about the identity of parties to a contract when they act for a corporation.[1] Further, they should also be careful when they themselves are parties to contracts with the corporation. Where a director or officer is unduly advancing his or her own interests, or acting maliciously, he or she will be held personally liable for any resulting damages. In *Tongue v. Vencap Equities Alberta Ltd.*,[2] directors were held liable for insider trading and for breaching fiduciary duties towards the selling shareholders to whom the directors did not disclose pertinent information.

[1] See *Watfield International Enterprises Inc. v. 655293 Ontario Ltd.* (1995), 21 B.L.R. (2d) 158 (Ont. Ct. (Gen. Div.)).

[2] (1994), 17 Alta. L.R. (3d) 103 (Q.B.); affd (1996), 39 Alta. L.R. (3d) 29 (C.A.).

§20.110 Usually extracontractual or tort liability[1] will not be of concern to directors or officers of a corporation unless they have personally acted so as to cause damage to another party or accord a gain to themselves, as opposed to acting strictly in the course of their duties and in the best interests of the corporation. However, in certain cases a director or officer will be liable if he or she knew or ought to have known of the corporation's wrongdoing.[2]

[1] That is, liability arising out of extra-contractual responsibility in Quebec, tort or negligence in other jurisdictions. See *Immeubles G.L.M.C. c. Tremblay*, J.E. 95-522 (C.Q.) where directors were held not responsible for non-fraudulent actions performed in the course of their duties and *WBD Bank, Canada v. Dofasco Inc.*, unreported, March 27, 1997 (Ont. Ct. (Gen. Div.)).

[2] In *St. Mary's Cement Corp. v. Construc Ltd.* (1997), 32 O.R. (3d) 595 (Ont. Ct. (Gen. Div.)), the director was liable for the corporation's breach of trust, both statutorily and at common law.

§20.111 If a director or officer breaches his or her statutory responsibilities, a court may consider such a contravention to be itself evidence of wrongdoing and he or she may, as a result, be required to pay any aggrieved party for the resulting damages.[1] Statutes may also act to mitigate or take away such a personal claim. In areas such as industrial accidents, an injured person's right to commence a civil action may be denied by statute,[2] although this may not be iron-clad. For example, although the Ontario *Workers' Compensation Act*[3] prohibits suits against an employer or fellow employees, the Ontario Court of Appeal held that executive officers are neither "employees" nor "employers" within the definition of the Act and that an injured employee could successfully claim against an executive officer who was found to have breached a personal duty of care owed to an employee which breach resulted in an injury in the workplace.[4]

[1] See *Morin v. Blais*, [1977] 1 S.C.R. 570; *R. v. Saskatchewan Wheat Pool*, [1983] 1 S.C.R. 205; and P.-G. Jobin, "La violation d'une loi ou d'un règlement entraîne-t-elle la responsabilité civile?" (1984), 44 R. du B. 222.

[2] E.g., the *Workers' Compensation Act*, R.S.O. 1990, c. W.11, ss. 10(9) and 16, and *An Act respecting Industrial Accidents and Occupational Diseases*, R.S.Q., c. A-3.001, s. 442.

[3] Ontario Bill 99 which repeals the *Workers' Compensation Act* and replaces it with the *Workplace Safety and Insurance Act, 1997* has passed third reading on October 9, 1997.

[4] *Berger v. Willowdale A.M.C.* (1983), 23 B.L.R. 19 (Ont. C.A.), leave to appeal to S.C.C. refused 41 O.R. (2d) 89n.

§20.112 Most labour and employment laws other than the B.C. and Ontario employment standards legislation already discussed, and the Ontario *Occupational Health & Safety Act*, discussed at §20.16, do not provide for the personal liability of directors of an employer which does not abide by their terms. Neither the Quebec *Act respecting Labour Standards*[1] nor the *Canada Labour Code*[2] provides for directors' personal statutory liability although section 122 of the *Act respecting labour relations, vocational training and manpower management in the construction industry*[3] does impose personal liability on directors for unpaid wages. Directors or officers of a delinquent corporation may, however, be found guilty of complicity or abetting in the commission of offences by the corporation under such statutes and therefore fined or jailed, as will be more fully discussed below. It should also be noted that directors who fail to comply with statutory requirements regarding their liability for employee wages may be found guilty of a penal offence and thereby be subject to fines.[4]

[1] R.S.Q., c. N-1.1.
[2] R.S.C. 1985, c. L-2.
[3] R.S.Q., c. R-20.
[4] Non-payment of such fines may also expose them to imprisonment. See, *e.g.*, QCA, s. 123 [am. 1990, c. 4, s. 305].

§20.113 Where a corporation incorporated under the QCA is dissolved, its directors may be held personally liable to unpaid creditors such as employees, even where the specific circumstances noted above are not met unless such creditors consent to the dissolution or the directors can prove good faith.[1] No comparable provision is found in the CBCA or OBCA.

[1] QCA, s. 29.

2. Liability for Excessive Executive Compensation

§20.114 The general rule is that, unless otherwise provided in the corporate articles, by-laws or a unanimous shareholders' agreement, directors of a corporation can establish the remuneration of executives without shareholder approval. However, directors and officers are, as has been mentioned, subject to both fiduciary duties including the duty to act in the company's best interests as well as statutory standards of reasonable care when exercising their powers and duties. Therefore, the establishment of compensation for executives must be done with a view to "the best interests of the corporation" as well as in accordance with appropriate care and skill.[1] In the context of conferring excessive executive compensation, the issue is whether directors have breached their fiduciary duties by overcompensating the executive and thus improperly using corporate assets or have acted oppressively towards one of their constituency.

[1] For an interesting British article on this issue see Andrew Griffiths, "Directors' Remuneration: Constraining the Power of the Board" (1996) Lloyds' Maritime and Commercial Law Quarterly, pp. 372-384.

§20.115 In the United States, the test of liability respecting appropriate compensation has been the "business judgment" rule which presumes that a director has not failed in his or her duties when exercising his or her sound business judgment. Courts generally held that the directors were not liable unless the compensation offered had no reasonable relation whatsoever to the benefit which the compensation might expect from the executive's accomplishments, or unless such compensation was so high as to represent a waste of corporate assets. Essentially courts would defer to a director's business decisions and not try to second-guess the advisability of the decision.[1] In other words, if the director exercised sound business judgment, in theory, no liability will attach to the decision. The extent to which this rule was sometimes applied revealed how low a standard was sometimes applied to a director's duty in this regard. Even gross mismanagement occasionally escaped condemnation.[2]

[1] See *Re R.J. Jowsey Mining Co.* (1969), 6 D.L.R. (3d) 97 (Ont. C.A.), at 101, leave to appeal refused, [1970] S.C.R. *v* and *Benson et al. v. Third Canadian General Investment Trust Ltd. et al.* (1993), 14 O.R. (3d) 493 (Ont. Gen. Div.).

[2] See *Re Five Minute Car Wash Service Ltd.*, [1966] 1 All E.R. 242 (Ch.), an English case, where accounts were not paid, unqualified staff was kept, business mistakes were left to simmer and the company's reputation had suffered accordingly and yet such mismanagement was held not to be oppressive.

§20.116 However, higher standards seem to be evolving. The business judgment presumption may be overturned in both the U.S. and Canada where the issue is just beginning to come before the courts if the court believes that the decision is being taken for an improper purpose,[1] is objectively *not* in the best interests of the corporation, or is being done with a view to oppressing another party. A brief review of the history of the issue and its early development in U.S. case law is instructive.[2]

[1] See *Teck Corporation Ltd. v. Millar* (1972), 33 D.L.R. (3d) 288 (B.C.S.C.), at pp. 312 and 315; *First City Fin. Corp. Ltd. v. Genstar Corp.* (1981), 33 O.R. (2d) 631 (Ont. H.C.J.) and *Re Olympia & York Enterprises v. Hiram Walker* (1986), 59 O.R. (2d) 254 for discussion of the proper purpose test for directors in other contexts.

[2] It is to be noted that the remarks just made and which follow apply as well to the establishment of "golden parachutes" which were discussed earlier. The same

principles of proper purpose and best interests of the corporation can come into play in deciding if the establishment of a golden parachute has been done appropriately by the directors.

§20.117   As mentioned, early case law in the United States developed the "waste test". The principle is that corporations are not allowed to waste their assets or spend substantial amounts that are unrelated to proper management of their affairs. A transaction will therefore not be condoned where "no person of ordinary business judgment would deem the benefit worth what the corporation paid".[1]

---

[1]   *Saxe v. Brady*, 184 A. 2d 602 (Del. Ch., 1962), at 610.

§20.118   The landmark case regarding executive compensation, in which the *waste test* was applied, is *Rogers v. Hill*.[1] In this case, which took place during the depths of the Depression, the United States Supreme Court had to determine whether a profit-sharing arrangement benefiting American Tobacco Company's top officers was so generous as to constitute a *waste*. The arrangement provided for the distribution of a given percentage of the company's net profits exceeding a certain amount. The plan was established by a by-law that had been ratified at an annual shareholders' meeting nearly twenty (20) years earlier. It had worked without controversy for many years but, by 1930, the president was receiving an annual salary of $168,000 and, pursuant to the by-law, a bonus of $842,507. Additionally, the vice-presidents were each being paid a salary of $50,000 and a bonus of $409,495.

---

[1]   289 U.S. 582 (1933).

§20.119   The court held that the by-law was valid and that the bonus formula was not unreasonable *per se*. Because the shareholders had allowed the bonus program to continue from year to year without changing it, the court presumed that the majority of the shareholders still supported it. Nevertheless, the court held that even majority will could not "justify payments of sums as salaries so large as in substance and effect to amount to spoliation or waste of corporate property". It found that the bonuses had "by reason of increase of profits, become so large as to warrant investigation in equity" and it ordered the District Court to determine whether and to what extent the payments constituted a waste of corporate funds. Unfortunately, the case was settled before the District Court held a hearing. While *Rogers* was never overruled and is seldom even criticized, it is almost entirely ignored, and is rarely cited in modern compensation cases. In the place of the principles introduced in *Rogers*, courts turned to the business judgment rule which, for decades, protected executive compensation from judicial review.

¹ 289 U.S. 582 (1933).

§20.120 The rash of take-overs in the United States in the 1980's forced American courts to re-examine closely the duties of directors and review the basic tenets of directors' liability in order to ascertain the rights of bidders, targets, shareholders and other constituencies. Such re-examination, of necessity, sought to clarify what would go beyond a proper show of business acumen by directors. The principles in these cases can and have been applied to executive compensation.

§20.121 A case upholding the business judgment rule is *Aronson v. Lewis*,¹ in which a shareholder failed in his efforts to bring a derivative action against Meyers Parking System Inc. challenging an employment agreement between the corporation and its principal shareholder, Leo Fink. Mr. Fink was 75 years old and was hired as a consultant at a salary of $150,000 a year for five years, plus a bonus equal to 5% of pre-tax profits over $2,400,000. The agreement provided that, upon termination, Fink was to remain as a consultant and receive from Meyers a minimum income of $100,000 per year for life, which was not to be affected by any incapacity preventing Fink from serving the corporation. The plaintiff charged that such a contract was a waste of corporate assets serving no valid business purpose and that Meyers' directors had acted under the control of Fink, who owned 47% of the stock.

¹ 473 A. 2d 805 (Del. S.C., 1984).

§20.122 The Supreme Court of Delaware fell back on familiar principles. Under American law (as under Canadian law), directors manage the business and affairs of the corporation and incur "certain fundamental fiduciary obligations to the corporation" but courts will also defer to the business judgment rule:

> It is a presumption that in making a business decision the directors of a corporation acted on an informed basis, in good faith and in the honest belief that the action taken was in the best interests of the company. . . . Absent an abuse of discretion, that judgment will be respected by the courts.¹

In the absence of articulated and particularized evidence of abuse, the court concluded that there was no ground to authorize a derivative action.

[1]   *Aronson v. Lewis*, 473 A. 2d 805 (Del. S.C., 1984), at 812. See also *Panter v. Marshall Field & Co.*, 646 F. 2d 271, at 293 (7th Circ., 1981), cert. denied 454 U.S. 1092.

§20.123 Similarly another American case sheds light on the question of what is acceptable director behaviour. In *Unocal Corp. v. Mesa Petroleum Co.*,[1] a take-over case, Mesa Petroleum's offer was deemed excessively coercive and Unocal's defensive measures (in effect, a self-tender of shares) were found reasonable and legal. The Supreme Court of Delaware emphasized that Unocal's board consisted of a majority of outside directors who came to their decision after lengthy consideration (a board meeting lasted over nine hours) of all relevant matters, including the contents of detailed presentations by legal counsel and the advice of their investment banker, on which they relied. The court added that it would not substitute its judgment for that of the board if the latter's decision could be "attributed to any rational business purpose". As the directors had reasonable grounds for acting and had shown good faith and reasonable investigation, their decision would stand as being in the best interests of the corporation's stockholders.

[1]   493 A. 2d 946 (Del. S.C., 1985).

§20.124 However, a number of U.S. cases have held that the executive compensation being paid was excessive and did not represent a proper exercise of the directors' business judgment. A brief review of a few of these U.S. cases will illustrate what sort of compensation has been considered excessive and the principles which courts have determined will enable them to judge when compensation would be considered to be reasonable and when excessive.

§20.125 A derivative action by minority shareholders seeking to recover damages allegedly resulting from actions taken by three corporate directors in violation of their fiduciary duties was upheld by the Supreme Court which held that the evidence supported the trial court's conclusion that the corporation's directors had failed to establish fairness to the corporation in connection with certain management fees in excess of $9,000 per month.[1] In *Owensby & Kritikos, Inc. v. C.I.R.*,[2] payments made to shareholder employees as compensation were unquestionably at the high end of the spectrum of compensation paid within this field of work, and therefore the Court of Appeal upheld a finding that the payments were disguised dividends and not compensation for services rendered. In *Rutter v. C.I.R.*,[3] the Tax Court's decision was upheld which had determined that salaries ranging from over $220,000 to over $430,000 paid to the corporation's principals from 1976 to 1979 were in part unreasonable, which part could not be deducted for purposes of the corporation's federal income taxes. This finding was upheld even though the principals were well qualified, made all the important decisions for the corporation, and were heavily involved in the daily management of the company. The principals were paid almost 50% of the corporation's before tax net income in 1976, their combined compensation decreased by only $11,250 in 1979 even though the corporation suffered net losses, they each received between 1.4 and 2.4 times the aggregate compensation of the top five middle management employees who were not family members, and the corporation had made dividend distributions to shareholders only three times in its history.

[1]   *Lynch v. Patterson*, 701 P.2d 1126 (Wyo. 1985).
[2]   819 F.2d 1315 (5th Cir. 1987).
[3]   853 F.2d 1267 (5th Cir. 1988).

§20.126   *Ferber v. American Lamp Corp.*[1] held that majority shareholders have a quasi-fiduciary duty to ensure that minority shareholders receive their proper share of profit and ordered the trial court to determine whether the minority was prejudiced by unreasonable compensation. *Berman v. Meth*[2] stated that the salary must bear a reasonable relation to the executive's ability and services. *Fendelman v. Fenco Handbag Mfg. Co.*[3] followed the rule that where officers, as directors, set their own salaries, they have the burden of showing reasonableness, and further, courts are obliged to determine the reasonableness of executive compensation even though the calculation cannot be established by a mathematical formula or hard and fast rules. *Crosby v. Beam*[4] permitted minority shareholders in a closed corporation to bring an action complaining of excessive compensation directly against the company's officers and directors rather than asserting a derivative claim.

[1]   469 A.2d 1046 (Pa. 1984).
[2]   258 A.2d 521 (Pa. 1969).
[3]   482 S.W.2d 461 (Mo. 1972). To the same effect, see *Soulas v. Troy Donut Univ., Inc.*, 460 N.E.2d 310 (Ohio 1983).
[4]   548 N.E.2d 217 (Ohio 1989).

§20.127   The factors which are to be considered in determining the reasonableness of a salary include the following: the employee's qualifications; the nature, extent, and scope of his or her work; the size and complexity of the business; comparison of salaries paid with the corporation's gross and net income; prevailing general economic conditions; comparison of salaries with distributions to shareholders; prevailing rates of compensation for comparable positions in comparable concerns; salary policy of the taxpayer as to all employees; the amount of compensation paid to particular employees in previous years; and profitability of the business.[1] The same case expressed the view that high compensation is more reasonable when there is a corresponding lack of fringe benefits, such as pension plans or stock options which might normally be expected. An employee's unusual capability, the extent of his or her responsibilities, and the results achieved are all important factors to be considered in determining the reasonableness of his or her salary.

[1]   *Kennedy v. C.I.R.*, 671 F.2d 167 (1982).

§20.128   Cases dealing with the reasonableness of executive compensation in Canada are sparse. In the case of *Cannaday v. McPherson*,[1] a president's compensation package which was regarded as excessive was struck down by the court.[2] In *Cannaday*, in the absence of Canadian authority, the United States' test for "fair and reasonable" was adopted. The court approved the test as being "whether or not under all the circumstances the transaction carries the earmarks of an arm's length bargain." The court found that the compensation agreement secured nothing for the company. The president, who was also a director, could have resigned one day after beginning his employment and received up to $300,000. The court concluded that the agreement was, in no way, fair and reasonable, did not have the earmark of an arm's length transaction and would probably not have been recommended by an independent Board of Directors acting in the best interests of the company.

[1]   (1995), 25 B.L.R. (2d) 75 (B.C.S.C.).
[2]   See also Edward Iacobucci, *Value for Money Executive Compensation in the 1990s*, (C.D. Howe Institute, 1996); *218125 Investments Ltd. v. Patel* (1995), 33 Alta. L.R. (3d) 245 (Q.B.); *Aquino v. First Choice Capital Limited* (1997), 148 Sask. R. 288, [1997] 3 W.W.R. 143; and *Chernoff v. Parta Holdings Ltd.* (1995), 13 B.C.L.R. (3d) 260 (S.C.).

§20.129   In the case of *Stech v. Davies*,[1] a director who decided unilaterally to increase his salary and pay himself management fees which bore no reasonable relation to the work performed for the corporation was found to have acted in an unfairly prejudicial manner. In the same vein, directors of the corporation involved in *Re Abraham and Inter Wide Investments Ltd.*[2] were found to have acted unfairly where they had voted themselves consulting and directors' fees which had no apparent business basis. In neither of these cases were directors required to repay the corporation or held liable to third parties. However, if this had been the remedy sought, it is likely that the directors would have been required to account for their gains to the corporations concerned.[3] In *Heap Noseworthy Ltd. v. Didham*,[4] a director who was repaid a loan, but no salary, after the corporation was sued by creditors, was ordered to repay the monies received after service of the claim.

[1] (1987), 53 Alta. L.R. (2d) 373 (Q.B.).
[2] (1985), 51 O.R. (2d) 460 (H.C.J.).
[3] See *Calmont Leasing Ltd. v. Kredl* (1993), 11 Alta. L.R. (3d) 232, affd (1995), 30 Alta. L.R. (3d) 16 (C.A.).
[4] (1996), 29 B.L.R. (2d) 279 (Nfld. T.D.).

§20.130 Mention may also be made of the Quebec case of *Tsuru v. Montpetit*,[1] in which advantages such as luxurious houses, cars, airplanes and boats bought and used at the expense of the corporation were found to constitute unreasonable compensation appropriated by Mr. Montpetit, who directed a series of thoroughly unsuccessful ventures. The abuse in this case was so blatant as to prevent any comparison with a corporation managed in a minimally reasonable fashion. Other cases may be cited in which excessive compensation paid to a dominant shareholder in small, closely held corporations was deemed oppressive.[2] In *Diligenti*, oppression was found when a director/manager was ousted by the three majority shareholders who began diverting a substantial sum of money by way of management fees to a company owned by the shareholders. In *National Building Maintenance*, a director was found to have acted oppressively in taking excessive management fees which represented almost all of the company's profits.

[1] [1989] R.J.Q. 2452 (S.C.), vard J.E. 90-996 (C.A.), leave to appeal to S.C.C. refused Dec. 20, 1990.
[2] *Diligenti v. RWMD Operations Kelowna Ltd.* (1976), 1 B.C.L.R. 36 (S.C.); *National Building Maintenance Ltd. v. Dove*, [1972] 5 W.W.R. 410 (B.C.C.A.). See also *Cannady v. McPherson* (1996), 25 B.L.R. (2d) 75 (B.C.S.C.) discussed at §20.123.

§20.131 In the case of *Michaud v. National Bank of Canada and Royal Bank of Canada*[1] the court was faced with a shareholder requesting that the Royal Bank and the National Bank include, in the circular which is required to be sent to their shareholders, five proposals that he intended to present to the upcoming shareholders' annual meeting. The applicant was relying on sections 143 and 144 of the *Bank Act*.[2] One of the proposals was to the effect that the global remuneration of the banks' most highly paid executives may not exceed twenty times the average remuneration of the banks' employees. The court considered the fact that the only way for the applicant to communicate with other shareholders directly was to include his proposals in the circular which must be sent to other shareholders by the banks, since only a minority of shareholders do, in fact, attend the shareholders' annual meeting.

¹ Unreported, Jan. 9, 1997, 500-05-025646-967 and 500-05-025647-965 (Superior Court of Quebec).
² S.C. 1991, c. 46.

§20.132 The court further stated that the legislator recognized for shareholders more than merely the right to be informed and that it protected their right to participate in the decision making on certain questions. Justice Rayle added that shareholders are entitled to present to the shareholders' annual meeting any relevant proposal, over and above the questions which are traditionally submitted by the Board of Directors. As a result, even if executive compensation falls within the Board of Directors' jurisdiction as per section 199(1) of the *Bank Act*, the court ruled that the proposals of the applicant should be included in the circulars to be sent to all shareholders.

§20.133 In *Michaud*,¹ the Quebec court refused to follow the decision rendered by the Ontario Court of Appeal in the 1928 case of *Wilson v. Woolatt*² to the effect that the president's remuneration did not fall within the shareholders' jurisdiction. Indeed, Justice Rayle noted that the social context has evolved since the time when the aforementioned decision was rendered. Justice Rayle added that section 123 of the *Bank Act* allowed shareholders to be the ultimate decision-makers, even on the question of executive compensation, if a proposal was duly voted by the shareholders at their annual meeting.

¹ *Michaud v. National Bank of Canada and Royal Bank of Canada*, Unreported, Jan. 9, 1997, 500-05-025646-967 and 500-05-025647-965 (Que. S.C.).
² (1928), 62 O.L.R. 620 (C.A.).

§20.134 In *Bell v. Canada Development Investment Corp.*,¹ the Ontario High Court was faced with a suit by the former president of the Canada Development Investment Corporation ("CDIC"), claiming damages for his dismissal, and failure to honour promises made to him. Mr. Bell had been enticed to leave Petro-Canada, where he had an income of $242,000 a year, for the presidency of CDIC on the promise that his situation would be at least as favourable at CDIC and that he would be provided reasonable protection on termination. Consultants recommended to CDIC that he be offered a salary ranging between $250,000 and $371,000. The government, which had the final word, capped Mr. Bell's income at $250,000. When the government changed, Mr. Bell was removed from his position by Order-in-Council. Emphasizing that Mr. Bell's successor at Petro-Canada earned $447,500 in

1987, the court found that the plaintiff was entitled to substantial compensation. The issue of reasonableness was not explicitly debated, but Holland J. noted at various points in his decision that the salary and advantages promised to Mr. Bell were not unusual, considering his position.

¹ (1990), 32 C.C.E.L. 16 (Ont. H.C.J.).

§20.135 The above cases indicate that compensation in Canada will be held to be reasonable if it bears some relationship to the market value of the services provided. They also show that terminated employees will be able to claim substantial amounts from their former employer and, in many jurisdictions, from its directors, if they were treated in an oppressive or unfairly prejudicial fashion. The decisive test remains that of the reasonable business person, that is, could a reasonable business person have made such a decision given all the circumstances at the time? If so, unless a party suffers direct material prejudice, the courts will most likely allow the decision to stand and not hold directors liable.

§20.136 On a final note, provincial legislatures are providing an indication that the issue of excessive executive compensation is of general concern. New regulations under the Ontario Securities Act ("OSA") provide increased disclosure to security-holders of the compensation paid by Ontario reporting issuers to their executive officers and directors. While it is not within the scope of this text to review the content of the new regulations, suffice it to say that the new executive compensation rules faithfully follow the current U.S. model, both in terms of format and content, adding requirements to provide disclosure in a hopefully more readily comprehensible tabular form, together with graphic disclosure of comparative stock market performance and detailed narrative disclosure of the policies and deliberations of the compensation (or other equivalent) committee in establishing executive compensation. The new regulations apply to "reporting issuers", with certain exemptions, as that term is used in the OSA and therefore small, private companies will not be subject to these rules. As one example of the content of these rules, a whole new category of disclosure has been created by the new regulations regarding the composition and activities of the issuer's compensation committee (or if the issuer has no compensation committee, the activities of the entire board in setting compensation levels). The new regulations require disclosure regarding persons responsible for executive compensation decisions (paying particular regard to the independence of such persons) and the basis on which compensation decisions were made. In particular, the compensation committee is required to prepare a report which, among other things, discloses the policies of the committee regarding the compensation of all executive officers (not just named executive officers) and includes a discussion of the emphasis placed by the issuer on the various factors relating to executive compensation. The report must include an analysis of the relationship between corporate performance and executive compensation and must provide details of any performance-based awards which were made despite the fact that the established criteria for such awards had not been met. Specific rules apply to CEO compensation. The new regulations require the compensation committee to explain the level of compensation paid to the CEO by setting out the factors considered, the criteria used and the relative weight assigned to each such factor. If competitive rates were considered in determining the CEO's compensation, the report is required to disclose, in detail, the method and basis for the comparison. The relationship of the issuer's performance to the CEO's compensation must also be reviewed. Disclosure of factors or criteria otherwise relevant to the determination of compensation, but which would require the disclosure of confidential business information is not required.

§20.137 Quebec has also enacted legislation requiring disclosure of compensation. *An Act respecting the disclosure of the compensation received by the Executive officers of certain legal persons,*[1] requires, among others, that any issuer subject to the Quebec *Securities Act* and which is thereby required to send out proxy solicitation circulars, must include in the circular, a statement of the compensation paid to its five most highly paid executives. Remuneration includes all forms of remuneration, options and any other advantages.

[1] S.Q. 1997, c. 61.

D. STATUTORY LIABILITIES

§20.138 A multitude of legal obligations are imposed by statute on a corporation acting as an employer. In some cases, directors and officers are also made personally liable to the Crown or to a third party if the corporation does not fulfil its obligations. In many other cases, the company and its directors and officers may be found guilty of statutory offences. The following summary of such provisions is not intended to be exhaustive but does provide an overview of those liabilities which should be of concern to the directors of any company with employees. The type of business activity will determine which provisions apply; therefore, appropriate advice should be sought in such cases.

1. Income and Other Tax Legislation

§20.139 Remittances or payroll deductions payable by an employer under the federal *Income Tax Act*[1] give rise to joint and several liability of directors who were in office when those sums were payable if they were not paid according to statutory requirements. Amounts withheld under the Act must be remitted to the Receiver General of Canada and are deemed to be held in trust for Her Majesty by the employer until so remitted. Should the employer default in withholding or remitting, its directors may be required to pay the sums due plus interest accrued thereon (at prescribed rates) plus a 10% penalty. Revenue Canada Information Circular 89-2, dated May 1, 1989 has clarified the Minister's intent to assess all directors with no distinction made between active, passive, nominee or outside directors although this distinction may be relevant when attempting to establish a due diligence offence.

[1] S.C. 1970-71-72, c. 63, as amended.

§20.140 Under the *Income Tax Act*, directors can incur liability only where a certificate specifying the amount payable has been registered before the Federal Court and such amount has not been paid, where the corporation is undergoing winding-up or dissolution, or where it becomes bankrupt. In the latter cases, the claim against the corporation must have been duly proved.[1] A claim against a director must be filed within two years after that person has left the board.[2]

[1] Under federal and Ontario tax law, the claim in cases of liquidation or bankruptcy must be filed within six months after the earliest act leading to those procedures. Under Quebec law, liquidation or bankruptcy must occur within one year from the day the amount has become payable.
[2] *Income Tax Act*, s. 227.1(4); Quebec *Act respecting the Ministry of Revenue*, R.S.Q., c. M-31, s. 24.0.2 [en. 1986, c. 16, s. 1]; Ontario *Income Tax Act*, R.S.O. 1990, c. I.2, s. 38(4).

§20.141 In Quebec, section 24 of the *Act respecting the Ministry of Revenue*[1] states that any person deducting, withholding or collecting an amount under provincial tax law, including payroll deductions and remittances made under the Quebec *Taxation Act*,[2] is required to pay the Minister of Revenue an equal amount. Where a company fails to do so, its directors become jointly and severally liable with it when it has not satisfied a judgment rendered in favour of the Deputy Minister of Revenue, or when the company is subject to a winding-up order or goes bankrupt.[3]

[1] R.S.Q., c. M-31.
[2] R.S.Q., c. I-3.

§20.142   Officers are not personally liable for sums which were not deducted or remitted under either the federal or Quebec Acts. Under the *Income Tax Act* of British Columbia, tax offences and liabilities apply to both directors and officers.[1] However, they could incur penal liability if they participated in some way in decisions which led to the commission of such acts, since attempts at evasion are themselves offences under the various tax statutes. It should also be noted that directors and officers are not personally liable for taxes payable by the corporation on its own income.

[1]   R.S.B.C. 1996, c. 215, ss. 57 and 66.

§20.143   A director will not be held liable for failure to deduct or remit employee deductions where that person has exercised the degree of care, diligence and skill[1] that a reasonably prudent person would have exercised in comparable circumstances in order to prevent such failure.[2] However, interpretative problems arise as to just how much "diligence" constitutes a sufficient defence.

[1]   *Income Tax Act*, s. 227.1(3), which uses the same formulation ("care, diligence and skill") as s. 122(1) of the CBCA, although the provisions have been distinguished in their application: *Merson v. M.N.R.*, [1989] 1 C.T.C. 2074 (T.C.C.), at 2083. See *Peters v. Canada*, 95 DTC 620 (T.C.C.) and *Hnatuk v. Canada*, unreported, Sept. 18, 1996 (T.C.C.).

[2]   Revenue Canada has set out its views on such matters in Information Circular 89-2, dated May 1, 1989, while Revenue Quebec has done the same in Interpretation Bulletin LMR.24.01-1/R1, dated December 21, 1990. These documents can easily be obtained from the Ministries of Revenue.

§20.144   Some decisions of the Tax Court of Canada have concluded that a high level of diligence is required while others have taken a more lenient stand especially to passive directors.[1] A director may, however, not be absolved of liability even if he or she was unaware of the corporation's statutory obligations under the *Income Tax Act*. Furthermore, complacent acceptance of assurances from officers of the corporation that prior defaults would be rectified is usually not sufficient to comply with statutory obligations, which include keeping deductions separate from other funds.[2] As a result, directors cannot blindly delegate the statutory responsibility of the corporation to officers, employees, or other directors and thereby wash their hands of such matters. Nevertheless, some more recent cases discussed below seem to indicate that a certain degree of reliance is permissible.

¹ D. Short, "Directors Beware!" (1989), 6 Business & the Law 73.
² R.L. Campbell, "Directors' Diligence under the Income Tax Act" (1990), 16 Can. Bus. L.J. 480, at 486; *Fraser v. M.N.R.*, 87 DTC 250 (T.C.C.).

§20.145 In order to fulfil their duty of diligence, some cases hold that directors must be able to demonstrate that they took positive steps to ensure that the corporation had appropriate accounting policies and procedures for the processing and payment of remittances and to verify from time to time that such policies and procedures were followed.[1]

¹ *Merson v. M.N.R.*, [1989] 1 C.T.C. 2074 (T.C.C.). See also *Barnett v. M.N.R.*, [1985] 2 C.T.C. 2336 (T.C.C.).

§20.146 In *Merson v. M.N.R.*,[1] it was held that when all reasonable measures had been taken and had been successful in the past, ongoing reliance on these measures on the part of a director could be reasonable.[2] What is considered to be a reasonable level of diligence varies according to, among other things, the corporation's financial position. When a corporation is in difficulty, a director should require specific information about conformity and should be particularly careful about delegating responsibility for complying with laws.[3] As the Tax Court of Canada has held:

> The degree of prudence required by subsection 227.1(3) leaves no room for risk. . . .
>
> . . . . .
>
> A director has an obligation to be aware of what is happening within the corporation of which he is director. Effective lines of communication between him and the corporation's responsible employees must be present to ensure the director does not fail his statutory obligations. However, when all reasonable measures are taken and these measures have been successful in the past, he may reasonably be expected to rely on the measures in the future.[4]

¹ [1989] 1 C.T.C. 2074 (T.C.C.), at 2084.
² See also T.S. Wach, "Directors' Liability for Taxes" (1989), 6 Business & the Law 1.
³ J.F. Grieve, "Directors Beware: Personal Liability for Employee Deductions Under the Income Tax Act" (1987), 4 Business & the Law 14.
⁴ *Merson v. M.N.R.*, [1989] 1 C.T.C. 2074 (T.C.C.) at 2083-84. Mr. Merson was found to have done all that could have been reasonably expected of him and was thus held not liable.

§20.147 However, as mentioned, it may be easier for an outside director to demonstrate that he or she fulfilled his duty of diligence than it would be for a director involved in the day-to-day management of the company.[1] In *Sheremeta v. M.N.R.*, 91 DTC 867 (T.C.C.), a schoolteacher who had become a director to accommodate her husband who controlled the company was absolved of liability. She was not involved with the company, had no knowledge of her responsibilities as a director and therefore was not held to a high standard of diligence. Similarly, in *Davies v. Canada*, 94 DTC 1716 (T.C.C.), three directors were retained to provide specialized services to a company: one to provide marketing services, and two to provide engineering services. Each of these directors relied on the other directors who were responsible for the company's daily financial matters. None of those directors were ever involved in the company's daily financial matters nor were they provided with the company's financial statements until November, 1988 when they found out that the company had failed to remit employee source deductions to Revenue Canada. The Court ruled that these three directors were not personally liable for the company's failure to remit the employee source deductions as they had arranged to establish their defence of due diligence. Most recently, in the case of *Sanford v. The Queen*,[2] the Tax Court absolved a director from responsibility for unpaid payroll deductions for income tax, unemployment insurance premiums and pension plan contributions because of her lack of experience and limited role she played in the management of the company, being a minimal director who had left administrative matters to the other directors. It was held that she had fulfilled the duty of care, diligence and skill to be expected of a reasonably prudent person in comparable circumstances because she was a person with no business training who was engaged by the company in order to expand sales. Most recently, the case of *Soper v. Canada*, 97 DTC 5407 (Fed. C.A.), comments on many of the cases discussed above and helps to clarify the law in this regard. An outside director was found responsible for unremitted tax, failing to establish his due diligence when he failed to make any enquiries after receiving a balance sheet showing the corporation was experiencing financial difficulties. A director may also establish that he or she was diligent by showing that all reasonable steps were taken to give specific instructions which were not obeyed, or that remittances were diverted through the undetectable fraud of a co-director.[3] Specific circumstances surrounding a case will therefore be given due consideration. Provincial authorities appear to hold the same view.

---

[1] See, *e.g.*, *Fitzgerald v. M.N.R.*, 92 DTC 1019 (T.C.C.), where a patriarch completely dominated the company and his son who sat on the board. See also *Vogt v. M.N.R.*, 91 DTC 1326 (T.C.C.).

[2] [1996] 1 C.T.C. 2016.

[3] *Edmondson v. M.N.R.*, [1988] 2 C.T.C. 2185 (T.C.C.), where the accused had done everything required to ensure that remittances would be duly made, including signing a cheque, but his co-director omitted to mail the cheque.

§20.148 Similar provisions also apply under the *Excise Tax Act*[1] with respect to remittance by the corporation of the federal Goods and Services Tax. Failure to remit GST could, in certain circumstances, result in the liability of directors of the corporation, subject to a defence of due diligence as discussed above.

[1] R.S.C. 1985, c. E-15, s. 323 [en. 1990, c. 45, s. 12; am. 1992, c. 27, s. 90(1)(*p*)]; am. 1997, c. 10, s. 239(1).

2. Employment Insurance

§20.149 Directors of a corporation are jointly and severally liable with it for payment of both the employees' and the employer's premium under the *Employment Insurance Act*[1] where the corporation neglects to remit premiums.

[1] S.C. 1996, c. 23, s. 83.

3. Statutory Health Insurance

§20.150 In Ontario and Quebec, employers are required by statute to contribute to provincial health insurance schemes and calculation of their contribution is based on the number of employees they hire and the gross amount of the payroll of the employer. This liability is therefore indirectly related to employment law.

§20.151 In Quebec, directors are jointly and severally liable for the payment of the employer's contribution to the health insurance program by virtue of sections 34 and 37 of the *Act respecting the Régie de l'Assurance-Maladie du Québec*[1] and of section 24.0.1 of the *Act respecting the Ministry of Revenue.*[2]

[1] R.S.Q., c. R-5.
[2] R.S.Q., c. M-31 [as am. 1986, c. 16, s. 1; 1991, c. 67, s. 568].

§20.152 In Ontario,[1] directors *and officers*[2] will, as of the date a contribution should have been remitted, be considered as joint and several debtors for the amounts in default if they knowingly concurred in the failure to remit, regardless of their intent. They will be held jointly and severally liable if the corporation goes into liquidation, is ordered to be wound up, becomes bankrupt or ceases to carry on its business regardless of whether or not they acquiesced in the corporation's failure to pay. Directors can also be fined if they direct, authorize, assent to, acquiesce in, or participate in a scheme to evade payment of the employer health tax.

[1]   *Employer Health Tax Act*, R.S.O. 1990, c. E.11, ss. 2 [am. 1996, c. 24, s. 2], 3 and 36.
See also *Health Insurance Act*, R.S.O. 1990, c. H.6, s. 41.
[2]   *Health Insurance Act*, R.S.O. 1990, c. H.6, s. 41.

§20.153   In general, directors and officers are not held personally liable for assessments payable by employers under labour accident legislation.[1]

[1]   See, *e.g.*, the *Act Respecting Industrial Accidents and Occupational Diseases*, R.S.Q., c. A-3.001, ss. 315-325. However, a director or officer of a company which prescribes or authorizes an act which is an offence under the Act (such as non-payment of an assessment by the company) is deemed to be a party to the offence and incurs penal liability: see, *e.g.*, s. 469. Similarly, under the Ontario *Occupational Health and Safety Act*, every director and officer has a duty to take reasonable care to ensure that the corporation complies with the Act, etc. and a failure to comply with this duty is an offence under which a director or officer can be fined up to $25,000 and given up to 12 months in jail.

4.   Pension Plans

§20.154   The law imposes on employers the obligation to contribute to pension plans related to statutory schemes, and to remit both the employees' contribution (if any) and its own. The *Act respecting the Quebec Pension Plan*[1] is a fiscal law for the purposes of the *Act respecting the Ministry of Revenue*. Therefore, as with unremitted provincial tax, directors are jointly and severally liable for unpaid Quebec Pension plan contributions under the same conditions as for tax. The *Canada Pension Plan*[2] provides that the directors of the corporation at the time when a failure to deduct or remit an amount under the Act occurred are jointly and severally liable with the corporation to the Crown.

[1]   R.S.Q., c. R-9. See §20.141.
[2]   R.S.C. 1985, c. C-8, ss. 9 [re-en. R.S.C. 1985, c. 30 (2nd Supp.), s. 3], 21 [am. R.S.C. 1985, c. 6 (1st Supp.), s. 1], 23 [am. R.S.C. 1985, c. 5 (2nd Supp.), s. 1; 1991, c. 49, s. 206(1); 1992, c. 27, s. 90(*d*)], 103(2) and principally 21.1 [en. R.S.C. 1985, c. 6 (1st Supp.), s. 2].

§20.155   In Quebec, directors of a corporation which is a party to a supplemental pension plan are jointly and severally liable for contributions which become due and remain unpaid during their term of office, with interest, for up to a period of six months.[1] Under the Ontario *Pension Benefits Act*, R.S.O. 1990, c. P-8, directors who acquiesce to or participate in a failure by the company to make contributions to an employee pension plan can be fined and the court may also order them to pay unremitted amounts. Failure to comply with the Act can expose a director to a fine of up to $25,000. As noted above, since the federal *Pension Benefits Standards Act* does not specifically provide for directors' liability for contributions to a supplemental pension plan, it is possible that such liability can be found under the general provisions providing for directors' liability for "debts" and "wages" under the CBCA and the Canada Labour Code. If pension plan contributions were held to be "wages" or "debts" for services to the corporation then director liability could, in theory, be found under these general provisions. However, there is no definitive case law on this subject.

[1] Supplemental Pension Plans Act, R.S.Q., c. R-15.1, s. 52.

5. Other Common Law Liabilities

§20.156 Directors and officers who commit acts in their capacity as directors or officers that cause physical or financial harm to others may be personally responsible for the loss which is suffered on the basis of common law principles. Directors and senior officers often find themselves as defendants in negligent or fraudulent misrepresentation suits[1] and suits for inducing breach of contract, interfering in economic relations or conspiracy to commit harm.[2] The fact that the directors and officers were acting as agents of the corporation or otherwise in a directorial capacity may or may not be a defence to this type of conduct.

[1] See, for example, *Toronto Dominion Bank v. Leigh Instruments Ltd.* (1991), 4 B.L.R. (2d) 220 (Ont. C.J. (Gen. Div.)) and *PWA Corp. v. Gemini Group* (1993), 10 B.L.R. (2d) 109 (Ont. C.A.), leave to appeal refused (1993), 16 O.R. (3d) xvi. What elements are required to ground a claim for negligent misrepresentation are set out in *Queen v. Cognos Inc.* (1993), 45 C.C.E.L. 153 (S.C.C.). See also *Hall-Chem v. Vulcan Packaging* (1994), 12 B.L.R. (2d) 274 (Ont. Gen. Div.) in which the Ontario Court (General Division) found an officer and employee liable for a negligent misrepresentation made in the course of his duties. The Court held that the fact that the representation was made in the best interests of the corporation and in the course of employment was not a defence to the claim. However, in *ScotiaMcLeod Inc. v. Peoples Jewellers Limited* (1995), 26 O.R. (3d) 481 (C.A.), leave to appeal dismissed, Sept. 12, 1996 (S.C.C.), the action against the directors for negligent misrepresentations was dismissed but the action against two senior officers was allowed to continue.

[2] Yet other recent cases to impose personal liability on corporate officers: *Cadbury Schweppes Inc. v. FBI Foods Ltd.*, [1994] 8 W.W.R. 727 (B.C.S.C.); *Brian Beattie Motors Ltd. (Trustee of) v. Booth*, unreported, Oct. 23, 1996 (Ont. Ct. (Gen. Div.)) supp. reasons Dec. 16, 1996; *Island Getaways Inc. v. Destinair Airlines Inc.* (1996), 29 B.L.R. (2d) 298 (Ont. Ct. (Gen. Div.)).

§20.157 As is discussed in detail in Chapter 21, directors or officers who are responsible for misleading statements in a press release, prospectus, offering memorandum, management proxy circular or any other document upon which other persons may rely may be individually responsible for the loss arising from their negligent or fraudulent misrepresentation (depending on the state of the director's or officer's knowledge of the falsity).

§20.158 As mentioned above, it is also actionable conduct in Canada to interfere in a contractual or economic relationship between other persons. On this basis, a director or officer could be liable for inducing a breach of contract between the corporation and a third person or otherwise interfering in that relationship. Where, however, the director or officer acts in the best interests of the corporation, it is unlikely that such a lawsuit will be successful although the oppression remedy discussed earlier may still be open to the complaining party.

§20.159 Prior to changes to securities legislation, neither the common law nor equitable principles prohibited directors or officers from trading in shares of the corporation using information obtained in their capacity as directors. Most Canadian jurisdictions now regulate this activity by prohibiting trades by persons in a special relationship with the issuer using special knowledge of undisclosed information of a material fact or change and by prohibiting passing on or "tipping" such information. Legislation also imposes reporting obligations on insiders. In Ontario, insider trading restrictions are found in both the Ontario *Securities Act* ("OSA")[1] and the OBCA. The OSA applies to widely held public corporations and the OBCA to those that are incorporated in Ontario but do not distribute their securities to the public. The CBCA provisions apply to insiders of CBCA companies and impose reporting obligations only on companies that distribute their securities to the public and trading prohibitions applicable to all companies.[2] Under the CCQ, a director is forbidden to use, for his or her own profit or that of a third person, any information he obtains by reason of his duties, unless he is authorized to do so by the shareholders of the corporation.[3] Similarly the rules of mandate which apply to directors and officers of Part 1A companies forbid a mandatary from using any information he obtained in carrying out his mandate unless the mandator, the corporation, consents.[4] Quebec securities legislation imposes insider trading restrictions as well.

[1] R.S.O. 1990, c. S.5.
[2] For a more detailed discussion of liabilities under the OSA and the QSA, see Chapter 21.
[3] C.C.Q., article 323.
[4] C.C.Q., article 2146.

PENAL AND CRIMINAL LIABILITIES
AND EMPLOYMENT

A. INTRODUCTION

§20.160 A vast number of provisions which potentially impose penal and criminal liability on directors and officers already exist in Canada, and the list is growing constantly.[1] We will not attempt to provide an exhaustive survey of such provisions in the following pages, nor will we attempt an analysis of the liability under such provisions in areas other than employment. However, it is important to note that directors and officers may incur penal or criminal liability as a result of their decisions in the course of their employment.

  [1] Authors have counted as many as 200 statutes imposing personal liability on directors: D. Saxe, *Environmental Offences: Corporate Responsibility and Executive Liability* (Aurora: Canada Law Book, 1990), p. 71.

§20.161 Under the general principles of penal and criminal law, a director or an officer who is a party to an offence may be found guilty. Plotting, inciting or attempting to commit an offence are offences in their own right. Moreover, various statutes expressly provide for directors' and officers' liability where they direct, authorize, or acquiesce in statutory violations by a corporation. Penal liability is therefore added to the personal civil liability of officers, most notably in the areas of employment law and environmental protection. A director or officer of a polluting corporation, for example, may not only be fined or jailed as a result of the corporation's offence, but may also be liable for the costs of cleaning up. A director may also attract criminal liability under the *Criminal Code* in certain circumstances.

§20.162 This part focuses on the potential penal and criminal liability of officers and/or directors, liability which obviously carries a more significant risk than monetary fines or damages. The provisions examined in the following pages sometimes apply only to officers but in most cases apply to both directors and officers.

B. PERSONS AT RISK

§20.163 In various Acts dealing with labour standards and practices, the "employer" is defined as including any person acting directly or indirectly in the interest of an employer in relation to an employee.[1] Such a wide category may include an agent or mandatary (the civil law equivalent of an "agent") of a corporation and, usually, its officers and directors. Principles governing agency or mandate would normally exempt the agent from personal liability where the impugned act took place within the scope of the agent's engagement and authority, and the principal or mandator (that is, the corporation) would bear the brunt of any accusation in this context. However, statutory provisions frequently state explicitly that directors and officers of an alleged offending corporation may be sued personally if they have been involved, however peripherally, in illegal behaviour on the part of the corporation. Legislatures have therefore explicitly chosen in many cases to look beyond the rules of mandate where the liability of the "directing minds" of a corporation is concerned and where they believe such personal liability is necessary to ensure compliance.

[1]   See, *e.g.*, Ontario's *Employment Standards Act*, R.S.O. 1990, c. E.14, s. 1.

§20.164   Although this section is mainly concerned with directors' and officers' liability, it is noteworthy that various statutes extend liability to other categories of agents or employees such as a corporation's manager,[1] chief executive officer, clerk, member or "whomever acts on behalf of the company".[2] Under legislation such as the Quebec *Labour Code*,[3] any director, officer, manager or executive who has approved or acquiesced in an illegal act such as interfering with an association of employees, refusing to employ any person because that person exercises a right arising from the *Labour Code*, or failing to acknowledge the representatives of a certified association of employees and to negotiate in good faith a collective labour agreement with them may personally be found guilty of an offence. Federal legislation is similarly drafted and is usually aimed at any "officer", "director", or "agent" of the company.[4] For instance, section 149(2) of the *Canada Labour Code*[5] provides:

> Where a corporation commits an offence under this Part, any officer, director or agent of the corporation who directed, authorized, assented to, acquiesced in or participated in the commission of the offence is a party to and guilty of the offence and is liable on conviction to the punishment provided for the offence, whether or not the corporation has been prosecuted or convicted.

[1]   *Labour Code*, R.S.Q., c. C-27, s. 145.
[2]   See, *e.g.*, in Quebec *An Act respecting Industrial Accidents and Occupational Diseases*, R.S.Q., c. A-3.001, s. 469; the *Charter of Human Rights and Freedoms*, R.S.Q., c. C-12, s. 88 [renumbered as s. 135 by 1989, c. 51, s. 21; am. 1989, c. 51, s. 19]; *An Act respecting the Ministry of Revenue*, R.S.Q., c. M-31, s. 68 [re-en. 1991, c. 67, s. 593]; *An Act respecting Labour Standards*, R.S.Q., c. N-1.1, s. 142; *Consumer Protection Act*, R.S.Q., c. P-40.1, s. 282; *Environment Quality Act*, R.S.Q., c. Q-2, s. 109.3 [en. 1988, c. 49, s. 24; am. 1990, c. 26, s. 11]; *An Act respecting Occupational Health and Safety*, R.S.Q., c. S-2.1, s. 241; *Securities Act*, R.S.Q., c. V-1.1, s. 205.
[3]   R.S.Q., c. C-27, s. 145.

[4] See, *e.g.*, the *Bankruptcy and Insolvency Act*, R.S.C. 1985, c. B-3, s. 204 [re-en. 1992, c. 27, s. 77] [am. 1997, c. 12]; *Bank Act*, S.C. 1991, c. 46 [am. 1996, c. 6, s. 167(1)(a)], ss. 210 and 567; *Canada Labour Code*, R.S.C. 1985, c. L-2, s. 149(2) [re-en. R.S.C. 1985, c. 9 (1st Supp.), s. 4]; *Canada Pension Plan*, R.S.C. 1985, c. C-8, s. 103(2); *Canadian Environmental Protection Act*, R.S.C. 1985, c. 16 (4th Supp.), s. 122; *Competition Act*, R.S.C. 1985, c. C-34, s. 65(4) [re-en. R.S.C. 1985, c. 19 (2nd Supp.), s. 38]; *Consumer Packaging and Labelling Act*, R.S.C. 1985, c. C-38, s. 20(3) [am. 1997, c. 6, s. 40]; *Customs Act*, R.S.C. 1985, c. 1 (2nd Supp.), s. 158; *Excise Tax Act*, R.S.C. 1985, c. E-15, s. 96(3) [re-en. R.S.C. 1985, c. 7 (2nd Supp.), s. 43(1)]; *Hazardous Products Act*, R.S.C. 1985, c. H-3, s. 28(2) [en. R.S.C. 1985, c. 24 (3rd Supp.), s. 1]; *Immigration Act*, R.S.C. 1985, c. I-2, s. 99(1); and the *Transportation of Dangerous Goods Act, 1992*, S.C. 1992, c. 34, s. 39.

[5] R.S.C. 1985, c. L-2 [as am. R.S.C. 1985, c. 9 (1st Supp.), s. 4].

§20.165 Depending on the particular wording of the statute involved, the liability of any of these persons may be triggered when they have "directed", "assented to", "prescribed", "authorized", "consented to", "approved", "acquiesced in", "participated in", "accepted", "ordered", "advised" or "encouraged" activities prohibited by the statute. Furthermore, under most of the statutes previously mentioned, a person holding any of the above positions may be prosecuted and convicted even if the corporation has not been tried or convicted of the offence.[1]

[1] See, for example, Ontario's *Employment Standards Act*, R.S.O. 1990, c. E.14, s. 79, *Pension Benefits Act*, R.S.O. 1990, c. P.8, the *Health Insurance Act*, R.S.O. 1990, c. H.6, *Employer Health Tax Act*, R.S.O. 1990, c. E.11, *Retail Sales Tax Act*, R.S.O. 1990, c. R.31.

§20.166 In some cases, mere knowledge of the commission of illegal activities is sufficient to create a presumption that its commission has been authorized, even in the absence of evidence of such authorization. Such is the case under the Quebec *Consumer Protection Act*.[1] In these cases, the executive has the onus of demonstrating to the court that he or she did not acquiesce in the commission of the offence of which the corporation is guilty.

[1] R.S.Q., c. P-40.1, s. 282.

C. AREAS OF RISK

1. Discrimination

§20.167 Various statutory provisions prohibit discrimination against an employee where, for example, the employee has made a complaint or is about to testify at an inquiry, investigation or proceeding against his or her *employer* for alleged violations of labour/employment standards legislation.[1] An employer or its agents may not dismiss or otherwise discriminate against an employee for these reasons. Beyond statutory liability, it may be noted that both at common law and under the CCQ, officers who intentionally participate in the infringement of civil rights can be held personally liable for resulting damages under general tort and civil responsibility principles. Moreover, insofar as they have acted in a discriminatory fashion prohibited by the Quebec *Charter of Human Rights and Freedoms*,[2] officers or directors can be liable for punitive damages.

[1] See, *e.g.*, the *Employment Standards Act*, R.S.B.C. 1996, c. 113, s. 83; *Occupational Health and Safety Act*, R.S.O. 1990, c. O.1, s. 50 [am. 1992, c. 21, s. 63]; *An Act respecting Labour Standards*, R.S.Q., c. N-1.1, s. 122 [am. 1980, c. 5, s. 10; 1982, c. 12, s. 5; 1990, c. 73, s. 55].

[2] R.S.Q., c. C-12, s. 49.

2. Immigration

§20.168 An officer or director of a corporation may be held liable if the corporation hired persons in violation of the *Immigration Act*.[1]

[1] R.S.C. 1985, c. I-2, ss. 96 and 99.

3. Occupational Health

§20.169 Under the Ontario *Occupational Health and Safety Act*,[1] directors and officers of a corporation are required to take reasonable care to ensure that the corporation complies with the Act, its regulations, and ministerial orders.[2] Such obligations are extensive and include requirements that equipment, material and safety devices prescribed by regulation be provided to workers and kept in good condition, obligations to provide information, supervision and instruction to an executive for safety purposes and the obligation to appoint only competent persons to supervisory positions.[3] A violation of the Act exposes an officer to a fine of not more than $25,000, or imprisonment for a term of not more than one year, or both.[4]

[1] R.S.O. 1990, c. O.1.

[2] R.S.O. 1990, c. O.1, ss. 9, 26 and 66(3).

[3] R.S.O. 1990, c. O.1, ss. 24, 25, 26 and 32.

[4] R.S.O. 1990, c. O.1, s. 66. Recently, a director of a company called Raglan Industries Inc. was fined $10,000 following an accident on May 12, 1992 to a worker who suffered severe burns. Contrary to the requirements of the regulations, the light used to illuminate the working space of the tank was not explosion proof.

§20.170 Where a corporation commits an offence contrary to the Quebec *Act respecting Occupational Health and Safety*,[1] a director, chief executive officer, employee or representative of the corporation who played a part in the offence may be found guilty. Offences contemplated by the Act include:

- doing anything that will directly and seriously compromise the health of a worker;
- failing to offer to a worker appropriate training and counselling services in occupational health and safety matters;
- failing to reassign a worker to another duty when that worker furnishes a certificate attesting to the fact that exposure to a contaminant threatens that worker's health, or similarly failing to reassign a pregnant worker;
- failing to ensure that the workplace, the organization of the work and the working procedures and techniques are safe, healthy and sanitary and to use methods, techniques and measures intended for the identification, control and elimination of risks to the safety or health of the worker;
- failing to supply free safety equipment and to ensure that it is kept in good condition;
- failing to ensure that no contaminant or dangerous substance adversely affects the health or safety of any person at the workplace; and
- manufacturing, supplying, selling, leasing, distributing or installing any product, process, equipment, material, contaminant or dangerous substance unless it is safe and conforms to the applicable regulations.[2]

[1] R.S.Q., c. S-2.1, s. 241.
[2] R.S.Q., c. S-2.1, ss. 32, 40 *et seq.*, 51, 63, 236 and 237 [as am.].

§20.171 Needless to say, this list is far from exhaustive. It does indicate, however, that the area of occupational health and safety has a crucial impact on an employer's activities and on the potential liability of its directors and officers. Similar statutory provisions exist in British Columbia.[1]

[1] *Workers' Compensation Act*, R.S.B.C. 1996, c. 492. See also Ontario's *Workers' Compensation Act*, R.S.O. 1990, c. W.11.

4. Competition Law

§20.172 Various types of business activities are prohibited by the *Competition Act*[1] and any person who is a party to the commission of such activities, such as a corporate officer or director, may be found guilty of an offence under general principles of penal and criminal law. Moreover, the Act expressly provides for directors' and officers' liability in specific cases.

    [1] R.S.C. 1985, c. C-34, as amended.

§20.173 Offences under the *Competition Act* include:

- entering into agreements in restraint of trade by which one agrees with another party to prevent, limit or unduly lessen competition in the supply, purchase or sale of a product;[1]
- entering into an agreement not to submit a bid in response to a call for bids or to submit bids arrived at by agreement between two or more bidders;[2]
- if a supplier is involved, granting a discount or other advantage to one customer over and above that which is granted to a competing customer in respect of a sale of articles of like quality and quantity,[3] or entering into other price discrimination practices;[4]
- engaging in a policy of selling products at unreasonably low prices for the purpose of reducing competition or eliminating a competitor;[5]
- attempting, as a supplier, to influence upward or to discourage the reduction of the prices at which any other person supplies or advertises a product in Canada;[6]
- making a representation to the public that is false or misleading in a material respect[7] or representing to the public that a test as to the performance, efficacy or length of life of a product has been made or a testimony has been given with respect to the product, unless the representation or testimony was previously made and the person making the representation approved in writing its publication.[8] It should be noted that, as of December 1996, significant revisions to the misleading advertising regime are before Parliament and are expected to become law imminently. (See Bill C-67 for details.); and
- advertising a product at a bargain price when a person does not have a reasonable quantity of the product,[9] supplying a product at a price higher than the advertised price,[10] or violating the rules of the Act or its regulations with respect to any promotional contest.[11]

    [1] R.S.C. 1985, c. C-34, ss. 45-49 [am. R.S.C. 1985, c. 19 (2nd Supp.), ss. 30-34; 1991, c. 45, s. 548; 1991, c. 46, s. 591; 1991, c. 47, s. 715(1); 1993, c. 34, s. 51(1)].
    [2] R.S.C. 1985, c. C-34, s. 47(1).
    [3] R.S.C. 1985, c. C-34, s. 50(1)(*a*).

[4] R.S.C. 1985, c. C-34, s. 51.
[5] R.S.C. 1985, c. C-34, s. 50(1)(c).
[6] R.S.C. 1985, c. C-34, s. 61 [am. R.S.C. 1985, c. 19 (2nd Supp.), s. 36; 1990, c. 37, s. 30].
[7] R.S.C. 1985, c. C-34, s. 52.
[8] R.S.C. 1985, c. C-34, s. 53.
[9] R.S.C. 1985, c. C-34, s. 57.
[10] R.S.C. 1985, c. C-34, s. 58 [am. R.S.C. 1985, c. 27 (1st Supp.), s. 189].
[11] R.S.C. 1985, c. C-34, s. 59.

§20.174 Any director or officer who has been involved in such practices can be arraigned before a court. Moreover, section 65(4) of the Act[1] provides that when a corporation is guilty of an offence amounting to obstructing the administration of the Act or investigations undertaken pursuant to its provisions, any officer, director or agent of the corporation who directed, authorized, acquiesced in or participated in the offence is guilty of the same offence.

[1] R.S.C. 1985, c. C-34 [am. R.S.C. 1985, c. 19 (2nd Supp.), s. 38].

5. Environmental Law

(a) The Importance of Environmental Law

§20.175 Directors and officers must be aware of the increasing possibility that, through their actions or failure to act, they may be held liable for the environmental consequences of corporate activities. This section briefly describes the rules generally applicable to directors' and officers' personal liability in relation to the environment. Readers should review current specialized textbooks on environmental law and consult with environmental experts, as the legislation in this area is rapidly changing and cannot be discussed in detail here. Rather, this section provides only a broad overview which is intended to alert interested parties to potential liabilities. It goes without saying that any corporation doing business in Canada should familiarize itself with the various environmental statutes applicable to it.

§20.176 The *Canadian Environmental Protection Act* ("CEPA"),[1] Quebec's *Environment Quality Act* ("EQA"),[2] Ontario's *Environmental Protection Act* ("EPA")[3] and British Columbia's *Waste Management Act* ("WMA")[4] are but a few examples of legislation specifically dealing with the personal liability of directors and officers in this area. These statutes, which include express powers to impose heavy fines (which increase rapidly in cases of subsequent offences) and even imprisonment, rely heavily on deterrence to achieve their ultimate goal of a cleaner environment.

¹   R.S.C. 1985, c. 16 (4th Supp.).
²   R.S.Q., c. Q-2.
³   R.S.O. 1990, c. E.19.
⁴   R.S.B.C. 1996, c. 482.

§20.177   The area of environmental law, in particular, reflects the legislature's changing ideas towards a director's or officer's personal responsibility, and the historic protection of the "corporate veil". The theoretical distinction between a corporation and those who run its day-to-day operations is increasingly viewed as antithetical to the effective protection of the environment. Legislation has therefore been enacted to hold those persons who control corporate decision-making personally accountable for the environmental impact of their decisions.[1]

[1]   The Ontario Court of Appeal decision in *R. v. Fell* (1981), 64 C.C.C. (2d) 456 clearly holds that the theory of "corporate veil" has no application in determining the statutory or criminal responsibility of a director or officer of a company.

(b)   The Prohibitions

§20.178   Provisions of statutes dealing with environmental law are usually broadly drafted and, as will be seen below, the duties imposed on corporations (and subsidiarily their officers and directors) are becoming increasingly serious. Basically, under the EQA, for example, every director or officer of a corporation who, by means of an order or authorization or through his or her advice or encouragement, leads the corporation to:

(1)   refuse or neglect to comply with an order, or
(2)   emit, deposit, release or discharge a contaminant into the environment in contravention of the provisions of the EQA or its regulations,

commits an offence,[1] and can be personally charged. The EPA goes even further, explicitly imposing on directors and officers of corporations that engage in activities that "may" result in a contaminating discharge, the positive duty to "take all reasonable care" to prevent the corporation from causing or permitting the discharge.[2] Moreover, section 194(3) of the EPA permits prosecution and conviction of a director or an officer whether or not the corporation has been prosecuted or convicted. In general, the federal (discussed below) and Quebec statutes tend to impose liability based on direct or active involvement of directors and officers in offences while Ontario has imposed a personal duty of care on directors and officers to ensure that their corporations comply with the law. However, there has been little judicial interpretation of such provisions.

[1] EQA, s. 109.3 [en. 1988, c. 49, s. 24; am. 1990, c. 26, s. 11].
[2] EPA, s. 194.

§20.179 Section 20 of the EQA contains a key prohibition against emitting or allowing the emission of a contaminant into the environment in a quantity greater than that provided for by regulation, or where it is likely to affect the comfort of human beings or otherwise impair the quality of the environment in general. A similar prohibition exists in Ontario.[1] Section 22 of the EQA and section 9 of the EPA add that no person may, in the case of Quebec, alter the environment in any way, or, in the case of Ontario, construct or alter any equipment which may discharge into the environment, without having obtained a certificate of authorization from the respective Minister of the Environment.

[1] EPA, ss. 6 and 14.

§20.180 Moreover, a corporation has a legal duty to advise the Minister without delay of any spill or accidental presence of a contaminant in the environment.[1] It must also follow the environmental impact assessment and review procedure when applicable.[2] It cannot sell, transport, deposit, store, eliminate or treat waste in contravention of any applicable regulation[3] and it cannot neglect to obey an order given by the Minister under the relevant Act.[4]

[1] EQA, s. 21; EPA, Part X.
[2] EQA, ss. 31.1 et seq. [en. 1978, c. 64, s. 10, as amended by 1995, c. 45, 1996, c. 2, c. 53]; Environmental Assessment Act, R.S.O. 1990, c. E.18 [am. 1996, c. 27].
[3] EQA, ss. 54, 66-68, 70 and 106; EPA Regulation, R.R.O. 1990, Reg. 347 [am. O. Reg. 512/95 (Gaz. 30/12/95, p. 901)].
[4] EQA, s. 106.1 [en. 1988, c. 49, s. 18]; EPA, s. 186.

§20.181 Federally, pursuant to section 122 of the CEPA, officers, directors and agents of, plus other persons associated with, a corporation which committed an offence may be found guilty of that offence if that person "directed, authorized, consented to, acquiesced in or participated in the commission of the offence". The scope of the CEPA is therefore wider than that of the EQA or EPA in that it makes persons other than just directors or officers (such as lenders, tenants, employees and consultants) personally liable for environmental crimes and clean-ups. A person convicted of an offence under the CEPA is liable, in the case of a prosecution made on summary conviction, to a fine not exceeding $300,000, or to imprisonment for a term not exceeding six months, or both. A person who is indicted is liable to a fine not exceeding $1,000,000, or to imprisonment for a term not exceeding three years, or both.

§20.182 Mere inactivity may trigger a director's or officer's liability under the CEPA, the EPA and the EQA if that person allows or tolerates the corporation's contravention of applicable laws and regulations without trying to remedy the situation. Especially in light of the wording of the EPA, such behaviour may be interpreted as an implicit consent to the commission of the offence, particularly if the person was aware or should have been aware of the contravention and was in a position to influence the corporation's conduct.

§20.183 Under both the EQA and the EPA, the Minister may act to protect the environment by doing the work set out in an order or decision against a corporation or other person.[1] Under the EQA, the Minister may recover such costs from officers or directors, who are jointly and severally liable, if they:

(1) authorized, encouraged, ordered or advised the corporation to refuse or to neglect to do something that was ordered; or
(2) tolerated the corporation's refusal or neglect to do what was ordered.

A similar right of recovery is provided under the EPA.

[1] EQA, ss. 31.43 [en. 1990, c. 26, s. 4] and 113 [am. 1984, c. 29, s. 20; 1990, c. 26, s. 12]; EPA, s. 150.

(c) The Implementation of Policies Respecting Environmental Law

§20.184 Directors and officers cannot take comfort from their ignorance of the corporation's environmental policies or practices. Where the director or officer has or should have concerns about the corporation's environmental conduct, he or she cannot avoid environmental liability by neglecting to obtain additional information on the subject or by wilfully ignoring the facts.

§20.185 Virtually all Canadian cases in which environmental liability has been imposed on persons related to a corporation concern inside directors, that is, directors who were also officers, employees or major shareholders of the corporation. It is very likely that officers who are not directors would be treated identically. Thus, inside directors and officers, given their greater knowledge of and influence and control over corporate operations, are more likely to incur liability than outside directors.

§20.186 Recent Ontario cases serve to illustrate an inside director's risk and also demonstrate that directors' and officers' liability is no longer merely a theoretical possibility. In *R. v. Blackbird Holdings Ltd.*,[1] the corporation owned property on which hazardous waste was discovered. The Environmental Appeal Board held that, of the three directors of Blackbird, only one was a managing director who exercised real decision-making powers; it was this director who was held liable for non-compliance with administrative control orders issued by the Ministry of the Environment. Similarly, in *R. v. Consolidated Maybrun Mines Ltd.*,[2] only the director who had actual management and control of the defendant corporation was found liable for non-compliance with a clean-up order.

[1] The Ontario Environmental Appeal Board's decision, unpublished, is dated July 24, 1990. A penal trial and appeals related to the same facts are reported as *R. v. Blackbird Holdings Ltd.* (1990), 6 C.E.L.R. (N.S.) 119 (Ont. Prov. Offences Ct.), vard *loc. cit.* p. 138 (Prov. Div.), leave to appeal to C.A. refused *loc. cit.* p. 116.

[2] (1992), 73 C.C.C. (3d) 268 (Ont. Ct. (Prov. Div.)), add. reasons (1992), 76 C.C.C. (3d) 94 (Prov. Div.)); affd (1993), 86 C.C.C. (3d) 317 (Ont. Ct. (Gen. Div.)).

§20.187 In the case of *R. v. Bata Industries Ltd.*,[1] an Ontario trial court endeavoured to set out the criteria relating to directors' and officers' liability for corporate contraventions of environmental laws and regulations. The court concluded that a person must be able to prove that he or she took concrete action to ensure corporate compliance with the relevant environmental standards and norms. This judgment marks a turning point for two reasons: directors were convicted despite the fact that no blatant offence was committed by some of them; and the decision sets out, for the first time, the elements that must be proven in order to establish a "due diligence" defence and thereby avoid personal liability for environmental infractions.

[1] (1992), 70 C.C.C. (3d) 394 (Ont. Ct. (Prov. Div.)), vard (1993), 11 C.E.L.R. (N.S.) 208 (Ont. Ct. (Gen. Div.)), vard (1995), 18 C.E.L.R. (N.S.) 11 (C.A.).

§20.188 The facts of the *Bata* case were as follows. In August 1990, Bata Industries Ltd. was charged with a number of offences relating to the storage of barrels containing used chemical products at its shoe manufacturing plant in Ontario. A large number of rusty containers were found, many of which had been left uncovered, and there was evidence of staining on the ground. The corporation was found to have discharged liquid industrial waste in contravention of applicable environmental laws. Three directors were also charged with having failed to take all reasonable steps to prevent the corporation from causing or allowing the discharge of a contaminant into the environment. These three directors also held the offices of chairman of the board, president and plant general manager, respectively.

§20.189 The corporation was convicted of causing or permitting a discharge of contaminants into the groundwater and into the environment in general. Although the corporation established that it had adopted a "Technical Advisory Circular" providing for environmental safety measures to be implemented in its plants, the court found that it had not complied with the guidelines set out in the document and that it had not established an adequate pollution prevention system. Consequently, the judge concluded that Bata had not adopted the necessary steps which would allow it to benefit from a defence of due diligence.

§20.190 Two of the three directors charged were also convicted and fined $6,000 each. The only acquitted director, the chairman of the board, was able to show that he had the least personal contact with the site, that he had played a major role in the implementation of the corporation's environmental policy and that he had always reacted promptly when an environmental problem was brought to his attention. The judge concluded that, due to this director's physical remoteness from the plant, he was justified in relying on the information provided to him by the general manager (who was found guilty) concerning potential or actual environmental problems. The other two directors, on the other hand, did not meet the requirements of a due diligence defence because they had personal knowledge of the storage problem and had not taken any particular steps to remedy it.

§20.191 The Bata case clearly indicates that directors and officers of a corporation can no longer avoid responsibility through a vague promise of good environmental behaviour. Directors and officers may not simply adopt an environmental policy and then consider their task complete. They must take all appropriate measures to put the environmental policy into effect and to verify its implementation and effectiveness. It should be noted that the trial judge attempted to impose, as a condition of the probation order, a prohibition against the company indemnifying the directors for their fines. On appeal, the court held that this was improper and that if a director is eligible for indemnification pursuant to the relevant corporate statute, in this case, s. 136 of the OBCA, then a court cannot forbid indemnification. Since there was no finding that the directors had not acted honestly, in good faith and in the reasonable belief that their conduct was lawful as set out in s. 136, the directors were entitled to indemnification.

D. DEFENCES

1. General Principles

§20.192 Clearly, Canadian federal and provincial laws providing for personal liability of directors and officers impose a heavy burden on presumably well-meaning managers.[1] In most cases, the director or officer is liable for a fine, the amount of which may vary greatly[2] according to the specific offence and the facts of the case. Where a fine is not paid within a prescribed period, the convicted person's property may be seized, or compensatory work or a prison term may be imposed.[3] Various offences related to employment law also provide for imprisonment for periods of up to one year where subsequent offences are committed. Such is the case, for instance, in the field of occupational health and safety.

[1] Maurice Martel and Paul Martel, *La compagnie au Québec: Les aspects juridiques* (Montréal: Wilson & Lafleur, Martel Ltée, 1994), p. 580.
[2] Fines in this area tend to range between $1,000 and $20,000 for individuals, with subsequent offences attracting higher fines.
[3] Where the offence stems from a Quebec statute: see the *Code of Penal Procedure*, R.S.Q., c. C-25.1, ss. 333 *et seq.*

§20.193 The situation is not, necessarily, as gloomy as it appears. In order for a director or officer to be found guilty of a penal offence, the Crown[1] must prove beyond a reasonable doubt that the director or officer committed all the required elements of the offence. However, in cases of "strict liability" offences such as environmental offences, the Crown is typically not required to prove an intention to commit the offence, or even a recklessness as to its commission. It is in this sense that strict liability offences are different from most true penal offences.

[1] Or other entity authorized to bring penal charges.

§20.194 The accused may, of course, raise various defences. Whether a given defence, such as ignorance of the facts surrounding the offence, can be invoked in a specific case raises matters of penal law which go beyond the scope of this summary. It is clear, however, that ignorance of the law is never a defence, and a director or officer who wishes to plead ignorance of his or her legal duties should not expect a sympathetic hearing.

§20.195 Other possible defences which are available in many situations include proof that the alleged contravention could not have been foreseen or guarded against; that the officer or director honestly and reasonably believed in a mistaken set of facts which, if true, would have rendered his or her omission or commission innocent or reasonable in the circumstances; and that the alleged contravention was undertaken as a result of advice provided by a government official and reasonably acted upon.

§20.196 As was noted earlier, due diligence may also be pleaded in defence especially in respect of environmental offences. Indeed, some statutes explicitly provide for this means of defence.[1] The availability of the due diligence defence is meant to balance the fact that the Crown typically does not need to prove intent or recklessness in strict liability offences. In many cases, a claim of "due diligence" is likely to be an officer's defensive weapon of choice. No person is likely to be convicted of a serious offence[2] if he or she used his or her best efforts to avoid its occurrence, given the circumstances. In general, directors and officers will be released from any liability if they successfully establish that they took all reasonable steps under the circumstances to prevent the offence from occurring. However, proving "best efforts" and "reasonable steps" may still remain a difficult task for the individual charged.

---

[1] As to due diligence as a defence in the context of statutory offences, see *R. v. Wholesale Travel Group Inc.*, [1991] 3 S.C.R. 154, which indicates that such a defence should always be available where an offence is punishable by imprisonment. Whether due diligence should also be a defence in other cases remains a complex question of constitutional and penal law.

[2] As opposed to offences such as parking tickets, where even a defence of due diligence would be likely to fail if the impugned act was in fact committed.

2. A Practical Case: Due Diligence in Environmental Law

§20.197 This last section will provide an overview of strategies recommended to be taken by directors and officers in order to establish a "due diligence" defence in an environmental law context. It can serve as an example of how a director or officer can avoid potential personal liability in various areas by demonstrating that he or she acted with "due diligence".

§20.198 Insofar as it is part of their responsibilities, directors and officers should see to it that the corporation conducts an environmental audit in order to determine the extent to which the corporation is complying with the various laws and regulations concerning environmental and occupational health and safety matters. The manager of a plant or the head of a division would do well to obtain such information, or, at the very least, press the corporation to conduct such an audit.

§20.199 An environmental policy must then be introduced together with firm commitments and specific action plans. Monitoring and control mechanisms must be put in place to ensure the implementation of the policy with the support of the board of directors and of the employees. All employees must understand that the environmental policy will serve as a guideline for corporate activity at all levels. Officers should actively monitor and apply the policy in their area of responsibility. The policy should be reviewed regularly, and updated as necessary.

§20.200 An adequate pollution prevention system should be set up and regularly evaluated. Officers must periodically ascertain that the corporation uses a state-of-the-art system which ensures:

(1) that environmental laws are complied with;
(2) that the officers submit to the board of directors periodic reports relating to the application and operation of such system; and
(3) that the officers prepare reports relating to any material violation or situation of non-compliance as soon as possible and that they submit such reports to the board of directors.

§20.201 Officers must obtain adequate information relating to the operation of the system and relay such information to their superiors and they must respond promptly and efficiently to any environmental problem. Officers and executives may reasonably rely on reports prepared by consultants, legal counsel or other qualified experts. Indeed, they should seek such expertise when it would be reasonable to conclude that they are not themselves in a position to adequately deal with a situation raising environmental issues.

§20.202 Directors and officers should be aware of the usual practices or standards used in industries having similar commercial activities, facing similar environmental risks or using similar contaminants. A comparison with industrial standards was used in *R. v. Bata Industries Ltd.*,[1] for example, to substantiate the finding that Bata's overall environmental performance was not adequate, given its environmental situation.

---

[1] (1992), 70 C.C.C. (3d) 394 (Ont. Ct. (Prov. Div.)), vard (1993), 11 C.E.L.R. (N.S.) 208 (Ont. Ct. (Gen. Div.)), vard (1995), 18 C.E.L.R. (N.S.) 11 (C.A.). See, *supra*, §§20.187 *et seq.*

§20.203   Obviously, directors and officers should react immediately and personally when a defect in the system is brought to their attention or if they personally notice such a failure. In the *Bata* case, the court recognized that directors and officers of a corporation with a complex structure must delegate part of their work and cannot participate in all environmental decisions. However, directors and officers cannot delegate all decision-making powers to other employees and thereby seek to avoid all responsibility for environmental problems.

§20.204   In summary, in order to avoid incurring personal liability and to show that they acted diligently, officers and directors must take concrete measures to ensure that the corporation they manage complies with environmental laws. Blissful ignorance is not a defence. Nor will they avoid their environmental liability if they delegate all their environmental duties or are wilfully blind to problems. The same level of care should be brought to the fulfilment of a director's or officer's environment-related duties as is brought to all of his or her other duties, from ensuring compliance with occupational health and safety measures to monitoring the proper remittance of sums due to government agencies.

E.   CRIMINAL CODE LIABILITY

1. Introduction

§20.205   Directors and officers should be aware that certain wrongdoing may also attract *Criminal Code* liability in addition to the civil liability canvassed earlier in this chapter and the penal liability just surveyed. In most cases, the intent to commit the offence or *mens rea* is required but there are also "absolute liability" offences where liability arises upon proof of the elements of the offence (the *actus reus*) and no particular state of mind is a prerequisite to guilt, and "strict liability" offences which only require proof of the *actus reus* but are subject to the defence of due diligence. Further, as with some of the penal statutory offences described earlier, certain *Criminal Code* offences will attract liability not only to the principal perpetrator of the offence, but to those aiding and abetting in the offence or merely standing by and not preventing its commission.

§20.206   Below is a non-exhaustive review of some of the provisions of the *Criminal Code* for which directors and officers may attract liability. An indictable offence will generally carry terms of imprisonment from two to ten years while a summary conviction offence, under Part

XXVII, except where otherwise provided, is generally punishable by a fine of not more than $2,000 or imprisonment for six months or both.[1] All references in this part are to sections of the *Criminal Code*.

   [1] R.S.C. 1985, c. C-46, s. 787(1).

2. Aiding and Abetting a Criminal Offence

§20.207 Under section 21 of the *Criminal Code*, anyone who aids or abets in a criminal offence can be held liable for such offence. Thus, where a corporation is charged with an offence, any director or officer who participated in or encouraged the offence can be charged as being a party to the offence. Normally, a director or officer would only be charged where he directed, encouraged or actively participated in the offence, but obviously there is a risk involved where a director has knowledge of the intended commission of an offence and the authority to prevent it and fails to do so.

The general principles required to prove this offence can be stated as follows:

- to be a party to an offence, the person must have assisted or encouraged the conduct that constituted an offence. In general, simply failing to prevent an offence does not constitute aiding or abetting and liability does not follow from mere knowledge of the offence.[1]
- to aid or abet the commission of an offence, a person must know he or she is helping or encouraging the acts which constitute the offence. However, it is not necessary that the person be aware that such conduct constitutes an offence. As with other offences, ignorance of the law, *e.g.* that some kind of behaviour constituted an offence under the *Criminal Code*, is not a defence to this offence.[2]
- it is not enough that a person's actions have the effect of aiding or abetting: the person must intend to assist or encourage the conduct constituting the offence.[3] If a person omits to do something with the intention of assisting or encouraging the conduct that constitutes an offence, the person will have aided or abetted the commission of an offence.[4]
- Even with offences of strict liability, the alleged aider or abettor must have intended to aid or abet, and he or she must have knowledge of the circumstances that constitute the offence.[5]

It is to be noted that the aiding and abetting provisions of the *Criminal Code* have been applied to offences under other federal statutes such as the *Combines Investigation Act*[6] (now the *Competition Act*[7]), which have provisions with criminal sanctions.[8]

[1]   *Dunlop and Sylvester v. The Queen* (1979), 47 C.C.C. (2d) 93 (S.C.C.).
[2]   *R. v. F. W. Woolworth* (1974), 18 C.C.C. (2d) 23 (Ont. C.A.).
[3]   *R. v. Morgan* (1993), 80 C.C.C. (3d) 16 (Ont. C.A.).
[4]   *R. v. Nixon* (1990), 57 C.C.C. (3d) 97 (B.C.C.A.).
[5]   *R. v. F. W. Woolworth* (1974), 18 C.C.C. (2d) 23 (Ont. C.A.).
[6]   R.S.C. 1970, c. C-23.
[7]   R.S.C. 1985, c. C-34.
[8]   *R. v. Campbell*, [1964] 3 C.C.C. 112, affd (1966), 58 D.L.R. (2d) 673 (S.C.C.).

§20.208   The principles of aiding and abetting apply equally to the corporation itself, with the *mens rea* component being determined by the "directing mind" test set out in *Canadian Dredge & Dock Co. Ltd. et al v. R.*[1] "Directing mind" is used to describe any person in a corporation who has some level of authority and discretionary power to bind the corporation. As *Canadian Dredge* indicated, there can be more than one directing mind including "the board of directors, the managing director, the superintendent, the manager or anyone else delegated [executive authority] by the board of directors."[2] A corporation will be found to have aided or abetted the commission of an offence if a directing mind of that corporation has the requisite knowledge and intent, and causes the corporation to assist or encourage the commission of the offence.[3]

[1]   (1985), 19 C.C.C. (3d) 1 (S.C.C.).
[2]   *Canadian Dredge & Dock Co. Ltd. et al v. R.* (1985), 19 C.C.C. (3d) 1 (S.C.C.) at 23.
[3]   *Canadian Dredge & Dock Co. Ltd. et al v. R.* (1985), 19 C.C.C. (3d) 1 (S.C.C.).

3.   Secret Commissions

§20.209   Pursuant to section 426, it is an offence, punishable by imprisonment for up to five years, to

(a) corruptly [which means secretly or without the requisite disclosure[1]],
   (i)   give or agree to give to an agent or,
   (ii) being an agent, demand, accept, or agree to accept,
   any reward, advantage or benefit for doing or not doing something relating to the affairs or business of his principal or for showing or not showing favour or disfavour to any person in relation to the affairs or business of his principal; or
(b) with intent to deceive a principal, give to an agent of the principal, or being an agent, use, with intent to deceive his principal, a receipt, account or other writing

(i)   in which the principal has an interest
(ii) that contains any statement that is false or erroneous or defective in any material particular; and
(iii) that is intended to mislead the principal.

¹ *R. v. Kelly*, 14 C.R. (4th) 181 (S.C.C.).

§20.210 Section 426(2) makes it also an offence to be "knowingly privy to the commission of an offence" under section 426(1) extending the general principle of section 21 described above that anyone who aids or abets in an offence will be guilty of the same offence. In order to prove section 426(2), one must prove both knowledge and privity on the part of the defendant.

§20.211 The three elements of the offence in section 426(1)(*a*) are:

- the existence of an agency relationship;
- the accepting by an agent of a benefit or consideration for doing or forbearing to do any act in relation to the affairs of the agent's principal; and
- the failure by the agent to make adequate and timely disclosure of the source, amount and nature of the benefit.

In order to establish the guilt of an agent, the mental element must be proved for each element of the offence, that is, the agent must know of the agency status, knowingly accept the secret commission, and be aware of the extent of disclosure to the principal or lack thereof.

4. Manipulation of Stock Exchange Transactions

§20.212 Section 382 creates a number of offences for those who, through the facility of a stock exchange, curb market or other market, and: (i) with the intent to create a false or misleading appearance of active public trading in a security; or (ii) with intent to create a false or misleading appearance with respect to the market price of a security, effect certain security transactions. These indictable offences are punishable by imprisonment up to five years. This offence requires the intent to create a false or misleading appearance of active public interest in the security but proof of conspiracy or trading by nominees is not required. The offence itself prejudices the integrity of stock exchanges and the financial community.¹ In *R. v. Jay*,² it was held that accumulating a large stock position for control purposes or to become a director, or to stabilize prices are all legitimate purposes and not a criminal offence under this section.

[1]   *R. v. MacMillan*, [1969] 2 C.C.C. 289 (Que. C.A.).
[2]   [1965] 2 O.R. 471 (C.A.).

5.   Affecting the Public Market

§20.213   Section 380(2) of the *Criminal Code* makes it an offence for anyone to, by deceit, falsehood or other fraudulent means and with intent to defraud, affect the public market price of stocks, shares, merchandise or anything that is offered for sale to the public. This is an indictable offence which carries a penalty of imprisonment for up to ten years. Proof of intent to defraud is necessary to establish this offence. In *R. v. McMaughton*,[1] the accused was convicted of this offence when he and several others traded shares of a listed company between two companies so as to give the illusion of trading and the impression that the shares were increasing in value.

[1]   (1976), 33 C.R.N.S. 279 (Que. C.A.).

6.   False Prospectus, Statement or Account or False Statement Concerning Financial Status

§20.214   Issuance of a prospectus, statement or account with material carrying false information, knowing the information to be false and with the intent to induce persons to: (a) purchase securities or become shareholders; or (b) deceive or defraud shareholders or creditors of a company constitute criminal offences under section 400. These offences require establishing that when the prospectus (or other document) was published, it contained statements which were false in some material particular, the accused knew of the falsity and the false statements were made with the intent to induce persons to become shareholders or partners (section 400(1)(*a*)) or with intent to defraud (section 400(1)(*b*)). The false information may be found in a statement of purposes which the author never had any intention of carrying out.[1]

[1]   *Cox and Paton v. R.*, [1963] 2 C.C.C. 148 (S.C.C.).

§20.215   In *R. v. McCleod*,[1] a misdescription by a director of loans as cash fell within this provision. In *R. v. Scallen*,[2] the accused was a director, president, and treasurer of a company and also operating head and largest shareholder of a U.S. company. He was convicted of both publishing a false prospectus to induce the public to become shareholders, and theft under the *Criminal Code* when, between the date of the prospectus and the closing date of the underwriting, he had intended to pay off the debt of the U.S. company with the proceeds of the underwriting. This fact was not disclosed in the prospectus and consequently, the prospectus was false in a material way.

[1] [1941] S.C.R. 228.
[2] (1974), 15 C.C.C. 441 (B.C.C.A.).

§20.216 Criminal liability for false declarations related to the financial situation of a company with the intent of: (a) obtaining a personal benefit or benefit to the company; (b) payment of an amount of money; or (c) an extension of credit is an offence under section 362(1)(c) carrying a maximum term of imprisonment of ten years.[1]

[1] *Pelland v. R.*, J.E. 95-946 (Que. C.A.); *Allard v. Verdon*, [1995] R.J.Q. 1203 (Que. S.C.).

7. Fraud

§20.217 Pursuant to section 380(1) of the *Criminal Code,* any person may be found guilty of fraud who defrauds the public or any person, of any property, money or valuable security, or any service. To establish fraud, there must be proof of dishonest deprivation. Using the assets of a corporation for personal purposes can constitute dishonesty and proof of some detriment, prejudice or risk of prejudice to the economic interests of the victim can constitute deprivation without proof of actual economic loss.[1] There must be proof that the accused intentionally committed the prohibited act.[2] The penalties for this offence vary from fines on summary conviction, to two to ten years as an indictable offence.

[1] *R. v. Olan*, [1978] 2 S.C.R. 1175.
[2] See *R. v. Littler* (1972), 41 D.L.R. (3d) 523 (Que. C.S.P.).

8. Criminal Liability for Theft

§20.218 Everyone commits theft who fraudulently and without colour of right, converts to his use or to the use of another person, anything whether animate or inanimate, with intent to deprive the owner of the use of it.[1]

[1] s. 322.

§20.219 In *Smith v. R.,*[1] officers of a corporation who had issued bank countercheques in fraud of the company were found guilty of theft. Directors were found guilty of theft when they pledged shares bought in the name of a corporation as security for personal loans.[2] A president's pledge of a controlling interest in a subsidiary and use of the proceeds to pay off personal debts was also held to be theft.[3]

[1]   (1961), 131 C.C.C. 403 (S.C.C.).
[2]   *R. v. Smith*, [1963] 1 O.R. 249 (C.A.).
[3]   *R. v. Winchell*, [1980] OSCB 238.

9.   Criminal Liability in Gaming in Stocks or Merchandise

§20.220   Under section 383(1) of the *Criminal Code*, gaming in stocks or merchandise is a criminal offence. In general, one must prove not only the intent to enter into such an agreement without the *bona fide* intention to acquire or dispose of the goods, but further, the specific or ulterior motive to make a gain or profit by the rise or fall in price of the stock, goods, wares or merchandise. Section 383(2) establishes a rebuttable presumption of unlawful intention when there is proof of a prohibited agreement or a participation in such an agreement.

10.   Criminal Liability for Forging Trademarks

§20.221   Sections 406 and 407 make it an offence to forge a trade mark, with intent to deceive or defraud the public or any person, whether ascertained or not.

11.   Criminal Liability Concerning Trade Unions

§20.222   Every one who, being an employer or the agent of an employer, wrongfully and without lawful authority: (a) refuses to employ or dismisses from his employment, any person for the reason only that the person is a member of a lawful trade union; or (b) seeks by intimidation or threat of loss of position to prevent that person from being a member of a trade union; or (c) conspires with an employer to do (a) or (b).[1] This is a summary conviction offence. In *Canadair Ltd. v. R.*,[2] the court held that the principal or real or determining cause of dismissal must be proven to be the membership in a lawful trade union to fall within this provision.

[1]   s. 425.
[2]   (1947), 5 C.R. 67 (Que. C.A.).

12.   Falsification of Books and Documents

§20.223   It is an offence under section 397(1) to falsify books or documents, sanctioned by imprisonment for a term not exceeding five years. Further, section 398 makes it a specific offence, punishable on summary conviction, to falsify an employment record with intent to deceive. The offence requires the specific intent to deceive, most often manifested by an intent to defraud.

CHAPTER 21

LIABILITY OF SENIOR EXECUTIVES UNDER SECURITIES LEGISLATION

A. INTRODUCTION

§21.1 An important source of potential liability of directors and officers referred to earlier remains to be discussed, namely, securities legislation. Such potential liability includes civil liability for damages, fines and penal sanctions. Our discussion of such potential liabilities in this chapter is limited to Ontario and Quebec securities legislation. However, analogous provisions apply in other jurisdictions and the present discussion therefore provides useful indications to "senior executives", as that term is defined below, throughout Canada.

§21.2 In this chapter, the expression "senior executive" means in the context of Quebec securities law any person exercising the functions of a director, president, vice-president, secretary, treasurer, controller or general manager of a corporation, or similar functions.[1] Where used in the context of Ontario securities law, also it includes the assistant secretary and assistant treasurer (but not specifically the controller) and "any other person designated an officer of a company by by-law or similar authority, or any individual acting in a similar capacity".[2] For definitions of a prospectus, take-over bid, take-over bid circular, etc., we would refer you to the relevant provincial securities legislation. "Issuer" means the corporation which has outstanding issues or prepares to issue a security.

[1] Quebec *Securities Act* ("QSA"), R.S.Q., c. V-1.1, s. 5.
[2] Ontario *Securities Act* ("OSA"), R.S.O. 1990, c. S.5, s. 1(1).

§21.3 Securities legislation does not generally govern closed or private corporations which, pursuant to restrictions contained in their constating documents, do not sell their securities to the public. Senior executives of a private corporation may, however, incur liability arising from securities legislation, if the private corporation engages in a transaction involving securities of a public corporation, such as a take-over bid, or if the private corporation holds more than 10% of the securities of a public corporation.

§21.4 Civil, penal or even criminal sanctions can arise principally from: (1) failure to prepare, file or deliver a prospectus or a take-over bid circular, an exchange bid circular or an insider bid circular when required, (2) the presence of misrepresentations in, or omissions of material facts from, documents used to carry out securities transactions, and (3) the use of privileged information. These sanctions, as well as the principal defences available to senior executives, the damages and the fines to which the senior executives may be exposed and the limitation periods related to these sanctions are briefly described below.

§21.5 This chapter does not purport to exhaustively describe the obligations or duties of senior executives under securities laws, but will describe those circumstances where the senior executives could incur personal liability in connection with these obligations and duties. This chapter will *not* discuss the potential liability (whether civil or criminal) of senior executives who act fraudulently or make fraudulent misrepresentations or who assist or abet an issuer in carrying out fraudulent acts or making fraudulent misrepresentations.

B. POTENTIAL LIABILITY ARISING FROM ISSUER'S DISCLOSURE OBLIGATIONS

1. Civil Liability

(a) Failure to Deliver a Prospectus or a Bid Circular

§21.6 Failure to prepare or file a prospectus in Ontario does not attract civil liability; however, a purchaser of a security who does not receive a prospectus from a dealer or offeror who was required to deliver such document has a right of action for rescission or damages against the dealer or offeror.[1] Similarly, where an offeror fails to deliver a take-over bid circular, an issuer bid or an issuer bid circular, or a notice of change or variation to a target shareholder where required to do so under the OSA, such shareholder has a right of action for rescission or damages against the dealer of offeror.[2] This would even apply in a situation where the offeror did not deliver the circular because it mistakenly believed that the bid was exempt from the take-over bid provisions.

---

[1] OSA, ss. 71 and 133.
[2] OSA, ss. 95, 98 and 133.

§21.7 Where an issuer of securities or a holder of securities has an obligation to prepare a prospectus, deliver it to potential investors and file it with the Quebec Securities Commission, its senior executives may be held liable for damages incurred by every person who subscribes for, or acquires securities from, that issuer or holder if the prospectus is not prepared and filed.[1] In Quebec, if the prospectus is prepared and filed but not delivered to the investor, then the investor generally will have a claim in damages against the dealer required to send the prospectus to him or her; the senior executives will not generally be exposed to potential liability for failure to deliver the prospectus to the investor unless the issuer is carrying out the distribution without a registered dealer.[2]

[1] QSA, s. 214 [am. 1990, c. 77, s. 36].
[2] QSA, ss. 29 and 214 [am. 1990, c. 77, s. 36].

§21.8 Similarly, under Quebec securities legislation where a corporation must prepare, deliver and file a take-over bid circular, an exchange take-over bid circular or an issuer bid circular, the senior executives of the offeror or of the issuer may be held liable for damages incurred by every person who should have received the circular if the offeror or the issuer fails to prepare, deliver and file the circular, or if the holder of securities who has a right to receive the circular has not received the circular.[1]

[1] QSA, s. 215.

§21.9 A senior executive in Quebec who is a defendant in an action for damages arising from transactions effected without a prospectus or bid circular when one was required may be held liable for damages unless it is proven that the absence of such prospectus or bid circular was not imputable to any act on his or her part.[1]

[1] QSA, s. 216.

§21.10 The quantum of damages which may be claimed by a plaintiff when a prospectus or bid circular has not been prepared, filed and delivered is not specifically addressed in the securities legislation in Quebec. Consequently, damages will be assessed by the court in accordance with ordinary principles of civil liability.

§21.11 There are many difficulties inherent in assessing the quantum of damages in most civil liability cases involving securities transactions. The primary remedy in the case of a distribution of securities where the purchaser has not resold the security is usually the rescission of the subscription agreement and the return of the investor's subscription funds to the investor. Senior executives in Quebec may be held liable for damages incurred by the investor which are beyond the amount of the subscription funds, such as damages arising from the loss of use of the funds.

§21.12 Damages are often difficult to assess, however, where rescission is not the principal remedy and the loss of value associated with the securities must be assessed. This is particularly the case if the securities in question are listed on an exchange and consequently fairly liquid, since the fluctuation of the market price of the securities may be influenced by many factors other than the failure to deliver a prospectus or a bid circular. Courts are often reluctant to award damages when asked to estimate damages based on a hypothetical alternate course of action available to a plaintiff, and particularly so in cases involving securities because the effect of the market on the value of the security or the behaviour of the security holder is not easily determined or evaluated.[1]

---

[1] P.P. Côté, "The Brokerage Function in the Securities Industry, Civil Liability and Investor Protection" (1975), 10 R.J.T. 255, at 286.

§21.13 In the only reported court case in Quebec discussing civil liability of officers in the absence of a required prospectus, the court held that the purchaser cannot sue officers for reimbursement of the purchase price, but rather only for damages in excess of the purchase price. This is true even if the corporation that issued the shares is unable to make the reimbursement.[1]

---

[1] *Cumulative Index Corp. v. Quadrex Information Systems Ltd.*, [1989] R.J.Q. 2555 (S.C.).

§21.14 In Ontario, no action can be commenced for rescission more than 180 days after the date of the transaction that gave rise to the cause of action. In a case where the plaintiff is seeking damages, the limitation for the period for the commencement of an action is the earlier of 180 days after the plaintiff first had knowledge of the facts giving rise to the cause of action or three years after the date of the transaction that gave rise to the cause of action.[1] In Quebec, no action for damages pursuant to a failure to deliver a securities disclosure document can be commenced more than one year after the time that the plaintiff obtains knowledge of the facts giving rise to the cause of action. If it is proved that the plaintiff did not have knowledge because of his or her own negligence, the plaintiff may be deemed to have had knowledge of the relevant facts earlier than he or she actually received them.[2] An action for damages in Quebec pursuant to a failure to deliver a securities disclosure document also cannot be commenced more than three years after the relevant transaction.[3]

1 OSA, s. 138.
2 QSA, s. 235.
3 QSA, s. 236 [am. 1990, c. 77, s. 37].

(b) Securities Transactions Effected with Documents Containing a Misrepresentation

§21.15 Under Ontario securities legislation, a prospectus is required to contain a certificate stating that the prospectus provides full, true and plain disclosure of all material facts relating to the securities offered thereby.[1] This certificate must be signed by the chief executive officer, the chief financial officer, and, on behalf of the board of directors, any two directors of the issuer, and any other person or company who is a promoter of the issuer.[2] Where a prospectus contains a misrepresentation, any purchaser of such securities during the period of distribution, who did not purchase the securities with knowledge of the misrepresentation, is deemed by the legislation to have relied on such misrepresentation and has a right of action for damages against the issuer and every other person who signed the prospectus. Such purchaser may also elect to exercise a right of rescission against the issuer or the underwriter, in which case the purchaser has no right of action for damages against such person, company or underwriter.[3]

1 OSA, s. 56.
2 OSA, s. 58.
3 OSA, s. 130(1).

§21.16 A prospectus in Ontario includes a short form prospectus issued pursuant to National Policy Statement Number 47 of the Canadian Securities Administrators, which incorporates by reference certain specific disclosure documents from the documents required to be filed by the issuer pursuant to the Ontario Continuous Disclosure Regime. Liability of officers and directors with respect to misrepresentations contained in the short form prospectus, and, by extension, documents incorporated by reference, is no different from that attaching to a "long form prospectus", as the certificate for a short form prospectus must state that the information contained in the short form prospectus, "*together with the documents incorporated herein by reference,* constitutes full, true and plain disclosure of all material facts...*"[1] Accordingly, officers and directors of a corporation must take special care before approving a short form prospectus to make their own investigations and become comfortable that the information in the short form prospectus and the information in the material incorporated by reference contain no misrepresentation.

> [1]   National Policy 47, Appendix B, Item 20.

§21.17 In Ontario, the OSA also provides that where a take-over bid circular sent to the security holders of an offeree issuer contains a misrepresentation, every such security holder shall be deemed to have relied on the misrepresentation and will have a right of action against every person who at the time the circular was signed was a director, and each person who signed the circular. Such individuals will also have a right of action for rescission or damages against the offeror. As with a prospectus, no person or company is liable if the person or company proves that the security holder had knowledge of the misrepresentation.[1]

> [1]   OSA, s. 131.

§21.18 Quebec securities legislation provides that a subscriber or acquiror of securities may claim damages against the senior executives of the issuer or the holder of securities whose securities are being distributed if a misrepresentation is contained in: (1) a prospectus;[1] (2) the permanent information record of such issuer or holder, if it is incorporated in a simplified prospectus;[2] (3) an offering memorandum required in connection with a prospectus exemption, including, *inter alia*, the exemptions for the distribution of seed capital securities, tax-shelter securities, rights to existing holders of securities to purchase further securities, shareholder subscription plans and employee share purchase plans;[3] or (4) any other document authorized by the Quebec Securities Commission for use in lieu of a prospectus.[4]

> [1]   QSA, ss. 217 and 218.
> [2]   QSA, s. 221(1) [am. 1984, c. 41, s. 52].
> [3]   QSA, s. 221(2) [am. 1984, c. 41, s. 52].
> [4]   QSA, s. 221(3) [am. 1984, c. 41, s. 52].

§21.19 In Quebec, where an investor has sold securities under a take-over bid, an exchange take-over bid, an issuer bid or a stock exchange bid and the bid circular (or, in the case of a stock exchange bid, the disclosure document required by the exchange) contains a misrepresentation, the investor may claim damages from the senior executives of the offeror or the issuer which has prepared the circular.[1] Also in the case of a take-over bid, a holder of securities of the target corporation may claim damages from the signatory or signatories of any circular of the board of directors, any dissenter's circular of a senior executive or any analogous document prepared for a stock exchange take-over bid[2] if it contains a misrepresentation.

[1] QSA, ss. 222 [am. 1984, c. 41, s. 53], 223 and 225.1 [en. 1987, c. 40, s. 24].
[2] QSA, ss. 225 [am. 1984, c. 41, s. 54] and 225.1 [en. 1987, c. 40, s. 24].

§21.20 Under Quebec and Ontario securities legislation, there is no statutory basis for civil liability of the senior executives of an issuer for misrepresentations contained in any of the following:

(1) an offering memorandum used by the issuer (for example, an offering memorandum used for a private placement pursuant to the "$150,000 investor" or "sophisticated purchaser" exemptions) other than an offering memorandum required by Quebec securities legislation;

(2) the annual report or the annual information form of the issuer or any other part of the issuer's permanent information record, except to the extent incorporated by reference in a simplified prospectus or "short-form" prospectus under National Policy Statement No. 47;

(3) the annual, semi-annual or quarterly financial statements of the issuer (except to the extent incorporated in one of the disclosure documents for which the senior executives may incur personal civil liability);

(4) a press release of the issuer;

(5) in Ontario, a material change report; or

(6) a proxy solicitation circular of the issuer.

§21.21 Senior officers may, however, incur personal liability for misrepresentations in these documents under statutory offences provided for in provincial securities legislation, and possibly also under civil liability suits based on general principles of the civil law of Quebec and the common law in Ontario (see below).

§21.22 A "misrepresentation" is defined in the OSA as an untrue statement of material fact or an omission to state a material fact that is required to be stated or that is necessary to make a statement not misleading in light of the circumstances in which it was made. "Material fact", where used in relation to securities issued or proposed to be issued means a fact that significantly affects, or would reasonably be expected to have a significant effect on, the market price or value of such securities.[1] The liabilities of the parties specified above are joint and several; however, the amount recoverable cannot exceed the price at which the securities were offered to the public.[2]

¹   OSA, s. 1(1).
²   OSA, ss. 130(8), (9).

§21.23   "Misrepresentation" is defined in Quebec securities legislation as any misleading information concerning a material fact as well as any omission of a material fact.¹ Although the concept of a "material fact" is not specifically defined in Quebec securities legislation some assistance as to the meaning is derived from statutory provisions which require that a prospectus disclose all facts "likely to affect the value or market price of securities to be distributed".² Relying on principles developed in American case law, the Quebec Superior Court has held that an omitted fact is material if there is a substantial likelihood that a reasonable shareholder would consider it important in deciding how to vote.³ Thus, it is not significant whether somebody in fact was misled but only whether there was a substantial likelihood that someone would be misled.

¹   QSA, s. 5 [am. 1987, c. 40, s. 1; 1990, c. 77, s. 2].
²   QSA, s. 13.
³   *Investissements Oxdon Inc. v. Corp. d'Acquisition Socanav-Caisse Inc.*, [1989] R.J.Q. 2387 (S.C.), at 2405.

§21.24   In Ontario, in order to establish a cause of action for damages, the plaintiff only needs to show the existence of a misrepresentation at the time of purchase of securities and the occurrence of damages. The plaintiff does not need to prove that he or she relied upon the misrepresentation.¹ The defendant bears the onus of proving that damages claimed do not represent depreciation in the value of a security as the result of the misrepresentation.²

¹   OSA, s. 130(1).
²   OSA, s. 130(7).

§21.25   Under Ontario securities legislation, directors and officers are not liable for representations contained in a circular or prospectus if: (1) it can be proven that the document was sent without their knowledge; (2) upon discovering any misrepresentation in any such document, such individual withdrew the consents thereto and gave reasonable general notice of the withdrawal and the reason therefor;¹ or (3) if the misrepresentation contained in a false statement purporting to be a statement made by an official person was a correct and fair representation of the statement and such individual had reasonable grounds to believe and did believe that the statement was true.²

¹   In order to meet the requirement of "general notice", the withdrawing party should file a written notice with the securities administrators who have been fur-

nished with the prospectus, the stock exchanges and major daily newspapers in the jurisdictions in which the offering is planned. V.P. Alboini, *Securities Law and Practice* (Toronto: Carswell, looseleaf) pp. 23-24–23-25.

² OSA, s. 131(3).

§21.26 In Quebec, the senior executive who is a defendant in a civil action for damages in respect of a securities transaction made following delivery of a required disclosure document which contains a misrepresentation will generally be held liable unless it is proven that: (1) the plaintiff knew, at the time of the securities transaction, of the misrepresentation; or that (2) the defendant acted with prudence and diligence.[1]

¹ QSA, ss. 220, 224 and 225 [am. 1984, c. 41, s. 54]; OSA, ss. 130 and 131.

§21.27 It should be noted that the first defence is very narrow in scope. The senior executive will not be able to raise a defence based on the fact that the misrepresentation was not an important influence on the plaintiff's decision to effect the securities transaction or to buy or sell the securities in question since there is no necessity for the plaintiff to prove reliance. Similarly, the senior executive will not be able to argue that he or she should not be held liable because the plaintiff could have detected the misrepresentation. In fact, it is irrelevant whether the plaintiff read the relevant disclosure document at all.

§21.28 The leading Canadian case on defence of prudence and diligence, *Nesbitt, Thomson & Co. v. Piggott*,[1] dealt with the liability of underwriters for misrepresentation in a prospectus. The Supreme Court of Canada stated that the existence of false statements in a prospectus does not, of itself, necessarily render the defendant liable in damages. Rather, the falsehood must be made "knowingly, or without belief in its truth, or with reckless disregard of whether it is true or false".[2] The court held that the indifference of the defendant as to the truth of the statements contained in the document was a sufficient basis for civil liability.

¹ [1941] S.C.R. 520.
² [1941] S.C.R. 520, at 530.

§21.29 Although the principles set out in *Nesbitt* are not binding in Quebec, it is likely that Quebec courts would recognize the principles set out there as part of the requirement of Quebec securities legislation that the senior executive exercise "prudence and diligence".

§21.30 In addition to liability arising from statutory provisions concerning misrepresentations, senior executives should also be aware that a separate ground for possible liability could arise under the general provisions of the Quebec Civil Code. Quebec courts have not been called upon to determine the scope of this alternate ground of liability, probably because of the breadth of the specific statutory provisions in Quebec securities legislation which make the plaintiff's case considerably easier by the presumption of reliance. Although this has not been the basis for any finding of liability, it is worth noting that the Quebec Superior Court has referred to the analogous common law ground of liability for negligent misrepresentation with approval.

> An offeree who relies on a take-over bid circular or a directors' circular which is misleading may have a cause of action for damages for negligent misrepresentation on the basis of the principle enunciated in *Hedley Byrne & Co. Ltd. v. Heller & Partners Ltd.*[1] by the House of Lords. The case "held" that a person in a position which would lead others to rely on his skill, judgment or ability to make a careful inquiry and who provides information or advice to another person whom he knows [or] ought to know will rely on it owes to the latter person a duty to take reasonable care that the information given is accurate.[2]

Consequently there is a possibility, at least in theory, that senior executives could incur personal civil liability for misrepresentations in securities documents other than in the circumstances specifically provided for in Quebec securities legislation.

[1] [1964] A.C. 465 (H.C.).
[2] *Behar v. Golden Pond Resources Inc.*, [1986] R.J.Q. 3064 (S.C.), at 3070, quoting from P. Anisman, *Takeover Bid Legislation in Canada* (Don Mills: CCH, 1974), pp. 308-9.

§21.31   In Ontario, directors or officers who are responsible for misleading statements in a press release, prospectus, offering memorandum, management proxy circular or any other document upon which other persons may rely may be individually responsible for the loss arising from their negligent or fraudulent misrepresentation (depending on the state of the directors' or officers' knowledge of the falsity). The grounds for a tort action in negligent misrepresentation arise from *Hedley Byrne*, discussed above. These issues were discussed in the case of *Montreal Trust v. ScotiaMcLeod Inc.*,[1] where the plaintiff sought to find a number of directors personally liable for damages arising from a misrepresentation in a prospectus which had been prepared for a previous transaction and which had been provided to the plaintiff as part of the company's disclosure record. At trial, Justice Farley for the Ontario Court General Division held that:

> Given that the statements were made in their capacity as officers and directors of [the corporation], it would not seem that there was any *personal* voluntary as-

sumption of liability. I think it a fair observation of business reality that a reasonable person would recognize that the statements being made were those of [the corporation] and not those of a director or officer in a personal capacity.[2]

Justice Farley ultimately concluded that the directors could not be held personally liable for the damages sought since they were not "involved in conduct or acts which could be considered as being so deliberate and reckless so as to make it his or her own as distinct from it being the conduct of or act of [the corporation]".[3] On appeal, the court concurred with the findings respecting the directors but allowed the appeal against two executive officers who were allegedly personally involved in the marketing of the debenture and made negligent misrepresentations. The court was not prepared to dismiss the action against them at this stage.[4]

As well, some authors are of the view that translating the Hedley Byrne principle into an action for negligently misleading disclosure is a stretch since the issuer will not normally be in the business of providing advice, and this may preclude recovery.[5]

[1] (1994), 15 B.L.R. (2d) 160 (Ont. Ct. (Gen. Div.)).
[2] *Montreal Trust v. ScotiaMcLeod Inc.* (1994), 15 B.L.R. (2d) 160 (Ont. Ct. (Gen. Div.)) at 197.
[3] *Montreal Trust v. ScotiaMcLeod Inc.* (1994), 15 B.L.R. (2d) 160 (Ont. Ct. (Gen. Div.)) at 209.
[4] *Montreal Trust v. ScotiaMcLeod Inc.* (1995), 23 B.L.R. (2d) 165 (Ont. C.A.).
[5] K.A. Groskaufmanis & R.R. Sorell, "Continuous Disclosure Liability" in *Securities Forum '95* (Toronto: Insight Educational Services, 1995), Vol. 2, Tab 1, p. 9.

§21.32 As mentioned, in order to ensure that he or she can rely on the "due diligence defence", a senior executive should conduct a reasonable investigation to verify the accuracy of the issuer's securities documents. What constitutes a "reasonable investigation" will depend on the circumstances of the case and the involvement of the particular senior executive. A reasonable investigation should involve, in all cases, verification by senior executives involved in the preparation of the relevant disclosure document of all statements made in the document and of the completeness of the document, and confirmation of satisfactory completion of this process to the directors. Furthermore, directors should read proofs of the disclosure document and follow up on what appear to be matters of possible concern. It is likely that a court would hold that mere attendance at the board meeting to approve the disclosure document or periodic questioning of other senior executives on various matters is insufficient.[1]

[1] V.P. Alboini, *Securities Law and Practice* (Toronto: Carswell, 1984), p. 23-17.

§21.33 The assessment of the quantum of damages which may be claimed by a plaintiff in respect of a securities transaction effected with a document containing a misrepresentation is subject to the same difficulties as those described above in respect of a securities transaction effected without a required prospectus or bid circular.

§21.34 The limitation periods in Ontario and in Quebec for an action in damages based on the use of a document containing a misrepresentation are the same as the limitation periods where a required prospectus or bid circular was not prepared.[1] In Quebec, however, the three-year period starts as of the filing of the disclosure document with the Quebec Securities Commission instead of the date of the transaction.[2]

[1]   See §21.14.
[2]   QSA, ss. 235 and 236 [am. 1990, c. 77, s. 37].

2. Statutory Offences

§21.35 Under the statutory offences provided for in provincial securities legislation, the prosecution must prove beyond a reasonable doubt that the defendant committed the offence. Consequently, the burden of proof is higher than for a civil action. Once the elements of the offence are proven, however, the defences which may be raised by the accused are very limited.

§21.36 Under Ontario securities law, every person or company that makes a statement in any material submitted to the Ontario Securities Commission that is misleading in a material respect or makes a statement to the Ontario Securities Commission in any document[1] required to be filed or furnished under security law that is misleading in a material respect is guilty of an offence and on conviction is liable to a fine of not more than $1,000,000 or to imprisonment for a term of not more than two years, or to both.[2] These sanctions are also applicable for every director or officer who authorizes, permits, or acquiesces in the commission of such an offence.[3] In addition, every person or company that contravenes "Ontario securities law", or any director or officer of such a company or person who authorizes, permits or acquiesces in such contravention of Ontario securities law is also subject to a fine of not more than $1,000,000 or to imprisonment for a term of not more than two years, or to both. "Ontario securities law" is defined as the OSA, the regulations under the OSA and any decision of the Ontario Securities Commission or one of its Directors to which the person or company is subject.[4]

[1] "Document" includes any application, release, report, preliminary prospectus, prospectus, return, financial statement, information circular, take-over bid circular and issuer bid circular and any other document required to be filed with the Commission.

[2] OSA, ss. 122(1)(a) and (b). See Ontario Securities Commission, Press Release, "Re: Gregory McGroaty" (26 April 1991) (1991), 14 O.S.C.B. 2031; Ontario Securities Commission, Press Release, "Re Plastic Engine Technology Corporation" (26 August 1991) (1991), 14 O.S.C.B. 4232; Ontario Securities Commission Press, Press Release, "Re: Plastic Engine Technology Corporation" (2 October 1991) (1991), 14 O.S.C.B. 4683; *Queen v. Plastic Engine Technology, Gerald McKendry and Larry Woods* (1992), 15 O.S.C.B. 2637 (Ont. Ct. (Prov. Div.)).

[3] OSA, s. 122(3).

[4] OSA, s. 1(1).

§21.37 In Ontario, no person or company is guilty of the offences described above if the person or company did not know and in the exercise of reasonable due diligence could not have known that the statement was misleading.[1] However, the OSA does not make this defence available to the directors or officers of such person or company. Notwithstanding this, in *R. v. Gilson*[2] it was determined that an offence under s. 122(3) of the OSA against an officer or director is a strict liability offence, making it "a defence is available to the accused if he can prove that he took all reasonable care and he had an honest and reasonable, but mistaken, belief as to the facts involved."[3]

[1] OSA, s. 122(2).

[2] (1989), 12 O.S.C.B. 3001.

[3] V.P. Alboini, *Securities Law and Practice* (Toronto: Carswell, looseleaf), p. 22-10.

§21.38 Legislation and case law have not established what actions or inactions by a senior executive would be considered "authorizing" or "permitting" for the purposes of the offences under provincial securities legislation. It is clear, however, that the more the senior executive knows about the relevant facts, and the more directly responsible the senior executive is for the matters which give rise to the issuer's offence, the more likely it is that a court would find he or she had authorized or permitted the documents or transactions which give rise to the offence. The senior executive who is a director of a corporation has obligations both under corporate law and, in some cases, under securities law to carry out his or her duties with prudence and diligence. In that case it is more likely that the senior executive may be considered to have authorized or permitted acts or omissions of the corporation even if the senior executive is not directly responsible for the matters which give rise to the issuer's offence.

§21.39 The notion of "prudence and diligence" has been discussed above under "Civil Liability".[1] It is unclear what scope can be given to the notion of "reasonable error". One example might be if the senior executive relies on advice from legal counsel with recognized expertise in securities law who advise that no prospectus is required for a transaction. If that advice was wrong, the senior executive would probably be able to invoke "reasonable error". The availability of this defence is less clear, however, if the legal counsel has no securities expertise.

[1]   See §§21.6 *et seq.*

§21.40   Under Quebec securities law, it is an offence for senior executives of a corporation to authorize or permit the corporation to effect a securities transaction by means of any of a variety of documents containing misrepresentations,[1] or to acquiesce in the corporation so doing,[2] if the misrepresentation is likely to affect the value or the market price of the securities concerned. These documents are the following:

(1)   any prospectus (preliminary, final or simplified) or offering memoranda required by Quebec securities legislation in connection with any distribution of securities;

(2)   the annual report of the issuer, if it is incorporated by reference in a simplified prospectus of the issuer and the annual information form of the issuer;

(3)   the annual, semi-annual and quarterly financial statements of the issuer filed under Quebec securities legislation and any press releases made by the issuer with respect to material changes;

(4)   any proxy solicitation circular and, if the senior executive is a director who delivers a dissident's circular with respect to a meeting of shareholders, that dissident's circular; and

(5)   any take-over bid circular, exchange take-over bid circular or issuer bid circular required by Quebec securities legislation.

[1]   QSA, ss. 196 and 205.
[2]   OSA, s. 122.

§21.41   It is also an offence if the senior executive, in any manner not provided for above, makes a misrepresentation: (1) in respect of a transaction in a security; (2) in the course of soliciting proxies or sending a circular to security holders; (3) in the course of a take-over bid, an exchange take-over bid or an issuer bid; (4) in any document or information filed with the Quebec Securities Commission or one of its agents; or (5) in any document forwarded to, or record kept by, any person pursuant to Quebec securities legislation.[1]

[1]   QSA, ss. 197 and 205.

§21.42 The senior executives of a corporation who authorize or permit the corporation to effect a securities transaction without a prospectus or bid circular where one is required commit an offence under Quebec securities legislation.[1] The senior executives can raise as a defence only that they acted with prudence and diligence or on the basis of a reasonable error.[2]

[1] QSA, ss. 202 [am. 1990, c. 4, s. 897; 1992, c. 35, s. 11] and 205.
[2] QSA, s. 206.

§21.43 A senior executive in Quebec who is accused of an offence in respect of a securities transaction effected with a document containing a misrepresentation will be acquitted if he or she proves that he or she acted with prudence and diligence or on the basis of reasonable error.[1]

[1] QSA, s. 206.

§21.44 Under Quebec securities law, a senior executive who is found guilty of an offence in respect of a securities transaction effected without a prospectus where one is required or with a document containing a misrepresentation is liable for a fine of not less than $5,000[1] or more than $1,000,000.[2]

[1] QSA, s. 204 [re-en. 1987, c. 40, s. 22; am. 1990, c. 4, s. 898; 1992, c. 35, s. 12].
[2] QSA, s. 204, OSA, s. 122.

§21.45 A senior executive who is found guilty of an offence in Quebec in respect of a take-over bid, an exchange take-over bid or an issuer bid made without the required bid circular is liable for a fine in Quebec of between $1,000 and $20,000.[1] In determining the amount of the fine, Quebec securities legislation provides that the court must take particular note of the harm done to investors and the advantages derived from the offence by the miscreant.

[1] QSA, s. 202 [am. 1990, c. 4, s. 897; 1992, c. 35, s. 11].

§21.46 In Quebec, every person who solicits proxies (or the withholding or revocation of proxies) for a meeting of holders of voting securities of a reporting issuer commits an offence if he or she does not deliver a proxy circular in prescribed form;[1] the maximum fine is $20,000.[2]

[1] QSA, ss. 82 [am. 1984, c. 41, s. 31] and 195(3).
[2] QSA, s. 202 [am. 1990, c. 4, s. 897; 1992, c. 35, s. 11].

§21.47 It appears, although it is not certain, that every senior executive or employee who authorizes or permits an offence by a corporation under Quebec securities legislation may be held liable for the same penalties as the corporation.[1] Generally, the senior executive will be able to raise a defence that he or she has acted with prudence and diligence or on the basis of reasonable error,[2] except in the case of insider trading or tipping offences (discussed separately below), certain illegal short sales transactions and certain false representations.[3] The maximum fine the senior executive may face is generally $20,000, except in the case of offences for misrepresentations (discussed above) and offences for insider trading or tipping.[4]

[1]   QSA, s. 205.
[2]   QSA, s. 206.
[3]   QSA, ss. 206 and 198.
[4]   QSA, ss. 202 [am. 1990, c. 4, s. 897; 1992, c. 35, s. 11] and 204 [re-en. 1987, c. 40, s. 22, am. 1990, c. 4, s. 898; 1992, c. 35, s. 12].

§21.48 It is also an offence for any person to conspire to commit an offence under the QSA, or to aid a person in the commission of an offence.[1]

[1]   QSA, ss. 207 and 208 [re-en. 1987, c. 40, s. 23].

§21.49 In Quebec, actions for statutory offences may not be taken after the expiry of a five-year statutory limitation period from the date of the offence.[1] In Ontario, no proceeding may be commenced later than five years from the date of the occurrence of the last event on which the proceeding is based.[2]

[1]   QSA, s. 211 [re-en. 1990, c. 77, s. 35].
[2]   OSA, s. 129.1.

3. Criminal Liability

§21.50 In the case of a misrepresentation in a prospectus, senior executives also face the possibility of criminal liability. A variety of offences under the *Criminal Code*[1] can be relevant to securities transactions, but most offences turn on the occurrence of fraudulent behaviour. Note, however, section 400(1) of the *Criminal Code*, which provides as follows:

> 400(1) Every one who makes, circulates or publishes a prospectus, a statement or an account, whether written or oral, that he knows is false in a material particular, with intent

(*a*) to induce persons, whether ascertained or not, to become shareholders or partners in a company,

(*b*) to deceive or defraud the members, shareholders or creditors, whether ascertained or not, of a company,

(*c*) to induce any person to entrust or advance anything to a company, or

(*d*) to enter into any security for the benefit of a company,

is guilty of an indictable offence and liable to imprisonment for a term not exceeding ten years.

[1] R.S.C. 1985, c. C-46.

§21.51 The case of *R. v. Bourdelais*[1] gives us an indication of the persons and behaviour targeted by section 400(1)(*a*). The prospectus in this case contained false financial information, such as a declaration of a profit of $90,000 when the company had actually suffered a loss of $679,122. A letter in which the company's bank demanded repayment was not disclosed. The defendant was found guilty under section 400(1)(*a*) because he was the "instigator" of the issue of shares in question. He had been "in charge of preparing" the prospectus; he had initiated resolutions at board of directors meetings to issue the shares; he had represented the company in meetings with brokers, the Quebec Securities Commission and securities lawyers; and he had personally answered all but one question put to the company at the due diligence meeting.

[1] [1986] R.J.Q. 1627 (C.S.P.).

§21.52 Under *Criminal Code* offences, the prosecutor must prove beyond a reasonable doubt that the defendant committed the offence.

C. USE OF PRIVILEGED INFORMATION

§21.53 Senior executives are generally prohibited from profiting from trading in securities on the basis of information that they have received about the corporation or its securities as a result of their position as directors or officers. In fact, they can incur personal liability for transactions involving securities of a reporting issuer (*i.e.*, usually a public corporation).[1] All transactions by senior executives in the securities of a reporting issuer in Ontario and Quebec are the subject of various provisions of the OSA and the QSA respectively and are generally referred to as insider trading. The effect of these provisions is generally to prohibit insider trading in certain circumstances and in others to require the filing of a report with the relevant provincial securities commissions. In discussing situations where insider trading is prohibited, former Supreme Court Chief Justice Brian Dickson once defined insider trading as the purchase or sale of the securities of a corporation by a person who, by reason of his or her position in such corporation, had access to confidential information not known to other shareholders or the general public.[2]

> [1] See the definition of "reporting issuer" in s. 1(1) of the OSA. Similar provisions apply in connection with transactions in the securities of a "distributing corporation" under the CBCA; compare CBCA, ss. 126-131.
> [2] *Multiple Access Ltd. v. McCutcheon*, [1982] 2 S.C.R. 161, at 164.

§21.54 Under Ontario securities legislation, the potential liability for insider trading arises in respect of a "person or company in a special relationship with a reporting issuer". The definition of a person or company in a special relationship with a reporting issuer is extensive and includes an insider, a person or a company who has knowledge of a material fact or change as a result of providing business or professional services to or on behalf or the reporting issuer, or a person or company who learns of the material fact or change from someone whom they knew or ought to have known was in a special relationship with the reporting issuer.[1] The Ontario securities legislation prohibits any person or company in a special relationship with a reporting issuer from buying or selling securities of the reporting issuer with knowledge of any undisclosed material fact or material change ("insider trading") and from passing on such information to people other than in the necessary course of business ("tipping").[2]

> [1] OSA, s. 76(5).
> [2] OSA, ss. 76 and 134.

§21.55 Potential liability for insider trading can also arise under Quebec securities law for persons who are considered "insiders" in various circumstances involving the use of "privileged information" and for persons who otherwise have access to privileged information.

§21.56 Under Ontario and Quebec securities legislation, the following are "insiders" of a reporting issuer:

(1) the directors, senior officers (Ontario) and the senior executives (Quebec) of a reporting issuer, of the subsidiaries of the reporting issuer and of any corporation which exercises control over more than 10% of the reporting issuer's voting or participating securities;[1]

(2) where another issuer (the "first issuer") becomes an insider of a reporting issuer, the directors and senior officers or senior executives of the first issuer are deemed to have been insiders of

the reporting issuer for the preceding six months or for such shorter period as they were directors, senior officers or senior executives of the first issuer;[2]

(3) if the first issuer is itself a reporting issuer, then the directors and senior officers or senior executives of the investee reporting issuer are also deemed to have been insiders of the first issuer for the preceding six months or for such shorter period as they were directors, senior officers or senior executives of the investee reporting issuer;[3]

In addition, in Quebec, in the case of an amalgamation of issuers or a purchase by an issuer of all or substantially all of the assets of another issuer or of a subsidiary of another issuer (at least one of which is a reporting issuer), the senior executives of each issuer involved in the amalgamation or reorganization are deemed to have been insiders of the reporting issuer for the preceding six months or for such shorter period during which they have been senior executives of the issuer.[4]

---

[1] QSA, s. 89 [am. 1984, c. 41, s. 34] and OSA, s. 1(1). It should be noted that according to s. 1(1) of the OSA, a senior officer also includes each of the five highest paid employees of an issuer. As well, according to the OSA the definition of insider includes the affiliates of any corporation which exercises control over more than 10% of the reporting issuers' voting or participating securities by virtue of s. 1(6) which provides that a company shall be deemed to own securities beneficially owned by its affiliates. Section 1(2) of the OSA states that a company is deemed to be an affiliate of another company if one of them is a subsidiary of the other, if both are subsidiaries of the same company, or if each of them is controlled by the same person or company.

[2] QSA, s. 94 and OSA, s. 1(8).

[3] QSA, s. 94 and OSA, s. 1(9).

[4] QSA, s. 95.

§21.57 As discussed above, securities laws in Ontario and Quebec prohibit certain persons or companies who are insiders with respect to a reporting issuer from insider trading and tipping. However, the securities legislation actually imposes these restraints on a much broader group of persons and companies, of which insiders constitute just one part, and includes persons or companies in a special or insider-like relationship with a reporting issuer.

§21.58 For instance, in Ontario, persons who are in a special relationship with the reporting issuer are prohibited from trading and tipping as discussed below. These individuals or companies include the following:

(1) a person or company that is an insider, affiliate or associate of: i) the reporting issuer; ii) a person or company that is proposing

to make a take-over bid of the reporting issuer; or iii) a person or company that is proposing to become party to a combination involving the reporting issuer;

(2) a person or company that is engaging in or proposing to engage in any business, or professional activity with or on behalf of the reporting issuer, or with or on behalf of a company described in part (1) above;

(3) a person who is a director, officer or employee of the reporting issuer or of a person or a company who: i) is proposing to make a take-over bid of the reporting issuer; ii) is proposing to become party to a combination involving the reporting issuer; or iii) is engaging or proposing to engage in any business or professional activity with the reporting issuer;

(4) a person or company that learned of the material fact or material change with respect to the reporting issuer while the person or company was a person or company described in parts (1), (2) or (3) above; and

(5) a person or company that learns of a material fact or material change with respect to the issuer from any other person or company described above in parts (1), (2), (3) or (4), and knows or ought reasonably to have known that the other person or company is a person or company in a special relationship with the reporting issuer.[1]

[1] OSA, s. 76(5).

§21.59 In Quebec, the following persons (who can be called "insider-like persons"), in addition to insiders, are subject to the prohibitions on trading and tipping based on undisclosed confidential information:

(1) affiliates of the reporting issuer;

(2) mutual fund managers and advisers, with respect to the mutual fund which they manage or advise;

(3) persons who acquire privileged information in the course of their business functions;

(4) persons who have privileged information disclosed by any other person bound by the tipping prohibition;

(5) persons who have information they know to be privileged, regardless of how it was obtained; and

(6) the associates of any person bound by the tipping prohibition.[1]

[1] QSA, s. 189 [am. 1984, c. 41, s. 47].

§21.60 The trading and tipping prohibitions in the Ontario securities legislation apply to transactions involving undisclosed material facts or material changes. The OSA defines "material fact" as follows:

> "Material fact", where used in relation to securities issued or proposed to be issued, means a fact that significantly affects, or would reasonably be expected to have a significant effect on, the market price or value of such securities.[1]

[1] OSA, s. 1(1).

§21.61 On the other hand, the OSA defines "material change" as follows:

> "Material change", where used in relation to the affairs of an issuer, means a change in the business operations or capital of the issuer that would reasonably be expected to have a significant effect on the market price or value of any of the securities of the issuer and includes a decision to implement such a change made by the board of directors of the issuer or by senior management of the issuer who believe that confirmation of the decision by the board of directors is probable.[1]

[1] OSA, s. 1(1).

§21.62 An important difference in the definitions of material fact and material change is that the definition of material change applies only to changes "in the business operations or capital of the issuer", whereas the definition of material fact applies to any "fact" affecting the specific securities. Thus, the definition of material fact appears to apply to facts and changes in them, whether internal or external to the business affairs of the issuer, that significantly affect or would reasonably be expected to have a significant effect on the market price or value of specific securities. Not only must those in a special relationship with a reporting issuer concern themselves with inside information relating to the affairs of the reporting issuer, they must also be concerned with external facts that have not been generally disclosed that have somehow come to their attention. The existence of undisclosed material facts was an issue in the decision of the Ontario High Court in *Re Royal Trustco Ltd. v. OSC.*[1] Here the court found that there had been a violation of the tipping prohibitions of the OSA. In its reasons, the High Court found that the information imparted by two senior officers of Royal Trustco to senior officers of a major shareholder of Royal Trustco to the effect that approximately 60% of the shares of Royal Trustco were owned by persons or companies whom such officers knew would not tender to the Campeau bid, constituted material facts. It was not suggested that such information should have been the subject-matter of a press release and timely disclosure report presumably because such facts were not material changes.

[1]   (1983), 42 O.R. (2d) 147 (H.C.).

§21.63 Quebec securities legislation defines "privileged information" as "any information not yet known to the general public and that could affect the decision of a reasonable investor".[1] Any information which could affect the decision of a reasonable investor to purchase or sell securities is privileged information, whether or not this information, when and if disclosed to the general public, would materially affect the value or the market price of such securities.

[1]   QSA, s. 5 [am. 1987, c. 40, s. 1; 1990, c. 77, s. 2].

§21.64 Under both Ontario and Quebec securities legislation, insiders of a reporting issuer are generally required to make public disclosure of the insiders' securities transactions.

§21.65 In Ontario, insiders of a reporting issuer have an obligation to make public disclosure of any of such insiders' transactions involving securities of a reporting issuer, assuming that none of the transactions involves undisclosed material facts or material changes. For example, according to the OSA, an insider is obligated to disclose in prescribed form any direct or indirect beneficial ownership of or control or direction over securities of the reporting issuer within ten days after the end of the month in which he or she became an insider.[1] As well, the OSA further provides that a person or company that has filed an insider report and whose direct or indirect beneficial ownership of or control or direction over the securities of a reporting issuer has changed from that shown in the latest report filed by the insider, must file within ten days following the end of the month in which the change took place, a report giving details of the change if the party was an insider at any time during the month in which the change took place. Again this report must be filed in prescribed form.[2]

[1]   OSA, s. 107(1).
[2]   OSA, s. 107(2).

§21.66 The OSA generally restricts the activities of insiders by prohibiting an insider of a reporting issuer from transferring or causing to be transferred any securities of the reporting issuer into the name of an agent, nominee or custodian without delivering to the Ontario Securities Commission a report of this transfer.[1] Similar to the Quebec legislation, the acquisition or the disposition by an insider of a put, call or other transferable option with respect to a security shall be deemed a change in the beneficial ownership of the security to which such put, call or other transferable option relates.[2] Furthermore, according to the

OSA, where voting securities are registered in the name of a person or company other than the beneficial owner and that person or company knows that they are beneficially owned by an insider and that the insider has failed to file a report of such ownership with the Ontario Securities Commission as required by the OSA, then that person or company shall file a report in accordance with the regulation except where the transfer was for the purpose of giving collateral for a genuine debt.[3]

---

[1] OSA, s. 108.
[2] OSA, s. 106(2)(*b*).
[3] OSA, s. 109.

§21.67 The OSA contains a variety of exceptions specifically aimed at these reporting duties of insiders. For instance, a person or company is not required to file a report on becoming an insider of an issuer where the person or company does not own or exercise, control or direction over securities of the issuer.[1] An exception for affiliate reporting is also available. Where a company files an insider report and includes securities beneficially owned, or deemed to be beneficially owned by an affiliate, the affiliate need not file a separate report and the report is deemed to be the report of the affiliate. Thus, it is sufficient if such changes are reported in a single report.[2] Ontario *Policy Statement* 10.1 offers an exception to the directors and senior officers of insider companies and affiliates of insiders of reporting issuers. These individuals may be exempted by the Ontario Securities Commission from the reporting requirements under the OSA provided that the companies involved do not control the reporting issuer and do not supply the reporting issuer with services or material which could have a significant effect on the price of the reporting issuer's securities. The decisive test is whether the directors and senior officers receive knowledge of material facts or material changes with respect to the reporting issuer prior to the general disclosure of such information. Finally, *Uniform Act Policy* 2-10 of the OSA provides that where an individual is an insider by virtue of being a director or senior officer of a principal company, and is also an insider by virtue of being a director or senior officer of a company that is itself an insider of that principal company, it is sufficient for the individual to file one insider trading report. The report must describe the two or more capacities under which the individual is required to report.

---

[1] Ontario *Securities Regulation* 1015, R.R.O. 1990 ("OSR"), s. 166.
[2] OSR, s. 170.

§21.68 In Quebec, where no privileged information is involved, insid-

ers of a reporting issuer have a similar obligation to file a report in prescribed form disclosing the number of securities of the reporting issuer
which the insider owns or controls: (1) within ten days after becoming
an insider; and (2) within ten days of any change in the number of securities the insider owns or controls.[1] However, a senior executive
deemed to be an insider of one company only because he is a senior
executive of another company which is an insider of the first company,
has ten days after the month in which any change occurs.[2] If a person
exercises voting rights attaching to securities as he or she sees fit, then
that person is deemed to control those securities.[3] Similarly, if an insider acquires or disposes of an option in respect of a security, the insider is deemed to have changed his or her control of the security.[4] An
insider must file a report with respect to any securities held in the
name of a nominee, and if he or she does not do so the nominee must
file the report.[5]

[1] QSA, ss. 96, 97 [re-en. 1987, c. 40, s. 6] and s. 174 of the Regulation regarding secu-
     rities.
[2] QSA, s. 98.
[3] QSA, s. 91.
[4] QSA, s. 92.
[5] QSA, ss. 102 and 103.

§21.69 The QSA also contains a variety of exceptions specifically
aimed at the reporting duties of insiders. For instance, the QSA exempts the senior executives of a mutual fund or of an unincorporated
mutual fund from the insider reporting requirements to which they
would otherwise have been subject.[1]

[1] QSA, s. 100.

1. Liability

(a) Civil Liability

§21.70 Every person or company in a special relationship with a reporting issuer who breaches the insider trading prohibitions by purchasing or selling securities of the reporting issuer with knowledge of
a material fact or material change with respect to the reporting issuer
that has not been generally disclosed may be liable to compensate the
seller or purchaser of the securities, as the case may be, for damages as
a result of the trade, subject to certain exceptions.[1]

[1] OSA, s. 134(1).

§21.71 The OSA provides that every: (a) reporting issuer; (b) person or company in a special relationship with a reporting issuer; and (c) person or company that proposes (i) to make a take-over bid for the securities of a reporting issuer, (ii) to become a party to reorganization, amalgamation or a merger involving a reporting issuer, or (iii) to acquire a substantial portion of the property of a reporting issuer, and who informs another person or company of a material fact or material change with respect to the reporting issuer that has not been generally disclosed is liable to compensate for damages any person or company that thereafter sells securities of the reporting issuer or purchases securities of the reporting issuer from the person or company that received the information, subject to certain exceptions.[1]

---

[1] OSA, s. 134(2).

§21.72 Under the QSA, an insider of a reporting issuer who has privileged information in respect of the reporting issuer may not trade in the securities of the reporting issuer unless he or she is justified in believing that: (1) the privileged information is generally known to the public or known to the other party to the trade; or (2) the trade is pursuant to an automatic investment plan established before he or she learned the information.[1] If the insider trades in breach of this provision, he or she may be held liable for the harm suffered by the other party to the transaction,[2] and is accountable to the issuer of the securities for any benefit accruing to him or her from the prohibited transaction (after repairing the harm caused to the other party).[3]

---

[1] QSA, ss. 187 [re-en. 1987, c. 40, s. 21; am. 1990, c. 77, s. 33], 189 and 189.1 [am. 1984, c. 41, ss. 47, 48].
[2] QSA, s. 226 [re-en. 1984, c. 41, s. 55].
[3] QSA, ss. 187 [re-en. 1987, c. 40, s. 21; am. 1990, c. 77, s. 33], 189, 189.1 [am. 1984, c. 41, ss. 47, 48] and 228 [re-en. 1984, c. 41, s. 56].

§21.73 Under the QSA, no insider of a reporting issuer having privileged information relating to the securities of the issuer may disclose or tip this information to another person unless: (1) he or she is justified in believing that the information is generally known or known to the other party; or (2) he or she discloses the information in the course of business and there are no grounds to believe the information will be used for insider trading.[1] Any insider or tippee who breaches this provision may be held liable for damages caused to any third party as a result of any trade in the securities of the reporting issuer by the recipient or any other person who uses the information disclosed.[2]

---

[1] QSA, s. 187 [re-en. 1987, c. 40, s. 21; am. 1990, c. 77, s. 33].

² QSA, s. 227.

(b) Statutory Offences

§21.74 Every person or company in a special relationship with a reporting issuer who violates the insider trading prohibition under the OSA by trading securities of a reporting issuer with the knowledge of a material fact or a material change that has not been generally disclosed, or who has violated the tipping prohibition by informing, other than in the necessary course of business, another person or company of a material fact or a material change with respect to the reporting issuer before that fact or change has been generally disclosed, subject to certain exceptions, commits a statutory offence under Ontario securities legislation.[1]

[1] OSA, s. 122(1).

§21.75 Under Quebec securities law, any insider, insider-like person or tippee of a reporting issuer who has privileged information in respect of the reporting issuer and who trades in the securities of the reporting issuer or who discloses such privileged information to another party commits a statutory offence under Quebec securities legislation.[1] The mere proof of a contravention entails conviction subject to grounds of defence (discussed below).[2]

[1] QSA, ss. 187 [re-en. 1987, c. 40, s. 21; am. 1990, c. 77, s. 33], 188 [am. 1984, c. 41, s. 46] and 189.1 [en. 1984, c. 41, s. 48].
[2] QSA, s. 198.

2. Defences

§21.76 Both the Ontario and Quebec securities legislation provide for defences in respect of breaches of its insider trading and tipping prohibitions.

§21.77 The OSA provides for certain defences to insider trading, both as to civil liability and to the statutory offences. The first defence is that the person or company in a special relationship reasonably believed that the material fact or material change had been generally disclosed.[1]

[1] OSA, ss. 76(4) and 134(1)(*a*).

§21.78 The second defence to insider trading in Ontario is available where the person or company in a special relationship with a reporting issuer reasonably believed that the other party to the purchase or sale had knowledge of the material fact or material change.[1] In a notable Ontario case, however, the Ontario Court of Appeal appears to set high standards as to how much the other party must know for the defendant insider to be able to rely on this "known to the other party" defence.[2] In that case, an insider of the reporting issuer wrote a letter to the seller of the securities informing him that there were "preliminary discussions" regarding a take-over bid, and that this "conceivably might result in an offer being made".[3] Nevertheless, the Ontario Court of Appeal held that the purchaser-insider was still in possession of specific confidential information and that he had not made adequate disclosure. The court noted that he had not disclosed information as to the "state of the negotiations", as well as the company's earnings.[4] The court did not speculate, however, on exactly how much detail would have been required for the defence to have been available.

[1] OSA, s. 134(1)(*b*) and OSR, s. 175(5)(*a*).
[2] *Green v. Charterhouse Group Canada Ltd.*, [1973] 2 O.R. 677 (H.C.J.), affd 12 O.R. (2d) 280 (C.A.).
[3] 12 O.R. (2d) 280 (C.A.) at 296.
[4] 12 O.R. (2d) 280 (C.A.) at 306.

§21.79 The OSA contains exceptions which apply to the prohibition on insider trading. For example, the OSA provides that a person or company that purchases or sells securities of a reporting issuer with the knowledge of a material fact or a material change relating to the reporting issuer that has not been generally disclosed is exempt from the insider trading prohibition and from civil liability under the OSA, if that person or company proves that:

1. no director, officer, partner, employee or agent of the person or company who made or participated in making the decision to purchase or sell the securities of the reporting issuer had actual knowledge of the material fact or material change; and
2. no advice was given with respect to the purchase or sale of the securities to the director, officer, partner, employee or agent of the person or company who made or participated in making the decision to purchase or sell the securities by a director, partner, officer, employee or agent of the person or company who had actual knowledge of the material fact or the material change.[1]

This exception, however, is not available to an individual who had actual knowledge of the material fact or change.

[1] OSR, s. 175(1).

§21.80 As well, the OSA provides that in determining whether a person or company has sustained the burden of proof under the above noted exception, it is relevant whether and to what extent the person or company has implemented and maintained reasonable policies and procedures to prevent contraventions of a trading prohibition by a person making or influencing investment decisions on its behalf, and to prevent transmission of information concerning a material fact or material change contrary to the tipping prohibition under the OSA.[1]

[1] OSR, s. 175(3).

§21.81 A further exception to insider trading in Ontario is available where a person or company in a special relationship that trades in securities of a reporting issuer with an undisclosed material fact or change proves that the purchase or sale was:

(1) entered into as agent of another person or company pursuant to a specific unsolicited order from that other person or company to purchase or sell; or

(2) made pursuant to participation in an automatic dividend reinvestment plan, share purchase plan or other similar automatic plan that was entered into by the person or company prior to the acquisition of the knowledge of the material fact or material change; or

(3) made to fulfil a legally binding obligation entered into by the person or company prior to the acquisition of knowledge of the material fact or material change.[1]

[1] OSR, s. 175(2).

§21.82 There are four defences which may be used in Ontario as to civil liability and to the statutory offences for tipping. The first defence is available where the person or company in a special relationship with the reporting issuer believed the material fact or material change had been generally disclosed.[1]

[1] OSA, ss. 76(4) and 134(2)(*d*).

§21.83 The second defence is available where the material fact or material change was known or ought reasonably to have been known to the seller or purchaser, as the case may be.[1] As discussed earlier, the *Green* case suggests that there is a very high threshold with respect to how much the other party must know for the defendant insider to be able to rely on this defence.

[1] OSA, s. 134(2)(*e*) and OSR, s. 175(5).

§21.84 The third defence to tipping in Ontario is available where, in the case of an action against a reporting issuer or a person in a special relationship with a reporting issuer, the information was given in the necessary course of business.[1] In *Royal Trustco Ltd. v. OSC*,[2] it was alleged that certain parties had revealed to a major shareholder, other than in the necessary course of business, certain material facts in relation to the affairs of Royal Trustco that had not been generally disclosed, including: (1) that approximately 60% of the shares of Royal Trustco were owned by persons or companies who the parties knew or had reason to believe would not tender pursuant to the bid; and (2) that Royal Trustco management was considering recommending to the board that the dividends payable on the Royal Trustco shares be increased. The court had no difficulty in concluding that the information disclosed fell easily within the category of material facts and that such material facts had been made available to such shareholder not "in the necessary course of business" from Royal Trustco's perspective.

[1] OSA, ss. 76(2) and 134(2)(*f*).
[2] (1983), 42 O.R. (2d) 147 (H.C.).

§21.85 Finally, the fourth defence to the tipping prohibitions is available where, in the case of an action against a person or company that proposes a take-over bid, a combination or an acquisition involving the reporting issuer, the information was given in the necessary course of business to effect the take-over bid, business combination or acquisition.[1]

[1] OSA, ss. 76(3) and 134(2)(*g*).

§21.86 Quebec securities legislation provides two defences in respect of insider trading. These defences may be used against both civil liability based on statutory provisions and statutory offences.

§21.87 The first defence is that the insider is justified in believing that the information is generally known or known to the other party.[1] In light of the Ontario Court of Appeal decision in *Green*, however, which is of some persuasive authority in Quebec, it appears that an insider or an insider-like person must disclose to the other party all potentially relevant details of the privileged information known in order to avail himself or herself of the "known to the other party" aspect of this defence.

[1] QSA, s. 187(1) [re-en. 1987, c. 40, s. 21] and s. 188(1).

§21.88 The second aspect of the "knowledge" defence is that the insider is justified in believing the information to be generally known.

Since information disclosed to the public ceases to be privileged information for the purposes of insider trading, this defence is limited to circumstances where the insider believes the information to be generally known (on reasonable grounds), but is mistaken.

§21.89 There is some doubt as to when information becomes "generally known". Any information fully disclosed in an information or continuous disclosure document or a press release of a reporting issuer would certainly be "generally known". Where, however, information is leaked through unofficial channels and published, and there has been no confirmation by the issuer, the accuracy of the information may still be questionable. In these circumstances it is unclear whether the information is "generally known" for the purposes of the defence.

§21.90 The second statutory defence in respect of insider trading in Quebec is that the insider of the reporting issuer had an automatic plan for the acquisition or sale of securities established before he or she learned of the privileged information.[1] In *Commission des valeurs mobilières du Québec v. Blaikie*,[2] the court held that the word "plan" when used for the purpose of this defence should have its ordinary dictionary meaning. The meaning adopted for that case may be translated from French as "a developed project involving an ordered sequence of transactions done with a view to attaining a goal; a set of steps established for the purpose of executing a project".

[1] QSA, s. 187(2).
[2] [1988] R.J.Q. 1461 (C.S.P.).

§21.91 With respect to the tipping prohibitions, where an insider of a reporting issuer or a tippee discloses privileged information to another party, two defences are available in Quebec securities legislation, both as to civil liability and as to the statutory offence.[1] The first, that the insider or tippee is justified in believing that the information is generally known or known to the party, has been discussed above.[2] The second is that the information was disclosed in the course of business and the insider or tippee had no grounds to believe that it would be used, whether directly or indirectly, in an insider trading transaction or disclosed by the recipient in a manner which would constitute insider tipping.[3]

[1] QSA, s. 188 [am. 1984, c. 41, s. 46].
[2] QSA, s. 188(1).
[3] QSA, s. 188(2) [re-en. 1984, c. 41, s. 46].

§21.92 An insider or tippee of a reporting issuer accused of the statutory offences of insider trading or insider tipping may also raise a third defence, that he or she acted with prudence and diligence or on the basis of reasonable error.[1] The concept of "prudence and diligence" has been discussed above. Although the meaning of "reasonable error" is not entirely clear, it would probably include the situation where the insider reasonably believed that the privileged information was known to the public at the time he or she effected the insider trading transaction or at the time he or she participated in insider tipping.

[1]   QSA, s. 206.

3. Damages and Fines

(a) Damages

§21.93 The OSA provides that an insider trader is liable to compensate the seller or purchaser of the securities for damages incurred as a result of the trade.[1] In addition, the insider trader must remit to the reporting issuer any benefit accruing to the insider from the prohibited transaction.[2] With respect to tipping, the OSA further provides that the insider is liable to compensate for damages any person or company that thereafter sells securities of the reporting issuer, or purchases securities of the reporting issuer from the person or company that received the information.[3] In assessing damages, with respect to insider trading or tipping, the court must consider the price paid or received, as the case may be, by the plaintiff for the security less the average market price of the security in the 20 days following general disclosure of the material fact or material change.[4]

[1]   OSA, s. 134(2).
[2]   OSA, s. 134(1).
[3]   OSA, s. 134(2).
[4]   OSA, s. 134(6).

§21.94 As mentioned earlier, under the QSA, insider trading transactions raise two types of civil liability: (1) liability for the harm suffered by the other party to the transaction; and (2) liability to remit to the reporting issuer any benefit accruing to the insider from the prohibited transaction.

§21.95 The first type of liability raises a number of questions as to the quantum of damages to be paid in respect of the harm suffered by the other party.[1] The time frame in which to measure a rise or fall in the price of the security traded is not clearly established. If, for example, the security is listed on an organized market, it is possible that the market value of the securities could rise over time to equal or exceed the purchase price, in which case there would appear to be no loss. Presumably, however, the damage should be measured on the basis of the drop in market value attributable to the information becoming generally known. The insider, insider-like person or tippee may be held liable for the harm suffered by the other party, whether or not the other person would have acted differently (for example, not bought or sold the security, or bought or sold at a different time) if he or she had knowledge of the privileged information.

[1] QSA, s. 226.

§21.96 The second type of liability, the liability of the insider to account to the reporting issuer for all of the benefit accruing to him or her in respect of the prohibited trade, is a strict liability.[1] It is sufficient that the transaction occurred, privileged information was available and there was a benefit to the insider. There need not be any proof of a detriment to the reporting issuer.

[1] QSA, s. 228.

§21.97 Since Quebec securities legislation allows for recovery both by the reporting issuer and by those who trade with the insider, there is a real possibility of double liability. The question may, however, be moot, since if a damaged third party is successful in his or her suit against the insider, the defendant could argue that he or she did not profit or benefit and thus there is nothing for which to account.

§21.98 Where the transaction involves insider tipping, Quebec securities legislation establishes that the insider is liable for damages caused to (as opposed to the harm suffered by) a third person as a result of a transaction effected with the tippee.[1] It remains unclear whether "damages caused" is intended to have a different meaning than "harm suffered".

[1] QSA, s. 227.

(b) Fines

§21.99 Under the OSA, an insider or tippee who is found guilty of an insider trading offence or an insider tipping offence is liable for a fine that shall not be less than any profit made, or loss avoided, by reason of the contravention and not more than the greater of (a) $1,000,000 and (b) triple the amount of such profit made, or loss avoided.[1] Under the OSA "profit made" means:

(1) the amount by which the average trading price of the security in the 20 trading days following general disclosure of the material fact or material change exceeds the amount paid for the security purchased in contravention of the trading prohibition;

(2) in respect of a short sale, the amount by which the amount received for the security sold in contravention of the trading prohibition exceeds the average trading price of the security in the 20 trading days following general disclosure of the material fact or material change, or

(3) the value of any consideration received for informing another person or company of a material fact or material change with respect to the reporting issuer in contravention of the tipping prohibition.[2]

---

[1] OSA, s. 122. In *Ignac Saliga* (Ontario Securities Commission, Press Release: Re: "Ignac Saliga" (11 June 1992) (1992), 15 O.S.C.B. 2789), a special relationship person of Corby Distilleries Limited was convicted of insider trading. The profit made was about $18,000 and the fine was $36,000.

[2] OSA, s. 122(6).

§21.100 "Loss avoided" means the amount by which the amount received for the securities sold in contravention of the trading prohibition exceeds the average trading price of the security in the 20 trading days following general disclosure of the material fact or the material change.[1]

---

[1] OSA, s. 122(6).

§21.101 Under the QSA, an insider or tippee who is found guilty of an insider trading offence or an insider tipping offence is liable for a maximum fine of the greater of $1,000,000 or four times the profit realizable by the insider (as described below) and a minimum fine of the greater of twice the profit of the insider and $5,000.[1]

---

[1] QSA, s. 204 [re-en. 1987, c. 40, s. 22; am. 1990, c. 4, s. 898; 1992, c. 35, s. 12].

§21.102 Where the insider or tippee who committed the offence traded in a security relying on privileged information, the "profit realizable" generally means the difference between the price at which the initial trade was effected and the average market price of the security in the ten trading days following general disclosure of the information; if the securities are sold within those ten trading days, however, the average market price is replaced by the price actually obtained if it is higher than the average market price.[1] Where the insider communicated privileged information, "profit realizable" means the consideration received for having communicated the information.[2] As well, every senior executive or employee of the principal offender including a person remunerated on commission who authorizes or commits an offence under the QSA is liable to the same penalties as the principal offender.[3]

---

[1] QSA, s. 204 [re-en. 1987, c. 40, s. 22; am. 1990, c. 4, s. 898; 1992, c. 35, s. 12].
[2] QSA, s. 204 [re-en. 1987, c. 40, s. 22; am. 1990, c. 4, s. 898; 1992, c. 35, s. 12].
[3] QSA, s. 205.

4. Statutory Limitation Periods

§21.103 Both the Ontario and Quebec securities legislation provide for statutory limitation periods with respect to actions in damages arising from violations of trading and tipping prohibitions.

§21.104 The OSA provides that unless otherwise provided therein, no action shall be commenced to enforce a right:

(a) in the case of an action for rescission, 180 days after the date of the transaction that gave rise to the cause of action; or
(b) in a case of any action, other than an action for rescission, the earlier of (i) 180 days after the plaintiff first had knowledge of the facts giving rise to the cause of action, or (ii) three years after the date of the transaction that gave rise to the cause of action.[1]

---

[1] OSA, s. 138.

§21.105 In Quebec, an action in damages in respect of insider trading or insider tipping is subject to the same statutory limitation period as that which applies to securities transactions effected without a required prospectus or bid circular.[1] The QSA provides that any action for damages is prescribed by the lapse of one year from knowledge of the facts giving rise to the action, except on proof that tardy knowledge is imputable to the negligence of the plaintiff.[2] However, these prescriptive periods are subordinate to a three-year limitation from the transaction in the case of actions for damages provided for in the tipping and trading prohibitions provisions.[3] The statutory offences are also limited by the same period as the offence for securities transactions effected without the required prospectus or bid circular and securities transactions effected with a document containing a misrepresentation, that is five years from the date that the investigation record relating to the offence was opened.[4]

[1] QSA, ss. 235 and 236 [am. 1990, c. 77, s. 37].
[2] QSA, s. 235.
[3] QSA, s. 236.
[4] QSA, s. 211 [re-en. 1990, c. 77, s. 35].

CHAPTER 22

DEFENSIVE STRATEGIES

A. INTRODUCTION

§22.1 Generally, the first and best defence against any of the liabilities described in the previous two chapters is diligence in discharging each and every one of a director's duties. Due diligence involves, generally, that a director exercise an appropriate degree of supervision and control over management. The final section in Chapter 20 illustrated how this might be done with respect to duties imposed by environmental laws. A director should keep abreast of the corporation's activities and should, to the extent possible, question and ensure its conformity with all statutory requirements. Sometimes, however, this may not suffice to prevent claims or accusations of negligence or other wrongdoing, and other lines of defence should be prepared well in advance.

B. UNANIMOUS SHAREHOLDER AGREEMENT

§22.2 Through a unanimous shareholder agreement, some of the powers and duties normally attributed to the directors of a corporation are transferred to shareholders. With this transfer of responsibilities comes a transfer of the liabilities accompanying them. The corporate statutes provide that directors will therefore be relieved from liability imposed by the statute of incorporation to the extent that such an agreement restricts the directors' management powers in respect of those duties or decisions which have become the shareholders' responsibility. However, the statutes provide little guidance as to how such transfer of responsibility is to operate, except in limited cases.[1] Where, for instance, budget and employment matters have become the province of the shareholders, directors would not as such be liable for unpaid wages.[2] However, in the same case, directors might nonetheless remain liable for amounts such as income tax remittances, even though they have no effective control over expenditures because such a penalty derives from the federal *Income Tax Act*. Most statutes imposing penalties on directors personally do not provide for the exoneration of directors simply because a unanimous shareholder agreement has been ratified. Therefore, whether a director so dispossessed of his or her powers could raise a valid defence to such a penal claim remains to be determined by the courts.

> [1] *Canada Business Corporations Act* ("CBCA"), R.S.C. 1985, c. C-44, s. 146(5); Ontario *Business Corporations Act* ("OBCA"), R.S.O. 1990, c. B.16, s. 108(5); Quebec *Companies Act* ("QCA"), R.S.Q., c. C-38, s. 123.92.
>
> [2] Section 146(5) of the CBCA is explicit as to relief of liability under s. 119. (See also ss. 108(5) and 131 of the OBCA.) Where directors are also shareholders, they could of course be held liable *qua* shareholders. (See also s. 136 of the OBCA.)

§22.3 Unanimous shareholder agreements therefore may not constitute a very effective shield and indeed may be a double-edged sword for the director. A director may still be liable in cases where he or she is powerless to compel the corporation to respect statutory provisions and not in possession of vital information because of the transfer of responsibility to the shareholders.[1] Moreover, a director who is also a shareholder will be liable as a shareholder in any case.

> [1] A defence of due diligence may succeed in such a case, depending on the circumstances.

§22.4 A person should weigh very carefully the pros and cons of accepting an appointment to the Board of Directors of a corporation in which a unanimous shareholder agreement which transfers wide powers from the board has been executed, unless he or she has a shareholder's vote. He or she should certainly ensure that appropriate indemnification measures, such as an indemnification agreement between shareholders and directors, are in place, as well as liability insurance, and keep careful notes of all matters concerning his or her directorship. He or she should continue to monitor as closely as possible the business of the corporation in matters where liability is not removed from the directors' shoulders.[1]

> [1] See *National Banking Law Review*, Vols. 3, 4, 5 (1995) for articles on basic issues in shareholder agreements.

C. INDEMNIFICATION

§22.5 Most incorporating statutes now contain provisions permitting, and in some cases requiring, the indemnification of directors and officers by the corporation and third parties when they are sued for a reason related to the proper exercise of their functions. Under the CBCA and the OBCA, the corporation may indemnify a director or officer with respect to all costs reasonably incurred in the defence of any action or proceeding based on events where the director or officer acted honestly and in good faith with a view to the best interests of the corporation. Thus, a director who successfully demonstrates that he or she acted honestly and lawfully will be indemnified for the cost of his or her defence; a director who is unsuccessful will not be indemnified.

§22.6 More specifically, the CBCA[1] states that the corporation *must* indemnify a director or officer for all reasonable expenses in connection with any civil, criminal or administrative action to which that person is a party as a result of his or her functions as a director or officer of the corporation[2] if that person acted in good faith, had reasonable grounds to believe his or her actions lawful[3] and was substantially successful in his or her defence of the action or proceeding. As mentioned above, the Ontario Court of Appeal in *R. v. Bata Industries Ltd.*[4] overturned the trial judge's prohibition on indemnifying directors who had been found guilty of certain environmental offences but who were not found to have acted in bad faith. Therefore, fulfillment of the statutory criteria concerning indemnification is sufficient for entitlement to it. Similarly, in *Blair v. Consolidated Enfield Corp.,*[5] the director was held to be entitled to indemnification under s. 136(1) of the OBCA since he acted in good faith in the best interests of the corporation in accordance with legal advice. The fact that the decision benefitted the director personally did not detract from the bona fides of the decision.

[1] CBCA, s. 124. The OBCA provisions are very similar to the CBCA ones. See OBCA, s. 136.
[2] CBCA, s. 124. The section's coverage is in fact slightly broader than what is indicated in this summary.
[3] The "reasonable grounds" aspect applies only where criminal and administrative actions are involved.
[4] (1995), 25 O.R. (3d) 321 (C.A.), revg 14 O.R. (3d) 354 (Gen. Div.).
[5] (1993), 15 O.R. (3d) 783 (C.A.), affd (1995), 128 D.L.R. (4th) 73 (S.C.C.).

§22.7 Moreover, the corporation *may* indemnify its director or officer for expenses, including a reasonable settlement, in respect of any proceeding to which he or she is made a party if that person acted honestly and in good faith with a view to the best interests of the corporation and, in the case of penal proceedings, if he or she had reasonable grounds for believing the impugned conduct to be lawful. When the corporation itself sued the officer or director, however, it may only indemnify with the approval of a court. Because of the wording of the sections in the CBCA (and the OBCA), it is probable that the corporation is not permitted to indemnify the director unless the statutory criteria have been met.

§22.8 Different statutory provisions relating to indemnification of directors are found in British Columbia.[1] Under the BCCA, a corporation may, with the approval of the court, indemnify a director if he or she acted honestly and in good faith with a view to the best interests of the corporation. In the case of a criminal or administrative action, the director must also have had reasonable grounds for believing the conduct to be lawful. Further, it is provided that the court may, on application of the corporation or director, make an order approving an indemnity, and the court may make any further order it considers appropriate in the circumstances. There is therefore no statutory indemnification as of right under the BCCA and courts have a broader discretion to do as they think fit. Moreover, statutory indemnification in British Columbia is limited to directors, although indemnification of officers is not expressly prohibited.

[1] British Columbia *Company Act* ("BCCA"), R.S.B.C. 1996, c. 62, s. 128.

§22.9 Provisions similar to those found in the CBCA were adopted in the QCA,[1] although under the latter statute, the company is obliged to assume the defence of an officer or director who is being sued and to indemnify the director or officer for any damages awarded against him or her even if his or her defence to an action or proceeding was unsuccessful, unless that person has committed a grievous offence or a personal offence separable from the exercise of his or her duties. However, in a criminal or penal proceeding, indemnification shall be made only if the director or officer had reasonable grounds to believe that his or her conduct was lawful or if he or she has been freed or acquitted. In addition to the QCA, provisions regarding statutory indemnification in Quebec are also found in the Civil Code, which stipulates that the mandator (the corporation) is bound to reimburse the expenses and charges which the mandatary (a director or officer) has incurred in the execution of the mandate.[2] As well, the mandator is obliged to indemnify the mandatary who is not at fault for losses caused by execution of the mandate.[3]

[1] Sections 123.87 and 123.88 [re-en. 1980, c. 28, s. 14].
[2] C.C.Q., art. 2150.
[3] C.C.Q., arts. 2154 and 2155.

§22.10 It is important to remember that lawsuits against directors or officers may be brought not only by third parties, but also by the corporation itself. As mentioned above, a director or officer sued by the corporation may, with the approval of the court as requested in his or her pleadings, obtain indemnification for the costs of defending such an action, from the corporation if he or she acted in good faith.[1] One situation in which a corporation may wish to sue a director (or former director) is where the director has been hired as an employee while controlling the corporation and has provided excessive compensation for himself or herself, thereby breaching his or her fiduciary duties.

[1] CBCA, s. 124(2); OBCA, s. 136(2). Under s. 123.88 of the QCA, the company will be liable to a director or officer for such costs if it loses its case in whole. In the case of partial victory, it is left to the discretion of the court.

§22.11 Statutory indemnification does not offer complete protection to directors and officers from potential costs and liabilities. However, the CBCA and similar provincial statutes do not prohibit (as some American states do) additional indemnification through the articles, by-laws or contracts.[1] It is therefore considered to be possible to extend protection by way of additional indemnification, absent explicit statutory prohibition. Similarly, officers and directors could seek additional indemnification by way of a contract with one or more shareholders, unless such contracts violated public policy or contravened the statute as set out below.

[1] For instance, California, while Delaware law includes a non-exclusive clause. See L.H. Richard, "La Protection des administrateurs de compagnies" (1989), 35 McGill L.J. 117, at 144.

§22.12 If possible, a director or officer should require, upon election or appointment, that the corporation sign an indemnification contract with him or her. Such an agreement offers a superior protection because it cannot be varied without the director's or officer's approval as can articles and by-laws.

§22.13 However, additional indemnification will not always provide protection to directors or officers against every liability found in every circumstance. Indemnification agreements that go beyond statutory limits will only be valid insofar as the courts hold that they do not violate "public policy".[1] Protection cannot extend to situations explicitly excluded by statute, such as violation of the duties of loyalty and good faith, or the existence of gross negligence.[2] Care should therefore be exercised in drafting such contracts.

[1] L.H. Richard, "La Protection des administrateurs de compagnies" (1989), 35 McGill L.J. 117, at 149.
[2] L.H. Richard, "La Protection des administrateurs de compagnies" (1989), 35 McGill L.J. 117, at 152.

§22.14 The British Columbia statute is specific in limiting the ability of a corporation to indemnify a director. The BCCA states that the provisions of a contract, the memorandum or the articles, or the circumstances of his or her appointment shall not relieve a director from the duty to act in accordance with the Act, or from any liability that by virtue of any rule of law would otherwise attach to him or her in respect of any negligence, default, breach of duty or breach of trust of which he or she may be guilty in relation to the corporation.[1] (As mentioned, the indemnification provisions in the corporate statutes of British Columbia do not relate to officers.)

[1]   BCCA, s. 119.

§22.15   Obviously, the success of indemnification as a mechanism of protection for a director or officer is premised on the corporation's solvency. As it may well be that the reason an individual is pursuing action against a director, such as for non-payment of wages or remittances, is the corporation's financial ill health, indemnification may often be a hollow mechanism. Therefore, if possible, the director should ensure that insurance is in place as described in the next section.

D.   INSURANCE

§22.16   Directors' and officers' liability insurance is another increasingly important means of protection becoming especially necessary where the corporation experiences financial difficulties. Moreover, its coverage is usually broader than that of the statutory indemnification provisions described in the preceding section.

§22.17   Both the CBCA and the OBCA specifically provide that a corporation has the right to purchase and maintain insurance for the benefit of directors or officers against any liability incurred in such capacity, except where such liability relates to failure to act honestly and in good faith with a view to the best interests of the corporation.[1] Insurance may also be purchased by a corporation for the benefit of a person who acts as a director of another corporation (*e.g.*, a subsidiary) at the request of that corporation.[2] Although the QCA does not expressly provide for the purchase of insurance of that nature, certain authors are of the view that a Part 1A corporation can validly take out such insurance under Quebec law especially given the obligatory indemnification of directors acting in good faith.[3]

[1]   CBCA, s. 124(4); OBCA, s. 136(4).
[2]   CBCA, s. 124(4); OBCA, s. 136(4).

³ Martel, Maurice et Paul, *La Compagnie au Québec: Les Aspects juridiques*. Montréal, Wilson & Lafleur, 1994, p. 488.

§22.18 In addition, directors and officers may wish to purchase insurance themselves so as to cover their liability in areas where the company is statutorily barred from providing them with insurance protection or where it elects not to insure them. This also gives them additional assurance that the insurance is maintained when needed.

§22.19 Specific matters of insurance law cannot be covered here but some of the important issues should be noted. Firstly, it is clear that some risks cannot be insured due to public policy considerations and the reluctance of insurers. Exclusions which are standard in directors' and officers' insurance policies include claims arising from dishonest or illegal behaviour, obtaining personal profit, punitive damages, and libel and slander. In addition, such insurance would only cover the acts done by the beneficiary in his or her capacity as a director or officer. The giving of legal advice by a lawyer who also happens to be a director would probably not be covered by such insurance, for example.[1] Moreover, insurance coverage may be unavailable for directors or officers of companies which are considered to be a substantial risk. Insolvency of the corporation may also terminate coverage at a time when it would become most useful. Close attention should always be paid to compliance with ongoing insurance requirements and obligations (such as reporting significant corporate changes) while an insurance policy is in force.

¹ R. McDowell and M. Newton, "Directors' and Officers' Liability Insurance" (1989), 7 Can. J. of Ins. L. 35, at 41.

E. RELIANCE ON EXPERTS

§22.20 Reliance on experts is a statutory defence available to directors in certain circumstances. Section 123(4) of the CBCA provides that a director (but not an officer) will escape liability from certain statutory offences if he or she relies in good faith on financial statements of the corporation represented to him or her by an officer of the corporation or in a written report of the auditor of the corporation, or relies on the report of a lawyer, accountant, engineer, appraiser or other person whose profession lends credibility to his or her statements. However, this exoneration from statutory liability is limited to certain provisions of the CBCA only and therefore does not provide a blanket defence to all liabilities or contraventions of all statutes.[1] In Ontario, exoneration through reliance on experts is limited to general duties of directors vis-à-vis employees.[2]

---

[1]   Under the CBCA, exoneration related to reliance on experts is limited to offences related to ss. 118, 119 and 122 of the CBCA: share issuances, wages and compliance with constituting documents and the Act.

[2]   The OBCA, s. 135(4), limits exoneration to ss. 130 and 134.

§22.21   By demonstrating good faith and reliance on expert advice, a director of a corporation in British Columbia can also avoid liability in various cases,[1] while in Quebec a director who relies on the advice of an expert is presumed to have acted with appropriate skill and care.[2]

---

[1]   S. Hebenton, "Limiting Directors' Liability" (1987), 4 Business & the Law 4.

[2]   QCA, s. 123.84.

§22.22   Directors are not experts in all fields and *must* therefore rely on the advice of specialists when circumstances so require. In fact, failure to consult specialists when needed could be deemed to be a breach of directors' general duties, such as the duty of diligence, prudence and care. However, when outside advice is sought or experts are relied on, the director should ensure that such an expert is qualified to give the advice sought in a relevant discipline, such as law, accounting or engineering.[1] Wainberg suggests several criteria necessary to entitle directors to rely on the advice of experts, such as the expert being independent of the directors; appearing qualified to give advice; and the directors continuing to exercise judgment in addition to relying on the advice given.[2]

---

[1]   Maurice Martel and Paul Martel, *La compagnie au Québec: Les aspects juridiques* (Montréal: Wilson & Lafleur, Martel Ltée, 1990), p. 543.

[2]   J.M. Wainberg and Mark I. Wainberg, *Duties and Responsibilities of Directors in Canada* (Don Mills: CCH, 1987), p. 24.

F.   DILIGENCE

§22.23   Directors' and officers' constant diligence remains their best defence. This requires that they be familiar with the requirements and potential liabilities of their positions and that they take positive steps to comply with their duties and to ensure the compliance of others. Written opinions from legal, accounting and other experts should be requested when important decisions are being made. As well as sometimes providing a statutory defence to a director who relies on such opinions, they also provide proof that a director or officer is properly discharging his or her duties.

§22.24 Directors and officers should also implement appropriate accounting and other control procedures to ensure adequate withholdings and remittances to governmental authorities and others. One author has suggested that in order not to be held personally liable for a corporation's failure to deduct and remit tax to Revenue Canada or other public entities, a director or officer should take the following positive action:

(1) controls should be established to account for withholdings from employees and remittances;

(2) financial officers of the corporation should be required to report regularly on the continued implementation of such controls; and

(3) regular confirmation that withholdings and remittances have been made should be consistently requested on an ongoing basis.[1]

In general, a director should keep well informed of the corporation's business and how the enterprise is faring, especially any financial difficulties. It is when corporations are facing financial difficulties that tax deductions and remittances are most often neglected.[2]

[1] D. Short and M. Eagles, "Directors Beware!" (1989), 6 Business & the Law 73.

[2] T.S. Wach, "Directors' Liability for Taxes" (1989), 6 Business & the Law 3.

§22.25 In general, close attention should be paid to any delegation of powers to officers of the corporation.[1] Directors may be held liable for the acts or omissions of officers or other directors even if the related duties and responsibilities were delegated. As Wainberg writes:

> A director cannot shirk his responsibilities by leaving everything to others. He relies on other directors at his own risk. The reliance on co-directors and officers should [therefore] not be unquestioning.[1]

In the absence of specific grounds for suspicion, a director should, however, be justified in trusting that officers (and co-directors) are honest.[2]

[1] J.M. Wainberg and Mark I. Wainberg, *Duties and Responsibilities of Directors in Canada* (Don Mills: CCH, 1987), p. 20.

[2] *Re City Equitable Fire Ins. Co.*, [1925] Ch. 407 (C.A.); *Soper v. Canada* (1997), 97 DTC 5407 (F.C.A.).

§22.26 A director may avoid liability for a decision to which he or she was not a party but must be diligent to so exculpate him or herself. Under the CBCA and the OBCA, a director is deemed to have participated in a board meeting and to have consented to any resolution if his or her dissent is not recorded in the minutes, even if he or she was absent from the meeting. Reading the minutes of board meetings is therefore imperative and dissent should be duly registered as soon as possible[1] and directors should insist on the speedy distribution of board meeting minutes. In Quebec, although the QCA deems an absent director not to have participated in a meeting, it is prudent to file a formal dissent where a director disagrees with a decision, in order to avoid an appearance of implicit ratification.

[1] Section 123(3) of the CBCA requires that dissent be registered within seven days after the director becomes aware of the resolution. Dissent would probably not diminish liability for unpaid wages: Bruce L. Welling, *Corporate Law in Canada: The Governing Principles*, 2nd ed. (Toronto: Butterworths, 1991), p. 377.

§22.27 In some cases, when a corporation faces financial difficulties, a court may require that it establish a distinct payroll account into which the gross payroll would be deposited, for subsequent disbursement to employees with the difference being remitted to the Crown when due.[1] Even where no court order is sought, it may be appropriate to use a separate bank account for the payment of wages and remittances, in order to segregate those funds. Such steps help to avoid situations where directors' or officers' liability might arise.

[1] In provinces other than Quebec, a trust account would be established for that purpose. The Quebec Civil Code has just introduced the notion of a "trust", into its legal system. Although not the exact analogue of the common law trust, presumably the establishment of such a Quebec trust could accomplish this purpose. Previously, Quebec corporations had to take special care to ensure that, if a separate account were opened in a financial institution which was a creditor of the company, that the institution would agree not to appropriate those funds by means of legal compensation. Preferably, an account should be opened in another institution altogether, such as a trust company. In general, where a company experiences difficulties, agreement should be sought from its bankers that they will honour any cheque for wages or unpaid wages and for remittances, irrespective of the banks' own interest.

§22.28 It bears repeating that directors and officers should ensure that they always act within the scope of their statutory and contractual authority and advance the best interests of the corporation. They should also do everything reasonably possible to ensure that the corporation does not cause illicit damage to third parties and that any third party is aware that it is dealing and contracting with the corporation, and not with the director or officer personally. Directors should not make misstatements to creditors of the corporation about the corporation's financial health to avoid the possibility of a later action based on negligent or fraudulent misrepresentations.

§22.29 Directors and officers should also familiarize themselves with employment-related legal requirements that are of concern to the corporation, such as those of occupational health and safety legislation.[1] In fact, a prudent person would be well advised to inquire into corporate policies in such matters even before accepting an appointment to a board of directors.

> [1] Such concerns may relate to education and training, compliance with safety standards, supervision, etc.; obviously, that area should be even more closely monitored in high-risk fields of activity.

§22.30 What "diligence" actually involves remains difficult to determine precisely and it is a concept which is constantly evolving over time. As statutes and case law impose heavier and heavier demands on directors, proving diligence becomes even more demanding. Directors and officers should be proactive and keep up-to-date with legal trends.

G. CONCLUSION

§22.31 It is imperative that a director be at all times vigilant in his or her supervision of the corporation's activities in order to be able to first detect and (where possible) reduce risks affecting his or her own liability and later to be able to prove due diligence in the performance of his or her duties.

§22.32 An officer's liability to third parties is in general less onerous, unless that person misuses his or her power or opportunities, although more and more provisions of the law are imposing joint and several liabilities on both officers and directors. As officers are often the persons who determine and implement the day-to-day policy of the corporation, they may, however, be more readily found liable in matters such as failure to make income tax remittances or the commission of offences by the corporation and less able to prove due diligence defences.

§22.33 Directors and officers are given the opportunity to achieve substantial personal and corporate success in the business world. With such an opportunity comes important responsibilities and attendant liability. It is not possible for a director or officer to eliminate completely the risk of his or her personal liability in connection with the responsibilities related to employment law and the other areas covered in this book. However, a director's and an officer's knowledge of the extent of his or her responsibilities and due diligence in this regard, together with the implementation of the suggested protective measures can measurably limit and even avoid much of such liability. Hopefully, these chapters, which have briefly summarized and outlined many of the areas in which directors or officers may incur liability, will assist in protecting them from unpleasant surprises.

CHAPTER 23

CORPORATE GOVERNANCE*

A. GENERAL PRINCIPLES

1. Introduction

§23.1 Corporate governance has become a very popular topic in business today. Indeed, both the Toronto Stock Exchange (hereinafter the TSE) and the Montreal Exchange (hereinafter the ME) have adopted listing requirements making it mandatory for listed corporations to disclose their approach to corporate governance on an annual basis, in respect of fiscal years ending on or after June 30, 1995. This new requirement was one of the main recommendations made by the TSE Committee on Corporate Governance in Canada in its report *"Where Were The Directors — Guidelines for Improved Corporate Governance in Canada"*.[1]

---

* The authors wish to thank Mélanie Hébert, student-at-law, for her valuable contribution to this chapter.
[1] Report of the Toronto Stock Exchange Committee on Corporate Governance in Canada (*Guidelines*), December 1994.

§23.2 So what exactly does corporate governance mean? The TSE Committee defines corporate governance as:

> the process and structure used to direct and manage the business and affairs of the corporation with the objective of enhancing shareholder value, which includes ensuring the financial viability of the business. The process and structure define the division of power and establish mechanisms for achieving accountability among shareholders, the board of directors and management. The direction and management of the business should take into account the impact on other stakeholders such as employees, customers, suppliers and communities.[1]

In other words, corporate governance aims at the establishment of an effective decision-making process within a corporation.

---

[1] Report of the Toronto Stock Exchange Committee on Corporate Governance in Canada (*Guidelines*), December 1994, p. 7.

§23.3 This chapter is divided into three major sections: the first section will introduce the general principles of corporate governance, including a brief history of the concept; the second section will describe in detail the recommendations contained in the Recommendations and Guidelines put forward by the TSE Committee (the *"Guidelines"*) and the implementation of these *Guidelines*; the third and final section will provide practical advice to assist a corporation in improving its corporate governance practices.

2. History of the Concept

§23.4 In 1991 the unexpected failure of certain major British (and foreign) companies suddenly raised questions about the workings of the English corporate system. In response to these questions, the Financial Reporting Council, the London Stock Exchange and the accountancy profession in the U.K. set up a committee to address the financial aspects of corporate governance in the United Kingdom. Following its study of corporate governance, the committee established a *"Code of Best Practice"*, directed towards the Board of Directors of all listed companies registered in the United Kingdom.[1] Today, disclosure regarding compliance with the 19 Recommendations included in this *Code* is a listing requirement for the London Stock Exchange.

---

[1] Report of the committee on the *Financial Aspects of Corporate Governance — The Code of Best Practice*, Burgess Science Press, 1992, hereinafter called the "Cadbury Report". For an interesting follow-up to the Cadbury Report, see Brian R. Cheffins, "Corporate Governance in the United Kingdom: Lessons for Canada" (1997), 28 Canadian Business Law Journal 69-106.

§23.5 Similarly, the recent failures of major Canadian companies in the midst of recessionary times (*e.g.*, Campeau, Lavalin, Royal Trustco, Coopérants, Confederation Life), made corporate governance a "hot" topic in Canada. Again, following these failures, questions began to arise from many different sources about the role and effectiveness of directors and management in Canadian business, and how one could re-establish investor confidence in the depressed market. Among the first groups to concretely address the issue of corporate governance in Canada were certain Canadian institutional investors such as la Caisse de dépôt et de placement du Québec (CDPQ), the Pension Investment Association of Canada (PIAC), the Ontario Teacher's Pension Plan Board (OTPPB), and the Ontario Municipal Employees' Retirement System (OMERS). Indeed, from the activism of these large institutional shareholders came the first Canadian guidelines on corporate governance which were specifically directed towards the corporations in which these shareholders habitually invested. These guidelines were aimed at informing these particular corporations of the corporate governance methods which these investors considered necessary for the corporations to implement, such as, for example, particular rules respecting proxy voting.

§23.6 Later, in the summer of 1993, the TSE, with the goal of improving investor confidence in the capital market, sponsored a committee to provide an in-depth evaluation of the state of corporate governance in Canada and to make recommendations for improvement. It is of note that, following its study, the Committee was of the opinion that with more effective governance, the risk of these failures and the magnitude of the losses that occurred would have been significantly reduced.[1] In December 1994, the Committee released a report containing 14 specific *Guidelines* for improved corporate governance (sometimes referred to as the Dey Report). On February 23, 1995, the TSE Board of Governors adopted the recommendation that Canadian corporations listed on the TSE annually disclose their approach to corporate governance. The Montreal Stock Exchange adopted similar measures soon after.

[1] Report of the Toronto Stock Exchange Committee on Corporate Governance in Canada (*Guidelines*), December 1994, p. 1.

§23.7 Response to the TSE report has been generally favourable. On March 8, 1995, *The Globe and Mail* (Toronto) reported the results of a survey done on 52 corporations and prepared by the firm of Ernst & Young, which solicited their reaction to the *Guidelines*. The only recommendation which received the support of less than 70% of the polled corporations was that which recommended that the Nominating Committee be composed solely of outside directors. All of the other guidelines received more than 70% approval. The survey also revealed that, although many of the guidelines were already company policy, many were not in place in these corporations. Among the recommendations of the guidelines which did not appear to have been implemented by most corporations were the following: the composition of the Nominating Committee, the existence of an evaluation process for directors, constitution of a Committee on Corporate Governance, description of a director's functions, nomination of an independent Chairman of the Board, and regular meetings of the Board without management. The report does, however, have its detractors. Donald H. Thain in an article in the *Business Quarterly* of Autumn 1994, in response to a draft of the guidelines circulated in 1994 (which differs in certain ways from the final report), felt that the report failed to recognize the seriousness of the problems involved and "falls short of recommendations that promise any significant improvements for shareholders". However, Thain did feel that the TSE report would stimulate an "interesting and worthwhile dialogue" on the important issue of corporate governance.

Appointing, training and monitoring the performance of senior management:

The key to this responsibility is the appointment of the best CEO for the job. The Board should ensure that the CEO's performance be measured against criteria established by the Board and the CEO, and that the CEO's remuneration be reviewed against such criteria.

Ensuring the highest calibre of management through appointment, training, assessment and providing for succession must be a priority of the Board. In addition, the Board must ensure that adequate training programs, both within and outside the corporation, are offered to management. Finally, the Board must ensure that specific criteria are established against which management's performance can be measured.

Communication policy:

The Board must also ensure that an effective communication policy is in place between the corporation and its shareholders, other stakeholders and the public. As specified by the TSE Committee, an effective policy must "interpret the operations of the corporation to shareholders and must accommodate feedback from shareholders".

Implementation and maintenance of effective control systems and information systems:

The Board must ensure that an effective self-evaluation control system is in place to make sure the Board has met all its responsibilities.

Analysis of the TSE view of the Board's responsibilities clearly indicates that the Board's duty is not the day-to-day running of the corporation. Rather, its principal function is to supervise the overall management of the business.[2]

---

[1] This section summarizes and quotes from recommendations in the *Guidelines* found at pp. 17 and 18.

[2] The Canadian Institute of Chartered Accountants has prepared its own series of recommendations for directors, focusing on the role of the board of directors as a control mechanism charged with overseeing management. Their report, "Guidance for Directors — Governance Processes for Control", addresses all facets of an organization's control mechanisms put in place to ensure the proper realization of any given objective, be it regarding financial information, conformity with laws and regulations, or efficiency of the organization in general.

§23.11 (b)   The composition of the Board of Directors:[1]

Bearing in mind the heavy responsibilities imposed upon a Board of Directors, it is clear that the composition of the Board and the process used to constitute it are central to an effective governance system. In appointing its Board of Directors, a corporation should pay attention to the following six factors:

(i) The composition of the Board:

The main goal is to establish a Board which is both capable and perceived as being capable of exercising independent judgment. To achieve this task, the Board should be composed of a majority of individuals who are "unrelated" or "independent" of management. To be considered "unrelated" or "independent", a director must be:

> ... a director who is independent of management and is free from any business or other relationship which could, or could reasonably be perceived to, materially interfere with the director's ability to act with a view to the best interests of the corporation, other than interests and relationships arising from shareholding.

Accordingly, former or actual employees, members of management or their relatives and people having an economic link with the corporation are not "unrelated".

The definition of an "unrelated or independent director" is not to be confused with the concept of "outside director" which is found in Canadian corporate law. An outside director can either be an unrelated director or a related director. For example, a representative of a minority shareholder of a corporation who is not employed or is not part of management of such corporation will be considered as an outside director and an unrelated director since he or she is independent of management and his or her relationship with the corporation is the result of a relationship arising from shareholding. However, a lawyer, whose firm provides services on a continuous basis to a corporation, will be an outside director, but may be considered as a related director depending on the level of his or her firm's economic relationship with the corporation. An unrelated director will not always be an outside director. For example, the CEO or vice-president of a corporation which is a significant shareholder holding in excess of 51% of the shares who is not employed or part of management of the corporation listed on the TSE could be an unrelated director but would not be an outside director since he or she is employed by the parent corporation, an affiliate of the Canadian subsidiary. As seen above, in the example of the lawyer whose firm provides legal services to the corporation, a related director can sometimes be an outside director.

If the corporation has a significant shareholder, the Board should include not only a majority of "unrelated" directors, but should also include directors who are independent from both the corporation and the significant shareholder. The TSE Committee defines a significant shareholder as "a shareholder with the ability to exercise a majority of the votes for the election of directors attached to the outstanding shares of the corporation". Thus, for example, if a significant shareholder owns two-thirds of the corporation's shares and the Board is composed of nine directors, at least five of those directors should be unrelated to the corporation and at least three should be unrelated to the corporation and to the significant shareholder.

The Board must determine which directors are unrelated and disclose annually the composition of the Board, indicating which Board members are unrelated, along with an explanation of the application of the principles supporting this conclusion. To assist in this determination, the TSE report contains examples of its interpretation of what is an unrelated director or related director. For example, an officer of one of the corporation's lenders might not be regarded as unrelated because of the interest he or she might have in protecting his or her employer's loan. The former CEO of a corporation would probably not be considered unrelated until an appropriate period of time had passed.

Before turning to the size of the Board, one should note, as did the TSE Committee, that having a majority of unrelated directors on a Board is no guarantee of independent judgment.

(ii) The size of the Board:

The effectiveness of the Board can be influenced by its size. Obviously, there are no fixed numbers that suit all circumstances, since each corporation is different. Therefore, each Board should review its size to determine the impact of the number of directors on effectiveness and, if necessary, undertake to reduce the number of directors in order to maximize effectiveness.[2] Conversely, certain Boards could benefit from an expansion in order to gain a wider range of expertise and experience.

(iii) The nomination of directors:

The Board of Directors must establish a set of criteria which nominees to the Board must meet. Naturally, these criteria will vary from Board to Board. The Board may appoint a Nominating Committee "... composed exclusively of outside directors, a majority of whom are unrelated directors, with the responsibility for proposing new nominees to the Board and for assessing directors on an ongoing basis". The delegation of this primary nomination and assessment responsibility is meant to limit any real or perceived concern about control over the appointment of nominees to the Board by, for example, a significant shareholder or the CEO. The Nominating Committee would use the criteria established by the Board to guide its decisions. During this process, the CEO should be consulted. Once the new candidates are identified, the Nominating Committee would report its recommendations to the full Board, which is responsible for all final decisions regarding nominations.

(iv) Director's development:

To improve the effectiveness of each individual director, a corporation should have in place an orientation and education program for its new directors which explains the business activities of the corporation, its strategy, relevant problems and questions, and the corporation's expectations of its directors. The TSE Committee also supported the development of external courses to educate directors on their responsibilities and effective corporate governance.

(v) Assessing the Board's performance:

Every Board of Directors should implement, at a minimum, an annual assessment of the effectiveness of the Board, of the different committees of the Board, of the CEO, and of the individual directors. This assessment can be carried out by the Nominating Committee or such other committee as the Board deems appropriate. The method of assessment should be fashioned to suit the needs of the corporation, but should include a discussion by the entire Board and a review with management.

(vi) Remuneration of directors:

Every Board should review the adequacy and form of directors' compensation and ensure that the compensation realistically reflects the responsibilities and risks involved in being an effective director. In conducting this review, the Board should be cognizant of the fact that excessive remuneration may raise questions about a director's dependence on the position and his or her ability to provide an independent view. Conversely, token remuneration may promote a tendency to think that the position is not to be taken seriously.

[1] This section is found at pp. 24-33 of the *Guidelines*.
[2] The TSE Committee recommends that a Board be composed of ten to 16 directors.

§23.12 (c) The functioning of the Board:

The functioning of the Board of Directors is also an important aspect of a good corporate governance practice. To function adequately and improve its effectiveness, the Board must, among other things, delegate some of its functions to committees and ensure their independence.

(i) The Committees:

Committees of the Board of Directors should be composed of outside directors (directors who are neither officers nor employees of the corporation or its affiliates), a majority of whom are unrelated directors.[1] However, it may be desirable to have one or more inside directors on certain committees, such as an executive committee.

In this section, rather than identifying possible committees, particular functions performed by the Board which can be delegated to Board committees will be highlighted.

Developing the corporation's approach to governance issues:

As was seen above, the Board has a responsibility to develop the corporation's approach to corporate governance. This function could easily be delegated to a "Governance Committee". This committee could propose necessary changes to the Board of Directors in response to the TSE Committee's governance *Guidelines* and could provide an explanation for any deviation from those *Guidelines*. In addition, this committee could also provide a forum for concerns of individual directors about topics that are not discussed in a full Board meeting. Such topics could include "the performance of management, or members of management or the performance of the Board or individual members of the Board".

Relationship of the Board to management:

To clarify the relationship between the Board of Directors and management, the Board, together with the CEO, should develop job descriptions for both Board members and the CEO. These descriptions should include corporate objectives which the Board expects the CEO to meet and the limits of management responsibility. This function could certainly be delegated to a committee of the Board, always reserving subsequent Board approval.

The Audit Committee:

This committee should only be composed of outside directors. The TSE Committee endorsed a recommendation made in one of the submissions concerning the functions of this committee as follows:

> The roles and responsibilities of the audit committee should be specifically defined so as to provide appropriate guidance to audit committee members as to their duties. The audit committee should have direct communication channels with the internal and external auditors to discuss and review specific issues as appropriate. The audit committee duties should include oversight responsibility for management reporting on internal control. While it is management's responsibility to design and implement an effective system of internal control, it would be the responsibility of the audit committee to ensure that management has done so.

(ii) The Board's independence:

The Board of Directors should implement procedures and develop structures to ensure that it operates independently of management. In order to promote this objective, the Board should either appoint a chair who is not a member of management or adopt alternate means to achieve the same goal.

The chair of the Board is responsible for setting the agenda. In so doing, he or she must make certain that all the necessary information needed to deal with issues on the agenda is provided to each individual director. In addition, to ensure that all the needed information is available, the Board should implement a system which enables an individual director to engage outside advisors, at the expense of the corporation, in appropriate circumstances. To prevent abuse, the engagement of an outside advisor should be subject to the approval of an appropriate committee of the Board.

[1] Pages 39-42 of the *Guidelines.*

3. Implementation of the TSE Committee's *Guidelines*

(a) Compliance with the disclosure requirement

§23.13 As mentioned above, the TSE and the ME require listed Canadian corporations to disclose in the annual report or information circular of the corporation for each fiscal year ending on or after June 30, 1995 their system of corporate governance with reference to the *Guidelines* set out in the TSE Report and similar guidelines adopted by the ME, and to explain any differences between the company's system and the *Guidelines*. This corporate governance report should address at least the following points:[1]

- The mandate of the Board, including its duties and objectives.
- The composition of the Board: whether the Board has a majority of unrelated directors and the basis for this analysis; if the company has a significant shareholder; whether the composition of the Board reflects the investment of minority shareholders in the corporation and the basis for this analysis.
- If the Board does not have a chair separate from management, the structures and processes which are in place to facilitate the functioning of the Board independently of management.
- Description of the Board committees, their mandates and their activities.
- Description of the decisions requiring prior approval by the Board.
- Procedures in place for recruiting new directors and other per-

formance-enhancing measures, such as assessment of Board performance.
- Measures for receiving shareholder feedback and measures for dealing with shareholder concerns.
- The Board's expectations of management.

¹ TSE Company Manual, Part IV, Section M, ME Policy I-15.

§23.14 To date, the disclosure requirement applies only to corporations incorporated under Canadian law whose shares are listed on the TSE or the ME.

(b) Non-compliance with the disclosure requirement

§23.15 It should be emphasized that the disclosure requirement does not mandate compliance with the *Guidelines*. However, there are three possible consequences which may result from a corporation's non-compliance with the disclosure requirement: i) ordering a temporary halt to trading in listed securities of the corporation; ii) a suspension; iii) withdrawal of the listing. Even though these sanctions exist, it is highly unlikely that the TSE or the ME would use such drastic measures. Indeed, the TSE Committee aims, in its report, to improve corporate governance in Canadian corporations without increasing the legislation to which Canadian corporations are subject. In fact, the TSE report does not purport to change the principal Canadian legislation on corporations. Instead, the *Guidelines* proposed by the TSE Committee establish a standard against which shareholders may evaluate the effectiveness of the Board of Directors.

C. PRACTICAL ADVICE

§23.16 The purpose of this section is to provide practical steps and procedures to help the Board of Directors to assess its present governance system and to comply with the new listing requirement on corporate governance.

1. Steps to be taken by the Chairman

§23.17 The following steps should be considered:

- *Provide a copy of the TSE Report or an executive summary of the Report to each member of the Board with a request that each Board mem-*

ber become familiar with the guidelines for improved corporate govern-ance contained in the TSE Report.

The TSE Report provides a comprehensive analysis of corporate governance issues in Canada as well as a detailed summary to the statutory liabilities of directors under Canadian law. It also contains suggested guidelines to improve corporate governance and the effectiveness of the Board of Directors.

- *Put corporate governance and the guidelines for improved corporate governance contained in the TSE Report on the agenda of the next Board meeting(s).*

  Consider inviting a senior officer or an expert in these matters (general counsel, for example) to such Board meeting to make a presentation as to the practical implications and principal rec-ommendations of the TSE Report.

- *Consider setting up a committee that will examine and report to the Board on corporate governance issues.*

  The TSE Report recommends that such a committee be com-posed exclusively of outside directors.

  The Committee's mandate could consist of:

  — a review of current corporate governance practices of the Corporation;
  — a comparison of such practices with the *Guidelines* and ex-planation of the differences;
  — initially making recommendations in a preliminary report to the Board as to amendments or improvements that should be implemented by the Board and providing a real-istic timetable to implement such changes;
  — preparing the required disclosure in the annual report or in-formation circular for approval by the Board;
  — defining its ongoing role as a permanent committee of the Board.

- *Fix a reasonable timetable for the Committee to make a preliminary re-port to the Board.*

  Such deadline could be tied to the end of the fiscal year and the preparation of the annual report and proxy materials.

2. Steps to be taken by the Committee

§23.18 In order to fulfil its mandate, the Committee should consider the following steps:

(a) *Examine and assess the constitution and the duties of the Board.* Consider the following:

(i) Constitution

- How many unrelated directors are on the Board?
- If there is a significant shareholder, who represents the minority shareholders?
- What is the size of the Board? Is it too big or too small?

(ii) Duties

- What are the duties and responsibilities of the Board?
- The Committee should, in its preliminary report to the Board, describe its current mandate, *i.e.*, to describe the current duties and responsibilities of the Board of the corporation and its constitution, to explain the differences with the above *Guidelines*, and to make appropriate recommendations should changes be deemed appropriate in light of such guidelines.

(b) *Look at how comparable companies within the corporation's industry, including in the U.S., have dealt with similar corporate governance issues.*

- Certain corporations are publishing their Board Guidelines on corporate governance issues.

(c) *Review and consider the principles and guidelines adopted by major Canadian institutional investors such as, for example, the corporate governance guidelines published in October 1994 by Caisse de dépôt et placement du Québec.*

- Such guidelines will express their views on acceptable corporate governance practices for companies in which they invest. As a general rule, although differences exist, the principal recommendations contained in the TSE Report have been endorsed by such institutional investors.

(d) *Prepare and deliver a yearly report to the Board which will be substantially included in the annual report or information circular and which will address the following points with reference to the Guidelines in the TSE Report.*

- mandate of the Board, which should set forth duties and objectives;
- the composition of the Board, whether the Board has a majority of unrelated directors and the basis for this analysis; if the corporation has a significant shareholder whether the corporation satisfied the requirement for fairly reflecting the investment of minority shareholders in the corporation and the basis for this analysis;
- if the Board does not have a chair separate from management, the structure and processes which are in place to facilitate the functioning of the Board independently of management;
- description of the Board committees, their mandates and their activities;
- description of decisions requiring prior approval by the Board;
- procedures in place for recruiting new directors and other performance-enhancing measures, such as assessments of Board performance;
- measures for receiving shareholder feedback and measures for dealing with shareholder concerns; and
- the Board's expectations of management.

D. CONCLUSION

§23.19   The TSE study and report found that major changes were necessary to improve the state of corporate governance in Canada. It is to be hoped that Canadian corporations will take this report seriously and adopt strategies to implement the changes that the TSE felt were necessary. The 14 *Guidelines* in the TSE report provide an excellent beginning for a corporation seeking to establish its own corporate governance policy. Hopefully, these *Guidelines* will be adopted and adapted by many major Canadian corporations over the next few years. The Conference Board of Canada published a report on the corporate governance practices of 200 companies, entitled *Canadian Director Practices 1995: A New Era in Corporate Governance*. The report found that while many companies were conforming with the *Guidelines*' recommendations on unrelated directors, there was "some work to do" in areas such as the nomination of new directors, ensuring independence from management, ongoing assessment of the Board and the chief executive officer, and basic orientation and training. Further, it is clear that changes in the area of corporate law may be necessary to harmonize the duties and responsibilities set out in corporate statutes with those in the securities legislation. Even now the federal government is looking towards amending the *Canada Business Corporations Act*[1] and one of the areas which it will be analyzing is the whole subject of corporate governance.

[1]   R.S.C. 1985, c. C-44.

§23.20   It is quite possible that real improvement in corporate governance may come from the influence of a wholly non-governmental and non-legislative source. Major Canadian institutional investors seem more and more willing to exert their considerable influence upon the Boards of Directors of corporations in which they propose to invest (or on the corporation as a whole) to require them to implement sound corporate governance policies. The reason is simple and pragmatic: these investors wish to place their money in well-governed corporations. As mentioned, before the TSE report was published, some institutional investors had already requested that certain targeted corporations follow a recommended approach to corporate governance. There is every reason to believe that corporations will pay attention to the recommendations of these investors.

§23.21   There is still much work to be done in this area but several excellent initiatives to improve Canadian corporate governance are under way. Only time will tell how well these measures succeed in reaching their common goal.

INDEX

(References are to paragraph numbers.)

A

Authority and responsibilities
    constructive dismissal, changes amounting to, 6.19-6.22
    work provided by employer, 6.15-6.22

B

"Ball Park" doctrine, 12.68-12.69
Benefits, employment. *See* Remuneration; Tax considerations
Breach of employment contract. *See* Employment contract; Written
    employment contract

C

Confidentiality. *See* Loyalty; Written employment contract
Constructive dismissal
    changes amounting to, 6.19-6.22
        authority and responsibilities, 6.6; 6.9; 12.77
        corporate downsizing, 6.18
        generally, 6.4-6.14; 6.19-6.22
        hostile work environment, 6.36
        modification of remuneration, 7.9-7.15
        reduction of salary or benefits, 6.8; 7.11; 12.74
        removal of tools, materials, equipment and space, 6.37-6.39
        removal of work, 6.13-6.14; 6.22
        reporting structure, 6.10-6.12; 6.19-6.21; 12.83
    duties and responsibilities, 12.77-12.82
    employer conduct, 12.91
    generally, 12.70-12.73
    geographical transfer, 12.85-12.90
    remuneration and benefits, 6.8; 7.9-7.15; 12.74-12.76; *See also*
        Remuneration
    sale of undertaking, 6.11.1
    status, 12.83-12.84
Contract of employment. *See* Employment contract
Contract, law of; *See also* Employment contract

Roman origins, 1.14-1.16
Copyright, 10.130-10.139
Corporate executives. *See also* Corporate governance
   civil law obligations of, 1.12
   custom and obligations of, 1.57-1.64
   defensive strategies for. *See* Defensive strategies
   defined, 1.8
   early notions of, 1.32-1.33
   loyalty. *See* Loyalty
   master and servant, as, 1.65-1.67
   power of, 1.4; 1.47-1.50
   role in law —
      civil law, 1.42-1.46
      common law, 1.40-1.41.1
      within employer's organization, 9.4-9.5
   safety of. *See* Health and safety
   security legislation, liability under. *See* Securities legislation liability
   "Usage" and, 1.60-1.64
   work, obligation to execute. *See* Work, execution of
Corporate governance
   changes, implementation, issues, 23.19-23.21
   defined, 23.2
   generally, 23.1-23.3
   historical background, 23.4-23.7
   present systems, assessment, 23.17-23.18
   Toronto Stock Exchange Committee —
      guidelines, board of directors
         composition, 23.11
         functioning, 23.12
         implementation, disclosure requirements, 23.13-23.15
         responsibilities, 23.10
         scope, 23.9
      recommendations, 23.8
Corporations
   limited liability joint-stock companies, 1.27-1.31
   New France, development in, 1.20-1.26
Curriculum vitae
   employee representation, 3.28; *See also* Just cause—dishonesty

D

Damages. *See* Wrongful dismissal
Defensive strategies
   diligence, 22.23-22.31

generally, 20.192-20.196
indemnification, 22.5-22.15
insurance, 22.16-22.19
reliance on experts, 22.20-22.22
unanimous shareholder agreement, 22.2-22.4
vigilance, 22.31
Dignity, 8.43
Directors. *See* Duties and liabilities of directors and officers
Disability
benefits received during, 16.52
deductibility from wrongful dismissal award, 16.52-16.53.6
just cause, 9.52-9.54
tacit renewal during, 9.58
termination during, 9.55-9.57; 9.59
Dismissal. *See* Constructive dismissal; Termination; Wrongful
dismissal
Duties and liabilities of directors and officers. *See also* Corporate
governance
Civil Code, amendments to, 20.106-20.107
criminal liabilities —
aiding and abetting, 20.207-20.208
falsifying books or documents, 20.223
forging trademarks, 20.221
fraud, 20.217
gaming in stocks or merchandise, 20.220
generally, 20.205-20.206
secret commissions, 20.209-20.211
stocks, offences concerning, 20.212-20.216; 20.220
theft, 20.218-20.219
trade unions, activities concerning, 20.222
defensive strategies. *See* Defensive strategies
directors —
concept of, 20.11-20.16
duties of —
civil law definition, 1.37-1.39; 10.1
common law definition, 1.34-1.36
independent directors and liability, 20.17-20.19
general principles, 20.1-20.10
inducement to breach contract, liability for, 20.103-20.105
legal duties —
exercise of care, diligence and skill —
Civil Code, 20.30, 20.35
generally, 20.29-20.30
standards of, 20.31-20.35

fairness to shareholders and creditors, 20.36-20.38
fiduciary —
   conflicts of duty and interest, 20.43-20.46
   generally, 20.39-20.42
   misappropriating corporate opportunities, 20.47-20.49.1
  framework, 20.25-20.28
liabilities towards employees —
  directors' liability for wages —
   creditors, employees as, 20.60-20.68
   debtor, 20.53-20.59.1
   debts claimable —
    alternate liability, 20.93-20.94
    golden parachutes, 20.79-20.92
    joint and several liability, 20.95
    statutory limitation periods, 20.96-20.99
    termination and severance payments, 20.77
    types of remuneration, 20.67-20.77
   generally, 20.51-20.52
   wrongful dismissal, 20.100-20.102
officers, 20.20-20.24
penal liabilities —
  areas of risk —
   competition law, 20.172-20.174
   discrimination, 20.167
   environmental law —
    due diligence defence, 20.197-20.204
    implementation of, 20.184-20.191
    importance of, 20.175-20.177
    prohibitions, 20.178-20.183
   immigration, 20.168
   occupational health, 20.169-20.171
  defences to —
   due diligence, 20.197-20.204
   general principles, 20.192-20.196
  generally, 20.160-20.162
  persons at risk, 20.163-20.166
securities legislation, under. *See* Securities legislation liability
shareholders, liability to —
  excess executive compensation, 20.114-20.137
  general rules, 20.109-20.113
statutory liabilities —
  income and other tax legislation, 20.139-20.148
  miscellaneous common law liabilities, 20.156-20.159
  pension plans, 20.154

statutory health insurance, 20.150-20.153
employment insurance, 20.149
wrongful dismissal liability, 20.100-20.102

E

Employee
identifying —
director or officer, 4.40-4.41
partner, 4.39
shareholder, 4.42
immigration. *See* Immigration
liability in tort for incompetence or non-performance, 15.17-15.19
obligations —
execute the work. *See* Work, execution of
loyalty. *See* Loyalty
mobility. *See* Place of work
Employer
authority to represent, 4.43-4.46
duty of care —
health and safety, 8.2
hiring process, 5.13-5.15
identifying —
companies with same administration, 4.16-4.22
employees on loan, 4.24-4.32
generally, 4.14
joint venture, 4.35-4.36
limited partnership, 4.33-4.34
personnel agencies, 4.23
seconding agreements, 4.24-4.32
third party control, 4.23
liability —
deductions. *See* Duties and liabilities
harassment. *See* Harassment
wrongful dismissal. *See* Wrongful dismissal
obligations —
provide a safe workplace. *See* Health and safety; Harassment
provide remuneration. *See* Remuneration
provide the work. *See* Work, provision of
Employment
defined, 1.09
elements, 4.3-4.13
remuneration, 4.6-4.7
subordination, 4.8-4.13

work for another, 4.3-4.5
historical analysis, 1.14 *et seq.*
immigration, 17.24-17.26
jurisdictional issues, 2.1-2.3
termination of. *See* Termination; Wrongful dismissal
Employment contract
  breach of by executive —
    acceptance of repudiation by employer, 15.15-15.16
    damages for premature resignation, 15.3-15.14
    liability in tort, 15.17-15.19
    profits and expenses wrongfully acquired, 15.20-15.21.1
  Civil Code, article 1024, 1.12; 1.54-1.60; 8.6; 10.89; 13.50; 20.23
  content —
    generally, 3.36-3.37
    policies and manuals, 3.13-3.18
  duration —
    fixed-term contract —
      automatic renewal clause, 6.49-6.50
      premature termination, 6.47.01; 6.47.1
      project, 6.46
      renewal during sick leave or disability, 9.58
      tacit renewal, 6.51-6.54
      termination of, employer liability, 12.41; 13.4-13.5
    generally, 6.42
    indeterminate contract —
      termination of, employer liability, 12.42; 13.6-13.7
    principles, 6.42-6.48
    term contract —
      automatic renewal clause, 6.49
      tacit renewal, 6.51-6.54
  enterprise, contract of, 4.11
  European origins, 1.17-1.19
  executive, and, 1.51-1.53
  formation of —
    consent, defects in —
      duress/undue influence, 3.33
      fraud, 3.26-3.32
      mistake/error, 3.21-3.25
      unconscionability, 3.34
      violence, 3.35
    consideration —
      negotiated terms, 3.7-3.12
      non-negotiated terms, 3.13-3.18
    content, 3.36-3.37

intention to create legal relationship, 3.19

introduction, 3.1

offer and acceptance, 3.2-3.6

pre-employment representations —

  employee misrepresentations, 3.26-3.31

  employer obligation not to mislead, 3.32; 5.5-5.20

proper law of —

  Civil Code, 2.7-2.9

  common law, 2.10-2.11

  constitutional law principles, 2.14-2.20

  generally, 2.4-2.6

  pensions, 2.13

  statutory requirements, 2.12

remuneration. *See* Remuneration

repudiation. *See* Termination

requirements of formation, 1.9-1.10

retirement income. *See* Retirement income provisions

taxation. *See* Tax considerations

termination. *See* Termination

validity, 3.2-3.19

  consideration, 3.7-3.12

  intent, 3.19

  offer and acceptance, 3.2-3.6

void or voidable, 3.20-3.35

  defects in consent, 3.20-3.35

    duress, 3.33-3.35

    error, 3.21-3.25

    fraud, 3.26-3.32

    mistake, 3.21-3.25

    unconscionability, 3.33-3.35

written. *See* Written employment contract

Employment law

  jurisdiction, 2.1-2.21

    Civil Code, 2.7-2.9

    common law, 2.9-2.11

    constitutional law, 2.14-2.21

    private international law, 2.4-2.13

  sources, 2.22-2.31

    case law, 2.30

    doctrine, 2.31

    legislation, 2.23-2.29

      Civil Code, 2.23-2.24

      statutes, 2.25-2.29

        health and safety, 2.28

human rights, 2.27
labour standards, 2.26
workers' compensation, 2.29
Environmental law liability
due diligence defence, 20.197-20.204
implementation of, 20.184-20.191
importance of, 20.175-20.177
prohibitions, 20.178-20.183
Execute the work. *See* Work, execution of
Executives. *See also* Corporate executives
role —
defined, 1.8, 1.40-1.46
distinguished from employee, 1.45
generally, 1.20
practically, 1.47-1.50
within employer's organization, 9.4-9.5

F

Fiduciary duty. *See* Duties and liabilities of directors and officers;
Loyalty
Free Trade Agreement, immigration exception, 17.41-17.47

G

Golden parachute
agreement —
advantages of, 11.75-11.79
criticism of, 11.80
elements of —
change in control, 11.70-11.71
loss of employment or resignation for good reason, 11.72-11.74
enforceability of, 11.87
judicial scrutiny of, strategy for surviving —
alternative employment, obligation to search for, 11.95
origin of proposal, 11.93
relationship to services performed, 11.94
timing, 11.92
taxing provisions re —
Canada, in, 11.90
U.S.A., in, 11.88-11.89
as claimable debt, 20.93-20.94
compensation —
business judgment rule, 11.82

fiduciary duty, 11.83-11.86
directors' and officers' liability, 20.81-20.92

H

Harassment
  defined, 8.27-8.29
  employer liability, 8.34-8.38
  health and safety, 8.34
  just cause, 8.40
  personal relations, 8.41-8.42
  prohibited forms (examples), 8.31-8.34
  sexual, 8.28-8.42.1
Health and safety, 2.28;
  employer's obligation to provide —
    duty of care, 8.2
    generally, 8.1-8.4
    legal basis, 8.5-8.26
    statutory basis, 8.13-8.26
      due diligence defence, 8.20-8.26
      employee's duties, 8.15
      employer's duties, 8.12
      generally, 8.11
      officer's and supervisor's duties, 8.14
      strict liability, 8.18-8.25
    vicarious liability, 8.7-8.10
      Civil Code basis, 8.10
      common law basis, 8.7-8.9
Human rights, 2.27
  hiring phase, 5.2-5.4

I

Immigration
  admissibility to Canada, 17.19-17.21
  employment —
    authorization requirement, 17.27-17.33
      exceptions to, 17.30-17.33
    "employment" defined, 17.24-17.26
    validation requirement. *See infra*, validation requirement
  generally, 17.1-17.4.1
  passport requirements, 17.22
  penal liability re, 20.168
  permanent residence in Canada —

    family class, 17.58-17.59
    independent applicants —
       entrepreneurs, 17.63-17.65
       generally, 17.60-17.62
       investors, 17.66-17.72
          government-administered venture capital fund, 17.71
          privately administered investment syndicate, 17.70
          Quebec, in, 17.72
       maintaining, 17.76-17.78
       overview, 17.51-17.55
       persons with arranged employment in Canada, 17.73-17.75
       Quebec, in, 17.56-17.57
    responsibilities of Canadian employer, 17.5-17.9
    right to enter and remain, 17.10
    validation requirement, 17.34-17.50
      selected exceptions — 17.45-17.47
        intra-company transferees, 17.39-17.47
          Free Trade Agreement, 17.41-17.47
        professional category, 17.48-17.50
    visa requirements, 17.16-17.18
    visitors vs. immigrants, 17.10-17.15
Indemnification, 22.5-22.15
Independent contractor
    defined, 4.10-4.13
    loyalty, 10.50-10.53
    taxation, 18.11-18.15
Insider trading. *See* Securities legislation liability
Insurance, 22.16-22.19

J

Just Cause
    defined, 12.22-12.23
    employer recourses. *See* Employment contract, breach by executive
    evaluation of —
       condonation, 12.39-12.40
       corporate culture, 9.31; 9.36-9.37
       duty to investigate before terminating, 10.11
       duty to warn, 12.16
       factors, 12.24
       service, 9.65
    examples of —
       absenteeism, 9.45-9.48
       adultery, 10.18

ambition, 9.13

dishonesty, theft or fraud, 10.6-10.9; 12.29-12.31

disloyalty, 12.36-12.37

failure to comply with employer's directives, 9.23-9.37

failure to improve despite warnings, 9.75

failure to maintain equipment, 9.26

failure to respect employer's policies, 9.15; 9.28; 9.33; 12.34

harassment, 8.40

incompetence, 12.35

insubordination, 9.29-9.30; 12.32

intoxication, 12.33

mental or physical incapacity, 9.52-9.54

misuse or misappropriation of employer's property, 10.10

negligence, 9.75

off-duty conduct, 9.18-9.21; 10.15; 10.17-10.20

other causes, 12.38

personality conflicts, 9.38-9.40

poor interpersonal skills, 9.11-9.13

refusal to relocate. *See* Place of work

substance abuse. *See* Substance abuse

L

Loyalty

    after employment. *See infra*, fiduciary duty

    Canaero decision, 10.27-10.31

    client lists, 10.101

    confidentiality, duty of —

        generally, 10.106-10.107

        information of trivial nature, 10.109

        limited confidential information, 10.110-10.111

        trade secrets —

            characteristics of, 10.114

            generally, 10.112-10.113

            springboard theory, 10.116-10.119

    conflict of interest, 10.55-10.69

    copyrights, 10.130-10.139

    dishonesty, 10.5-10.12

        false allegations, 10.11-10.11.1

    during employment. *See infra*, fiduciary duty

    employer's interests and reputation, damage to, 10.13-10.21

    fiduciary duty —

        after termination of employment —

            Canaero decision, 10.85-10.93

post-employment competition, 10.94-10.105
Canaero decision, 10.27-10.31
contract, created by, 10.47-10.49
directors' and officers' liability, 20.39-20.49.1
    conflict of duty and interest, 20.43-20.46
    misappropriation of corporate opportunities, 20.47-20.49.1
during employment —
    conflict of interest, 10.55-10.69
    fellow employees' harmful conduct, duty to report, 10.76-10.80
    generally, 10.54
    obligation to account, 10.81-10.84
    whistle-blowing, 10.70-10.75
generally, 10.22-10.26
independent contractors, 10.50-10.53
mere employees vs. top management, 10.32-10.36
who owes, 10.32-10.36
    tests to determine —
        breach by association, 10.46
        contract, 10.47-10.48
        employer's vulnerability, 10.39-10.44
        key person in department, 10.38
        key personnel, 10.37
        length of employment, 10.45
generally, 10.1-10.4
insurance brokers, 10.101-10.102
patents and other intellectual property rights —
    assignment contracts, 10.125-10.128
    generally, 10.120-10.123
    Industrial Design Act, 10.140-10.142
    Integrated Circuit Topography Act, 10.143-10.144
    Public Servants Invention Act, 10.145-10.146
    validity of inventions, 10.129
post-employment competition, 10.94-10.105

M

Misuse or misappropriation of employer's property, 10.10
Mitigation
    anticipated mitigation, 16.44.2
    employee's duty to —
        alternative employment, 16.20-16.29
        employment with same employer, 16.24-16.26
        geographic area of search, 16.30-16.35
        self-employment, 16.36-16.43

References are to paragraph numbers

employer's duty to, 15.8
nature of obligation, 16.9-16.19
termination provision, 16.44

N

Near cause/contributory fault. *See* Wrongful dismissal
Non-competition clause. *See* Written employment contract
Non-solicitation clause. *See* Written employment contract
Notice
  abuse of rights, 11.56.1
  benefits received during —
    disability, 16.52-16.53
    employment insurance, 16.54-16.58
    pension, 16.45-16.51
  during sick leave or disability, 9.55
  factors determining length of —
    age, 12.48-12.48.1
    "ball park" doctrine, 12.68-12.69
    economic climate, 12.56-12.57; 12.61
    finding similar employment, 12.52-12.58
    generally, 12.43-12.45
    geographic location, 12.55
    induced to leave stable employment, 12.49-12.51
    length of service, 12.59-12.60
    manner, 12.58
    other factors, 12.61-12.67
    position, 12.46-12.47
    representations, 12.64-12.65
    spouse, 12.54
  fixed-term contract, 13.4-13.5
  length of —
    fixed-term employment contract, 13.4-13.5
    generally, 13.2-13.3
    indeterminate employment contract, 13.6-13.7
  maximum, 12.45
  mitigation. *See* Mitigation
  purpose, 12.44
  written provisions, 11.55-11.56

O

Obligations of executive. *See also* Corporate executives; Employee
  good faith, 1.55-1.56
  historically, 1.53-1.64

role within employer's organization, 9.4-9.5
Officers. *See* Duties and liabilities of directors and officers

P

Patents and inventions
   assignment contracts, 10.125-10.128
   generally, 10.120-10.122
   validity of inventions, 10.129
Penal liability. *See* Duties and liabilities of directors and officers
Pensions. *See* Retirement income provisions
Personal services corporations, 18.16-18.24
Place of work, 6.23-6.29, 11.14-11.15
   relocation, 9.43-9.44
   tax considerations, 18.36. *See also* Tax considerations
Policies and manuals, 3.13-3.18
Pre-employment obligations
   generally, 5.1
   recruitment phase —
      advertisements/applications/interviews, 5.2-5.4
      negligent misrepresentation, 5.5-5.20

R

"Reading down", 11.31-11.34
   covenant, 11.11
Registered retirement savings plan
   creditor protection, 19.13-19.14
   group RRSP, 19.10-19.14
   individual RRSP, 19.7-19.9
Release. *See* Termination payment
Remuneration
   components of —
      advances, 7.29-7.32
      benefits, 7.55-7.60
      bonuses, 7.39-7.40
      commissions, 7.33-7.38
      company car, 7.65
      disability benefits, 7.60
      expatriate allowances, 7.61
      expense accounts, 7.64
      generally, 7.16-7.21
      loans, 7.69
      pension benefits, 7.56-7.58

post-termination benefits, 7.58-7.59
private club memberships, 7.62-7.63
profit sharing, 7.50-7.51
salary, 7.16-7.21
salary increases, 7.22-7.24
  red-circling, 7.24
sick days, 7.60.1
statutory holidays, 7.25-7.28
stock purchase and option plans, 7.52-7.54
subsidized housing, 7.67-7.68
vacation pay, 7.25-7.28
defined, 7.3-7.8
element of employment relationship, 4.6-4.7
employer's obligation to provide, 7.1-7.2
modification of, 7.9-7.15
Residence. *See* Immigration; Tax considerations
Resignation
constructive, 12.19-12.20
damages for premature —
  employer's duty to mitigate, 15.8
  generally, 15.1-15.3
  purpose, 15.6
generally, 12.13-12.18
validity of, 12.17
Restrictive covenant. *See* Written employment contract
Retirement income provisions
generally, 19.1-19.2
post-retirement insurance coverage, 19.51-19.52
retirement counselling services, 19.50
supplementary executive retirement plans —
  generally, 19.35-19.37
  retirement compensation arrangement, 19.38-19.41
  secular trust, 19.42-19.43
  unfunded retirement income arrangement, 19.43-19.49
tax-sheltered retirement savings vehicles —
  generally, 19.3-19.6
  registered pension plan —
    deferred profit sharing plan, 19.33
    generally, 19.15-19.17
    individual plan, 19.28-19.32
    standard plan —
      contribution limits, 19.18-19.21
      enrolment, 19.22
      portability, 19.25

residual surplus entitlement on termination, 19.26-19.27
vesting and locking-in, 19.23-19.24
registered retirement savings plan —
creditor protection, 19.13-19.14
group RRSP, 19.10-19.14
individual RRSP, 19.7-19.9
RRSP. *See* Retirement income provisions
RSP. *See* Retirement income provisions

S

Safety. *See* Health and safety
Salary. *See* Remuneration; Tax considerations
Securities legislation liability
generally, 21.1-21.5
insider trading. *See infra*, privileged information, use of
issuer's disclosure obligations —
civil liability —
documents containing misrepresentation, 21.15-21.34
prospectus or bid circular, failure to deliver, 21.6-21.14
criminal liability, 21.50-21.52
statutory offences, 21.35-21.49
privileged information, use of —
civil liability, 21.70-21.73
damages, 21.93-21.98
defences, 21.76-21.92
fines, 21.99-21.102
generally, 21.53-21.69
statutory limitation periods, 21.103-21.105
statutory offences, 21.74-21.75
Shareholder
employee as —
generally, 4.42-4.50
taxation considerations —
generally, 18.115-18.119
phantom stock plans, 18.126-18.130
share appreciation rights, 18.131
stock option plans, 18.120-18.124
stock purchase plans, 18.125
liability to —
excessive executive compensation, 20.114-20.137
general rules, 20.109-20.113
Substance abuse
illness or disability, 9.60; 9.67-9.68

References are to paragraph numbers

just cause, 9.61-9.68
  revelation of character, 9.63

T

Tax considerations
  allowances, 18.102-18.103
  deferred compensation, 18.108-18.114
  departure from Canada, 18.136-18.140
  director's fees, 18.104
  employee profit sharing plans, 18.105-18.107
  employment benefits —
    aircraft, 18.63
    automobiles, 18.58-18.62
    child care, 18.67
    club memberships, 18.64-18.65
    counselling services, 18.91-18.92
    employer-paid vacations, 18.68-18.69
    employment-related costs, reimbursement of, 18.97-18.101
    flexible benefit plans, 18.87-18.90
    generally, 18.51-18.56
    health and welfare trusts, 18.84-18.86
    insurance premiums, 18.71-18.72
    legal services plans, 18.66
    loans and advances, 18.74-18.78
    private health services plans, 18.80-18.82
    relocation expenses, 18.93-18.96
    retirement plans, 18.79
    sales for less than fair market value, 18.73
    sickness/accident/disability income, 18.70
    unemployment benefit plans, supplementary, 18.83
  employment income, taxation of. *See infra*, salary, wages and other
    remuneration
  entering Canada, 18.141-18.143
  golden parachute —
    Canada, in, 11.90
    U.S.A., in, 11.88-11.89
  independent contractor —
    common law jurisdictions, 18.11-18.12
    contractual implications, 18.14-18.15
    Income Tax Act considered, 18.7-18.10
    Quebec, in, 18.13
  international tax treaties, 18.39-18.41
  residence, place of —

domestic rules of residency, 18.34-18.38
generally, 18.29-18.33
international tax treaties, 18.39-18.41
salary, wages and other remuneration —
basic inclusion rules, 18.43-18.46
indirect payments, 18.50
timing of income inclusion, 18.47-18.49
shareholder or quasi-shareholder, employee as —
generally, 18.115-18.119
phantom stock plans, 18.126-18.130
share appreciation rights, 18.131
stock options plans, 18.120-18.124
stock purchase plans, 18.125
situs of employment, 18.25-18.28
"sojourner rule", 18.31
tax planning checklist, 18.3
taxpayer —
employee or independent contractor —
common law jurisdictions, 18.11-18.12
contractual implications, 18.14-18.15
Income Tax Act considered, 18.7-18.10
Quebec, in, 18.13
generally, 18.5-18.6
personal services corporations, 18.16-18.24
terminating employment, 18.132-18.135
withholding and contribution obligations, 18.144-18.145
Termination. See also Wrongful dismissal
asset sale, 12.8
frustration/impossibility of performance —
change of employer, 12.8-12.10
death, 12.11-12.12
fortuitous event and financial difficulties, 12.5-12.7
generally, 12.3
illness, 12.4
generally, 12.1
notice. See Notice
obligation to search for work, 16.13.1
repudiation —
employer, by —
constructive dismissal. See also Constructive dismissal
duties and responsibilities, 12.77-12.82
employer conduct, 12.91
generally, 12.70-12.73
geographical transfer, 12.85-12.90
remuneration and benefits, 12.74-12.76

status, 12.83-12.84

dismissal, 12.21

dismissal for cause, 12.22-12.40. *See also* Just cause

dismissal without cause —

    fixed-term contract, 12.41

    indeterminate-duration contract, 12.42

    reasonable notice of termination, 12.43

executive, by —

    constructive resignation, 12.19

    resignation. *See* Resignation

sale of business, 12.8-12.9

share sale, 12.8

term, expiry of, 12.2

Termination payments

  termination package and release, 16.58-16.68

  termination provision, 16.44. *See also* Notice

U

Unanimous shareholder agreement, 22.2-22.4

W

Wages, directors' liability for

  creditors, employees as, 20.60-20.68

  debtor, 20.53-20.59.1

  debts claimable —

    alternate liability, 20.93-20.94

    golden parachutes, 20.79-20.92

    joint and several liability, 20.95

    statutory limitation periods, 20.96-20.99

    termination and severance payments, 20.77

    types of remuneration, 20.67-20.77

  generally, 20.51-20.52

Whistle-blowing, 10.70-10.75

Work, execution of

  components of the obligation —

    behaviour —

      attitude, 9.10-9.13

      conduct, 9.4-9.22

      obedience to directives, 9.23-9.37

      personality conflict, 9.38-9.40

    competence, 9.69-9.80

      defined, 9.70-9.71

      extent of obligation, 9.72-9.74

    generally, 9.6-9.9

    physical component —

absenteeism, 9.45-9.48
    mental or physical incapacity, 9.49-9.59
    presence at work, 9.41-9.44
    substance abuse, 9.60-9.68
generally, 9.1-9.3
just cause. *See* Just cause
relocation. *See* Place of work
revelation of character, 9.21; 9.63
role within the organization, 9.4-9.5
Work, provision of
    assistance, 6.30-6.34
    authority and responsibilities, 6.15-6.22
    change in terms and conditions, 6.19-6.22. *See also* Constructive
        dismissal
    constructive dismissal, 6.19-6.22. *See also* Constructive dismissal
    directives, 6.30-6.34
    duration of the obligation —
        fixed-term or indeterminate contract, 6.42-6.54
        generally, 6.3-6.14
    geographic location. *See* Place of work
    hours of work, 6.40-6.41;
    respect, 6.35-6.36;
    tools, materials, equipment and space, 6.37-6.39
    transfers, 6.26-6.29
    type of work, 6.13-6.14
Workers' compensation, 2.29
Written employment contract
    arbitration provisions, 11.97-11.105
    breach of, remedies for —
        breach of contract, 11.47
        injunction, 11.46
        "liquidated damages" clause, 11.48
        rights to relief, 11.49-11.50
    change in control, protection from. *See also* Golden parachutes
        generally, 11.67-11.68
        golden parachute agreement —
        advantages of, 11.75-11.79
        criticism of, 11.80
        elements of —
            change in control, 11.70-11.71
            loss of employment or resignation for good reason,
                11.72-11.74
        enforceability of, 11.87
        judicial scrutiny of, strategy for surviving —

alternative employment, obligation to search for, 11.95
origin of proposal, 11.93
relationship to services performed, 11.94
timing, 11.92
taxing provisions re —
Canada, in, 11.90
U.S.A., in, 11.88-11.89
golden parachute compensation —
business judgment rule, 11.82
fiduciary duty, 11.83-11.86
Civil Code approach to, 11.5-11.6
common law approach to, 11.3-11.4
confidentiality provisions, 11.42-11.45
defining executive's position, 11.11
duration provisions, 11.12-11.13
generally, 11.1-11.2
golden parachutes. *See* Golden parachutes
illegal, void or unenforceable clauses —
generally, 11.7
independent legal advice, 11.9
severability, 11.8
non-competition clause —
civil law position, 11.17
common law position, 11.18
defined, 11.16
reasonableness —
duration, 11.22-11.24
generally, 11.19-11.21
nature of prohibited activities, 11.27-11.30
onus of proving covenant unreasonable, 11.31-11.34
territory, 11.25-11.26
non-solicitation of clients, 11.35-11.40
non-solicitation of employees, 11.41
place of work, 11.14-11.15
reading down, 11.31-11.34
remuneration and benefit clauses, 11.51-11.54
termination and severance pay, notice of —
contracting out of notice requirements, 11.57
monetary indemnity in lieu of notice, 11.58-11.60
obligation to mitigate damages, 11.61-11.62
scope of contract, 11.55-11.56
termination payment, 11.63-11.66
validity of, 11.3-11.4
Wrongful dismissal. *See also* Termination

aggravated/moral damages —
    anxiety and mental distress, 14.24-14.28
    communication of dismissal, 14.35-14.36
    generally, 14.1-14.3
    humiliation, 14.21-14.23
    legal basis of award, 14.6-14.20
    loss of reputation, 14.29-14.34
contributory fault. *See infra,* near cause/contributory fault
deductibility of benefits from damage award, 16.52-16.57
discharge transactions. *See infra,* termination packages
exemplary damages, 14.37-14.45
heads of damages —
    alternative employment expenses, 13.39-13.43
    bonus and profit sharing, 13.20-13.25
    business expenses personally incurred, 16.7-16.8
    club membership fees, 13.36
    commissions, 13.17-13.19
    company car/car allowance, 13.37-13.38
    director's fees, 13.54
    expense accounts, 13.45
    generally, 13.8-13.11
    income tax deduction benefits, 13.55
    increase in salary, 13.14-13.16
    insurance and medical plans, 13.31-13.35
    miscellaneous claims, 13.56
    pension, 13.26-13.30
    salary, 13.12-13.13
    severance pay, 13.46-13.50
    share option/purchase plan, 13.51-13.53
    termination pay, 13.46-13.50
    vacation pay, 13.44-13.45
liability for, 20.101-20.103
mitigation. *See* Mitigation
moral damages, 14.4. *See also, supra,* aggravated/moral damages
near cause/contributory fault, 16.1-16.6
notice, defined. *See* Notice
notice period. *See* Notice
personal liability of terminating person, 16.69-16.70
punitive and exemplary damages, 14.37-14.45
termination packages, 16.58-16.68